Sardinia

Gregor Clark, Kerry Christiani, Duncan Garwood

PLAN YOUR TRIP

CHIESA DI SAN MICHELE, ALGHERO P115

TRADITIONAL MAMUTHONE MASK P187

ON THE ROAD

Contents

BOSA P106

UNDERSTAND

SURVIVAL GUIDE

SPECIAL FEATURES

Welcome to Sardinia

Sardinia captivates with its wild hinterland, out-of-this-world beaches and endearing eccentricities. Here coastal drives thrill, prehistory puzzles and four million sheep rule the roads.

Beach Beauties

Sardinia has some of the dreamiest beaches you'll find without stepping off European shores. Yes, the sand really is *that* white, and the sea the bluest blue. Imagine dropping anchor in Costa Smeralda's scalloped bays, where celebrities and supermodels frolic in emerald waters; playing castaway on the Golfo di Orosei's coves, or sailing to La Maddalena's cluster of granite islands. Whether you're walking barefoot across the dunes on the wave-lashed Costa Verde or lounging on the Costa del Sud's silky smooth bays, unroll your beach towel and you'll never want to leave.

Outdoor Adventures

Whether you go slow or fast, choose coast or country, Sardinia is one of Europe's last great island adventures. Hike through the lush, silent interior to the twilight of Tiscali's nuraghic ruins. Walk the vertiginous coastal path to the crescent-shaped bay of Cala Luna. Or ramble through holm oak forests to the mighty boulder-strewn canyon of Gola Su Gorropu. The sea's allure is irresistible to windsurfers on the north coast, while divers wax lyrical about shipwrecks off Cagliari's coast, the underwater Nereo Cave and Nora's submerged Roman ruins.

Island of Idiosyncrasies

As DH Lawrence so succinctly put it: 'Sardinia is different'. Indeed, where else but here can you go from near-alpine forests to snow-white beaches, or find wildlife oddities such as the blue-eyed albino donkeys on the Isola dell'Asinara. The island is also a culinary one-off, with distinct takes on pasta, bread and *dolci,* its own wines and cheeses – including maggoty *casu marzu pecorino,* stashed away in barns in the mountainous interior. In every way we can think of Sardinia is different, and all the more loveable for it.

Time Travel

Sardinia has been polished like a pebble by the waves of its history and heritage. The island is scattered with 7000 *nuraghi,* Bronze Age towers and settlements, *tombe dei giganti* ('giant's grave' tombs) and *domus de janas* ('fairy house' tombs). Down every country lane and in every 10-man, 100-sheep hamlet, these remnants of prehistory are waiting to be pieced together like the most puzzling of jigsaw puzzles. Sardinia is also an island of fabulously eccentric festivals, from Barbagia's carnival parade of ghoulish *mamuthones,* said to banish winter demons, to the death-defying S'Ardia horse race in Sedilo.

Why I Love Sardinia

By Kerry Christiani, Writer

Sardinia was love at first sight for me. No matter how often I return, I find new coastal trails to explore and mountains to climb, hidden bays to kayak to and little-known *agriturismi* tucked away in the silent hinterland. The island is deceptive – it looks small on paper, but unravel it and it is huge. It's like a continent in miniature, shaped by its own language and fierce traditions, its own cuisine and culture, its own history and the mystery that hangs over it like a shroud. Sardinians are proud of their island, and so they should be.

For more about our writers, see p288

Above: Masua (p73), west coast

Sardinia

0 50 km
0 25 miles
Parco Nazionale dell'Asinara
Island wilderness (p130)
Costa Smeralda
Where the sun-kissed high life is lived (p155)
Grotta di Nettuno
Descend 654 steps to this fairy-tale grotto (p128)
Orgosolo
Political murals in the former bandit capital (p184)
Alghero
Spanish-style walled city (p114)
Tiscali
An ancient archaeological enigma (p200)
Bosa
Postcard-pretty riverside town (p106)
Gola Su Gorropu
Europe's Grand Canyon and explorers' playground (p199)
8°E
9°E
10°E
41°N
Santa Teresa di Gallura
Isola Maddalena
Isola Caprera
Parco Nazionale dell'Arcipelago di La Maddalena
Porto Pollo
Palau
Baia Sardinia
Romazzino
Porto Rotondo
Golfo Aranci
Arzachena
Parco Nazionale dell'Asinara
Torre Pelosa
Stintino
Golfo dell' Asinara
Castelsardo
Tempio Pausania
Olbia
Porto Torres
Marina di Sorso
Platamona
Sorso
Sassari
Coghinas
Lago di Coghinas
Monti
Tyrrhenian Sea
Porto Ferro
Monte Timidone (361m)
Grotta di Nettuno
Fertilia
Alghero
Cala Bona
Ozieri
Siniscola
Villanova Monteleone
Torralba
Tirso
Orune
Orosei
Monte Ortobene (955m)
Mare di Sardegna
Bosa
Nuoro
Dorgali
Macomer
Oliena
Cala Gonone
Tiscali
Torre
Cuglieri
Mamoiada
Orgosolo
Gola Su Gorropu

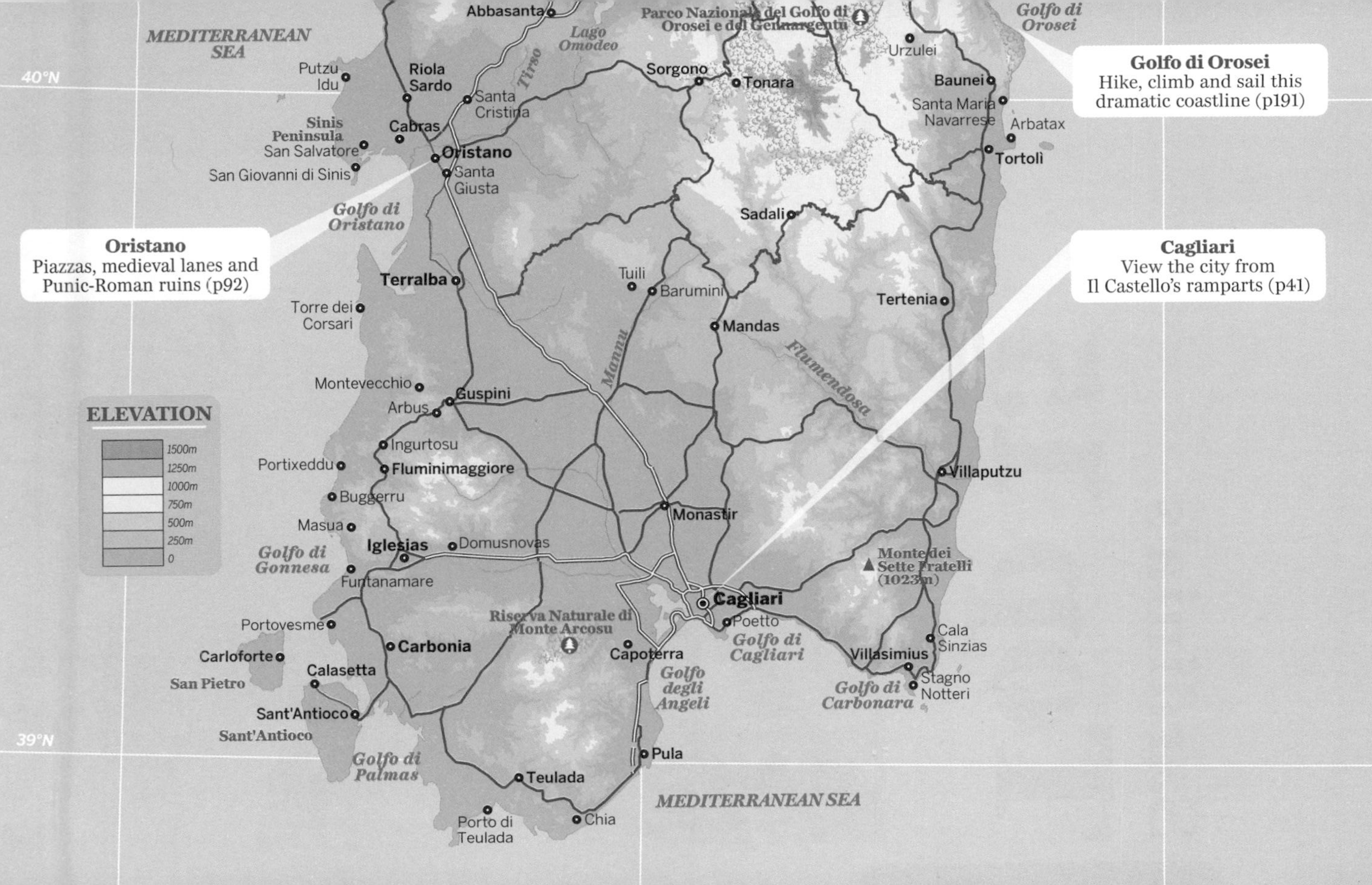

Golfo di Orosei
Hike, climb and sail this dramatic coastline (p191)
Cagliari
View the city from Il Castello's ramparts (p41)
Oristano
Piazzas, medieval lanes and Punic-Roman ruins (p92)
ELEVATION
1500m
1250m
1000m
750m
500m
250m
0
MEDITERRANEAN SEA
MEDITERRANEAN SEA
40°N
39°N
Abbasanta
Lago Omodeo
Tirso
Parco Nazionale del Golfo di Orosei e del Gennargentu
Golfo di Orosei
Urzulei
Baunei
Santa Maria Navarrese
Arbatax
Tortolì
Putzu Idu
Riola Sardo
Santa Cristina
Sorgono
Tonara
Sinis Peninsula
San Salvatore
San Giovanni di Sinis
Cabras
Oristano
Santa Giusta
Golfo di Oristano
Sadali
Terralba
Tuili
Barumini
Tertenia
Torre dei Corsari
Mandas
Flumendosa
Mannu
Montevecchio
Guspini
Arbus
Ingurtosu
Portixeddu
Fluminimaggiore
Villaputzu
Buggerru
Monastir
Masua
Iglesias
Domusnovas
Golfo di Gonnesa
Funtanamare
Monte dei Sette Fratelli (1023m)
Cagliari
Poetto
Riserva Naturale di Monte Arcosu
Portovesme
Carbonia
Capoterra
Golfo di Cagliari
Cala Sinzias
Villasimius
Carloforte
Calasetta
San Pietro
Golfo degli Angeli
Golfo di Carbonara
Stagno Notteri
Sant'Antioco
Sant'Antioco
Golfo di Palmas
Pula
Teulada
Porto di Teulada
Chia

Sardinia's Top 15

Golfo di Orosei

1 We can wax lyrical about sparkling aquamarine waters, blindingly white sands and sheer limestone cliffs but, trust us, seeing is believing when it comes to the Golfo di Orosei. Where the mountains collide spectacularly with the sea, this huge, sweeping crescent forms the seaward section of the Parco Nazionale del Golfo di Orosei e del Gennargentu (p191). Set your spirits soaring by hiking its clifftop trails, exploring its sea grottoes in a kayak, or boating along the gulf to hidden coves – each more mind-blowingly beautiful than the last.

Tiscali

2 Held hostage in the twilight of a collapsed limestone cave, the archaeological site of Tiscali (p200) is an enigma. Though only skeletal ruins remain, with a little imagination you can picture this nuraghic village as it was back in the Bronze Age. Every bit as enchanting as Tiscali itself is the trail through the lush green valley that takes you there – mighty rock faces loom above you, birds of prey wheel overhead and only the sound of your footsteps interrupts the overwhelming sense of calm that blankets this valley.

ZAKAZ86/SHUTTERSTOCK ©

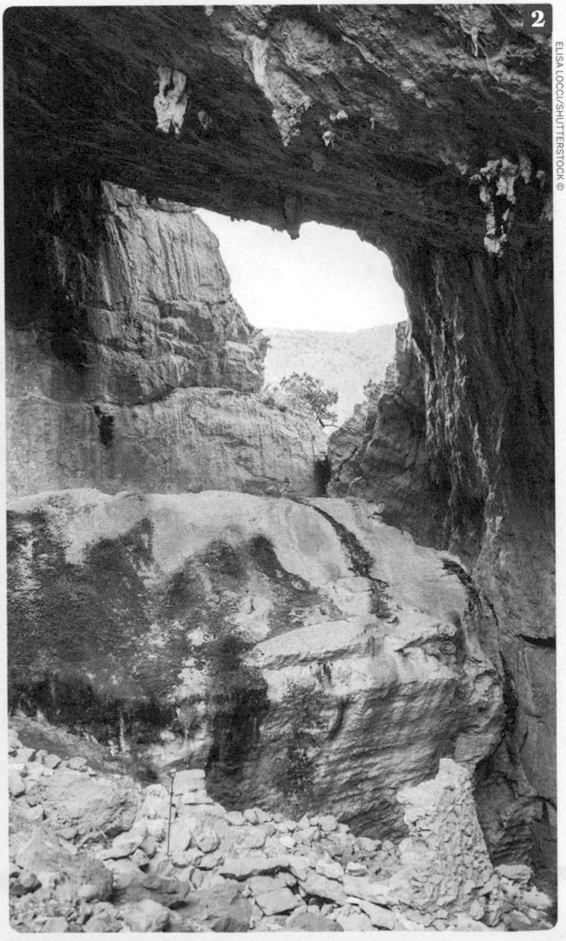

2

ELISA LOCCI/SHUTTERSTOCK ©

Il Castello, Cagliari

3 Perched on a rocky peak, Cagliari's Il Castello (p43) is never more captivating than at dusk on a warm summer's evening. Rimmed by imposing ramparts, this hilltop neighbourhood spells out the Sardinian capital's history in artefacts. As the softening light paints the sky purple-pink, the citadel's walls, *palazzi* and Pisan towers glow gold. Capture the moment by heading to the laid-back terrace of a bar on the ramparts, where sundowners are served with dress-circle views of the illuminated city.

Costa Smeralda

4 Believe the hype: the Costa Smeralda (p155) is stunning. Here the Gallura's granite mountains tumble down to fjordlike inlets, and an emerald sea fringes a coast that is necklaced with bays like the Aga Khan's favourite, Spiaggia del Principe, a perfect crescent of frost-white sand smoothed by gin-clear water. Marvel at the mega-yachts in millionaires' playground resorts, or eschew the high life to seek out secluded coves, embedded in fragrant *macchia* (Mediterranean scrubland), where the views are simply priceless.

Gola Su Gorropu

5 The first glimpse of Gola Su Gorropu (p199) on the scenic hike down from the Genna 'e Silana pass is mesmerising. Dubbed Europe's Grand Canyon, this mighty ravine boasts 400m-high rock walls and enormous boulders scattered like a giant's marbles. At its narrowest point – just 4m wide – the gorge seems to swallow you up, blocking out the sun and silencing the world outside. Were it not for the occasional fellow trekker or climber, the chasm would have the eerie effect of seeming totally lost in time and space.

Alghero

6 To see Alghero (p114) at its most atmospheric, come in the early evening when crowds fill its maze of dark, medieval lanes and people-watch from the grand cafe terraces on Piazza Civica. Tables are set up along the honey-coloured ramparts, softly lit by lanterns, for al fresco dining with uninterrupted views of the sea and stars. Never mind the expense, you must try Alghero's famous *aragosta alla catalana* (lobster with tomato and onion), a lingering taste of the city's past as a Catalan colony.

Bosa

7 Like many great works of art, Bosa (p106) is best admired from afar. From a distance you can take in the whole picture: the elegant houses in a fresco painter's palette of colours, the fishing boats bobbing on the Fiume Temo and the medieval Castello Malaspina perched on a steep hillside. Linger until evening to see one of Sardinia's prettiest towns without the crowds, walking its narrow alleyways and stopping to sample some of the freshest fish on the west coast at family-run restaurants.

Nuraghi & Tombe dei Giganti

8 Defensive watchtowers, sacred ritual sites, prehistoric community centres...the exact purpose of Sardinia's 7000 *nuraghi* is unknown. Yet the island's Bronze Age past is still tangible within the semicircular walls of these stone towers and fortified settlements. Most famous and best preserved is the beehive complex of Nuraghe Su Nuraxi (p87), a Unesco World Heritage Site. Equally mysterious are the island's *tombe dei giganti* (giants' tombs), megalithic mass graves sealed off by stone stele.

7

8

STEFANO GUIDI/SHUTTERSTOCK ©

MNSTUDIO/SHUTTERSTOCK ©

ELISA LOCCI/SHUTTERSTOCK ©

Grotta di Nettuno

9 Whether you glide in by boat from Alghero or take the vertiginous 654-step staircase that zigzags down 110m of sheer cliff, arriving at the Grotta di Nettuno (p128) is unforgettable. Enter the immense, cathedral-like grotto and it really is as though the forces of Neptune, god of the sea, have been at work. All around you are forests of curiously shaped stalactites and stalagmites, reflected in still pools of water. Nothing – not even the midday crowds – can detract from the magic of this underground fairyland.

Hilltop Villages

10 You're lost on a hairpin-bend-riddled road in the mountains that seemingly leads to nowhere, and no sat nav, map or passing flock of sheep can help you. But then, suddenly, you crest a hill and a tiny village slides into view, surrounded by titanic mountains and sweeping forests. It happens all the time in Sardinia's wild Barbagia and Ogliastra provinces. If you're up for an offbeat adventure, get behind the wheel for a head-spinning drive to gloriously remote villages such as Aritzo (p189), pasted high on a mountain slope.

Top right: Castelsardo (p135)

Parco Nazionale dell'Asinara

11 Dangling off the northwestern tip of the island in splendid isolation, the rugged green Parco Nazionale dell'Asinara (p130) is one of Sardinia's greatest coastal wildernesses. The unique *asino bianco* (albino donkey) is at home in this outstanding national park, as are peregrine falcons, mouflon, wild boar and loggerhead turtles. For close-up wildlife encounters, join one of the guided walking or cycling tours that take in the island's remote corners. Or go diving in the crystal-clear waters that lap its granite cliffs and dreamy beaches.

MILOSK50/SHUTTERSTOCK ©

EMMANUELE CONTINI/SHUTTERSTOCK © / GETTY IMAGES ©

Oristano & the Sinis Peninsula

12 One of Sardinia's great medieval cities is Oristano (p92), the capital of the 14th-century province of Arborea. History seeps through the centre's baroque lanes and piazzas, presided over by the graceful domed *duomo*. Slow the pace and follow the locals to the Piazza Eleonora d'Arborea to stroll and chat in front of the ornate *palazzi*. Or base yourself here to explore the Punic-Roman ruins of Tharros and the snow-white beaches and bird-filled lagoons of the Sinis Peninsula.

Festive Sardinia

13 Be it the death-defying horse races of S'Ardia or *mamuthones* (costumed carnival figures) exorcising winter demons in Mamoiada, Sardinians celebrate in weird and wonderful ways. Time your visit to catch standouts like the medieval tournament Sa Sartiglia (p96, pictured above) in Oristano in February, Cagliari's Festa di Sant'Efisio in May or the folkloric parades of Nuoro's Sagra del Redentore in August. Hungry? Check out our line-up of seasonal food festivals, where you can indulge in everything from chestnuts to sea urchins.

Orgosolo

14 Social commentary, politics, end-of-the-world prophecy – all are writ large on the shabby exteriors of houses and cafes in Orgosolo (p184). Once a byword for banditry, today Orgosolo is an enormous canvas for some of the most emotionally charged graffiti you'll ever see. Along the Corso Repubblica, vivid murals recall the big events of the 20th and 21st centuries, from the creation of the atomic bomb to the fall of Baghdad – events that seem a million miles away from this small village in the heart of the tough, mountainous Barbagia.

Opposite top right: Che Guevara wall mural

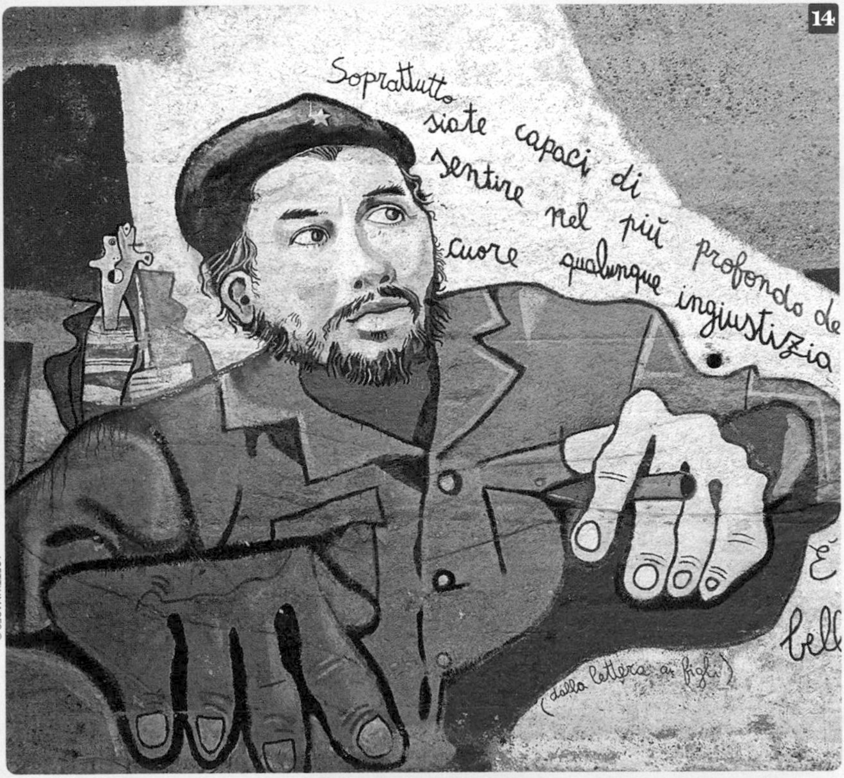

/ GETTY IMAGES ©

Foodie Sardinia

15 'Organic' and 'slow food' are modern-day buzzwords for what Sardinia has been doing for centuries. Trawl the interior for farms selling their own *pecorino*, salami and full-bodied Cannonau red wines; buy artistic-looking loaves and almondy sweets from bakeries and confectioners in Cagliari and Nuoro; and tuck into a smorgasbord of seafood. Or sample the lot at a rustic *agriturismo*, such as Li Mori (p154), where your hosts will ply you with course after course, including antipasti and slow-roasted suckling pig.

Right: Pasta with clams

IULIA KARNAUSHENKO/SHUTTERSTOCK ©

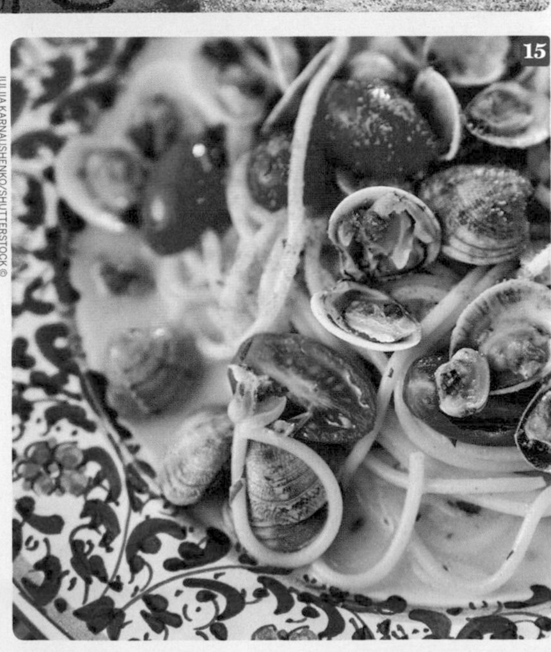

Need to Know

For more information, see Survival Guide (p259)

Currency
Euro (€)

Language
Sardinian (Sardo), Italian

Visas
Generally not required for stays of up to 90 days (or at all for EU nationals); some nationalities need a Schengen visa.

Money
ATMs are widely available (daily withdrawal limit €250). Major hotels and restaurants usually accept credit cards, but at some smaller places it's cash only.

Mobile Phones
As of June 2017, roaming charges no longer apply in the EU. Australian mobiles must be set up for international roaming.

US cell phones that operate on the 900 and 1800 MHz frequencies work in Sardinia.

Buy SIM cards at phone and electronic stores.

Time
Central European Time (GMT/UTC + one hour)

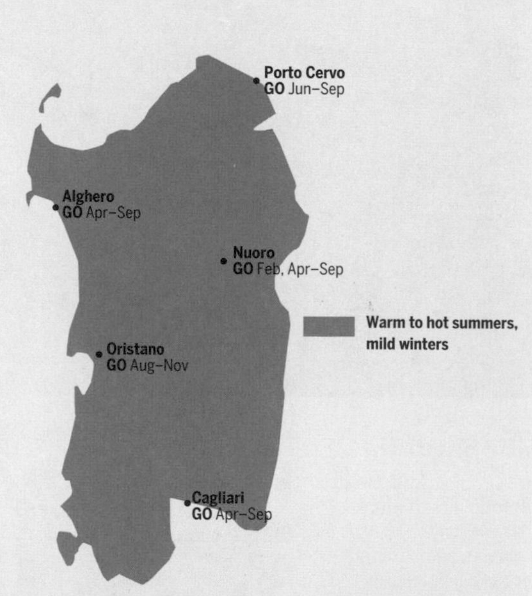

High Season (Jul & Aug)
- Crowds flock to coastal resorts and room rates skyrocket.
- Prices also rise over Easter and school holidays.
- Roads are at their most congested.
- Hot days good for the beach.

Shoulder Season (Apr–Jun & mid-Sep–Oct)
- Room rates are significantly lower.
- The weather is changeable and the sea chilly.
- Excellent for hiking, cycling and climbing.
- Sights and beaches are less crowded.

Low Season (Nov–Mar)
- Days are shorter, weather is colder and wetter.
- Many sights, hotels and restaurants are closed.
- Prices up to 50% less than high season.
- Carnevale is reason to visit in February.

Useful Websites

Sardegna Turismo (www.sardegnaturismo.it) The official tourist board website is your first port of call for activities, culture, itineraries, events and accommodation.

ENIT (www.enit.it) The Italian State Tourist Board has some background on what to see, do and eat.

Lonely Planet (www.lonelyplanet.com/sardinia) Destination information, hotel bookings, traveller forum and more.

ARST (www.arst.sardegna.it) Regional transport; find timetables and plan your journey.

Trenitalia (www.trenitalia.com) For timetables and prices of rail journeys in Sardinia.

Sardegne.com (www.sardegne.com) The lowdown on accommodation, restaurants, transport and weather.

Important Numbers

To dial listings from outside Italy, dial your international access code, Italy's country code and then the number (including '0').

Country Code	☎39
International access code	☎00
Europe-wide emergency	☎112
Ambulance	☎118
Fire	☎115
Police	☎113

Exchange Rates

Australia	A$1	€0.66
Canada	C$1	€0.66
Japan	¥100	€0.80
NZ	NZ$1	€0.63
UK	UK£1	€1.14
US	US$1	€0.89

For current exchange rates see www.xe.com.

Daily Costs

Budget: Less than €120

➡ Dorm bed: €20–25

➡ Double room in a budget hotel or B&B: €60–100

➡ Fixed-price lunches: €15–20

➡ Takeaway pizza: €4–7.50

Midrange: €120–250

➡ Double room in a midrange hotel: €100–200

➡ Dinner in a local restaurant: €25–45

➡ Cocktail: €5–8

➡ Boat tour: €15–30

Top end: More than €250

➡ Double room in a five-star hotel: €200–350

➡ Restaurant meal: €50–60

➡ Boat/yacht charter: €800 per day

Opening Hours

Opening hours vary throughout the year. We've provided high-season opening hours; hours will generally decrease in the shoulder and low seasons.

Banks 8.30am to 1.30pm and 2.45pm to 4.30pm Monday to Friday

Bars 7pm to 1am Monday to Saturday

Cafes 7am or 8am to 10pm or 11pm Monday to Saturday

Clubs 10pm to 3am, 4am or 5am Thursday to Saturday

Post offices 8am to 6.50pm Monday to Friday, 8am to 1.15pm Saturday

Restaurants noon to 2.30pm or 3pm and 7.30pm to 10pm or 11pm

Shops 9am to 1pm and 4pm to 8pm Monday to Saturday

Arriving in Sardinia

Cagliari Elmas Airport Trains run from the airport to Cagliari station (€1.30) approximately every 20 to 30 minutes between 6.37am and 11.07pm. The journey takes six to 10 minutes. A taxi will set you back around €20.

Aeroporto di Olbia Costa Smeralda Local bus lines 2 and 10 (€1, or €1.50 if ticket is bought on-board) run half-hourly between the airport to central Olbia. The journey takes 10 minutes. A taxi costs around €15.

Alghero Airport Hourly buses run from the airport to Via Catalogna (€1, or €1.50 on-board) between 5.20am and 11pm. The journey takes about 25 minutes. A taxi from the airport will cost around €25.

Cagliari Ferry Port Tirrenia ferries link Cagliari to Civitavecchia (€53, 13 hours), Naples (€50, 13½ hours) and Palermo (€50, 12 hours).

Etiquette

Hospitality Accept offers of a glass of wine, beer or *mirto* when offered.

Dress Don't go around dressed scantily for the beach in mountain areas where people can be quite conservative.

Language Remember that Sardo is not a dialect of Italian; it is a separate language.

Greetings Shake hands and say *buongiorno* (good day) or *buona sera* (good evening) to strangers; kiss both cheeks and say *come stai* (how are you) to friends.

For much more on **getting around**, see p28 & p266

If You Like...

Islands & Beaches

Sardinia's islands, beaches and wind-sculpted seascapes are captivating. Dive into barracuda-filled waters, anchor in hidden bays and find your own patch of whiter-than-white sand.

Parco Nazionale dell'Arcipelago di La Maddalena Explore pink granite islands, sugar-fine sands and gin-clear water. (p167)

Spiaggia di Piscinas Remote and stunning, this 3.5km beach has memorable sunsets. (p75)

Isola dell'Asinara This wildlife-rich island, home to albino donkeys, is best discovered on foot or by bicycle. (p130)

Cala Mariolu Be dazzled by the shimmering white pebbles and aquamarine waters of this tucked-away bay. (p194)

Spiaggia del Principe The Aga Khan loves this gorgeous white crescent lapped by startlingly blue water. (p156)

Spiaggia della Pelosa A ravishing, frost-white sweep of a beach guarded by a Spanish watchtower. (p130)

Is Aruttas A perfect arc of sparkly quartz sand, turquoise sea and total peace. (p99)

Cala Domestica Beach Bounded by rugged crags, this astonishing beach has shallow blue waters for blissful swims. (p73)

Archaeological Digs

Stage your own archaeological explorations on this mysterious island, home to 7000 *nuraghi* (Bronze Age settlements), *pozzi sacri* (sacred wells) and *tombe dei giganti* ('giants' tombs').

Nuraghe Su Nuraxi Sardinia's sole World Heritage Site, and its most famous *nuraghe*, dates to 1500 BC. (p87)

Tiscali Ponder the meaning of this ruined *nuraghe*, hidden in a collapsed cave in the limestone Supramonte. (p200)

Nuraghe di Santa Cristina A beautiful nuraghic complex centred on a Bronze Age *tempio a pozzo*. (p105)

Serra Orrios Find mystery in the ruined huts and temples of this nuraghic settlement nestled in olive groves. (p200)

Nuraghe di Palmavera A 3500-year-old *nuraghe* with a complex system of dwellings. (p127)

Necropoli di Montessu A prehistoric cemetery set in a rocky amphitheatre. (p77)

Coddu Ecchju A fine example of a *tombe dei giganti*, sealed off by stone stele. (p160)

Nuraghe Is Paras This *nuraghe* stands out for its 11.8m *tholos* (conical tower). (p191)

Great Outdoors

Climb sea cliffs, breeze across the Med on a board or hike into forest-cloaked mountains; Sardinia thrills with exhilarating landscapes, unique wildlife and boundless outdoor pursuits.

Gola Su Gorropu Strike into the wilderness of the island's grandest canyon, a place of primordial beauty. (p199)

Cardedu Kayak Paddle in off-the-radar spots along the red granite coastline. (p203)

Golfo di Orosei Walk the gulf's shores or sail its sparkling waters in search of little-known bays, grottoes and sea stacks. (p191)

Sporting Club Sardinia The beautiful breezes that pummel this north-coast resort are irresistible to windsurfers. (p170)

Parco Nazionale del Golfo di Orosei e del Gennargentu Hike, bike, canyon, kayak, dive, cave and climb in Sardinia's largest national park. (p191)

Capo Galera Diving Centre Dive into the deep blue in search of frilly red coral in Nereo Cave, the Mediterranean's largest underwater grotto. (p126)

La Giara di Gesturi Hike this lush tabletop plateau in search of wild horses. (p88)

Top: Church in Iglesias (p67)

Bottom: Roccia dell'Elefante, Castelsardo (p135),

Authentic Agriturismi

Go slow with a stay or dinner at an *agriturismo*. Sprinkled across the island, these middle-of-nowhere farmsteads are the ultimate escape, often nestled among oak woods, olive groves and sheep-speckled fields.

Agriturismo Guthiddai This whitewashed retreat sits at the foot of rugged mountains, surrounded by olive trees. (p223)

Agriturismo Su Boschettu Serene farm in Sardinia's agricultural heartland. (p213)

Agriturismo Montiferru Time your visit for a Sunday lunch to remember at this *agriturismo* tucked away in the hills. (p103)

Agriturismo Testone Sneak away from the crowds at this rustic abode snuggled away in holm oak woods. (p222)

Agriturismo Nuraghe Mannu Gaze out across Cala Gonone at this *agriturismo*, with a super-friendly welcome and home-grown food. (p222)

Agriturismo La Colti Feast on organic produce and grilled-to-perfection meats at this rustic farm above Cannigione. (p159)

Agriturismo Sa Mandra The perfect country escape near Alghero, this farm is a tranquil escape with bang-on-the-money home cooking. (p216)

Coastal Walks & Rides

Sardinia's soaring cliffs, wild gorges and a coast necklaced with crescent-shaped coves beg exploration on foot or by bicycle.

Selvaggio Blu Go east for the big one – an epic seven-day hike taking in Sardinia's most dramatic coastlines. (p192)

Cala Goloritzè Walk from the other-worldly Golgo plateau to this beautiful bay, with unbelievably blue water. (p196)

Funtanamare Cycle to the remote Costa Verde, taking in glassy waters, rugged cliffs and sea stacks. (p73)

Cala Luna Hike from Cala Fuili along clifftops and through fragrant scrub to this captivating half-moon bay. (p192)

Hilltop Towns & Villages

Winding roads and rivers wend through the patchwork fields, forests and mountains of Sardinia's silent hinterland. Visit hill towns and villages for back-in-time flavour, soul food and swoon-worthy views.

Castelsardo A beautiful medieval centre perched on a hilltop overlooking the sea. (p134)

Ulassai A road corkscrews up to this tiny village beneath jagged mountains. (p205)

Montiferru Explore the wonderful nature of this region's villages, but most of all the magnificent local beef and olive oil. (p102)

Orgosolo From the creation of the atomic bomb to the destruction of the twin towers – the murals here pack a powerful political punch. (p184)

San Pantaleo Tiptoe away from the Costa Smeralda's glitz to this pretty stone village surrounded by granite peaks. (p161)

Laconi Peace reigns in this mountain town, where cobbled lanes twist to a verdant woodland park. (p190)

Tempio Pausania A charming grey-stone town nestled amid cork oak woods in the cool, hilly heart of the Gallura. (p171)

Natural Wonders

Nature has worked wonders in Sardinia – the coastline is indented with bays, honeycombed with grottoes and punctuated by granite rock formations, while canyons carve up the interior.

Grotta di Nettuno Descend 654 steps to this cathedral-like grotto. (p128)

Belvedere Dominating the seascape views is Sugarloaf Rock, the largest of several *faraglioni* (rock towers) rearing out of glassy blue waters. (p73)

Grotta di Ispinigoli Find a forest of stalagmites (including the world's second tallest) in this mammoth cave. (p200)

Roccia dell'Elefante Bet you didn't think you'd find an elephant near Castelsardo... Novelty factor aside, this rock wonder conceals two neolithic tombs. (p135)

Il Golgo Peering into the depths of this 270m abyss is enough to bring on vertigo. (p201)

Food from the Source

Sardinian food is all about simple pleasures – family-run wine cellars, farms selling fresh *pecorino,* honey and salami, and towns celebrating their bounty at vivacious food festivals.

Cantine Surrau A super-slick winery near the Costa Smeralda, famous for its tangy Vermentino whites and full-bodied Cannonau reds. (p159)

Il Caminetto Try salty, flavoursome *muggini* (mullet) and *bottarga* (mullet roe) in the fishing town of Cabras. (p99)

Durke A fantasy of homemade Sardinian sweets, the best made with just sugar, egg whites and almonds. (p60)

Formaggi Gruthas Buy locally produced ricotta, *pecorino* and goat cheese at this working farm. (p202)

Alghero Feast on local rock lobster and spiky *ricci* (sea urchins) from the briny blue. (p114)

Vivaio I Campi Fill your bags with zesty citrus fruits at this pick-your-own in Milis. (p104)

Historic Cities

Carthaginians, Romans, Aragonese and Pisans – all have left their indelible stamp on Sardinia. Rewind the clocks when strolling along ramparts, clambering up to citadels and relaxing on church-dotted piazzas.

Alghero The *centro storico* is a shady labyrinth of honey-coloured *palazzi*, buffered by walls that on summer evenings are crowded with diners. (p114)

Cagliari Wander the lanes of the medieval citadel Il Castello, lingering as the setting sun lights up its ramparts. (p41)

Oristano The charming historic centre is full of good eateries and fun bars. (p92)

Iglesias The Iberian atmosphere of Iglesias and its collection of churches make it a fascinating place to explore. (p67)

Olbia Be catapulted back to Roman times while contemplating the mighty ships in the Museo Archeologico. (p148)

Month by Month

TOP EVENTS

Carnevale, February

Pasqua, March/April

Festa di Sant'Efisio, May

S'Ardia, July

Festa del Redentore, August

January

Festa di Sant'Antonio Abate

Bonfires rage in Orosei, Orgosolo, Sedilo and Paulilatino at this festival from 16 to 17 January. Sinister half-human, half-animal *mamuthones* make a mad dash through Mamoiada. (p187)

February

Carnevale

Highlights include the burning of an effigy of a French soldier in Alghero (p117), the sinister *mamuthones* in Mamoiada (p187), costumed displays in Ottana (p185), and the townsfolk of Bosa (p109) inspecting each other's groins.

Sa Sartiglia

Medieval capers abound at Sa Sartiglia in Oristano, with jousting, horsemen in masquerade and knightly challenges in the lead-up to Shrove Tuesday. (p92)

March

Lunissanti

The Monday after Palm Sunday, Lunissanti, is marked by heartfelt processions in the medieval hilltop centre of Castelsardo. (p135)

Settimana Santa

Holy Week in Sardinia is a big deal, with solemn processions and Passion plays all over the island. The celebrations in Alghero (p117), Castelsardo (p198), Cagliari (p54), Oliena (p198), Iglesias (p71) and Tempio Pausania (p171) are particularly evocative.

Sagra del Torrone

Forget eggs: Tonara in the Barbagia di Belvi gorges on the deliciously nutty local *torrone* (nougat) at Easter Monday's Sagra del Torrone. (p185)

April

Sagra degli Agrumi

Get juiced at Sagra degli Agrumi, a feast of oranges and lemons at Muravera's zesty Citrus Festival, which happens in mid-April. (p63)

Festa di Sant'Antioco

Costumed processions, dancing, concerts and fireworks are held over four days at the Festa di Sant'Antioco to celebrate the town's namesake patron saint. (p83)

May

Festa di Sant'Efisio

On 1 May a wooden statue of St Ephisius is paraded around Cagliari on a bullock-drawn carriage amid the colourful celebrations of Festa di Sant'Efisio. The saint is carried to Nora, from where he returns on 4 May for yet more festivities. (p54)

Cavalcata Sarda

On the second-last Sunday of May, hundreds of locals in traditional costume gather at Sassari to celebrate victory over the Saracens in AD 1000 at the Cavalcata Sarda. Horsemen charge through the streets at the parade's end. (p138)

June

Girotonno

Cooking competitions, tastings, concerts and nautical events celebrate Carloforte's *mattanza* (tuna catch) at Il Girotonno. (p80)

July

S'Ardia

In this ferocious horse race an unruly pack of horsemen race around the chapel at Sedilo. (p105)

Festa della Madonna del Naufrago

This mid-July procession takes place off the coast of Villasimius, where a submerged statue of the Virgin Mary is given a wreath of flowers in honour of shipwrecked sailors. (p64)

August

Festa di Santa Maria del Mare

Bosa's fishermen pay homage to the Virgin Mary with a river parade of boats bearing her image on the first weekend in August at this festival. (p109)

Sa Coia Maurreddina

On the first Sunday of August, Santadi's costumed townsfolk re-enact a Moorish wedding. (p78)

I Candelieri

Sassari's must-see festival, I Candelieri, takes place on 14 August. The high point is the *faradda,* when the city's nine trade guilds, parade giant votive candles through the streets. (p138)

Sagra del Redentore

Horsemen and dancers accompany Sardinia's grandest costumed parade. A torch-lit procession winds through Nuoro on 28 August and an early-morning pilgrimage to the statue of Christ the Redeemer on Monte Ortobene takes place the following day. (p182)

Festa dell'Assunta

Processions of religious fraternities, men on horseback and women in traditional costume make this mid-August festival in Orgosolo a must. (p185)

Time in Jazz

This is Berchidda's big music fest in the second week of August, with jazz jams, dance happenings and dawn concerts. (p176)

Narcao Blues Festival

Top blues and jazz performers take to the stage in a small mining village for the Narcao Blues Festival, one of Sardinia's top music events, in late August. (p78)

September

Festa di San Salvatore

At the Festa di San Salvatore, several hundred young fellows clothed in white set off from Cabras on the Corsa degli Scalzi (Barefoot Race), an 8km dash to the hamlet and sanctuary of San Salvatore. (p99)

October

Sagra delle Castagne

The mountain town of Aritzo enlivens late October with a Chestnut Fair, folk music and shows. (p189)

November

Rassegna del Vino Novello

Sniff, swirl and drink new wine at this festival held in the piazzas of Milis in early November. (p105)

December

Natale

Processions and religious events are held in the run-up to Christmas. Many churches set up elaborate cribs or nativity scenes, known as *presepi*. Fireworks displays and concerts ring in the New Year in Alghero.

Itineraries

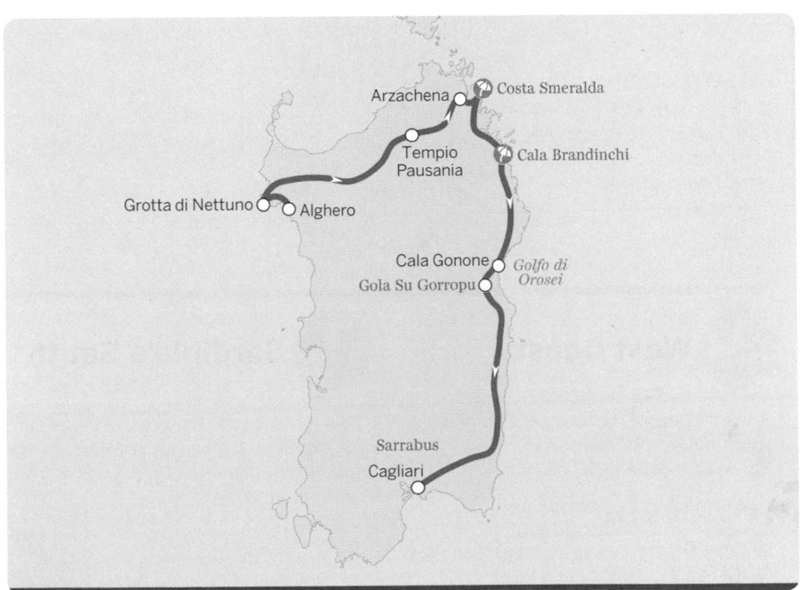

Essential Sardinia

This best-of-the-best itinerary brings together island's most seductive coastlines, culture and flavours in one easy route.

Warm up with two days in Spanish-style, sea-splashed **Alghero**, unravelling the old town and ramparts, then hop in a boat to head to the cathedral-like **Grotta di Nettuno**.

On day three, wend your way east, pausing for a slice of laid-back village life in **Tempio Pausania** and forays into prehistory at the nuraghic sites around **Arzachena**. Wake up at a rural *agriturismo* in the nearby granite mountains of Gallura, then spend a couple of days lounging on blissfully secluded coves on the **Costa Smeralda**.

Day six takes you further south, with a picnic break at the utterly sublime **Cala Brandinchi**, then continue on to the magnificent arc of the Golfo di Orosei. Base yourself in **Cala Gonone** and strike out on foot or by car to dramatic, cliff-backed bays, archaeological sites and the immense **Gola Su Gorropu**.

On day nine, swing south through the mountains of the Sarrabus to capital **Cagliari**. Devote your final day to must-see museums and strolls in the hilltop Il Castello district and Marina dining.

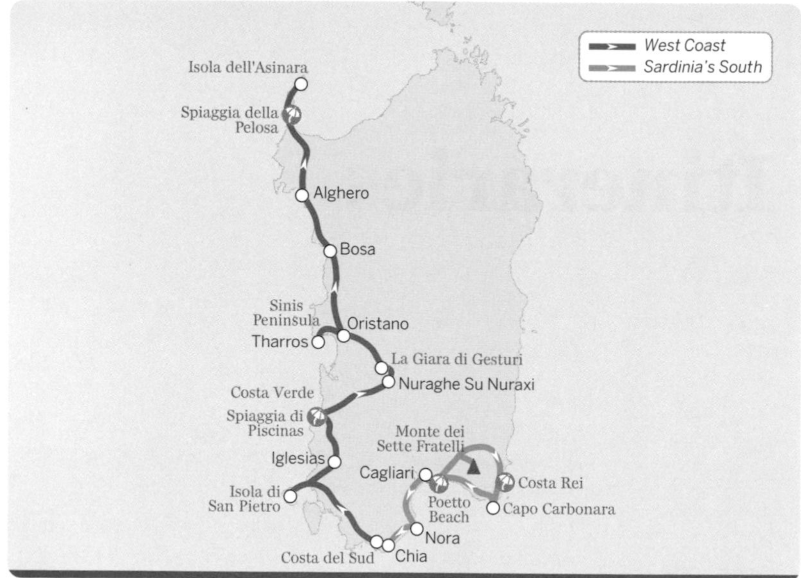

7 DAYS West Coast

A week's tour of the west coast reveals some of Sardinia's most remarkable *nuraghe* and off-the-radar beaches.

Warm up with a day lazing on the beaches of the **Costa del Sud**, or hop across to the ravishing **Isola di San Pietro** for coastal walks and a lunch of freshly caught local tuna. Head north on day two via Sardinia's mining heart, **Iglesias**, to spend a couple of days on the **Costa Verde** and its deserted beaches – barefoot dune hiking at **Spiaggia di Piscinas** is a must.

On day four, detour to the hinterland to admire the Unesco-listed, prehistoric **Nuraghe Su Nuraxi** and glimpse wild horses on the lonesome **La Giara di Gesturi** plateau. Push north on the following day to discover **Oristano** and the Phoenician ruins at **Tharros**, a short hop away on the wild **Sinis Peninsula**.

Day six takes you up to **Bosa** and its crowning-glory castle, then on a dramatic coastal drive to **Alghero** in time for dinner on the sea walls. Wind out your trip on the silky sands of **Spiaggia della Pelosa** or spotting albino donkeys on the serene **Isola dell'Asinara**.

7 DAYS Sardinia's South

This south-coast tour contrasts the buzz of the capital with the calm of the mountains and beaches, making for a perfect mix of culture and coast.

Kick off with two days in soulful **Cagliari**, wandering the steep, winding lanes of the medieval Il Castello district and lounging on **Poetto beach**. Besides checking off trophy sights like the Pisan towers, allow time simply to stroll its cafe-rimmed piazzas and boutique-lined lanes.

Day three whisks you on a serpentine coastal drive east; the landscape is splashed gold with flowering blooms in spring. Tiptoe off the map for a spell in the lushly forested heights of **Monte dei Sette Fratelli**. On day four, dive into the iridescent water of the **Capo Carbonara** marine reserve, or simply bliss out on the flour-white beaches at **Costa Rei**.

Spend your last few days swinging west of Cagliari, perhaps taking in the Phoenician ruins of **Nora** before more chilled time on the lovely pine-flanked coves of the **Costa del Sud** – **Chia** is the go-to beach for windsurfing, flamingo spotting and dune walking.

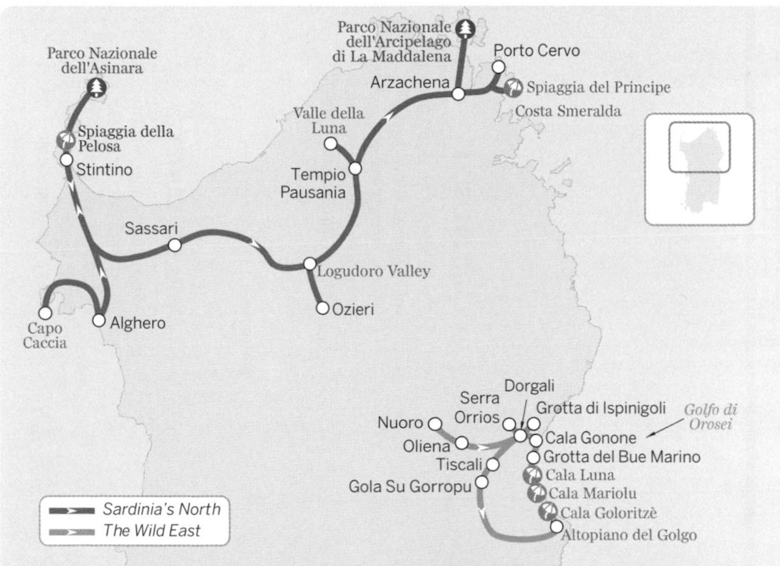

7 DAYS Sardinia's North

With a week, you can tick off some of the island's most alluring towns and beaches.

Begin with **Alghero**, a city characterised by its Catalan heritage. Take a day trip to the dramatic cliffs of **Capo Caccia**.

On day three, meander north to isolated **Stintino** and dreamy **Spiaggia della Pelosa**. Or visit the wild **Parco Nazionale dell'Asinara**. See university city **Sassari** on day four, before heading east to tour the **Logudoro Valley** and learn about the neolithic treasures of **Ozieri**.

Continue your drive northeast on the SS127 to the quaint hill town of **Tempio Pausania**, then on to the other-worldly, boulder-strewn **Valle della Luna**.

In the northeast explore the *nuraghi* (Bronze Age fortified settlements) around **Arzachena**, or squeeze in a day's island-hopping around the pristine **Parco Nazionale dell'Arcipelago di La Maddalena**. Spend your last day or two on the **Costa Smeralda**, mingling with celebs in **Porto Cervo** and beach-hopping along its cove-laced coastline to gorgeously secluded bays like **Spiaggia del Principe**.

7 DAYS The Wild East

Be seduced by Sardinia's exhilarating landscapes on this route through the wild Parco Nazionale del Golfo di Orosei e del Gennargentu.

Get set in **Nuoro**, capital of the Barbagia hill country, before heading for **Oliena** to taste its ruby-red Cannonau wine. Swing east to **Dorgali**, a fine base for visiting the **Grotta di Ispinigoli**, home to the world's second-tallest stalagmite, and the nuraghic village of **Serra Orrios**.

From Dorgali, it's a head-spinning drive down to the bay of **Cala Gonone**, where you can easily spend two days rock climbing, diving or exploring the **Golfo di Orosei** on foot or by kayak. Boat across aquamarine waters to the sea cave **Grotta del Bue Marino** and sublime bays such as **Cala Luna** and **Cala Mariolu**.

Return inland and spend two days striking out into the wilderness. Hike to the enigmatic nuraghic village of **Tiscali** and to the **Gola Su Gorropu**, a vast rock chasm. From the weird highland plateau of **Altopiano del Golgo**, further north, mule trails thread down to **Cala Goloritzè**, thrashed by astonishingly blue waters.

Off the Beaten Track: Sardinia

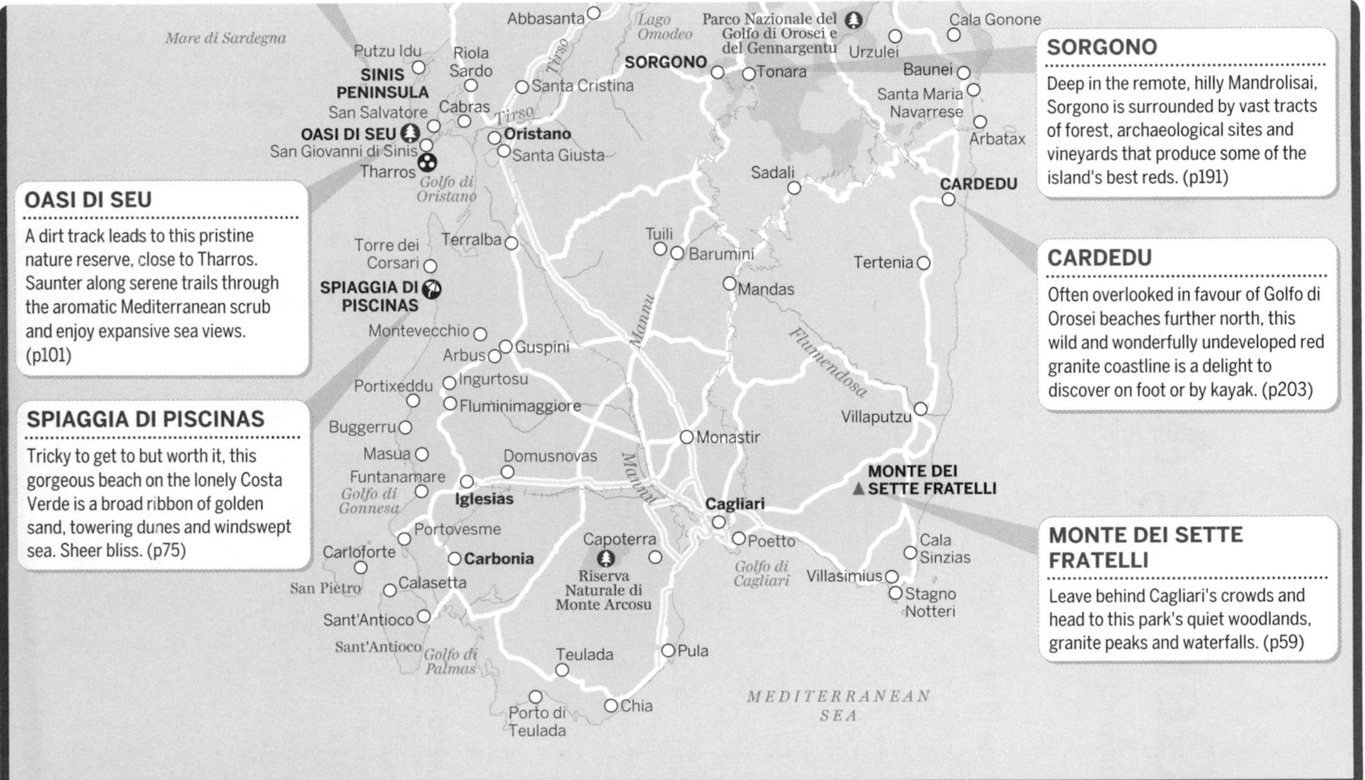

OASI DI SEU

A dirt track leads to this pristine nature reserve, close to Tharros. Saunter along serene trails through the aromatic Mediterranean scrub and enjoy expansive sea views. (p101)

SPIAGGIA DI PISCINAS

Tricky to get to but worth it, this gorgeous beach on the lonely Costa Verde is a broad ribbon of golden sand, towering dunes and windswept sea. Sheer bliss. (p75)

SORGONO

Deep in the remote, hilly Mandrolisai, Sorgono is surrounded by vast tracts of forest, archaeological sites and vineyards that produce some of the island's best reds. (p191)

CARDEDU

Often overlooked in favour of Golfo di Orosei beaches further north, this wild and wonderfully undeveloped red granite coastline is a delight to discover on foot or by kayak. (p203)

MONTE DEI SETTE FRATELLI

Leave behind Cagliari's crowds and head to this park's quiet woodlands, granite peaks and waterfalls. (p59)

Getting Around

For more information, see Transport (p266)

Travelling by Car

To fully explore Sardinia's remote beaches, archaeological sites and off-the-beaten-track wonders, you'll benefit greatly from having your own wheels.

Car Hire

Major car-rental firms have offices at Sardinia's three main airports, in Cagliari, Alghero and Olbia. You'll find downtown rental agencies in these same cities, and in provincial capitals such as Oristano, Sassari and Nuoro.

Even if your credit card company normally provides automatic LDW (loss and damage) insurance for international car rentals, it may not cover you in Sardinia; check with your provider before renting.

Driving Conditions

Fast multi-lane highways such as the SS131 make for easy travel between the island's main cities, including Cagliari, Sassari, Olbia, Oristano and Nuoro. Once you exit the *superstrada* (SS) and get onto the network of smaller *strade provinciali* (SP), things slow down considerably – especially in places such as Nuoro province, where narrow village streets and sinuous mountain roads make it challenging to average more than 50km per hour.

Main roads, even between small towns, are generally paved and reasonably well maintained, but there are plenty of places – for example, access roads to beaches – where you'll find yourself leaving the pavement behind.

RESOURCES

Automobile Club d'Italia (ACI; www.aci.it) Italy's motoring organisation. Foreigners do not have to join but instead pay a fee in case of breakdown assistance (€115 to €138, 20% more on weekends and holidays). Further charges apply if your car needs to be towed away. Check the website for details.

Touring Editore (www.touringclubstore.com) Does an excellent island map at a scale of 1:200,000. It's available online or at bookshops in Sardinia.

Tuttocittà (www.tuttocitta.it/traffico/sardegna) Online map displaying current traffic conditions all around the island.

Parking

Parking in Sardinian cities and at popular beaches can be a headache.

- Blue lines denote pay-and-display parking – buy tickets at the coin-operated meters, from tobacconists or from parking assistants.
- Rates run about €1 per hour, typically charged only between 8am and 1pm and then from 4pm to 8pm.
- White lines denote free parking and yellow lines indicate spaces reserved for drivers with specific passes.
- Some historic city centres are off-limits to unauthorised traffic during certain hours. If you slip into a ZTL (*zona a traffico limitato*, or limited traffic zone) you risk being caught on camera and fined.

No Car?

Public transport in Sardinia is reasonably priced but it can be difficult and time-consuming to use. Services slow to a trickle in the low season. In most cases buses are preferable to trains.

Bus

Azienda Regionale Sarda Trasporti (p268) operates an impressively vast network of intercity buses, with services covering much of the island. In smaller towns, service may be restricted to a bus or two per day, so unless you have unlimited time, planning an entire vacation around bus travel is impractical.

Fares for bus travel are quite reasonable; short trips cost as little as €1.30 and even multi-hour jaunts across the island rarely exceed €20.

Train

Sardinia's rail network is limited. The island's only major line, operated by Italy's national railway, runs north from Cagliari via Oristano to Ozieri-Chilivani, where it branches northeast to Olbia/Golfo Aranci and northwest to Sassari/Porto Torres. See Trenitalia (www.trenitalia.com) for timetables.

Regional operator ARST (www.arst.sardegna.it) also runs a few trains on shorter routes, including Nuoro to Macomer and Sassari to Alghero.

In summer, the tourist-oriented – and very slow – Trenino Verde (www.treninoverde.com) also operates along a few scenic routes between the coast and the interior.

Bicycle

Sardinia lends itself well to cycling. Roads are rarely busy outside of high summer and the scenery is magnificent. But bear in mind that the hilly (sometimes mountainous) terrain will take it out of you and your bike.

Bike hire (available in most resorts and towns) costs €10 to €25 per day.

DRIVING FAST FACTS

- **Right or left?** Right
- **Manual or automatic?** Manual
- **Top speed limit:** 110km/h
- **Signature car:** Fiat 500
- **Legal driving age:** 18

Road Distances (km)

	Cagliari	Oristano	Sassari	Nuoro
Oristano	94			
Sassari	217	126		
Nuoro	180	90	123	
Olbia	265	173	106	105

Plan Your Trip
Activities

Sardinia's stunning coastline and mountainous interior provide the perfect backdrop for a whole host of activities, from hiking and multi-pitch climbing to caving, road cycling and mountain biking. Offshore, pristine waters tempt kayakers, divers, surfers and kite-surfers. When it's time to unwind, virtually everyone will appreciate Sardinia's beaches, wineries and scenic train rides.

Sardinia's Best Outdoor Adventures

Cardedu Kayak (p203)

For prime perspectives on Sardinia's gorgeously rugged Ogliastra coast, paddle the shoreline on a guided kayak tour.

Cala Gonone (p191)

Swoon over sensational sea views wriggling up the steep limestone cliffs and overhangs in this climbing mecca.

Gola Su Gorropu (p199)

Don hiking boots or grab your climbing gear to explore this deep limestone ravine – one of Europe's greatest gorges.

Arcipelago di La Maddalena (p167)

With its crystal clear waters and sheltered bays, this sprinkling of beautiful islands and islets makes for some of Sardinia's finest sailing and diving.

Is Benas Surf Club (p99)

Go fly a kite and surf the waves off the white sands of Putzu Idu on the island's west coast.

On the Land

Hiking

With its lushly wooded, mountainous interior, utterly gorgeous coastline and extensive network of trails, Sardinia is fabulous hiking country. There is a huge variety of routes, from tough mountain tracks to cliff-hugging coastal paths, and whatever your level of fitness you'll find something to suit. Only by hitting the trail can you appreciate how big, wild and boundlessly beautiful Sardinia really is.

Halfway up the east coast, the Parco Nazionale del Golfo di Orosei e del Gennargentu (p191) offers terrific walking, with trails threading precariously along clifftops that plunge to seas of bluest blue and a truly rugged hinterland. Justifiably popular half-day hikes head deep into the mighty gorge of Gola Su Gorropu (p199) and up to the ruined prehistoric village of Tiscali (p200) in the twilight of the limestone overhang. For something more hard-core and coastal, the seven-day Selvaggio Blu (p192) is a once-in-a-lifetime hike for the experienced, involving some scrambling, abseiling and navigational skills. It's often hailed as Europe's toughest trek.

Further north, there's great walking on the pine-clad summit of Monte Limbara (p171) (1359m), near Tempio Pausania, and through Gallura's other-worldly, wind-licked granite rockscapes – Capo Testa (p162), for instance. Near Alghero, Le Prigionette Nature Reserve (p128) is a fine choice for coastal walks, with its rocky shoreline, woodlands and abundant wildlife.

To the south, you can hike through the empty, verdant countryside around Montiferru (1050m) and on La Giara di Gesturi (p88), a huge table-top plateau where wild horses roam.

For a gentle coastal ramble, and the chance to spot Eleonora's falcons, head to lighthouse-topped Capo Sandalo (p81) on the serene Isola di San Pietro.

Climbing

With its vertiginous coastline and marvellously craggy interior, Sardinia is climbing heaven, whether multi-pitch, bouldering or Deep Water Soloing (DWS) is your bag. The island is bolted with some 4000 sport and 1000 multi-pitch routes, which teeter up rock faces of granite, limestone and basalt.

Bring your own rope, a head for heights, and a copy of Maurizio Oviglia's definitive *Pietra di Luna* climbing guide (the website www.pietradiluna.com also provides a useful overview).

Other handy resources including the websites Climb Europe (www.climb-europe.com) and www.sardiniaclimb.com will give you a head start. For courses and camps, check out Climbing Sardinia (www.climbingsardinia.com).

Climbing hot spots include Cala Gonone and Ulassai in the east, Capo Caccia in the northwest, and Domusnovas in the southwest.

GUIDED HIKES

Sardinia is peppered with footpaths but routes are often unmarked and tricky to navigate solo. If you're wary about striking out alone, consider taking a guided walk with a local hiking cooperative; a half-day hike will typically set you back around €40 to €50.

Reputable companies include Cooperative Ghivine (p201), based in Dorgali, which offers day hikes (Tiscali and Gola Su Gorropu) as well as multi-day itineraries in the Supramonte. If you're serious about tackling the Selvaggio Blu (p192), you could enlist the services of one of the island's best – guide and pro climber Corrado Conca (p192), who really knows his stuff.

Cycling

Big skies, sea breezes and your bum in a saddle – ah, there's no better way to escape the crowds, blitz the back roads and see the real Sardinia, say cyclists.

Road cycling is big here, especially in the spring and autumn when traffic thins, the island bursts into bloom and temperatures are pleasantly mild. On the hot list for road cyclists, the SS125 provides a challenging ride as it corkscrews through rugged mountain country between Dorgali and Santa Maria Navarrese. Over on the west coast, take to the spectacular coastal road that runs south of Alghero to Bosa.

If mountain biking is more your scene, test your mettle on the remote peaks of the Ogliastra where hurtling descents plunge to the glistening Med. There are stacks of wonderful backcountry, cross-country and single track options for those willing to climb a little. Some head through beautiful forgotten forests of holm oak and pine; others zip along old mule tracks once plied by the island's shepherds and charcoal burners.

Cycling is also a laid-back way of exploring Sardinia's offshore islands, including the Isola di San Pietro and the uninhabited Isola dell'Asinara.

Useful cycling websites include Bike Tour Sardinia (www.biketoursardinia.com) and Sardinia Cycling (www.sardiniacycling.com).

Horse Riding

Sardinia has some fine horse-riding opportunities. The island's biggest equestrian centre is the Horse Country Resort (p214) near Arborea, which offers an extensive range of riding packages. Alternatively you can explore the verdant Isola Caprera on horseback, or the glorious coast around San Teodoro on a beach hack with Maneggio La Cinta (p154).

Expect to pay around €35 for a 1½ hour hack.

On the Water

Windsurfing

Windsurfers from across Europe flock to Porto Pollo (p170), on Sardinia's northeastern coast, to pit themselves against the fierce winds that whistle through the channel between Sardinia and Corsica. Beginners can also try their hand here in the safe, sheltered bay waters.

Other windsurfing hot spots include the beautiful Spiaggia della Pelosa (p130) on the northwestern coast, the protected waters of Spiaggia Mugoni (p129) near Alghero, San Teodoro (p153) on the northeast coast, the Sinis Peninsula (p98) in the west and Cagliari's Poetto beach (p45).

You'll find windsurf centres across the island offering rig hire and lessons for all levels – bank on up to €20 per hour for rentals and about €160 for a two-day course.

Kitesurfing

Thanks to the stiff winds that pummel the more exposed coastlines of the island, Sardinia offers world-class kitesurfing that is way up there among Italy's best. Various schools cater to newbies and hardened vets. If you're keen to go fly a kite, make your way west to the lovely white-sand strand of Putzu Idu on the remote Sinis Peninsula. Is Benas Surf Club (p99) makes the most of those fabulous waves here. In September the region hosts the **Open Water Challenge Oristano** (www.eolowindsurf.com), a three-day kitesurfing, windsurfing and SUP event.

Another hot area for kitesurfing is Porto Pollo at the island's northern tip, where there are consistent winds and dazzling views out across the azure Strait of Bonifacio and over to Corsica. Pro Center MB (p170) offers rentals and courses, as does Sporting Club Sardinia (p170). Edging east, San Teodoro is another fine spot to launch a kite – the kite school Wet Dreams (p154) makes it happen. In September, it hosts the Extreme Fun Games (p154).

ALTERNATIVE ACTIVITIES

Ready for a change of pace? Beyond Sardinia's plethora of adrenaline-packed adventure sports, you'll find a slew of more sedentary pursuits.

Wine-Tasting

Sardinia is renowned for its Cannonau reds, Vermentino whites and sweet Malvasia and Vernaccia wines, which can be tasted at the source in wineries and tasting rooms all over the island. Wine-tasting hot spots include Bosa in the west, Jerzu and Sorgono in Nuoro province, Serdiana and Santadi in the south, the Riviera del Corallo in the northwest and the Gallura region in northeastern Sardinia.

Boat Tours

Kick back and enjoy Sardinia's magnificent coastal scenery in between bouts of dolphin-watching, snorkeling and/or swimming on an organised boat trip. Operators all around the island offer day excursions, often with lunch and drinks included in the ticket price. Prime destinations include the Blue Crescent (from Cala Gonone), the islands of the Maddalena archipelago (from Palau, Poltu Quatu or La Maddalena) and Capo Caccia (from Alghero).

The Trenino Verde Tourist Train

If you're not in a rush, one of the best ways of exploring Sardinia's interior is on the Trenino Verde, a slow, narrow-gauge train that runs through some of the island's most inhospitable countryside, stopping at isolated rural villages en route. As a means of public transport, it's of limited use – it's extremely slow – but it's an excellent way of glimpsing corners of the island that you otherwise probably wouldn't see.

Between mid-June and early September, the Trenino Verde operates multiple lines in various parts of the island. See www.treninoverde.com for full route and price details.

Surfing

Sardinia's position means that it gets small- to medium-sized waves throughout the year, particularly on the west coast where swells sweep in from the Med. Winter is the best time but there's also reliable action in spring and autumn.

Committed surfers should make a beeline for the Sinis Peninsula northwest of Oristano, where waves can reach 4m around the wild Capo Mannu. Elsewhere, there's action on the beaches around Chia, and at Buggerru and Masua on the Iglesiente coast. In the north, Porto Ferro, a small bay north of Alghero, is popular with local surfers.

Board rentals go for around €20 per day.

Diving

One look at Sardinia's azure waters, among the clearest in the Mediterranean, and divers are itching to take to the deep to investigate hidden grottoes and sunken wrecks. Caves, gorges and cliffs give way to an underwater Eden full of coral and sunken ruins. Tuna, barracuda, groupers, and even turtles, dolphins and (harmless) sharks can sometimes be spotted.

Some of the best diving is off Sardinia's rocky islands, such as the Isola di San Pietro in the southwest, Isola Tavolara in the northeast, and the protected waters of Arcipelago di La Maddalena in the north.

There are plenty of schools offering courses and guided dives for all levels from April to October. Expect to pay roughly €40 for a single tank dive, €420 for a PADI open-water course and €20 per day for equipment hire.

Sailing

Sailing Sardinia's crystal-clear seas is a classic summer holiday experience. Pick up a boat in Carloforte and set sail for the secluded coves of the Isola di San Pietro, or head north to the granite isles and protected, marine-life-rich waters of the Parco Nazionale dell'Arcipelago di La Maddalena (p167). Sailing is also the best, and sometimes the only, way of getting to the otherwise off-the-radar bays and coves of the shimmering Blue Crescent, the magnificent stretch of coastline south of Cala Gonone.

For lessons, the Sporting Club Sardinia (p170) in Porto Pollo offers a range of courses, as does the Club della Vela (p129) near Alghero. Reckon on from €250 for a basic five-lesson sailing course. To charter a sailing boat, you'll be looking at around €1500 per week, while it should cost between €100 and €150 to hire a lightweight rubber boat *(gommone)* for a day.

A reliable, up-to-date source of information is Sailing Sardinia (www.sailing sardinia.it), which has links to individual charter companies.

BEST BEACHES

A magnet for summer sun-seekers, Sardinia's beaches are among the finest in the Med.

Chia (p84) Windsurfers, dune walkers and flamingo-seeking birdwatchers all rave about Chia's sandy beaches, sheltered by aromatic juniper bushes.

Cala Goloritzè (p196) Descend an old mule trail through a cleft in the Supramonte highlands to discover the soaring limestone pinnacles and Curacao-blue waters of this astonishingly lovely beach.

Spiaggia della Pelosa (p130) This heavenly frost-white strip of sand fringed by electric-blue waters is backed by a Spanish watchtower atop a craggy islet.

Spiaggia di Piscinas (p75) Walking barefoot across the 30m-high sand dunes that frame this wild, remote beach is a magical sunset experience.

Kayaking

Few experiences in Sardinia beat paddling in quiet exhilaration to hidden coves at your own speed. In the island's east, Cala Gonone makes a cracking base for sea kayakers keen to strike out along the cove-dotted Golfo di Orosei; Prima Sardegna (p193) rent out kayaks. Alternatively, venture slightly south to Cardedu to take in the dramatic sea stacks and coves of the Ogliastra coast with Cardedu Kayak (p203). It arranges excursions and rents out equipment should you prefer to go it alone.

Kayak rental costs around €25 per day.

Plan Your Trip

Travel with Children

Ah, bambini! The Sardinians just love them, so expect pinched cheeks, ruffled hair and warm welcomes galore. And with the island's easygoing nature, gently shelving beaches, caves to explore and prehistoric mysteries straight out of a picture book, travelling here with kids in tow is child's play.

Best Regions for Kids

Eastern Sardinia

Cave exploring, climbing, biking and all kinds of activities for older kids and teens, plus family-friendly campgrounds.

Northeastern Sardinia

Excellent beaches with entertainment for kids, wildlife excursions, gentle hiking and dolphin-spotting boat trips.

Northwestern Sardinia

Fantastic child-friendly beaches for all ages, nature parks, fascinating caves and wildlife-watching and an array of water sports for older kids and teens.

Southeastern Sardinia

A long town beach, dizzying tower climbing in the historic centre, fun shops and the wonderful *trenino verde* train ride in the countryside.

Southwestern Sardinia

Cavallini (mini-horses) roaming on the mountain plateau of La Giara di Gesturi, excellent beaches, eerie mines and wondrous caves.

Western Sardinia

Water-sport-heavy beaches for teens, sandy beaches for tots and beautiful bird life for all ages.

Sardinia for Kids

Like all of Italy, Sardinia is wonderful for kids of all ages. Babies and toddlers are cooed over everywhere, while older kids and teenagers can unleash their energy with a host of outdoor activities – from horse riding on the beach to learning to dive and snorkel, kayaking to climbing, wildlife spotting to coastal hiking. Most resorts have tree-fringed promenades suitable for buggies, as well as playgrounds and gelaterie.

Wherever you base yourself, discounts are available for children on public transport and for admission to sights.

Children's Highlights

Beach Fun

Sinis Peninsula (p98) Long sandy beaches and tiny pebble beaches, perfect for toddlers.

Cala Gonone (p191) Low-key family-oriented resort, with a pine-fringed *lungomare* (seafront promenade), a shady campground and several playgrounds.

Costa del Sud (p84) Stretches of sand and shallow, limpid waters along Sardinia's southwest coast.

Cala Battistoni, Baia Sardinia (p158) Hair-raising rides and water madness, plus fine sandy beaches.

Riviera del Corallo, Alghero (p125) Greenery, umbrellas, sunloungers and kids' play areas.

Costa Verde (p75) Gorgeous, dune-backed beaches off the beaten track. Not many facilities but plenty of space to run around.

Energy Burners

Cardedu Kayak (p203) Kayaking and nautical camping on a remarkable stretch of red granite coast.

Horse Country Resort (p214) This huge horse-riding resort in Arborea offers lessons and treks along the beach or through pine woods.

Golfo di Orosei (p191) Canoeing, biking, caving, diving and canyoning, all great for teens.

Palau and Porto Pollo (p165) These north-coast neighbours offer water sports galore – from windsurfing and kayaking to kids' diving courses.

Laguna di Nora (p85) Canoe expeditions and basic snorkelling.

Capo Carbonara & Villasimius (p64) Shallow water and sandy beaches for play and snorkelling.

Nature & Wildlife Encounters

Sinis Peninsula (p98) Salt lakes and pink flamingos in spring.

Parco Nazionale dell'Asinara (p130) Albino donkeys steal the show at this wildly beautiful national park in the north.

Parco Naturale Regionale Molentargius (p54) Protected reed-fringed wetlands with abundant bird life – flamingos, herons and little egrets.

Stagno S'Ena Arrubia (p97) Keep binoculars handy to spot flamingos, herons, coots and ospreys.

La Giara di Gesturi (p88) Try to spy the shy miniature wild horses that roam this tabletop plateau.

Capo Carbonara (p64) A marine reserve with flamingo-filled lagoons and boat trips to the islands.

Riserva Naturale di Monte Arcosu (p77) A WWF reserve home to wild boar, martens, wildcats, weasels and birds of prey.

Rock Stars & Cave Capers

Roccia dell'Orso, Palau (p165) Wind-blasted granite formation in the shape of a bear.

Grotta di Nettuno, Capo Caccia (p128) Count the 656 steps to the bottom of this glittering, cathedral-like cave.

Le Grotte Is Zuddas, Santadi (p78) Marvel at helictites in this spectacular cave system.

Roccia dell'Elefante, Castelsardo (p135) Seen the bear rock? Go check out the elephant.

Grotta di Ispinigoli, Dorgali (p200) Underground fairyland of stalagmites, including the world's second tallest.

Planning

When to Go

- The best time to visit Sardinia with children is from April to June and in September, when the weather is mild, accommodation is plentiful and crowds are fewer.
- In July and August, temperatures soar, prices sky-rocket and tourist numbers swell.
- If you are tied to school holiday dates, check out alternatives to the packed coastal resorts.

Where to Stay

- Coastal resorts are well geared towards families. Hotels and camp sites often have pools, kids' clubs organising activities and special children's menus.
- Apartment rentals are often a good bet, too, providing space and freedom – and they often work out cheaper than hotels.
- *Agriturismi* (farm stays) are great for giving the masses the slip; here you'll find space for the kids to play freely, farm animals, trails to explore and a genuinely warm welcome.
- Book in advance whenever possible, and be sure to ask about the hotel's kid policy – many places will squeeze in a cot for free or an extra bed for a nominal charge.

What to Pack

- Most airlines allow you to carry on a collapsible pushchair for no extra charge.

FOOD, GLORIOUS FOOD

Eating out with the kids is pretty stress-free in Sardinia, where *bambini* are made very welcome. There are few taboos about taking children to restaurants, even if locals with little ones in tow stick to the more popular trattorias – you'll seldom see children in an expensive restaurant.

➡ Even if there is no children's menus, most places will cheerfully tailor a dish to appeal and serve a *mezzo porzione* (half portion).

➡ Very few restaurants have *seggioloni* (high chairs), so bring a fabric add-on or stick your wiggly toddler on your knee and hope for the best.

➡ Baby-changing facilities are few and far between, though the staff will usually find a space for you (sometimes rolling a tray table into the toilets for you!).

➡ Food-wise, most kids are in heaven. Spaghetti, pizza and ice cream abound, as do Sardinian takes on pasta like ravioli-style *culurgiones*.

➡ For additional items such as booster seats and travel cots, they often levy a fee of around £10 to £20 per flight.

➡ You can take baby food, milk and sterilised water in your hand lugguage.

Baby Essentials

➡ Baby formula, disposable nappies (diapers; *pannolini*) and sterilising solutions are widely available at *farmacie* and supermarkets.

➡ Fresh cow's milk is sold in litre and half-litre cartons in supermarkets, *alimentari* (food shops) and in some bars. Carry an emergency carton of *lunga conservazione* (UHT).

Car Hire

➡ It is possible to hire car seats for infants and children (usually for a daily fee) from most car-rental firms, but book them well in advance.

➡ Most compact cars are short on space, so you may struggle to squeeze in your luggage and pushchair in the boot.

➡ Check the car's dimensions before booking or consider upgrading to a bigger model.

Getting Around

➡ Under-fours generally travel for free on trains and ferries, but without the right to a seat or cabin berth; for children between four and 12, discounts of 50% are usually applied.

➡ Sardinian trains are seldom busy, but in high season it's advisable to book seats.

➡ Note that coastal and mountain roads can be very curvy and travel sickness is a serious prospect, so be prepared.

➡ Kids love the Trenino Verde (p268), a narrow-gauge train that chugs through some of Sardinia's most spectacular and inaccessible countryside.

Resources

➡ Lonely Planet's *Travel with Children* is packed with practical tips, while the *Kids' Travel Guide – Italy*, published by FlyingKids, is a fun take on the country.

➡ Lots of general advice, though nothing specific to Sardinia, can be found at www.travelwithyourkids.com.

➡ Tots Too (www.totstoo.com) is an online agency specialising in upmarket, kid-friendly properties.

Regions at a Glance

Sardinia may be an island, but it sure is a big one. Even with your own wheels you may be surprised how long it can take to get from A to B, so careful route planning helps.

The capital, Cagliari, strikes perfect balance with its blend of culture and coast. Swinging southwest brings you to the Costa del Sud, the dune-dotted Costa Verde, and verdant countryside with must-see *nuraghi* (Bronze Age fortified settlements). The northwest seduces with Spanish soul in Alghero, as well as shimmering white beaches and grottoes. Hop over to the island's northeast for celebrity glamour on the gorgeous, cove-speckled Costa Smeralda and to tour Gallura's granite heartland. In the mountainous east, the cliffs, peaks and the bluest of seas will have you itching to climb, hike, cycle and kayak.

Cagliari & the Sarrabus

Culture
Food
Outdoors

Medieval Palazzi

Nothing says Cagliari like the medieval Il Castello citadel, with its grandstand views, Pisan towers and pastel-fronted *palazzi*. Rococo churches, a Roman amphitheatre and a stellar archaeological museum reveal the island's past.

Shellfish & Sweets

Enjoy fresh fish in Marina's buzzing restaurants, al fresco shellfish on Poetto beach, Sardinian sweets at pavement cafes and award-winning wines in Serdiana.

Coastal Adventures

A coastal road threads through to the 6km sands of Poetto beach. The fine beaches, crystal-clear waters and cape diving around Villasimius entice further east.

p40

Iglesias & the Southwest

History
Beaches
Islands

Time Travel

Revisit the Bronze Age at Unesco-listed Nuraghe Su Nuraxi, explore Phoenician and Roman history by diving to Nora's submerged ruins, and tour the *domus de janas* (fairy houses) at Necropolis del Montessu.

Hidden Coastlines

This swathe of coastline is wildly beautiful: from the Costa Verde's 30m-high dunes to the silky beaches of the Costa del Sud – and not least the gorgeous Spiaggia della Piscinas.

Island-Hopping

On Isola di San Pietro, gaze at Eleonora's falcons at Cala Fico and explore *palazzi*-dotted Carloforte. Sardinia's great seafaring past is evoked in Phoenician ruins studded along Isola di Sant'Antioco.

p66

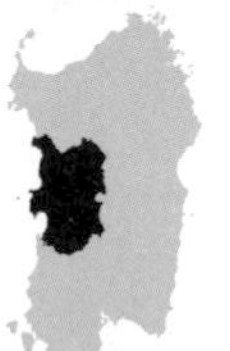

Oristano & the West

Beaches
Food
Outdoors

Beautiful Bays

Flour-white beaches and bluer-than-blue water: few coastlines are as compelling as the Sinis Peninsula. Escape the world on Is Aruttas' bleached sands or on Isola di Mal di Ventre (Stomach Ache Island).

Local Flavours

Cabras for the *bottarga* (mullet roe), Seneghe for its olive oil and *bue rosso* beef, Milis for its sweet oranges, the vineyards for crisp Vernaccia wines – Sardinia's west is foodie heaven.

Summits & Surf

On this western swathe of the island, clamber up volcanic Montiferru, surf Putzu Idu and trot through Arborea's flatlands and pine woods on horseback. The lagoons teem with bird life, from herons to flamingos.

p91

Alghero & the Northwest

History
Coast
Outdoors

Catalan Culture

Long part of Catalonia, Alghero radiates a Spanish air, its honey-coloured sea walls enclosing cobbled lanes and Gothic *palazzi*.

Natural Wonders

The coastal road weaves around to broad bays and Capo Caccia, where cliffs plunge to the fairy-tale Grotta di Nettuno. Go north to Spiaggia della Pelosa, a gorgeous lick of white sand.

Unique Wildlife

Grab your binoculars and head to Isola dell'Asinara to spot *asini bianchi* (albino donkeys), silky-haired mouflon and falcons; Bosco di Monte Lerno to spy Giara horses; and Le Prigionette Nature Reserve's forests for a Noah's Ark of wildlife.

p111

Olbia, the Costa Smeralda & Gallura

High Life
Coast
Interior

Celebrity Sands

The Costa Smeralda is the place to daydream about a billionaire's lifestyle as you float in an emerald sea past palatial villas. Porto Cervo and Porto Rotondo are celeb-spotting central.

Crystal Waters

The Costa Smeralda is scalloped with beautiful coves and fjordlike inlets. Beach-hop south to San Teodoro's frost-white beaches, or north to the ravishing Arcipelago di La Maddalena.

Vineyards & Hill Towns

Gallura's rugged interior is a staggering contrast to the coast. Weave through thick woods and vineyards to hill towns such as San Pantaleo, Tempio Pausania and Aggius.

p145

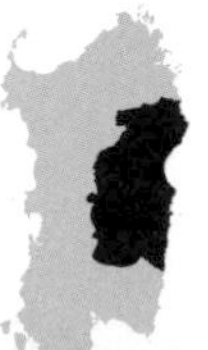

Nuoro & the East

Outdoors
Coast
Mountains

Cliffs & Canyons

This is hiking and climbing paradise. Cala Gonone's cliffs are a must-climb, while hikers won't want to miss a trek deep into the cavernous Gola Su Gorropu canyon and the nuraghic enigma of Tiscali.

Dazzling Coves

Half-moon Cala Luna, breathtaking Cala Goloritzè – everyone has their favourite Golfo di Orosei cove. The dreamiest bays are best discovered on foot, or by boat or kayak.

Peak Performance

In the remote interior, brooding mountains rear above deep valleys, forests and stuck-in-time villages. A helter-skelter of roads leads you to the Gennargentu's lofty peaks and Barbagia's wilds.

p177

On the Road

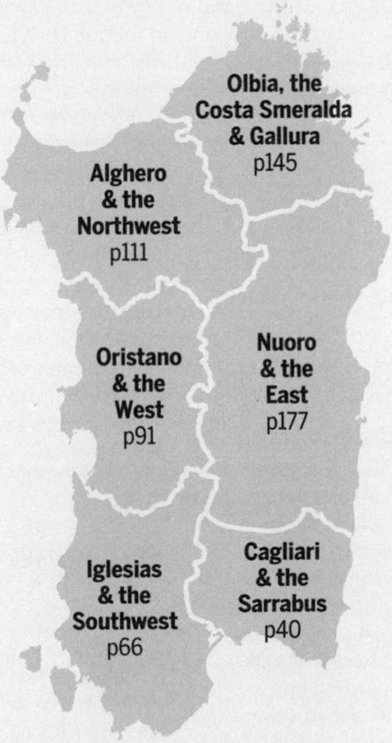

Olbia, the Costa Smeralda & Gallura
p145

Alghero & the Northwest
p111

Oristano & the West
p91

Nuoro & the East
p177

Iglesias & the Southwest
p66

Cagliari & the Sarrabus
p40

Cagliari & the Sarrabus

Includes ➡

Best Places to Eat

- ➡ Luigi Pomata (p58)
- ➡ Dal Corsaro (p59)
- ➡ Per Bacco (p58)
- ➡ La Pola (p55)
- ➡ Martinelli's (p58)

Best Places to Sleep

- ➡ Hotel Miramare (p209)
- ➡ Hotel Nautilus (p209)
- ➡ Il Cagliarese (p208)
- ➡ Hotel Mariposas (p210)

Why Go?

From urban clamour and cultural gems to wild, inhospitable mountains and thrilling coastlines, Sardinia's southeast makes for a wonderful introduction to the island.

The main gateway is Cagliari, Sardinia's largest city. Cultured and cosmopolitan, the island's historic capital is a joy to explore with its bristling waterfront, colourful alleyways and formidable hilltop citadel. Its museums, galleries and baroque churches are among Sardinia's best, harbouring innumerable treasures. Yet for all its riches, Cagliari remains a busy working port and a trip here is as much about the simple pleasures as sightseeing: seafood dinners in neighbourhood trattorias, people-watching at pavement cafes, strolling through medieval alleyways.

East of Cagliari, the landscape becomes increasingly wild as urban sprawl gives way to the verdant, wooded mountains of the Sarrabus. This great unspoilt wilderness boasts inspiring scenery and magnificent white beaches at Villasimius and the Costa Rei, two of the area's most popular summer destinations.

When to Go

- ➡ Summer sees an annual influx of visitors heading for the area's glorious beaches. Resorts such as Villasimius and the Costa Rei are at their busiest, particularly in August when many Italian families take their holidays.
- ➡ Cagliari is at its best in spring and early autumn when it's still pleasantly warm but not so hot that sightseeing becomes hard physical labour.
- ➡ The first few days of May means party time in Cagliari as thousands take to the streets to partake in the city's great annual celebration.
- ➡ For the best hiking conditions in the Sarrabus, spring and early autumn are generally the best times.

CAGLIARI

☎070 / POP 154,460

Forget flying: the best way to arrive in Sardinia's historic capital is by sea, the city rising in a helter-skelter of golden-hued *palazzi,* domes and facades up to the rocky centrepiece, Il Castello. Although Tunisia is closer than Rome, Cagliari is the most Italian of Sardinia's cities. Vespas buzz down tree-fringed boulevards and locals hang out at busy cafes tucked under arcades in the seafront Marina district.

Like many Italian cities, Cagliari wears its history on its sleeve and everywhere you go you come across traces of its rich past: ancient Roman ruins, museums filled with prehistoric artefacts, centuries-old churches and elegant *palazzi.*

Edging east of town brings you to Poetto beach, the hub of summer life with its limpid blue waters and upbeat party scene.

History

The Phoenicians established themselves in the area in the 8th century BC, but it wasn't until the Carthaginians took control of what they called Karel or Karalis (meaning 'rocky place') around 520 BC that a town began to emerge.

It remained a Carthaginian stronghold until the Romans occupied it in the First Punic War (218–201 BC). Julius Caesar later declared it a full Roman municipality in 46 BC, paving the way for a golden age as a prosperous port. But with the eclipse of Roman power came more turbulent times.

Vandals operating out of North Africa stormed into the city in AD 455, only to be unseated by the Byzantine Empire in 533. By the 11th century, weakening Byzantine influence (accentuated by repeated Arab raids) led Cagliari and the other districts to become virtually autonomous.

In 1258 the Pisans took the town, fortified the Castello area and replaced the local population with Pisans. A similar fate awaited them when the Catalano-Aragonese took over in 1326. The Black Death swept through in 1348, with frequent repeat outbreaks in the succeeding decades.

With Spain unified at the end of the 15th century, the Catalans were subordinated to the Spaniards. Cagliari fared better than most of the island under Spanish inertia, and in 1620 the city's university opened its doors.

The dukes of Savoy (who in 1720 became kings of Sardinia) followed the Spanish precedent in keeping Cagliari as the viceregal seat, and it endured several anxious events (such as the 1794 anti-Savoy riots). From 1799 to 1814 the royal family, forced

CAGLIARI IN...

Two Days

Get off to an uplifting start by summitting the **Torre dell'Elefante** (p44) and enjoying fabulous city views. Suitably inspired, follow the narrow, twisting lanes of the **Castello district** (p43) up to the **Cattedrale di Santa Maria** (p44). In the afternoon, bone up on Sardinia's prehistoric past at the **Museo Archeologico Nazionale** (p43) before seeing out the day over cocktails at the **Caffè Libarium Nostrum** (p59).

On day two, breakfast at **Antico Caffè** (p59) before heading up to the **Galleria Comunale d'Arte** (p44) for a blast of modern art. Afterwards, clear your head in the green confines of the **Orto Botanico** (p47). Lunch on seafood in the Marina district, perhaps at **Antica Cagliari** (p58), and spend the afternoon mooching around the shops on Via Giuseppe Garibaldi and Via Sulcis. Round things off with an al fresco aperitif on **Piazza Yenne** (p46).

Four Days

Rise early on day three and stock up on picnic goodies at the **Mercato di San Benedetto** (p61). Then head out to **Poetto beach** (p45) for a day of sunbathing, swimming and windsurfing.

On day four, take a day trip, choosing between the pristine beaches of Villasimius (p64) or a visit to the **Cantine Argiolas** (p62), one of Sardinia's top wineries in Serdiana. Alternatively, strap on your walking boots for some hiking in the wooded mountains around **Monte dei Sette Fratelli** (p59).

Cagliari & the Sarrabus Highlights

❶ **Il Castello** (p43) Exploring the nooks and crannies of Cagliari's medieval citadel.

❷ **Cala Giunco** (p64) Gazing at a vision of near beach perfection near Capo Carbonara, Sardinia's most southeasterly point.

❸ **Monte dei Sette Fratelli** (p59) Hiking the thickly wooded mountains at the heart of the remote Sarrabus district.

❹ **Museo Archeologico Nazionale** (p43) Coming face-to-face with prehistoric giants at Cagliari's artefact-packed archaeology museum.

❺ **Caffè Libarium Nostrum** (p59) Admiring sweeping panoramas as you sip cocktails at this hilltop cafe.

❻ **Cantine Argiolas** (p62) Sampling the pick of the region's wines during a cookery class at this famous Serdiana winery.

❼ **Festa di Sant'Efisio** (p54) Joining the crowds to watch costumed processions parade through Cagliari during its great annual festival.

❽ **Poetto Beach** (p45) Sunbathing by day and partying at night on Cagliari's fabulous beach.

out of Piedmont by Napoleon, spent time in Cagliari protected by the British Royal Navy.

Cagliari continued to develop slowly throughout the 19th and 20th centuries. Parts of the city walls were destroyed and the city expanded as the population grew. Heavily bombed in WWII, Cagliari was awarded a medal for bravery in 1948.

Reconstruction commenced shortly after the end of the war and was partly complete by the time Cagliari was declared capital of the semi-autonomous region of Sardinia in the new Italian republic in 1949. A good deal of Sardinia's modern industry, especially petrochemicals, has since developed around the lagoons and along the coast as far as Sarroch in the southwest.

Sights

Cagliari's key sights are concentrated in four central districts: Il Castello, Stampace, Marina and Villanova. The obvious starting point is the hilltop Castello area (p43), home to a group of fine museums at the Cittadella dei Musei (p50) and affording terrific views of the city's skyline.

To the west, high up the hill, is **Stampace**, where most of the action spirals around Piazza Yenne (p46). Elsewhere in this district you'll find a number of important churches, a botanical garden and Cagliari's rocky Roman amphitheatre.

Stampace was Cagliari's medieval working-class district, home to the city's impoverished Sards, who lived huddled in the shadow of the mighty castle. In the 14th century, when the Aragonese were in charge, the Sards were forbidden to enter the castle after nightfall. If caught they were thrown off the castle walls, with the benediction *stai in pace* (rest in peace), a phrase that over time gave rise to the neighbourhood's name, Stampace.

Bordered by Largo Carlo Felice to the west and seafront Via Roma, the characterful **Marina district** is a joy to explore on foot, not so much for its sights, of which there are few, but for the atmosphere of its dark, narrow lanes crammed with artisanal shops, cafes and trattorias.

Extending east of Marina, the 19th-century **Villanova district** boasts some of the city's most picturesque streets – the area around Piazza San Domenico is particularly alluring – as well as wide traffic-clogged roads and imposing piazzas. Its star sight is the hard-to-miss Santuario & Basilica di Nostra Signora di Bonaria (p45).

★Il Castello AREA

(Map p52) This hilltop citadel is Cagliari's most iconic image, its domes, towers and *palazzi,* once home to the city's aristocracy, rising above the sturdy ramparts built by the Pisans and Aragonese. Inside the battlements, the old medieval city reveals itself like Pandora's box. The university, cathedral, museums and Pisan palaces are wedged into a jigsaw of narrow high-walled alleys. Sleepy though it may seem, the area harbours a number of boutiques, bars and cafes popular with visitors, students and hipsters.

The neighbourhood is known to locals as Su Casteddu, a term also used to describe the whole city. The walls are best admired (and photographed) from afar – good spots include the Roman amphitheatre across the valley to the northwest and Bonaria to the southeast.

★Museo Archeologico Nazionale MUSEUM

(Map p48; ☎070 6051 8245; http://museoarcheocagliari.beniculturali.it; Piazza Arsenale; adult/reduced €5/2.50, incl Pinacoteca Nazionale €7/3.50; ⏰9am-8pm Tue-Sun) Of the four museums at the Cittadella dei Musei (p50), this is the undoubted star. Sardinia's premier archaeological museum showcases artefacts spanning thousands of years of history, from the early neolithic, through the Bronze and Iron Ages to the Phoenician and Roman eras. Highlights include a series of colossal figures known as the Giganti di Monte Prama and a superb collection of *bronzetti* (bronze figurines), which, in the absence of any written records, are a vital source of information about Sardinia's mysterious nuraghic culture.

In all about 400 nuraghic bronzes have been discovered, many in sites of religious importance, leading scholars to conclude that they were probably used as votive offerings. Depicting tribal chiefs, warriors, hunters, mothers and animals, the pint-sized figurines are stylistically crude but remarkably effective.

Just as the Giganti di Monte Prama are. These 2m-high sculptures, on the 3rd floor, are the only nuraghic stone statues to have been discovered in Sardinia, and among the oldest examples of their type in the Mediterranean. Dating to the 8th and 9th centuries BC, they all represent men, mainly as boxers, archers or wrestlers. More are on display in the Museo Civico in Cabras near where they were originally unearthed.

The ground floor provides a chronological history of the island from the neolithic age through to the early Middle Ages. Its fine stash of finds includes pre-nuraghic stone implements and obsidian tools, rudimentary ceramics and funny round fertility goddesses. You'll also find a model *tophet* (sacred Phoenician or Carthaginian burial ground for children and babies) and delicate debris such as terracotta vases, glass vessels, scarabs and jewellery from ancient Karalis (Cagliari), Sulcis, Tharros and Nora.

The 1st and 2nd floors contain more of the same but are divided by region and site rather than by age. Among the highlights are some Roman-era mosaics, a collection of statues, busts and tombstones from Cagliari, and coin displays.

★Cattedrale di Santa Maria CATHEDRAL
(Map p52; ☎070 864 93 88; www.duomodicagliari.it; Piazza Palazzo 4; ⏲8am-noon & 4-8pm Mon-Sat, 8am-1pm & 4.30-8.30pm Sun) Cagliari's graceful 13th-century cathedral stands proudly on Piazza Palazzo. Except for the square-based bell tower, little remains of the original Gothic structure: the clean Pisan-Romanesque facade is a 20th-century imitation, added between 1933 and 1938. Inside, the once-Gothic church has all but disappeared beneath a rich icing of baroque decor, the result of a radical late-17th-century makeover. Bright frescoes adorn the ceilings, and the side chapels spill over with exuberant sculptural whirls.

The third chapel on the right, the Cappella di San Michele, is perhaps the most baroque of all, with its ornate sculptural depiction of a serene-looking St Michael casting devils into hell.

At the central door, note the two stone pulpits, sculpted by Guglielmo da Pisa between 1158 and 1162. They originally formed a single unit, which stood in Pisa's Duomo until the Pisans donated it to Cagliari in 1312. It was subsequently split into two by the meddlesome Domenico Spotorno, the architect behind the 17th-century baroque facelift, and the big stone lions that originally formed its base were removed to the altar where they now stand.

Beneath the altar is the **Santuario dei Martiri** (Sanctuary of Martyrs), the only one of several underground rooms open to the public. Carved out of rock, the sanctuary, which is named after the 179 martyrs whose relics are kept here, is an impressive sight with its sculptural decoration and intricate carvings.

Torre dell'Elefante TOWER
(Map p52; www.beniculturalicagliari.it; Via Santa Croce, cnr Via Università; adult/reduced €3/2; ⏲10am-7pm summer, 9am-5pm winter) One of only two Pisan towers still standing, the Torre dell'Elefante was built in 1307 as a defence against the threatening Aragonese. Named after the sculpted elephant by the vicious-looking portcullis, the 42m-high tower became something of a horror show, thanks to the severed heads the city's Spanish rulers used to adorn it with. The crenellated storey was added in 1852 and used as a prison for political detainees. Climb to the top for far-reaching views over the city's rooftops to the sea.

The Spaniards beheaded the Marchese di Cea here and left her head lying around for 17 years. They also liked to festoon the portcullis with the heads of executed prisoners, strung up in cages like ghoulish fairy lights.

Galleria Comunale d'Arte GALLERY
(Map p48; ☎070 677 75 98; www.museicivicicagliari.it; Giardini Pubblici; adult/reduced €6/2.50; ⏲10am-9pm Wed-Mon summer, to 6pm winter) Housed in a neoclassical villa in the Giardini Pubblici (Public Gardens) north of the Castello, this terrific gallery focuses on modern and contemporary art. Works by many of Sardinia's top artists are on show, alongside paintings and sculptures from the Collezione Ingrao, a formidable collection of 20th-century Italian art.

Highlights include the haunting sculpture *La madre dell'ucciso* (Mother of the Killed) by important Nuoro artist Francesco Ciusa, and *La Mattanza,* a stylised and vividly defined rendition of a tuna kill by the neorealist painter Foiso Fois.

Once finished in the gallery, visit the gardens, which command sweeping views over Cagliari's modern skyline.

Bastione di Saint Remy VIEWPOINT
(Map p52) This vast neoclassical structure, comprising a gallery space, monumental stairway and panoramic terrace, was built into the city's medieval walls between 1899 and 1902. The highlight is the elegant Umberto I terrace, which commands sweeping views over Cagliari's jumbled rooftops to the sea and distant mountains. To reach the terrace, which was recently reopened after a two-year restoration, you can try the stairway (closed at the time of research) on Piazza Costituzione or take the elevator from the Giardino Sotto Le Mure (p51).

Chiesa di San Michele CHURCH
(Map p52; Via Ospedale 2; ⏲8-11am & 7-8.30pm Mon-Sat, 9am-noon & 7-9pm Sun) Although consecrated in 1538, this Jesuit church is best known for its lavish 18th-century decor, considered the finest example of baroque styling in Sardinia. The spectacle starts outside with the ebullient triple-arched facade

WORTH A TRIP

POETTO BEACH

An easy bus ride from the city centre, Cagliari's fabulous **Poetto beach** is one of the longest stretches of sand in Italy. Extending 7km beyond the green Promontorio di Sant'Elia, it's an integral part of city life, particularly in summer when much of the city's youth decamps here to sunbathe by day and party by night. The long, sandy strip is lined with bars, snack joints and restaurants, known locally as *chioschi* (kiosks), many of which also act as *stabilmenti balneari* (private beach clubs). These offer various facilities, including showers and changing cabins, and rent out beach gear (prices start at around €15 for an umbrella and two sunloungers).

The southern end of the beach is the most popular, with its picturesque Marina Piccola. Looming over the marina is the craggy Promontorio di Sant' Elia, known as the **Sella del Diavola** (Devil's Saddle). According to local legend, the headland was the scene of an epic battle between Lucifer and the Archangel Michael. In the course of the struggle Satan was thrown off his horse and his saddle fell into the sea where it eventually petrified atop what was to become the headland. Although much of the headland is now owned by the military and closed to the public, you can access it via a scenic walking path.

To get to Poetto hop on bus PF or PQ from Piazza Matteotti.

and continues through the vast colonnaded atrium into the magnificent octagonal interior. Here six heavily decorated chapels radiate out from the centre, capped by a grand, brightly frescoed dome. Also of note is the sacristy, with its vivid frescoes and intricate inlaid wood.

Before you go inside, take a minute to admire the massive four-columned pulpit in the atrium. This was built and named in honour of the Spanish emperor Carlos V, who is said to have delivered a stirring speech from it before setting off on a fruitless campaign against Arab corsairs in Tunisia.

★Santuario & Basilica di Nostra Signora di Bonaria CHURCH

(Map p48; ☎070 30 17 47; Piazza Bonaria 2; donations welcome; ⏰6.30-11.45am & 4.30-8pm summer, 6.30-11.45am & 4-7pm winter) Crowning the Bonaria hill, around 1km southeast of Via Roma, this religious complex is a hugely popular pilgrimage site. Devotees come from all over the world to visit the 14th-century Gothic church (sanctuary) and pray to *Nostra Signora di Bonaria,* a statue of the Virgin Mary and Christ that supposedly saved a ship's crew during a storm. To the right of the sanctuary, the towering basilica still acts as a landmark to returning sailors.

The sanctuary, the historic seat of the Mercedari order of monks, was originally part of a fortified compound built by the Catalano-Aragonese. The Spaniards arrived in Cagliari in 1323 intent on wresting the city from the Pisans, but when they saw what they were up against, they set up camp on the fresh mountain slopes of Montixeddu, which over time came to be known as Bonaria for its clean air – from the Italian *buon'aria* meaning 'good air'. A three-year siege ensued, during which the camp grew to become a fortress with its own church.

Nowadays little remains of the fortress, apart from its Gothic portal, a truncated bell tower, which initially served as a watchtower, and the church. And it's in the church that you'll find the revered Virgin Mary and Christ. Legend has it that the statue had a magical calming effect on the sea after it was cast overboard by Spanish seamen during a storm in the 14th century, and still today mariners pray to it for protection on the high seas. Above the church altar hangs a tiny 15th-century ivory ship, whose movements are said to indicate the wind direction in the Golfo degli Angeli.

You'll find yet more model boats, as well as other ex-voto offerings and a golden crown from Carlo Emanuele I in the sanctuary's **museum**, accessible through the small cloister. There are also the mummified corpses of four plague-ridden Catalano-Aragonese nobles whose bodies were found miraculously preserved inside the church.

Adjacent to the sanctuary is the hulking neoclassical basilica. Construction started on this in 1704 but the money ran out and it wasn't officially completed until 1926.

MUSEUM PASS

If you're planning on visiting more than one of Cagliari's Musei Civici (Civic Museums), consider investing in a museum pass (adult/reduced €8/4). Valid for seven days, the pass covers admission to the **Galleria Comunale d'Arte** (p44), the **Museo d'Arte Siamese** (p51) and **Palazzo di Città** (p51).

A second, more extensive week pass (€13) is also available, covering the above mentioned museums as well as the **Torre dell'Elefante** (p44), **Torre di San Pancrazio** (p46), **Villa di Tigellio** (p50), **Cripta di Santa Restituta** (p47) and **Grotta della Vipera**.

For further details see www.museicivicicagliari.it.

Pinacoteca Nazionale GALLERY

(Map p48; ☎070 65 69 91; www.pinacoteca.cagliari.beniculturali.it; Piazza Arsenale; adult/reduced €3/1.50, incl Museo Archeologico Nazionale €7/3.50; ⏲9am-8pm Tue-Sun) Cagliari's principal gallery showcases a prized collection of 15th- to 17th-century art. Many of the best works are *retablos* (grand altarpieces), painted by Catalan and Genoese artists. Of those by known Sardinian painters, the four 16th-century works by Pietro Cavaro, father of the so-called Stampace school and arguably Sardinia's most important artist, are outstanding. They include a moving *Deposizione* (Deposition) and portraits of St Peter, St Paul and St Augustine.

Also represented is the painter's father, Lorenzo, and his son Michele. Another Sardinian artist of note is Francesco Pinna, whose 17th-century *Pala di Sant'Orsola* hangs here. These images tend to show the influence of Spain and Italy, rather than illuminating the Sardinian condition, but there some 19th- and early-20th-century Sardinian painters here as well, such as Giovanni Marghinotti and Giuseppe Sciuti.

Torre di San Pancrazio TOWER

(Map p48; www.beniculturalicagliari.it; Piazza Indipendenza; adult/reduced €3/2) Rising above the skyline by the Castello's northeastern gate, this 36m-high tower is the twin of the Torre dell'Elefante (p44). Completed in 1305, it is built on the city's highest point and commands expansive views of the Golfo di Cagliari. It is currently closed for renovations.

Palazzo Viceregio PALACE

(Map p52; Piazza Palazzo 2; €1.50; ⏲10am-6.30pm Tue-Sun) Just steps from the cathedral, this pale lime *palazzo* was once home to the city's Spanish and Savoy viceroys. Today it serves as the provincial assembly and stages regular exhibitions and summer music concerts. Inside, you can visit several richly decorated rooms culminating in the Sala del Consiglio, the assembly's main meeting chamber.

Piazza Yenne PIAZZA

(Map p52) The focal point of the Marina district, and indeed of central Cagliari, is Piazza Yenne. The small square is adorned with a statue of King Carlo Felice to mark the beginning of the SS131 cross-island highway, the project for which the monarch is best remembered. On summer nights, the piazza heaves as a young crowd flocks to its bars, gelaterie and pavement cafes.

Chiesa di Sant'Anna CHURCH

(Map p52; Piazza Santa Restituta; ⏲7.30-10.30am & 5-8pm Tue-Sun) Largely destroyed by bombing in 1943 but painstakingly rebuilt afterwards, Chiesa di Sant'Anna rises grandly above a wide staircase in the Stampace district. More impressive outside than in, it's fronted by a towering two-tier baroque facade topped by a pair of matching bell towers.

Museo del Tesoro e Area Archeologica di Sant'Eulalia MUSEUM

(Map p52; ☎070 66 37 24; www.mutseu.org; Vico del Collegio 2; adult/reduced €5/2.50; ⏲10am-1pm & 4-7pm Tue-Sun) In the heart of the Marina district, this museum contains a rich collection of religious art, as well as an archaeological area beneath the adjacent Chiesa di Sant' Eulalia. The main drawcard is a 13m section of excavated Roman road (constructed between the 1st and 2nd centuries AD), which archaeologists think would have connected with the nearby port.

In the upstairs treasury you'll find all sorts of religious artefacts, ranging from exquisite priests' vestments and silverware through to medieval codices and other precious documents. Fine wooden sculptures abound, along with an *Ecce homo* painting, depicting Christ, front and back, after his flagellation. The painting has been attributed to a 17th-century Flemish artist.

Chiesa di Santo Sepolcro CHURCH

(Map p52; Piazza del Santo Sepolcro 5; ⌚10am-noon & 5-7pm) The most astonishing feature of this church is an enormous 17th-century gilded wooden altarpiece housing a figure of the Virgin Mary. From the church, stairs lead down to the crypt, a creepy grotto consisting of two cave-like rooms gouged out of bare rock. In one you'll find a skull and crossbones on the wall.

Cripta di Santa Restituta CRYPT

(Map p52; ☎070 667 01 68; Via Sant'Efisio 14; adult/reduced €2/1; ⌚10am-1pm) This crypt has been in use since pre-Christian times. It's a huge, eerie, natural cavern where the echo of leaking water drip-drips. Originally a place of pagan worship, it became the home of the martyr Restituta in the 5th century and a reference point for Cagliari's early Christians. The Orthodox Christians then took it over – you can still see remnants of their frescoes – until the 13th century, when it was abandoned.

In WWII the crypt was used as an air-raid shelter, a task it wasn't up to, since many died while holed up here in February 1943. It's interesting to make out the wartime graffiti that covers the walls.

Chiesa di Sant'Efisio CHURCH

(Map p52; Via Sant'Efisio; ⌚closed to the public) Despite its unassuming facade, the Chiesa di Sant'Efisio is of considerable local importance – not for any artistic or architectural reasons but rather for its ties to St Ephisius, Cagliari's patron saint. A Roman soldier who converted to Christianity and was later beheaded for refusing to recant his faith, St Ephisius is the star of the city's big 1 May festivities (p54). The effigy of the saint that is paraded around the city on a beautifully ornate *carozza* (carriage) is kept here.

Over the centuries, the saint has stood the city in good stead, saving the populace from the plague in 1652 – when the church got its marble makeover – and repelling Napoleon's fleet in 1793 by stirring up the storm that sent the fleet packing.

At the side of the church is the entrance to the crypt where St Ephisius was supposedly held before being executed in Nora (near Pula). It's marked in stone – *Carcer Sancti Ephysii M* (Prison of the Martyr St Ephisius) – and retains the column where Ephisius was tied during his incarceration.

Anfiteatro Romano ARCHAEOLOGICAL SITE

(Map p48; Viale Sant'Ignazio da Laconi) Cagliari's most significant Roman monument is this 2nd-century amphitheatre. Currently resembling a messy construction site (it's closed for restoration), the structure is carved into the rocky flank of the Buon Cammino hill, near the northern entrance to Il Castello. Over the centuries much of the original theatre has been cannibalised for building material, but enough survives to stir the imagination.

In its heyday, crowds of up to 10,000 people – practically the entire population of Cagliari – would gather in the steeply stacked stands to watch gladiators battle each other and the occasional wild animal.

Orto Botanico GARDENS

(Botanic Gardens; Map p48; ☎070 675 35 22; www.ccb-sardegna.it; Viale Sant'Ignazio da Laconi 11; adult/reduced €4/2; ⌚9am-6pm Tue-Sun summer, to 2pm winter) Established in 1858, the Orto Botanico is one of Italy's most famous botanical gardens. Today it extends over 5 hectares and nurtures 2000 species of flora. Leafy arches lead to trickling fountains and gardens bristling with palm trees, cacti and *ficus* trees with huge snaking roots.

Specimens from as far afield as Asia, Australia, Africa and the Americas sidle up to the local carob trees and oaks. Littering the gardens are a Punic cistern, a Roman quarry and an aqueduct.

Basilica di San Saturnino BASILICA

(Map p48; Piazza San Cosimo; ⌚9am-7pm Sat & 1st Sun of month) One of the oldest churches in Sardinia, the Basilica di San Saturnino is a striking example of Paleo-Christian architecture. Based on a Greek-cross pattern, the domed basilica was built over a Roman necropolis in the 5th century, on the site where Saturninus, a much-revered local martyr, was buried. According to legend, Saturninus was beheaded in AD 304 during emperor Diocletian's anti-Christian pogroms.

In the 6th century San Fulgenzio da Ruspe, a bishop in exile from Tunisia, built a monastery here. In 1098 this was reworked into the current Romanesque church by a group of Vittorini monks from Marseille. Since then the basilica has undergone various refurbishments, most notably after it was stripped in 1662 to provide building material for the Cattedrale di Santa Maria and, more recently, after it sustained severe bomb damage in WWII.

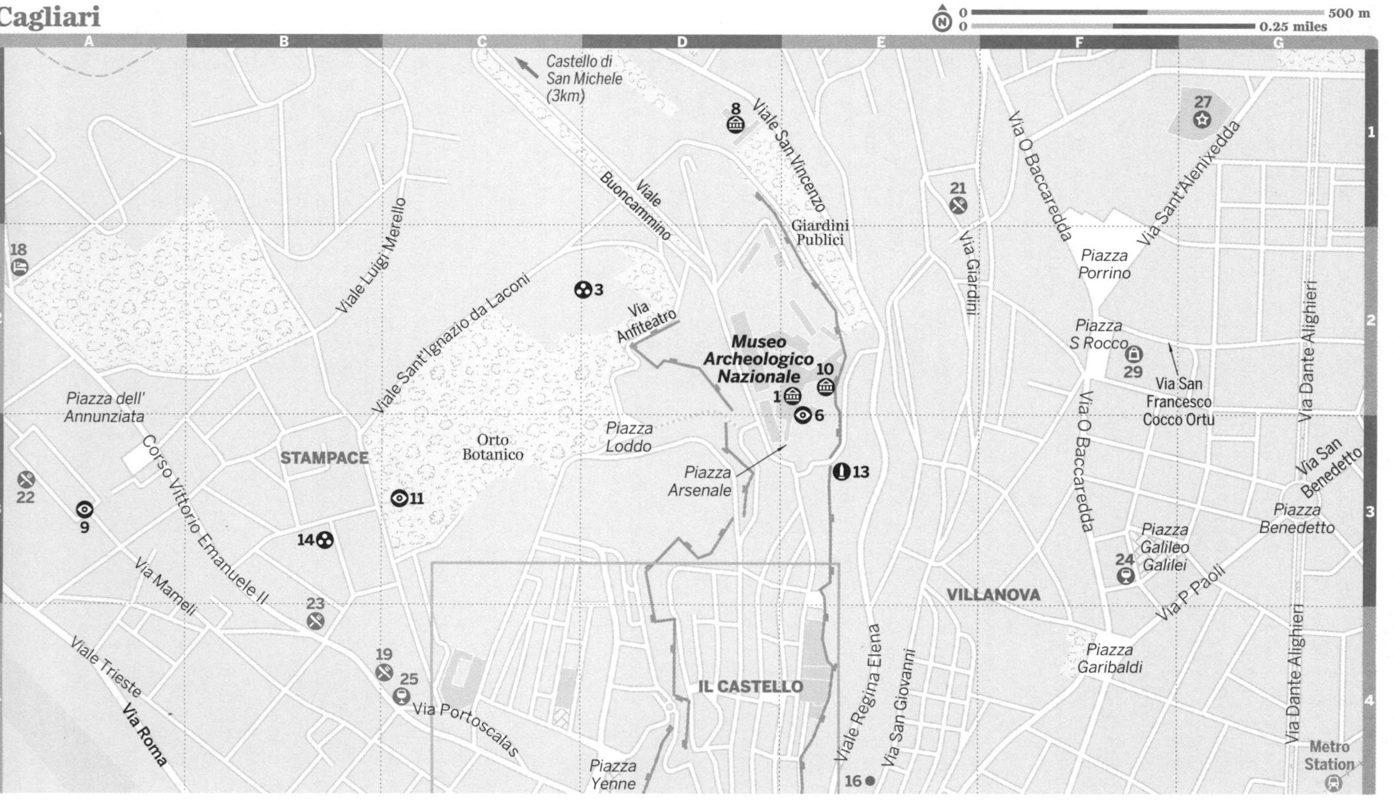
Cagliari
0 500 m
0 0.25 miles
A
B
C
D
E
F
G
1
2
3
4
Castello di San Michele (3km)
8
Viale San Vincenzo
Viale Buoncammino
Giardini Publici
21
Via Giardini
Via O Baccaredda
27
Via Sant'Alenixedda
Piazza Porrino
18
Viale Luigi Merello
3
Via Anfiteatro
Viale Sant'Ignazio da Laconi
Museo Archeologico Nazionale
10
1
6
Piazza S Rocco
29
Via San Francesco Cocco Ortu
Via Dante Alighieri
Piazza dell' Annunziata
Corso Vittorio Emanuele II
STAMPACE
Orto Botanico
Piazza Loddo
Piazza Arsenale
13
Via San Benedetto
Piazza Benedetto
22
9
11
14
Piazza Galileo Galilei
24
Via P Paoli
Via Mameli
23
VILLANOVA
Viale Trieste
Via Roma
19
25
Via Portoscalas
IL CASTELLO
Viale Regina Elena
Via San Giovanni
Piazza Garibaldi
Piazza Yenne
16
Metro Station

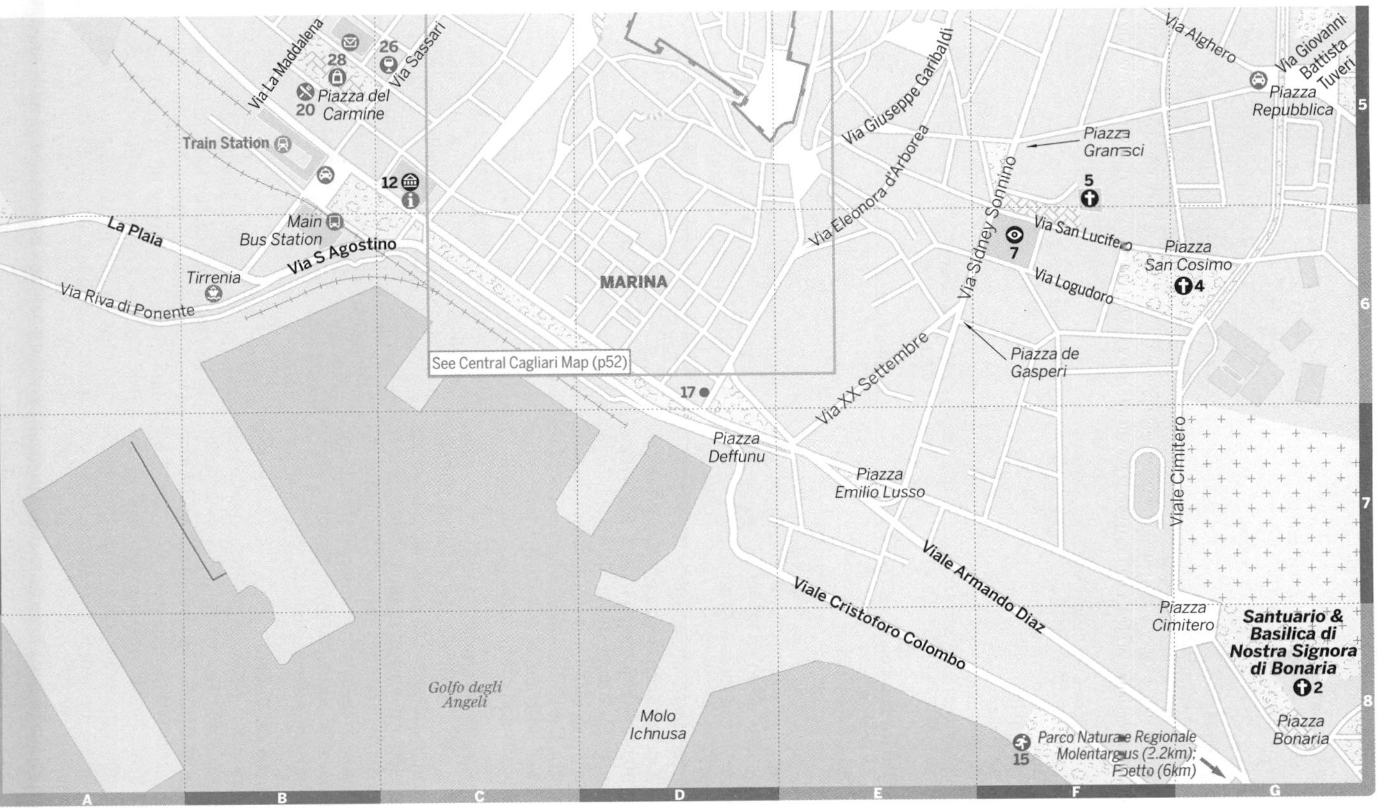

Via La Maddalena
28
26
Via Sassari
Piazza del Carmine
20
Train Station
12
Main Bus Station
La Plaia
Via S Agostino
Tirrenia
Via Riva di Ponente
MARINA
See Central Cagliari Map (p52)
17
Via Giuseppe Garibaldi
Via Eleonora d'Arborea
Via Alghero
Via Giovanni Battista Tuveri
Piazza Repubblica
Piazza Gramsci
5
Via Sidney Sonnino
7
Via San Lucifero
Piazza San Cosimo
4
Via Logudoro
Piazza de Gasperi
Via XX Settembre
Piazza Deffunu
Piazza Emilio Lusso
Viale Cimitero
Viale Armando Diaz
Viale Cristoforo Colombo
Piazza Cimitero
Santuario & Basilica di Nostra Signora di Bonaria
2
Piazza Bonaria
Golfo degli Angeli
Molo Ichnusa
15
Parco Naturale Regionale Molentargius (2.2km); Poetto (6km)
A
B
C
D
E
F
G
5
6
7
8

Cagliari

Top Sights
1 Museo Archeologico Nazionale E2
2 Santuario & Basilica di Nostra Signora di Bonaria G8

Sights
3 Anfiteatro Romano D2
4 Basilica di San Saturnino G6
5 Chiesa di San Lucifero F5
6 Cittadella dei Musei E3
7 Exmà F6
8 Galleria Comunale d'Arte D1
9 MEM A3
10 Museo d'Arte Siamese E2
11 Orto Botanico C3
12 Palazzo Civico C5
Pinacoteca Nazionale .... (see 10)
13 Torre di San Pancrazio E3
14 Villa di Tigellio B3

Activities, Courses & Tours
15 Boardwalk F8
16 L'Accademia E4
17 One World Language Centre D6

Sleeping
18 Locanda dei Buonoi e Cattivi A2

Eating
19 Crackers C4
20 Gocce di Gelato e Cioccolato B5
21 L'Opoz E1
22 Man.Gia A3
23 Pizzeria Nansen B4

Drinking & Nightlife
24 Cucina eat F3
25 Il Merlo Parlante C4
26 Inu C5

Entertainment
27 Teatro Lirico G1

Shopping
28 Cagliari Antiquaria B5
29 Mercato di San Benedetto F2

Exmà CULTURAL CENTRE
(Map p48; ☎070 66 63 99; www.exmacagliari.com; Via San Lucifero 71; admission varies, typically €3-5; ⏲10am-1pm & 4-9pm Tue-Sun summer, 9am-1pm & 4-8pm Tue-Sun winter) Housed in Cagliari's 18th-century *mattatoio* (abattoir) – hence the sculpted cow's head over the entrance and around the internal courtyard – Exmà is a delightful cultural centre. Check the website for details of its varied program of events, performances, concerts and exhibitions.

Cittadella dei Musei AREA
(Map p48) Cagliari's main museum complex occupies the site of the city's former arsenal at the northern end of the Castello district. It's home to several museums, including the Museo Archeologico Nazionale (p43) and Pinacoteca Nazionale (p46), as well as several university departments.

Museo del Duomo MUSEUM
(Map p52; ☎333 594 85 49; www.museoduomodicagliari.it; Via del Fossario 5; adult/reduced €4/2.50; ⏲10am-1pm & 4.30-7.30pm Sat & Sun) Treasures from the Cattedrale di Santa Maria (p44) are displayed at this compact museum just around the corner from the cathedral. One standout is the 15th-century *Trittico di Clemente VII,* which was moved here from the cathedral for safe keeping. This precious painting in oil on timber has been attributed to either the Flemish painter Rogier van der Weyden or to one of his disciples. Another important work is the 16th-century *Retablo dei Beneficiati,* produced by the school of Pietro Cavaro.

Palazzo Civico HISTORIC BUILDING
(Map p48; ☎070 677 80 14; Via Roma) Overlooking Piazza Matteotti, the neo-Gothic Palazzo Civico, also known as the Municipio, is home to Cagliari's municipal council as well as the city's tourist office (p62). Capricious, pompous and at the time of research half-covered by scaffolding, it was built between 1899 and 1913, and faithfully reconstructed after bombing in 1943. The upstairs chambers contain works by a number of Sardinian artists, including Pietro Cavaro. Admission is by appointment only.

Villa di Tigellio ARCHAEOLOGICAL SITE
(Map p48; www.beniculturalicagliari.it; Via Carbonazzi; adult/reduced €2/1; ⏲9am-5pm) These remains of three Roman houses date to the 1st century BC. Legend has it that Tigellio Ermogene – a famous Sardinian poet and musician, and a close a friend of Julius Caesar – lived here. Today the ruins are pretty overgrown and surrounded by houses, so you'll need to use your imagination to picture the

magnificent mosaics, columns and baths that once stood here.

Chiesa di San Lucifero CHURCH

(Map p48; ☎070 65 69 96; Via San Lucifero 78; ⏰closed to the public) Below this baroque church is a 6th-century crypt where the tomb of the early Archbishop of Cagliari, St Lucifer, rests. In earlier times the area had been part of a Roman burial ground. The church is rarely open, but its austere 17th-century facade is worth a quick look from the outside.

Castello di San Michele CASTLE

(☎070 50 06 56; Via Sirai; adult/reduced €3/2; ⏰10am-1pm & 4-7pm Tue-Sun summer, 10am-1pm & 3-6pm Tue-Sun winter) Lifted by a hill high above the city, this stout three-tower Spanish fortress northwest of the centre commands incredible city and sea views. Set in serene grounds, the 10th-century castle was built to protect Santa Igia, capital of the Giudicato of Cagliari, but is most famous as the luxurious residence of the 14th-century Carroz family. It now hosts exhibitions and cultural events. To get here, take bus 5 from Via Roma to the foot of the hill and then walk 800m to the castle.

MEM CULTURAL CENTRE

(Mediateca del Mediterranea; Map p48; Via Mameli 164; ⏰cafe 8.30am-9pm Mon-Fri, to 3am Sat & Sun) Opened in 2011, this contemporary glass and steel pavilion has given a new lease of life to a former food market. It's now a cultural complex housing two libraries, the city's historical archives and the Sardinian film library. As a visitor, the main attraction is the structure itself, but its cafe is a popular place to while away an hour or two on a slow afternoon.

Giardino Sotto Le Mure PARK

(Map p52; Viale Regina Elena; ⏰7am-9pm winter, longer hours summer) A small strip of park in the shadows of the Castello's mighty walls, this 500m-long green space is home to seven works by leading Sardinian sculptor Pinuccio Sciola. You'll also find the lift up to the Bastione di Saint Remy (p44).

Palazzo di Città MUSEUM

(Map p52; ☎070 677 64 82; www.museicivici-cagliari.it; Piazza Palazzo 6; adult/reduced €4/2.50; ⏰10am-9pm Tue-Sun summer, to 6pm winter) Cagliari's town hall from medieval times to the 19th century, the beautifully restored Palazzo di Città has been converted into a small museum. It contains a well-edited collection of Sardinian textiles, ceramics, paintings and engravings. The basement level displays contemporary art.

Museo d'Arte Siamese MUSEUM

(Map p48; ☎070 65 18 88; www.museicivicicagliari.it; Piazza Arsenale; adult/reduced €2/1; ⏰10am-8pm Tue-Sun, to 6pm winter) Cagliari's medieval heart is an unlikely place for a collection of Asian art, but that's exactly what you'll find here. Donated to the city by local engineer Stefano Cardu, who had spent many years in Thailand, the collection is highly eclectic. Alongside Ming- and Qing-era Chinese porcelain vases, there are silk paintings, Japanese statuettes, Burmese sculpture and some truly terrifying Thai weapons.

Ghetto degli Ebrei AREA

(Jewish Ghetto; Map p52) Cagliari's medieval Ghetto degli Ebrei was situated in the cramped area between Via Santa Croce and Via Stretta. The city's Jewry lived here until they were expelled from Sardinia by the island's Spanish rulers in 1492. Today virtually nothing remains of

WORTH A TRIP

SAN SPERATE

San Sperate, a small town just over 20km northwest of Cagliari, is worth a quick detour for its colourful murals. These present a Daliesque tableau of traditional country life as well as depicting more modern urban trends (skateboards stretching down a wall like an array of colourful tongues). Check out Pinuccio Sciola's epic **Storia di San Sperate** (History of San Sperate; Via Sassari, San Sperate) and the surreal pop-art works on Via Concordia and Via Decimo.

If you're in need of a break, **Ada** (☎070 960 09 72; Via Cagliari 21, San Sperate; meals €30-35; ⏰12.30-3pm & 7.30-11pm Mon-Sat) is a fine Sardinian restaurant serving antipasto of *crudi* (raw seafood), homemade pasta with truffles, local wine and artisanal beer.

Hourly buses serve San Sperate from Cagliari (€1.90, 30 minutes).

Central Cagliari

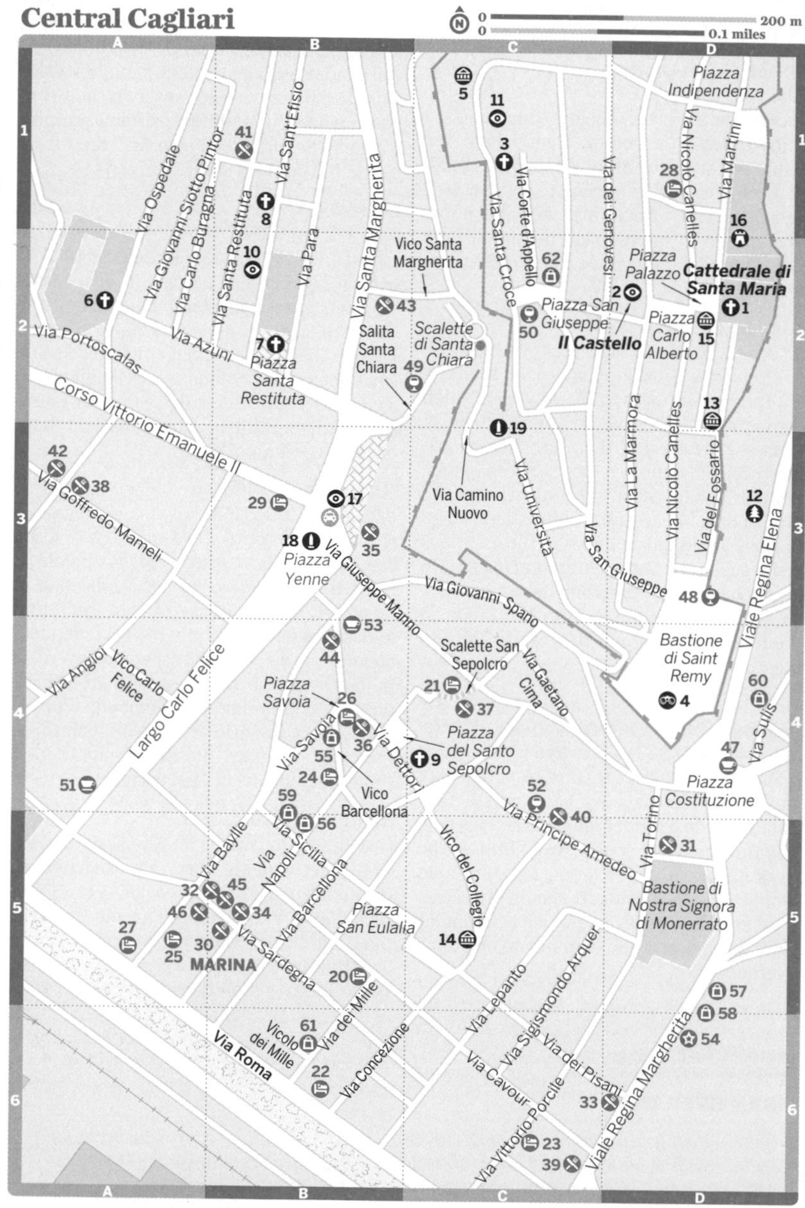

the Ghetto except its name, applied to a restored former barracks, the **Centro Comunale d'Arte e Cultura Il Ghetto** (Map p52; ☎070 667 01 90; Via Santa Croce 18; adult/reduced €3/2; ⏰9am-1pm & 4-8pm Tue-Sun), which hosts temporary exhibitions.

In the wake of the Jewish expulsion, the **Basilica di Santa Croce** (Map p52; Piazzetta Santa Croce; ⏰9am-noon & 4-7pm) was built over the ghetto's former synagogue.

Central Cagliari

Activities

Not surprisingly, water sports are big at Poetto beach (p45), where you can generally hire canoes at the beach clubs. Offshore, the Golfo di Cagliari is littered with the wrecks of WWII ships, which makes it an excellent place for divers to explore.

Windsurfing Club Cagliari WATER SPORTS
(☎070 37 26 94; www.windsurfingclubcagliari.org; Viale Marina Piccola; 6-lesson surfing/windsurfing/catamaran course €120/180/220) From its base at Marina Piccola, this centre offers a range of water-sports courses. Special courses with reduced rates are available for children aged six to 15. See the website for details.

Harry S Tours BOATING
(☎338 377 40 51; www.harrystours.com; half-day cruise €45, full day incl lunch €85) Operating out of Marina di Capitana, 14km east of Cagliari, this outfit offers a range of boat tours, including day and half-day cruises, sunset sails, even a wine-tasting jaunt.

Boardwalk PROMENADE
(Map p48) Cagliari's seafront boardwalk offers breezy views back to the Marina district as it hugs the waterfront from Molo Ichnusa to Su Siccu. It's a relaxed place for a jog, stroll or bike ride away from the buzz of the city centre.

WORTH A TRIP

CALLING ALL BIRDWATCHERS

The protected reed-fringed wetlands of the **Parco Naturale Regionale Molentargius** (www.parcomolentargius.it; ⌚6.30am-9pm summer, 7am-6pm winter) lie slightly east of Cagliari towards Quartu Sant'Elena. A housing estate forms an incongruous backdrop to these freshwater and brackish pools, which attract nesting, migrant and wintering birds in their thousands. With a little luck you may well spot pink flamingos, purple herons, little egrets, marsh harriers, sandwich terns and black-winged stilts from the observation points.

The reserve is best explored on foot or by bicycle. Before heading out you can get information at the **InfoPoint** (☎070 3791 9201; www.parcomolentargius.it; Edificio Sali Scelti, Via La Palma; ⌚8.30am-8pm Mon-Fri, 9am-8.30pm Sat & Sun) on the eastern fringes of town. Dawn and dusk are prime-time viewing for twitchers.

Courses

One World Language Centre LANGUAGE
(Map p48; ☎070 67 02 34; www.oneworldcagliari.com; Viale Regina Margherita 6; 1-week course €199, plus subscription fee €60, individual lessons per hr €30) Brush up your Italian with a course at this reputable language school, which takes an interactive approach and offers lessons for all levels. The centre can help arrange homestays (from €210 per week) and apartment rooms (from €160 per week).

L'Accademia LANGUAGE
(Map p48; ☎328 8811464; www.laccademia.com; Via San Giovanni 34; 15/20hr course €230/260, individual class per hr €35) This school takes a hands-on approach to learning Italian, offering the chance to combine language skills with cultural immersion activities such as city tours, Italian movie screenings and traditional Sardinian dinners.

Tours

Sardinia Tourist Guide TOURS
(☎349 4558367; www.sardiniatouristguide.it; 3½hr tour for 2-4 people €200) Based in Selargius, 12km northeast of town, these expert guides run tours of Cagliari, which takes in highlights including Poetto beach, Sella del Diavola (Devil's Saddle), Basilica di Bonaria and Il Castello. Archaeological tours (such as to Nora) and outdoor excursions such as canyoning in the Flumendosa and trekking on Monte Corrasi can also be arranged.

Festivals & Events

Cagliari puts on a good show for Carnevale, generally in February, and during the Easter Holy Week, when hooded processions pass by its historic churches. The city's main headline event, though, is the Festa di Sant'Efisio (p54), held each year in May.

Festa di Sant'Efisio RELIGIOUS
(www.festadisantefisio.com; ⌚1-4 May) Visitors descend in droves for this saintly celebration in May. On the opening day the effigy of St Ephisius, Cagliari's patron saint, is taken from the Chiesa di Sant'Efisio and paraded through the streets on a bullock-drawn carriage before being carried to Nora, 40km away, and back again. Tickets for the stands (€15 to €25) are sold at **Box Office Tickets** (Map p52; ☎070 65 74 28; www.boxofficesardegna.it; Viale Regina Margherita 43; ⌚10am-1pm & 5-8pm Mon-Fri winter, plus 10am-1pm Sat summer).

Get the best views from the grandstand seating around Piazza Matteotti and Largo Carlo Felice.

Sardegna Pride PARADE
(www.sardegnapride.org; ⌚Jun) This colourful, rainbow flag-waving parade fills the seafront streets of Cagliari's Marina district in late June.

Eating

It's not difficult to eat well in Cagliari. The city offers everything from classy fine-dining restaurants to humble neighbourhood trattorias, pizzerias, bars and takeaways. Marina is chock-full of places, some of which are obviously touristy but many that are not and are popular with locals. Other good eat streets include Via Sassari and Corso Vittorio Emanuele.

Dulcis PASTRIES €
(Map p52; ☎070 67 40 43; www.dulcispasticceria.it; Via Baylle 25; cake €2.50; ⌚7.30am-midnight summer, 8am-11pm winter) For a taste of traditional Sardinian cakes and pastries, Dulcis is the place to go. Part shop, part cafe, part

wine bar, it's a lovely spot to relax over tea and a slice of *pan di sapa* (a sticky island speciality made with almonds, honey, orange peel and raisins). There's also a carefully selected choice of island wines you can sample.

Stefino GELATERIA €
(Map p52; Via Dettori 30; gelato €1.50-5.40; noon-11.30pm Thu-Mon, to 9pm Tue & Wed;) This organic gelateria is ideally placed for a mid-afternoon treat or post-dinner dessert. There's not a huge choice but quality is high and there are some exciting flavours including ginger-infused chocolate and pear and cinnamon.

Pizzeria Nansen PIZZA €
(Map p48; 070 667 03 35; Corso Vittorio Emanuele II 269; pizzas €5-10; 11.30am-2.30pm & 6.30-11.30pm Tue-Sun) For a slice of *delizioso* pizza and a cool bottle of Ichnusa (Sardinian beer), head to this super-friendly pizzeria. The pizzas, served ready cut on a tray, are finger-lickingly good with light fluffy bases and flavour-packed toppings, and the setting – high stools, paper napkins and framed Roma football shirts (!) – is suitably relaxed.

L'Opoz ITALIAN €
(Map p48; 070 858 48 94; www.facebook.com/lopozrestaurant; Via Giardini 145; meals €20-25; 7pm-2am Wed-Mon) Snuggled away north of the centre in the Villanova district, this artsy, red-walled bistro-pub is a chilled pick for a Guinness and a bite to eat – the *tagliata* (steak) stands out, but it also knocks up simple pasta dishes, hamburgers and salads.

Trattoria Ci Pensa Cannas SARDINIAN €
(Map p52; 070 66 78 15; www.cipensacannas.it; Via Sardegna 37; meals €19-25; noon-3pm & 7-10.30pm Mon-Sat) A trattoria from the traditional no-frills school. It's far from a looker with its bright white lighting and basic decor, but the welcome is genuine and the food modestly priced and generous, be it pasta dishes like *gnocchetti alla campidanese* (Sardinian gnocchi with a tomato and sausage sauce), steaks or seafood.

★**La Pola** SEAFOOD €€
(Map p52; 070 65 06 04; Vico Barcellona 10; meals €30; 7-11pm Mon-Sat, plus 1-3pm Sat & Sun) There are many seafood restaurants in the Marina district but few bring in the crowds like this local favourite. To look at, it's nothing out of the ordinary with its murals and orange and yellow walls, but once the food starts arriving you'll appreciate why it's so often packed: multi-dish starters, luxurious lobster mains, beautifully seared tuna.

DON'T MISS

FAVOURITE SNACK SPOTS

Le Patate & Co (Map p52; Scalette San Sepolcro 1; meals €10; 11.30am-3pm & 6pm-midnight) If you get the urge for something uncomplicated, head to this fast-food joint for a satisfying fill-up of fried snacks. Sit on the terrace at the top of the steps and choose between fish 'n' chips, mozzarella balls, battered vegetables or fried seafood.

Isola del Gelato (Map p52; Piazza Yenne 35; ice cream €1.50-4; 7am-2am) A hugely popular hang-out on Piazza Yenne. Join the young crowd to linger over a drink and gelato, semifreddo or sorbet.

Gocce di Gelato e Cioccolato (Map p48; Piazza del Carmine 21; gelato €1.70-4.50; noon-10pm Mon-Fri, to 11pm Sat, 10.30am-1.30pm & 4.30-10pm Sun, longer hours summer) Stop by for divine handmade gelati, desserts (try the millefeuille), spice-infused pralines and truffles.

Locanda Caddeo (Map p52; 070 68 04 91; www.facebook.com/locandacaddeocagliari; Via Sassari 75; meals €5-20; noon-3.30pm & 6.30-11pm Mon-Sat) A cool, gallery-style eatery that hums at lunchtime as shoppers, students, visitors and business folk pack into its black, glass-plated interior to chat over focaccias, sliced pizza, grilled steaks and freshly prepared salads. Takeaway available.

I Sapori dell'Isola (Map p52; Via Sardegna 50; 7.30am-1.30pm & 4.30-8.30pm Mon-Sat) It's all in the name – 'Island Flavours'. This friendly deli specialises in top-quality Sardinian delicacies: breads, pastries, cured meats, cheeses, olive oils, wine and *bottarga* (cured dried mullet roe that's generally grated onto pasta dishes).

SEAN PAVONE/SHUTTERSTOCK ©

1. Cityscape, Cagliari (p41)
Boasting ancient Roman ruins and centuries-old churches, Sardinia's capital wears its history on its sleeve.

2. Bastione di Saint Remy (p44)
The Bastione's terrace commands sweeping vistas over Cagliari to the sea and distant mountains.

3. Festa di Sant'Efisio (p54)
Visitors descend on Cagliari in droves for this saintly celebration in May

ALXPIN/SHUTTERSTOCK ©

★Luigi Pomata SEAFOOD €€
(Map p52; ☎070 67 20 58; www.luigipomata.com; Viale Regina Margherita 14; meals restaurant €40-50, bistrot €25-30; ⏰1-3pm & 8-11pm Mon-Sat) There's always a buzz at chef Luigi Pomata's minimalist seafood restaurant, with pared-down decor and chefs skilfully preparing super-fresh sushi. For a more casual eating experience, try the Pomata Bistrot, beneath the main restaurant, where you can dine on dishes such as stuffed squid with broccoli cream in a tranquil, relaxed setting.

Da Marino al St Remy SARDINIAN €€
(Map p52; ☎070 65 73 77; www.stremy.it; Via Torino 16; meals €40; ⏰1-2.30pm & 8-10.30pm Mon-Sat) Tucked away on a side street, St Remy keeps the mood intimate in a vaulted, lime-washed space with stone arches. The menu puts a creative spin on Sardinian flavours, with homemade pasta preluding mains like grilled beef with herb butter or fish of the day with cream of broccoli and anchovies – all cooked to a T and presented with panache.

Per Bacco SARDINIAN €€
(Map p52; ☎070 65 16 67; www.enoperbacco.it; Via Santa Restituta 72; meals €25-35; ⏰8.30-11.30pm Tue-Sat) Hidden in the alleys of Stampace is this friendly restaurant, with stone walls, cheek-by-jowl tables and a refined, low-key atmosphere. Chef-owner Sabrina allows ingredients to shine in her simple, seasonal dishes. Start with, say, stewed octopus and creamed potatoes, and follow up with a *primo* such as *fregola sarda ai sapori di mare* (semolina pasta with seafood).

Martinelli's ITALIAN €€
(Map p52; ☎070 65 42 20; www.martinellis.it; Via Principe Amedeo 18; meals from €35; ⏰8.30pm-midnight Mon-Sat) Simplicity is the ethos underpinning this intimate, subtly lit bistro in the Marina district. Service is friendly without being overbearing, and the menu plays up seasonal, winningly fresh seafood along the lines of *tagliolini* (flat spaghetti) with octopus ink and sea bass cooked in Vernaccia wine.

EATING ON THE HOOF

For a delicious packed lunch go into one of the neighbourhood *salumerie* (delicatessens) and ask for a thick cut of *pecorino sardo* (Sardinian *pecorino* cheese) and a slice or two of prosciutto (ham) in a freshly baked *panino* (bread roll).

Antica Cagliari SARDINIAN €€
(Map p52; ☎070 734 01 98; www.anticacagliari.it; Via Sardegna 49; meals €30-40; ⏰12.30-3pm & 7.30-11.30pm) A cut above most restaurants in the Marina district, this vaulted restaurant always has a good buzz. Diners come for its traditional seafood, which stars in dishes such as spaghetti *vongole e bottarga* (with clams and mullet roe) and sea bass cooked with Vermentino white wine, olives and laurel. Reserve ahead for one of the few outdoor tables.

Crackers ITALIAN €€
(Map p48; ☎070 65 39 12; Corso Vittorio Emanuele 195; meals €40; ⏰12.45-3pm & 8-11.30pm Thu-Tue) A corner of Piedmont in Sardinia, Crackers specialises in northern Italian cuisine with a wide range of risottos, including a classic *risotto al Barolo* (risotto with Barolo wine), and a selection of steaks and traditional meat dishes. There's also seafood and a thoughtfully curated wine list.

Ristorante Ammentos SARDINIAN €€
(Map p52; ☎070 65 10 75; Via Sassari 120; fixed-price menu €15-30; ⏰1-3pm & 8-11pm Wed-Mon) Dine on authentic southern Sardinian fare in rustic surrounds at this traditional old-school trattoria. *Malloreddus* (typical Sardinan gnocchi) with gorgonzola cheese is a delicious lead to succulent meat dishes such as wild pork and sausages.

Fork Easy Restaurant RISTORANTE €€
(Map p52; ☎070 664318; www.stefanodeidda.it; Viale Regina Margherita 28; fixed-price lunch menu €15, meals €35-40; ⏰12.45-3pm & 7.45-11pm Tue-Sun) The younger and less formal sibling of Dal Corsaro (p59), Fork Easy is the brainchild of Michelin-starred chef Stefano Deidda. An elegant, soberly styled restaurant, it serves modern Italian fare with an onus on fresh seafood. For a taste, the €15 lunch menu is an outstanding bargain.

Sa Piola SARDINIAN €€
(Map p52; ☎070 66 67 14; www.sapiolaristorante.it; Vico Santa Margherita 3; meals €35-40; ⏰noon-4pm & 7.30pm-midnight) Classical Sardinian cooking is celebrated at this rustic backstreet restaurant near Piazza Yenne. A menu highlight is prize *bue rosso* beef which is married with Cannonau and Vermentino wines to make meatballs and hearty stews. Seafood and seasonal vegetables also appear in various tasty guises.

WORTH A TRIP

A WALK IN THE WOODS

A world away from the urban hustle of Cagliari, the **Monte dei Sette Fratelli** is the highest point of the remote Sarrabus district. Its granite peaks and woodlands bristling with cork and holm oak, juniper, oleander and myrtle are a haven to wild boar, hawks and golden eagles, and it's one of only three remaining redoubts of the *cervo sardo* (Sardinian deer). Accessible by the SS125, it offers some magnificent hiking, with routes ranging from straightforward strolls to a tough 12km ascent of **Punta Sa Ceraxa** (1016m).

You can pick up a trekking map from the **Caserma Forestale Campu Omu**, a forestry corps station near the Burcei turn-off on the SS125.

From Burcei, a lonely road crawls 8km up to **Punta Serpeddi** (1067m), from where you can gaze out across the whole Sarrabus to Cagliari and the sea.

Taverna dai Matti RISTORANTE €€
(Map p52; 070 66 64 37; www.tavernadaimatti.it; Via Sardegna 44; meals €30-35; 12.30-3pm & 7.30-10.30pm) One of the better places on the Marina district's main restaurant strip, the Taverna sets itself apart with a bright minimalist look and casual vibe. The menu is similarly modern, and although dishes can be a bit hit and miss, there are some wonderful creations, including a flavoursome ravioli with *burrata,* sea urchins and artichoke.

Man.Gia PIZZA €€
(Map p48; 070 204 19 50; www.mangiasenzaglutine.it; Via Mameli 196; pizzas €4-11, meals €25-30; 6.30pm-midnight Tue-Sat) Waving the flag for gluten-free dining, Man.Gia does a roaring trade in pizzas, as well as serving a short menu of uncomplicated pastas and main courses. The look and vibe are laid-back, and they even do gluten-free beer.

Dal Corsaro RISTORANTE €€€
(Map p52; 070 66 43 18; www.stefanodeidda.it; Viale Regina Margherita 28; fixed-price menus €70-80; 7.45-11pm Tue-Sun) One of only two Michelin-starred restaurants in Sardinia, Dal Corsaro has long been a bastion of high-end culinary creativity. Calling the shots is chef Stefano Deidda whose artistic brand of cuisine marries technical brilliance with a passion for seasonal Sardinian ingredients. Typical of his style is his *maialino da latte, topinambur e aglio* (roast pork with Jerusalem artichoke and garlic). Bookings required.

Drinking & Nightlife

Head up to Il Castello for sundowners with a dress-circle view of Cagliari. Elsewhere, there's plenty of bar action on buzzy Piazza Yenne and nearby Corso Vittorio Emanuele, and in the busy lanes of Marina. In summer the party scene shifts to the bars and seafront joints at Poetto beach.

★**Cucina eat** WINE BAR
(Map p48; 070 099 10 98; www.shopcucina.it; Piazza Gallileo Galilei 1; 10.30am-11.30pm Mon-Sat) A bookshop, a bar, a bistrot? Cucina eat is pretty much all these things with its central bar and ceiling-high shelves stocked with wines, olive oils, cookbooks and kitchen gadgets, all of which are available to buy. Cool and relaxed, it's a fine spot to spend an evening over a bottle of wine and a light meal (around €20 to €25).

★**Caffè Libarium Nostrum** BAR
(Map p52; 346 5220212; Via Santa Croce 33; 7.30am-2am Tue-Sun) Offering some of the best views in town, this modish Castello bar has panoramic seating on top of the city's medieval ramparts. If the weather's being difficult, make for the brick-lined interior and order yourself an Alligator, a formidable cocktail of Calvados and Drambuie created in honour of the hero of Massimo Carlotto's novels (p61).

Antico Caffè CAFE
(Map p52; www.anticocaffe1855.it; Piazza Costituzione 10; 7am-2am) DH Lawrence and Grazia Deledda once frequented this grand old cafe, which opened its doors in 1855. Locals come to chat over leisurely coffees, crêpes and salads. There's a pavement terrace, or you can settle inside amid the polished wood, marble and brass.

Emerson LOUNGE
(070 37 51 94; www.emersoncagliari.it; Viale Poetto 4; 9am-1am summer, 10am-5pm winter) A swank beachside hang-out, Emerson is one of the more glamorous of the *chioschi* that line the seafront at Poetto. Part cocktail lounge, part restaurant and

part beach club, it dishes up everything from pasta to *aperitivi,* live music and sunloungers. It's near the fourth bus stop on the beach access road.

Caffè Svizzero CAFE

(Map p52; ☎070 65 37 84; Largo Carlo Felice 6; ⏰7am-9pm Mon-Sat) At the bottom of Largo Carlo Felice, this Liberty-style place has been a stalwart of Cagliari cafe society since the early 20th century. Anything from tea to cappuccinos and cocktails is on offer in its polished wood and brick-vaulted interior.

Tiffany CAFE

(Map p52; ☎070 732 47 87; Via Baylle 133; ⏰6am-9pm Mon-Sat) The outside tables at this handsome brick-vaulted cafe are *the* place to be for an early evening aperitif. Come around 6.30pm and you'll find every seat taken as Cagliari's fashionable drinkers congregate to catch up on gossip, sip on *spritz* and look beautiful.

Hop Corner PUB

(Map p52; ☎070 67 31 58; www.hopcornerbirreria.com; Via Principe Amedeo 14; ⏰7pm-1am Tue-Sat) This vaulted pub carved out of rock is an atmospheric spot for speciality craft beers and ales, which pair nicely with the excellent hamburgers and platters of local cheeses and cured meats. It hosts occasional live music evenings with a retro vibe.

Inu WINE BAR

(Map p48; ☎070 667 04 14; www.inusardinianwinebar.it; Via Sassari 50; ⏰7pm-1am Tue-Sun) Get versed in Sardinian wine at this contemporary, high-ceilinged wine bar, which pairs throaty Cannonau reds and tangy Vermentino whites with platters of top-quality Sardinian cured meats and cheeses, prepared at the well-stocked counter.

Caffè degli Spiriti BAR

(Map p52; ☎070 311 03 73; www.facebook.com/caffedeglispiriti; Bastione San Remy; ⏰10am-2am) This long-standing lounge bar boasts alfresco seating on the panoramic Bastione di Saint Remy, one of Cagliari's prize locations. Recently reopened after the Bastione's long restoration, it sets a memorable stage for lingering over cool summer drinks.

Il Merlo Parlante PUB

(Map p48; ☎333 9774573; Via Portoscalas 69; ⏰8pm-3am) One for beer fans, this is an unpretentious, no-frills pub, little changed over the past two decades. It has a fine selection of guest beers, bottled and on tap, and tasty *panini* to go with them. Expect basic wooden tables and boisterous, happy drinkers.

Caffè dell'Elfo BAR

(Map p52; ☎070 68 23 99; www.facebook.com/elfo.caffe; Salita Santa Chiara 4-6; ⏰7pm-2am Mon-Sat) Named after the elves that populate its small, stone-clad interior, this relaxed wine bar is a popular evening hang-out, serving decent cocktails and a small food menu.

☆ Entertainment

Cagliari has a lively performance scene, comprising classical music, dance, opera and drama. The season generally runs from October to May, although some places also offer a summer line-up of events. For information on up-coming events ask at the tourist office (p62), check online at Box Office Tickets (p54), or pick up a copy of the local newspaper *L'Unione Sarda*.

Teatro Lirico THEATRE

(Map p48; ☎070 408 22 30; www.teatroliricodicagliari.it; Via Sant'Alenixedda) This is Cagliari's premier venue for classical music, opera and ballet. The line-up is fairly traditional but quality is high and concerts are well attended. Tickets range range from €10 to €35 for concerts, from €15 to €75 for opera and ballet.

Shopping

Cagliari has a refreshing absence of overtly touristy souvenir shops, although they do exist. Style-conscious shoppers will find plenty to browse on Via Giuseppe Manno and Via Giuseppe Garibaldi. Nearby Via Sulis is another good area with several fashion boutiques and jewellery stores. You'll also find various artisanal shops tucked away, particularly in the Marina district. Sunday is best for flea market and antique finds.

★Durke FOOD

(Map p52; ☎347 2246858; www.durke.com; Via Napoli 66; ⏰10.30am-1.30pm & 4.30-8pm Mon-Sat) In Sardinian, *durke* means 'sweet', and they don't come sweeter than this delightful old-fashioned store. Its *dolci* (sweets) are all made according to age-old recipes, often with nothing more than sugar, egg whites and almonds. Indulge in fruit-and-nut *papassinos,* moist *amaretti di sardegna* biscuits and *pardulas* (delicate ricotta cheesecakes flavoured with saffron).

★**Mercato di San Benedetto** MARKET
(Map p48; Via San Francesco Cocco Ortu; 7am-2pm Mon-Sat) Cagliari's historic morning food market is exactly what a thriving market should be – busy, noisy and packed with fresh, fabulous produce: fish, salami, heavy clusters of grapes, *pecorino* the size of wagon wheels, steaks, sushi, you name it.

Cagliari Antiquaria ANTIQUES
(Map p48; Piazza del Carmine; 8am-2pm 1st, 2nd & 4th Sun of month) Three Sundays a month, Cagliaritani go bargain hunting at Cagliari Antiquaria, an antique and collectors market on Piazza del Carmine.

Enoteca Biondi 1959 WINE
(Map p52; 070 667 04 26; www.enotecabiondi.it; Viale Regina Margherita 83; 10am-1.30pm daily & 5-9.30pm Mon-Sat) One of Cagliari's best stocked bottle shops, Enoteca Biondi sells wine and beer from all over the world, as well as a selection of Italian gourmet specialities: balsamic vinegar from Modena, Sicilian *torrone* (nougat), conserves, cheeses and truffles.

Bistimentas CLOTHING
(Map p52; 070 289 20 74; www.facebook.com/bistimentas; Vico Barcellona 16; 10.30am-1pm & 5.30-8.30pm, closed Wed morning & Sun) Add a touch of Sardinian style to your wardrobe with a trip to Bistimentas. The shop is a celebration of island costumes and customs with everything from corduroy jackets and woollen waistcoats to masks, bags and embroidered dresses, all made by island artisans.

Intrecci ARTS & CRAFTS
(Map p52; 070 332 87 08; www.intrecciart.com; Viale Regina Margherita 63; 10am-1pm & 4.30-8.30pm Mon-Sat) There are plenty of souvenir shops in Cagliari but this airy showroom is a cut above them all. It showcases a range of products made by island artisans, including hand-crafted jewellery, paintings, ceramic work and objets d'art.

Love Retrò FASHION & ACCESSORIES
(Map p52; 070 800 50 25; www.loveretro.it; Via Sulis 26; 10am-1pm Tue-Sat & 5-8.30pm Mon-Sat) Local designer Alice Tolu displays her vintage-inspired fashions at her chic boutique on trendy Via Sulis. Alongside her seasonal creations, you'll find a range of elegant accessories and jewels carefully selected to complement the clothes.

Sapori di Sardegna FOOD & DRINKS
(Map p52; 070 684 87 47; www.saborescagliari.com; Via dei Mille 1; 9.30am-1pm & 3.30-8.30pm Mon-Sat) Roberto, his brother and their enthusiastic team do a brisk trade in glorious Sardinian food at this breezy Marina emporium. Stop by for the finest *pecorino*, salami, *bottarga* (mullet roe), bread, wine and prettily packed *dolci* (sweets). If you've got

MASSIMO CARLOTTO'S ALLIGATOR

Cagliari resident Massimo Carlotto's life reads like the plot of one of his crime novels because, quite simply, it is the plot of one of his books.

At 19, during Italy's 'years of lead', he witnessed the murder of Margherita Magello, a 25-year-old student who was stabbed 59 times. The events that followed became the novel *Il Fuggiasco* (The Fugitive). Covered in Magello's blood, Carlotto ran to get the police, who accused him of the killing. He was subsequently sentenced to 18 years' imprisonment. In 1993, after an international campaign, he was released with a full pardon from the president of Italy.

While in prison, Carlotto found the true-life material for the explicit crime novels he now writes. His most famous series is the Alligator, which Carlotto claims was developed from real legal cases.

The protagonist is loosely modelled on Carlotto himself; he even drives the Škoda Carlotto once drove (because many people say it is the least-stopped car in Italy). The nickname comes from the character's (and Carlotto's) favourite cocktail – seven parts Calvados to three parts Drambuie, crushed ice and a slice of apple – invented by a barman at the Caffè Libarium Nostrum (p59) in Cagliari. The cocktail's fame has since spread to bars in Rome, Milan and Naples. It's said that nobody can drink more than four.

Several of Carlotto's books have been translated into English, including *Gang of Lovers* (2015), *Band Love* (2010), *The Fugitive* (2008), *Death's Dark Abyss* (2007) and *The Goodbye Kiss* (2006).

no room in your luggage, staff can arrange to ship orders worldwide.

Sorelle Piredda FASHION & ACCESSORIES
(Map p52; ☎334 21 57 266, 349 55 00 528; www.sorellepiredda.com; Piazza San Giuseppe 4; ⏲10am-7.30pm Mon-Sat) For haute couture with history, search out this oh-so-stylish Castello boutique. The shop itself is a sight, set over a Punic cistern and ancient Roman streets, but it's the imaginative designs of the Piredda sisters that steal the limelight: slinky evening dresses, capes and intricate shawls inspired by ancient Sardinian motifs and traditional island costumes.

Loredana Mandas JEWELLERY
(Map p52; ☎070 66 76 48; www.loredanamandas.com; Via Sicilia 31; ⏲9.30am-1pm & 5-8.30pm Mon-Sat summer, 9.30am-1pm & 4.30-8pm Mon-Sat winter) For something very special, seek out this jewellery workshop where artisan Loredana Mandas creates the exquisite gold filigree for which Sardinia is so famous. Her designs, which often incorporate precious or semi-precious gemstones, cost from around €220 to €2000 plus.

ℹ Information

Guardia Medica (☎070 52 24 58; Via Talete 4; ⏲8pm-8am Mon-Fri, 10am-8am Sat, 8am-8am Sun) For overnight or weekend non-emergency medical assistance. It's located northeast of the city centre; take bus 1 from the train station (get off at Via Flavio Gioia).

Lamarì (Via Napoli 43; per hr €3; ⏲8am-9pm Mon-Sat) Speedy internet and wi-fi with cheap snacks and drinks on the side.

Ospedale Brotzu (☎070 53 92 10; www.aobrotzu.it; Piazzale Ricchi 1) Hospital with accident and emergency department. It's located northwest of the city centre; take bus 1 from Via Roma if you need to make a non-emergency visit.

Post Office (Map p48; ☎070 605 41 64; Piazza del Carmine 27; ⏲8.20am-7.05pm Mon-Fri, to 12.35pm Sat)

Tourist Office (Map p48; ☎070 677 81 73; www.cagliariturismo.it; Via Roma 145, Palazzo Civico; ⏲9am-8pm summer, 10am-1pm & 2-5pm Mon-Sat winter) Helpful English-speaking staff can provide city information and maps. The office is just inside Palazzo Civico's main entrance, on the right.

ℹ Getting There & Away

AIR

Cagliari Elmas Airport (☎070 21 12 11; www.cagliariairport.it) is 9km northwest of the city centre, near Elmas. Flights connect with mainland Italian cities, including Rome, Milan, Bergamo, Bologna, Florence, Naples, Rome, Turin and Venice. There are also flights to/from European destinations including Barcelona, London, Paris and Frankfurt. In summer, there are additional charter flights.

A number of major international airlines serve Cagliari, such as easyJet, Eurowings and Ryanair, as well as Italy's national carrier **Alitalia** (☎892010; www.alitalia.it) and **Meridiana** (☎892928; www.meridiana.it).

Trains run from the airport to Cagliari station approximately every 20 to 30 minutes between 6.37am and 11.07pm. The journey takes six to 10 minutes; tickets cost €1.30. A taxi will set you back around €20.

BOAT

Cagliari's **ferry port** is located just off Via Roma. **Tirrenia** (Map p48; ☎892 123, agency 070 66 95 01; www.tirrenia.it; Via Riva di Ponente 1; ⏲agency 9am-noon Mon-Sat, plus 4-7pm Mon-Wed, 5-8pm Thu, 4.30-7.30pm Fri, 5-7pm Sat) is the main ferry operator serving Cagliari, with year-round services to Civitavecchia (€56–€66 per person with a *poltrona* seat), Naples (€56–

WORTH A TRIP

SERDIANA

A pretty but otherwise undistinguished agricultural town about 25km north of Cagliari, Serdiana is home to one of Sardinia's most celebrated wine producers, the award-winning **Cantine Argiolas** (☎070 74 06 06; www.argiolas.it; Via Roma 28-30, Serdiana; tour with tasting €13-28; ⏲enoteca 10am-1pm & 3-6pm Mon-Fri, 9am-1pm Sat). You can stock up at the winery's *enoteca* or, with more time, take a guided tour. There are several to choose from, including a 1½-hour visit with tastings and a two-hour tour of local vineyards (€20). Cookery lessons are also available for €90 to €95 per person. Reservations required.

By car, take the SS554 north from Cagliari and after about 10km follow the SS387 for Dolianova. After another 10km take the turn-off for Serdiana. Alternatively, there are regular ARST buses (€2.60, 45 minutes).

€98 per person) and Palermo (€58–€70 per person). Book tickets at the port agency, online or at travel agencies.

BUS

From the **main bus station** (Map p48; Piazza Matteotti) , **ARST** (Azienda Regionale Sarda Trasporti; ☎800 865042; www.arst.sardegna.it) buses serve Pula (€3.10, 50 minutes, hourly), Chia (€3.70, 1¼ hours, up to 10 daily) and Villasimius (€4.30, 1½ hours, at least six daily), as well as Oristano (€6.70, two hours, two daily), Nuoro (€12.50, 2¾ hours, two daily) and Iglesias (€4.30, 1½ hours, daily weekdays).

Turmo Travel (☎0789 2 14 87; www.grupoturmotravel.com) has services to Olbia (€16.50, 4½ hours, twice daily) and Santa Teresa di Gallura (€19.50, 5½ hours, daily).

CAR & MOTORCYCLE

The island's main dual-carriage, the SS131 'Carlo Felice', links the capital with Porto Torres via Oristano and Sassari; a branch road, the SS-131dcn, runs from Oristano to Olbia via Nuoro. The SS130 leads west to Iglesias.

The coast roads approaching from the east and west get highly congested in the summer holiday season.

TRAIN

The main train station is located on Piazza Matteotti. Direct trains serve Iglesias (€4.30, one hour, 11 daily), Carbonia (€4.90, one hour, eight daily), Sassari (€16.50, 2¾ hours, three daily), Porto Torres (€18, 3½ hours, one daily), Oristano (€6.70, 50 minutes to 1½ hours, 15 daily) and Olbia (€18, 3¼ hours, three daily).

ARST (p63) runs a light rail service from Piazza Repubblica to Monserrato, where you can connect with trains for Dolianova, Mandas and Isili. A single ticket costs €1.30.

Getting Around

The centre of Cagliari is small enough to explore on foot. The walk up to Il Castello is tough, but there's an elevator at the bottom of the Scalette di Santa Chiara behind Piazza Yenne.

BUS

CTM (Consorzio Trasporti e Mobilità; ☎800 078870; www.ctmcagliari.it; single/daily ticket €1.30/3.30) bus routes cover the city and surrounding area. You might use the buses to reach a handful of out-of-the-way sights, and they come in handy for Calamosca and Poetto beaches. Tickets are valid for 1½ hours.

The most useful lines:

Bus 7 Circular route from Piazza Yenne up to Il Castello and back.

Bus 30 or 31 Along the seafront to near the sanctuary at Bonaria.

Bus PF or PQ From Piazza Matteotti to Poetto beach.

WORTH A TRIP

MURAVERA'S CITRUS CELEBRATION

On the first or second weekend before Easter, the workaday agricultural centre of Muravera celebrates its fabled citrus fruit crop during the annual **Sagra degli Agrumi** (Citrus Fair; www.sagradegliagrumi.it; ⏲Mar/early Apr). Events include tastings, concerts, workshops and a colourful parade of folk groups from all over Sardinia in their traditional costumes.

ARST runs up to nine buses daily from Cagliari to Muravera (€5.50, 1¾ to three hours). By car, take the SS125 northeast 74km towards Tortoli.

CAR & MOTORCYCLE

Driving in the centre of Cagliari is a pain, although given the geography of the town (one big hill), you might consider renting a scooter for a day or two.

Parking in the city centre from 9am to 1pm and 4pm to 8pm Monday to Saturday means paying. On-street metered parking (within the blue lines) costs €1 per hour. Alternatively, there's a 24-hour car park next to the train station, which costs €1 per hour or €10 for 24 hours. There's no maximum stay.

There's a **Hertz** (☎070 65 10 78; www.hertz.it; Piazza Matteotti 8; ⏲8.30am-7.30pm Mon-Fri, 8.30am-1pm & 4-7.30pm Sat, 9am-1pm & 4-7.30pm Sun) in town and several car rental agencies at the airport including **Auto Europa** (☎800 334440; www.autoeuropa.it; Cagliari Elmas Airport; ⏲8am-11pm).

TAXI

Many hotels and guesthouses arrange airport pick-ups. There are taxi ranks at **Piazza Matteotti** (Map p48; Via Sassari), **Piazza Repubblica** (Map p48) and on **Largo Carlo Felice** (Map p52; Piazza Yenne). Otherwise you can call the radio taxi firms **Radio Taxi 4 Mori** (☎070 40 01 01; www.cagliaritaxi.com) and **Rossoblù** (☎070 66 55; www.radiotaxirossoblu.com).

THE SARRABUS

The Sarrabus, the triangular-shaped territory that covers Sardinia's south-eastern corner, is one of the island's least-populated and least-developed areas. It might only be an hour or two by car from Cagliari but it feels like another world with its remote, thickly wooded mountains and snaking, silent roads. Its high point, Monte dei Sette Fratelli, is a miraculously unspoilt wilderness, home to some of the island's last remaining deer. The coastal scenery is every bit as impressive, featuring high cliff-bound coves and endless swathes of sand fronted by transparent azure waters.

Most people visit in summer, sticking to the well-known beach destinations of Villasimius and the Costa Rei, but venture inland and you'll discover there's some great hiking to be had in its mountainous hinterland.

Villasimius & Capo Carbonara

Once a quiet fishing village surrounded by pines and *macchia* (Mediterranean shrubland), Villasimius has grown into one of Sardinia's most popular southern resorts. The town itself is about 1.5km inland but it makes a handy base for exploring the fabulous beaches and transparent waters that sparkle on the nearby coast. In summer it's a lively, cheerful place, but activity all but dies out in winter.

Sights

★Capo Carbonara NATURE RESERVE

(www.ampcapocarbonara.it) If you embark on just one excursion from Villasimius, make it the 15-minute drive south to Capo Carbonara, a protected marine park. The promontory dips spectacularly into the crystal-clear waters of the Med. Besides perfect conditions for divers, the area has some gorgeously secluded bays with white quartz sand, backed by cliffs cloaked in *macchia* and wildflowers. Walking trails teeter off in all directions. Note that parts of the promontory are off-limits to the public due to the presence of a military weather station.

★Cala Giunco BEACH

The pick of Villasimius' *spiagge* (beaches), Cala Giunco is a vision of beach perfection: a long strip of silky white sand sandwiched between azure waters and a silvery lagoon, the Stagno Notteri (p64), where pink flamingos congregate in winter. To the north, *macchia*-clad hills rise on the blue horizon.

Museo Archeologico MUSEUM

(☎070 793 02 90; Via Frau 5; adult/reduced €3/1.50; ⏰10am-1pm & 6-9pm Tue-Sun summer, 9am-1pm & 4-6pm Tue-Sun winter) This museum harbours a small but interesting collection of Roman and Phoenician artefacts, as well as various odds and ends recovered from a 15th-century Spanish shipwreck.

Fortezza Vecchia HISTORIC SITE

(☎070 793 02 71; adult/reduced €3/1.50; ⏰5-8pm) Perched on cliffs close to Capo Carbonara, this ruined 14th-century fortress dates back to the time the Aragonese controlled the island. The views over the bay to the green, *macchia*-tufted mountains are more striking than the stronghold itself.

Activities

In town the main activity is browsing shops and enjoying the holiday atmosphere. Boat tours are a popular summer activity, with operators running cruises along the coast between May and September.

Fiore di Maggio BOATING

(☎345 6032042; www.fioredimaggio.eu; per adult/child incl lunch €45/35) These daily boat tours are a superb way to see the hidden bays and islands of the Capo Carbonara marine reserve. Take your bathers if you fancy a dip.

Festivals & Events

Festa della Madonna del Naufrago RELIGIOUS

(⏰3rd weekend Jul) The Festa della Madonna del Naufrago, Villasimius' big annual event, is held towards the end of July. The highlight is a boat procession to a spot off the coast where a statue of the Virgin Mary lies on the seabed. Wreaths of flowers are left in honour of shipwrecked sailors.

DON'T MISS

VILLASIMIUS BEACHES

Villasimius boasts some of Sardinia's finest beaches. The easiest to get to is **Spiaggia Simius**, which is walkable from the town centre along Viale Matteotti. Further to the south is **Cala Giunco** (p64), a fabulous strip of sand on the seaward side of the **Stagno Notteri**. On the other side of the peninsula, north of the Porto Turistico, **Spiaggia del Riso** and the smaller **Spiaggia Campulongu** are also popular hang-outs.

DON'T MISS

DIVING OFF CAPO CARBONARA

Although parts of the cape are a military zone off-limits to visitors, the azure waters around Capo Carbonara (p64) are a marine reserve. This protected area, which includes the Isola dei Cavoli, Secca dei Berni and Isola di Serpentara, is accessible with an authorised diving company. Both **Morgan Diving** (☎337 564354; www.morgandiving.com; Marina di Capitana; dives €40-110) and **Air Sub** (☎070 79 20 33; www.airsubdiving.com; Via Roma 121; single dive from €40, full kit hire €20) in Villasimius lead dives to a number of sites, including an underwater mountain known as the Secca di Santa Caterina. Reckon on €40 to €110 for a dive, depending on location and level of difficulty.

Eating

In Villasimius, you'll find several pizzerias, bars and restaurants, many serving local seafood. Action is concentrated on the main drag, Via del Mare, its continuation Via Umberto I, and Via Roma. With your own transport, there are also various summer-only restaurants dotted around the coastal areas south of town. Many resort hotels also have restaurants open to nonguests.

Ristorante Le Anfore MEDITERRANEAN €€
(☎070 79 20 32; www.hotelleanfore.com; Via Pallaresus 16; meals €30-40; ⏰noon-2.30pm Tue-Sun & 7.30-10.30pm daily) The chef's love of fresh local produce shines through in Sardinian dishes such as *bottarga di muggine* (mullet roe) and *fregola con le vongole* (couscous-like pasta with clams) at this highly regarded hotel-restaurant. Adding to the experience is the al fresco verandah overlooking the hotel gardens.

Ristorante La Lanterna RISTORANTE, PIZZERIA €€
(☎070 79 00 13; Via Roma 64; meals €35; ⏰12.30-2.30pm & 6.50-10.30pm daily summer, Thu-Tue winter) A warm and welcoming restaurant-cum-pizzeria with a sunny outdoor terrace and genuine island food, this is one of the best places in the town centre. The menu covers all bases with a range of classic seafood dishes alongside traditional Sardinian pastas, steaks and pizzas.

Information

Tourist Office (☎070 793 02 71; Piazza Giovanni XXIII; ⏰10am-11.30pm summer, shorter hours winter) In the town centre just off the central Via Umberto I.

Getting There & Around

ARST buses run to and from Cagliari (€4.30, 1½ hours, at least six daily) throughout the year.

If you want to rent your own wheels (a good idea, as most of the beaches are a few kilometres out of town), **Rent A Car Simius** (☎070 792 80 37; www.rentacarsimius.com; Via Roma 77) hires out bikes, scooters and cars.

Costa Rei

Stretching along Sardinia's southeastern seafront, the Costa Rei extends from Cala Sinzias, about 25km north of Villasimius, to a rocky headland known as Capo Ferrat. Its lengthy beaches are stunning with pearly-white sands and glorious azure waters.

Approaching from Villasimius, the first beach you hit is Cala Sinzias, a pretty sandy strip some 6km south of the main Costa Rei resort. The resort is typical of many in Sardinia, a functional holiday village of villas, shops, bars and eateries that's dead in winter but packed in the summer holiday months.

North of the resort, the beaches continue up to the road's end at Capo Ferrato, beyond which drivable dirt trails lead north.

Sights

Spiaggia Costa Rei BEACH
In front of the eponymous resort, the Spiaggia Costa Rei is a lengthy strip of dazzling white sand lapped by astonishingly clear blue-green waters.

Spiaggia Piscina Rei BEACH
To the north of Costa Rei, this fabulous beach impresses with its blinding-white sand and turquoise water. A couple more beaches fill the remaining length of coast up to Capo Ferrato.

Getting There & Away

Throughout the year, three weekday ARST buses connect the Costa Rei with Villasimius (€1.90, 45 minutes). In summer, there are at least a couple more services.

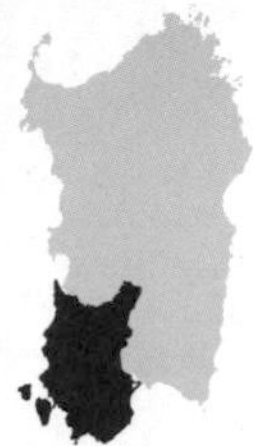

Iglesias & the Southwest

Includes ➡

Best Places to Eat

➡ Agriturismo Su Boschettu (p89)

➡ Cibus (p79)

➡ Osteria Della Tonnara da Andrea (p80)

➡ Agriturismo L'Oasi del Cervo (p76)

➡ Rubiu (p83)

Best Places to Sleep

➡ Nichotel (p211)

➡ Agriturismo Su Boschettu (p213)

➡ B&B Mare Monti Miniere (p210)

➡ Hotel Baia di Nora (p212)

➡ Hotel Luci del Faro (p212)

Why Go?

Silky beaches, prehistoric treasures, haunting mines – Sardinia's southwest is rich in history and natural beauty. The main drawcard is its thrilling coastline, which stretches from the great untamed sands of the Costa Verde to the cliff-bound coves of the Iglesiente and the seductive bays of the Costa del Sud. Offshore, the Isola di San Pietro and Isola di Sant'Antioco boast their own distinctive charms: San Pietro with its animated and instantly likeable atmosphere, and Sant'Antioco with its earthy character and rich archaeological legacy.

Inland, there's a rather melancholy feel to the area around Iglesias, the southwest's charming main town. This was once the island's mining heartland and the silent hills are today pitted with abandoned mines, many of which have been resurrected as museums and visitor attractions. Further in, the Marmilla's voluptuous green countryside harbours rich archaeological pickings, including Sardinia's greatest *nuraghe,* the Unesco-listed Nuraghe Su Nuraxi.

When to Go

➡ Sardinia goes to town for Easter (March or April), celebrating Holy Week with processions and parades. Iglesias excels at this with a series of hooded processions accompanied by deathly drumming.

➡ Foodies should pencil in late May or early June when the Isola di San Pietro goes wild for tuna at its big annual festival, the Girotonno.

➡ August is perfect for beach parties on the southern coast and exploring the remote dunes of the Costa Verde.

➡ For hiking on the Iglesiente coast, April, May, September and early October are prime periods with good weather and beautiful colours.

IGLESIAS

☎0781 / POP 27,190

Surrounded by the skeletons of Sardinia's once-thriving mining industry, Iglesias is a historic town that bubbles in the summer and slumbers in the colder months. Its historic centre, an appealing ensemble of lived-in piazzas, sun-bleached buildings, churches and Aragonese-style wrought-iron balconies, creates an atmosphere that's as much Iberian as Sardinian – a vestige of its time as a Spanish colony. Visit at Easter to experience the city's extraordinary Settimana Santa (Holy Week) processions, featuring trains of sinister, white-robed celebrants parading through the skinny lanes of the *centro storico*.

History

Although named after its churches – Iglesias means churches in Spanish – the town has a long history as a mining centre. The Carthaginians are known to have mined the surrounding area, as did the Romans who extracted silver and lead, and established a mining town, Metalla, in the hills south of modern-day Fluminimaggiore.

Iglesias itself was founded in the 13th century by Ugolino della Gherardesca. A Pisan noble with a shrewd head for business, Ugolino reopened the Roman mines and organised the town, which was originally called Villa di Chiesa, as a Tuscan-style *comune* (self-regulating town) with its own currency, rights and laws. These laws were subsequently codified and recorded in a book known as the Breve di Villa di Chiesa.

The city thrived but in 1324 it fell to the Catalan-Aragonese, who promptly renamed it Iglesias. More seriously, they closed its mines, and for the next 500 years the pits lay abandoned until private entrepreneurs, such as Quintino Sella, revived their fortunes in the 19th century. As a nascent industrial centre in a resurgent and soon-to-be-united Italy, Iglesias once again flourished until WWII and modern economics tolled its death knell in the 1970s.

Sights

Much of the pleasure of visiting Iglesias lies in the medieval centre. There are no great must-see sights, but the narrow lanes and suggestive piazzas are in good nick and are much appreciated by locals who flock here to browse the shops and hang out in its bars. It's also here that you'll find many of the churches that give the city its name.

Chiesa di San Francesco CHURCH

(Piazza San Francesco; ⌚8.30am-11.30am & 5-7pm) From Piazza del Municipio, Via Pullo leads to the dainty rose-red trachyte of the Chiesa di San Francesco. Built over a 200-year period between the 14th and 16th centuries, this small church is a wonderful example of Catalan Gothic architecture with its simple austere facade, circular windows and single-nave interior. Flanking the nave is a series of chapels squeezed between the buttresses.

Cattedrale di Santa Chiara CATHEDRAL

(Duomo; Piazza del Municipio; ⌚9am-12.30pm & 3-8pm) Dominating the eastern flank of Piazza del Municipio, the Cattedrale di Santa Chiara boasts a lovely Pisan-flavoured facade and a checkerboard stone bell tower. The church was originally built in the late 13th century, but it was given a comprehensive makeover in the 16th century, which accounts for its current Catalan Gothic look. Inside, the highlight is a gilded retable that once held the relics of St Antiochus.

This was originally on the Isola di Sant'Antioco but it was bought to Iglesias in the 17th century to protect it from the threat of pirate raids. And although the clerics were later forced to return the relics, they managed to hold on to the altarpiece.

Flanking the cathedral on the piazza is the bishop's residence, the **Palazzo Vescovile**, and opposite is Iglesias' neoclassical **Municipio**. Both buildings are closed to the public.

Chiesa di Santa Maria delle Grazie CHURCH

(Piazza Manzoni 7; ⌚9am-12.30pm & 3-8pm) Originally constructed at the end of the 13th century, the modest Chiesa di Santa Maria delle Grazie retains little of its original form. About the only surviving element is the base of the medieval facade, which is topped by a pinky baroque structure, added in the 17th and 18th centuries.

Piazza Quintino Sella PIAZZA

Iglesias' focal square, Piazza Quintino Sella was laid out in the 19th-century in what was at the time a field outside the city walls. It soon became a central meeting place and

Iglesias & the Southwest Highlights

❶ **Spiaggia di Piscinas** (p75) Escaping the coastal crowds on this remote beach on the Costa Verde.

❷ **Nuraghe Su Nuraxi** (p87) Delving into the mysteries of Sardinia's nuraghic culture.

❸ **Capo Sandalo** (p81) Revelling in inspiring coastal views on the Isola di San Pietro.

❹ **Strada Panoramica della Costa del Sud** (p84) Driving this stunning coastal road.

❺ **Cala Domestica Beach** (p73) Sneaking off the radar for a day at this magnificent secluded beach.

❻ **La Giara di**

Gesturi (p88) Coming face to face with wild horses on Sardinia's Table Mountain.

7 **Tempio di Antas** (p86) Poking around Roman ruins at this bucolic site, north of Iglesias.

8 **Settimana Santa** (p71) Giving yourself over to the sombre atmosphere of Iglesias' Easter processions.

9 **Porto Flavia** (p73) Marvelling at the engineering ingenuity of this cliffside port.

10 **Necropoli di Montessu** (p77) Peering into the long-dead past at this prehistoric necropolis.

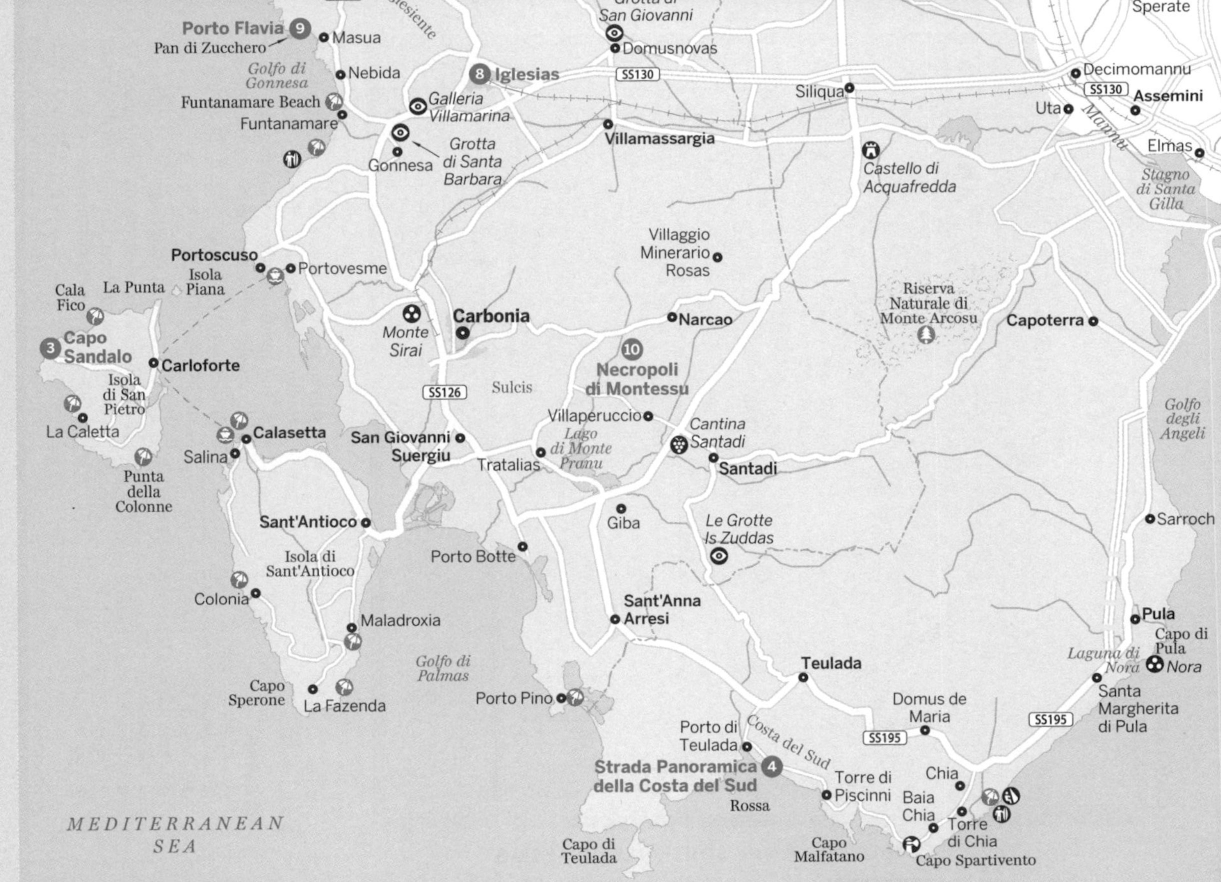

Iglesias

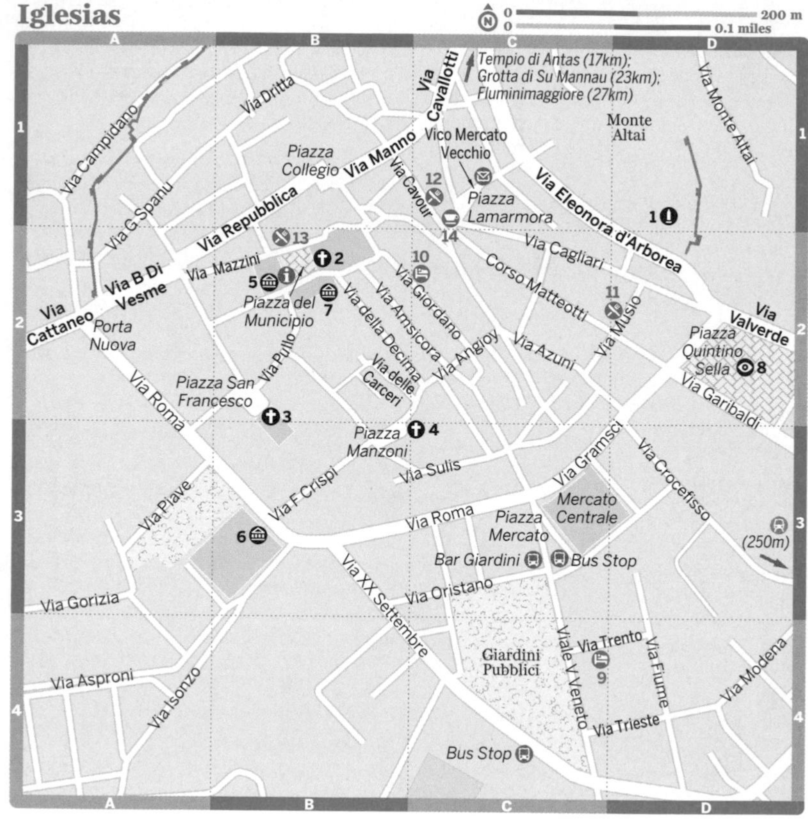

Iglesias

Sights

1 Castello Salvaterra D1
2 Cattedrale di Santa Chiara B2
3 Chiesa di San Francesco B2
4 Chiesa di Santa Maria delle Grazie C3
5 Municipio B2
6 Museo dell'Arte Mineraria B3
7 Palazzo Vescovile B2
8 Piazza Quintino Sella D2

Sleeping

9 B&B Mare Monti Miniere C4
10 La Babbajola B&B C2

Eating

11 Gazebo Medioevale D2
12 Pizzeria Il Quinto Moro C1
13 Villa di Chiesa B2

Drinking & Nightlife

14 Caffè Lamarmora C1

still today it throngs with people during the evening *passeggiata* (evening stroll). The statue in the centre commemorates Quintino Sella (of Sella e Mosca wine fame), a 19th-century statesman and champion of the area's mining industry.

Museo dell'Arte Mineraria MUSEUM
(☎347 5176886; www.museoartemineraria.it; Via Roma 47; adult/reduced €5/4; ⏲6.30-8.30pm Sat & Sun summer, by appointment rest of year) Just outside the historic centre, Iglesias' main museum is dedicated to the town's mining heritage. It displays up to 70 extraction machines, alongside tools and a series of thought-provoking B&W photos. But to get a real taste of the claustrophobic conditions in which the miners worked, duck down into the recreated tunnels. These were dug by mining students and were used to train senior workers until WWII when they were used as air-raid shelters.

Castello Salvaterra TOWER
(Via Monte Artai) Just off Piazza Quintino Sella, stairs lead to a stout square tower. This is all that remains of the Castello Salvaterra, the once-mighty Pisan fortress of Ugolino della Gherardesca. Behind it a path leads along a short section of the town's original crenellated wall.

To get a better idea of what the city looked like before the walls came down, head to Via Campidano, where a stretch of 14th-century wall remains defiantly in place, complete with towers.

Monteponi Mine MINE
(0781 27 45 05; Monteponi Mine; adult/reduced €10/6.50; by appointment only) About 2km west of Iglesias, the sprawling Monteponi mining complex, now abandoned, was once one of Sardinia's most important producers of lead, zinc and silver. Extraction on the site started in around 1324 and continued on and off until 1992, when the entire operation transferred to Campo Pisano across the valley. Guided visits take in the Galleria Villamarina, an underground tunnel that connected the mine's two main shafts: the Pozzo Vittorio Emanuele and Pozzo Sella.

Festivals & Events

Settimana Santa RELIGIOUS
(Holy Week; Mar/Apr) In the week before Easter, Iglesias celebrates its Spanish roots and traditions in a series of dramatic religious processions. Every night between Holy Tuesday and Good Friday, white-hooded participants bear effigies of the Virgin Mary and Christ through the historic centre to the sound of drums and heavy wooden rattles. Events culminate in the Good Friday procession, a sombre re-evocation of Christ's funeral.

Estate Medioevale Iglesiente CULTURAL
(Aug) Iglesias' Medieval Summer comprises a series of themed events that involve much dressing up and flag-waving. Highlights include a huge costumed procession through the *centro storico* on 13 August.

Eating & Drinking

Pizzeria Il Quinto Moro PIZZA €
(0781 186 08 86, 349 4927035; www.facebook.com/pizzeriaquinto.moro.7; Via Cavour 18; pizzas from €4.70; 6-11pm Wed-Mon) For a delicious pizza, search out this busy little place in the *centro storico*. It's decidedly no-frills with wooden tables, paper tablecloths and plastic cutlery, but the wood-fired pizzas are the business with their thick, Neapolitan-style bases. Unusually, they're sold in different sizes, either to eat in or takeaway.

Villa di Chiesa RISTORANTE, PIZZERIA €€
(0781 3 16 41; Piazza del Municipio 9-10; meals €30; 12.30-3pm & 7.30-11pm Tue-Sun) The elegant confines of Piazza del Municipio set the stage for alfresco dining at this long-standing summer favourite. In winter, diners move inside to feast on pizza, pasta and seafood while being serenaded by local crooners. Menu stalwarts include *ravioli di cernia* (ravioli filled with grouper) and *sebadas* (light pastry filled with cheese and honey).

Gazebo Medioevale SARDINIAN €€
(0781 3 08 71; www.facebook.com/gazebomedioevale; Via Musio 21; meals €30-35; noon-3pm & 8-11.45pm Mon-Sat) A long-standing restaurant in the historic centre, Gazebo Medioevale looks the part with its exposed brick walls, stone arches and Sardinian masks. The food is fresh and authentic, with dishes ranging from cheese and cured meat platters to seafood pastas and hearty grilled steaks. No credit cards.

Caffè Lamarmora CAFE
(Piazza Lamarmora 6; 6am-1pm & 3-9.30pm winter, longer hours summer) Occupying a towering 19th-century *palazzo* covered in Liberty-style advertising – these were added in 1904 – this landmark cafe is ideally placed for a quick coffee fix. In summer, linger at tables in the small square outside.

Information

Banco BNL (Via Roma 29) Bank with an ATM.

Post Office (Vico Mercato Vecchio; 8.20am-1.35pm Mon-Fri, to 12.35pm Sat)

Tourist Office (0781 27 45 05; Piazza del Municipio; 10am-noon & 4-8pm Mon-Sat) Helpful tourist office located on the ground floor of the main Municipio building.

Getting There & Away

BUS

ARST buses run to Cagliari (€4.50, one to 1½ hours, two daily) and Carbonia (€2.50, 50 minutes, nine daily) as well as closer destinations on the Iglesiente coast such as Funtanamare (€1.30, 20 minutes, at least six daily).

DON'T MISS

CLIMBING & CAVING

Rock Climbing

About 10km east of Iglesias, the town of Domusnovas is at the centre of one of Sardinia's top rock-climbing areas. The outlying countryside is peppered with limestone rocks, cliffs and caves, many of which are ideal for sports climbing. There are about 500 routes for both novice and experienced climbers ranging from simple, single-pitch walls to tough overhangs. Experts say climatic and rock conditions are at their best between early autumn and late spring.

For more technical information, see www.climb-europe.com/rockclimbingsardinia.html.

Caving

Several caves near Iglesias also merit a visit.

Grotta di San Giovanni Four kilometres north of Domusnovas, the Grotta di San Giovanni, an 850m-long natural cave-gallery adorned with stalactites and stalagmites, is worth checking out. It's free to enter and is illuminated between 9am and 9pm. If you're feeling peckish there's a bar-restaurant by the car park at the entrance.

Grotta di Santa Barbara (☎0781 27 45 07; adult/reduced €15/12; ⌚guided tours 9am, 10.15am, 11.30am, 12.45pm Sat, plus 2.15pm & 3.10pm Sun) The Grotta di Santa Barbara lies deep within the abandoned San Giovanni mine some 4km west of Iglesias. The walls of the single enormous chamber are pockmarked with dark-brown crystals and white calcite, while stalactites and stalagmites give the impression of a ghostly underground forest. To ensure a spot on a guided tour, it's advisable to book through the tourist office (p71) in Iglesias.

Grotta di Su Mannau (☎0781 58 04 11; www.sumannau.it; adult/reduced €10/6; ⌚9.30am-5.30pm Easter-Jun & mid-Sep–Oct, to 6.30pm Jul–mid-Sep, by appointment Nov-Easter) A few kilometres south of Fluminimaggiore off the SS126, this is the largest cave system of its sort so far discovered in the Iglesiente. The standard hour-long tour passes through several lake chambers and the Archaeological Room, so-called because it's thought to have once housed a water temple. Finally you'll reach the Pozzo Rodriguez (Rodriguez Well), home to an impressive 7m column formed by a stalagmite and stalactite fusing together, and beyond that, the Rodriguez Room.

Intercity buses arrive at and depart from **Via XX Settembre** and **Piazza Mercato** near the Giardini Pubblici.

Get timetable information and tickets from **Bar Giardini** (Piazza Mercato 10; ⌚5.30am-8.30pm Mon-Sat) across the road from the Piazza Mercato stop.

CAR & MOTORCYCLE

From Cagliari, it's 55km to Iglesias on the SS130, a dual carriageway. Alternatively, you can take the SS195 coastal road and connect with the SS126.

From the north, the SS126 drops south from Oristano to Guspini and then winds through the hills via Arbus and Fluminimaggiore.

TRAIN

Up to 10 direct trains run daily to/from Cagliari (€4.30, one hour).

THE IGLESIENTE

To the north and west of Iglesias, the mountainous landscape of the Iglesiente is picturesque and strangely haunting. Wild green scrub cloaks the silent hills in a soft, verdant down and abandoned mines, many of which can now be visited, serve as a poignant reminder of the industry that once thrived here. The coast is dramatic, one of southern Sardinia's most beautiful, with plunging cliffs and superb seascapes at every turn.

To explore the coast, the SP83 coastal road dips and weaves its way northwards from Funtanamare, passing through the former mining villages of Nebida, Masua and Buggerru before petering to a halt at Portixeddu. Inland, the SS126 snakes through thickly wooded hills south of Fluminimaggiore leading to two of the area's main sights: the Tempio di Antas and Grotta di Su Mannau.

Southern Iglesiente Coast

West of Iglesias, the SP83 coastal road affords spectacular views as it snakes its way northwards from Funtanamare to Cala Domestica, passing through the former mining communities of Nebida and Masua.

Sights

Sights below (listed from south to north) are all easily accessible from the SP83.

Funtanamare Beach BEACH

The nearest beach to Iglesias is at Funtanamare (which is also spelt Fontanamare), about 12km west of town. A long strip of golden sand backed by dunes and fertile farmland, it's a hugely popular spot, though it rarely gets too crowded, if nothing else because it's so long. Strong winds make it a surfer favourite, particularly when the *maestrale* (northwestly wind) is blowing.

At least six daily buses run from Iglesias to the beach (€1.30, 20 minutes), and there's plenty of parking if you want to drive. Buses also continue to a second beach known as **Plage Mesu**, further south along the same strand.

★Belvedere VIEWPOINT

(Nebida) This panoramic terrace, accessible by a cliffside path from Nebida's southern entrance, commands fabulous views. Dominating the seascape is the 133m-high Pan di Zucchero, the largest of several *faraglioni* (sea stacks) that rise out of the glassy blue waters against a backdrop of sheer white cliffs. The gutted shell of a building you see beneath you is the Laveria Lamarmora, a former mineral washing plant.

Pan di Zucchero NATURAL FEATURE

(Sugarloaf) A vast white *scoglio* (rock) rising out of the glassy blue seas in front of Masua, the Sugarloaf is one of the coast's great postcard sights. Named because of its resemblance to the more famous Pão de Açúcar hill in Rio de Janeiro, its distinctive bulk, which tops off at 133m, is visible from miles around.

★Porto Flavia PORT

(☎0781 27 45 05; Masua; adult/reduced €10/6.50; ⊙guided tours 9.30am, 10.30am, 11.30am & 12.30pm Mon-Fri summer, plus 2.30pm & 3.30pm Sat & Sun year-round) A marvel of early-20th-century engineering, Porto Flavia is a port dug into cliffs 50m above the sea. Consisting of two 600m tunnels and an ingenious mechanical arm, it was used to load zinc and lead ore directly onto cargo ships waiting in the waters below. To find it, head towards Masua's beach from where a road leads back uphill and around the coast for about 2.5km. Visits are by guided tour only; it's best to book through the tourist office (p71) in Iglesias.

Built in 1924, Porto Flavia revolutionised the system of shipping minerals from Masua. Before it was built, the mined ore had to be loaded onto boats that had been hauled up onto the beach. These then sailed to Carloforte to transfer their loads to larger cargo vessels. However, Porto Flavia enabled the ore to be transported directly from underground depots to the cargo ships by means of a conveyor belt (in the lower of the two tunnels).

Spiaggia di Masua BEACH

Beyond the unsightly remnants of Masua's mine, this lovely little sandy beach provides memorable close-ups of the Pan di Zucchero (p73) rock stack.

★Cala Domestica Beach BEACH

A sensational sandy beach wedged into a natural inlet between craggy rocks, Cala Domestica is a heavenly spot. Its shallow blue waters are ideal for swimming and surfers

HIKING THE IGLISIENTE COAST

The Iglesiente coast provides a dramatic setting for some wonderful hiking. Trails and dirt tracks hug the coastline, leading through green-capped slopes to hidden beaches and old mines, many of which can be visited on guided tours. A popular, though tough, route is the stretch from Nebida to Buggerru, via Masua and Cala Domestica beach. Best done over two, or even three, days, it's approximately 30km and involves some serious hill work.

GUIDED MINE VISITS

A number of mines and industrial sites in the Iglesias hinterland can be visited on guided tours. These include **Porto Flavia** (p73) in Masua, **Galleria Henry** (p74) in Buggerru and the **Monteponi Mine** (p71) near Iglesias.

For information or to book a spot on a tour, either call the site directly or contact the **tourist office** (p71) in Iglesias.

can take to the waves that sometimes curl up here. A walk along the rocky path to the right of the beach brings you to a smaller, more sheltered side strand. The beach is situated north of Masua, about 5km from Buggerru.

Facilities are thin on the ground here, besides a pay car park and a small snack bar. Bring your own shade in summer.

Eating

906 Operaio PIZZA €

(☎338 9165388; Belvedere, Nebida; pizzas €5.50-12; ⏱7.30am-midnight Easter-Oct) For once the food plays second fiddle. A meal at this casual, laid-back pizzeria is all about its magical setting at Belvedere (p73). Tables are laid out on a covered cliffside path offering extraordinary views over the plunging coastline and, in the distance, the famous Pan di Zucchero sea stack. The pizzas are pretty good too.

Buggerru & Portixeddu

Set within the natural stone walls of a steep valley, Buggerru is a popular resort with a small harbour and a rash of holiday apartments. Like many villages in the area, it started life as a mining centre and today its mine (aka the Galleria Henry) is a major visitor attraction. Mining aside, the village makes a convenient base for exploring the Iglesiente coast. Just a couple of kilometres to the north, the tiny tourist village of Portixeddu boasts one of the coast's best beaches, a gloriously unspoilt swathe of sand backed by remote green hills.

History

The largest village on the Iglesiente coast, Buggerru was established in 1860 and by the early 20th century had become an important mining centre. For a long time it was accessible only by sea, a fact that forced it into enterprising self-sufficiency – it had its own electricity supply before Cagliari and Sassari, as well as a hospital and small theatre. It wasn't all roses though, and in 1904 Buggerru's miners downed tools and went on strike – the first ever recorded in Sardinia. Later the closure of mines in WWI and the 1930s forced many workers to leave and the local population to plummet.

Sights & Activities

Spiaggia di Portixeddu BEACH

About 2km north of Buggerru, Spiaggia di Portixeddu is one of the best beaches in the area. A gloriously unspoilt strip of sand backed by swathes of rolling olive-green *macchia*, it extends for 3km up to the Rio Mannu, the river marking the end of the Iglesiente coast.

Galleria Henry MINE

(☎388 9323529; www.comune.buggerru.ci.it; Via Roma 52, Buggerru; adult/reduced €10/6; ⏱hours vary) A remnant of Buggerru's day as a mining centre, the Galleria Henry is a 1km-long tunnel that was dug in 1865 to allow a small train to transport minerals from underground depots to washing plants. A highlight of the hour-long gallery tour is the view down to the sea 50m below. Call between 10am and noon to check opening hours or head to the website of the Comune di Buggerru.

Mormora BOATING

(☎340 2727524; Porto Turistico; tours per person from €30) To take to the local waters, this outfit runs boat tours and hires out boats (from €90 per half-day plus fuel) from Buggerru's Porto Turistico (Tourist Harbour).

Eating

L'Ancora SEAFOOD €€

(☎0781 5 49 03; Via degli Asfodcli 6, Località Portixeddu; meals €25-35; ⏱12.30-3.30pm & 8.30-11pm summer, 12.30-3.30pm Thu-Tue winter) L'Ancora is a small family-run trattoria overlooking the beach at Portixeddu. Its sea-facing terrace is a charming spot to chow down on mussels and clams, shellfish pastas and grilled fish of the day. It's open year-round but if coming in winter it pays to call ahead.

Getting There & Away

Buggerru is about 15km north of Masua on the SP83. The only way to get here by public transport is to take a bus from Iglesias (€3, 70 minutes, six daily Monday to Saturday).

Three daily ARST buses connect Buggerru with Portixeddu (€1.30, 15 minutes).

Costa Verde

Extending from Capo Pecora in the south to the small resort of Torre dei Corsari in the north, the Costa Verde (Green Coast) is one of Sardinia's great untamed coastlines, an unspoilt stretch of wild, exhilarating sands and windswept dunes. Inland, woods and *macchia* (Mediterranean scrubland) cover much of the mountainous hinterland.

The area's main drawcards are its two magnificent beaches – Spiaggia di Scivu and Spiaggia di Piscinas – and the former mining complex of Montevecchio. Elsewhere, keen hikers can summit Monte Arcuentu (785m), one of the last preserves of the *cervo sardo* (Sardinian deer), and lovers of quirky museums can learn about Sardinian knives at Arbus, a small mountain town sprawled along the slopes of Monte Linas.

Sights

★Spiaggia di Piscinas BEACH

This magnificent beach is a picture of unspoilt beauty. A broad band of golden sand, it's sandwiched between a windswept sea and a vast expanse of dunes flecked by hardy green *macchia*. These towering dunes, known as Sardinia's desert, rise to heights of up to 60m. The beach is signposted off the SS126 and accessible via Ingurtosu and a 9km dirt track.

Once you exit the SS126 for Ingurtosu, the road descends through a valley lined with the abandoned buildings and machinery of a crumbling 19th-century mining settlement.

Facilities at the beach are limited but in summer one or two beach bars offer showers, umbrellas and sunloungers.

Spiaggia di Scivu BEACH

A 3km lick of fine sand backed by towering dunes and walls of sandstone, Spiaggia Scivu is the most southerly of the Costa Verde's beaches. To get there take the SS126 and head towards Arbus (if heading north) or Fluminimaggiore (if heading south) and follow the signs about 12km south of Arbus.

These direct you onto a narrow mountain track that leads into the scrub-covered southern heights. After about 13km you eventually arrive at a parking area, where there's a kiosk and freshwater showers in summer. From here, it's a few hundred metres walk to the beach.

Miniera Montevecchio MINE

(☎070 97 31 73; www.minieramontevecchio.it; adult/reduced €5/3.50; ⏰10am-1pm & 3.30-6.30pm summer, Sat & Sun or by appointment winter) Surrounded by woods and granite peaks, Montevecchio was once home to a massive mining complex. At its height in 1865, it was Italy's most important zinc and lead mine, employing up to 1100 workers. It remained operative until 1991, and since then has been kept alive as a visitor attraction.

Forty-five-minute guided tours take in the mines as well as the Palazzo della Direzione (Management Building), machinery workshops and workers' housing. For the monthly visiting times check the website.

Torre dei Corsari VILLAGE

Marking the northernmost point of the Costa Verde, Torre dei Corsari is the area's main resort. In itself, it's not an especially attractive place, with bland modern buildings and an ugly concrete piazza, but it does have a good beach. This broad band of golden sand is sandwiched between an emerald-green sea and a range of mountainous dunes, which mushroom back into green scrubland. Overlooking the beach is a ruined watchtower after which the town is named.

WORTH A TRIP

CASCATA SA SPENDULA

The wooded countryside around Villacidro, an agricultural town best known for its saffron-based liqueur, harbours a number of striking waterfalls. Chief among these is the Cascata Sa Spendula, where the waters of the Rio Coxinas crash down an imposing rock face en route to the Campidano plain. To get to the Cascata from Villacidro, head north for Gonnosfanadiga and follow the signs; it's about 1.5km from Villacidro.

The top end of the beach, known as Pistis, is a good long walk away or an 8km drive via Sant'Antonio di Santadi.

There's pay parking at both ends.

Museo del Coltello Sardo MUSEUM
(☎349 0537765; www.museodelcoltello.it; Via Roma 15, Arbus; ⏲9am-12.30pm & 4-8pm Mon-Fri, by appointment Sat & Sun) FREE In Arbus's hilltop centre, just off Piazza Mercato, the Museo del Coltello Sardo is dedicated to the ancient Sardinian art of knife-making. The museum was founded by Paolo Pusceddu, whose *s'arburesi* (from Arbus) knives are among Sardinia's most prized. Check out Signor Pusceddu's historic knife collection, which includes one of the world's largest penknives.

Eating

Agriturismo L'Oasi del Cervo SARDINIAN €€
(☎347 301 13 18; www.oasidelcervo.com; Località Is Gennas; meals €25-30) This rural *agriturismo* is as authentic as it gets. Once you've successfully navigated the 2.5km dirt track (follow the signs off the SP65) and are safely seated at the long wooden table, you're treated to an abundant farmhouse spread of tangy cheeses, cured meats, pastas, succulent roasts and homemade *dolci* (sweets). By reservation only.

Agriturismo L'Aquila SARDINIAN €€
(☎347 822 24 26; www.agriturismolaquila.com; Località Is Gennas; meals €25-30) An isolated farm in the green hills northwest of Montevecchio, this welcoming place serves bumper meals with cold cuts, ravioli with ricotta, lemon and saffron, and traditional Sardinian desserts. To reach the farm, follow the signs off the SP65 and head up the dirt track for about 2km. By reservation only.

Getting There & Away

Travelling in this area is difficult without a car. You can get to Arbus by bus from Cagliari (€5.50, two hours, up to 11 daily weekdays) and Oristano (€4.90, 1¼ hours, up to seven daily weekdays), but beyond that you're pretty much on your own.

Access to the area by road is via the inland SS126 which runs to Guspini and Arbus, from where Montevecchio is a short hop to the west. Continuing from Montevecchio, the SP65 winds northwards to Torre dei Corsari.

SULCIS

Named after Sulci, the ancient city the Phoenicians established on the Isola di Sant'Antioco, the Sulcis area encompasses Sardinia's southwestern corner and its two offshore islands. Attention here is largely focused on its beaches and coastal splendours but venture inland and you'll discover a mountainous interior speckled with historical interest.

The area has been inhabited since prehistoric times and traces of its complex past are to be found everywhere – a nuraghic necropolis at Montessu, Phoenician tombs in Sant'Antioco, Roman ruins at Nora. Harking to more recent times, remnants of its once thriving mining industry offer a sobering insight into what life was once like in these parts.

But however much you travel the area, the call of the sea is always there. Even outside summer, the Costa del Sud is a glorious sight, and the Isola di San Pietro charms with its laid-back port and wild scenery.

Carbonia

☎0781 / POP 28,755

A modern town fallen on hard times, Carbonia was constructed by Mussolini between 1936 and 1938 to house workers from the nearby Sirai–Serbariù coalfield. But since mining ceased in the area in 1972 it has struggled and there's really little reason to stop off in the town centre. Rather head out to the Grande Miniera di Serbariù and the Museo del Carbone, a museum dedicated to the town's mining heritage. Slightly further away, but also worth investigating, is Monte Sirai, where the remnants of an ancient Phoenician fort lie littered around a panoramic mountaintop.

Sights

Museo del Carbone MUSEUM
(☎0781 6 27 27; www.museodelcarbone.it; Grande Miniera di Serbariù; adult/reduced €8/6, incl Monte Sirai €15; ⏲10am-7pm summer, to 6pm Tue-Sun winter) Housed in Carbonia's decommissioned coalmine, the Grande Miniera di Serbariù, this fascinating museum provides a chastening look into the life of Carbonia's miners. The main exhibition hall displays a collection of machines, photos, equipment and documents. Tours into

WORTH A TRIP

EXPLORING THE SULCIS INTERIOR

With your own vehicle you can reach several noteworthy attractions along the back roads west of Cagliari.

Necropoli di Montessu (☎0781 6 40 40; www.mediterraneacoop.it; adult/reduced €5/3; ⏲10am-7pm summer, to 5pm winter) One of Sardinia's most important archaeological sites, this ancient necropolis occupies a natural rocky amphitheatre in the verdant countryside near Villaperuccio. It dates to the Ozieri period (approximately 3000 BC) and is peppered with primitive tombs known as *domus de janas* (literally 'fairy houses'). Many of these appear as little more than a hole in the wall, though some harbour wonderful relief carvings.

From the ticket booth it's a 500m walk up to the main site. When you first arrive up the stairs from the roadway, to your immediate right is a **Tomba Santuario**, a rectangular foyer followed by three openings into a semicircular tomb area behind. Follow the trail to its right to see a cluster of tombs and then the **Tomba delle Spirali**, where you can clearly make out the raised relief of spiralsnd symbolic bulls.

To get to the site from Villaperuccio, take the road for Narcao and follow the signs off to the left. It's about 2km.

Castello di Acquafredda (☎349 1564023; www.castellodiacquafredda.it; adult/reduced €4/3.50; ⏲9.30am-6.30pm) Approaching Siliqua on the SS293 road, you'll see the fairy-tale image of castle ruins atop an extraordinary craggy mountain. These belong to the Castello di Acquafredda, a 13th-century castle that served as a temporary hideout for Guelfo della Gherardesca when his father, Ugolino, the reviled ruler of Iglesias, was imprisoned in Pisa and the family banished. Nowadays, little more than the castle walls remain.

Riserva Naturale di Monte Arcosu (☎0783 55 20 35; www.wwf.it/oasi/sardegna/monte_arcosu; Località Sa Canna; adult/reduced €4/free; ⏲8am-7pm Sat & Sun summer, 9am-6pm Sat & Sun winter) Encompassing some 3600 hectares, the Riserva Naturale di Monte Arcosu is a WWF reserve and one of the few remaining habitats of the *cervo sardo* (Sardinian deer). Covering the peak of Monte Arcosu (948m), it also harbours wild boar, wildcats and plenty of birds of prey. From mid-July to mid-September access is only possible on a guided tour.

the claustrophobic mine shafts give a good idea of what it must have been like to work at the coalface.

Monte Sirai ARCHAEOLOGICAL SITE
(☎320 5718454, 0781 6 35 12; www.mediterraneacoop.it; Località Sirai, SS126 Sulcitana; adult/reduced €6/5, incl Museo del Carbone €15; ⏲9am-7pm Tue-Sun summer, 10am-3pm Wed-Sun winter) Monte Sirai, 4km northwest of Carbonia, is crowned by the remnants of a 7th-century-BC fort. Built by the Phoenicians of Sulci (modern-day Sant'Antioco) in 650 BC, it was taken over a century later by the Carthaginians. Not a lot now remains but among the ruins you can make out the placement of the Carthaginian acropolis and defensive tower, a necropolis and a *tophet* (a sacred burial ground for children).

As well as the regular entry ticket, cumulative tickets are also available (€15) covering Monte Sirai and four other museums in Carbonia, including the Museo del Carbone (p76).

ℹ Getting There & Away

Carbonia is located on the SS126. ARST buses arrive at and depart from Via Manno in Carbonia's hilltop centre; for tickets go to Bar Balia at Viale Gramsci 4. Regular services connect with Iglesias (€2.50, 50 minutes, nine daily) and a host of local towns, including Portovesme (€1.90, 35 minutes, up to 11 daily), the ferry port for the Isola di San Pietro.

Tratalias

☎0781 / POP 1080

Now a sleepy backwater, Tratalias was once the religious capital of the entire Sulcis area. When Sant'Antioco was abandoned in the 13th century, the Sulcis archdiocese was transferred to the village and the impressive

DON'T MISS

NARCAO BLUES FESTIVAL

One of Sardinia's top musical events, the **Narcao Blues Festival** (☎0781 87 50 71; www.narcaoblues.it; ⏲Jul) is held in the second half of July. The sleepy Sulcis town of Narcao stages blues, funk, soul and gospel concerts, performed by a cast of top international performers.

Chiesa di Santa Maria was built. The church today presides over Tratalias' lovingly renovated *borgo antico,* the medieval part of town, which was abandoned in the 1950s after water from the nearby Lago di Monte Pranu started seeping into the subsoil. The *borgo* is east of the modern town, off the SS195.

Sights

Chiesa di Santa Maria CHURCH
(Piazza Chiesa; incl Museo del Territorio Trataliese €2.50; ⏲9am-1pm & 3-5pm Wed-Sun winter, longer hours summer) This lovely church, the centrepiece of Tratalias' *borgo antico,* is a prime example of Sardinia's Romanesque-Pisan architecture. Consecrated in 1213, it features a simple facade punctuated by a classic rose window and an austere columned interior. To enter, you'll have to buy a ticket at the nearby Museo del Territorio Trataliese. Note also that the visiting times change monthly – for the latest, check www.trataliasturismo.it.

Eating

Locanda Monserrat SEAFOOD €€
(☎0781 68 83 76, 340 4668760; www.locandamonserrat.it; Borgo Antico; meals €35; ⏲noon-2.30pm & 7.30pm-midnight summer, Tue-Sun winter) Tratalias' medieval *chiesa* sets a memorable backdrop for alfresco dining at the sole restaurant in the *antico borgo*. Refined and casually elegant, it specialises in seafood with exemplary dishes such as *tagliolini con ricci di mare* (thin pasta ribbons with sea urchins).

Getting There & Away

A couple of weekday buses stop in Tratalias en route between Carbonia and Cagliari (€1.90, 35 minutes). There are also a couple of afternoon buses from Sant'Antioco (€1.90, 25 minutes) during the school term.

Note, however, that the *borgo antico* is someway east of the modern town centre.

Santadi

☎0781 / POP 3470

Wine buffs can come to grips with the local Carignano wine at Santadi, a small agricultural centre in the hilly countryside east of Tratalias. The village, known locally for its annual Moorish Wedding festival, is home to the biggest winery in the southwest, as well as a small museum illustrating how its rural workers once lived. A few kilometres to the south, the Is Zuddas caves are well worth a visit.

Sights

Cantina Santadi WINERY
(☎0781 95 01 27; www.cantinadisantadi.it; Via Cagliari 78; ⏲8am-1pm Mon-Sat, plus 4.30-6.30pm Tue & Fri) On the road between Santadi and Villaperuccio, this award-winning winery is the place to stock up on local wines. Particularly good are the highly rated reds Terre Brune and Grotta Rossa, both made with Carignano grapes.

Le Grotte Is Zuddas CAVE
(☎0781 95 57 41; www.grotteiszuddas.com; Località Is Zuddas; adult/reduced €10/7; ⏲10am-12.15pm & 2.30-6pm summer, shorter hours spring & autumn, closed winter) Five kilometres south of Santadi, the Grotte Is Zuddas is a fascinating cave system. Of particular note are the helictites in the main hall. No one really knows how these weirdly shaped formations were created, although one theory suggests that wind in the cave may have acted on drops dripping off the stalactites.

Museo Etnografico 'Sa Domu Antiga' MUSEUM
(☎0781 94 10 10; Via Mazzini 37; adult/reduced incl Museo Archeologico €5/3; ⏲8am-2pm Wed & Thu, 8.30am-1.30pm & 3.30-6.30pm Fri-Sun) To give an idea of how villagers lived in the early 20th century, this small museum recreates the home of a relatively well-off rural worker. Admission also covers Santadi's modest archaeology museum (same hours) at Via Umberto I 17.

Festivals & Events

Sa Coia Maurreddina CULTURAL
(Matrimonio Mauritano; ⏲Aug) Like many rural towns, Santadi celebrates its traditions in high style. On the first Sunday of August,

townspeople gather for Sa Coia Maurreddina (the Moorish Wedding), a costumed rite accompanied by folk dancing, eating and drinking. At the centre of events, the blushing bride and groom are transported to the main square on a *traccas* (cart) drawn by red bulls.

Eating

★Cibus OSTERIA €€
(☎349 3925289; Via Umberto I 24; meals €25; ⊙12.30-2.30pm & 7-11pm Tue-Sun, daily Aug) Santadi's local wines provide the ideal accompaniment to rustic country fare at this delightful *osteria* not long open. Handsomely decorated with wooden wine barrels, exposed brick and a sloping timber roof, it serves generous portions of uncomplicated favourites such as bruschetta, cured sausages and homemade pasta with rich, meaty *ragù*.

Getting There & Away

Regular weekday ARST buses serve Santadi from Carbonia (€2.50, one to 1½ hours). There are also a couple of weekday services from Cagliari (€4.30, 1¾ hours).

By car, the village is about 20km north of Teulada on the SP70.

Isola di San Pietro

Boasting an elegant main town (Carloforte) and magnificent coastal scenery, the Isola di San Pietro is a hugely popular summer destination. A mountainous island about 15km long and 11km wide, it's named after St Peter who, legend has it, was marooned here during a storm on the way to Karalis (now Cagliari). The Romans had previously called it Accipitrum after the falcons that nest here.

Laid-back and friendly, San Pietro owes its unique character to its past as a Genoese colony. It was settled in 1736 by a group of Ligurian coral fishers who arrived after their previous home, the island of Tabarka, had been taken over by the Tunisian *bey* (governor). North African pirates subsequently raided the island in 1798, making off with 1000 prisoners. These eventually returned to the island after the Genoese Savoys paid a ransom for them. Today islanders still speak *tabarkino,* a 16th-century version of Genoese.

Carloforte

☎0781 / POP 6190

The very image of Mediterranean chic, Carloforte offers a refined introduction to the Isola di San Pietro. Graceful *palazzi,* crowded cafes and palm trees line the busy waterfront while, behind, a creamy curve of red-roofed buildings rises in a half-moon up the green hillside. There are no great sights as such, but a slow wander through the quaint, cobbled old town makes for a pleasant prelude to an aperitif and fine seafood meal at one of the town's wonderful restaurants.

A short drive south of Carloforte, beach-goers can take to the sand at the Spiaggia La Bobba, one of a series of small beaches in the south of the island.

Sights & Activities

Museo Civico MUSEUM
(☎0781 85 58 80; Via Cisterna del Re; adult/reduced €2/1; ⊙10am-1pm & 4-8pm Tue, 9am-1pm Wed & Fri, 4-8pm Thu, 5-8pm Sat, 10am-1pm Sun) Uphill from the seafront, this small museum is housed in an 18th-century fort, one of the first masonry buildings to be erected on the island. Of chief interest is the Tonnara Room, dedicated to the island's tradition of tuna fishing. Continuing the nautical theme, there's an assortment of boating bric-a-brac and a small collection of Mediterranean seashells.

Isla Diving DIVING
(☎328 5673136, 335 462502; www.isladiving.it; Viale dei Cantieri) This outfit offers a full range of dives and snorkelling excursions around the island. Bank on from €70 for a dive (including equipment hire) and €35 for a snorkelling trip.

Carloforte Sail Charter BOATING
(☎0781 85 50 55, 342 1433106; www.cscharter.it; c/o Tabarka Viaggi e Turismo, Corso Battellieri 24; ⊙9.15am-1pm & 4.30-8pm Mon-Fri, 9.15am-1pm Sat) If you want to take to the sea, this operator has a fleet of sailing boats available for charter with or without a skipper (from €1500 per week). It also runs day tours of the island (€40 to €60 per person) and sailing courses (from €120 for a weekend course).

Tours

Cartur BOATING
(☎329 8586318; Molo No 3; tour per person €30) Operating out of a booth on the *lungomare*

WORTH A TRIP

VILLAGGIO MINERARIO ROSAS

In the country near Narcao, the **Villaggio Minerario Rosas** (☎0781 185 51 39; www.ecomuseominiererosas.it; Località Rosas, Narcao; €8; ⊙9am-7pm summer, 9am-1pm & 2-6pm winter) is a fascinating museum complex housed in what was once an important lead, copper and zinc mine. The site's rusty minehead and heavy timber structures set the scene for exhibits illustrating village life and the workings of the mine. Visits take in the pit's former Laveria (Washing Plant), the underground mine shafts and a display of minerals, which showcases samples of rosasite, a mineral discovered on the site in 1908.

There are also nature trails to explore, an on-site pizzeria, and accommodation (p211) in the former miners cottages.

(seafront), Cartur is one of several outfits offering three-hour boat tours of the island.

Festivals & Events

Girotonno FOOD & DRINK

(www.girotonno.it; ⊙May/Jun) Dedicated to the tuna catch of the *mattanza,* the island's main annual event features cooking competitions, tastings, seminars, concerts and various nautical-themed events. It's held over four days in late May or June.

Creuza de Mà MUSIC

(www.musicapercinema.it) This annual three-day festival is dedicated to cinema music with concerts and screenings of films and documentaries. The dates vary from year to year – in 2016, it was in October – so check the website for details.

Eating

Tuna is the king of *tabarkina* cuisine, as island cooking is known. It's on menus throughout the year, but it is only available fresh from May to August/September. You'll also be able to sample *cuscus,* a local variety of North African couscous, which is a staple of the town's many restaurants and trattorias.

Güštèn TAPAS €

(Corso Battellieri; meals €15-20; ⊙noon-3.30pm Fri-Sun, plus 7pm-1am Thu-Tue) For a change in atmosphere, head to Güštèn, a recently opened eatery and wine-bar. A good-looking place with exposed stone walls, chandeliers and an L-shaped bar, it takes a casual, contemporary approach with relaxed service and a blackboard menu of tapas (meatballs, mini quiches etc), gourmet hamburgers and local Sardinian wines.

★**Osteria Della Tonnara da Andrea** SEAFOOD €€

(☎0781 85 57 34; www.ristorantedaandrea.it; Corso Battellieri 36; meals €40; ⊙12.30-2.30pm & 8-10.30pm Thu-Tue, closed mid-Jan–early Mar) Located at the waterfront's southern end, this charming restaurant is one of the best places to taste the local tuna (though it's only available in the tuna-fishing season). Signature dishes include *lasagnetta di tonno con gocce di pesto* (tuna and pesto lasagne) and *ventresca di tonno* (succulent red tuna steaks grilled and served with aromatic olive oil).

Al Tonno di Corsa SEAFOOD €€

(☎0781 85 51 06; www.tonnodicorsa.it; Via Marconi 47; meals €35-45; ⊙12.30-2.30pm & 8-10.30pm Tue-Sun) With its summery dining rooms and terrace overlooking Carloforte's rooftops, this refined restaurant specialises in fresh seafood. The star of the menu is the local tuna, which appears in various guises – smoked, grilled, in *ragù* and as tripe. Tuna tripe, known as *belu,* is a much appreciated local speciality that's served here in a casserole with potatoes and onions.

Ristorante L'Oasi SEAFOOD €€

(☎0781 85 67 01; Via Gramsci 59; meals €25-30; ⊙noon-2.30pm & 7-10.30pm summer, closed Sun dinner winter) Dig into honest, home-style island cooking at this friendly unpretentious restaurant. The menu, like many on the island, focuses on classic tuna and shellfish dishes, while the ambience is pleasantly rustic with exposed stone walls and a wooden ceiling.

Da Nicolo RISTORANTE €€€

(☎0781 85 40 48; Corso Cavour 32; meals €55; ⊙8-11pm Mon-Thu, 1-3pm & 8-11pm Fri-Sun May-Sep) A bastion of San Pietro cuisine, this island institution sits in elegant splendour on the seafront. Tables are laid out with starched formality in a glass pavilion, ready for diners who come to try sophisticated dishes showcasing locally caught fish, often coupled with aromatic herbs and zesty citrus flavours.

Drinking & Nightlife

The *lungomare* is the place where it's at. The seafront is lined with bars and cafes, particularly the part around Piazza Carlo Emanuele.

Bar Napoleone CAFE
(☎0781 85 47 73; Corso Cavour 5; ⊙7am-2am) The most popular of the bars lining Carloforte's palm-lined seafront. Its pavement tables are a top spot to hang out over an early evening sundowner and lap up the holiday atmosphere.

Barone Rosso BAR
(Via XX Settembre 26; ⊙noon-3.30pm & 7pm-2am summer, closed Tue winter) Just off the seafront, Barone Rosso is an island institution, a long-standing bar with a kitsch interior, lively tunes and a few streetside tables.

Information

Banca Intesa SanPaolo (Corso Cavour 1) Bank with an ATM.

Tourist Office (☎0781 85 40 09; Corso Tagliafico 2; ⊙10am-1pm & 5-8pm Mon-Sat summer, shorter hours winter) Can provide island maps and tips on what to do and see.

Around the Island

Sights

★**Capo Sandalo** VIEWPOINT
The westernmost point of the island, Capo Sandalo is a superb vantage point, commanding breathtaking views down the cliff-bound coast. From the car park near the lighthouse, a marked trail (the *Sentiero Rosso*) heads through the rocky, red scrubland that carpets the clifftops.

Cala Fico BEACH
On the island's northwest coast, the rocky inlet of Cala Fico is one of the island's hidden beauty spots and, along with **Isola del Corno**, home to a nesting colony of Eleonora's falcons. The bay, resembling a tiny fjord, is flanked by a wall of chipped and cracked white-grey rock that catches the late afternoon sun and reflects the light onto the seawater, lending it a lovely turquoise colour.

La Punta VIEWPOINT
A quick 5.5km drive north of Carloforte brings you to La Punta, a desolate, windswept point with sea views over to the offshore Isola Piana. In May and June crowds gather to witness the *mattanza,* the seasonal tuna slaughter, in front of the Tonnara, the island's abandoned tuna-processing plant.

Beaches

All of the Isola's beaches are in the south of the island, accessible by the SP103 and SP102. The nearest to Carloforte is **Spiaggia La Bobba**, about 6km from town. A small strip of sand, it's situated near two sea columns (Le Colonne) that give the island's southernmost point its name, Punta delle Colonne. Continue westwards and you come to the island's most popular beach, **Spiaggia La Caletta** (also known as Spiaggia Spalmatore), a relatively modest arc of fine sand flanked by boulders. Further south you can detour to view the spectacular coastline of La Conca.

Getting There & Away

Regular **Delcomar** (☎800 195344; www.delcomar.it; Carloforte; ⊙ticket office 5am-9pm) ferries sail to Carloforte from Portovesme (per person/midsize car €4.90/13.70, 30 minutes, at least 13 daily) and Calasetta (per person/midsize car €4.50/10.80, 13 daily) on the neighbouring Isola di Sant'Antioco. Buy tickets directly at the ports.

Getting Around

From Carloforte, four main roads branch out across the island: the SP101 which heads north to La Punta; the SP102 and 103, which serve the south and the beaches; and the picturesque SP104, which cuts across the island to Capo Sandalo.

BICYCLE

If you haven't got a car, the ideal way to explore the island is by bike. You can hire bikes (from €10 per day), as well as scooters (from €20) and cars (from €40) at **D & G Motors** (☎329 9429628; Viale Osservatorio Astronomico 13; bike/scooter/car hire from €10/20/40; ⊙8.30am-1.30pm & 3.30-8pm Mon-Sat) in Carloforte.

BUS

On weekdays three daily buses run from Carloforte to La Punta (12 minutes), La Caletta (20 minutes) and Capo Sandalo (18 minutes). Tickets cost €1.30. Services are increased between mid-June and mid-September.

Isola di Sant'Antioco

Larger and less exuberant than the Isola di San Pietro, Isola di Sant'Antioco is Italy's fourth-largest island (after Sicily, Sardinia and Elba). Unlike many Mediterranean islands it's not dramatically beautiful – although it's by no means ugly – and it exudes no sense of isolation. Instead it feels very much part of Sardinia, both in character and look. The main town, Sant'Antioco, is an authentic working port, and the green, rugged interior looks like much of southern Sardinia. In fact, since Roman times, the island has been physically linked to the Sardinian mainland by bridge – the ruins of the Roman structure lie to the right of the modern road bridge.

Sant'Antioco

☎0781 / POP 11,310

A working fishing port that transforms into an animated summer hang-out, Sant'Antioco is the main town of the island that bears its name, the Isola di Sant'Antioco.

The island has been inhabited since prehistoric times, but the town was founded by the Phoenicians in the 8th century BC. Known as Sulci, it was Sardinia's industrial capital and an important port until the demise of the Roman Empire more than a millennium later. It owes its current name to St Antiochus, a Roman slave who brought Christianity to the island when exiled here in the 2nd century AD.

Evidence of the town's ancient past is not hard to find – the hilltop historic centre and northern outskirts are riddled with Phoenician tombs and fascinating archaeological litter.

Sights

★Museo Archeologico MUSEUM

(☎0781 8 21 05; www.archeotur.it; €6, incl tophet €7; ⌚9am-7pm) This great little museum is one of the best in southern Sardinia. It has a fascinating collection of local archaeological finds, as well as models of nuraghic houses and Sant'Antioco as it would have looked in the 4th century BC. Highlights include an impressive pair of stone lions that once guarded the town gates, as was customary in Phoenician towns, and a panther mosaic taken from a Roman *triclinium* (dining room).

Basilica di Sant'Antioco Martire Catacombs CATACOMB

(☎0781 8 30 44; www.basilicasantantiocomartire.it; guided tours adult/reduced €5/3; ⌚9am-noon & 3.30-5.30pm Mon-Sat, 11am-noon & 3.30-6.30pm Sun summer, shorter hours winter) According to legend, St Antiochus was condemned to work in the island's lead mines by the Romans after he refused to recant his faith. But he escaped, hidden in a tar barrel, and was taken in by an underground Christian group who hid him in these catacombs beneath the **Basilica di Sant'Antioco** (☎0781 8 30 44; www.basilicasantantiocomartire.it; Piazza Parrocchia 22; ⌚8.30am-noon & 3-8pm summer, to 6.30pm winter).

Accessible by guided tour, the catacombs consist of a series of burial chambers, some dating to Punic times, that the Christians used between the 2nd and 7th centuries.

The dead members of well-to-do families were stored in elaborate, frescoed family niches in the walls – a few fragments of fresco can still be seen – while middle-class corpses wound up in unadorned niches, and commoners' bodies were placed in ditches in the floor. A few skeletons lying in situ render the idea a little more vividly.

Villaggio Ipogeo TOMB

(www.archeotur.it; Via Necropoli; €2.50; ⌚9am-8pm summer, 9.30am-1pm & 3-6pm winter) Sant'Antioco's Punic necropolis and its cavernous tombs were taken over by islanders in the Middle Ages as a safe haven from marauding Arab raiders. Here you can explore the grotto houses where they lived and where the island's poor continued to live well into the 20th century – it's reckoned up to 700 people were living in them in the 1930s.

Museo Etnografico MUSEUM

(☎389 0505107; www.archeotur.it; Via Necropoli 24a; €2.50; ⌚9am-8pm summer, 9.30am-1pm & 3-6pm winter) At this small museum in the historic centre, you can investigate age-old living habits, as illustrated by an assortment of traditional farm tools and household implements.

Tophet ARCHAEOLOGICAL SITE

(€4, incl Museo Archeologico €7; ⌚9am-7pm) Dating to the 8th century BC, the *tophet* was an ancient sanctuary used by the Phoenicians and Carthaginians to cremate and bury their children and still-born babies. Before visiting, it's worth checking out the *tophet* display at the Museo Archeologico to see how the tombs were laid out.

Forte Su Pisu FORT
(www.archeotur.it; Via Castello; €2.50; ⌚9am-8pm summer, 9.30am-1pm & 3-6pm winter) Also known as the Forte Sabaudo, this 19th-century Piedmontese fort marks the highest point in town. Its most famous action took place in 1815 when the garrison stationed here failed to fight off a party of North African Saracen raiders. In the ensuing battle, many islanders were killed and more than 130 were taken prisoner.

Festivals & Events

Festa di Sant'Antioco CULTURAL
(⌚Apr) Held over four days around the second Sunday after Easter, this festival celebrates the town's patron saint with processions, traditional music, dancing, fireworks and concerts. It's one of the oldest saint's festivities on the island, dating to 1359.

Eating & Drinking

The summer crowds lend Sant'Antioco's bars and cafes a lively holiday atmosphere. Cafe-goers sit out on sidewalk tables on tree-lined Corso Vittorio Emanuele and drinkers swarm to the waterfront bars on the Lungomare Cristoforo Colombo.

★**Rubiu** PIZZA €
(☎346 7234605; www.rubiubirra.it; Via Bologna; pizzas €5-11.50; ⌚7pm-1am) Craft beer, creative pizzas and a laid-back warehouse vibe await at this contemporary microbrewery. Housed in an industrial grey building, complete with bar and shiny aluminium brewing tanks, it has a terrific selection of home-brewed beers and does a nice line in original pizzas.

I Due Fratelli SEAFOOD €€
(☎366 8397107; Lungomare Cristoforo Colombo 71; fixed-price menu €22-27; ⌚12.30-3pm & 7.45-11pm) If the sight of heaped fishing nets and boats bobbing on the waterfront puts you in the mood for seafood, head to this modest sea-facing trattoria. Its eggshell-blue interior – or sunny outdoor terrace – is just the place to try humble fishing fare such as marinated sardines, spaghetti with prawns, and fried fish.

Renzo e Rita RISTORANTE, PIZZERIA €€
(☎0781 80 04 48; www.renzoerita.com; Via Nazionale 42; pizzas from €4, meals €25-30; ⌚7pm-midnight Thu-Tue) A steady stream of locals keeps the *pizzaioli* (pizza-makers) busy at this cheerful pizzeria-cum-restaurant. Many buy takeaway but if you decide to eat in, it has a big, bright dining room and a comprehensive menu of pizzas, pastas and tempting seafood offerings.

Around the Island

Sights

Much of the island's hilly hinterland is cloaked by *macchia* (Mediterranean shrubland) with the occasional white house dotted around the empty slopes. Most of the better beaches lie to the south of Sant'Antioco.

About 5km out of Sant'Antioco town, **Maladroxia** is a small resort with a couple of hotels and a pleasant beach and port. Further south, **Spiaggia Coa Quaddus** is a wild and beautiful beach about 3km short of **Capo Sperone**, the island's panoramic southernmost point.

On the windy west coast, bathing hot spots include **Cala Lunga** and **Cala Sapone** with wonderful crystal clear waters.

Calasetta, the island's second town, which was founded by Ligurian families from Tabarka in 1769, is 10km northwest of Sant'Antioco. There are several beaches in the vicinity, including the lovely dune-backed **Spiaggia delle Saline** (Salina).

Eating

Outside of Sant'Antioco, you'll find a cluster of restaurants and eateries around the harbour in Calasetta, mostly specialising in seafood. Many island hotels also have in-house restaurants and offer rates for half-board (room plus breakfast and dinner).

Da Pasqualino TRATTORIA €€
(☎0781 8 84 73; Via Regina Margherita 85, Calasetta; meals €35; ⌚12.45-3pm & 7.45-11pm Wed-Mon) In the grid of white streets that extend back from Calasetta's harbour, this popular trattoria is an ever-reliable choice for fresh seafood. Menu stalwarts include delicate fish couscous and *fregula* (couscous-like pasta) with mussels, clams, squid and prawns.

Getting There & Away

There are two ways of approaching the island. By car, Sant'Antioco town is accessible by the SS126 road bridge. By sea, car ferries sail to Calasetta from Carloforte on the Isola di San Pietro.

BOAT

Delcomar (☎800 195344, Calasetta ticket office 342 1080330; www.delcomar.it; Calasetta; ⏰7.15am-5.50pm Mon-Sat, to 7pm Sun) ferries sail between Calasetta in the north of the island and Carloforte (per person/midsize car €4.50/10.80, 13 daily) on the Isola di San Pietro. In Calasetta, get tickets from the small office at the port.

BUS

Buses run to Sant'Antioco town from Carbonia (€1.90, 50 minutes) and Iglesias (€3.10, 1¾ hours).

Getting Around

Euromoto (☎0781 84 09 07, 347 8803875; www.euromoto.info; Via Nazionale 57; ⏰9am-1pm & 4-8pm Mon-Sat) hires out bikes (€12 to €25 per day), scooters (€30 to €45 per day) and cars (from €40 per day), as well as running a shuttle service to/from Cagliari airport (€10 per person). It also organises guided excursions led by volunteers; there's no fixed rate, although you're welcome to leave a tip.

Porto Pino & Around

Porto Pino, a *frazione* (ward) of Sant'Anna Arresi, is a small resort nestled among pine groves, lagoons and beaches. A popular day-trip destination, it boasts a good-looking beach and a ready supply of casual restaurants and pizzerias.

Just south of the resort's main beach, Spiaggia Porto Pino, there's a second beach, Spiaggia Sabbie Bianche, famous for its soft, silky dunes. However, it's on military land and is off-limits outside of July and August.

Much of the area southeast of Porto Pino, including Capo di Teulada, Sardinia's southernmost point, is also owned by the military and inaccessible to the public. You can get to some beaches, though, including Cala Piombo and Porto Zafferano, albeit only in July and August, and only by boat. You can pick up a boat at the small marina at Porto di Teulada near Porto Tramatzu beach.

Sights

Spiaggia Porto Pino BEACH

The best and busiest of the beaches in this neck of the woods, Spiaggia Porto Pino is at the eponymous resort near Sant'Anna Arresi. A favourite with weekending locals, it's a broad swath of creamy sand lapped by lovely, shallow waters ideal for tentative toddlers and nervous swimmers. There's ample parking and a string of cheerful eateries near the parking lot.

Eating

La Medusa SEAFOOD, PIZZA €€

(☎380 2434429, 0781 188 48 38; Via Porticciolo 16, Località Porto Pino; meals €25-30; ⏰noon-3pm & 7-midnight summer, Sat & Sun only winter) A white villa with its own gated courtyard, La Medusa is one of several restaurants on Via Porticciolo, a short hop from the beach. It's a relaxed place where service is leisurely and the food, mainly seafood, simple and flavoursome. A menu highlight is *orecchiette* (pasta ears) with prawns, mussels and courgettes.

Getting There & Away

To reach Porto Pino by car take the SS195 to Sant'Anna Arresi and then follow the signs.

A couple of summer-only ARST buses run to Carbonia (€2.50, one hour).

Costa del Sud

Extending from Porto di Teulada to Chia, the Costa del Sud is one of southern Sardinia's most beautiful coastal stretches. The main hub is Chia, a popular summer hang-out centred on two glorious beaches. Elsewhere, you'll find several swimming spots on the Strada Panoramica della Costa del Sud, the stunning road that dips and twists its way along the rocky coastline.

Sights & Activities

Chia VILLAGE

More a collection of hotels, holiday homes and campsites than a traditional village, Chia is surrounded by rusty-red hills tufted with tough *macchia*. Its beaches are hugely popular, drawing an annual influx of sun-seekers, windsurfers and water-sports enthusiasts. To see what all the fuss is about, head up to the Spanish watchtower and look down on the **Spiaggia Sa Colonia**, the area's largest and busiest beach, to the west, and the smaller **Spiaggia Su Portu** to the east.

★**Strada Panoramica della Costa del Sud** SCENIC DRIVE

Running the 25km length of the Costa del Sud, this panoramic road – known more prosaically as the SP71 – snakes along the spectacular coastline between Porto di Teulada and Chia. It's a stunning drive whichever way you do it, with jaw-dropping views at every turn and a succession of bays capped by Spanish-era watchtowers.

Starting in Porto di Teulada, the first stretch twists past several coves as it rises to the high point of **Capo Malfatano**. Along the way, **Spiaggia Piscinni** is a great place for a dip with incredible azure waters.

Beyond the cape, the popular **Cala Teuradda** beach boasts vivid emerald-green waters, summer snack bars and a conveniently situated bus stop.

From here the road climbs inland away from the water. For great coastal views, turn off along the narrow side road at Porto Campana and follow the dirt track to the lighthouse at **Capo Spartivento**. From here a series of beaches stretch north – watch out for signposts off the main coastal road to **Cala Cipolla**, a gorgeous spot backed by pine and juniper trees, **Spiaggia Su Giudeu** and **Porto Campana**.

At the end of this stretch you'll see another Spanish watchtower presiding over Chia, the small resort that marks the end of the road.

Eating

Crar 'e Luna SEAFOOD **€€**

(☎070 923 00 41; www.crareluna.it; Viale Chia 41, Chia; meals €30; ⏲noon-3.30pm & 6.30pm-midnight Tue-Sun summer, Sat & Sun winter) Set in its own verdant grounds with an alfresco dining area and a rustic, stone-clad dining room, this restaurant is a lovely setting for classy seafood. Try island classics such as *bottarga* (mullet roe) and *burrida* (dogfish) or play it safe with fried *calamari* (squid) or pizza (evenings only).

Getting There & Away

Chia is located off the SS195, the main road that runs between Cagliari and Teulada. Regular ARST buses connect Cagliari with Chia (€4.30, 1¼ hours).

Pula & Around

Some 32km southwest of Cagliari, the village of Pula makes a good base for exploring the southern beaches and nearby site of Nora. There's little to see in the village itself, but in summer, visitors throng to its vibrant cafes and restaurants lending it an infectious holiday atmosphere.

From Pula, the SS195 road follows the coast southwest towards Chia. However, unless you're staying at one of the self-contained resort hotels that hog much of this part of the coast, you're unlikely to glimpse the sea around here. Which is a shame because the coastline is quite magnificent: a string of glorious sandy beaches lapped by crystalline waters and backed by fragrant pine woods.

Sights

Nora ARCHAEOLOGICAL SITE

(☎070 920 91 38; http://nora.beniculturali.unipd.it; adult/reduced €7.50/4.50; ⏲10.30am-7pm Apr-Sep, 10.30am-5.30pm Oct, 10am-4pm Nov–mid-Feb, 8.30am-5pm mid-Feb–Mar) About 4km from Pula, Nora's ruins are all that remain of what was once one of Sardinia's most powerful cities. Founded by Phoenicians in the 8th century BC, it later became an important Punic centre, and in the 3rd century AD, the island's Roman capital. It was eventually abandoned in the 8th century as the threat of Arab raids got too much for its nervous citizens. Highlights of the site, which is accessible by guided tour only, include a Roman theatre and an ancient baths complex.

Upon entry, you pass a single melancholy **column**. This is all that's left of a temple dedicated to Tanit, the Carthaginian Venus, who was once worshipped here. Beyond this is a small 2nd-century Roman **theatre** facing the sea. Towards the west are the substantial remains of the **Terme al Mare** (Baths by the Sea). Four columns (a tetrastyle) stand at the heart of what was a patrician villa; the surrounding rooms retain their mosaic floor decoration. More remnants of mosaics can be seen at a temple complex towards the tip of the promontory.

Overlooking the ruins, the **Torre del Coltellazzo** is a 17th-century watchtower set on the site of the Phoenician city's acropolis.

Regular shuttle buses run to Nora from Piazza Municipio in Pula.

Laguna di Nora LAGOON

(☎070 920 95 44; www.lagunadinora.it; adult/reduced €8/6, excursions €25/15; ⏲visitor centre 10am-8pm Jun-Aug, to 7pm Sep) On the western side of the Nora promontory, you can often spy pink flamingos stalking around the Laguna di Nora. To learn more about the lagoon and its aquatic fauna, pop into the visitor centre, which has a small aquarium and displays dedicated to whales and dolphins. There are also nature trails and, in summer, you can sign up for snorkelling tours and canoe outings.

Near the entrance to the lagoon are two beaches: the pleasant **Spiaggia di Nora** and, a little further around, the bigger **Spiaggia Su Guventeddu**.

Chiesa di Sant'Efisio CHURCH
(☎340 485 18 60; ⊙4-7pm Sat, 10am-noon & 4-7pm Sun) Before heading up to the archaeological site at Nora, take a moment to stop at this pint-sized Romanesque church. Dating to the 12th century, it marks the spot where the disgraced Roman commander Ephysius was executed for his Christian beliefs in AD 303. Despite its modest dimensions, it's the scene of great celebrations on 1 May as pilgrims bring the effigy of St Ephysius here as part of Cagliari's Festa di Sant'Efisio (p54).

Eating

S'Incontru RISTORANTE, PIZZA €€
(☎070 920 81 28; www.sincontru.it; Piazza del Popolo 69; meals €15-30; ⊙noon-4.30pm & 7pm-midnight) The liveliest of the popular eateries on Piazza del Popolo, this casual square-side haunt buzzes on warm summer evenings. Diners swarm to its outdoor tables as waiters slide through the crowds bearing plates of wood-fired pizzas, grilled steaks and colourful seafood pastas.

Su Furriadroxu SARDINIAN €€
(☎070 924 61 48, 338 7317096; www.sufurriadroxu.it; Via XXIV Maggio 11; meals €25-30; ⊙8-10pm Mon & Thu-Sat, 1-2.30pm Sun) The flavours of the Campidano district are celebrated at this good-looking restaurant near Piazza del Popolo. Housed in a farm-style building, complete with a well and cobbled courtyard, it serves wholesome country food such as *malladdedus* (spiralled Sardinian gnocchi) with *pecorino* (sheep's milk cheese) and asparagus, and boar in red wine sauce.

Zia Leunora SEAFOOD €€
(☎070 920 95 59; Via Trieste 19; meals €35-40; ⊙7-11.30pm Mon, Tue & Thu-Sat, 1-3pm Sun) Tucked away in a backstreet in Pula's historic centre, Zia (Aunty) Leunora specialises in seafood and serves a full range of classic staples, including fried fish and sea bream roasted in salt. Its spacious wood-beamed hall is an attractive place to dine.

Information

Tourist Information Point (☎070 920 93 33; Corso Vittorio Emauele, cnr Piazza Municipio; ⊙9.30am-12.30pm & 4-7pm, longer hours summer) Kiosk with maps and printed material in English.

Getting There & Away

From Cagliari, there are hourly buses to Pula (€3.10, 50 minutes), many of which continue onto Santa Margherita di Pula (€3.70, one hour and 10 minutes, nine daily).

LA MARMILLA

Some 55km north of Cagliari, the dusty plains of the Campidano district give

WORTH A TRIP

TEMPIO DI ANTAS

An impressive Roman temple set in bucolic scenery 9km south of Fluminimaggiore, the **Tempio di Antas** (☎0781 58 09 90; www.startuno.it; adult/reduced €4/3; ⊙9.30am-7.30pm summer, to 5.30pm spring & autumn, to 4.30pm Tue-Sun winter) has stood in isolation since the 3rd century AD. Built by the emperor Caracalla, it was constructed over a 6th-century-BC Punic sanctuary, which was itself set over an earlier nuraghic settlement. In its Roman form, the temple was dedicated to Sardus Pater, a Sardinian deity worshipped by the nuraghic people as Babai and by the Punic as Sid, god of warriors and hunters.

After lying abandoned for centuries, the temple was discovered in 1836 and extensively restored in 1967. Most impressively, the original Ionic columns were excavated and re-erected. At the foot of these columns you can make out remains of the temple's Carthaginian predecessor, which the Romans cannibalised to erect their version.

From the site several paths branch off into the surrounding countryside. One of them, the **Strada Romana**, leads from near the ticket office to what little remains of the original nuraghic settlement and on to the Grotta di Su Mannau, 2.5km away.

WINDOWS TO THE PAST

For centuries, the locals thought little about the stone towers scattered across the island and many were used as humble shepherds' shelters. Then, 70 years ago, carbon footage revealed that they were in fact Bronze Age fortified settlements, most built between 1800 and 500 BC. In the absence of any written records – a fact that has led scholars to assume that the early Sards never had a written language – the *nuraghi* (stone towers) and *tombe dei giganti* (literally 'giants' tombs'; ancient mass graves) provide one of the few available windows into the mysterious nuraghic civilisation.

There are said to be up to 7000 *nuraghi* across the island, probably twice that many if you count those still underground. Their exact function has long been debated, but the consensus is that they served as watchtowers and sacred sites for religious rites, as well as being used for celebrations and commercial exchanges.

Early *nuraghi* were simple free-standing structures with internal chambers. Over time, they became bigger – the Nuraghe Santu Antine (p143) at Torralba is the tallest remaining *nuraghe*, at 25m – and increasingly complex with elaborate rooms and labyrinthine passages. Walls were raised around the watchtowers and villagers began to cluster within the walls' protective embrace. The most spectacular example of this is the beehive complex of the Nuraghe Su Nuraxi (p87).

way to the undulating green hills of La Marmilla. Named after these low-lying mounds – *marmilla* is derived from *mammellare,* meaning 'breast shaped' – La Marmilla is an area of bucolic scenery and quiet, rural life. It's also one of Sardinia's richest archaeological regions, and it's here, in the shadow of the table-topped high plain known as La Giara di Gesturi, that you'll find the island's best-known nuraghic site, the Unesco-listed Nuraghe Su Nuraxi.

Barumini & Nuraghe Su Nuraxi

A tiny stone village, Barumini has blossomed into a major tourist draw thanks to the nearby Nuraghe Su Nuraxi, Sardinia's largest and best-known prehistoric site. Once you've visited the *nuraghe* and Barumini's charming museum you've pretty much exhausted the village's attractions, but it makes a tranquil base for exploring the surrounding countryside and Giara dei Gesturi.

Sights

★Nuraghe Su Nuraxi ARCHAEOLOGICAL SITE
(☎070 936 81 28; www.fondazionebarumini.it; adult/reduced €11/7; ⏲9am-7pm summer, to 4pm winter) In the heart of the voluptuous green countryside near Barumini, the Nuraghe Su Nuraxi is Sardinia's sole World Heritage Site and the island's most visited *nuraghe.* The focal point is the 1500 BC tower, which originally stood on its own but was later incorporated into a fortified compound. Many of the settlement's buildings were erected in the Iron Age, and it's these that constitute the beehive of circular interlocking buildings that tumble down the hillside.

The Nuraxi tower, the oldest part of the complex, originally rose to a height of 18.6m and had three floors, each housing a single *tholos* (internal chamber). It was subsequently strengthened in around 1200 BC with the addition of four subsidiary towers and a massive curtain wall.

The first village huts arrived in the Bronze Age, between the 11th and 9th centuries BC, though many of the ruins you see today date to a later phase of construction in the 6th and 7th centuries BC. As the village grew, a more complex defensive wall was built around the core, consisting of nine towers with arrow slits. Weapons in the form of massive stone balls have also been unearthed here.

In the 7th century BC the site was partly destroyed but not abandoned. In fact it grew and it was still inhabited in Roman times. Elements of basic sewerage and canalisation have even been identified.

The site was rediscovered by Giovanni Lilliu (Sardinia's most famous archaeologist) in 1949, after torrential rains eroded the compact earth that had covered the *nuraghe* and made it look like just another Marmilla hillock. Excavations continued for six years and today the site is the only entirely excavated *nuraghe* in Sardinia. You can get an inkling of the work involved by seeing how many square bricks have been incorporated into the structure – these were deliberately made to stand out so they could be distinguished from the original basalt.

Visits are by guided tour only. Queues are the norm in summer when it can get extremely hot on the exposed site.

Casa Zapata MUSEUM
(☎070 936 84 76; www.fondazionebarumini.it; Piazza Giovanni XXIII; adult/reduced incl Nuraghe Su Nuraxi €11/7; ⏰10am-1hr before sunset) This attractive museum complex occupies the 16th-century residence of the Spanish Zapata family, La Marmilla's 16th-century rulers. The whitewashed villa was originally built over a 1st-millennium-BC nuraghic settlement, which has been skilfully incorporated into the museum's display. You'll also find artefacts from the Nuraghe Su Nuraxi, a section dedicated to the Zapata dynasty, and a small collection of traditional musical instruments.

Parco Sardegna In Miniatura AMUSEMENT PARK
(☎070 936 10 04, 370 1357035; www.sardegnainminiatura.it; adult/reduced €15/12; ⏰9am-7pm Apr-Nov) A kilometre west of Barumini, the Parco Sardegna in Miniatura is a family-friendly theme park centred on a miniature reconstruction of Sardinia. Other attractions include a dinosaur park, a recreated nuraghic village, a biosphere, planetarium and plenty of picnic tables. Note that there are various admission prices depending on what you want to visit.

Castello di Marmilla CASTLE
(Las Plassas) Lording it over the electric green landscape, the scant ruins of the 12th-century Castello di Marmilla sit atop a perfectly pyramidal hill near the hamlet of Las Plassas, 3km southwest of Barumini. The castle was originally part of a defensive line that the medieval rulers of Arborea built on the frontier with the province of Cagliari.

To get to the castle from Las Plassas, follow the road for Tuili and you'll soon see a path on your left rising up the hill.

Getting There & Away

Two weekday buses run from Cagliari to Barumini (€4.90, 1½ to two hours) via Sanluri. Once in the village you'll need to walk out to the Nuraghe Su Nuraxi, about a kilometre away.

La Giara di Gesturi

Looming over the countryside northwest of Barumini is the *altopiano* (high plain) known as La Giara dei Gesturi – *Sa Jara* in local dialect. The result of volcanic activity millions of years ago, the plateau is a beautiful natural wilderness, stretching for about 12km by 4km at an average height of 550m. Wildlife thrives in the area, which is home to Sardinia's last population of wild ponies, the so-called *cavallini*.

The principal gateway to the Giara, a protected area off-limits to cars, is Tuili, though you can also reach it from Setzu or Gesturi.

Sights

★La Giara di Gesturi AREA
(Altopiano della Giari) Rising above the rolling green landscape, La Giara di Gesturi is a high basalt plateau famous for its wild horses and uncontaminated natural beauty. The 45-sq-km plain, much of which is carpeted by *macchia* (Mediterranean scrubland) and woods of ancient oak and cork trees, offers excellent walking and wonderful wildlife watching.

Approaching the Giara from Tuili, the road climbs in a series of steep switchbacks to a car park at the Giara's southernmost entrance.

From here, a well-trodden trail leads to a small lake called the **Pauli Mauri**. This is one of several seasonal *paulis* (pools) on the Giara where you just might spot one of the area's indigenous *cavallini* (ponies) as they come out to drink. The best time to try for a sighting is the early morning or late afternoon.

The plateau also has its own microclimate, which fosters an array of unusual flora, best seen in spring when the ground is covered in heather and the wild orchids are in bloom.

Chiesa di Santa Teresa d'Avila CHURCH
(Via Fra Nicola, Gesturi) On the Giara's southeastern flank, the town of Gesturi is dominated by the 30m-high bell tower of the Chiesa di Santa Teresa d'Avila. The faithful flock to this 17th-century parish church to celebrate Gesturi's greatest son, Fra Nicola 'Silenzio' (1882–1958), a Franciscan friar revered for his wisdom and simple life.

Activities

Parco della Giara Escursioni OUTDOORS
(☎348 2924983, 070 936 42 77; www.parcodellagiara.it; Via Tuveri 16, Tuili) Operating out of Tuili, this local outfit leads guided tours of the Giara. A standard two-hour tour costs €50 for a group of one to five adults.

Getting There & Away

One weekday bus runs from Cagliari to Tuili (€4.90, 2½ hours) via Sanluri, although you'll need your own transport for the final leg up to the Giara.

Villanovaforru & Nuraghe Genna Maria

POP 640

On the southern fringes of La Marmilla, Villanovaforru is a manicured, pretty little village famous for its archaeological sites. The village itself boasts a worthwhile museum, while a short hop to the west is the important *nuraghe* of Genna Maria.

Sights

Museo Archeologico MUSEUM
(☎070 930 00 50; www.gennamaria.it; Piazza Costituzione 4; €3.50, incl Complesso Nuragico di Genna Maria €5; ⏰9.30am-1pm & 3.30-7pm Tue-Sun summer, to 6pm winter) Housed in a yellow 19th-century *palazzo* in the village centre, the Museo Archeologico provides a good overview of the area's prehistoric past with finds from many local sites, including Su Nuraxi and Genna Maria. Exhibits include some enormous amphorae and pots, metal and stone tools, oil lamps, jewellery and coins.

Complesso Nuragico di Genna Maria ARCHAEOLOGICAL SITE
(www.gennamaria.it; €2.50, incl Museo Archeologico €5; ⏰9.30am-1pm & 3.30-7pm Tue-Sun summer, to 6pm winter) This nuraghic complex, signposted as the Parco Archeologico, is set on a panoramic wooded hilltop about 1km out of the village on the road to Collinas. One of the most important *nuraghi* in Sardinia, it consists of a central tower, around which was raised a three-cornered bastion. Much later an encircling wall was built to protect an Iron Age village, of which little has survived.

Museo Sa Corona Arrubia MUSEUM
(Museo Naturalistico del Territorio Giovanni Pusceddu; ☎070 934 10 09; www.sacoronarrubia.it; Località Sa Corona Arrubia; adult/reduced €6/4; ⏰3-7pm Mon, 9am-1pm & 3-7pm Tue-Thu, 9am-7pm Fri-Sun) To the northeast of Villanovaforru near Lunamatrona, this excellent museum showcases the area's flora and fauna, as well as illustrating its ancient history and rural culture. Recreations of prehistoric sites and dioramas of local habitats bring the subjects to life, while information panels explain what you're looking at. The museum also hosts temporary art exhibitions, many dedicated to local artists.

Eating

★**Agriturismo Su Boschettu** AGRITURISMO €€
(☎070 93 98 84, 333 4797401; www.suboschettu.it; Località Pranu Laccu, Pauli Arbarei; meals €25; ⏰by reservation) Come hungry, take a seat and wait for the fun to begin. Out will come an array of delicious antipasti – seasonal vegetables, salami, cheeses – all accompanied by warm home-baked bread. Next up is pasta, perhaps ravioli filled with lemon-infused ricotta, followed by grilled meat and a selection of unpronounceable desserts. It's quite magnificent, especially if capped with a glass of local *mirto*.

Getting There & Away

One weekday bus runs to Villanovaforru from Cagliari (€4.30, 1¾ hours). There are also services to/from Sardara (€1.30, 30 minutes, five Monday to Saturday) and Sanluri (€1.90, 45 minutes, one Monday to Saturday).

Sardara

☎070 / POP 4080

Sardara, about 8km southwest of Villanovaforru, is a sleepy town with an attractive stone centre and several interesting archaeological sights. It's also known for its curative waters. The Romans built thermal baths in the nearby locality of Santa Maria de Is Acquas and people still come to indulge themselves at the local spa facilities.

Sights

Sardara's thermal waters have been attracting visitors to the town since ancient times. To treat yourself to a soothing day in the wet stuff you can buy a day's entrance to one of the spa hotels in Santa Maria de Is Acquas. A typical package costs €40 (€50 at weekends) and covers access to the thermal swimming pool and lunch.

Area Archeologico ARCHAEOLOGICAL SITE
(☎070 938 61 83; www.coopvillabbas.sardegna.it; Piazza Sant'Anastasia; €2.60, incl Civico Museo €4.50; ⌚9am-1pm & 5-8pm Tue-Sun summer, 9am-1pm & 4-7pm Tue-Sun winter) A few hundred metres from Sardara's museum, the Gothic **Chiesa di Sant'Anastasia** sits in the midst of what was once a much larger nuraghic temple. An important place of worship between the 11th and 7th centuries BC, the temple features an underground well, known as *Sa funtana de is dolus* (Fountain of Pain), whose waters were supposed to have had curative properties.

Civico Museo Archeologico Villa Abbas MUSEUM
(☎070 938 61 83; www.coopvillabbas.sardegna.it; Piazza Liberta 7; €2.60, incl Area Archeologico €4.50; ⌚9am-1pm & 5-8pm Tue-Sun summer, 9am-1pm & 4-7pm Tue-Sun winter) At the top of the historic centre, this modest museum showcases a collection of finds from local archaeological sites. Among the finest pieces are two 8th-century-BC bronze statuettes found on the edge of Sardara in 1913.

Getting There & Away

Sardara is just off the SS131 about halfway between Cagliari and Oristano. Regular buses serve Sardara from Cagliari (€4.30, 1¼ hours) and Sanluri (€1.90, 15 minutes). Buses also connect with Villanovaforru (€1.30, 30 minutes, three daily weekdays).

Sanluri

☎070 / POP 8530

One of the biggest towns in the Medio Campidano province, Sanluri is a bustling agricultural centre. In the 14th century Queen Eleonora d'Arborea lived here for a period and the town was a key member of her opposition to Catalan-Aragonese expansion. In 1409 island resistance was finally crushed at the Battle of Sanluri, paving the way for centuries of Iberian domination. Unfortunately, little remains to vouch for the town's former glory apart from Eleonora's squat, brooding castle.

Sights

Castello di Sanluri MUSEUM, CASTLE
(☎070 930 71 05; www.castellodisanluri.it; Via Generale Nino Villa Santa 1; adult/reduced €5/2.50; ⌚10am-1pm & 3.30-7pm) Just off Via Carlo Felice, the main road through town, Sanluri's 14th-century castle houses the **Museo Risorgimentale Duca d'Aosta** and its eclectic collection of assorted military paraphernalia. Outside in the garden, you'll see a medieval catapult, while inside you're treated to an extraordinary display of objects, ranging from period furniture and military mementos to an assortment of almost 400 wax figurines.

Eating

Bistrot Il Castello TRATTORIA €
(☎347 7378339; Piazza Castello; meals €25; ⌚8am-3.30pm & 5.15-11.30pm Tue-Sun) After visiting the Castello, decamp to this attractive stone-clad bar-trattoria near the castle entrance. Relaxed and informal, it's good for a classic meal of cured meats and cheeses, seasonally driven pastas and grilled steaks, all accompanied by a carafe of fortifying local wine.

Getting There & Away

Sanluri is well served by bus with regular connections to/from Cagliari (€3.70, one to 1¼ hours). There are also a couple of weekday services to Barumini (€2.50, 35 minutes) and Villanovaforru (€1.90, 25 to 45 minutes).

Oristano & the West

Includes ➡

Best Places to Eat

- ➡ Essenza del Gusto (p109)
- ➡ Desogos (p103)
- ➡ Agriturismo Montiferru (p103)
- ➡ Locanda di Corte (p109)
- ➡ Agriturismo Sinis (p100)

Best Places to Sleep

- ➡ Antica Dimora Del Gruccione (p214)
- ➡ Hotel Lucrezia (p214)
- ➡ Eremo del Cavaliere (p214)
- ➡ La Torre di Alice (p215)
- ➡ Hotel Regina d'Arborea (p214)

Why Go?

This part of central Sardinia boasts much of what makes the island such a beautiful and intriguing place: sublime beaches, verdant hills, ancient ruins and mysterious nuraghic temples.

In the heart of it all is Oristano, one of Sardinia's great medieval cities. It's a lively place with a gracious historic centre and laid-back atmosphere. A short hop away, the Sinis Peninsula harbours gorgeous beaches and ancient Roman ruins, while, to the north, Bosa charms with its riverside *centro storico* (historic centre).

For an altogether different experience, venture inland for a taste of rural Sardinia. The villages and soaring slopes of Monti Ferru are ripe for foodie touring with their prized local specialities, most notably *bue rosso* beef and extra-virgin olive oil.

Festival-goers will also enjoy the area. Oristano hosts colourful carnival celebrations, and the village of Sedilo stages one of Sardinia's most exhilarating events, the extraordinary S'Ardia horse race.

When to Go

- ➡ January is prime time for spotting pink flamingos on the Sinis Peninsula.
- ➡ In February, you can thrill to the acrobatic horsemanship of Oristano's Sa Sartiglia, the most colourful carnival on the island.
- ➡ Head to western Sardinia's beaches in June, to bask in the warm sun without the peak summer crowds.

ORISTANO

☎0783 / POP 31,600

With its elegant shopping streets, ornate piazzas, popular cafes and some good restaurants, Oristano's refined and animated centre is a lovely place to hang out. Though there's not a huge amount to see beyond some churches and an interesting archaeological museum, the city makes a good base for the surrounding area.

History

The flat, fertile countryside around Oristano was an important nuraghic centre, but it was the Phoenicians who first put the area on the map. Arriving in the latter half of the 8th century BC, they established the city of Tharros, which later thrived under the Romans and became the de facto capital of western Sardinia.

The city was eventually abandoned in 1070 when its citizens, fed up with continuous Saracen raids, decamped to a more easily defensible inland site, Aristianis (present-day Oristano). This new city became capital of the Giudicato d'Arborea, one of Sardinia's four independent provinces, and the base of operations for Eleonora of Arborea (c 1340–1404). A heroine in the Joan of Arc mould, Eleonora organised the 14th-century war against the Spanish and wrote the Carta de Logu (Code of Laws) before succumbing to the plague. With her death, anti-Spanish opposition crumbled and Oristano was incorporated into the rest of Aragonese-controlled Sardinia. It wasn't a good time for the city. Trade collapsed and the city suffered from plague and famine.

The construction of the Cagliari–Porto Torres highway in the 1820s, and Mussolini's land-reclamation programs, gave Oristano a much-needed boost.

Sights

Oristano's main sights are in the *centro storico* (historic centre), a pretty area of stone houses, sunny piazzas and baroque streets.

★Piazza Eleonora d'Arborea PIAZZA

Oristano's elegant outdoor salon sits at the southern end of pedestrianised Corso Umberto I. An impressive, rectangular space, it comes to life on summer evenings when townsfolk congregate and children blast footballs against the glowing *palazzi*. The city's central square since the 1800s, it's flanked by grand buildings, including the neoclassical Municipio. In the centre stands an ornate 19th-century statue of Eleonora raising a finger as if about to launch into a political speech.

Bargain hunters should drop by on the first Saturday of the month when the piazza hosts an antique market.

Cattedrale di Santa Maria Assunta CATHEDRAL

(Duomo; Piazza del Duomo; ⊙9am-7pm summer, to 6pm winter) Lording it over Oristano's skyline, the Duomo's onion-domed bell tower is one of the few remaining elements of the original 14th-century cathedral, itself a reworking of an earlier church damaged by fire in the late 12th century. The free-standing *campanile* (bell tower), topped by its conspicuous majolica-tiled dome, adds an exotic Byzantine feel to what is otherwise a typical 18th-century baroque complex.

Centro di Documentazione sulla Sartiglia MUSEUM

(www.biblioteca.oristano.it; Via Sant'Antonio 9; ⊙9am-2pm & 3.30-7pm Mon-Thu, 9am-2pm Fri, 9am-1pm Sat) FREE For a visceral taste of Oristano's headline festival, **Sa Sartiglia** (⊙Feb), pop into this free museum adjacent to the city's Pinacoteca. Look out for various depictions of the Mamuthones, the sinister costumed characters that feature in many Sardinian carnival festivities, and peruse the collection of festival memorabilia, which includes masks, costumes and an interesting selection of historic photos dating as far back as 1864.

Pinacoteca Carlo Contini GALLERY

(Via Sant'Antonio 9; adult/reduced €4/2; ⊙10am-1pm & 4.30-7.30pm) Oristano's municipal art gallery has a small but interesting permanent collection of Sardinian paintings, together with rotating exhibits by local artists.

Museo Antiquarium Arborense MUSEUM

(☎0783 79 12 62; www.antiquariumarborense.it; Piazza Corrias; adult/reduced €5/2.50; ⊙9am-8pm Mon-Fri, 9am-2pm & 3-8pm Sat & Sun) Oristano's principal museum boasts one of the island's major archaeological collections, with prehistoric artefacts from the Sinis Peninsula and finds from Carthaginian and Roman Tharros. There's also a small collection of *retabli* (painted altarpieces), including the 16th-century *Retablo del Santo Cristo*, by the workshop of Pietro Cavaro, which depicts a group of apparently beatific

Oristano & the West Highlights

1. **Is Aruttas** (p99) Topping up your tan on this blinding white beach.
2. **Tharros** (p101) Giving your imagination a workout at windswept ancient ruins.
3. **Sa Sartiglia** (p96) Throwing yourself into Oristano's carnival madness.
4. **Castello Malaspina** (p106) Marvelling at Bosa's brooding hilltop castle.
5. **Museo Civico** (p98) Facing up to the Giants of Monte Prama at Cabras' fine archaeological museum.
6. **Montiferru** (p102) Revelling in soaring mountainous views.
7. **Nuraghe di Santa Cristina** (p105) Taking in this impressive nuraghic site.
8. **S'Ardia** (p105) Cheering on the riders at Sedilo's famous summer horse race.
9. **San Salvatore** (p100) Perfecting your spaghetti-western swagger in this former film set of a village.

Oristano

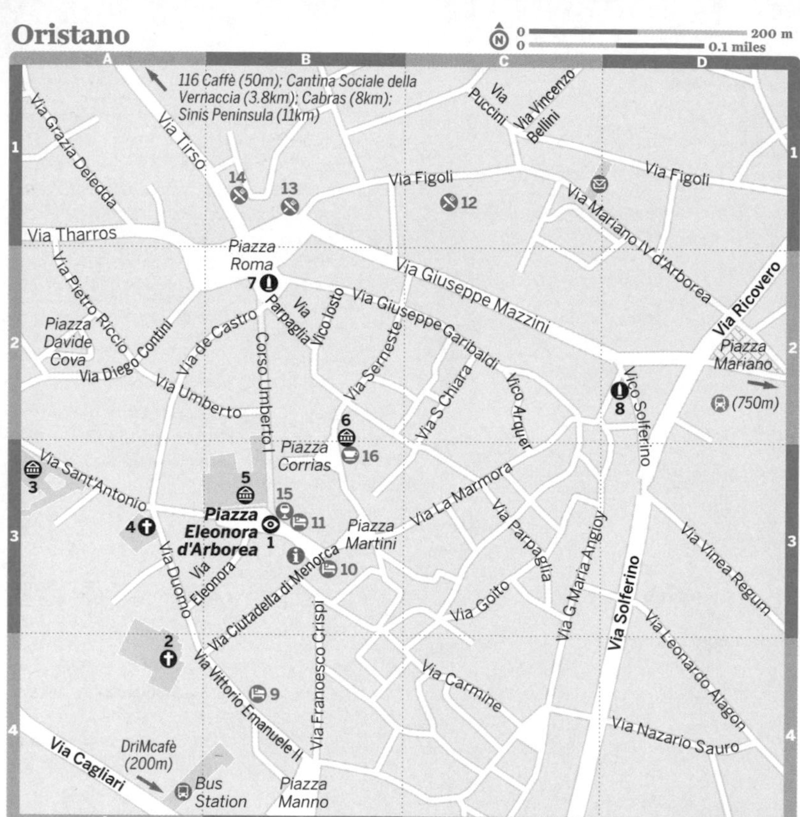

saints. But look closer and you'll see they all sport the instruments of their torture slicing through their heads, necks and hearts.

Chiesa di San Francesco CHURCH
(Via Sant'Antonio; ⏲Mass only) The 14th-century *Crocifisso di Nicodemo,* considered one of Sardinia's most precious carvings, is the highlight of this 19th-century neoclassical church designed by Cagliari architect Gaetano Cima. Also take a look at the sacristy's 16th-century altarpiece by Pietro Cavaro.

Torre di Mariano II TOWER
(Piazza Roma) Little survives of the medieval walled town except for a pair of towers. This 13th-century beauty, known also as the Torre di Cristoforo, was the town's northern gate and an important part of the city's defences. The bell was added in the 15th century.

Torre di Portixedda TOWER
(⏲variable) This tower, just off Via Giuseppe Mazzini, was part of the city's medieval walls, most of which were pulled down in the 19th century. It's now used to stage temporary exhibitions.

Eating

Eating in Oristano is a pleasure. There's a good range of reasonably priced restaurants, and the nearby Stagno di Cabras and Golfo di Oristano provide plentiful fresh seafood. Local staples include *muggine* (mullet), which often appears on menus as *mrecca* (boiled, wrapped in pond grass and then dried and salted). Grilled eel is popular, as are *patelle* (limpet-like dark clams).

★DriMcafè CAFE €
(☎078 330 37 50; Via Cagliari 316; light snacks & meals €4-9; ⏲8.30am-8pm Mon-Sat; 📶✍) This delightful, laid-back hang-out brings a slice

Oristano

Top Sights

Sights

Sleeping

Eating

Drinking & Nightlife

of boho warmth to Oristano, with its rust-red walls, mishmash of vintage furnishings, book shelves and chipper service. Besides speciality teas (including Moroccan mint) and homemade cakes, it rustles up day specials – from vegetarian and vegan offerings to rosemary-rubbed lamb with seasonal vegetables.

La Torre PIZZA €
(0783 30 14 94; Piazza Roma 52; pizzas €4.50-10, meals €20-25; noon-3pm & 6.30-11pm Tue-Sun) This place doesn't look like much from the outside; in fact, it's not so amazing inside either. No matter, it serves the best pizza in town. If you're off pizza but just want to enjoy the hectic atmosphere, there's a full menu of pastas and grilled main courses.

★ **Trattoria Gino** TRATTORIA €€
(0783 7 14 28; Via Tirso 13; meals €25-33; 12.30-3pm & 8-11pm Mon-Sat) For excellent food and a bustling, authentic vibe, head to this old-school trattoria. Since the 1930s, locals and visitors alike have been squeezing into Gino's simple dining room to feast on tasty seafood and classic pastas. Don't miss the seafood antipasto, the butter-soft roast *seppie* (cuttlefish) and the scrumptious *seadas* (fried dough pockets with fresh *pecorino*, lemon and honey) for dessert.

La Brace SARDINIAN €€
(0783 7 33 28; Via Figoli 41; lunch specials €15-20, meals €25-35; 1-3pm & 8-11pm Tue-Sun) This restaurant's name refers to the glowing embers of a wood fire, and grilled meats and fish are indeed its speciality – but you'll also find a full range of Sardinian appetisers, homemade pastas and desserts. The weekday lunch special is a big draw at €15 for two courses, or €20 for three.

Drinking & Nightlife

Oristano's liveliest and most atmospheric drinking spots are concentrated in the historic centre near Piazza Eleonora d'Arborea and Piazza Roma.

Librid BAR
(www.facebook.com/libridoristano; Piazza Eleonora d'Arborea; 10am-midnight Wed-Mon) This appealing new cafe, bar and arts space fills the interior courtyard and stone-and-brick-vaulted former stables of a *palazzo* on Oristano's main square. It's a great spot for everything from *aperitivi* to Sardinian craft beers to morning coffee and freshly squeezed juices. Ongoing cultural offerings include an evening film series and an attached bookstore.

Lola Mundo CAFE
(Piazza Corrias 14; 7am-midnight Mon-Sat) With its piazza seating, bright modern interior and perfect *centro storico* location, this popular cafe is a great spot to hang out over a coffee or aperitif.

116 Caffè CAFE
(Via Tirso 116; 6.30am-1am Mon-Sat) This modern cafe – think bare wooden floorboards and black and grey tones – is the place for an early evening *aperitivo* accompanied by a predinner snack from the ample buffet spread.

Shopping

Cantina Sociale della Vernaccia WINE
(0783 3 33 83; www.vinovernaccia.com; Via Oristano 6/A, Rimedio; 8am-1pm & 3.30-6.30pm Mon-Fri, 8am-1pm Sat) Oristano is famous for its fortified Vernaccia wine, and this cantina about 3km north of the city centre is the place to buy it. Most of Oristano's local producers bring their grapes here to be crushed, so you can be assured of the quality.

SA SARTIGLIA: ORISTANO'S MARDI GRAS

Sa Sartiglia is Sardinia's most colourful and carefully choreographed festival. Its origins are unknown, but its godlike central figure, the Su Cumpoidori, hints at pagan ritual. The jousts and costumes are undoubtedly Spanish, probably introduced by the *giudici* (provincial governors), who were trained at the Court of Aragon. The word Sartiglia comes from the Castilian *sortija,* meaning 'ring', and the central event is a medieval joust in which the Su Cumpoidori, the King of the Sartiglia, must pierce a star (ring) suspended overhead. The virgin brides who dress the Su Cumpoidori, along with his effeminate, godlike status and the throwing of grain, all suggest older fertility rites heralding spring.

The event is held over two days, Sunday and *martedì grasso* (Shrove Tuesday or Mardi Gras). At noon the Su Cumpoidori is 'born'. He sits on a table (the altar) and is reverently clothed and masked by the *sas massaieddas* (young virgins). From this point on he cannot touch the ground and is carried to his horse, which is almost as elaborately dressed as he is. The Su Cumpoidori's white mask is framed by a stiff mantilla, on top of which he wears a black top hat. In his hand he carries a sceptre decorated with violets and periwinkles with which he blesses the crowd. It is his task to start the Sartiglia, the race to the star, which he does with two other knights, his *segundu* (second) and *terzu* (third), who all try to pierce the star. The more times they strike it, the more luck they bring to the coming year. The last ritual the Su Cumpoidori performs is the Sa Remada, where he gallops along the course lying on his back. Then the games are open to acrobatic riders who perform feats that draw gasps from the crowd.

Information

Ospedale San Martino (☎0783 31 71; Via Rockefeller) Hospital south of the centre.

Post Office (☎0783 36 80 28; Via Mariano IV d'Arborea; ⏱8.20am-7.05pm Mon-Fri, to 12.35pm Sat)

Tourist Office (☎0783 368 32 10; www.gooristano.com; Piazza Eleonora d'Arborea 18; ⏱9am-1pm Mon-Fri, plus 3-6pm Mon & Wed) Oristano's tourist office is helpful and centrally located on the main square.

Getting There & Away

BUS

From the main **bus station** (Via Cagliari), direct buses run to/from Santa Giusta (€1.30, 15 minutes, half-hourly), Cagliari (€6.70, two hours, two daily), Bosa (€4.90, two hours, five daily) and Sassari (€8.10, two hours, three daily).

CAR & MOTORCYCLE

Oristano is just off the SS131, which connects Cagliari with Sassari and Porto Torres. Branch highways head off to the northeast for Nuoro and Olbia.

TRAIN

The main train station is in Piazza Ungheria, east of the town centre. Up to 15 daily trains, some of which involve a change, run between Oristano and Cagliari (€6.70, 50 to 80 minutes). Direct trains serve Sassari (€11, two to 2¼ hours, two to three daily) and Olbia (€12.50, 2½ hours, two to three daily); there are additional services but they require a change at Ozieri-Chilivani.

Getting Around

BUS

The town centre is easily covered on foot, although you'll probably want to use buses to get in from the train station. Take a line 3 bus to Piazza Roma in the historic centre.

Various buses run from Via Cagliari to Marina di Torregrande (€1.30, 15 minutes).

CAR & MOTORCYCLE

Parking is not too difficult if you leave your car a little out of the centre. Blue lines denote pay-and-display parking. Near the centre it costs €0.80 per hour between 9am and 1pm and then from 4pm to 8pm Monday to Saturday. Outside these hours it's free.

TAXI

There are taxi stands at the train station and on Piazza Roma. Alternatively call ☎0783 7 02 80 or ☎0783 7 43 28.

SOUTH OF ORISTANO

South of Oristano, flat plains extend in a patchwork of wide, open fields interspersed with canals, lagoons and the odd pocket of pine forest. Until Mussolini launched an ambitious drainage and reclamation program in 1919, the area was largely covered with malarial swampland and thick cork forests. Nowadays it's a featureless, and sometimes strange, landscape dotted with sleepy villages and agricultural towns.

Santa Giusta

0783 / POP 4810

A bustling agricultural town, Santa Giusta lies on the shores of the Stagno di Santa Giusta, Sardinia's third-largest lagoon. Once the Punic town of Othoca, it is best known for its extraordinary basilica, one of the first, and finest, examples of Romanesque architecture in Sardinia.

Sights

★Basilica di Santa Giusta CHURCH

(7.30am-6.30pm) This landmark Romanesque church is one of Sardinia's architectural jewels. Dating to the early 12th century, it sports a severe sandstone exterior punctuated by blind arcades and a typically Tuscan portal. Inside, three naves are divided by rows of marble and granite columns, several of which probably came from ancient Tharros. Beneath the presbytery, a vaulted crypt houses the relics of St Justa, a 2nd-century martyr who is said to have been executed here during the reign of Diocletian.

For four days around 14 May, the basilica takes centre stage during celebrations of the town's annual **Festa di Santa Giusta**.

Stagno S'Ena Arrubia LAGOON

Six kilometres to the south of Santa Giusta, the Stagno S'Ena Arrubia is a paradise for birdwatchers – flamingos, herons, coots and ospreys are regularly sighted.

Getting There & Away

Santa Giusta is a 10-minute drive down the SP56 from Oristano. Half-hourly buses make the run to/from Oristano's bus station (€1.30).

Arborea

0783 / POP 3960

Founded by Mussolini in 1928, the quiet town of Arborea bears all the hallmarks of its Fascist inception – severe grid-patterned streets, an immaculate central piazza and an array of fantastical architectural styles. Just a few kilometres northwest, the coastal hamlet of Marina di Arborea is home to a notable equestrian centre.

Sights & Activities

Piazza Maria Ausiliatrice PIAZZA

Arborea's showcase square, Piazza Maria Ausiliatrice is a beautifully tended space that wouldn't look out of place in a Swiss alpine village. Overlooking it is the clocked facade of the Tyrolean-style **Chiesa del Cristo Redentore** and, over the road, the art-nouveau **Municipio** (Town Hall).

MUB Museo della Bonifica MUSEUM

(0783 80 20 05; Corso Italia 24; adult/reduced €2/1; 10.30am-1pm Mon-Wed, 10.30am-1pm & 4.30-7pm Thu-Sat) Housed in a renovated mill, this civic museum charts Arborea's Mussolini-era origins, including its architectural planning, the influx of new residents from northeastern Italy and the reclaiming *(bonifica)* of land from the surrounding malarial wetlands. There's also a small archaeological section displaying nuraghic and ancient artefacts unearthed at the Necropoli di S'Ungroni and other sites in the vicinity.

Spiaggia di Marina di Arborea BEACH

The tiny settlement of Marina di Arborea gives onto this long and rarely busy beach. Backed by dense pine woods, the sandy strip extends northwards for several kilometres to the Stagno S'Ena Arrubia lagoon.

Horse Country Resort HORSE RIDING

(0783 8 05 00; www.horsecountry.it; Strada a Mare 24; riding lessons per person from €20) Hidden behind a thick pine wood at Marina di Arborea, 2km northwest of Arborea, this is Sardinia's largest equestrian centre and one of the most important in Italy, with a stable of Arabian, Andalucian and Sardinian horses. You can choose from a number of riding packages, with lessons starting at €20 per person. Accommodation (p214) at the resort is also available.

Getting There & Away

It's a 20-minute drive from Oristano to Arborea via the SP49. ARST operates hourly buses along this route (€1.90, 25 minutes).

Marceddi

This tiny fishing village overlooks the mouth of the Stagno di Marceddi, a wildlife-rich lagoon that separates the Arborea plains from the Costa Verde, providing important habitat for flamingos, cormorants and herons. For much of the year Marceddi is a sleepy place, where the only signs of modern life are a few battered cars and ragged electricity lines flapping over dirt roads. Visitors who make the detour will be rewarded with fresh seafood, wide-open vistas and an authentic slice of local life.

Eating

Da Lucio SEAFOOD €€

(☎0783 86 71 30; www.ristorantedalucio.it; Via Lungomare 40; meals around €35; ⏲12.30-2.45pm & 8.30-10.45pm Fri-Wed) The pick of Marceddi's waterfront restaurants, this is a relaxed spot for a seafood feast. Try the octopus salad, or, if they're available, fleshy little sea urchins, followed by *fregola con arselle nera* (small semolina pasta with black clams). For a main course, you can't go wrong with grilled fish.

Getting There & Away

You'll need your own wheels to get to Marceddi. The drive from Oristano, via the SP49 and SP69, takes about 35 minutes.

SINIS PENINSULA

Spearing into the Golfo di Oristano, the Sinis Peninsula feels like a world apart. Its limpid lagoons – the Stagno di Cabras, Stagno Sale Porcus and Stagno Is Benas – and snow-white beaches lend it an almost tropical air, while the low-lying green countryside appears uncontaminated by human activity. In fact, the area has been inhabited since the 5th century BC. *Nuraghi* litter the landscape and the compelling Punic-Roman site of Tharros stands testament to the area's former importance. Sports fans will enjoy great surfing, windsurfing and some fine diving.

Although summer is the obvious time to visit, early spring is also wonderful as wildflowers brighten the verdant landscape and flocks of migrating birds swarm to the lagoons. The queen of the show is the gorgeous pink flamingo.

Cabras

☎0783 / POP 9210

Sprawled on the southern shore of the Stagno di Cabras, Cabras is best known for its archaeology museum and its fine seafood. Beyond these attractions, there's little reason to linger.

Sights

★Museo Civico MUSEUM

(☎0783 29 06 36; www.museocabras.it; Via Tharros 121; adult/reduced €5/4, incl Tharros €8/5; ⏲9am-1pm & 4-8pm daily Apr-Oct, 9am-1pm & 3-7pm Tue-Sun Nov-Mar) Cabras' cultural highlight is the Museo Civico, and the real superstars here are the so-called Giants of Monte Prama (p98), a series of towering nuraghic figures depicting archers, wrestlers and boxers. Also of interest are finds from Tharros and the prehistoric site of Cuccuru Is Arrius, along with obsidian and flint tools said to date back to the neolithic cultures of Bonu

THE GIANTS OF MONTE PRAMA

A group of vast nuraghic figures, the Giants of Monte Prama saw the light of day for the first time in almost 3000 years when they went on display in March 2014 at the archaeological museums in Cabras and Cagliari.

The sandstone statues, which stand up to 2.5m high, are among the oldest of their type ever discovered in the Mediterranean, dating to the 8th or 9th century BC. They depict archers, boxers and warriors, and have strange, haunting faces with pronounced eyebrows and well-defined noses. Their most distinguishing feature, however, are their hypnotic eyes, which are represented by two concentric circles, thought to symbolise power and magic.

As they stand today, the statues are the result of a painstaking four-year project to piece them together from fragments found at Monte Prama, a low-rising hill between San Salvatore and Riola Sardo. The first fragments were accidentally discovered by a local farmer in 1974, but over the next five years more than 5000 pieces were unearthed, including 15 heads and 22 torsos. So far archaeologists have assembled 25 statues and 13 models of *nuraghi*, and identified pieces for three more figures.

Excavation of the site is ongoing, and new discoveries are constantly being made. As of 2017, the archaeological museum in Cabras was expanding to accommodate some of the new finds.

SINIS PENINSULA BEACHES

Within easy striking distance of Oristano, the beaches on the Sinis Peninsula are among the best on the island. Ideally you'll need your own car to get to them, but limited bus service is available in July and August.

Is Aruttas One of the peninsula's most famous beaches, Is Aruttas is a pristine arc of white sand fronted by translucent aquamarine waters. For years its quartz sand was carted off to be used in aquariums and on beaches on the Costa Smeralda, but it's now illegal to take any. From San Salvatore on the main Oristano–Tharros road, follow signs 2km north along the SP7 then continue 5km west on the SP59 to reach the beach.

Putzu Idu Backed by a motley set of holiday homes and beach bars, Putzu Idu's beach sits near the north of the peninsula. It's a picturesque strip of sand that's something of a water-sports hot spot with excellent surfing, windsurfing and kitesurfing. To the north, the **Capo Mannu** promontory is scalloped with a tantalising array of more secluded beaches – and battered by some of the Mediterranean's biggest waves.

Isola di Mal di Ventre This bare, rocky island 10km off the coast owes its strange name (Stomach-ache Island) to the seasickness that sailors often suffered while navigating its windy waters. Now uninhabited, it was home to a primitive nuraghic settlement and later used by Saracen pirates. The only people who now visit are holidaymakers keen to search out the beaches on its eastern shores. **Maremania** (☎348 0084161; www.maluentu.it; tours adult/reduced €25/15; ⌚9am-1pm & 3-7pm Jun-Sep) is one of several operators running boat tours from Putzu Idu between June and September.

Is Benas Surf Club (☎0783 192 53 63; www.isbenas.com; Lungomare S'Arena Scoada, Putzu Idu) In business for more than 20 years, the Sinis Peninsula's top surf school has it all – from lessons to equipment to accommodation to professional advice – for surfers, kitesurfers and stand-up paddleboarders. The main branch is just south of Putzu Idu at Arena Scoada beach, while the affiliated Capo Mannu Kite School is a few kilometres northwest at Sa Rocca Tunda.

Ighinu and Ozieri. As of 2017, the museum was expanding to accommodate additional finds from the Monte Prama excavations.

Festivals & Events

Festa di San Salvatore RELIGIOUS

(⌚Sep) To mark the Festa di San Salvatore on the first weekend in September, hundreds of young men participate in the **Corsa degli Scalzi**, a traditional barefoot dash between Cabras and San Salvatore. The run, which is spread over two days, commemorates an episode in 1506, when townspeople rushed to San Salvatore to save a statue of the Holy Saviour from Moorish sea raiders.

Events kick off on the Saturday when the runners, all barefoot and clad in white, accompany the statue along 8km of dusty paths to San Salvatore. But this is only the halfway point, and the next day they retrace their steps and haul the statue back to Cabras for safekeeping at the Chiesa di Santa Maria Assunta.

Eating

Expect to eat well in Cabras, an important fishing town that is known throughout Sardinia for its mullet fisheries. The local *bottarga* (mullet roe) is much sought after and well worth trying.

Il Caminetto SEAFOOD €€

(☎0783 39 11 39; www.ristorante-ilcaminetto.com; Via Cesare Battisti 8; meals €25-35; ⌚12.45-2.45pm & 8-10.30pm Tue-Sun) Hidden away in the historic centre, this is one of the best-known seafood restaurants in the area. Sit down to island classics such as *muggine affumicato* (smoked mullet) followed by spaghetti *alle arselle* or *alla bottarga* (spaghetti with clams or mullet roe) and a *grigliata mista* (mixed grill of today's fresh fish).

Sa Pischera 'e Mar 'e Pontis SEAFOOD €€

(☎0783 39 17 74; www.consorziopontis.it; Strada Provinciale 6; menus €27-32; ⌚1-2.30pm & 8-9.30pm) Fronting the Pontis fishing cooperative on the waterfront between Cabras and Tharros, this is an atmospheric spot to sample fresh seafood. The menu changes according to the daily catch, but pride of place goes to the local *muggine* (mullet) and prized *bottarga* (mullet roe). Booking recommended.

Getting There & Away

Buses run every hour to/from Oristano (€1.30, 15 minutes). By car or motorcycle, Cabras is a 10-minute drive from Oristano via the SP56, SP1 and SP3.

Marina di Torregrande

0783 / POP 780

About 4.5km south of Cabras, the small summer resort of Marina di Torregrande is a favourite hang-out for Oristano's beach-goers. Behind the long, sandy beach, the village presents a familiar seaside scene, with suntanned locals parading down a palm-flanked *lungomare* (promenade) and music emanating from bars. Out of season it's a different story and you'll find the holiday homes shuttered and most of the restaurants closed.

The village's one and only building of any historical note is the stout 16th-century **Aragonese watchtower**, after which the resort is named. Once you've seen that, there's not much to do except don your swimmers and head to the beach. You can hire sun-loungers and umbrellas there – expect to pay from about €11 per day.

Activities

Eolo WINDSURFING
(327 5609844; www.eolowindsurf.com; Lungomare Eleonora d'Arborea; 9am-6pm Jun-Sep, 10am-6pm May & Oct, noon-4pm Nov-Apr) Eolo organises sailing and windsurfing courses, along with beach tennis and equipment rental (windsurf packages start at €18 per hour).

Eating

Ittiturismo Sapori di Mare SEAFOOD €€
(0783 2 20 34; Via Colombo 8; meals €25-35; 12.30-3pm & 7.30-11pm Tue-Sun) Its tables draped in multiple shades of sea blue, this restaurant a couple of blocks in from the waterfront serves an unabashedly fish-focused menu. Expect daily specials such as seafood lasagne with artichokes, followed by prawns sautéed in Vernaccia wine, swordfish or tuna steak, or perfectly grilled catch of the day.

Getting There & Away

From Oristano buses run from various stops along Via Cagliari (including the main terminal) to Marina di Torregrande (€1.30, 15 minutes). By car it's an easy 10km drive via the SP1.

San Salvatore

0783 / POP 10

A spaghetti-western film set during the 1960s, the tiny hamlet of San Salvatore is centred on a dusty square and surrounded by rows of minuscule terraced houses, known as *cumbessias*. For much of the year these simple abodes are deserted, as is the rest of the village, but in early September they're opened to house pilgrims for the Festa di San Salvatore, a nine-day celebration focused on the village's pint-sized church.

Sights

Chiesa di San Salvatore CHURCH
(9.30am-1pm year-round, plus 3.30-6pm Mon-Sat summer) In the centre of the village, the 17th-century Chiesa di San Salvatore stands over a stone *ipogeo* (underground vault) dating to the nuraghic period. This originally housed a pagan sanctuary linked to the cult of water, and you can still see a well in the main chamber. It was later converted into a Roman-era church, and the dark stone walls still bear traces of 4th-century graffiti and faded frescoes.

Eating

★**Agriturismo Sinis** SARDINIAN €€
(0783 39 26 53, 328 9312508; www.agriturismoilsinis.it; Località San Salvatore; meals €20-32; booking required) Just north of San Salvatore, this working farm has a superb restaurant. The menu varies daily, but the vegetables and fruit are always home-grown and the meat is cooked to perfection on a big outdoor grill. When there's a big enough crowd, you may be lucky enough to sample its delectable home-bred *porcetto* (suckling pig). Bookings required.

Getting There & Away

San Salvatore is an easy 20-minute drive west of Oristano via the SP6. The town is not served by public transport.

Tharros & San Giovanni di Sinis

Straddling a dramatic headland framed by blue-green Mediterranean waters, the Area Archeologica di Tharros is one of Sardinia's most thrilling archaeological sites. Tharros was a major city in ancient times and its ruins today make for a haunting sight as they tumble down the promontory to Capo San Marco, the southernmost point of the Sinis Peninsula. Try to visit early in the morning or just before sunset when the site is at its quietest and most atmospheric.

Access to Tharros is via the small town of San Giovanni di Sinis, 1km to the north, which is home to one of Sardinia's oldest churches.

Sights

★Area Archeologica di Tharros ARCHAEOLOGICAL SITE

(☎0783 37 00 19; www.tharros.sardegna.it; adult/reduced €5/4, incl tower €6/5, incl Museo Civico Cabras $8/6; ⏲9am-7pm Jun, Jul & Sep, to 8pm Aug, to 6pm Apr, May & Oct, to 5pm Nov-Mar) The choppy blue waters of the Golfo di Oristano provide a magnificent backdrop to the ruins of ancient Tharros. Founded by the Phoenicians in the 8th century BC, the city thrived as a Carthaginian naval base and was later taken over by the Romans. Much of what you see today dates to the 2nd and 3rd centuries AD, when the basalt streets were laid and the aqueduct, baths and other major monuments were built.

As you approach the site it's impossible to see the ruins until you reach the hilltop ticket office. From here follow a brief stretch of *cardo* (the main street in a Roman settlement) until you reach, on your left, the *castellum aquae,* the city's main water reserve. Two lines of pillars can be made out within the square structure. From here the **Cardo Massimo**, the city's main thoroughfare, leads to a bare rise topped by a Carthaginian **acropolis** and a **tophet**, a sacred burial ground for children. Also here are remains of the original nuraghic settlement.

From the bottom of the Cardo Massimo, the **Decumano** runs down to the sea passing the remains of a **Punic temple** and, beyond that, the Roman-era **Tempio Tetrastilo**, marked by its two solitary columns. These are, in fact, reconstructions, although the Corinthian capital balanced on the top of one is authentic.

Nearby is a set of **thermal baths** and, to the north, the remains of a **palaeo-Christian baptistry**. At the southernmost point of the settlement is another set of baths, dating to the 3rd century AD.

For a bird's-eye view of the site, head up to the late-16th-century **Torre di San Giovanni watchtower** (adult/reduced €3/2, incl Tharros €6/5), occasionally used for exhibitions. Here you can look down on the ruins, as well as the **Spiaggia di San Giovanni di Sinis**, a popular beach that extends on both sides of the tower. There is nothing to stop you wandering down the dirt tracks to Capo San Marco and the lighthouse.

Chiesa di San Giovanni di Sinis CHURCH

(⏲9am-5pm) Near the southern tip of the Sinis Peninsula, just beyond the car park at the foot of the Tharros access road, you'll see the sandstone Chiesa di San Giovanni di Sinis, one of the two oldest churches in Sardinia (Cagliari's Basilica di San Saturnino is older). It owes its current form to an 11th-century makeover, although elements of the 6th-century Byzantine original remain, including the characteristic red dome. Inside, the bare walls lend a sombre and surprisingly spiritual atmosphere.

Getting There & Away

Tharros is a 25-minute drive from Oristano. Take the SP6 to San Giovanni di Sinis, then continue south another 1km to the parking area (€2 for two hours, €4 per day).

In July and August, there are five daily buses from Oristano to San Giovanni di Sinis (€2.50, 35 minutes), from where it's a straightforward 10-minute walk south to Tharros. In other months there are no bus services.

OFF THE BEATEN TRACK

OASI DI SEU

A few kilometres out of Tharros, and signposted off the main road, the Oasi di Seu is a veritable Eden of Mediterranean flora. Once you've navigated the 3km dirt track to the entrance, you enter a silent world of sandy paths and undisturbed nature. Herby smells fill the air, rising off fragrant masses of *macchia* (scrub), rosemary, dwarf palms and pine trees.

MONTIFERRU

North and inland of the Sinis Peninsula, western Sardinia's landscape is dominated by the wooded slopes of Montiferru. Reaching its highest point at Monte Urtigu summit (1050m), this vast volcanic massif is a beautiful and largely uncontaminated area of ancient forests, verdant pastures, natural springs and small market towns. Lonely roads snake over rocky peaks covered in a green down of cork, chestnut, oak and yew trees, while falcons and buzzards float on warm air currents overhead. Mouflon and Sardinian deer are slowly being introduced back to their forest habitats after coming close to extinction.

Santu Lussurgiu & Around

☎0783 / POP 2380 / ELEV 503M

On the eastern slopes of Montiferru, Santu Lussurgiu lies inside an ancient volcanic crater. The main point of interest is the small *centro storico* (historic centre), a tight-knit huddle of stone houses banked up around a natural amphitheatre.

Sights

Museo della Tecnologia Contadina MUSEUM

(Museum of Rural Technology; ☎349 6868600; www.museotecnologiacontadina.it; Via Deodato Meloni 1; adult/reduced €4/3; by appointment) Santu Lussurgiu has long been known for its crafts and remains a production centre for ironwork, woodwork and leatherwork. Explore the town's rural culture and traditions at this 10-room museum, which has a comprehensive, locally donated collection of more than 2000 ingenious tools, utensils and machines. Guides Mauro and Maria help interpret the museum's unique gems: eel-catching shears, a bow-and-arrow mouse trap, a miniature WWI monument sculpted by a returning soldier, 19th-century cognac distillery equipment and more. Advance booking essential.

Chiesa di San Leonardo de Siete Fuentes CHURCH

This charming 12th-century Romanesque church, which once belonged to the Knights of St John of Jerusalem, forms the centrepiece of the tiny woodland hamlet of San Leonardo de Siete Fuentes, famous for its gurgling spring waters. The town's grandiose Spanish name refers to the seven fountains through which the water gushes. Above the church, easy trails (ideal for parents with little 'uns) continue uphill through oak and elm woods. It's 6km north of Santu Lussurgiu via the SP19 and SP20.

Santuario di Santa Maria Madonna di Bonacattu CHURCH

According to an edict issued by Pope Pius VII in 1821, anyone who confesses at this tiny church between 14 and 28 September will receive full plenary indulgence. The delightfully simple sanctuary is little more than a rudimentary chapel capped by a simple dome, constructed of brick and volcanic stone in the 7th century on the site of an ancient Roman bath, then modified some 800 years later. There are no official opening hours, but you'll usually find it open.

Eating

Many local accommodation places have their own excellent restaurants and offer *mezza pensione* (half-board) to guests. A local speciality well worth sampling is beef from russet-red *bue rosso* cows, bred only

HIKE MONTIFERRU

The best way of exploring Montiferru is to ditch the car and walk. This scenic route leads up to the summit of Monte Entu, which, at 1024m, is one of the highest peaks in western Sardinia. It's not especially demanding, although you should allow about four hours.

You'll need a car to get to the start, which is by the Nuraghe Ruju, outside of Seneghe. From Seneghe, head towards Bonarcado and after a few hundred metres follow the sign for S'iscala. Continue up the road for about 8km to the Nuraghe Ruju picnic area and join the path a few metres down from the car park, in the wood to the left of the stone wall. Heading upwards you'll arrive at an opening, marked by a holm-oak tree, where you should go left. Carry on past the wooden gate until you reach a second metal gate. Go through it and continue until you reach a fork in the trail. Head left for some marvellous views of the coast, as far as Alghero on a clear day. From here you can continue onwards to the foot of the volcanic cone that marks the summit of Monte Entu.

here and in Modica, Sicily. Gourmets consider the meat to be among the finest in Italy.

Sas Benas SARDINIAN €€
(☎0783 55 08 70; Via Cambosu 6; meals €30-40; ⏱1-2.30pm & 8-11.30pm Tue-Sun) Spread across several stone-walled dining rooms in the hotel of the same name, Sas Benas mixes elegance with rusticity, serving fixed-price menus of traditional country fare. Dishes, which showcase seasonal ingredients and local meats, include much-loved classics such as *pasta con funghi e salsiccia* (pasta with mushrooms and sausage) and *tagliata di bue rosso* (steak of *bue rosso* beef).

Information

Tourist Office (☎0783 55 10 34; Via Santa Croce 9; ⏱variable) Small tourist office in the historic centre.

Getting There & Away

The drive from Oristano to Santu Lussurgiu takes about 40 minutes via the SS131 and SP65. ARST also runs six weekday buses between Santu Lussurgiu and Oristano (€3.10, 45 minutes to 1½ hours).

Cuglieri

☎0785 / POP 483M

Perched high on the western face of Montiferru and surrounded by lovely mountain scenery, the farming village of Cuglieri makes an excellent lunch stop.

Sights

Basilica di Santa Maria della Neve CHURCH
A landmark for miles around, the hulking, silver-domed Basilica di Santa Maria della Neve marks the high point of the village. According to local tradition it stands on the spot where a bull-drawn cart deposited a statue of the Madonna that had mysteriously washed up on the beach at Santa Caterina di Pittinuri in the early 14th century. More than the church, though, it's the vast views down to the sea that are the real highlight here.

Eating

★**Desogos** TRATTORIA €€
(☎0785 3 96 60; Via Cugia 6; meals €30; ⏱12.30-2.30pm & 8-11pm daily, reservation required for dinner in winter) Run by the Desogos family for more than 70 years, this welcoming, old-school trattoria in the historic centre is perfect for a fill-up of hearty mountain fare. Forget the menu and surrender yourself into the hands of sisters Pina and Andreina, who will ply you with an abundant array of lip-smacking cured meats, marinated vegetables, tangy cheeses, pastas and wild game.

OFF THE BEATEN TRACK

LUNCH IN THE COUNTRYSIDE

For an authentic taste of rural Montiferru life, head for the wonderful **Agriturismo Montiferru** (☎333 5704060; www.facebook.com/agriturismo.montiferru; Località Monte Sant'Antonio; meals €35; ⏱1-5pm Sun) way out in the hills. It opens only once a week, for Sunday lunch – but what a lunch it is! The feasting lasts for hours as you move from *aperitivi* through massive spreads of antipasti, two kinds of homemade pasta, grilled meats and scrumptious homemade Sardinian desserts.

Reservations are essential. The farm is 30 to 40 minutes' drive from Bosa, Cuglieri or Santu Lussurgiu.

Shopping

Azienda Olearia Peddio FOOD
(☎0785 36 92 54; www.oliopeddio.it; Corso Umberto 87; ⏱8.30am-1pm & 3-8pm) On the main road through the village, this is the place to stock up on local olive oil. A litre costs between €8 and €9.

Getting There & Away

Cuglieri is on the SS292, 41km north of Oristano and 22km south of Bosa. There are five weekday buses between Cuglieri and Oristano (€3.70, one hour) and, in July and August, two Sunday services.

Santa Caterina di Pittinuri

☎0785 / POP 380

Santa Caterina di Pittinuri is the main resort on the northern Oristano coast, and while the town itself is largely made up of summer holiday homes, the surrounding coastline is lovely, ranging from dramatic cliffs and sea arches to long sweeps of untrammeled sand.

Sights

Spiaggia dell'Arco BEACH

On the northern fringe of the beachside community of S'Archittu, the Spiaggia dell'Arco features a dramatic stone arch that rises 6m above the emerald-green waters.

Is Arenas BEACH

About 3km south of S'Archittu, just outside the town of Torre del Pozzo, tracks lead off the SS292 to Is Arenas beach, which at 6km is one of the longest in the area.

Getting There & Away

From Oristano it's about a 30-minute drive up the SS292 to Santa Caterina di Pittinuri. ARST runs buses from Oristano to S'Archittu and Santa Caterina (€2.50, 40 minutes, five Monday to Saturday, plus two on Sunday in July and August).

Seneghe

0783 / POP 1760 / ELEV 310M

Seneghe is an essential stop on any gastronomic tour of central Sardinia. A dark stone village with little obvious appeal, it is famous for its extra-virgin olive oil, a one-time winner of the prestigious Premio Nazionale Ercole Olivario award (the Oscars of the Italian olive-oil industry). The village also provides food for the soul, hosting an annual poetry festival.

Festivals & Events

Settembre dei Poeti LITERATURE

(www.settembredeipoeti.it; Aug/Sep) Held in late August or early September, the Settembre dei Poeti is a four-day celebration of local and international poetry with readings, Q&A sessions and a poetry slam competition – a thoroughly entertaining, dramatic performance in which adversaries improvise rhyming responses to each other, much like a freestyle rap battle.

Shopping

Alimentari Marina FOOD

(Corso Umberto 126a; 9am-1pm Mon-Sat, plus 5.30-8pm Mon & Fri) Seneghe's award-winning olive oil comes in containers of every shape and size at this market in the heart of town. Grab an ultra-portable 250mL bottle (€5), or go all out with a 5L can (€43).

Getting There & Away

Seneghe is about half an hour north of Oristano by car or motorcycle via the SS131 and SP15. ARST also operates a few daily buses between Oristano and Seneghe (€2.50, 45 minutes).

Milis

0783 / POP 1590

A one-time Roman military outpost (its name is a derivation of the Latin word *miles,* meaning soldier), Milis is a small and prosperous farming village, surrounded by the orange orchards that have brought it wealth. Its low-key attractions include the lovely Tuscan-Romanesque Chiesa di San Paolo and the stately but decaying Palazzo Boyl.

Sights & Activities

Chiesa di San Paolo CHURCH

Near the eastern entrance to town, the Tuscan-Romanesque Chiesa di San Paolo has a lovely stone exterior and harbours some interesting paintings by 16th-century Catalan artists inside.

Palazzo Boyl HISTORIC BUILDING

(0783 5 16 65; Piazza Martiri; by appointment only 9am-1pm Mon-Sat) FREE A fine example of Piedmontese neoclassicism, 18th-century Palazzo Boyl dominates Milis' manicured village centre. Originally a summer residence for the aristocratic Boyl family, it became something of a literary meeting place in the late 19th and early 20th centuries – Gabriele D'Annunzio, Grazia Deledda and Honoré de Balzac all spent time here. Nowadays it houses a small, rather neglected museum dedicated to traditional Sardinian costumes and jewellery. You'll need to call the town hall in advance to arrange a visit.

Vivaio I Campi FOOD

(393 9040081; www.vivaioicampi.it; Loc Perdiesi; by appointment) Where's the best spot to sample Milis's famous citrus? At this wonderful pick-your-own orchard just southwest of town. Plant-lover Italo has converted his 3-hectare yard into a wonderland of multi-hued flowers interspersed with clementine, orange and mandarin orchards. Locals flock here on Sundays from November to March when the fruit is at its peak, but you can visit anytime by arrangement.

In March, Italo also hosts one of Italy's most spectacular flower festivals, Primavera in Giardino (www.primaveraingiardino.it).

Festivals & Events

Rassegna del Vino Novello WINE
(Festival of Young Wine; www.vininovelli.com; ⌚Nov) In early November, Milis holds the Festival of Young Wine, a chance for Sardinia's wine producers to show off their best products. You can do the rounds sampling the wines and grazing the food stalls that line the streets.

Getting There & Away

Milis is an easy 21km drive from Oristano via the SS131, SS292 and SP56. To continue north into the Montiferru region, take the SP15 to Santu Lussurgiu (14km).

INLAND ORISTANO PROVINCE

Inland, the countryside of Oristano province is sparsely populated and rich in archaeological interest, with two of central Sardinia's most important nuraghic sites. You'll find Lago Omodeo, Sardinia's largest artifical lake, surrounded by the green hills of the Barigadu. Some 22km long and up to 3km wide, the lake was created between 1919 and 1924 to supply water and electricity to the agricultural lands around Oristano and Arborea.

Sights

★Nuraghe di Santa Cristina ARCHAEOLOGICAL SITE
(www.archeotour.net; adult/reduced incl Museo Archeologico-Etnografico Paulilatino €5/2.50; ⌚8.30am-sunset) Just off the SS131 north of Oristano, the Nuraghe Santa Cristina is an important nuraghic complex. Its extraordinary Bronze Age *tempio a pozzo* (well temple) is one of the best preserved in Sardinia. The worship of water was a fundamental part of nuraghic religious practice, and there are reckoned to be about 40 sacred wells across the island.

On entering the site, the first area you come to is a small village centred on the **Chiesa di Santa Cristina**, an early Christian church dedicated to Santa Cristina. The church and the terraced *muristenes* (pilgrims' huts) that surround it are opened

S'ARDIA

On 6 and 7 July Sedilo hosts Oristano's most exciting festival, S'Ardia, when nearly 50,000 people pack themselves into the tiny village to see Sardinia's most reckless and dangerous horse race.

It celebrates the Roman Emperor Constantine, who defeated the vastly superior forces of Maxentius at Rome's Ponte Milvio in AD 312. Since then the festival has received a Christian gloss. Legend has it that Constantine received a vision before the battle, in which he saw a cross inscribed with the words, '*In Hoc Signo Vinces*' ('In this sign you will conquer'). He took the sign as the insignia for his forces, and the following year he passed an edict granting the Christians religious freedom. So, locally, although not officially, he was promoted to St Constantine (Santu Antinu in the local dialect).

The race circles the Santuario di San Costantino and the stone cross bearing his insignia. One man – the Prima Pandela (First Flag) – is chosen to bear Constantine's yellow-brocade standard. He selects two of the best horsemen to ride with him, and they choose three cohorts each. These men will be the Prima Pandela's guard and, armed with huge sticks, they will strive to prevent the 100 other horsemen from passing him. To be chosen as the Prima Pandela is the highest honour of the village. Only a man who has proven his courage and horsemanship and substantiated his faith can carry the flag.

On 6 July the procession prays in front of the stone cross and the riders are blessed by the parish priest. In theory the priest should start the race, but in practice it is the Prima Pandela who chooses his moment and flies off at a gallop down the hill. The other horsemen are after him in seconds, aiming to pass him before he reaches the victory arch. Hundreds of riflemen shoot off blanks, exciting the horses. The stampede towards the narrow entrance of the victory arch is the most dangerous moment, as any mistake would mean running into the stone columns at top speed. In 2002 one rider was killed. If all goes well, the Prima Pandela passes through the arch and races on to circle the sanctuary, to deafening cheers from the crowd.

Sedilo sits 40km northwest of Oristano, on the SS131.

for only 20 days a year – 10 days preceding each of the twin feast days of Santa Cristina (second Sunday in May) and San Raffaele Arcangelo (fourth Sunday in October).

From the church, a path leads about 150m to the **well temple**. Dating back to the late Bronze Age (11th to 9th century BC), the *tempio a pozzo* is accessible through a finely cut keyhole entrance and a flight of 24 superbly preserved steps. When you reach the bottom you can gaze up at the perfectly constructed *tholos* (conical tower), through which light enters the dark well shaft. Every 18 years, one month and two days, the full moon shines directly through the aperture into the well. Otherwise you can catch the yearly equinoxes on 21 March and 23 September, when the sun lights up the stairway down to the well.

Over on the other side of the Christian village is the Nuraghe di Santa Cristina, a single 7m-high **tower** set in a peaceful olive grove. This once stood at the heart of a nuraghic village, which was inhabited until the early Middle Ages and whose remains lie littered around the woody glades.

Museo Archeologico-Etnografico Palazzo Atzori MUSEUM
(www.archeotour.net; Via Nazionale 127, Paulilatino; adult/reduced incl Nuraghe Santa Cristina €5/2.50; 9.30am-1pm & 4.30-7pm Tue-Sun Jul-Sep, 9.30am-1pm & 3.30-6pm Tue-Sun Oct-Jun) Spread over three floors, this museum in Paulilatino focuses on traditional rural life, with exhibits dedicated to baking, lacework, equestrian gear, glassware, basketry, farm and domestic implements and more. The museum also owns a collection of finds from the Santa Cristina archaeological site 5km down the road, but these are only intermittently on display.

Nuraghe Losa ARCHAEOLOGICAL SITE
(www.nuraghelosa.net; adult/reduced €5/2.50; 9am-1hr before sunset) Off the SS131 just north of Paulilatino, the Nuraghe Losa is one of Sardinia's most impressive *nuraghi*. The site's centrepiece is a three-sided keep surrounded by three circular towers, two joined by a wall and one standing alone. A rough-hewn spiral staircase lets you climb to the 13m summit of the partially destroyed central keep, which dates to the Middle Bronze Age (about 1500 BC). Guided tours (included in price) are available in English, French or Italian with advance notice.

Eating

Su Carduleu SARDINIAN €€
(0785 56 31 34; www.sucarduleu.it; Via Sant' Agostino 1, Abbasanta; meals €35-45; 12.30-3pm & 8-10.30pm Thu-Tue) For a locally sourced gourmet feast, stop in at this Slow Food–acclaimed restaurant run by hometown success story Roberto Serra. Presentation and flavour are both paramount in dishes such as marjoram-scented roast quail and lavender-marinated kid with figs and rock salt.

BOSA

0785 / POP 7930

Bosa is one of Sardinia's most attractive towns. Seen from a distance, its rainbow townscape resembles a vibrant Paul Klee canvas, with pastel houses stacked on a steep hillside, tapering up to a stark, grey castle. In front, moored fishing boats bob on a glassy river elegantly lined with palm trees.

Bosa was established by the Phoenicians and thrived under the Romans. During the early Middle Ages it suffered repeat raids by Arab pirates, but in the early 12th century a branch of the noble Tuscan Malaspina family moved in and built their huge castle. In the 19th century, the Savoys established lucrative tanneries here, but these have since fallen by the wayside.

At the mouth of the Fiume Temo, about 2.5km west of Bosa proper, Bosa Marina is the town's seaside satellite, a busy summer resort set on a wide, 1km-long beach overlooked by a 16th-century Aragonese defensive tower.

Sights

Most of Bosa's sights lie on the north bank of the river Temo. The main strip, Corso Vittorio Emanuele, is one block north of the riverfront and leads to the two central piazzas: Piazza Costituzione and Piazza IV Novembre. South of the river, Via Nazionale runs 3km west to Bosa Marina.

★**Castello Malaspina** CASTLE
(0785 37 70 43; adult/reduced €4/3; 10am-1hr before sunset Apr-Oct, 10am-1pm Sat & Sun Nov-Mar) Commanding huge views, this hilltop castle was built in the 12th and 13th centuries by the Tuscan Malaspina family. Little remains of the original structure except for its skeleton – imposing walls and a series of

WORTH A TRIP

FORDONGIANUS

Southwest of Lago Omodeo, the small spa town of Fordongianus was founded by the Roman emperor Trajan in the 1st century AD. Forum Traiani, as it was then known, was an important commercial centre and site of a major baths complex, the remains of which can still be visited.

Terme Romane (☎0783 6 01 57; www.forumtraiani.it; adult/reduced incl Casa Aragonese €4/2; ⊙9.30am-1pm & 3-6.30pm) The impressive remains of Fordongianus' 1st-century Terme Romane sit on the banks of the river Tirso. In the centre of the complex you'll see a rectangular pool, which originally was covered by a barrel-vaulted roof and flanked by an imposing portico, a section of which still stands. The 54°C spring water that used to feed the pool has long since been diverted to meet the modern town's needs.

Casa Aragonese (adult/reduced incl Terme Romane €4/2; ⊙9.30am-1pm & 3-6pm Tue-Sun) A characteristic of Fordongianus is the rusty-red trachyte stone of which so many of its buildings are made. As red as the rest is the lovely late-16th-century Casa Aragonese, a typical Catalan noble house with a columned loggia and Gothic windows and portal. The strange statues outside, also fashioned from the ubiquitous trachyte, are the result of an annual sculpture competition held here.

Fordongianus is most easily reached by car or motorcycle along the SS388 from Oristano. Up to eight weekday buses also connect with Oristano (€2.50, 35 minutes).

stone towers. Inside, a humble 14th-century chapel, the **Chiesa di Nostra Signora di Regnos Altos**, is adorned with an extraordinary 14th-century fresco cycle depicting saints ranging from St George slaying the dragon to St Lawrence in the middle of his martyrdom on the grill.

★Museo Casa Deriu MUSEUM

(☎0785 37 70 43; Corso Vittorio Emanuele 59; adult/reduced €4.50/3; ⊙10.30am-1pm & 3-5pm Tue-Fri, to 6pm Sat & Sun) Housed in an elegant 19th-century townhouse, Bosa's main museum showcases local arts and artisanal crafts. Each of the three floors has a different theme relating to the city and its past: the 1st floor hosts temporary exhibitions and displays of traditional hand embroidery; the 2nd floor displays the *palazzo*'s original 19th-century decor and furnishings; and the top floor is dedicated to Melkiorre Melis (1889–1982), a local painter and one of Sardinia's most important modern artists.

Your ticket also grants access to the small Pinacoteca across the street, which houses a collection of paintings by the 20th-century Sardinian artist Antonio Atza.

Cattedrale di San Pietro Extramuros CATHEDRAL

(€2; ⊙9.30am-12.30pm & 3.30-5.30pm, shorter hours winter) Two kilometres upstream from the Chiesa di Sant' Antonio Abate is this 11th-century cathedral, said to be the oldest Romanesque church in Sardinia. Originally built in 1073, it was subsequently modified with changes made to the apse in the 12th century and a Gothic facade added a century or so later.

Ponte Vecchio BRIDGE

Spanning the Temo River near the heart of the old town, Bosa's main bridge is a handsome three-arched affair, built from the region's characteristic red trachyte stone. Cross to the southern side for a perfect photo of Bosa's multicoloured houses stacked up below the Castello Malaspina.

Museo Delle Conce MUSEUM

(☎0785 37 70 43; Via Sas Conzas 62; adult/reduced €3.50/2.50; ⊙10am-1pm & 3-6pm Sat & Sun, 10am-1pm Tue-Fri) On the south bank of the river, this museum occupies Bosa's former tanneries, which remained in business until after WWII. On the ground floor you can see the original stone tanks where the leather hides were washed; upstairs, explanatory panels and a small collection of photos and old tools illustrate the whole tanning process. English-language handouts offer interesting historical details.

Cattedrale dell'Immacolata CATHEDRAL

(Piazza Duomo; ⊙10am-noon & 4-7pm) Bosa's cathedral dates to the early 19th century when it was built over an earlier Romanesque church. A rare, if not overly riveting, example of rococo (officially called Piedmontese

Bosa

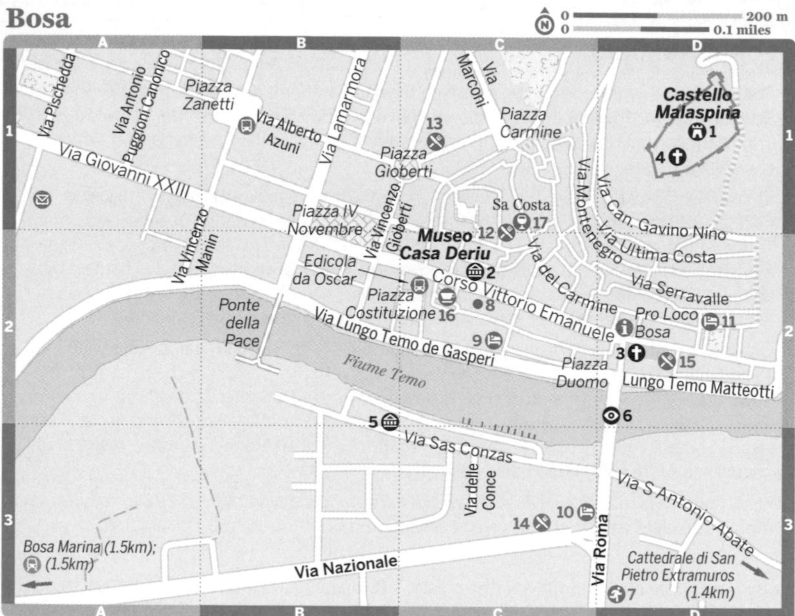

Bosa

Top Sights

1 Castello Malaspina D1
2 Museo Casa Deriu C2

Sights

3 Cattedrale dell'Immacolata D2
4 Chiesa di Nostra Signora di Regnos Altos D1
5 Museo Delle Conce B2
6 Ponte Vecchio D2

Activities, Courses & Tours

7 Cuccu D3
8 Esedra Sardegna C2

Sleeping

9 Corte Fiorita C2
10 Hotel Sa Pischedda C3
11 La Torre di Alice D2

Eating

12 Locanda di Corte C2
13 Pizzeria da Giovanni C1
14 Sa Pischedda C3
15 Trattoria Biancospino D2

Drinking & Nightlife

16 Caffè I Portici C2
17 Cantina G Battista Columbu C1

baroque), it boasts an imposing marble altar and several frescoes by the 19th-century artist Emilio Scherer.

Activities

Bosa is an important wine centre, renowned for its dessert wine, Malvasia. With advance notice, tastings can be arranged at major local producers, including **G Battista Columbu** (www.malvasiacolumbu.com), **Emidio Oggianu** (www.malvasiaoggianu.it), **Zarelli** (www.zarellivini.it) and **Angelo Angioi** (www.saltodicoloras.com).

Bosa Diving DIVING

(☎335 8189748; www.bosadiving.com; Piazza Paul Harris Banchina Commerciale Foce del Temo, Bosa Marina) This established operator offers a series of packages, including guided dives (from €45) and snorkelling excursions (€25). It also hires out canoes (single/double €7/10 per hour) and dinghies (for four people from €150 per day).

Cuccu CYCLING

(☎0785 37 32 98; Via Roma 5; ⏰9am-1pm & 4-8pm Mon-Sat) To explore out of town, you can hire scooters (€40 per day) and bikes (€10 per day) at this mechanic's shop on the southern side of the river.

Tours

Trenino Verde RAIL

(www.treninoverde.com; return fare Bosa Marina to Tresnuraghes/Macomer €15/18; ⊙mid-Jun–early Sep) For a different take on the area, the summer-only *trenino verde* (little green train) runs, slowly, between Bosa Marina, Tresnuraghes and Macomer. Travel times from Bosa Marina are one hour to Tresnuraghes and 2½ hours to Macomer. Schedules vary from year to year; see the website for details.

Esedra Sardegna TOURS

(☎0785 37 42 58; www.esedrasardegna.it; Corso Vittorio Emanuele 64; ⊙9.30am-1pm & 4.30-8pm Mon-Sat, 10.30am-1pm Sun) A reliable local operator that offers a wide range of packages, including river cruises, birdwatching excursions, boat tours, guided shop visits and train trips on the trenino verde. Prices vary, but are usually between €25 and €35 per person.

Festivals & Events

Carnevale CARNIVAL

(Carrasegare Osincu; ⊙Feb) Carnevale kicks off with a burning pyre outside the Chiesa di Sant'Antonio Abate and follows with days of parades, culminating in boisterous celebrations on *martedi grasso* (Shrove Tuesday).

On the Tuesday morning, townsfolk dress in black to lament the passing of Carnevale, while in the evening, groups of locals dress in white to hunt the *giolzi,* a manifestation of the carnival that is said to hide in people's groins. To find it people hold lanterns up to each other's nether regions shouting '*Giolzi! Giolzi! Ciappadu! Ciappadu!*' (Giolzi! Giolzi! Gotcha! Gotcha!).

Festa di Santa Maria del Mare RELIGIOUS

(⊙Aug) For four days around the first Sunday of August, Bosa celebrates the Festa di Santa Maria del Mare. Fishers form a colourful procession of boats to accompany a figure of the Virgin Mary from Bosa Marina to the cathedral. Fireworks and folkloristic performances add to the fun.

Festa di Nostra Signora di Regnos Altos RELIGIOUS

(⊙Sep) In the second week of September, streets in the old town are bedecked with huge palm fronds, flowers and *altarittos* (votive altars) to celebrate the Festa di Nostra Signora di Regnos Altos.

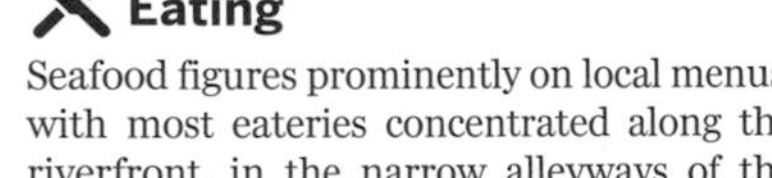

Eating

Seafood figures prominently on local menus, with most eateries concentrated along the riverfront, in the narrow alleyways of the historic centre, or out on the coast at Bosa Marina.

Pizzeria da Giovanni PIZZA €

(Via Ginnasio 6; pizza slices €1.30-2.50; ⊙noon-2pm & 6-10pm, closed lunch Wed & Sun) For a quick bite on the hoof, head to this humble, no-frills takeaway and join the ever-present queue of locals for a taste of Giovanni's fabulous sliced pizza.

★**Locanda di Corte** SARDINIAN €€

(☎340 2474823; www.facebook.com/LocandaDiCorte; Via del Pozzo 7; meals €30-35; ⊙12.30-2.30pm & 7.30-10pm Wed-Mon) Wriggle through Bosa's backstreets to discover this sweet local trattoria on a secluded cobblestoned square. Owners Angelo and Angela work the small collection of tables adorned with red-and-white-checked cloths, while their son Nicola cooks up scrumptious Sardinian classics such as fregola pasta with mussels, clams and cherry tomatoes, or pork chops in Cannonau wine.

Trattoria Biancospino TRATTORIA €€

(☎0785 37 41 58; www.facebook.com/trattoriabiancospino; Corso Vittorio Emanuele 6; meals €35; ⊙noon-3pm & 7-11pm) A cosy little spot near the cathedral, Biancospino offers inventive menus that take liberties with traditional recipes – for example, recasting Sardinia's classic cheese-and-honey *seadas* dessert as a savoury appetiser with Gorgonzola, bacon and asparagus, or combining grilled squid with green tomatoes, fennel and orange.

Sa Pischedda SEAFOOD €€

(☎0785 37 30 65; www.hotelsapischedda.com; Via Nazionale; meals €30-40, pizzas €7-9; ⊙noon-3pm & 7.30-11pm) At the hotel of the same name, Sa Pischedda is one of Bosa's top restaurants. With tables laid out on a romantic verandah and in a stylish back garden, it specialises in fish (both fresh-water and salt-water), but also does excellent pasta and pizza.

★**Essenza del Gusto** SEAFOOD €€€

(☎0785 37 30 13; www.facebook.com/nannisolinas65; Viale Mediterraneo 48; meals €40-50; ⊙1-3pm & 8-11pm Tue-Sun) For some of Bosa's best seafood – and a Mediterranean view to boot – make a beeline for this high-end local favourite in Bosa Marina. Fresh fish is exquisitely presented in dishes that range from a jazzed-up *frittura mista* (fried shrimp and calamari in a feather-light tempura-like batter) to fresh tuna tataki with sesame seeds, all accompanied by top local wines.

The atmosphere may feel a tad formal for some, but the food is as good as you'll find anywhere on this stretch of coast.

Drinking & Nightlife

Cantina G Battista Columbu WINE BAR
(☎339 5731677; www.malvasiacolumbu.com; Via del Carmine 104; ⌚10.30am-1.30pm & 5.30-9pm) A wonderful venue for sampling Bosa's renowned Malvasia, this attractive cantina is operated by the Columbu family, which has been producing wine in the region for three generations. Sip glasses (€3 to €4) of their smooth-as-silk, sherry-like Malvasia di Bosa and aromatic Alvariga along with wines from other Sardinian vintners, accompanied by local *salumi* and *formaggi* (cold cuts and cheeses).

Visits to local vineyards can also be arranged upon request.

Caffè I Portici CAFE
(Piazza Costituzione 6; ⌚7am-9pm, later in summer) Perfect for a leisurely evening drink, Caffè I Portici is a bustling cafe with outdoor tables on Piazza Costituzione, a prime people-watching spot.

Information

Banco di Sardegna (Piazza IV Novembre)

Farmacia (☎0785 37 31 32; Corso Vittorio Emanuele 51; ⌚9am-12.30pm & 4-7.30pm Mon-Fri)

Post Office (Via Pischedda 1; ⌚8.20am-7.05pm Mon-Fri, to 12.35pm Sat)

Pro Loco Bosa (☎349 9360900; www.facebook.com/prolocobosa.info; Corso Vittorio Emanuele 33b; ⌚10am-1pm & 3.30-7pm) Conveniently located tourist office on Bosa's main pedestrian thoroughfare, just north of the Ponte Vecchio.

Getting There & Away

BUS

There are weekday services from the **bus stops** (Piazza Zanetti) to Alghero (€3.70, 55 minutes, two daily), Sassari (€4.30, 2¼ hours, three daily) and Oristano (€5.50, two hours, five daily). Buy tickets at **Edicola da Oscar** (Corso Vittorio Emanuele 80; ⌚6am-8pm Mon-Sat, to 1pm Sun).

CAR & MOTORCYCLE

Bosa is connected to Oristano and Cuglieri by the SS292 and Alghero by the scenic coastal roads SP49 and SP105. The SS129 offers access to Macomer and other inland destinations.

Look for free street parking west of the centre in the modern town, or along the riverbank just south of Bosa's main bridge.

Alghero & the Northwest

Includes ➡

Best Places to Eat

- ➡ Agriturismo Sa Mandra (p127)
- ➡ Agriturismo Porticciolo (p129)
- ➡ Trattoria Lo Romanì (p119)
- ➡ San Gavino (p133)
- ➡ La Botteghina (p119)

Best Places to Sleep

- ➡ Hotel El Faro (p216)
- ➡ Agriturismo Sa Mandra (p216)
- ➡ Angedras Hotel (p215)
- ➡ Villa Las Tronas (p216)

Why Go?

Inspiring natural beauty goes hand-in-hand with history and urban charm in Sardinia's northwestern corner.

The obvious belle of the ball is the coastline with its brilliant sandy beaches, heady cliffs and hidden rocky coves. But head inland and surprises await – architectural and archaeological gems litter the green, stony countryside. Most notably, a string of Pisan Romanesque churches testify to medieval glories and tumbledown ruins attest to the presence of thriving prehistoric communities.

A history of foreign rule has left an indelible mark on the area, not only in bricks and mortar but also in spirit. Alghero, the northwest's main gateway and a one-time Catalan stronghold, has a distinctly Spanish feel, while Sassari owes its cosmopolitan outlook to its past as a Genoese colony. In many ways, the entire area seems less Sardinian than other parts of the island, less rural and less reserved, but is no less enchanting for it.

When to Go

- ➡ Join the masses to chow down on sea urchins at Alghero's Sagra del Bogamari food festival, usually held between February and March.
- ➡ The best months to tour the hinterland and its cultural and archaeological sites are April and May – the weather's warm and sunny, the roads are quiet and the countryside is blooming with spring colour.
- ➡ One of Sardinia's most prestigious festivals, Sassari's Cavalcata Sarda, draws huge crowds. Thousands flock to the city in May to watch costumed processions and displays of acrobatic horse riding.
- ➡ The summer and autumn months of June, July, August and September are made for hanging out on the beach and cruising the rocky coastline. Expect crowds and high-season prices.

Alghero & the Northwest Highlights

❶ **Spiaggia della Pelosa** (p130) Diving into Caribbean-coloured waters at this idyllic beach, one of Sardinia's most spectacular.

❷ **Sea Walls** (p114) Revelling in dreamy sunset views on Alghero's historic *bastioni*.

❸ **Parco Nazionale dell'Asinara** (p131) Watching out for albino donkeys in the rocky wilds of this remote, deserted island.

❹ **Le Prigionette Nature Reserve** (p128) Walking and lapping up the scenery in this unspoiled pocket of aromatic Mediterranean scrubland.

❺ **Grotta di Nettuno** (p129) Going underground at Capo Caccia's fairy-tale cave complex.

❻ **Nuraghe Santu Antine** (p143) Boning up on Sardinia's prehistoric past at this extraordinary nuraghic site.

❼ **Castello** (p134) Strolling Castelsardo's hilltop *centro storico* and gazing seawards from its impregnable castle.

❽ **Cavalcata Sarda** (p138) Getting into the festive swing at Sassari's great headline festival.

0 20 km
0 10 miles
Portobello
Costa Paradiso
Isola Rossa
Golfo dell' Asinara
Badesi
Valle della Luna
Luras
Aggius
Tempio Pausania
Valledoria
Viddalba
Castelsardo 7
Nuraghe Paddaggiu
Santa Maria
Roccia dell'Elefante
Lago di Castel Doria
SS134
Tergu
Sedini
Bulzi
Coghinas
Marina di Sorso
Perfugas
SP81
Laerru
Monte Acuto (493m)
Berchidda
Sorso
Sennori
Martis
Nulvi
SS200
SS131
Chiaramonti
Osilo
Lago di Coghinas
8 Sassari
Logudoro
Oschiri
Basilica della Santissima Trinità di Saccargia
Ploaghe
Chiesa di Sant'Antioco di Bisarcio
Ossi
Usini
Codrongianos
Monte Lerno (1094m)
SS729
Uri
Ardara
Chilivani
Ittiri
Ozieri
Pattada
Siligo
Lago Lerno
Mores
Borutta
Bonnanaro
Ittireddu
Thiesi
Torralba
Dolmen Sa Coveccada
Nuraghe
6 Santu Antine
Lago di Temo
Monteleone Rocca Doria
Valle dei Nuraghi
Bultei
Benetutti
Monte Minerva (664m)
Rebeccu
Necropoli di Sant'Andrea Priu
Bonorva
Padria
Pozzomaggiore
Tirso
SS131
Montresta
Bolotana
Orotelli
Bosa
Silanus
SS129
Sindia
Suni
Macomer

ALGHERO

☎079 / POP 44,000

One of Sardinia's most beautiful medieval cities, Alghero is the main resort in the northwest. Although largely given over to tourism – its population can almost quadruple in July and August – the town retains a proud and independent spirit. Its animated historic centre is a terrific place to hang out, and with so many excellent restaurants and bars, it makes an ideal base for exploring the beaches and beauty spots of the nearby Riviera del Corallo.

The main focus of attention is the picturesque *centro storico* (historic centre), one of the best preserved in Sardinia. Enclosed by robust, honey-coloured sea walls, it's a tightly knit enclave of cobbled lanes, Gothic *palazzi* and cafe-lined piazzas. Below, yachts crowd the marina and long, sandy beaches curve away to the north. Presiding over everything is a palpable Spanish atmosphere, a hangover from the city's past as a Catalan colony.

History

A modern city by Sardinian standards, L'Alguerium (named after the algae that washed up on the coast) started life as an 11th-century fishing village. Thanks to its strategic position, it was jealously guarded by its Genoese founders who, despite a brief Pisan interregnum in the 1280s, managed to retain control until the mid-14th century.

They were finally ousted by the Catalan Aragonese, who took the city in 1353 after a naval battle at Porto Conte. Catalan colonists were encouraged to settle in the town, and after a revolt in 1372 the remaining Sardinians were relocated inland to Villanova Monteleone. From then on, Alghero became resolutely Catalan and called itself Alguer.

Under its Iberian rulers, the town thrived. It became the main Catalan port on the island and in 1501 was raised to the status of city. Fortifications were built to defend it against land and sea attacks. Further adding to its prestige was the arrival of the Holy Roman Emperor (and king of Spain) Charles V in 1541 to lead a campaign against the North African corsairs.

After about 350 years of Spanish rule, the city passed to the Piedmontese House of Savoy in 1720. The next couple of centuries proved hard for Alghero, and by the 1920s its population had fallen to just over 10,000. Heavily bombed in 1943, it remained in pretty poor shape until tourism arrived in the late 1960s, paving the way for the development of the modern new town.

Sights

Most of Alghero's sights are to be found in the *centro storico,* which, with its massive sea walls and narrow lanes, is ideal for leisurely strolling. Prime time is early evening when crowds parade their tans.

★Sea Walls WALLS

(Bastioni; Map p120) Alghero's golden sea walls, built around the *centro storico* by the Aragonese in the 16th century, are a highlight of the town's historic cityscape. Running from Piazza Sulis in the south to Porta a Mare and the marina in the north, they're crowned by a pedestrianised path that commands superb views over to Capo Caccia on the blue horizon. Restaurants and bars line the walkway, providing the perfect perch to sit back and lap up the holiday atmosphere.

To walk the walls, also known as the *bastioni,* start at **Torre di Sulis** (Map p120; Piazza Sulis) on the piazza of the same name. This 22m-high tower originally closed off the defensive line of towers to the south of the old town. Continuing northwards along the **Bastioni Cristoforo Colombo**, you'll pass the **Torre di San Giacomo** (Map p120) before arriving on the main stretch, the **Bastioni Marco Polo**, where most of the restaurants are lined up.

At the northern tip are two more towers, the **Torre della Polveriera** (Map p120) and **Torre di Sant'Elmo** (Map p120). The last stretch, the **Bastioni Magellano**, leads on to **Porta a Mare** (Map p120), the second of Alghero's medieval gateways, through which you can access Piazza Civica (p115) in the historic centre. Beyond the Porta, the Torre della Maddalena (p116) is incorporated into the Forte della Maddalena (p116), the only remnant of the city's land battlements.

★Campanile TOWER

(Bell Tower; Map p120; ☎079 973 30 41; Via Principe Umberto; adult/reduced €2.50/free; ⏰11am-1pm & 7-9pm Mon & Fri Jul & Aug, 11am-1pm Mon, Tue, Thu & Fri & 4-7pm Thu & Fri May, Jun, Sep & Oct, by request Dec & Jan, closed Feb-Apr) Rising above the historic centre, the Cattedrale di Santa Maria's 16th-century *campanile* (bell tower) is one of Alghero's signature landmarks. The tower, accessible through a Gothic doorway on Via Principe Umberto, is a fine example of Catalan Gothic architecture with its elegant octagonal structure and short pyramid-shaped spire. Climb to the top for amazing views.

★Chiesa di San Francesco CHURCH
(Map p120; ☎079 97 92 58; Via Carlo Alberto; ⊙9.15am-12.30pm Mon-Sat & 5-6.30pm Mon, Wed, Thu & Sat, 4.30-6.30pm Tue & Fri, 9.15-10.30am & 5-6.30pm Sun) Alghero's finest church is a model of architectural harmony. Originally built to a Catalan Gothic design in the 14th century, it was later given a Renaissance facelift after it partially collapsed in 1593. Inside, interest is focused on the 18th-century marble altar and a strange 17th-century sculpture of a haggard Christ tied to a column. Through the sacristy you can enter a beautiful 14th-century cloister, where the 22 columns connect a series of round arches.

The buttery sandstone used in the arcades and columns lends the cloister a special warmth, which makes it a wonderful setting for summer concerts.

Museo Archeologico della Città di Alghero MUSEUM
(Map p120; ☎079 98 07 29; Via Carlo Alberto 72; adult/reduced €6/4; ⊙11am-1.30pm & 5.30-8pm Thu-Tue) The history of human settlement in the Alghero area is charted at this gleaming new archaeological museum, inaugurated in December 2016. Artefacts discovered in nuraghic villages, neolithic caves and Roman shipwrecks are exhibited in thematic displays relating to the sea, ancient ways of life, and cults and death.

Piazza Civica PIAZZA
(Map p120) Just inside Porta a Mare, Piazza Civica is Alghero's showcase square. In a former life it was the administrative heart of the medieval city, but where Spanish aristocrats once met to debate affairs of empire, tourists now converge to browse jewellery displays in elegant shop windows, eat ice cream and drink at the city's grandest cafe – **Caffè Costantino** (Map p120; ☎079 98 29 29; Piazza Civica 31; ⊙7.30am-1.30am, closed Mon winter) occupies the ground floor of the Gothic Palazzo d'Albis, where the Spanish emperor Charles V famously stayed in 1541.

Torre Porta a Terra TOWER
(Map p120; Piazza Porta Terra 2; ⊙9.30am-1pm & 4-8pm Tue-Sun) FREE Near the Giardini Pubblici, the 14th-century Torre Porta a Terra is all that remains of Porta a Terra, one of the two main gates into the medieval city. A stumpy 23m-high tower known originally as Porta Reial, it has a panoramic terrace with terrific rooftop views over to the sea.

CENTRO STORICO DRIVING ALERT!

Note that most of Alghero's historic centre is out of bounds to non-authorised drivers. If, by mistake, you enter the ZTL (*zona a traffico limitato;* limited traffic zone) you risk a fine, payable to your car-hire company if you're in a rental car.

The ZTL restrictions are lifted between 8am and 10.30am and then again from 2.30pm to 4.30pm.

Cattedrale di Santa Maria CATHEDRAL
(Map p120; ☎079 97 92 22; Piazza Duomo 2; ⊙7am-7.30pm, later in summer) Overlooking Piazza Duomo, Alghero's oversized Cattedrale di Santa Maria appears out of place with its pompous neoclassical facade and fat Doric columns. An unfortunate 19th-century addition, the facade was the last in a long line of modifications the hybrid cathedral has endured since it was built, originally on Catalan Gothic lines in the 16th century. Inside it's largely Renaissance, with some late-baroque baubles added in the 18th century.

Chiesa di San Michele CHURCH
(Map p120; ☎079 97 92 34; Via Carlo Alberto; ⊙9.30am-1pm & 3.30-7.45pm Mon-Sat, 8.30am-1pm & 3.30-7.45pm Sun) On Via Carlo Alberto, the *carrer major* of the medieval town, the 17th-century Chiesa di San Michele is best known for its maiolica-tiled dome. The present tiles were laid in the 1960s, but this doesn't detract from their beauty. Inside, look out for a wooden sculpture of San Michele (St Michael) slaying Satan.

Just before you reach the church you cross Via Gilbert Ferret. This intersection is known as the *quatre cantonades* (four sides), and for centuries labourers would gather here in the hope of finding work.

Museo del Corallo MUSEUM
(Map p120; ☎079 973 40 45; Via XX Settembre 8, Villa Costantino; adult/reduced €6/4; ⊙10.30am-12.30pm & 4.30-7pm Tue-Sun) Housed in a Liberty-style villa, this small museum is dedicated to Alghero's coral trade. Information panels and exhibits, which include works of coral jewellery, illustrate how coral has been harvested over the years and the role it has played in local artisanal traditions.

Spiaggia di San Giovanni BEACH
(Map p118) The closest beach to the historic centre, Spiaggia di San Giovanni is part of a long stretch of sand that curves around the bay almost uninterrupted to Fertilia. In Alghero you can hire umbrellas and sunloungers for about €15 per day, as well as windsurfers and canoes.

Forte della Maddalena FORT
(Map p120) To the north of the old town, the Forte della Maddalena is the sole survivor of three forts built at the end of the 16th century to bolster the city's land battlements. Its tower, known as the **Torre della Maddalena** (Map p120) or Torre di Garibaldi, dates to an earlier medieval period.

Giardini Pubblici PARK
(Giardini Giuseppe Manno; Map p120; entrances Via Catalogna, Via Cagliari, Via Vittorio Emanuele, Via Lamarmora) At some point you'll probably find yourself passing by Alghero's public gardens. The verdant park, which effectively separates the medieval centre from the modern town, was created in the 19th century when the landward stretches of the city's defensive walls were torn down. Today it's frequented by everyone from tourists and street sellers to teens and chatting locals.

Beaches

North of Alghero's yacht-jammed marina, Via Garibaldi sweeps up to the town's long, sandy beaches: **Spiaggia di San Giovanni** and, beyond that, **Spiaggia di Maria Pia**. Nicer still are the beaches further around the coast near Fertilia (p126). In Alghero you can hire umbrellas and sunloungers for about €15 per day, as well as windsurfers and canoes.

Activities

Nautisub DIVING
(Map p118; ☎079 95 24 33; www.nautisub.com; Via Garibaldi 45; ⏰9am-1pm daily, plus 4-7.30pm Tue-Sat) Operating out of a dive shop on the seafront, this year-round outfit organises dives (from €45 or €60 with kit hire), snorkelling excursions (€35) and boat tours (€50 including lunch).

Courses

Italiano in Riviera LANGUAGE
(Map p118; ☎079 27 50 35; www.italianoinriviera.it; Via Gallura 14) This school runs a series of Italian-language courses for all levels. There's also the possibility of combining language studies with classes on the history of art, cookery, wine tasting and sport. Individual lessons cost €40 per hour; weekly courses start at €239 per person.

Pintadera LANGUAGE
(Map p120; ☎079 91 70 64; www.pintadera.info; Vicolo Adami 41) A small school based in the historic centre, Pintadera offers a range of language lessons as well as courses in Sardinian history and culture, food, wine tasting and drawing. Reckon on €60 for an evening's cookery class; a weeklong language course is €280.

Tours

Progetto Natura TOURS
(Map p118; ☎392 1404069; www.progettonaturasardegna.com; Lungomare Barcellona; tours adult/reduced €37/25) Take to Alghero's seas with a crew of marine biologists and environmental guides. Summer day tours, which run from June to October, combine dolphin watching with snorkelling in the protected waters of the Area Marina Protetta Capo Caccia-Isola Piana; winter tours, from November to May, are dedicated to dolphin watching. Note, its seafront kiosk is only operative May through October.

Linea Grotta Navisarda BOATING
(Map p120; ☎079 95 06 03; www.navisarda.it; Porto di Alghero; to Grotta adult/child return €16/8, cave entrance not included, day cruise €45/22; ⏰hourly 10am-3pm Jun-Sep, 11am & 3pm Mar-May & Oct) Take a boat trip along the impressive northern coast to Capo Caccia and the Grotta di Nettuno (p128) cave complex. Traghetti Navisarda is one of a number of operators running ferries up to the caves as well as day cruises with lunch and swimming stops. The round trip to the Grotta, including cave visit, lasts approximately two-and-a-half hours.

Cooperativa Itinera WALKING
(Map p120; ☎079 973 40 45; itinera.alghero@alice.it; Piazza Porta Terra 2, Torre Porta a Terra) Offers two-hour group guided tours of the city in various languages, including English, Italian, French and Catalan. Groups requiring a non-Italian-speaking guide should book five or six days in advance. It also rents out audio guides (€7.50 for the first one, then €5 for additional ones).

Linea Grotta Attilio Regolo BOATING
(Map p120; ☎368 3536824; www.grottedinettuno.it; to Grotta adult/child return €15/7, cave

entrance not included, day cruise €45/20; ⏲hourly 10.45am-3.45pm Jun-Sep, 10.45am, 11.45am & 1.45pm Apr, May & Oct) Runs boats up the coast to the Grotta di Nettuno (p128) and day cruises along the Riviera del Corallo.

Trenino Catalano TOURS
(Map p120; adult/reduced €5/3; ⏲10am-midnight Jul & Aug, to 8pm Mar-Jun, Sep & Oct) One for the kids, this miniature train chugs around the historic centre. Departures are half-hourly from the port; buy tickets at the departure point near Forta della Maddalena.

Trottolo BUS
(Map p120; ☎329 8755555; www.trottolo.it; 24/48hr €18/25) Trottolo runs panoramic hop-on, hop-off tours in an open-top bus. Routes start near the Alghero marina and run up the coast to Porto Conte and Capo Caccia, stopping off at various points en route, including the Grotta di Nettuno. There are up to six daily departures from May to mid-October, dropping to three in April and late October. Buy tickets onboard.

Festivals & Events

Alghero has a full calendar of festivals and events, though spring and summer are the best times to catch an event. To see what's on, check www.algheroturismo.eu.

Festa di Sant Miquel RELIGIOUS
(⏲Sep) The feast day of Alghero's patron saint, Sant Miquel (St Michael), is celebrated on 29 September as part of a larger program of religious, cultural and sporting events between late September and early October.

Sagra del Bogamarì FOOD & DRINK
(⏲Feb/Mar/Apr) Alghero locals pay homage to the humble sea urchin *(riccio di mare)* by eating mountainloads of the spiky molluscs. The exact dates vary from year to year, but it's usually held between February and March or early April.

Easter Holy Week RELIGIOUS
(⏲Mar/Apr) Figures of Christ and the Virgin Mary are borne through town in enactments of the Misteri (Passion of Christ) and Incontru (Meeting of the Virgin with Christ).

Ferragosto (Feast of the Assumption) RELIGIOUS
(⏲Aug) On 15 August, Alghero celebrates Ferragosto with fireworks, boat races and music.

Carnevale CARNIVAL
(Lo Carraixali de l'Alguer; www.sardegnaturismo.it; ⏲Feb) Alghero celebrates the run-up to Lent with a series of Carnival parades, kids in fancy dress, and much merry-making.

Eating

Eating out is a joy in Alghero. There are a huge number of restaurants, trattorias, pizzerias and takeaways, many in the historic centre, and standards are generally high. Menus feature the full range of Sardinian staples, but seafood is the star. A local speciality is Catalan-style lobster, *aragosta alla catalana,* served with tomato and onion.

Gelateria I Bastioni GELATO €
(Map p120; Bastioni Marco Polo 5; gelato €1.50-4; ⏲2-8pm Apr & Oct, noon-midnight Jun-Sep) It's only a hole in the wall, but this gem of a gelateria dishes up superb ice cream, as well as milkshakes and *granite* (flavoured ice drinks). Particularly fab are the fresh fruit flavours, perhaps mulberry or watermelon, ideally topped by a generous squirt of whipped cream.

Prosciutteria Sant Miquel SARDINIAN €
(Map p120; ☎348 4694434; Via della Misericordia 20; meals €20; ⏲11.30am-1am summer, shorter hours winter) A model wine bar complete with wooden ceiling, hanging hams and a menu of delicious Sardinian charcuterie and cheeses. Grab a table in the tiny, usually packed, interior and tuck into wafer-thin slices of ham and salami, wedges of aged *pecorino* and bowls of plump, glistening olives, all served on thick wooden boards.

Lu Furat PIZZA €
(Map p120; ☎079 973 60 52; Via Columbano 8; snacks €3-9; ⏲noon-3pm & 7-11pm) Duck down into this vaulted, hole-in-the-wall pizzeria and for a few euro you can snack on perfectly thin, crisp pizza or *fainè* (chickpea pancakes) followed by a classic *seadas* (fried pastry served with honey). If you can't bag one of the few tables, get a takeaway.

FISH ON THE MENU

Something to look out for when ordering lobster *(aragosta)* or fish at a restaurant is that most menus give the price of fresh fish per gram (or per *etto* – 100g), not for the dish as a whole. If in doubt, check with the waiter and ask to have the fish weighed before ordering.

Alghero

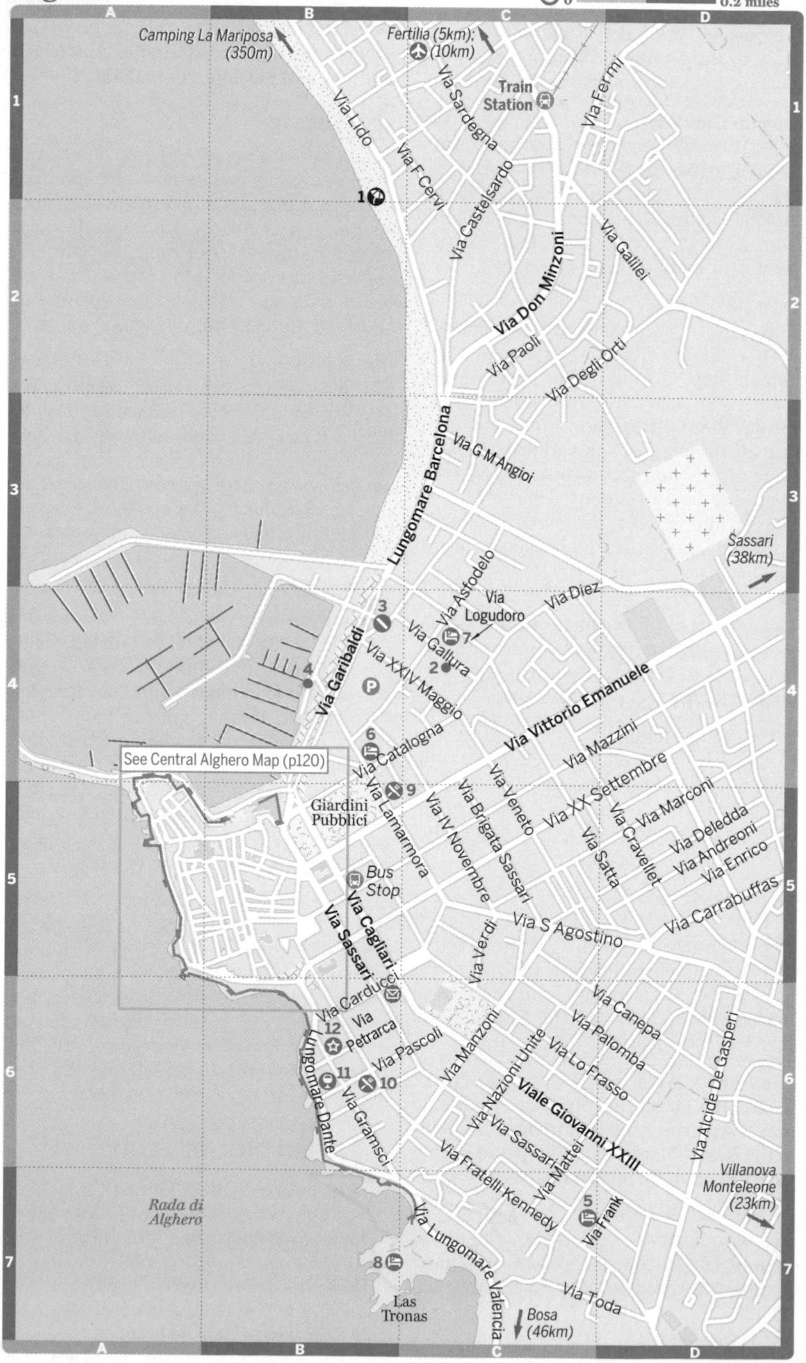

0 — 400 m
0 — 0.2 miles

Camping La Mariposa (350m)
Fertilia (5km); (10km)
Train Station
Via Lido
Via Sardegna
Via Fermi
Via F Cervi
Via Castelsardo
1
Via Galilei
Via Don Minzoni
Via Paoli
Via Degli Orti
Lungomare Barcelona
Via G M Angioi
Sassari (38km)
Via Asfodelo
Via Logudoro
Via Diez
3
7
Via Gallura
2
Via Garibaldi
4
Via XXIV Maggio
Via Vittorio Emanuele
6
Via Catalogna
Via Mazzini
See Central Alghero Map (p120)
9
Via Lamarmora
Via Brigata Sassari
Via Veneto
Via XX Settembre
Via Marconi
Giardini Pubblici
Via IV Novembre
Via Satta
Via Cravellet
Via Deledda
Via Andreoni
Via Enrico
Bus Stop
Via Cagliari
Via Sassari
Via Carrabuffas
Via S Agostino
Via Verdi
Via Carducci
Via Canepa
Via Petrarca
12
Via Palomba
Via Pascoli
Via Manzoni
Via Nazioni Unite
Via Lo Frasso
11
10
Lungomare Dante
Via Gramsci
Viale Giovanni XXIII
Via Alcide De Gasperi
Via Sassari
Via Mattei
Via Fratelli Kennedy
Villanova Monteleone (23km)
Rada di Alghero
5
Via Frank
Via Lungomare Valencia
8
Via Toda
Las Tronas
Bosa (46km)

Alghero

Sights

Activities, Courses & Tours

Sleeping

Eating

Drinking & Nightlife

Entertainment

★Trattoria Lo Romanì SARDINIAN €€
(Map p120; ☎079 973 84 79; Via Principe Umberto 29; meals €35; ⏲12.30-2.30pm Tue-Sun & 7.30-10.30pm daily) Many of Alghero restaurants serve *porcetto,* Sardinia's classic spit-roasted pork, but few places cook it to such buttery perfection. The crackling is spot on and the meat is sweet and packed with flavour. *Porcetto* apart, it's a delightful trattoria. Exposed sandstone walls and soft lighting create a warm, elegant atmosphere, service is attentive and the fresh island food is terrific.

★La Botteghina SARDINIAN €€
(Map p120; ☎079 973 83 75; www.labotteghina.biz; Via Principe Umberto 63; meals €35; ⏲7-11.30pm Wed-Fri, noon-3pm & 7-11.30pm Sat & Sun) Cool, casual dining in a stylish *centro storico* setting – think blond-wood decor and low sandstone arches – is what La Botteghina is all about. In keeping with the upbeat, youthful vibe, the food is simple, seasonal and local, so expect steaks of *bue rosso* beef, cured meats and Sardinian cheeses, alongside inventive pizzas and Sardinian wines and craft beers.

★Il Pesce d'Oro RISTORANTE, PIZZERIA €€
(Map p120; ☎079 95 26 02; www.pescedoroalghero.it; Via Catalogna 12; pizzas €5-12, meals €30-35; ⏲12.30-2.30pm & 7.30-11pm, closed Mon lunch & Wed) The modest demeanour of this Alghero favourite – locals come here for their weekend evening out – belies the quality of its excellent food. You can keep it simple with a wood-fired pizza, or push the boat out and feast on fab seafood, starting with the flavourful mixed-fish antipasto.

Mabrouk SEAFOOD €€
(Map p120; ☎079 97 00 00; http://mabroukalghero.com; Via Santa Barbara 4; meals €40; ⏲6pm-midnight Tue-Sat, 1-3.30pm Sun) Reserve a table at this cosy, low-ceilinged stone restaurant and you never know what you're going to get. What you do know is that it'll be fish, it'll be fresh, and it'll be excellent. Dinner, which is served as a set menu, depends on the day's catch, but with several antipasti, three pasta dishes and three main courses included, you won't go hungry.

Angedras Restaurant SARDINIAN €€
(Map p120; ☎079 973 50 78; www.angedrasristorant.it; Bastioni Marco Polo 41; lunch menu €16, meals €35; ⏲noon-2.45pm & 7-11.30pm Apr-Oct) Alghero's honey-coloured ramparts set a memorable stage for al fresco dining. This is one of the better restaurants on the walls, serving a regional menu of elegantly presented seafood and the occasional meat offering. At lunch, you can save by going for the €16 menu, which consists of two dishes chosen from the regular à la carte menu.

Al Tuguri RISTORANTE €€
(Map p120; ☎079 97 67 72; www.altuguri.it; Via Maiorca 113; tasting menus vegetarian/seafood/meat €40/48/48; ⏲12.30-2pm & 7.30-10pm Mon-Sat; ✎) A long-standing Alghero favourite, Al Tuguri impresses for all the right reasons. Decorated in traditional rustic style, it's a smart, intimate spot to dine on inventive local seafood and satisfying grilled meats and fish. For vegetarians, there's also the rare luxury of a dedicated veggie menu. Booking is advisable.

SELF-CATERING

You can stock up on picnic supplies, fresh meat and fish at Alghero's daily **market** (Map p120; Via Sassari 23; ⏲7am-1pm) near Torre Porta a Terra. Otherwise, there's a **Euro Spin supermarket** (Map p118; Via Lamarmora 26; ⏲8am-9.30pm Mon-Sat, 9am-1.30pm & 5-9pm Sun) by the Giardini Pubblici.

Central Alghero

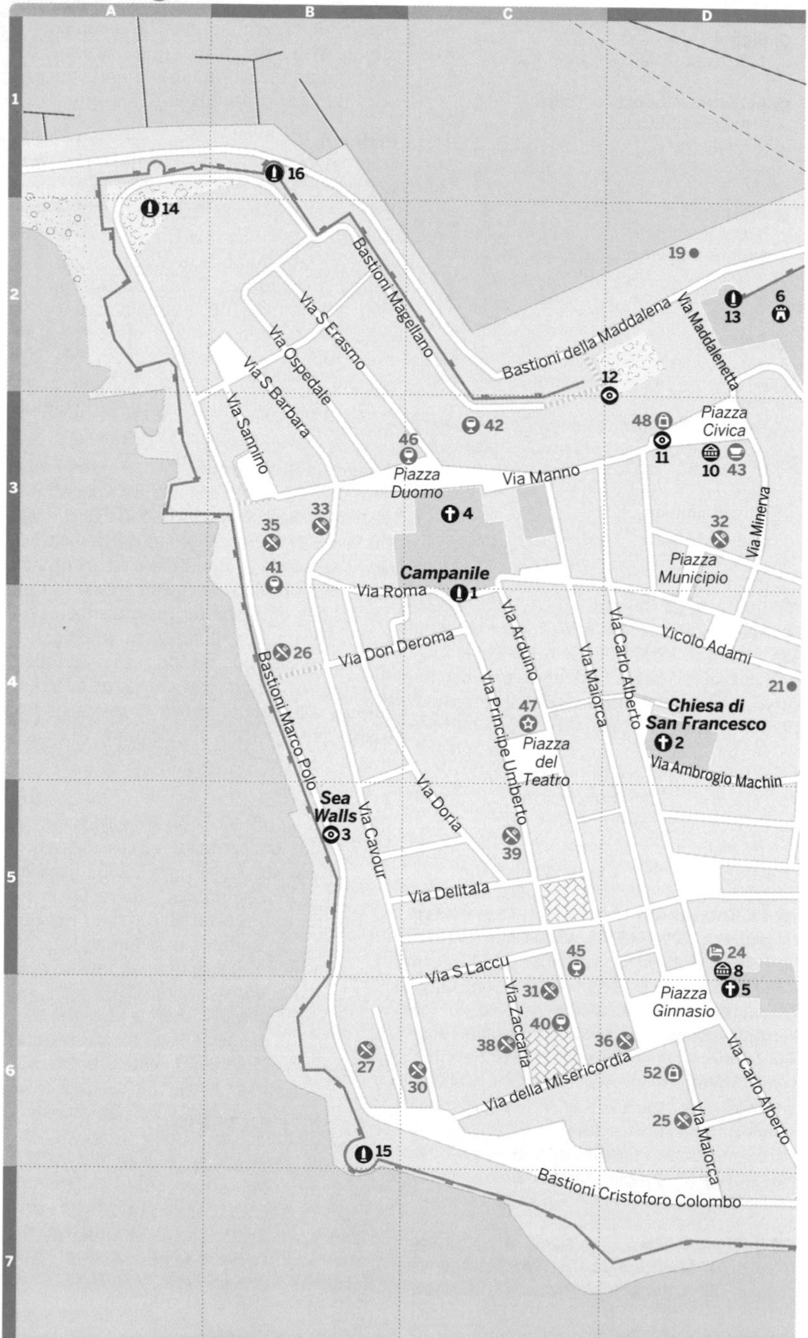

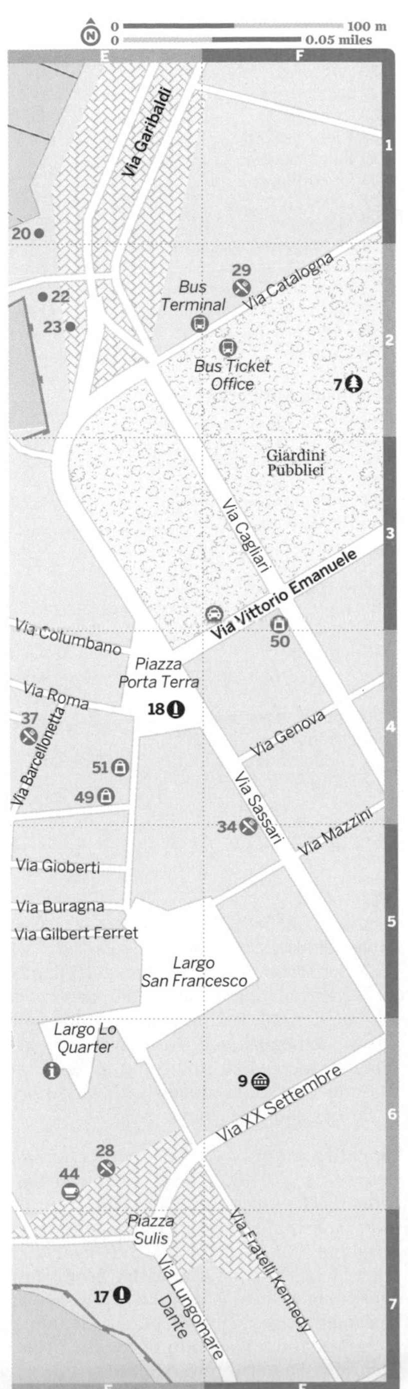

Trattoria Al Refettorio RISTORANTE €€
(Map p120; ☎079 973 11 26; Vicolo Adami 47; meals €35; ⏰noon-3pm & 7.30-10.30pm) Al Refettorio is a smart wine bar and restaurant with tables under a low stone arch and in a softly lit vaulted interior. Creative seafood is the headline act, along with a carefully curated selection of wines and craft beers, so sit down to oysters and smoked mussels, pasta with sea urchins and fresh fish of the day.

Osteria Macchiavello SARDINIAN €€
(Map p120; ☎079 98 06 28; www.osteriamacchiavello.it; Bastioni Marco Polo 57, Via Cavour 7; meals €35-40, fixed-price lunch menus €16-21; ⏰noon-2.45pm & 7-11.30pm Apr-Oct) A popular restaurant on the sea walls, this is a panoramic spot for a leisurely meal. The menu covers most tastes with a number of classic local dishes, including *baccalà* (salted cod) served in a sweet-and-sour stew and wild boar braised in red wine. Alongside the à la carte menu, there are also a couple of fixed-price lunch menus.

Trattoria La Saletta SARDINIAN €€
(Map p118; ☎079 412 57 48; Via Fratelli Kennedy 27; meals €25-30; ⏰7-11pm Tue-Sat, noon-3pm Sun) Sardinia's culinary traditions take centre stage at this popular trattoria. The menu features *pecorino* cheese, *fregula sarda* (a type of Sardinian-style pasta couscous), roast pork and stewed lamb, while the decor is rustic and cheerfully cluttered.

Trattoria L'Assassino TRATTORIA €€
(Map p120; ☎079 23 34 63; Via Zaccaria 12; meals €25-30; ⏰noon-3pm & 7pm-midnight summer, Sat & Sun winter) This humble *centro storico* trattoria offers a great location – it's housed in a former convent on an atmospheric piazza – and a menu of traditional Sardinian staples, including snails served with garlic, parsley and chilli, and gnocchi with fresh sausage.

Kings SARDINIAN €€
(Map p120; ☎079 97 96 50; www.thekingsrestaurant.it; Via Cavour 123, Bastioni Marco Polo 5; meals €40; ⏰7.30-11.30pm; ✎) With a sea-facing terrace on Alghero's golden ramparts, this restaurant cranks up the romance as day softens into dusk. Clean, bright Mediterranean flavours shine through in dishes such as lightly fried sea bass and mullet served on a bed of shellfish cream. There are also dedicated menus for kids and vegetarians, and handmade desserts.

Central Alghero

Top Sights
1 Campanile ... C4
2 Chiesa di San Francesco ... D4
3 Sea Walls ... B5

Sights
4 Cattedrale di Santa Maria ... C3
5 Chiesa di San Michele ... D6
6 Forte della Maddalena ... D2
7 Giardini Pubblici ... F2
8 Museo Archeologico della Città di Alghero ... D5
9 Museo del Corallo ... F6
10 Palazzo d'Albis ... D3
11 Piazza Civica ... D3
12 Porta a Mare ... D2
13 Torre della Maddalena ... D2
14 Torre della Polveriera ... A2
15 Torre di San Giacomo ... B6
16 Torre di Sant'Elmo ... B1
17 Torre di Sulis ... E7
18 Torre Porta a Terra ... E4

Activities, Courses & Tours
Cooperativa Itinera ... (see 18)
19 Linea Grotta Attilio Regolo ... D2
20 Linea Grotta Navisarda ... E1
21 Pintadera ... D4
22 Trenino Catalano ... E2
23 Trottolo ... E2

Sleeping
24 B&B Benebenniu ... D5

Eating
25 Al Tuguri ... D6
26 Angedras Restaurant ... B4
27 Gelateria I Bastioni ... B6
28 Il Pavone ... E6
29 Il Pesce d'Oro ... F2
30 Kings ... C6
31 La Botteghina ... C6
32 Lu Furat ... D3
33 Mabrouk ... B3
34 Mercato Civico ... F5
35 Osteria Macchiavello ... B3
36 Prosciutteria Sant Miquel ... D6
37 Trattoria Al Refettorio ... E4
38 Trattoria L'Assassino ... C6
39 Trattoria Lo Romanì ... C5

Drinking & Nightlife
40 Baraonda ... C6
41 Buena Vista ... B3
42 Cafè Latino ... C3
43 Caffè Costantino ... D3
44 Chez Michel ... E6
45 l'altra vineria ... C5
46 SardOa ... C3

Entertainment
47 Teatro Civico ... C4

Shopping
Agostino Marogna ... (see 10)
48 Boutique Marras ... D3
49 Calzoleria Naitana ... E4
50 Cyrano ... F3
51 Enodolciaria ... E4
52 l'altra isola ... D6

Il Pavone SARDINIAN €€€
(Map p120; ☎079 97 95 84; Piazza Sulis 3-4; meals €45-50; ⊙noon-3.30pm & 7-11.30pm summer, closed Sun dinner winter) A city institution, Il Pavone offers the best of both worlds – excellent food and a prime location on Piazza Sulis. Its sea-facing pavilion is a lovely spot to sit down to seafood hits such as fresh pasta with *bottarga* (mullet roe), artichokes and *pecorino* cheese.

Drinking & Nightlife

Alghero's drinking scene consists of elegant cafes, waterfront bars, hole-in-the wall cocktail joints, pubs and wine bars. Much of the action is in the historic centre, but you'll also find places on the sea walls and the seafront south of Piazza Sulis. Things quieten considerably outside of the summer season.

★**SardOa** WINE BAR
(Map p120; ☎349 2212055; Piazza Duomo 4; ⊙6pm-late daily summer, noon-2.30pm & 6pm-late Sat & Sun winter) The Basque country lands in Alghero at this chilled wine bar. Under a vaulted stone ceiling, happy punters sit on wooden crates and sip Basque and Sardinian wines while munching on *pintxos* (Basque-style tapas) made with glistening anchovies and Iberic ham.

★**l'altra vineria** CRAFT BEER
(Map p120; ☎079 601 49 54; Via Principe Umberto 66-68; ⊙7pm-late) A newcomer to Alghero's drinking scene, l'altra vineria is all about the pleasures of craft beer and island wine. The bar, run with warmth and infectious enthusiasm by Luca and Sonia, is a small, cosy place with barrels doubling as tables and a selection of terrific beers, including Sassari-brewed Speed.

Cafè Latino BAR

(Map p120; ☎079 97 65 41; Bastioni Magellano 10; ⏰9am-2am daily summer, to 9.30pm Wed-Mon winter) Revel in romantic harbour views over an evening *aperitivo* at this chic bar on the sea walls. Overlooking the marina, it has outside tables and an ample menu of drinks and snacks.

Buena Vista BAR

(Map p120; Bastioni Marco Polo 47; ⏰4pm-2am) Fabulous mojitos go hand-in-hand with stunning sunset views at this buzzing little bar on the western walls. Upbeat Latin tunes and a cavernous interior add to the friendly, laid-back vibe.

Baraonda WINE BAR

(Map p120; Via Principe Umberto 75; ⏰6pm-2am daily summer, Thu-Tue winter) Exposed stone walls, lilac hues and a low-key jazz soundtrack set the tone at this good-looking wine bar. In summer sit out on the cobbled piazza and watch the world parade by as you get to grips with the extensive wine list.

Blau Skybar ROOFTOP BAR

(Map p118; www.hotelcatalunya.it; Via Catalogna 22; ⏰10am-3pm & 4-10pm) This modern, glass-walled bar boasts some of the best views in town from its lofty position on the 9th floor of the four-star Hotel Catalunya. Arm yourself with a cocktail and enjoy the full sweep of the marina, historic centre and bay laid out before you.

L'Arcafè BAR

(Map p118; Lungomare Dante 6; ⏰8am-2am daily summer, 6pm-midnight Thu-Sun winter) This rocking music bar is an ever-popular hangout. Its seafront position and convivial atmosphere ensure a steady stream of drinkers, while party lovers come for the weekend DJ sets and live gigs.

Chez Michel CAFE

(Map p120; Piazza Sulis 2; ⏰7am-midnight summer, to 11pm winter) One of several cafes and bars offering ringside seats on Piazza Sulis, this is a prime spot for people-watching and evening drinks. Aperitifs (from €3.50) are served as well as coffees and cocktails.

Il Ruscello CLUB

(☎349 1244677; SS Alghero–Olmedo; ⏰11pm-late summer) One of Alghero's big-name clubs, the summer-only Ruscello attracts a young party-loving crowd with its three dance floors and DJ-fuelled soundtrack of house, pop and Latin beats. Admission is generally in the €10 to €15 range.

The club is about 2km northeast of town on the road to Olmedo.

☆ Entertainment

Poco Loco LIVE MUSIC

(Map p118; ☎079 98 36 04; www.pocolocoalghero.com; Via Gramsci 8; ⏰7.30pm-1am Tue-Sun) A historic multipurpose venue serving up cocktails, pizza by the metre and regular live music. Concerts, staged between October and June, cater to most tastes, although jazz and blues headline more than most. Admission to concerts generally costs €10.

Teatro Civico THEATRE

(Map p120; www.facebook.com/teatroalghero; Piazza del Teatro 1) Inaugurated in 1862, Alghero's main theatre hosts regular events, including an annual season of prose and dance performances. Program details are published on the Alghero tourist website (www.algheroturismo.eu).

Shopping

Streets throughout the historic centre are lined with shops selling foodie treats, designer threads, tourist tat and jewellery made from Alghero's famous red coral (p126). Most shops close over lunch, usually from around 1pm to 4.30pm, reopening in the evening until about 8.30pm. In summer many stay open late, closing only when the flow of passersby has dried up.

★Cyrano BOOKS

(Map p120; ☎079 973 83 03; Via Vittorio Emanuele 11; ⏰8.30am-midnight daily summer, 8.30am-1.30pm & 4-9.30pm Mon-Sat winter) A cool independent bookshop doubling as a cafe and cultural centre. Most books are in Italian, but in summer it stocks a small range of English-language titles. Books apart, it's a lovely spot to hang out over a coffee, *aperitivo* or glass of wine. Regular events are also held, including musical evenings, book presentations and wine tastings.

l'altra isola ARTS & CRAFTS

(Map p120; ☎079 97 51 71; www.altraisola.com; Via Maiorca 107; ⏰10am-1pm & 4.30-8pm winter, to 11.30pm summer) If you're looking for a souvenir, this well-stocked showroom specialises in traditional Sardinian craftwork. You'll find everything from rugs and handwoven linens to wicker baskets, painted ceramics, jewellery and pocket knives, all handmade by island artisans.

Agostino Marogna JEWELLERY
(Map p120; ☎079 98 48 14; www.marognacoralli.it; Piazza Civica 34; ⊙9.30am-1pm & 4.30-8pm) Coral has long been harvested in the waters off the Alghero coast (the aptly named Riviera del Corallo) and transformed into jewellery. Agostino Marogna is one of Alghero's finest coral shops, selling a dazzling range of jewellery, from delicate gold brooches to ornate necklaces with smooth blood-red beads. Prices start at around €100.

Calzoleria Naitana SHOES
(Map p120; ☎079 97 59 54; www.sandalinaitana.it; Via Ambrogio Machin 26; ⊙9am-1pm & 4.30-9.30pm Mon-Sat, daily in summer) This is one of the oldest shops in the *centro storico*. It has been selling its own handmade leather belts and sandals since 1945 and still today the smell of freshly cut leather permeates its cluttered interior. Bank on from €28 for a belt, and from €47 for a pair of sandals.

Boutique Marras FASHION & ACCESSORIES
(Map p120; ☎392 9242834; www.boutiquemarras.com; Piazza Civica 9; ⊙10am-1pm Mon-Sat & 4.30-9pm daily, to midnight summer) Antonio Marras is Alghero's most famous fashion designer – he has worked as artistic director for Kenzo and is the stylist behind the I'm Isola Marras line. His designs are among the stylish garments on sale here, at the Marras family's elegant boutique.

Enodolciaria FOOD & DRINKS
(Map p120; ☎079 97 97 41; Via Simon 24; ⊙9.30am-1pm & 4.30-midnight summer, 9.30am-1pm & 4.30-8pm Mon-Sat winter) A local landmark near the entrance to the *centro storico*, this foodie shop is a gourmet's treat, selling everything from local liqueurs and island wines to olive oils, honeys and packets of *fregola* (small couscous-like pasta) and *bottarga* (mullet roe).

Information

Airport Tourist Office (☎079 93 50 11; ⊙9am-11pm) In the arrivals hall.

BNL Banca (Via Vittorio Emanuele 5)

Farmacia Cabras (☎079 97 92 60; www.farmaciacabras.it; Via Fratelli Kennedy 10; ⊙9am-1pm & 4-8.30pm Mon-Fri) English-speaking pharmacy.

InfoAlghero Office (Map p120; ☎079 97 90 54; www.algheroturismo.eu; Largo Lo Quarter; ⊙9am-1pm & 3.30-6.30pm Mon-Fri, 9am-1pm & 4-7pm Sat year-round, plus 10am-1pm Sun summer only) The helpful English-speaking staff can provide information on the city and environs. Note that there's a possibility the office will relocate to the Giardini Pubblici.

Ospedale Civile (☎079 995 51 11; Via Don Minzoni) Alghero's main hospital.

Police Station (☎079 972 00 00; Via Fratelli Kennedy; ⊙8am-8pm Mon-Fri, to 2pm Sat & Sun)

Post Office (Map p118; Via Carducci 35; ⊙8.20am-7.05pm Mon-Fri, to 12.35pm Sat)

Getting There & Away

AIR

Alghero airport (Fertilia; ☎079 93 50 11; www.aeroportodialghero.it) is 10km northwest of town in Fertilia. It's served by **Alitalia** (☎892010; www.alitalia.com) and a number of low-cost carriers, including **Ryanair** (☎895 589 5509; www.ryanair.com), which operates flights to mainland Italy and destinations across Europe, including Brussels, Eindhoven, Frankfurt, London and Munich.

BUS

Intercity buses serve the **bus terminal** (Map p120; Via Catalogna) by the Giardini Pubblici. Note, however, that it's not much of a terminal, more a series of bus stops with a small **ticket office** (Map p120; Via Catalogna; ⊙6.25am-7.15pm Mon-Sat).

Up to 11 daily **ARST** (☎800 865042; www.arst.sardegna.it) buses run to Sassari (€3.10, one hour), where you can pick up connections to destinations across the island. There are also buses to/from Porto Torres (€3.70, one hour, five daily) and Bosa (€3.70, 1¼ hours, two daily with extra services in summer), as well as a single weekday service to Macomer (€5.50, two hours).

Logudoro Tours (☎079 28 17 28; www.logudorotours.it) runs two daily buses from the airport to Cagliari (€20, 3½ hours), via Oristano (€16, 2¼ hours) and Macomer (€12, 1¼ hours).

Redentours (☎0784 3 03 25; www.redentours.com) operates two daily buses from Alghero airport to Nuoro (€18, 2¼ hours).

There are no direct links with Olbia – you have to go via Sassari.

CAR & MOTORCYCLE

The fast-running SS291 connects with Sassari, 40km to the northeast, where you can pick up the SS131, the island's main north–south artery.

Snaking along the west coast, the scenic SP105 runs 46km southwards to Bosa.

TRAIN

The train station is 1.5km north of the old town on Via Don Minzoni. There are up to 12 daily trains to/from Sassari (€3.10, 35 minutes).

Getting Around

Your own feet will be enough to get you around the old town and most other places, but you may want to jump on a bus to get to the beaches.

ARRIVING IN ALGHERO

Alghero airport Hourly buses run from the aiport to Via Catalogna (€1, or €1.50 onboard, 25 minutes) between 5.20am and 11pm. A taxi from the airport will cost around €25.

Bus terminal Intercity buses arrive at the bus terminal on Via Catalogna. From Via Catalogna, walk to the historic centre, or pick up a taxi on nearby Via Vittorio Emanuele.

BICYCLE

A bike could be useful for exploring out of town and reaching the beaches. **Rentabike Raggi di Sardegna** (☎ 334 3052480; www.raggidis-ardegna.com; Via Maiorca 119; ⏱ 9.30am-1pm & 4-7pm Mon-Sat, 10am-1pm Sun) has an excellent range of bikes available for hire, costing from €5/8 per one/24 hours.

BUS

From the **bus stop** (Map p118; Via Cagliari), bus line AF runs along the seafront and up to Fertilia. Tickets, available at newspaper stands and *tabacchi* (tobacconists), cost €1, although you can also buy them on-board for €1.50.

CAR & MOTORCYCLE

The best place to park in Alghero is at the large free car park on Via Garibaldi; it rarely gets so crowded that there's no space.

All the major local and international car-hire companies have booths at Alghero airport.

Operating out of a hut on the seaward side of Via Garibaldi, **Cicloexpress** (☎ 079 98 69 50; www.cicloexpress.com; Via Garibaldi; ⏱ 9am-1pm & 4-7.30pm Mon-Sat, 9.30am-noon Sun) hires out cars (from €60 per day), scooters (from €30) and bikes (from €5).

TAXI

There's a **taxi rank** (Map p120) by the Giardini Pubblici at Via Vittorio Emanuele 1. Otherwise you can call for one by phoning **Alghero Radio Taxi** (☎ 079 989 20 28; www.taxialghero.it).

RIVIERA DEL CORALLO

The Riviera del Corallo (Coral Riviera), named after the red coral for which the area is famous, encompasses Alghero's northwest coast and hinterland. The main focus of interest is Porto Conte, a scenic bay sprinkled with hotels and discreet villas, and Capo Caccia, a rocky headland famous for its cave complex, the Grotta di Nettuno. For

ALGHERO TO BOSA BY CAR OR BIKE

Taking in sensational panoramas, mountain woods and one of Sardinia's great coastal roads, this 108km route offers the best of *il mare* (the sea) and *i monti* (the mountains). It involves some twisting mountain climbing and is best tackled as either a two-day bike ride or a day's drive.

From Alghero take the inland SS292 road and wind up towards Villanova Monteleone. Enjoy wonderful views across the water to Capo Caccia, before dipping over a ridge and plunging into deep woods. After 23km you'll reach **Villanova Monteleone** (567m), perched like a natural balcony on the slopes of the Colle di Santa Maria.

Continue on the high road beyond Villanova to enjoy yet more great coastal views as the road bobs and weaves through shady woods. The final 5km climb is far outweighed by the sizzling 10km descent to **Bosa**.

Overnight in Bosa (or, at the very least, stop to explore its attractive historic centre) before setting off on the return leg, via the spectacular 46km coastal road. There's only one significant climb of 6.2km to 350m, but if you're cycling the effort is offset by the stunning views, and with little to disturb you except for the jangle of goats' bells and the occasional sighting of a bird of prey, it's a superb ride.

There are two swimming spots along the way. The first is just south of **Torre Argentina**, about 4.5km out of Bosa – look for cars parked by the roadside and a path down to the beach. The second is **Spiaggia Speranza**, a lovely beach 8km south of Alghero, where you can lunch on fresh fish at **Ristorante La Speranza** (☎ 079 957 61 07; SP105 Alghero–Bosa, Km 8; meals €40; ⏱ 12.30-2.30pm & 7-10.30pm daily summer, Thu-Tue winter) before the final push into town.

sunseekers there are several great beaches, while history buffs can explore a couple of interesting archaeological sites. Inland, the landscape flattens and you'll find two of the island's main wine producers as well as a number of hospitable *agriturismi*.

Fertilia

079 / POP 1700

Sandy, pine-backed beaches fringe the coast around Fertilia, about 5km to the northwest of Alghero. A rather soulless little town, outside of summer at least, with ruler-straight streets and a striking rationalist church, its sleepy atmosphere comes as something of a surprise after Alghero's medieval hustle.

The town was built by Mussolini, who intended it to be the centre of a grand agricultural reclamation project, and who brought in farmers from northeastern Italy to populate it. Later, postwar refugees arrived from Friuli-Venezia Giulia, bringing with them an allegiance to the lion of St Mark, the symbol of Venice, which adorns a statue on the waterfront Piazzale San Marco.

Sights & Activities

There's not a great deal to see or do in Fertilia once you've pottered around the seafront, but there are a couple of excellent beaches nearby.

Spiaggia delle Bombarde BEACH

A couple of kilometres west of Fertilia, this is a favourite local beach, set amid greenery and well equipped with umbrellas and sunloungers. It's signposted off the main road, but if you don't have a car, the Capo Caccia bus from Alghero passes nearby.

Spiaggia del Lazzaretto BEACH

A lovely sandy beach framed by sandstone rocks and Mediterranean scrubland.

Capo Galera Diving Centre DIVING

(079 94 21 10; http://diving.capogalera.com; Località Capo Galera, Fertilia; dives from €20) Signposted off the main road to Capo Caccia, this place organises dives and courses for all levels, as well as superlative cave diving in the Nereo Cave, the largest underwater grotto in the Mediterranean. Dives start at €20, with full kit hire costing €20. Snorkelling excursions are from €20 per person. Accommodation (p216) is available at the centre.

Riviera del Corallo & Porto Conte

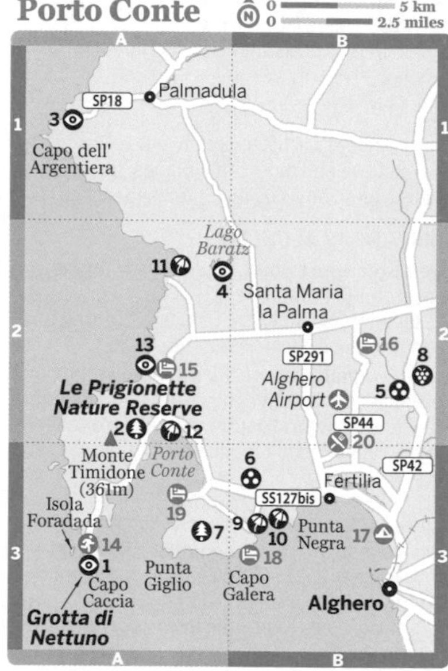

Eating

Better than Fertilia itself, which offers few good eating options, is the surrounding countryside, which is riddled with excellent *agriturismi* and rural restaurants. You will, however, need a car to get to them.

Il Paguro RISTORANTE €€

(079 93 02 60; Via Zara 13; meals €30-35; 12.30-2.30pm & 7.30pm-midnight Thu-Tue) One of the better places in Fertilia, Il Paguro specialises in fresh fish and seafood dishes. The restaurant is in a residential street about five minutes' walk from the town centre.

Getting There & Away

From Alghero, take the airport bus, which runs hourly from Via Catalogna, stopping at Fertilia (€1 or €1.50 onboard, 15 minutes) en route. Alternatively, catch local bus AF.

Around Fertilia

Sights

Necropoli di Anghelu Ruju ARCHAEOLOGICAL SITE

(Località I Piani; adult/reduced€6/4, incl Nuraghe di Palmavera €8/6; 9am-7pm Mon-Fri summer,

Riviera del Corallo & Porto Conte

Top Sights
1 Grotta di Nettuno A3
2 Le Prigionette Nature Reserve A2

Sights
3 Argentiera A1
4 Lago Baratz A2
5 Necropoli di Anghelu Ruju B2
6 Nuraghe di Palmavera B3
7 Parco di Porto Conte A3
8 Sella e Mosca B2
9 Spiaggia del Lazzaretto B3
10 Spiaggia delle Bombarde B3
11 Spiaggia di Porto Ferro A2
12 Spiaggia Mugoni A2
13 Torre del Porticciolo A2
Viewpoint .... (see 14)

Activities, Courses & Tours
Capo Galera Diving Centre .... (see 18)
Club Della Vela .... (see 12)
14 Via Ferrata del Cabirol A3

Sleeping
15 Agriturismo Porticciolo A2
16 Agriturismo Sa Mandra B2
17 Camping La Mariposa B3
18 Capo Galera Diving Centre B3
19 Hotel El Faro A3

Eating
20 Agriturismo Barbagia B2
Agriturismo Porticciolo .... (see 15)
Agriturismo Sa Mandra .... (see 16)

Shopping
Enoteca .... (see 8)

10am-2pm daily winter) Some 10km northwest of Alghero, just off the SP42 to Porto Torres, lie the scattered burial chambers of the Necropoli di Anghelu Ruju. The 38 tombs carved into the sandstone rock, known as *domus de janas* (fairy houses), date from between 3300 BC and 2700 BC. Most of the sculptural decor has been stripped off and removed to museums, but in some of the chambers you can make out traces of sculpted bull's horns, perhaps symbolising a funeral deity. Three weekday buses run from Alghero to near the *necropoli* (€1.90, 25 minutes).

Sella e Mosca VINEYARD
(☎079 99 77 00; www.sellaemosca.com; Località I Piani; guided tour free, tasting depends on wines; ⏰tour & tasting 10am & 4pm Mon-Fri, guided tour 5.30pm Mon-Sat summer, by request rest of year) FREE Sardinia's top wine producer has been based on this 650-hectare estate since 1899. To learn more about its history and production methods, join the free afternoon tour of the estate's historic cellars and lovingly tended museum. Afterwards, stock up at the beautiful **enoteca** (☎079 99 77 19; www.sellaemosca.it; Località I Piani; ⏰8.30am-8pm Mon-Sat summer, to 6pm winter). Private tastings can also be organised. From Alghero, three weekday buses pass by the turn-off for Sella e Mosca (€1.90, 25 minutes).

Nuraghe di Palmavera ARCHAEOLOGICAL SITE
(☎329 4385947; www.coopsilt.it; Località Monte Palmavera; adult/reduced €6/4, incl Necropoli di Anghelu Ruju €8/6; ⏰9am-7pm Mon-Fri summer, 10am-2pm daily winter) A few kilometres west of Fertilia on the SS127bis road to Porto Conte, the Nuraghe di Palmavera is a 3500-year-old nuraghic village. At its centre stands a limestone tower and an elliptical building with a secondary sandstone tower. The ruins of smaller towers and fortified walls surround the central edifice, beyond which are the packed remnants of circular dwellings, of which there may originally have been about 50.

The circular **Capanna delle Riunioni** (Meeting Hut) is the subject of considerable speculation. Its foundation wall is lined by a low stone bench, perhaps for a council of elders, and encloses a pedestal topped by a model *nuraghe*. One theory suggests there was actually a cult to the *nuraghi* themselves.

Between April and September a single weekday bus runs to the site from Alghero (€1.30); otherwise you'll need a bike or car to get there.

Eating

★ **Agriturismo Sa Mandra** SARDINIAN €€
(☎079 99 91 50; www.aziendasamandra.it; Strada Aeroporto Civile 21; meals €35-40; ⏰8-11pm Tue-Sun summer, 1-3pm Fri-Sun winter, reservations necessary; ✎) This smart, beautifully maintained *agriturismo* serves fantastic farmhouse food, inspired by the culinary traditions of the mountainous Barbagia region, from where the owners hail. For vegetarians there's a dedicated menu featuring aromatic

BLOOD-RED GOLD

Since ancient times the red coral of the Mediterranean has beguiled and bewitched people. Many believed it to be the petrified blood of Medusa, attributing to it aphrodisiac and other secret qualities.

Alghero's coast south of Capo Caccia is justifiably called the Riviera del Corallo (p125). The coral fished here is of the highest quality and glows a dark orangey-red. The strong currents around the headland mean the little coral polyps are short and dense to withstand the drag of the sea, which, in turn, means they have few air pockets – the sign of top-quality coral.

To protect the precious commodity, coral fishing is tightly regulated. It can only be harvested by 25 licensed divers in a season that runs from May or June to September, and at a depth of no less than 50m. Once harvested, it's sold in chunks, with its price varying according to colour, quality and size.

To learn more, head to the Museo del Corallo (p115) in Alghero, or Agostino Marogna (p124), one of Alghero's finest coral shops.

cheeses and home-grown roasted vegetables, while meat lovers can tear into island favourites such as spit-roasted pork or boar with wild fennel.

Much of what you eat is produced on the *agriturismo*'s farm, which you can visit before eating.

To get here head towards the airport – the *agriturismo* is signposted to the right of the SP44.

Agriturismo Barbagia SARDINIAN €€
(☎079 93 51 41; www.agriturismobarbagia.it; Località Fighera 26; meals €30-35; ⏲1-2.30pm & 8-11pm daily summer, Sat & Sun winter, reservations required) With its folkloristic murals and farmhouse decor, this rustic *agriturismo* is a fine spot for an authentic Sardinian feast. Think starters of cheese, cured hams and marinated vegetables, *malloredus* (semolina dumplings) with sausage in tomato sauce, and *porceddu* (pork) spit-roasted for five hours on the giant stone fireplace.

It also has six double rooms available, costing up to €90 in high summer.

From Fertilia head north on the SS291, take a right onto the SP44 and look for signs on the left.

Porto Conte & Capo Caccia

Known more poetically as the Baia delle Ninfe (Bay of Nymphs), Porto Conte is a lovely unspoiled bay, its blue waters home to an armada of bobbing yachts and its green shores thick with mimosa and eucalyptus trees.

Much of the bay, including Capo Caccia, the dramatic headland that marks its southernmost point, is covered by a regional nature reserve. The scenery around here is superb as towering white cliffs sheer up from impossibly blue waters and thrilling seascapes unfurl at every turn.

Sights

★Le Prigionette Nature Reserve NATURE RESERVE
(☎079 94 21 11; Località Prigionette; on foot or by bike €3, per person in car €5; ⏲9am-6pm summer, to 4pm winter) This reserve, just west of Porto Conte at the base of Monte Timidone (361m), is a beautiful pocket of uncontaminated nature. Encompassing 12 sq km of woodland, aromatic *macchia* (Mediterranean scrub) and rocky coastline, it offers wonderful scenery and excellent walking with a network of well-marked tracks, suitable for hikers and cyclists. Wildlife flourishes – deer, albino donkeys, Giara horses and wild boar roam the woods, while griffon vultures and falcons fly the skies.

For stirring coastal views head to **Cala della Barca**, a remote cliffside spot overlooking the **Isola Piana**. The easiest and quickest way of getting there is to drive from the reserve's entrance until you come to an open space by a hut – it takes about 20 minutes along the dirt track. Park here and continue on foot for the last kilometre or so.

★Grotta di Nettuno CAVE
(☎079 94 65 40; adult/reduced €13/7; ⏲9am-7pm May-Sep, 10am-4pm Apr & Oct, 10am-2pm Jan-Mar, Nov & Dec) Capo Caccia's principal crowd-puller is the Grotta di Nettuno, a haunting fairyland of stalactites and stalagmites. The easiest way to get to the caves is

to take a ferry from Alghero, but for those with a head for heights, there's a vertiginous 654-step staircase, the **Escala del Cabirol**, that descends 110m of sheer cliff from the car park at the end of the Capo Caccia road.

Tours of the caves last around 45 minutes and take you through narrow walkways flanked by forests of curiously shaped stalactites and stalagmites, nicknamed the organ, the church dome (or warrior's head) and so on. At its furthest point the cave extends back for 1km, but a lot is off-limits to the public, including several freshwater lakes deep inside the grotto. Note that in bad weather, visits to the grotto are suspended.

To get to the caves by public transport, a daily ARST bus departs from Via Catalogna (€2.50, 50 minutes) in Alghero at 9.15am and returns at midday. From June to September, there are two extra runs at 3.10pm and 5.10pm, returning at 4.05pm and 6.05pm.

Viewpoint VIEWPOINT
For a view to remember, stop off at this viewing point a few hundred metres short of Capo Caccia, and look down at the full sweep of the Baia delle Ninfe beneath you. On the other side, a wave-buffeted rock known as the Isola Foradada rises out of the azure waters.

Spiaggia Mugoni BEACH
The main focus of Porto Conte is Spiaggia Mugoni, a hugely popular beach that arcs around the bay's northeastern flank. With its fine white sand and protected waters, it makes an excellent venue for beginners to try their hand at water sports. The **Club della Vela** (☎338 1489583; www.clubdellavelaalghero.it; Località Mugoni) offers windsurfing, canoeing, kayaking and sailing courses, and also rents out boats.

Torre del Porticciolo BAY
On the coast north of Porto Conte, the Torre del Porticciolo is a tiny natural harbour backed by a small arc of beach and overlooked by a 16th-century watchtower on the northern promontory. High cliffs mount guard on the southern side, and you can explore adjacent coves along narrow walking trails.

Spiaggia di Porto Ferro BEACH
The Spiaggia di Porto Ferro is a fabulous, unspoiled beach, much loved by local surfers. Hidden behind thick tracts of pine woods about 6km north of Torre del Porticciolo, its 2km of sands and lovely azure waters rarely get as busy as the better-known beaches in the area. Buses run from Alghero (€3, 45 minutes) twice daily between April and September.

Lago Baratz LAKE
Surrounded by low wooded hills, Lago Baratz is Sardinia's only natural lake. It's a quiet spot that attracts some bird life, although the winged fellows tend to hang about the less accessible northern side. Paths circle the lake's marshy banks and there's a 3km dirt track connecting with the Spiaggia di Porto Ferro (p129).

Cantina Sociale di Santa Maria la Palma WINERY
(☎079 99 90 08; www.santamarialapalma.it; Località Santa Maria la Palma; ⊙8am-1pm & 3-8pm summer, 8am-1pm & 2.30-6.30pm Mon-Fri, 8am-1pm Sun winter) With some 700 hectares under vine, Santa Maria la Palma is the second-largest winery in the northwest. Head to its *enoteca* (wine bar) to browse its extensive selection of spumante, whites and reds, many made from the Cannonau and Cagnulari grape varieties. Guided tours can be arranged on request.

Activities

Via Ferrata del Cabirol CLIMBING
(www.ferratacabirol.it) Rock climbers can enjoy exclusive views of the sea on the Via Ferrata del Cabirol, a stunning cliffside route along a series of exposed rock faces. Of medium difficulty, the traverse mainly follows ledges around the rocks, but does involve some short vertical ascents. Conditions are best in spring and autumn, though it stays in the shade until 2pm during summer.

Eating

The best bet for a really good meal around here is to head for one of the many *agriturismi* hidden in the verdant countryside. Meals at these tend to be set menus, usually comprising starters of cured meats, cheeses and marinated vegetables, homemade pastas and roast meats.

★ **Agriturismo Porticciolo** SARDINIAN €€
(☎079 91 80 00, 347 5231024; www.agriturismoporticciolo.it; Località Porticciolo; set menus €25-35; ⊙1-3pm & 7.30-10.30pm daily summer, Sat & Sun winter) This welcoming *agriturismo* serves delicious home-grown fare in an echoing barn with timber beams and a huge fireplace. The set menus comprise

PARCO DI PORTO CONTE

The **Parco di Porto Conte** (www.parcodiportoconte.it), one of only two regional nature parks in Sardinia, covers 60km of coastline and 53.5 sq km of an area once described by French oceanographer Jacques Cousteau as one of the most beautiful in the Mediterranean.

Its diverse landscape, which ranges from woods and wetlands to tracts of low-lying *macchia* scrubland and soaring white cliffs, is an important natural habitat, providing sanctuary to 35 species of mammals and 150 of birds.

It offers great walking, particularly in Le Prigionette Nature Reserve (p128) and on the headland running down Porto Conte's eastern flank. One of the best routes leads from a park entrance just off the SS127 near Maristella to **Punta Giglio**, a panoramic point at the south of the promontory. It's about 6km there and back – allow at least three hours – but make the effort and you'll be rewarded with dazzling sea views over the bay to Capo Caccia.

For further details about the park and its network of paths and cycle tracks, check its website.

hot and cold antipasti, two pasta dishes and *porceddu* (Sardinian roast pork), so you'll need to pace yourself if you want to get through it all.

Getting There & Away

Regular ARST buses run between Alghero and Porto Conte (€1.30, 30 minutes, up to 10 daily between June and September, three to five daily rest of year).

THE NORTH COAST

Stintino & Isola dell'Asinara

Sardinia's remote northwestern tip boasts wild, unspoiled countryside and one of the island's most celebrated beaches, the stunning Spiaggia della Pelosa.

The only town of any note is Stintino, a former tuna-fishing village turned breezy summer resort and the main gateway to the Isola dell'Asinara. This small island, now a national park and wildlife haven, was for years home to one of Italy's most notorious prisons.

North of Stintino, the road continues to Capo Falcone, a rugged headland peppered with hotels and holiday homes, and the fabled Pelosa beach.

Outside of summer, the area is pretty deserted. Silence hangs over the empty landscape and the cold *maestrale* (northwesterly) wind blows through, blasting the tough *macchia* (Mediterranean scrubland) and bare rocks.

Sights

★Spiaggia della Pelosa BEACH

About 2.5km north of Stintino, the Spiaggia della Pelosa is a dreamy image of beach perfection: a salt-white strip of sand lapped by shallow, turquoise seas and fronted by strange, almost lunar, licks of rocky land. Completing the picture is a Catalan-Aragonese watchtower on the craggy Isola Piana. The beach gets extremely busy in July and August, but is popular throughout the year, especially with wind- and kitesurfers, who take to its waters when the *maestrale* wind whips through.

Year-round buses run to the beach from Stintino (€1.30, five minutes, four weekdays, two Sundays). In summer services are considerably increased.

If you have your own wheels, there's limited roadside parking near the beach (within the blue lines) for around €5 per half-day.

★Parco Nazionale dell'Asinara NATIONAL PARK

(www.parcoasinara.org) Named after its resident *asini bianchi* (albino donkeys), the Isola dell'Asinara encompasses 51 sq km of *macchia* (Mediterranean scrub), rocky coastline and remote sandy beaches. The island, Sardinia's second-largest, is now a national park, but for years it was home to one of Italy's toughest maximum-security prisons. The only way to reach it is with a licensed boat operator from Stintino or Porto Torres; you can explore independently, although there's no public transport and access is restricted to certain areas.

The smallest of Sardinia's three national parks, the island is a haven for wildlife, providing a habitat for an estimated 50 to 70 donkeys alongside 80 other animal species, including mouflon (silky-haired wild sheep) and peregrine falcons.

Dotted around its stark landscape is a series of abandoned buildings that were once part of the island's notorious *carcere* (prison). Built in 1885, along with a quarantine station for cholera victims, the jail was a kind of Italian Alcatraz and many of Italy's most dangerous criminals did time there, including Neapolitan gangster Raffaele Cutolo and the infamous mafia boss Totò Riina. The prison finally closed in 1997.

Spiaggia Le Saline BEACH

Just south of Stintino a signpost directs you to the abandoned *tonnara* (tuna processing plant) and the Spiaggia Le Saline, once the site of a busy salt works, now a beautiful white beach. Behind it, marshes extend inland to form the **Stagno di Casaraccio**, a big lagoon where you might see flamingos.

Museo della Tonnara MUSEUM

(☎345 9718686; www.mutstintino.com; Via Lepanto 36; adult/reduced €5/free; ⏲6-11pm daily Jul & Aug, 11am-1pm & 3.30-7pm Tue-Sun Jun & Sep, same hours Fri-Sun May, shorter hours winter) Stintino's history and tuna-fishing heritage are documented at this small museum. Videos, documents, old black-and-white photos and computer displays illustrate life in the village and the centuries-old fishing methods used by its hardy fishing folk.

Activities

Windsurfing Center Stintino WINDSURFING

(☎079 52 70 06; www.windsurfingcenter.it; Località l'Approdo, Le Saline) On the beach at Pelosa, this outfit rents out windsurf rigs (from €18 per hour) and canoes (from €10 per hour), as well as offering windsurfing and sailing courses. If that all sounds far too energetic, it can also sort you out with an umbrella and sunloungers (€17 to €33 per day).

Asinara Scuba Diving DIVING

(☎079 52 71 75; www.asinarascubadiving.com; Viale la Pelosa, Località Porto dell'Ancora) Just before Pelosa beach, near the Club Hotel Ancora, this diving centre offers a range of dives around Capo Falcone and the protected waters of the Parco Nazionale dell'Asinara. Reckon on €45-plus for a dive and €20 for kit hire.

OFF THE BEATEN TRACK

ARGENTIERA

A natural inlet about 11km north of Lago Baratz, the haunting backwater of Argentiera is dominated by the ghostly ruins of its silver mine, once Sardinia's most important. Argento (silver) was extracted here from Roman times right up to the 1960s, when the mine was finally abandoned. The dark-brick mine buildings, now held together by wooden scaffolding, rise in an untidy jumble from a small grey-sand beach. You can't go into them, but they make a stark and melancholy sight.

There's a second, nicer, beach accessible from the approach road to the mines.

Argentiera is at the end of the SP18, signposted from Palmadula.

Tours

Agenzia La Nassa TOURS

(☎079 52 00 60; www.agenzialanassa.it; Via Sassari 39; tours per person €18-65; ⏲8.30am-1pm & 4.30-8pm daily summer, Mon-Sat winter) This agency runs a number of tours around Parco Nazionale dell'Asinara. The cheapest option, available between June and September, covers your ferry passage only, leaving you free to walk or cycle on designated paths on the island – you can download a map from the agency's website. More expensive packages include boat tours and visits with 4WD or bus transport.

Linea del Parco TOURS

(☎349 2605023; www.lineadelparco.it; Porto Mannu, Stintino; ⏲ticket office 9am-12.30pm, longer hours summer) Linea del Parco offers a number of packages, including tours by bus or Land Rover, horse rides and boat excursions. Reckon on from €55 per person for the Land Rover tour. To go it alone you can take your own bike over to the island (€25) or hire one at Fornelli (€33 including return boat fare).

Mare e Natura TOURS

(☎339 9850435, 079 52 00 97; www.marenatura.it; Via Sassari 77, Stintino) Agency that organises land and boat tours of the Parco Nazionale dell'Asinara.

Eating

The main hub in these parts is Stintino, which has a few decent restaurants and waterfront eateries. Elsewhere you can grab a simple bite at one of the many bars and snack joints around the Spiaggia della Pelosa. Many resort hotels have their own restaurants.

Albergo Ristorante Silvestrino SEAFOOD €€
(☎079 52 30 07; www.hotelsilvestrino.it; Via Sassari 14; meals €35; ⊙12.30-2.30pm & 7.30-10.30pm daily summer, closed Thu winter) On Stintino's main drag, this evergreen hotel restaurant is a dependable choice for classic Sardinian seafood. Its sunny dining hall and small streetside terrace set the stage for timeless creations such as *spaghetti con vongole e bottarga* (with clams and mullet roe) and *fregola ai frutti di mare* (couscous-like pasta with mixed seafood).

Skipper ITALIAN €€
(☎079 52 34 60; Lungomare Cristoforo Colombo 57; panini €5, meals €25; ⊙11am-11pm daily summer, 10.30am-8pm Tue-Sun winter) A long-standing favourite, this casual bar-restaurant is a jack of all trades. You can sit down on the waterfront terrace and order anything from coffee and cocktails to *zuppa di cozze* (mussel soup), hamburgers, salads and *panini*.

Lu Fanali TRATTORIA, PIZZERIA €€
(☎079 52 30 54; www.lufanali.it; Lungomare Cristoforo Columbo 89; pizzas €8, meals €30; ⊙noon-midnight) Watch the boats bob by as you dig into reliably good pizzas and crowd-pleasing surf-and-turf dishes at Lu Fanali, a popular, unbuttoned kind of place with al fresco sea-facing tables near Porto Mannu.

SognAsinara SARDINIAN €€
(☎346 1737043; www.sognasinara.it; Cala Reale, Isola dell'Asinara; meals €30-40; ⊙by reservation Mar-Oct) If you want lunch on the Isola dell'Asinara, book at this bar-restaurant near the jetty at Cala Reale. Run by a local cooperative, it's a modest set-up specialising in classic Sardinian seafood. It also offers basic, no-frills accommodation, charging up to €60 per person for full board in a double room.

Getting There & Away

Between June and mid-September, **Sardabus** (☎079 51 05 54; www.sardabus.it) operates five daily buses to Stintino from Alghero and Alghero airport (€7, 50 minutes).

There are at least four weekday ARST buses (two on Sundays) to Stintino from Porto Torres (€2.50, 45 minutes) and Sassari (€3.70, 70 minutes). Services increase between June and September.

From May to October daily boats sail for the Isola dell'Asinara from the Porto Turistico in Stintino. Departures are generally around 9am to 9.30am, returning 5pm to 6pm. A simple return costs €18. Services are much reduced between November and April.

Porto Torres

☎079 / POP 22,310

A busy working port and industrial centre, Porto Torres harbours a couple of worthwhile sights: a small archaeological museum and, more impressively, the Basilica di San Gavino, one of Sardinia's most important Romanesque churches.

The town had its heyday under the Romans, who founded it as their main port on Sardinia's northern coast. Originally known as Turris Libisonis, it remained one of the island's key gateways until the Middle Ages and was capital of the Giudicato di Torres.

Sights

Basilica di San Gavino CHURCH
(☎348 8996823; www.basilicasangavino.it; admission/guided tour €3/4; ⊙9am-1pm & 3-6.45pm mid-May–Sep, to 5.45pm Apr & Oct, by reservation Nov-Mar) Porto Torres' modern, workaday streets provide the unlikely setting for Sardinia's largest Romanesque church. Built between 1030 and 1080, the basilica is an impressive and architecturally important structure, notable for its facing apses – it has no facade – and three lateral portals. Its austere interior is divided by 28 marble columns, pilfered by the Pisan builders from the ancient Roman city, while underneath, the crypt is lined with religious statuary and various stone tombs.

The church, which stands on an ancient pagan burial ground, is dedicated to one of the great Sardinian saints. Gavino (Gavinus in English) was the commander of the Roman garrison at Torres during the reign of the emperor Diocletian. According to legend, he was converted to Christianity by two priests, Protus and Januarius, and beheaded with them on 25 October 304. Evidence for these events is scanty, but the myth of

WORTH A TRIP

VISITING THE ISOLA DELL'ASINARA

Stintino, along with Porto Torres, is the main embarkation point for trips to the Isola dell'Asinara. Access to the island is strictly controlled and only possible with an authorised operator. In Stintino, licensed ferries operate out of Porto Mannu, generally sailing to the island at around 9am, and returning between 5pm and 6pm. Services are pretty regular from May to October, but outside of these months boats will only set out if there are enough people to justify the trip.

Agencies in Stintino offer a range of guided tours, which typically include the return boat fare and transport on the island, either in a bus or 4WD vehicle. Itineraries vary but most take in the prison at **Fornelli**, **Cala d'Oliva**, the panoramic high point of **Punta della Scomunica**, and the beach at **Cala Sabina**. As a rough guide, reckon on around €55 per person for a tour.

Alternatively, there are boat tours or you can go it alone. A return ferry ticket costs €18 and once you're on the island you're free to explore its paths and surfaced roads on foot or, better still, by bike. In Stintino, Agenzia La Nassa (p131) rents bikes and has a map of the island's paths that you can download from its website.

Note that many tours do not include lunch, so either take a picnic or book a meal at the SognAsinara (p132) restaurant at Cala Reale. If you want to overnight on the island, the restaurant also offers basic, no-frills hostel accommodation.

the *martiri turritani* (martyrs of Torres) is strongly rooted.

To get to the basilica follow Corso Vittorio Emanuele back from the port for about 1km; it's a block or so to the west.

Museo Antiquarium Turritano & Area Archeologica MUSEUM, ARCHAEOLOGICAL PARK
(☎079 51 44 33; www.facebook.com/antiquariumturritano; Via Ponte Romano 99; museum/antiquarium & area archeologica €2/3, 1st Sun of month free; ⏲9am-6pm Thu-Tue) This complex houses the excavated remains of Turris Libisonis, the ancient Roman port on which the modern city stands. The museum displays finds from the adjacent archaeological area, including a collection of ceramics, busts, marble statues and mosaics. Outside you can see the remains of an ancient bathing complex known as the Palazzo del Re Barbaro; a mosaic-decorated house, the Domus dei Mosaici; and an impressive Roman bridge. Note that visits to the archaeological area are by guided tour only.

Eating

★San Gavino SARDINIAN €€
(☎079 51 03 00; www.sangavino.it; Piazza Marconi 12A; meals €30-35; ⏲noon-3pm & 6-11.30pm Tue-Sun) Tucked into a leafy corner near the Basilica di San Gavino, this welcoming restaurant scores across the board. The regional food is fabulous – try the antipasto of cured meats and vegetables in olive oil – the setting is attractive, and service is friendly and efficient. Also does wood-fired pizzas.

Information

BNL (Corso Vittorio Emanuele 20) Bank with ATM.

Post Office (Via Ponte Romano 83; ⏲8.20am-1.35pm Mon-Fri, to 12.35pm Sat)

Tourist Office (☎079 504 80 08; Via Bassu, Stazione Marittima; ⏲9am-1pm & 3-6pm Sat & Sun) Near the train station.

Getting There & Away

BOAT

Tirrenia (p267) and Grandi Navi Veloci (p267) run ferries between Porto Torres and Genoa. Tirrenia services are year-round, while GNV operates between mid-May and September. High-season fares for the 12-hour crossing are around €100.

La Méridionale (p267) operates ferries to/from Marseille (with/without car €245/95, 17½ hours).

All ferry operators have offices at the Stazione Marittima (www.comune.porto-torres.ss.it/Comunicazione/Argomenti/Porto-Torres-Turismo/Come-arrivare/Arrivare-in-nave; Via Bassu).

BUS

Buses leave from Via Mare near the porticoes on the waterfront. There are regular buses to Sassari (€1.90, 30 minutes, hourly), Alghero (€3.70, one hour, five daily) and Stintino (€2.50, 45 minutes, at least four daily), with extra services in summer. Get tickets from the newsstand on Piazza XX Settembre.

TRAIN

Direct trains run to Sassari (€1.90, 15 minutes, five daily), where you can connect for Cagliari (€18, 3¾ hours). Trains for Olbia (€9.50, two to 3¾ hours) require a change at Sassari and some also at Ozieri-Chilivani.

Castelsardo

☎079 / POP 6005

An attractive and popular day-trip destination, Castelsardo huddles around the high cone of a promontory jutting into the Mediterranean. Towering over everything is its hilltop historic centre, a small, tightly packed ensemble of medieval alleyways and stone buildings seemingly melded onto the dark grey rock.

The town was originally designed as a defensive fort by a 12th-century Genoese family. Named Castel Genoese, it was the subject of much fighting and in 1448 it fell to the Spanish, who changed its name to Castel Aragonese. It later became part of the Kingdom of Sardinia under the Piedmontese Savoy dynasty and, in 1767, took its current name, which means Sardinian castle.

Inland, the verdant hills of the rural Anglona district harbour a number of interesting sights, including a much-loved roadside rock resembling a proud old elephant.

Sights

Castello CASTLE

(www.mimcastelsardo.it; Via Marconi; adult/reduced €3/2; ⌚9am-1am Aug, to midnight Jul, to 9pm May, Jun & Sep, to 7pm Easter-May & Oct, 10.30am-4.30pm rest of year) Lording it over the hilltop *centro storico* is the medieval Castello, the centrepiece around which the original town was built. Constructed in the 12th century by the Doria family and home to Eleonora d'Arborea for a period, it commands superb views over the Golfo dell'Asinara to Corsica. It also houses a small museum, the **Museo dell'Intreccio del Mediterraneo** (www.mimcastelsardo.it; Via Marconi; adult/reduced €3/2; ⌚9am-1am Aug, to midnight Jul, to 9pm May, Jun & Sep, to 7pm Easter-May & Oct, 10.30am-4.30pm rest of year), dedicated to the basket weaving for which the town is famous.

Chiesa di Santa Maria CHURCH

(Piazza della Misericordia; ⌚9am-7pm summer, shorter hours winter) Just below the Castello, the medieval Chiesa di Santa Maria is a much-loved church, venerated for its 14th-century crucifix. One of the oldest in Sardinia, it's known as Lu Cristu Nieddhu (Black Christ) because of the colour the juniper wood has taken on over the centuries. According to local lore, the crucifix helped the townsfolk beat off an attack by a French fleet in 1527.

Cattedrale di Sant'Antonio Abate CATHEDRAL

(Via Manganella; cathedral free, Museum Ampuriense €4; ⌚cathedral 7am-1pm & 3-8pm, Museum Ampuriense 10am-1pm & 3.30-7.30pm, shorter hours winter) Announcing the presence of the cathedral is its landmark bell tower, topped by a brightly tiled cupola. The cathedral itself, which sits on a panoramic terrace, was originally Gothic but a protracted 17th-century remodelling saw the addition of Renaissance and baroque elements. Inside, the main altar is dominated by the *Madonna in trono col Bambino,* a painting by the mysterious 15th-century Maestro di Castelsardo. More of his works can be seen in the **Museum Ampuriense** in the crypt.

A series of small rooms chiselled out of the living rock, the crypt is all that remains of the Romanesque church that once stood here.

Chiesa di Nostra Signora di Tergu CHURCH

(⌚closed to the public) Tergu, a small village 10km or so south of Castelsardo, is home to this fine 12th-century Romanesque church. Built out of wine-red trachyte and white limestone, it sits in a pleasant garden alongside the few visible remains of a monastery that once housed up to 100 Benedictine monks. You can't go into the church, but from outside you can admire its facade, a pretty ensemble of arches, columns, geometric patterns and a simple rose window.

Museo Domus de Janas MUSEUM

(☎349 8440436; Via Nazionale, Sedini; adult/reduced €2.50/1.50; ⌚9.30am-1pm & 3-6pm Mon-Fri, 10am-1pm Sat & Sun summer, by reservation winter) Head to the small, sleepy town of Sedini to see one of the area's best-known *domus de janas* (prehistoric tombs). Gouged out of a huge calcareous rock known as La Rocca, the prehistoric tomb was lived in by farmers in the Middle Ages and used as a prison until the 19th century. It now houses a small museum displaying traditional farming tools and household items. Four weekday buses run to Sedini from Castelsardo (€1.90, 25 minutes).

Festivals & Events

Lunissanti RELIGIOUS

(Mar/Apr) On the Monday after Palm Sunday, Castelsardo's townsfolk turn out for the Lunissanti, a solemn Easter parade through the old town from the Chiesa di Santa Maria.

Eating & Drinking

La Trattoria da Maria Giuseppe TRATTORIA, PIZZERIA €

(079 47 06 61; Via Colombo 6; pizzas €5.50-10, meals €25-30; 12.30-2.30pm & 7.30-11.30pm, closed Mon winter) For a relaxed meal, head to this unpretentious, neighbourhood trattoria near Piazza Pianedda. Locals come here for the excellent wood-fired pizzas, but you can also fill up on pasta classics such as spaghetti *ai frutti di mare* (with seafood), grilled meats and fresh local fish.

Il Cormorano SEAFOOD €€€

(079 47 06 28; www.ristoranteilcormorano.net; Via Colombo 5; meals €50; 12.30-2.30pm & 8-11pm daily Jun-Sep, Tue-Sun Apr, May & Oct, Sat & Sun Dec-Mar) Behind an unassuming roadside exterior, this smart restaurant enjoys a stellar reputation for high-end seafood. There's a creative edge to many of the dishes, which include standouts such as risotto with scampi and Sardinian myrtle, and stewed squid with seasonal artichokes.

Il Portico WINE BAR

(079 47 01 76; Via Vittorio Emanuele 12; 9.30am-9pm, to midnight summer) See out the end of the day with a glass of something cool at this handsome *centro storico* bar. With outside tables and a typically Mediterranean interior – all whites, stone arches and terracotta floor tiles – it's a fine place for a taste of island wine or a craft beer accompanied by nibbles. Aperitifs from €5.

Shopping

Castelsardo has long been famous for its artisanal basketwork and, as you wander through the old town, you'll see women on their doorsteps, creating intricate baskets and other wicker objects. Down in the modern town there are several emporia selling all manner of handcrafts.

DON'T MISS

ROCCIA DELL'ELEFANTE: A WONDER ROCK

From Castelsardo, the SS134 Sedini road leads to one of the area's most lovable landmarks, the **Roccia dell'Elefante** (Elephant Rock), a bizarre trachyte rock that looks just like an elephant raising its trunk towards the road. The monolith's shape is the result of nothing more mysterious than wind and rain erosion, but it's been the source of local interest for millennia, as witnessed by the presence of two neolithic tombs (known as *domus de janas* or 'fairy houses') in the hollow interior.

The upper tomb has been damaged by erosion, but the lower one is still in good shape, with four small rooms and a rock carving of a bull's horns.

Information

Tourist Office (079 47 02 20; www.castelsardoturismo.it) At the time of research, the office was without a home and was only taking phone enquiries.

Getting There & Away

ARST buses run to/from Sassari (€3.10, one hour, 11 services Monday to Saturday, four Sunday) and Santa Teresa di Gallura (€5, 1½ hours, three daily). Buy tickets from the *edicola* (newsstand) at the corner of Via Trieste and Via Roma.

SASSARI

079 / POP 127,525

Sassari, Sardinia's second-largest city, is a proud and cultured university town with a handsome historic centre and an unpretentious, workaday vibe.

Like many Italian towns it hides its charms behind an outer shell of drab apartment blocks and confusing, traffic-choked roads. But once through to the inner sanctum it opens up, revealing a grand centre of wide boulevards, impressive piazzas and stately *palazzi*. In the evocative and slightly rundown *centro storico* (historic centre), medieval alleyways hum with Dickensian activity as residents run about their daily business amid grimy facades and hidden churches.

History

The presence of *nuraghi* and ancient ruins in the area around Sassari attest to the presence of settlers long before the city came into being in the Middle Ages. Sassari, or Tathari as it was originally known, was founded by inhabitants of the ancient Roman colony of Turris Libisonis (modern-day Porto Torres), who fled inland to escape pirate raids.

It expanded rapidly in the 12th century, growing to become the largest city in the Giudicato di Torres. Eventually it broke away from the Giudicato and, with support from Genoa, declared itself an autonomous city state in 1294.

But the Sassaresi soon tired of Genoese meddling and in 1321 they appealed to the Crown of Aragon to help rid them of their mainland partners. The Catalan-Aragonese arrived in 1323, but Sassari soon discovered it had leapt from the frying pan into the fire. The first of many revolts against the city's new masters came two years later. It took another century for the Iberians to fully control Sassari.

For a time the city prospered, but waves of plague and the growing menace from Ottoman Turkey sidelined Sardinia, leaving Sassari to slide into decline in the 16th century. A century later the founding of the city's university, Sardinia's first, was a rare highlight in this otherwise grim period.

It wasn't until the middle of the 19th century that Sassari began to take off again, following the modernisation of Porto Torres and the laying of the Carlo Felice highway between the port, Sassari and Cagliari. Since 1945 the city has maintained a slow pace of economic growth. It has also been an industrious producer of national politicians, including former presidents Antonio Segni (1891–1972) and Francesco Cossiga (1928–2010), the charismatic communist leader Enrico Berlinguer (1922–84) and Beppe Pisanu (b 1937), a former interior minister under Silvio Berlusconi.

Sights

★Museo Nazionale Sanna — MUSEUM

(☎079 27 22 03; www.museosannasassari.beniculturali.it; Via Roma 64; adult/reduced €3/2, 1st Sun of month free; ⏲9am-8pm Tue-Sat & 1st Sun of month, to 1pm Sun) Sassari's premier museum, housed in a grand Palladian villa, boasts a comprehensive archaeological collection and an ethnographical section dedicated to Sardinian folk art. The highlight is the nuraghic bronzeware, including weapons, bracelets, votive boats and figurines depicting humans and animals.

Archaeological artefacts are displayed in chronologically ordered rooms, starting with the Sala Preistorica, which showcases finds from the Stone Age and neolithic periods. In this and the room dedicated to finds from the Copper Age temple of Monte d'Accoddi (p142), you'll find an array of fossils, pottery fragments and bone tools.

Beyond these, the museum opens up in a series of displays dedicated to megalithic tombs and *domus de janas* (fairy houses).

Sections dedicated to the Phoenician and Carthaginian eras reveal some exquisite pottery, gold jewellery and masks. Continuing on, the Roman collection is mostly made up of ceramics and oil burners, but there are also some statues and a sprinkling of coins, jewellery and household objects. Off to one side lies a stash of heavy Roman anchors.

The 1st floor is given over to the museum's nuraghic collection, with reconstructions of *nuraghi* and finds from sites around Sassari and Alghero. Ceramics, household items, and pottery are displayed but the star feature is the sophisticated bronzeware, including tools, jewellery and *bronzetti* (bronze figurines).

A separate ethnographic section has a small collection of Sardinian folk art plus an eclectic array of carpets, saddlebags, embroidered clothes and curious terracotta hot-water bottles.

★Piazza Italia — PIAZZA

Sassari's largest piazza is one of Sardinia's most impressive public spaces. Covering about a hectare, it is surrounded by imposing 19th-century buildings, including the neoclassical Palazzo della Provincia, seat of the provincial government and, opposite, the neo-Gothic Palazzo Giordano, now home to the Banca Intesa SanPaolo. Presiding over everything is a statue of King Vittorio Emanuele II.

The statue was unveiled in 1899 to much pomp and costumed celebration, in anticipation of the grand event that would become the city's main festival, the Cavalcata Sarda. The piazza also marks the starting point for Sassari's other big jamboree, I Candelieri.

Duomo — CATHEDRAL

(Cattedrale di San Nicola; Piazza Duomo; ⏲8.45am-noon Mon-Sat & 4.30-7pm Tue-Sat, 9-11.30am & 5-7pm Sun) Sassari's principal cathedral dazzles with its 18th-century baroque facade, a giddy free-for-all of statues, reliefs, friezes and busts. It's all a front, though, because inside the cathedral reverts to its true Gothic character. The facade masks a late-15th-century Catalan Gothic body, which was itself built over an earlier Romanesque church. Little remains of this, except for the 13th-century bell tower.

Museo della Brigata Sassari MUSEUM
(079 208 53 08; www.assonazbrigatasassari.it; Piazza Castello 9; 8am-4.30pm Mon-Fri, to 1pm Sat) FREE Sassari is home to one of Italy's most revered army regiments. The Sassari Brigade was established in 1915 and during WWI established a reputation for bravery in the face of appalling conditions. You can glean something of the suffering the brigade endured in this tiny museum in the regiment's city-centre barracks. Uniforms, photos, documents and other memorabilia testify to the bravery of the Sardinian soldiers, who were thrown into battle against the Austrians in northern Italy.

Corso Vittorio Emanuele II STREET
The main drag through the *centro storico*, Corso Vittorio Emanuele II follows the path of the ancient Roman road from Porto Torres to Cagliari. Little remains from its 13th-century heyday, but there are a few signs of past grandeur. At No 23, Casa Farris is a 15th-century townhouse, while a few metres up, the Casa di Re Enzo provides a Catalan Gothic setting for a clothes shop. Opposite, the Liberty-style Teatro Civico (p140) was a 19th-century addition.

Piazza Tola PIAZZA
Just north of Corso Vittorio Emanuele II, Piazza Tola was medieval Sassari's main square where condemned heretics were burned at the stake. Overlooking the piazza is the 16th-century **Palazzo d'Usini** (city library 9am-1.30pm Mon-Fri & 4-6.15pm Tue & Thu), one of the first Renaissance buildings to be constructed in Sardinia and now home to the city library.

Museo della Città MUSEUM
(www.comune.sassari.it/thamus/en; adult/reduced €3/2) This museum dedicated to Sassari's history is spread over three sites. Its main seat is **Palazzo di Città** (079 201 51 22; Corso Vittorio Emanuele II; adult/reduced €3/2; 10am-1pm Tue-Sun & 3-6pm Wed-Sat), where exhibits illustrate the city's urban development, festivals and traditions. A short walk away, **Palazzo Ducale** (331 4377156; Piazza del Comune; adult/reduced €3/2; 10am-1pm & 3-6pm Tue-Fri, 10am-1pm Sat) FREE, which also doubles as Sassari's city hall, has historical artefacts relating to the palace's former life as an aristocratic 18th-century residence and an interesting underground section. The third location is **Palazzo della Frumentaria** (079 20 03 45; Via delle Muraglie 1; adult/reduced €3/2; 10am-1pm Tue-Sun & 3-6pm Wed-Sat), a 16th-century grain warehouse that's used to stage temporary exhibitions.

Pinacoteca Nazionale di Sassari GALLERY
(079 23 15 60; www.facebook.com/PinacotecaSassari; Piazza Santa Caterina 4; adult/reduced €4/2; 9am-6pm Tue-Sat) Housed in a 16th-century Jesuit college, Sassari's municipal art collection boasts more than 400 paintings from the Middle Ages to the 20th century. Of the religious art on show, a highlight is Bartolomeo Vivarini's fine triptych, *Madonna con bambino* (1473). Upstairs, works by the likes of Giovanni Lanfranco and Guercino hang alongside landscapes and Flemish still lifes, while up on the 2nd floor you'll find paintings by 20th-century Sardinian artists.

Chiesa di Santa Maria di Betlem CHURCH
(Piazza di Santa Maria; Mass 6pm Mon-Sat, 8am, 10am,11am & 6pm Sun) With its distinctive dome and proud Romanesque facade, the much-loved Chiesa di Santa Maria di Betlem reveals a curious blend of architectural styles. The exterior sports Gothic and even vaguely Oriental elements. Inside, the Catalan Gothic vaulting has been preserved, but much baroque frippery has crept in to obscure the original lines of the building. In the lateral chapels stand some of the giant 'candles' the city guilds parade about town during the 14 August I Candelieri (p138) festivities.

Fontana di Rosello FOUNTAIN
(Piazza Mercato; guided tours €3; 10am-1pm Tue-Sun & 3-6pm Wed-Sat) FREE Sassari's most famous fountain sits in a sunken area by Piazza Mercato, a busy traffic junction just outside the city walls. A monumental marble box ringed by four statues and eight lion-head spouts, and topped by two fine marble arches, it was for a long time the focus of city life. Guided tours are available through the tourist office (p140).

Sassari

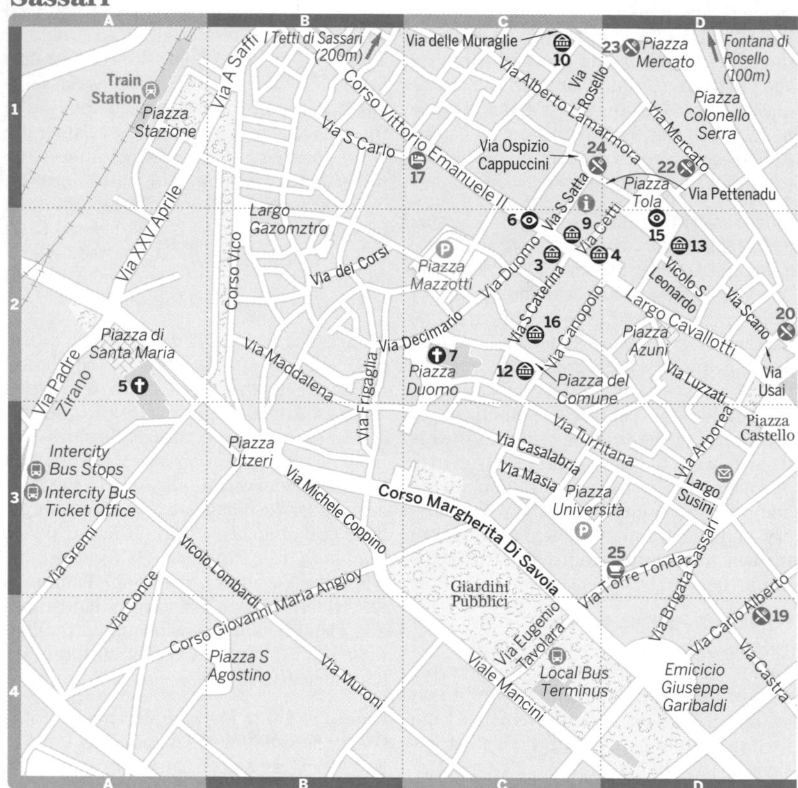

Festivals & Events

Cavalcata Sarda PARADE

(May) One of Sardinia's highest-profile festivals is held in Sassari on the second-last Sunday of May. Thousands of people converge on the city to participate in costumed processions, to sing and dance and watch fearless horse riders exhibit their acrobatic skills.

I Candelieri RELIGIOUS

(www.icandelierisassari.it; Aug) A big summer festival, which is held every 14 August. Teams wearing medieval costumes and representing various 16th-century guilds bear nine wooden columns (the 'candlesticks' in the festival's name) through town. The celebrations have their origins in 13th-century Pisan worship of the Madonna of the Assumption.

Eating

Eating in Sassari is a real pleasure. Eateries range from cheap student cafes to refined restaurants, and standards are universally high. A local speciality is *fainè,* a cross between a crêpe and a pancake made from chickpea flour.

Fainè alla Genovese Sassu SARDINIAN €

(079 23 64 02; Via Usai 17; meals €10-15; 7.30-11.30pm Mon-Sat) Modest, no-frills and much loved locally, this bare, white-tiled eatery is the place to try Sassari's famous *fainè.* There's nothing else on the menu, but with various types to choose from – sausage, onions, mushrooms, anchovies – they're ideal for a cheap, tasty fill-up.

Mercato Civico MARKET €

(Piazza Mercato; 8am-2pm Mon-Sat) Housed in a modern white building, Sassari's produce market is a thriving city institution.

Sassari

Top Sights

1 Museo Nazionale Sanna F4
2 Piazza Italia E3

Sights

3 Casa di Re Enzo C2
4 Casa Farris C2
5 Chiesa di Santa Maria di Betlem A2
6 Corso Vittorio Emanuele II C2
7 Duomo C2
8 Museo della Brigata Sassari E3
9 Museo della Città C2
10 Palazzo della Frumentaria C1
11 Palazzo della Provincia E3
Palazzo di Città ..... (see 9)
12 Palazzo Ducale C2
13 Palazzo d'Usini D2
14 Palazzo Giordano E3
15 Piazza Tola D2
16 Pinacoteca Nazionale di Sassari C2

Sleeping

17 Hotel Vittorio Emanuele C1
18 Tanina B&B F2

Eating

19 Bistrot Ristorante Sassari D4
20 Fainè alla Genovese Sassu D2
21 L'Antica Hostaria E4
22 Le 2 Lanterne D1
23 Mercato Civico D1
24 Trattoria L'Assassino C1

Drinking & Nightlife

25 Accademia D3
26 Caffè Italiano F4

Entertainment

27 Nuovo Teatro Verdi E2
Teatro Civico ..... (see 9)

Locals come here to browse stalls laden with squid and silvery-grey shellfish, oranges, aubergines, pungent *pecorino* cheese, freshly baked bread and much more. There's no better place to load up for a picnic.

Trattoria L'Assassino SARDINIAN €€
(☎079 23 34 63; www.trattorialassassino.it; Via Pettenadu 19; fixed-price menu €22, meals €25-30; ⏱12.30-3pm & 7.30pm-midnight) This is a model trattoria in a tiny back lane – go through the arch near the tourist office – specialising in traditional island cooking. Expect starters of cheese and cured meats, pastas with tomato sauce, grilled steaks and stuffed snails.

L'Antica Hostaria RISTORANTE €€
(☎079 20 00 66; www.lanticahostaria.eu; Via Cavour 55; meals €40; ⏱1-3pm & 8-11.30pm Mon-Sat) Hidden behind a chipped, low-key exterior, L'Antica Hostaria is a consistently top restaurant. In intimate, homey surroundings you're treated to inventive dishes rooted in Italian culinary traditions. Desserts are also impressive, and there's an excellent list of island and Italian wines.

Le 2 Lanterne SARDINIAN €€
(☎329 426 17 06; Via Mercato 28a; fixed-price menus €20-23, meals €25-30; ⏱noon-3pm & 7pm-midnight) Join the locals for a taste of authentic Sassarese home cooking at this laid-back trattoria near the city walls. The mustard-yellow and Pompeiian-red decor sets a cheerful mood for honest dishes of *culurgiones* (Sardinian ravioli) with tomato sauce, grilled meats and creamy ricotta desserts.

Bistrot Ristorante Sassari INTERNATIONAL €€
(☎079 492 03 00; Via Carlo Alberto 34; meals €30-35; ⏱1-3pm & 8-11pm Mon-Sat) Casual modern

dining is the byword at this good-looking bistro-restaurant near Piazza Italia. The daily menu, chalked up on a blackboard, features evergreen favourites such as red tuna and richly accessorised burgers of prime Tuscan beef. The wine list also impresses with a curated selection of island vintages.

Trattoria Da Gesuino TRATTORIA €€
(☎079 27 33 92; Via Torres 17; pizzas €5-8, meals €30-35; ⏱noon-3pm & 8-11pm Mon-Sat) A bit of a walk out from the centre, Da Gesuino hits all the right notes with its relaxed, unpretentious atmosphere, efficient service and decent food. The menu covers all the usual bases with pasta, risottos, fresh fish and terrific meat dishes. There's also pizza, served at both lunch and dinner.

Drinking & Nightlife

With its big student population and busy business community, Sassari has a vibrant cafe culture. You'll find a number of popular spots on Via Roma and Via Torre Tonda, a lively student strip. Another good bet is Piazza Tola, which comes alive on summer evenings. Many places stay open late and some offer occasional live music.

Accademia CAFE
(Via Torre Tonda 11; ⏱7.30am-midnight Mon-Thu, to 2am Fri & Sat) With al fresco summer tables, a vaulted interior and an enclosed wrought-iron verandah, this is a lively hang-out in the university district. It gets very busy at lunchtimes and on Friday and Saturday nights, when it often hosts gigs.

Caffè Italiano CAFE
(☎328 0057291; Via Roma 38-40; ⏱7am-11pm Mon-Fri, 8am-3pm & 5pm-2am Sat) One of the best places on Via Roma is this big, bustling bar with pavement tables and a stylish interior. Business folk lunch here, and young locals come most afternoons to chat over an aperitif. Cocktails from €5.

☆ Entertainment

Teatro Civico THEATRE
(☎079 200 80 72; Corso Vittorio Emanuele II 39) Sassari's neoclassical theatre in Palazzo di Città (p137) stages plays, classical music concerts, film projections and cultural events. Seasonal programs are generally posted around town.

Nuovo Teatro Verdi THEATRE
(☎079 23 94 79; Via Politeama) One of Sassari's historical theatres, the Nuovo Teatro Verdi hosts dance, opera, concerts, musicals, children's shows and cultural events.

Nuovo Teatro Comunale THEATRE
(☎079 37 12 73; Piazzale Cappuccini) Inaugurated in February 2012, Sassari's largest theatre stages opera, concerts and plays. Check local listings for upcoming performances, or visit www.cedacsardegna.it.

Information

Banca Intesa SanPaolo (Piazza Italia 19) In Palazzo Giordano.

Farmacia Piazza Castello (☎079 23 32 38; Piazza Castello 5; ⏱9am-1pm & 4.30-8pm, plus night shift 8pm-9am)

Movimento Omosessuale Sardo (MOS; ☎079 21 90 24; www.movimentomosessualesardo.org; Via Rockfeller 16c) Sardinian LGBT organisation.

Ospedale Civile SS Annunziata (☎079 206 10 00; Via De Nicola 14) Hospital south of the city centre.

Police Station (Questura; ☎079 249 50 00; Via Giovanni Palatucci 1; ⏱8am-2pm daily, plus 2-8pm Mon-Sat) The main police headquarters.

Post Office (Via Brigata Sassari 13; ⏱8.20am-7.05pm Mon-Fri, to 12.35pm Sat)

Tourist Office (☎079 200 80 72; www.turismosassari.it; Via Sebastiano Satta 13; ⏱9am-1.30pm & 3-6pm Tue-Fri, 9am-1.30pm Sat) The helpful staff can provide information on Sassari and the surrounding area.

Getting There & Away

AIR

Sassari shares Alghero airport (p124), about 28km west of the city at Fertilia.

Up to nine daily buses run from the airport to Via Padre Zirano (€3.10, 30 minutes).

BUS

Intercity buses depart from and arrive at **Via Padre Zirano**, near the Chiesa di Santa Maria di Betlem. There's a small **ticket office** (Via Padre Zirano; ⏱6.30am-8pm Mon-Sat, 8am-2pm & 5-8pm Sun) by the stops.

Services run to/from Alghero (€3.10, one hour, up to 10 daily), Porto Torres (€1.90, 30

SASSARI THEATRES

Sassari's theatres don't tend to move into gear until September or October, after the sting has gone out of the summer heat. For show information, check the local newspaper *La Nuova Sardegna* or contact the theatres directly.

minutes, hourly) and Castelsardo (€3.10, one hour, 11 weekdays, four Sundays). There are also buses to Nuoro (€8.10, 1¾ hours, six daily) and Oristano (€8.10, two hours, two daily).

CAR & MOTORCYCLE

Sassari is located on the SS131, the main road from Porto Torres to Cagliari. From Alghero, take the road north towards Porto Torres and then the SS291 east to Sassari. Take the same route from Alghero airport.

Car hire is available at **Maggiore** (079 26 04 09; Strada 18, 38, Zona Industriale Predda Niedda; 8.45am-12.45pm & 4-7pm Mon-Fri, 9am-12.30pm Sat), in the industrial zone northwest of the train station.

TRAIN

The main train station is just beyond the western end of the old town on Piazza Stazione. Direct trains run to Cagliari (€16.50, three to four hours, three daily), Oristano (€11, two to 2½ hours, four daily) and Olbia (€8.10, 1¾ hours, four daily). There are also daily services to these destinations via Ozieri-Chilivani.

Once a week, between mid-June and mid-September, the Trenino Verde (p268) departs from Sassari for the slow panoramic ride to Tempio Pausania (€24 return).

Getting Around

ARRIVING IN SASSARI

Alghero Airport Up to nine daily buses run from the aiport at Fertilia to Sassari, stopping at the bus stops on Via Padre Zirano (€3.10, 30 minutes).

Intercity Bus Stops Intercity buses arrive at Via Padre Zirano.

BUS

ATP (079 263 80 47; www.atpsassari.it) orange buses run along most city routes, although you're unlikely to need one in the small city centre. In summer there are also buses to the beaches north of Sassari from the **terminus** (Via Eugenio Tavolara; ticket office 7am-9.15pm Mon-Fri, 7.50am-2.10pm Sun). Tickets cost €1.30.

CAR & MOTORCYCLE

Parking in Sassari is generally a nightmare. Within blue lines, rates are up to €0.50 per 30 minutes. Get tickets from traffic wardens, roadside meters or newsagents.

Note also that much of the historic centre is a limited traffic zone (ZTL), out of bounds to non-authorised vehicles.

TAXI

To phone for a taxi, call **Cooperativa Taxi Sassari** (079 25 39 39).

AROUND SASSARI

Ozieri

079 / POP 10,680

A prosperous agricultural town, Ozieri sits in a natural hollow, its handsome 19th-century centre sloping upwards from a striking central piazza. The surrounding area has been inhabited since neolithic times and the town's name is now associated with a period in Sardinian prehistory – the Ozieri (or San Michele) culture, which spanned the years between 3500 and 2700 BC.

The town is also known for the Premio Ozieri per la Letteratura Sarda, one of Sardinia's major literary awards. The prize, which showcases the work of Italian and Sardinian writers, was originally inspired by the *gare poetiche* (poetry slams) held at many local festivals.

Sights

Museo Archeologico MUSEUM

(079 785 10 52; http://museo.comune.ozieri.ss.it; Piazza Micca; adult/reduced €5/4, incl Grotta di San Michele €6/5; 9am-1pm & 3-7pm Tue-Fri, 9am-1pm & 3-6pm Sat & Sun) Investigate Ozieri's rich archaeological legacy at the wonderful Museo Archeologico. Housed in the 18th-century Convento Clarisse, it has a small but rich collection, including a couple of copper ingots (nuraghic settlements were trading copper as far back as the neolithic age), some surprisingly modern-looking tools and a selection of fine ceramic fragments found in the nearby Grotta di San Michele.

Grotta di San Michele CAVE

(079 78 76 38; Vicolo San Michele; adult/reduced €3/2, incl Museo Archeologico €6/5; 10.30am-1pm & 3-6pm Tue-Sun summer, 10am-1pm & 2-5pm Tue-Sun winter) To the south of the town centre, this small cave complex was inhabited by nuraghic people, who also used it as a tomb and place of cult worship. Excavations in 1914 and then 1949 unearthed pottery, vases and figurines, many of which are now on display at the Museo Nazionale Sanna (p136) in Sassari.

Eating

La Torre RISTORANTE, PIZZERIA €€

(079 78 66 95; www.latorreozieri.it; Via Scarpata del Cantaro 1; meals €30; 12.30-2.30pm & 7.30-11.30pm Tue-Sun) With al fresco tables on

WORTH A TRIP

LAGO LERNO

About 24km east of Ozieri, Lago Lerno presents a bucolic picture. Although an artificial lake – it was created in 1984 by damming the Rio Mannu – it fits perfectly into the surrounding scenery, with grassy slopes gently rising from the still waters and rocky **Monte Lerno** (1094m) looming in the near distance. Nearby, deer, mouflon and wild horses roam in the **Bosco di Monte Lerno** (Monte Lerno Wood). To get to the wood, pass Ozieri, enter Pattada, some 15km east, and continue towards Oschiri. After about 11km, turn right and continue over the Rio Mannu into the northwest reaches of the forest.

a sunny cobbled terrace and a bright, light-filled dining room, La Torre is a handsome spot to sit down to wood-fired pizzas and stylishly presented seafood. Booking is recommended for weekends.

Getting There & Away

By public transport the easiest way to get to Ozieri is by ARST bus from Sassari (€3.70, one hour, five Monday to Saturday).

By car, Ozieri is about 45km southeast of Sassari via the SS127 and SS729.

Sennori, Sorso & the Sassari Riviera

Some 15km north of Sassari, the Sassari Riviera is centred on the small resort of Platamona Lido. A favourite with sun-seeking Sassaresi, who flock here on hot summer weekends, it's not really a town as such, more a smattering of bars, pizzerias and beach clubs strung along a lengthy strip of sand. Further east, Marina di Sorso offers more of the same.

Inland, the hilltop town of Sennori and neighbouring Sorso are famous for their wine and together they produce the sweet Moscato di Sorso-Sennori. To the west, Monte d'Accoddi is a strange and intriguing archaeological site well worth searching out.

Sights

★Monte d'Accoddi ARCHAEOLOGICAL SITE

(adult/reduced €3/2; ⌚9am-6pm Tue-Sun summer, to 2pm winter) Signposted off the SS131 between Sassari and Porto Torres, Monte d'Accoddi is a unique neolithic temple. Unlike anything else in the Mediterranean basin (the closest comparable structures are the Mesopotamian ziggurats), it originally dates to the 4th millennium BC. However, most of what you see survives from a later stage of construction dating to around 2800 BC. It went through several phases until it appears to have been abandoned around 1800 BC. Soon after, the first *nuraghe* began to be raised.

The central part of the structure is a rectangular-based platform (30m by 38m) that stands atop a grassy, walled mount linked to a long sloping ramp. Either side of the ramp are a menhir and a stone altar believed to have been used for sacrifices.

Spiaggia di Platamona BEACH

With its fine sand and clean waters, the beach at Platamona is a popular summer hang-out, and you'll find all the usual beach facilities: sunloungers, umbrellas, showers and a car park. It stretches for about 15km, so even on the busiest of August weekends you'll be able to find some space for yourselves.

Eating

Da Vito SEAFOOD €€€

(☎079 36 02 45; www.facebook.com/Ristorante-Da-vito-122998726112; Via Napoli 14, Sennori; meals €45; ⌚12.30-2.30pm Tue-Sun & 7-11pm Tue-Sat) In Sennori, off the main Sassari road above the historic centre, is this great place to sample the local wine and delicious fresh seafood. Particularly good are the abundant, multi-dish antipasti.

Getting There & Away

To get to Platamona Lido or Marina di Sorso from Sassari, take the BB bus from Via Eugenio Tavolara. Tickets cost €1.30.

Weekday ARST buses serve Sennori from Via XXV Aprile in Sassari, but services are limited and you'll find getting around much easier with your own wheels.

Valle dei Nuraghi

The Valle dei Nuraghi (Valley of the Nuraghi), some 40km south of Sassari, is a verdant area rich in archaeological interest. The hills and fields around the villages of Torralba, Mores, Borutta and Bonarva are littered with the ruins of prehistoric *nuraghi* and *domus de janas*, including one of Sardinia's top archaeological sites, the Nuraghe Santu Antine.

Sights

Nuraghe Santu Antine ARCHAEOLOGICAL SITE
(☎079 84 74 81; www.nuraghesantuantine.it; Torralba; adult/reduced €6/4; ⏰9am-8pm summer, to 5pm winter) One of the largest nuraghic sites in Sardinia, the Nuraghe Santu Antine sits 4km south of Torralba. The complex is focused on a central tower, which now stands 17.5m high but which originally rose to a height of 25m. Around this, walls link three bastions to enclose a triangular compound. The oldest parts of the *nuraghe* date to around 1600 BC, but much of it was built over successive centuries. Visits are by guided tour only.

You enter the compound from the southern side and can walk through the three towers, connected by rough parabolic archways. The entrance to the main tower is separate. Inside, four openings lead into the chamber from an internal hall. Stairs lead up from the hall to the next floor, where a similar but smaller pattern is reproduced. Apart from tiny vents there is no light, and the presence of the dark stone is overwhelming. You ascend another set of steps to reach the floor of what was the final, third chamber, now open to the elements.

On weekdays there are up to eight buses from Sassari to Torralba (€3.10, 45 minutes to 1½ hours), from where it's still a 4km walk to the *nuraghe*.

Basilica di San Pietro di Sorres CHURCH
(☎079 82 40 01; www.sanpietrodisorres.net; Località San Pietro di Sorres, Borutta; ⏰9am-12.30pm & 3.30-6.30pm) This 12th-century Romanesque church commands impressive views from its hillside position overlooking Borutta. The original Pisan

ROMANESQUE CHURCHES OF THE LOGUDORO

Extending south and east of Sassari, the fertile territory known as the Logudoro has been inhabited since prehistoric times. It was home to several nuraghic communities and later became an important granary for the Roman Empire; still today the landscape is a patchwork of rugged slopes and golden wheat fields – the name Logudoro means 'place of gold'. As the Giudicato del Logudoro, it enjoyed a medieval heyday, and it's to this period that it owes many of its impressive Romanesque churches.

Perhaps the most celebrated of its churches is the **Basilica della Santissima Trinità di Saccargia** (SS729 Sassari–Olbia km 2; admission €3; ⏰9am-6pm Apr-Oct), about 18km southeast of Sassari on the SS729 Olbia road. A local landmark with a stripy limestone and basalt campanile, this was supposedly built in 1116 on the site of a miraculous revelation. According to legend, the Giudice Constantino di Mariano and his wife camped the night here and received a vision telling them that they were going to have their first longed-for child. The Giudice, delighted by the news, built the church and a neighbouring monastery, which the pope subsequently gave to the Camaldolite monks. Little remains of the monastery, although the church is still in use.

Continuing from the basilica towards Olbia, you'll pass the abandoned **Chiesa di San Michele di Salvènero** as you push on to **Ardara**, 13km away. Ardara was once the capital of the Giudicato di Torres, and a quick turn to the left as you enter town leads to the brooding **Chiesa di Santa Maria del Regno** (Ardara; ⏰10am-1pm & 3.30-8pm summer, 3.30-7pm winter). Consecrated in 1107, this grey-basalt church features a columned interior and a fabulous 16th-century retable depicting episodes from the lives of Jesus, Mary and various prophets.

Further east along the SS729, you'll see a turn-off for the 12th-century **Chiesa di Sant'Antioco di Bisarcio** (guided tours per adult/reduced €3/2; ⏰10am-1pm & 2.30-7pm Tue-Sun summer, 10am-1pm & 2-5pm Tue-Sun winter), one of Sardinia's largest Romanesque churches. Its campanile was decapitated by a burst of lightning, and much of the facade's decoration has been lost, but the uniquely French-inspired porch and interior convey the impression of its one-time grandeur.

From here you can continue on the SS729 for the tiny **Chiesa di Nostra Signora di Castro** on the banks of **Lago di Coghinas**, or head north along the SS132 to the **Chiesa di San Pietro di Simbranos** at **Bulzi**.

SARDINIA'S CUTTING EDGE

Sardinia has a long tradition of knife-making. The most prized of the island's knives is known as *sa pattadesa* (the Pattada knife). The classic Pattada knife, first made in the mid-19th century, is the *resolza,* with a myrtle-leaf-shaped blade that folds into a handle made of horn.

Most of the best artisans only work to order and take at least two days to fashion such a knife, folding and tempering the steel for strength and sharpness. The handle is then carved from a single piece of mouflon (silky-haired wild sheep) horn. If you're looking at a handle made with two parts screwed together, you're not looking at a quality piece. A good knife will cost at least €10 a centimetre.

In the past such knives were made all over the island, but now only a few towns follow the traditional methods. **Pattada** is the most famous, although quality knives are also made in **Arbus**, **Santu Lussurgiu** and **Tempio Pausania**. The classic *s'arburesa* (from Arbus) knife has a fat, rounded blade and is used for skinning animals, while the *lametta* of Tempio Pausania has a rectangular blade good for stripping bark from cork oaks.

church and adjacent abbey had long been abandoned when a community of Benedictine monks moved here in 1955 and set about restoring them to their former glory. The white-and-grey-banded facade has three levels of blind arches and is decorated with some lovely elaborate stonework. Of note inside is an intriguing stone Gothic pulpit set on four legs.

Necropoli di Sant'Andrea Priu ARCHAEOLOGICAL SITE
(☎348 5642611; €6; ⏰10am-1pm & 3-5pm Mar-May & Oct, 10am-7pm Jun-Sep, by appointment Nov-Feb) About 7km east of Bonorva, the Necropoli di Sant'Andrea Priu is an isolated site, immersed in silence and accessible only by a narrow potholed road. It's made up of around 20 small grottoes carved into trachyte rock, some of which date as far back as 3000 BC.

Of the grottoes, the Tomba del Capo, accessible only with a guide, is by far the most interesting. In the early Christian period, three of the main rooms were transformed into a place of worship, and partly restored frescoes from the 5th century survive in two of them. Most striking is the fresco of a woman in the *aula* (hall) where the faithful heard Mass.

Dolmen Sa Coveccada ARCHAEOLOGICAL SITE
FREE To the south of Mores, the mighty Dolmen Sa Coveccada is said to be the largest dolmen (a megalithic chambered tomb) in the Mediterranean. Dating to the end of the 3rd millennium BC, the rectangular construction consists of three massive stone slabs, roofed by a fourth, weighing around 18 tonnes. As it stands, it reaches a height of 2.7m, is 5m long and 2.5m wide.

Rebeccu VILLAGE
Between the Necropoli di Sant'Andrea Priu and Bonarva is hilltop Rebeccu, a windswept and largely abandoned medieval hamlet carved into calcareous rock. It's worth taking an hour or so to explore the village. According to a local legend, the village was hit by malaria and abandoned after it had been cursed by a princess who had been accused of witchcraft and driven out by the villagers.

Eating

Agriturismo Sas Abbilas SARDINIAN €€
(☎347 6758725; www.sasabbilas.it; Località Mariani, Bonorva; fixed-price menus €15 & €30; ⏰by reservation) Things don't get much more off the beaten track than this *agriturismo,* ensconced in silent woods 1km or so beyond the Necropoli di Sant'Andrea Priu. Meals are typically abundant affairs featuring cheeses and cured meats, home-grown vegetables, roast meats and classic *seadas* desserts. Just how much you eat depends on whether you opt for the €15 menu or larger €30 option.

Getting There & Away

ARST buses serve the main villages (Mores, Torralba, Borutta, Bonorva) from Sassari but that's only half the battle as most of the archaeological sites are some way from the village centres.

To get the best out of the area, you really do need a car.

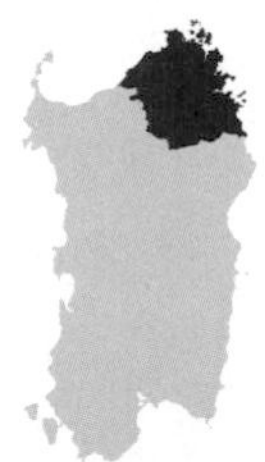

Olbia, the Costa Smeralda & Gallura

Includes ➡

Best Places to Eat

- Dolceacqua (p148)
- Il Portolano (p153)
- Agriturismo La Colti (p159)
- Li Mori (p154)
- I Frati Rossi (p156)
- Agriturismo Saltara (p164)

Best Places to Sleep

- B&B Lu Pastruccialeddu (p220)
- Agriturismo La Cerra (p221)
- La Murichessa (p219)
- Ca' La Somara (p220)
- Porto Romano (p217)
- S'Astore (p219)

Why Go?

The Costa Smeralda evokes Sardinia's classic images: pearly-white beaches and weird, wind-whipped licks of rock tapering into emerald seas. The dazzling coastal strip that the Aga Khan bought for a pittance is today the playground of millionaires and A-listers. Come summer, scandal-hungry paparazzi haunt the marinas, zooming in on oligarchs cavorting with bikini-clad beauties on yachts so big they eclipse the sun.

A few kilometres inland, a very different vision of the good life emerges. Here, vine-striped hills roll to deeply traditional villages and mysterious *nuraghi* (Bronze Age fortified settlements), silent cork-oak woods and granite mountains. Immune to time and trends, the hinterland offers a refreshing contrast to the coast, best appreciated during a multiday getaway at a country *agriturismo* (farm-stay).

Further north the Gallura coast becomes wilder, the preserve of the dolphins, divers and windsurfers who splash around in the startlingly blue waters of La Maddalena marine reserve.

When to Go

- In March and April, join traditional Easter processions in the ancient streets of Tempio Pausania.
- Stake your claim on northeastern Sardinia's legendary beaches in June before peak holiday crowds arrive.
- See the summer out in style at San Teodoro's annual windsports festival in September.

Olbia, the Costa Smeralda & Gallura Highlights

1 Costa Smeralda (p155) Hanging out with the bronzed, beautiful and super-famous on Sardinia's most exclusive coastline.

2 Parco Nazionale dell'Arcipelago di La Maddalena (p167) Island-hopping around the archipelago and diving into its jewel-coloured waters.

3 Cala Brandinchi (p154) Lounging on the frosty white sands of 'Little Tahiti.'

4 Tempio Pausania (p171) Exploring ancient stone streets and endless cork forests.

5 Porto Pollo (p170) Riding the wind through the wild waters between Sardinia and Corsica.

6 Olivastri Millenari di Santo Baltolu (p161) Taking refuge from the coastal glamour and clamour in the haunting silence of this magnificent ancient olive grove.

7 Capo Testa (p162) Clambering among weirdly sculpted boulders and looking for columns from an ancient Roman quarry.

8 Cantine Surrau (p159) Tasting crisp Vermentino whites and rich Cannonau reds at this contemporary winery.

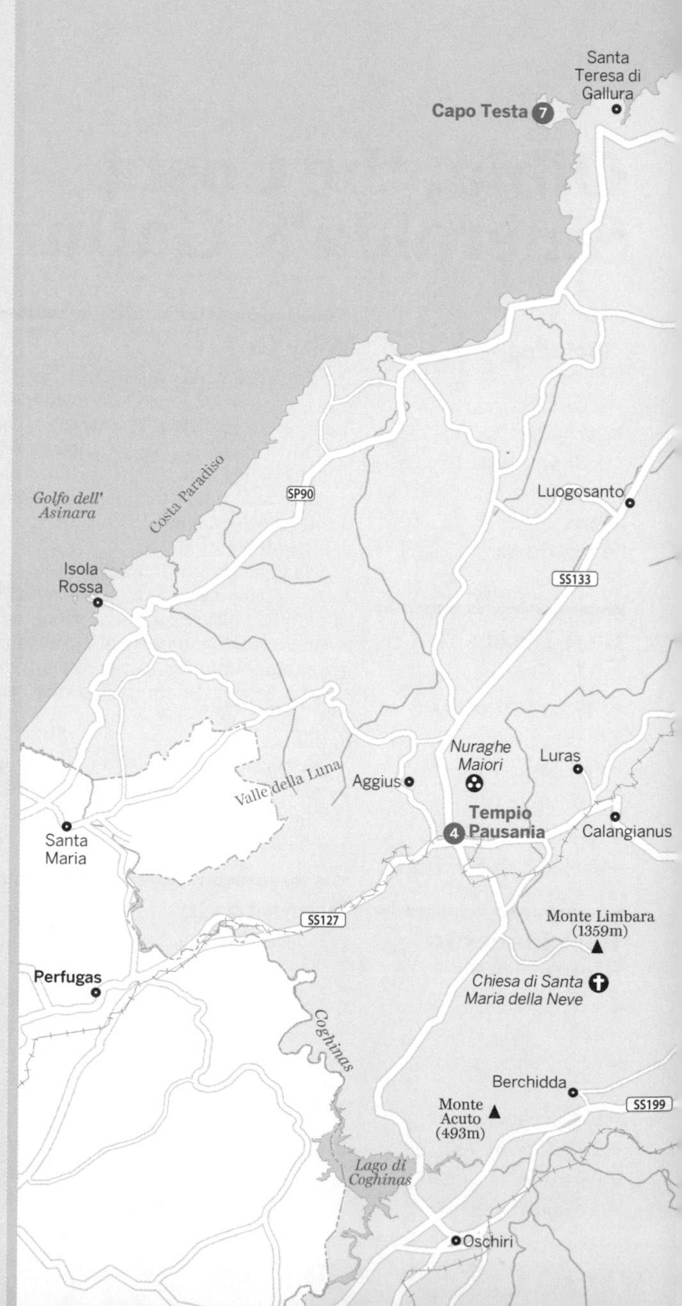

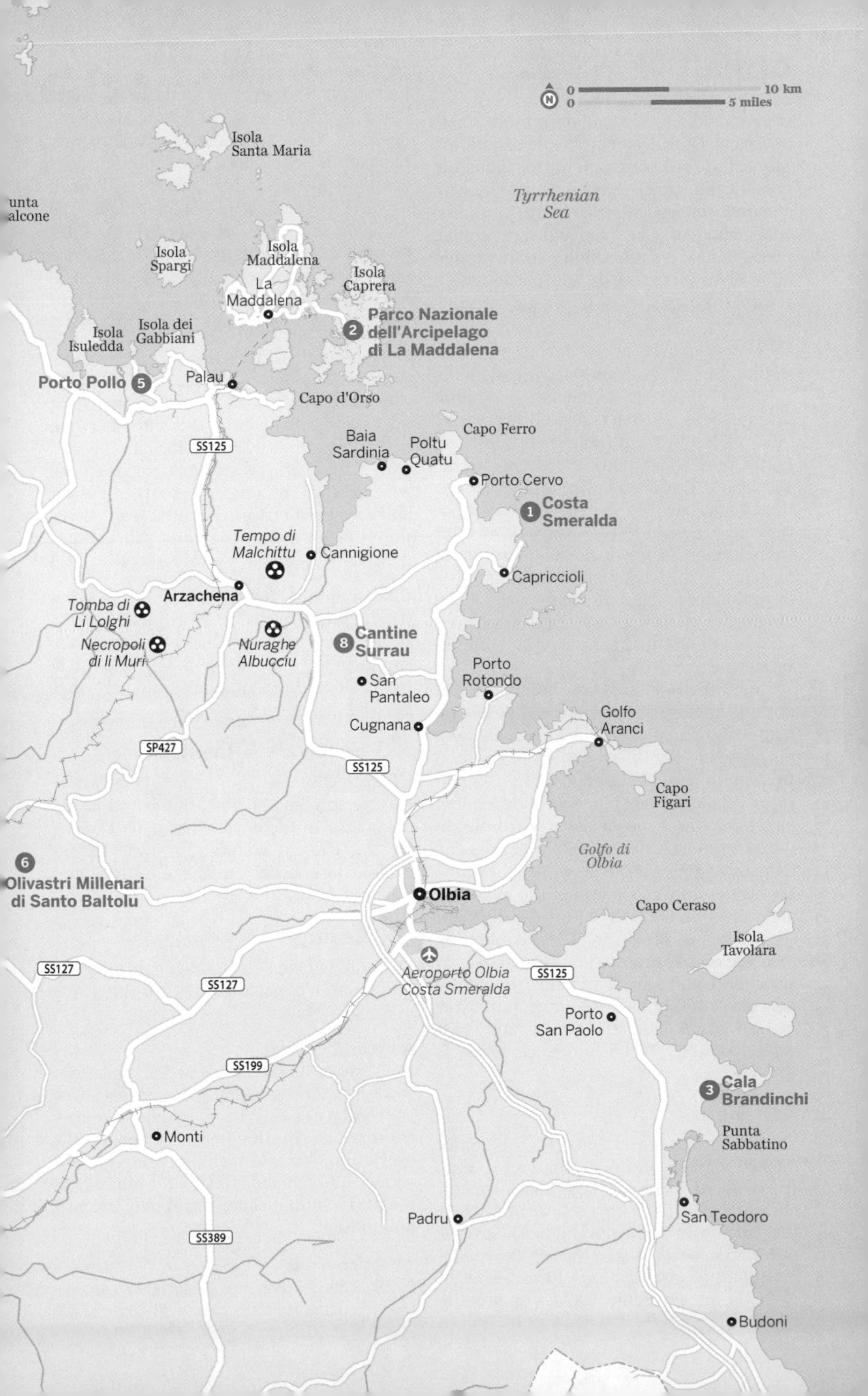

0 10 km
0 5 miles

Isola Santa Maria
unta alcone
Tyrrhenian Sea
Isola Spargi
Isola Maddalena
La Maddalena
Isola Caprera
Parco Nazionale dell'Arcipelago di La Maddalena
Isola Isuledda
Isola dei Gabbiani
Porto Pollo
Palau
Capo d'Orso
SS125
Baia Sardinia
Poltu Quatu
Capo Ferro
Porto Cervo
Costa Smeralda
Tempo di Malchittu
Cannigione
Capriccioli
Arzachena
Tomba di Li Lolghi
Necropoli di li Muri
Nuraghe Albucciu
Cantine Surrau
San Pantaleo
Porto Rotondo
Cugnana
Golfo Aranci
SP427
SS125
Capo Figari
Golfo di Olbia
Olivastri Millenari di Santo Baltolu
Olbia
Capo Ceraso
Isola Tavolara
SS127
SS127
Aeroporto Olbia Costa Smeralda
SS125
Porto San Paolo
SS199
Cala Brandinchi
Monti
Punta Sabbatino
SS389
Padru
San Teodoro
Budoni

OLBIA

☎0789 / POP 59,370

Often ignored in the mad dash to the Costa Smeralda, Olbia has more to offer than first meets the eye. Look beyond its industrial outskirts and you'll find a fetching city with a *centro storico* (historic centre) crammed with boutiques, wine bars and cafe-rimmed piazzas. Olbia is a refreshingly authentic and affordable alternative to the purpose-built resorts stretching to the north and south.

History

Archaeological evidence has revealed the existence of human settlement in Sardinia's northeast in the mid-neolithic period (about 4000 BC), but Olbia was almost certainly founded by the Carthaginians in the 4th or 5th century BC. Certainly Carthaginians had been present in the area since the mid-6th century BC as proved by their participation in the Battle of Mare Sardo (a naval battle between Greek colonists from Corsica and a combined Etruscan and Carthaginian fleet in 538 BC, considered by some to be the first ever naval battle in Western waters).

Under the Romans, Olbia became an important military and commercial port – remains of a dozen or so Roman vessels were unearthed in the 1990s. Known as Civita, it went on to become the capital of the Giudicato di Gallura, one of the four independent kingdoms that encompassed Sardinia in the 12th and 13th centuries. But when the Catalano-Aragonese took control, decline set in. Not until the arrival of the highways and railway in the 19th century did the town show signs of life again. The surrounding area was slowly drained and turned over to agriculture and some light industry, and the port was cranked back into operation. Now as a working industrial centre and joint capital of Olbia-Tempio province, Olbia is thriving.

Sights

To the south of Corso Umberto, the tightly packed warren of streets that represents the original fishing village has a certain charm, particularly in the evening when the cafes and trattorias fill with groups of hungry locals. A stroll along the *corso,* culminating in a drink on Piazza Margherita, is an agreeable way to spend the evening.

★Museo Archeologico MUSEUM

(Isolotto di Peddone; ⏲10am-1pm & 5-8pm Wed-Sun) FREE Architect Vanni Macciocco designed Olbia's strikingly contemporary museum near the port. The museum spells out local history in artefacts, from Roman amulets and pottery to nuraghic finds. The highlight is the relic of a Roman vessel discovered in the old port. A multimedia display recreates the scene of the Vandals burning and sinking such ships in AD 450. Free audio guides are available in English.

Chiesa di San Simplicio CHURCH

(Via San Simplicio; ⏲7.30am-1pm & 3.30-8pm) Considered to be Gallura's most important medieval monument, this Romanesque granite church was built in the late 11th and early 12th centuries on what was then the edge of town. It is a curious mix of Tuscan and Lombard styles with little overt decoration other than a couple of 13th-century frescoes depicting medieval bishops.

Chiesa di San Paolo CHURCH

(Via Cagliari; ⏲hours vary) Worth a look is the 18th-century granite Chiesa di San Paolo, spectacularly topped by a Valencian-style multicoloured tiled dome (added after WWII).

Festivals & Events

L'Estate Olbiese CULTURAL

During July and August, outdoor concerts are staged in the city centre as part of the L'Estate Olbiese, a cultural festival that includes concerts, performances, readings and cabarets.

Eating

The bulk of Olbia's restaurants are crowded into the web of narrow streets to either side of Corso Umberto.

Anticas Licanzias CAFE €

(Via Tigellio 12; snacks from €3; ⏲7.30am-midnight) A convenient place to recharge your batteries any time of day, this cosy corner cafe in the heart of town sells everything from morning pastries and coffee to homemade pasta and other light meals, including some vegan and vegetarian options.

★Dolceacqua ITALIAN €€

(☎0789 196 90 84; http://ristorantedolceacqua.com; Via Giacomo Pala 4; meals €30-40; ⏲12.30-2pm & 7.30-10.30pm Tue-Sun, 7.30-10.30pm only

Olbia

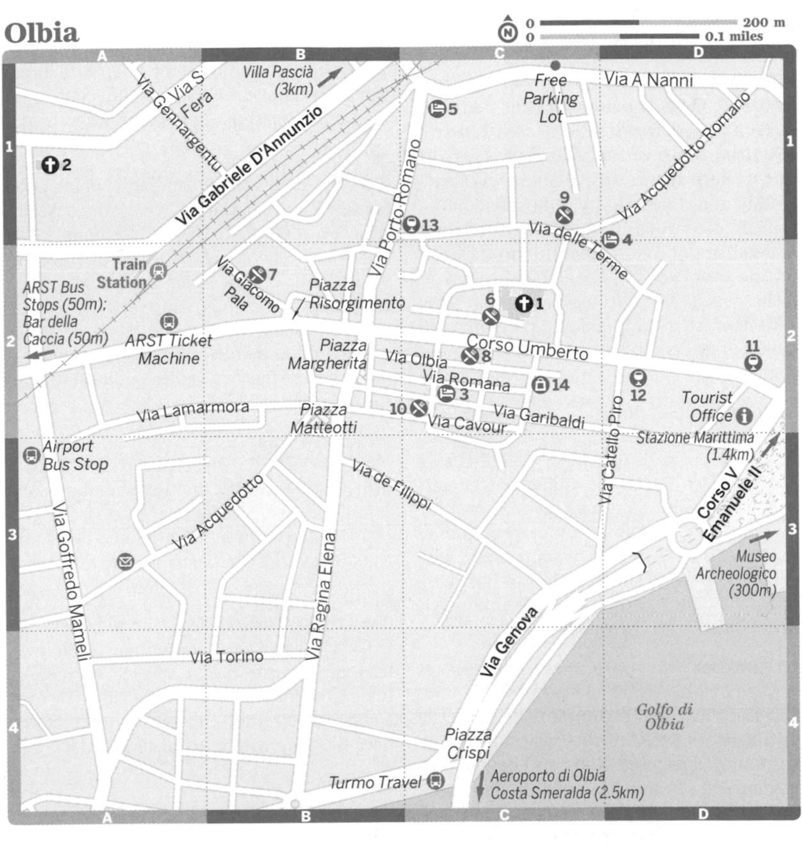

Olbia

Sights
1 Chiesa di San Paolo....C2
2 Chiesa di San Simplicio....A1

Sleeping
3 Hotel Panorama....C2
4 La Locanda del Conte Mameli....D1
5 Porto Romano....C1

Eating
6 Anticas Licanzias....C2
7 Dolceacqua....B2
8 La Lanterna....C2
9 L'Essenza Bistrot....C1
10 Ristorante da Paolo....C2

Drinking & Nightlife
11 In Vino Veritas....D2
12 KKult....D2
13 Movida Lounge....C1

Shopping
14 Disicios....C2

mid-Jun–mid-Sep) This smart, intimate bistro entices with a laid-back vibe, warm service and an appetising mix of Sardinian and Ligurian cuisine. Start with its decadent sampler of five seafood antipasti, then move on to Sardinian classics such as *culurgiones* or creative alternatives like *millefoglie di orata alla ligure* (bream cooked in oil, garlic, olives and wine, between thin pastry layers).

★ **Agriturismo Agrisole** SARDINIAN €€
(☎349 0848163; www.agriturismo-agrisole.com; Via Sole Ruiu 7, Località Casagliana; menu incl drinks €30; ⏰dinner daily by reservation Apr-Sep) Tucked serenely away in the countryside around 10km north of Olbia, this Gallurese *stazzo* (farmhouse) dishes up a feast of home cooking. Monica, your charming host, brings dish after marvellous dish to the table – antipasti, *fregola* (granular pasta), *porceddu* (roast suckling pig) and ricotta sweets. From Olbia,

take the SS125 towards Arzachena/Palau, turning left at the signs at Km 327.800.

L'Essenza Bistrot FUSION €€
(☎0789 2 55 94; www.essenzabistrot.it; Via delle Terme 10; meals around €45; ⊙noon-2.30pm & 6.30-11pm) For a classy night out, head for this modern bistro with romantic sidewalk seating and a beautifully remodelled stone-walled and wood-beamed interior. Local seafood and produce feature prominently on the ever-evolving chalkboard menu, in dishes such as saffron-scented fish stew with fried *carasau* bread and crunchy vegetables, or grilled prawns with asparagus and cognac sauce.

Ristorante da Paolo SARDINIAN €€
(☎0789 216 75; enter from Via Garibaldi 18 or Via Cavour 15; meals €30-40; ⊙noon-2.45pm & 7-10.30pm Mon-Sat) Stone walls, timber ceilings and coastal paintings give this restaurant a cheery air. Dig into soul food such as *zuppa gallurese* (a hearty soup made with bread, cheese and lamb broth), sea bass with artichokes, and *culurgiones* (Sardinian-style ravioli filled with cheese and potato).

La Lanterna ITALIAN €€
(☎0789 2 30 82; Via Olbia 13; pizzas €6-16, meals €30-45; ⊙6pm-midnight Thu-Tue) The Lanterna distinguishes itself with its cosy subterranean setting of exposed stone and beams. The menu ranges from pizza to Sardinian dishes such as handmade *gnochetti* sardi and saffron-infused *fregola* with scorpion-fish ragu.

Drinking & Nightlife

The vineyards that ribbon the hillsides on the outskirts of Olbia produce some of the finest Vermentino white wines, as well as a handful of noble reds from the cabernet, Cannonau, merlot and Bovale grapes. The city has some great drinking venues, from wine bars to trendy nightspots with occasional live music. Olbia's cafe life centres on Piazza Margherita and Piazza Matteotti.

★Movida Lounge BAR
(Via Porto Romano 4; ⊙10am-2am) Olbia's coolest new lounge bar draws locals for cocktails, wine, excellent food, DJs and live music. The vast space encompasses three distinct environments: a slick brick- and stone-walled resto-bar, a spacious courtyard under the palm trees out back (complete with sofas and a little AstroTurf terrace) and an underground wine bar in a vaulted cellar dating to the 17th century.

In Vino Veritas WINE BAR
(Corso Umberto 4; ⊙9.30am-midnight) Bottles line the walls at this inviting wine bar. Snag a table to taste Sardinian wines from Vermentinos to Cannonaus, artisanal beers and a tasting plate of local *salumi* and *formaggi*.

KKult BAR
(www.facebook.com/kkultolbia; Corso Umberto 39; ⊙7.30am-2am) This contemporary lounge bar–cafe hybrid has a terrace on Olbia's main drag for watching the world go by over a coffee or cocktail. On weekend nights, the pace picks up with live music and DJs.

Villa Pascià CLUB
(Via Corea 145; ⊙11pm-6am Sat) This glam club attracts a young, upbeat crowd on summer weekends. The pick of local DJs keeps the dance floor rammed, pumping out house, hip-hop and Latin beats. It's a five-minute taxi ride from the centre of town.

Shopping

Corso Umberto is a catwalk to designer labels and stylish Italian fashion. Explore its side streets for arts, crafts and Sardinian specialities.

Disicios FOOD & DRINKS
(☎340 6224234; Via Olbia 42; ⊙8am-9pm) This shop's name translates as 'desires', and you'll understand why once you see its tempting array of Sardinian food and drink. Choose from *pane carasau* (Sardinian flatbread), delectable Sardinian sweets from Oliena laced with almonds and honey, *panadas* (little meat-filled tarts) from Oschiri and a first-rate selection of wine, olive oil and typical Sardinian pastas such as *fregole*.

MUST-TRY GALLURESE DISHES

Zuppa gallurese Layers of bread and cheese drenched in broth and baked to a crispy crust.

Ortidas Fried sea anemones.

Capretto al mirto Roast kid infused with myrtle.

Fregola con cozze e vongole Sardinian granular pasta with mussels and clams.

Mazzafrissa Creamy fried semolina.

OFF THE BEATEN TRACK

TENUTE OLBIOS

Spread across 60 hectares, **Tenute Olbios** estate (☎0789 64 10 03; www.tenuteolbios.com; Via Loiri 83, Località Venafiorita; ⏰8.30am-1pm & 3-6pm Mon-Fri) whisks visitors through the winemaking process in 1½-hour guided tours (€10), which head down to the cellar and conclude with a three-wine tasting below the oak ceiling of the granite-walled tasting room. A slightly longer tour (€15) includes a walk through the vines. For an additional €5 per person, you can sample regional cheeses, *salumi* and antipasti. Tenute Olbios is 7km south of the city centre. Take the SP24 and follow the signs.

The tours are available in Italian and English and advance booking is recommended, though you are free to pop by to buy wine any time.

Besides a stroll among the vines, this is a beautiful area for an afternoon spent in the Gallura countryside, dappled with oak and pear trees, dotted with lakes and ablaze with wildflowers that bloom in spring.

Information

Post Office (Via Acquedotto 5; ⏰8.20am-7.05pm Mon-Fri, to 12.35pm Sat)

Tourist Office (☎0789 5 22 06; www.olbiaturismo.it; Piazza Terranova Pausania; ⏰9am-8pm Apr-Sep, reduced hours Oct-Mar) This helpful tourist office should be your first port of call for info on Olbia.

Unimare (☎0789 2 35 24; www.unimare.it; Viale Principe Umberto 1; ⏰8.30am-12.30pm & 3.30-7.30pm Mon-Fri, 8.30am-noon Sat) A central travel agent where you can book ferries and flights.

Getting There & Away

AIR

Olbia's **Aeroporto di Olbia Costa Smeralda** (☎0789 56 34 44; www.geasar.it) is about 5km southeast of the centre and handles flights from major Italian and European airports. It's the home airport for Meridiana, which flies to two dozen cities. Low-cost operators include Air Berlin, easyJet and Volotea. Destinations served include most mainland Italian airports as well as London, Paris, Madrid, Barcelona, Berlin, Amsterdam and Zurich.

BOAT

Olbia's ferry terminal, Stazione Marittima, is on Isola Bianca, an island connected to the town centre by the 1km Banchina Isola Bianca causeway. All the major ferry companies have counters here, including **Moby Lines** (☎199 30 30 40; www.moby.it), **Grimaldi Lines** (☎0789 183 55 64; www.grimaldi-lines.com) and **Tirrenia** (☎199 30 30 40; www.tirrenia.it). There are frequent services, especially during the summer months, to Civitavecchia, Genoa, Livorno and Piombino.

You can book tickets at any travel agent in town, or directly at the port.

BUS

Azienda Regionale Sarda Trasporti (ARST; ☎0789 5 53 00, 800 865042; www.arst.sardegna.it) buses run from Olbia to destinations across the island. Get tickets from **Bar della Caccia** (Corso Vittorio Veneto 28; ⏰5.30am-8pm Mon-Sat), just opposite the main bus stops on Corso Vittorio Veneto, or from the **self-service machine** (Corso Umberto 166E) behind Olbia's train station. Destinations include Arzachena (€2.50, 45 minutes, 12 daily) and Porto Cervo (€2.50, 1½ hours, five daily). Further afield you can get to Nuoro (€8.10, 2½ hours, eight daily), Santa Teresa di Gallura (€4.30, 1½ hours, seven daily) and Sassari (€8.10, 1½ hours, two daily) via Tempio Pausania (€3.70, 1¼ hours, seven daily). There are fewer connections on Sunday.

Turmo Travel (☎0789 2 14 87; www.grupoturmotravel.com) runs two buses from Olbia to Cagliari (€19, 4½ hours) – an early-morning weekday bus from Piazza Crispi, and a daily afternoon bus from Olbia's port that stops off at Olbia's airport en route. Get tickets at Stazione Marittima or on the bus.

Sun Lines (☎348 2609881, 0789 5 08 85; www.sunlineseliteservice.com) operates buses between Olbia and various destinations on the Costa Smeralda, including Porto Cervo, Baia Sardinia and Cannigione. Buses originate at Olbia's airport, passing through downtown Olbia (Piazza Crispi) and the port on their way north.

CAR & MOTORCYCLE

Car hire is available at the airport, where all the big international outfits are represented, and at the Stazione Marittima ferry terminal. Bank on about €50 per day for a Fiat Punto.

TRAIN

The station is off Corso Umberto. There are direct trains to Cagliari (€18, 3¼ hours, three daily), Oristano (€12.50, 2¼ hours, three daily), Sassari (€8.10, 1¾ hours, four daily) and Golfo Aranci (€2.50, 25 minutes, six daily).

Getting Around

BUS

You're unlikely to need local buses, except for getting to the airport and Stazione Marittima. You can save by buying tickets at tobacconists, some bars or the tourist office; they cost €1/2.80/10 for a single/day/week ticket.

Local buses are run by **ASPO** (☎0789 55 38 00, 800 191847; www.aspoolbia.it). Bus 9 runs every half-hour between Stazione Marittima and the town centre (Via San Simplicio).

CAR & MOTORCYCLE

Driving in Olbia is no fun thanks to a confusing one-way system and almost permanent roadworks. The main strip, Corso Umberto, is closed to traffic between Piazza Margherita and Via San Simplicio. There's limited free parking in a **lot** (cnr Via Nanni & Via Papandrea) just north of the centre and by the port; otherwise, metered parking is available (€0.80 per hour from 9am to 1pm and 4pm to 8pm).

TAXI

You can sometimes find taxis on Corso Umberto near Piazza Margherita. Otherwise call ☎0789 6 91 50.

GOLFO ARANCI

Perched on the northern tip of the Golfo di Olbia, Golfo Aranci is a port, straggling resort and fishing village rolled into one. Most people blaze through without a second glance as it's fairly nondescript on the face of things. It's worth considering as a cheaper alternative to the Costa Smeralda, however, if activities such as diving, speargun fishing and dolphin-spotting rock your boat.

Sights & Activities

There are three sandy white beaches in town – **Spiaggia Prima**, **Seconda** and the best of the three, **Terza** (they're translated to First Beach, Second and Third) – and with your own transport you can easily get to others. The town is also well equipped for families, with a number of public parks and well-maintained playgrounds.

Capo Figari NATURE RESERVE

Rising up behind the port are the craggy heights of Capo Figari (342m), which is now a minor nature reserve. Trails crisscross the *macchia* and lead up to an abandoned lighthouse on the summit, known as *il vecchio semaforo* (old traffic light). It was from here that Guglielmo Marconi sent the first radio signal to the Italian mainland in 1928.

Alpha Diving DIVING

(☎346 3509725; www.alphadiving.it; Piazzetta dei Pescatori 4) Operating out of the port, this European Scuba Agency–accredited diving outfit will set you up for dives around Capo Figari and Tavolara. A single dive will set you back €40, a new-diver course, €290. The centre also arranges boat excursions to Capo Figari (€40) and Isola Tavolara (€80), ecofriendly dolphin-watching excursions (€30), guided snorkelling (€30) and 'mermaiding' (from €35).

Eating

Seafood features heavily in the restaurants lined up around Via della Liberta and Via Colombo. Nearly everywhere closes from November to March.

La Spigola SEAFOOD €€

(☎0789 4 62 86; www.ristorantelaspigola.it; Via Colombo 19; meals €35-40; ⊙noon-10.30pm) Bag a table on the breezy terrace and go straight for the grilled fish and seafood – from a cracking spaghetti with clams to local lobster – at this friendly beachside restaurant with splendid sea views.

Getting There & Away

From Olbia it's a scenic 15-minute drive up the coast to Golfo Aranci.

Between June and September six daily ARST buses link Golfo Aranci with Olbia (€2.50, 25 minutes). Trains (€2.50, 25 minutes) also cover the same route, running six times daily year-round.

Sardinia Ferries (☎0789 4 67 80; www.sardiniaferries.com) operates daily ferries to Golfo Aranci from Livorno (€60 to €90, 6½ to 9½ hours) and less frequent ferries from Nice (€37 to €71, 11 to 16 hours).

SOUTH COAST

The coast reaching south of Olbia is peppered with resorts that heave in summer and slumber in winter. Typical of the type is Porto San Paolo, the main embarkation point for Isola Tavolara and, 11km further south, party-loving San Teodoro.

Porto San Paolo & Isola Tavolara

☎0789 / POP 3400

East of Olbia, the hulking form of Isola Tavolara rears dramatically out of the Tyrrhenian Sea, catching the attention of anyone within a 50km radius. The eastern half of the island is a NATO military facility and therefore off-limits to travellers, but curious souls can ferry across to the pretty beach on the island's western shores, or even climb to Tavolara's 565m summit. Access is by ferry from Porto San Paolo, a small beach town with a few hotels, holiday apartments and restaurants.

Sights & Activities

★Isola Tavolara ISLAND

Rising from the sapphire sea like some kind of giant sea creature, this rocky island is a sight to behold. The main draw is splashing about in the translucent water of the white-sand **Spiaggia Spalmatore**, and admiring the incredible views of Tavolara's heights and mainland Sardinia. You could wander down to the little **cemetery** to see the graves of Tavolara's kings (the title was bestowed by Carlo Alberto in 1848 after a successful goat-hunting trip).

The island – just 5km long and 1km wide – used to be known as the Island of Hermes, perhaps because you need wings to reach the plateau (565m), which is inhabited only by seabirds and falcons, as well as a few nimble-footed wild goats. The few people who live here reside on the western side, at **Spalmatore di Terra**, where the boats land and where there are a couple of beachside snack bars.

Tramontana Escursioni HIKING, CLIMBING

(☎335 8410380; putzu.massimo10@gmail.com; per person €50) For thrilling perspectives on Isola Tavolara, climb to the summit with experienced local guide Massimo Putzu. The rope-assisted climb takes about 2½ hours, with a class-three section near the top. Book seven to 10 days in advance. Massimo leads other trekking and canyoning trips throughout Sardinia, and maintains an excellent English-language blog (http://sardiniaisland.blog) about Sardinia's natural wonders.

Tavolara Diving DIVING

(☎340 8392154, 0789 4 03 60; www.tavoladiving.it; Via Molara 4) Tavolara's craggy coves and crystal-clear waters present some wonderful diving opportunities around the underwater mountain of **Secca del Papa**. If you're interested, reckon on €40 for a single dive and €400 for an open-water diver course.

Isola Molara Boat Excursions BOATING

Make the most of your beach day with an extended cruise (€26) from Tavolara Traghetti. Boats set off at 9am from Porto San Paolo for Isola Molara, where you can swim in the natural pools before proceeding to Isola Tavolara around noon. Take your pick of afternoon ferries (included in tour price) for return to the mainland.

Eating

★Il Portolano ITALIAN €€

(☎0789 4 06 70; www.ristoranteilportolano.it; Via Molara 11; meals €35-45; ⊙noon-2.30pm & 7-10.30pm mid-Apr–Oct) For dreamy sunset views of Isola Tavolara, book ahead at chic waterfront Il Portolano, run by Sardinian-Swiss couple Roberto and Claudia. Creatively prepared Mediterranean seafood is the star attraction, from octopus salad with fresh artichokes and Cabras *bottarga* to homemade lemon pasta with sea bass, almonds and courgette pesto – all beautifully complemented by island wines and tempting desserts such as mandarin-Campari sorbet.

Getting There & Away

Porto San Paolo is an easy 20- to 30-minute drive southeast of Olbia. Upon arrival follow signs for the port.

ARST buses run every 1½ hours between Olbia and Porto San Paolo (€1.90, 30 minutes).

Getting Around

At Easter time and from May through mid-October, **Tavolara Traghetti** (☎349 4465993; www.tavolaratraghetti.it) operates daily ferries from Porto San Paolo to Isola Tavolara. Outward-bound boats leave half-hourly between 9am and 1.30pm, and return trips set off between 1pm and 6.30pm. The return trip (25 minutes each way) costs €16 per person (€8 for kids under 13).

San Teodoro

☎0784 / POP 4930

Fun-loving San Teodoro lives to party in summer, with its glam beach bars and clubs providing an affordable alternative

DON'T MISS

SAN TEODORO BEACHES

San Teodoro has some truly glorious beaches, many of which can easily compete with the Costa Smeralda in the beauty stakes. Central **Cala d'Ambra** is pretty, but more striking still is **Spiaggia La Cinta**, 2km to the north, a ribbon of frosty-white sand strung between the topaz sea and the Stagno San Teodoro. It's a popular sports beach, particularly for kitesurfing. Or take your beach towel 9km further north to the stunning crescent-shaped bays of **Lu Impostu** or 1km further on to 'Little Tahiti' **Cala Brandinchi**, separated by a wooded spit of land. Commanding fine views of the limestone hump of Isola Tavolara, **Capo Coda Cavallo**, 13km north of San Teodoro, is a marine reserve and its transparent waters bubble with snorkellers and divers.

to the megabucks Costa Smeralda. The model resort is perfect, almost to the point of being characterless, but its pristine white-sand beaches are glorious. Water sports and boat excursions race you out to sea, while back on dry land, trekking, mountain biking and horse riding entice you from the beach towel.

Sights & Activities

Stagno San Teodoro NATURE RESERVE

Nestled amid fragrant *macchia* and wind-eroded granite formations, and backing onto La Cinta beach, this lagoon attracts ramblers and birdwatchers. Keep an eye out for bird life including pink flamingos, herons, cormorants, little egrets and kingfishers.

Wet Dreams WATER SPORTS

(☎347 9409356, 0784 85 20 15; www.wetdreams.it; Via Sardegna; ⏲9am-1pm & 4.30-8pm mid-Feb–Dec) Run by congenial local surfer Emerico Pala, this surf shop offers three-hour introductory kitesurfing sessions for €210. Private instruction starts at €80/100 per hour with/without your own equipment.

Dive Aquarius DIVING

(☎0784 83 41 24; www.diveaquarius.net; Località Capo Coda Cavallo, Villaggio Le Farfalle; dives from €45) If you fancy taking the plunge in the gin-clear waters of the Tavolara marine park, this place near Capo Coda Cavallo is a safe bet. It offers single dives, night dives, wreck dives, plus the whole shebang of PADI courses.

Maneggio La Cinta HORSE RIDING

(☎0784 85 10 07, 338 8228984; www.maneggiolacintasanteodoro.it; Località La Cinta; 👪) Saddle up here for a scenic 1½-hour hack (€35) along La Cinta beach. Pony rides for kids are also available.

Festivals & Events

Extreme Fun Games SPORTS

(www.extremefungames.com; ⏲Sep) San Teodoro embraces its role as a beach-sports capital with this late summer blowout. An international crowd convenes for four days of kitesurfing, windsurfing and stand-up paddleboarding competitions, interspersed with nightly beach parties and DJ contests.

Eating

There's no shortage of eateries in San Teodoro – options include everything from bars and restaurants in the town centre to beachside pizzerias through to *agriturismi* in the surrounding countryside. Bear in mind that nearly everywhere closes from mid-October to March.

Da Fabio PIZZA €

(☎0784 86 55 87; cnr Via Platani & Via Pes; pizzas €6-12; ⏲noon-2.30pm & 7-11.30pm) Bask in the scent of jasmine on the sweet back patio at this Neapolitan-owned pizzeria smack in the heart of town. The real-deal wood-oven pizzas come laden with DOP San Marzano tomatoes, Fior di Latte mozzarella and Sardinian seafood.

★**Li Mori** SARDINIAN €€

(☎348 8607678, 0784 85 10 00; www.agriturismolimori.it; Località Li Mori; meals incl drinks €35; ⏲8-11pm) A genuine slice of rustic island life, Li Mori dishes up a generous spread of Sardinian dishes in a convivial farm setting. Loosen a belt notch for specialities such as *malloreddus al sugo di cingiahle* (semolina pasta with wild boar sauce), ravioli, suckling pig roasted to crackling perfection and local *dolci* (sweets) – all washed down with free-flowing wine.

Bal Harbour INTERNATIONAL €€
(☎0784 85 10 52; www.balharbour.it; Via Stintino; meals €30-40; ⊙noon-midnight) This super-trendy beachside lounge-restaurant attracts gym-fit guys and girls, who come to pose by the palm-fringed pool by day and sip mojitos to DJ beats by night. The food is surprisingly good, whether you go for a sizzling steak from the Brazilian grill, a platter of sushi, or Italian dishes such as seafood risotto.

La Taverna degli Artisti ITALIAN €€
(☎0784 86 60 60; Via del Tirreno 17; pizzas €5-9, meals €30-40; ⊙noon-3pm & 7-11pm) Proximity to the waterfront is the main drawcard at this sprawling place out by La Cinta beach. The menu ranges from garlicky mussels to salt-crusted sea bass to handmade tagliatelle with scampi and pesto. There's also pizza to take away.

Drinking & Nightlife

San Teodoro is the south coast's party central, its lounge bars and clubs attracting the young, bronzed and beautiful in summer from June to September.

Luna Glam Club CLUB
(www.lalunadisco.it; Località Stirritoggiu; ⊙midnight-5.30am) Dress to impress the eagle-eyed bouncers and fit in with the glossy 30-plus crowd at this uber-trendy club. It rules its own small hilltop just south of town, off the exit road from the SS125.

L'Ambra Night CLUB
(www.ambranight.it; Via Cala d'Ambra; ⊙midnight-6am) Down by the beach, opposite Hotel L'Esagono, this club with an outdoor dance floor rocks to a mainly commercial beat. It occasionally welcomes DJ royalty to the decks.

Buddha del Mar BAR
(www.facebook.com/buddhasanteodoro; Via Toscana 1; ⊙5pm-2am) Summer evenings at this Asian-inspired lounge in the town centre can resemble an MTV beach party, with the fun fuelled by dancing, cocktails and good vibes.

Information

Tourist Office (☎0784 86 57 67; www.santeodoroturismo.it; Piazza Mediterraneo 1; ⊙9am-midnight daily summer, 9am-1pm & 4-7pm Mon-Sat winter) The efficient tourist office can provide information on local operators and tour guides.

Getting There & Away

ARST buses make the run up the coast to Olbia (€3.10, 45 minutes, six daily, up to nine on weekdays) and inland to Nuoro (€6.10, one hour 50 minutes, five daily). **Deplano** (☎0784 29 50 30; www.deplanobus.it) also runs five daily buses to/from Olbia airport (€2.50, 30 minutes) and Nuoro (€6.10, 1¼ hours).

COSTA SMERALDA & AROUND

Back in 1962, flamboyant millionaire Karim Aga Khan established a consortium to buy a strip of unspoiled coastline in northeastern Sardinia. Each investor paid roughly US$25,000 for a little piece of paradise, and the coast was christened Costa Smeralda (Emerald Coast) for its brilliant green-blue waters.

These days billionaire jet-setters cruise into Costa Smeralda's marinas in mega-yachts like floating mansions, and models, royals, Russian oligarchs and balding media moguls come to frolic in its waters.

Starting at the Golfo di Cugnana, 17km north of Olbia, the Costa stretches 55km northwards to the Golfo di Arzachena. The 'capital' is the yachtie haven of Porto Cervo, although Porto Rotondo, a second marina developed in 1963, attracts plenty of paparazzi with its Silvio Berlusconi connections and its attractive seafront promenade.

Inland from the Costa Smeralda, the mountain communities of San Pantaleo and Arzachena offer a low-key counterpoint to the coastline's glitz and glamour.

Porto Cervo

☎0789 / POP 420

Porto Cervo is a curious, artificial vision of Mediterranean beauty. The utopian village combines Greek, North African, Spanish and Italian architectural elements, and the overall effect is pseudo-Moorish with a touch of the Flintstones. Apart from the magnificent coastal scenery that surrounds it, there's nothing remotely Sardinian about Porto Cervo. Instead, it resembles exactly what it is: a purpose-built leisure centre for the super-rich – a kind of Disneyland for Gucci-clad grown-ups.

DON'T MISS

BEACHES SOUTH OF PORTO CERVO

Spiaggia del Grande & Piccolo Pevero This twinset of stunning bays, 3km south of Porto Cervo, fulfil the Sardinian paradise dream with their floury sands and dazzlingly blue, shallow water. There's a small beach bar, too.

Spiaggia Capriccioli Dotted with granite boulders and backed by fragrant *macchia*, this gorgeous half-moon bay has water that goes through the entire spectrum of blues and is shallow enough for tots. Umbrellas and sunbeds are available to rent.

Spiaggia del Principe Also known as Portu Li Coggi, this magnificent crescent of white sand is bound by unspoiled *macchia* and startlingly clear blue waters. Apparently it's the Aga Khan's favourite. It's around 2.5km northeast of Capriccioli.

Spiaggia Romazzino Less busy than some, this curving sandy bay has remarkably clear water and is named after the rosemary bushes that grow in such abundance. Look beyond the main bay to smaller coves for more seclusion.

Spiaggia Liscia Ruia Though busy in peak season, this beach is a beauty – a long arc of pale, fine sand and crystal-clear water. It's close to the neo-Moorish fantasy that is Hotel Cala di Volpe.

Sights

As nearly everyone in Porto Cervo has a boat (it has the best marine facilities on the island), most of the action takes place elsewhere during the day, in the paradisiacal inlets and on the silky beaches. Things begin to heat up in the early evening when the playboys and girls come out to browse the boutiques and pose in the piazzas.

Piazzetta PIAZZA

The place to be seen is the Piazzetta, a small square at the centre of a web of discreet shopping alleys. From the piazza, stairs lead to the Sottopiazza and La Passeggiata, both lined with fancy boutiques – Cartier, Gucci, Versace, Prada, Valentino, Moschino – you name it, they're all here.

Chiesa di Stella Maris CHURCH

(Piazza Stella Maris; 8.30am-8pm) Perched above Porto Cervo is Michele Busiri Vici's surreal white church with a funnel-shaped bell tower. The church hosts classical-music concerts in the summer. Unsurprisingly it's also done rather well in the donations department, receiving El Greco's impressive *Mater Dolorosa* as a Dutch aristocrat's bequest.

Louise Alexander Gallery GALLERY

(www.louise-alexander.com; Via del Porto Vecchio 1; 10am-1pm & 5pm-midnight Jun-Sep) Visit this gallery for temporary exhibitions showcasing works by contemporary artists, such as a recent one featuring Israeli sculptor Arik Levy. The gallery also sells modern art, so if you're in the market for a Warhol or Lichtenstein, drop it a line.

Eating

Porto Cervo's best restaurants are a quick drive or taxi hop out of town.

La Briciola MODERN ITALIAN €€

(0789 9 14 09; Liscia di Vacca; pizzas €6-14, meals €35-45; 12.30-2.15pm & 7.30-11pm;) You know you've struck gold when you find a restaurant frequented by locals in a purpose-built resort. With its garden terrace, pleasant service and spot-on pizzas, La Briciola gets it just right. Besides pizza, it does a fine line in pasta (for instance with *bottarga* and sea urchin), risotti and grilled fish.

Hivaoa MEDITERRANEAN €€

(0789 9 14 51; www.ristorantehivaoa.com; Via Della Marina Nuova; pizzas €8-14, fixed-price menus €15-22, meals €25-35; noon-midnight;) Fine dining it is not, but if you're seeking a cheerful, affordable, family-friendly place with decent food, Hivaoa hits the mark every time. Go for wood-oven pizza, good-value tourist menus or à la carte steaks, seafood and pasta dishes.

★**I Frati Rossi** ITALIAN €€€

(0789 9 43 95; www.fratirossi.it; Località Pantogia; meals €50-75; 7-10pm Mon, 12.30-2pm & 7-10pm Tue-Sun Jan-Oct) This rustic-chic restaurant has broad sea views from its hilltop perch, 3.5km south of Porto Cervo. Local ingredients shine in beautifully cooked and presented dishes such as black tagliatelle with squid and ripe cherry tomatoes. The fish and shellfish platters are astoundingly fresh. Follow the signs up a narrow country lane off the SP59.

Spinnaker MODERN ITALIAN **€€€**
(☎0789 9 12 26; www.ristorantespinnaker.com; Liscia di Vacca; meals €40-55; ⏲12.30-2.30pm & 7.30-10pm daily Jun-Sep, closed Wed Apr, May & Oct) This fashionable restaurant buzzes with a good-looking crowd, who come for the stylish ambience and fabulous seafood. Pair dishes such as calamari with fresh artichokes or rock lobster with a local Vermentino white. The restaurant is on the road between Porto Cervo and Baia Sardinia.

Drinking & Nightlife

Porto Cervo's nightlife is strictly a summer-only scene. People-watching is one of the few affordable options, although the moment you sit down at a bar on the Piazzetta you'll be looking at around €10 for a drink. To get in on the real clubbing action, however, dress to impress and head a couple of kilometres south of town.

Aqua Lounge LOUNGE
(☎0789 183 20 33; www.aqualounge.it; Piazza Azzurra; ⏲10.30am-2am May-Sep) Overlooking the marina, this swanky lounge bar is the place to celeb-watch and play spot the yacht over a cocktail or light bite to eat. Mellow DJ beats and sofa-filled nooks keep the mood relaxed.

Lord Nelson PUB
(Porto Cervo Marina; ⏲7am-3am) Strangely for such a swish resort, one of the favourite drinking hang-outs is this nautically themed English-style pub.

Billionaire CLUB
(www.billionairelife.com/portocervo; Via Rocce sul Pevero; ⏲11pm-5am) Launched two decades ago by former Formula One boss Flavio Briatore, this glitzy club in a three-story villa lures star DJs and a who's who of the absurdly rich and famous to its dance floor every summer. It can be difficult to get in unless you happen to know someone or book dinner at the swanky restaurant.

Sottovento CLUB
(www.sottoventoclub.it; Località Sottovento; ⏲midnight-5am) Bono, Craig David and Denzel Washington have all been spotted at this exclusive club. Getting in is no party and depends entirely on the whim of the stony-faced bouncers.

Getting There & Away

ARST has up to five daily bus connections between Porto Cervo and Olbia (€2.50, one to 1½ hours).

Between June and September, **Sun Lines** (☎348 2609881, 0789 5 08 85; www.sunlineseliteservice.com) buses run from Olbia airport to the Costa Smeralda, stopping at Porto Cervo and various other points along the coast. Tickets cost between €3 and €4.

Poltu Quatu

One of the Costa Smeralda's most exclusive destinations, Poltu Quatu sits astride a fjordlike inlet flanked by rugged granite cliffs. With its jumble of whitewashed, terracotta-roofed villas centred on a picture-perfect marina, the town is easier on the eye than many nearby resorts. Shopping in the boutiques and galleries, dining al fresco and soaking up the views are the main activities.

Activities

Orso Diving DIVING
(☎0789 9 90 01; www.orsodiving.com; ⏲Apr-Oct) Head to this harbourside outfit to dive in the marine parks of La Maddalena and Tavolara (single dives from €45), snorkel in the fish-filled waters around Isola Caprera (€45) or embark on an ecofriendly dolphin-watching (€45) or whale-watching (€120) excursion. The centre also offers the whole shebang of PADI courses.

Eating

Aruanã Churrascaria BRAZILIAN **€€**
(☎0789 90 60 85; www.aruana.it; Via Degli Oleandri; buffet €40; ⏲8pm-1am) With romantically lit tables set amid garden terraces that cascade down from a boulder-strewn hillside, this Brazilian steakhouse offers that rare combination of classy setting and top-notch food. Relocated to Poltu Quatu in 2017, Aruanã specialises in Brazilian-style grilled meats. Serve yourself at will from the all-you-can-eat buffet; drinks cost extra.

Getting There & Away

Poltu Quatu is 4km west of Porto Cervo via the SP59. ARST runs a few daily buses along this route (€1.30, five minutes).

Baia Sardinia

0789 / POP 160

Follow the meandering main road 3km west of Poltu Quatu and you reach Baia Sardinia, just outside the Costa Smeralda but for all intents and purposes a Costa resort like its more famous neighbours.

Activities

Cala Battistoni BEACH

Baia Sardinia's major draw is this beach, a fine sweep of pale sand massaged by translucent waters.

Aquadream WATER PARK

(www.aquadream.it; Località La Crucitta; adult/child €20/15; 10.30am-6pm mid-Jun–early Sep) A sure-fire winner with the kids, Aquadream has hair-raising slides, flumes and pools to keep children entertained all day.

Eating

In the town centre, just above Cala Battistoni, a slew of restaurants and bars caters to the beach-going crowds. Most places close from November to Easter.

News Café CAFE €

(Piazza Centrale; 8am-2am) In the seafront arcade, this cafe is a popular meeting point and good for a quick bruschetta at lunchtime and live music and drinks by night.

Casablanca ITALIAN €€

(339 2940837; www.ristorante-casablanca.it; Piazzetta Principale; meals €30-40; noon-2.30pm & 7-11pm) With a name like Casablanca, you wouldn't expect this restaurant to be any less than romantic. And with candlelit tables and dreamy views out to sea and La Maddalena, it doesn't disappoint. The chef places the accent on freshness and flavour – from salads through to pasta, fish and steaks. Get here for sunset.

Ristorante La Rocca SARDINIAN €€

(0789 93 30 11; www.ristorante-larocca.com; Loc Pulicinu; 12.30-2.30pm & 7pm-midnight) With black-clad waiters and impeccably fresh seafood ('choose any shellfish living in the aquarium'), La Rocca offers dependable quality with a resolutely old-school vibe. It's the kind of place where you'll find Sardinian families lingering over a long lunch or celebratory dinner. Look for it southwest of town along the main road towards Cannigione.

Drinking & Nightlife

Phi Beach BAR, CLUB

(www.phibeach.com; Via Forte Cappellini; 1pm-midnight) One of the coast's hottest venues, this is a great place to hang out and watch the sunset. By day it's a regular bathing club with sunloungers and umbrellas to hire, but as the sun goes down it transforms into a cool lounge bar and restaurant. All the while DJs spin chilled sounds in the background.

Ritual CLUB

(www.ritual.it; Località La Crucitta; 11.30pm-5.30am Tue-Sat, to 4.30am Sun & Mon) Just out of town on the road for Porto Cervo, this club is an old favourite. Even if you're not going to dance it's worth a look for the sexy cavernous interior gouged out of the rock side.

Getting There & Away

If you've got your own vehicle, Baia Sardinia is a scenic 10-minute (7km) drive along the SP59 west of Porto Cervo. **Sun Lines** (p151) operates buses from Baia Sardinia to Olbia, while **Caramelli** (079 67 06 13; www.caramellitours.it) heads north to Palau. Both companies offer service to Porto Cervo.

Cannigione

Some 12km southwest of Baia Sardinia, Cannigione sits on the western side of the Golfo di Arzachena, the largest *ria* (inlet) along this coast. Originally a fishing village established in 1800 to supply the Maddalena islands with food, it grew bigger when coal and cattle ships began to dock at its harbour in the 1900s, and it's now a prosperous and reasonably priced resort.

You'll find the best beaches north of Cannigione, including **Tanca Manna**, a good bet for families, with its soft sand and shallow water.

Activities

Consorzio del Golfo BOATING

(335 7742392, 0789 8 84 18; www.consorziodelgolfo.it; adult/child incl lunch €45/25) Down at the port, Consorzio del Golfo is one of several operators offering excursions to the Arcipelago di La Maddalena. Boats leave at 9.15am and return around 5pm.

Areamare DIVING

(338 8221135; www.areamare.com; Via Vespucci 52) Dive instructor Marco will take you to

WORTH A TRIP

CANTINE SURRAU

Cantine Surrau (☎0789 8 29 33; www.vignesurrau.it; Località Chilvagghja; ⏲10am-10pm May-Sep, to 9pm Apr & Oct, to 8pm Nov-Mar) Cantine Surrau takes a holistic approach to winemaking. Take a spin of the cellar and the gallery showcasing Sardinian art before tasting some of the region's crispest Vermentino white and beefiest Cannonau red wines.

The standard tasting (€25) gets you three different wines served with *pane carasau* (Sardinian flatbread), cheese, *salumi* (cured meats) and olives, while the €35 tasting consists of five wines, local cheese, salami, *bottarga* (mullet roe) and Sardinian sweets. Find the winery on the road between Arzachena and Porto Cervo.

some of the most beautiful spots around the Arcipelago di La Maddalena. A two-tank dive will set you back €80, six dives cost around €240 and an Open Water Diver course, €550. Discounts are available for advance online bookings.

Anthias DIVING
(☎0789 8 63 11, 345 4512689; www.facebook.com/anthias.diving; Villaggio Camping Golfo di Arzachena) This PADI dive centre offers snorkelling and diving excursions (from €50 each) along with a full range of courses, from the basic Discover Scuba (€125) to full-on Dive Master certification (€695).

Eating

★Agriturismo La Colti AGRITURISMO €€
(☎0789.8 84 40, 333 1437599; www.lacolti.it; Strada Arzachena–Cannigione; meals €35) Calling all carnivores (or anyone seeking a break from seafood)!: skip lunch and save your appetite for a full-on Sardinian feast at this rustic farmstead 2km outside Cannigione. The endless parade of courses begins with bread, cheese, olives and homemade *salumi,* followed by soup, salad and copious amounts of roast-ed-to-perfection meats, finished off with glasses of homemade *mirto* or *limoncino.*

Ristorante Acqua Marina SEAFOOD €€
(☎335 6634646; Via Lungomare; meals €35-45; ⏲noon-2.30pm & 7.30-10.30pm) Freshly caught seafood makes the short journey from the Gulf of Cannigione to your plate at this atmospheric floating restaurant on a boat moored in Cannigione's harbour. Opened in 2017, it's a spin-off from long-time local favourite Lu Jaddu and a perfect spot for a romantic dinner, with lights twinkling on the water and a good selection of Sardinian wines.

Information

Tourist Office (☎0789 8 85 10; www.cannigione.org; Via Nazionale 47; ⏲9.30am-12.30pm Apr–mid-Oct, plus 5.30-7.30pm Jun–mid-Sep) This helpful tourist office has bags of information on Cannigione and the surrounding area.

Getting There & Away

Cannigione is a 35-minute drive north of Olbia via the SS125. Regular ARST buses make the run to Olbia (€2.50, one hour), Arzachena (€1.30, 10 minutes), Baia Sardinia (€1.90, 20 minutes) and Porto Cervo (€1.90, 30 minutes).

Arzachena

☎0789 / POP 13,560

Tucked into rocky countryside a few kilometres inland from the Costa Smeralda, Arzachena is surrounded by pretty scenery and some interesting archaeological sites. The town itself is a rather workaday place, but with the Mediterranean's most exclusive resorts an easy drive away, and with some delightful rural accommodations just outside town, it has morphed from a humble shepherds' village in the 1960s to something of a tourist centre.

Sights

Most people use Arzachena as a base for exploring the Costa Smeralda, but if you want to hang around, action is focused on **Piazza del Risorgimento**, a small piazza with a couple of cafes and a stone church, the **Chiesa di Santa Maria delle Neve**. A short stroll away is the bizarre **Roccia Il Fungo Mont'Incappiddatu**, a mushroom-shaped granite rock at the end of Via Limbara. Archaeologists believe the overarching rock may have been used as a shelter for neolithic tribespeople as long ago as 3500 BC.

DON'T MISS

ARZACHENA'S NURAGHIC SITES

The mysterious countryside around Arzachena is littered with *nuraghi* and *tombe dei giganti* ('giants' tombs'; ancient mass graves). Most sites are open from 9am to 7pm daily from Easter to October and by request in winter. Entry costs €3 to €3.50 for a single site, or you can purchase a multi-site ticket (two/three/four/five/six sites €6/8.50/11/13.50/16). Free handouts in English, German, Spanish and French are available at all sites, as are guided tours with advance notice.

La Prisgiona (€3.50; 9am-7pm) Covering an area of several square kilometres, the partially excavated nuraghic ruins of La Prisgiona are among the most extensive in northeastern Sardinia. At the centre of the site are a main keep and two side towers, flanked by a 7m-deep well and the remains of a village containing the foundations of several dozen stone huts. To get here, drive 1km or walk the scenic nature trail from nearby Coddu Ecchju.

Tempio di Malchittu (€3; 9am-7pm) Accessible via a 2km track from the Nuraghe di Albucciu ticket office, this temple dating back to 1500 BC is one of a few of its kind in Sardinia. Experts can only guess at its original purpose, but it appears it had a timber roof and was closed with a wooden door. Just as engaging as the ruins is the trail to get here, which affords lovely views over the surrounding countryside, strewn with granite boulders.

Coddu Ecchju (€3; 9am-7pm) Taking the Arzachena–Luogosanto road south, you can follow signs to one of the most important *tombe dei giganti* in Sardinia. The most visible part of it is the oval-shaped central stele (standing stone). Both slabs of granite, one balanced on top of the other, show an engraved frame that apparently symbolises a door to the hereafter, closed to the living. On either side of the stele stand further tall slabs of granite that form a kind of semicircular guard of honour around the tomb.

Li Muri (€3; variable) This necropolis is a curious site made up of four interlocking megalithic burial grounds, possibly dating to 3500 BC. Archaeologists believe that VIPs were buried in the rectangular stone tombs. At the rim of each circle was a menhir or betyl, an erect stone upon which a divinity may have been represented.

To reach Li Muri, turn left (west) for Luogosanto on the Arzachena–Luogosanto road. After about 3km turn right and follow the signs to Li Muri along a dirt track.

This site keeps less dependable hours than others in the area; inquire about its current status at the Nuraghe di Albucciu ticket office in Arzachena.

Li Lolghi (€3; 11am-5pm) This *tomba di gigante* is quite striking. The central east-facing stele, part of which was snapped off and later restored, dominates the surrounding countryside from its hilltop location. To reach it, take the SS427 towards Calangianus, turn right after around 3km, then follow the signs.

Nuraghe di Albucciu (€3; 9am-7pm) This is the nearest *nuraghe* to town, and certainly the easiest to find, on the main Olbia road, about 3km south of Arzachena. It's unusual for several reasons, not least for its flat granite roof instead of the usual *tholos* (conical shape) and its warren of what appear to be emergency escape routes.

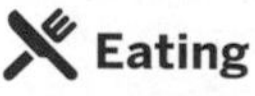

Eating

La Terrazza ITALIAN €
(0789 8 25 75; www.laterrazzaristorantepizzeria.it; Viale Costa Smeralda; pizzas €6-8, meals around €30; 12.15-2.30pm & 7.15-11pm Tue-Sun) Wood-fired pizza and cracking seafood are the hallmarks of this popular eatery. Locals come here to grab a bite to eat and chat with the *pizzaiolo* (pizza-maker) while out-of-towners sit down to huge helpings of fresh fish and grilled meat.

Jaddhu SARDINIAN €€
(0789 8 06 99; Località Capichera; meals €35-45; noon-3pm & 7-11pm Apr-Oct) Hidden in granite mountains, this *stazzu* (Gallurese stone-built country house) has a delightful garden terrace where you can settle in for a full-blown Sardinian feast, from *zuppa cuata* (bread and cheese soup) to swordfish with almonds and candied lime to spot-on *porceddu* (spit-roasted suckling pig) with rosemary potatoes.

The restaurant is part of the Jaddhu Country Resort, situated 5.5km off the SS427 south of Arzachena.

Getting There & Away

Arzachena has good bus connections. ARST services run to/from Olbia (€2.50, 45 minutes, 12 daily), Santa Teresa di Gallura (€3.10, one hour, five daily) and Palau (€1.90, 25 minutes, five daily). Regular buses also link with the Costa Smeralda resorts, namely Porto Cervo and Baia Sardinia.

Between mid-June and mid-September you can pick up the **trenino verde** (p268) to Tempio Pausania (€12, 1½ hours, one daily Monday to Saturday).

San Pantaleo

Although only about 16km from Porto Cervo, the rural village of San Pantaleo provides a welcome dose of authenticity after the sterile resorts on the coast.

The village sits high up behind the coast, surrounded by gap-toothed granite peaks, and has become something of an artists' haven, speckled with little galleries and craft shops. It is also one of the few Sardinian villages set around a piazza, with a sturdy little church at one end. In summer you'll often find a bustling Thursday market here, and in spring the blossoms make it more photogenic than ever. Year-round, it's an attractive place for an aimless amble.

Between 27 July and 30 July San Pantaleo holds its annual knees-up, a weekend of general jollity with traditional Sardinian dancing.

Eating & Drinking

Zara Cafe SARDINIAN €€

(Trattoria da Nicolino; ☎339 8852981; Via Zara 59; meals around €30; ⊙7.30pm-midnight) Abuzz with a steady mix of locals and tourists, this village-centre trattoria knows its way around all the Sardinian classics, from *guazzetto di cozze* (mussels stewed in a tomatoey broth) to *seadas* (fried dough stuffed with cheese and drizzled with honey) for dessert.

Caffè Nina CAFE

(Piazza della Chiesa; ⊙7.30am-2am) Grab a pew in Caffè Nina's cosy, stone-walled interior, or opt for the sprawling front terrace facing San Pantaleo's church square; either way, it's the perfect spot for morning cappuccino or an *aperitivo*-hour glass of Vermentino with *pecorino* and olives.

Getting There & Away

With your own vehicle, the 21km drive from Olbia to San Pantaleo takes about 25 minutes via the SS125 and SP73. ARST runs five daily buses to San Pantaleo from Olbia (€1.90, 30 minutes) and Arzachena (€1.90, 15 minutes).

NORTHERN GALLURA COAST

The northern Gallura coast is home to some of Sardinia's most gorgeous seascapes. From

OFF THE BEATEN TRACK

LAGO DI LISCIA & AROUND

From Arzachena, the SP427 heads inland into the undeveloped and utterly transfixing heart of Gallura. The road bobs and weaves through lush green fields and wood-crested hills as it twists its way up to the agricultural town of **Sant'Antonio di Gallura** en route to **Lago di Liscia**, one of Sardinia's unspoiled secrets. An 8km-long artificial lake, and the main source of water for Gallura's east coast, it is set beautifully amid granite-scarred hills and woods of billowing cork and oak trees.

The best place to admire this captivating landscape is at a picnic spot near the tiny off-the-beaten-track nature reserve known as **Olivastri Millenari di Santo Baltolu** (admission €2.50). The *olivastri* are a group of wild olive trees that have been growing for thousands of years. Scientists from the University of Sassari have calculated that the biggest, measuring 20m in circumference and reaching a height of 14.5m, is about 3800 years old. Certainly, it's quite a specimen, its gnarled and twisted trunk writhing upwards like something out of *Lord of the Rings*. To get to the site from Sant'Antonio di Gallura, follow the road for Luras and Tempio Pausania then take the turning marked *'olivastri millenari'*. After a further 10km or so, there's a short, steep dirt track up to the left – the *olivastri* are at the top.

the port town of Palau, ferries and small tour boats cross over to the Arcipelago di La Maddalena, a world of dreamy turquoise waters studded with islands and ringed by secluded beaches. Continuing north and west of Palau, the wind-whipped coast rises and falls like a rocky sculpture, culminating in the lunar-like headland of Capo Testa. Fine beaches stretch out towards Vignola in the west and sunny Santa Teresa di Gallura, the fashionable heart of the north coast's summer scene, in the east. The windy waters are a magnet for windsurfers and kitesurfers; competitions are often held here, some of which dash across the windy straits to Bonifacio in Corsica.

Santa Teresa di Gallura

0789 / POP 5230

Bright and breezy Santa Teresa di Gallura occupies a prime seafront position on Gallura's north coast. The resort gets extremely busy during high season, yet somehow manages to retain a distinct local character, making it an agreeable alternative to the more soulless resorts on the Costa Smeralda.

The town was established by Savoy rulers in 1808 to help combat smugglers, but the modern town grew up as a result of the tourism boom since the early 1960s. Santa Teresa's history is caught up with Corsica as much as it is with Sardinia. Over the centuries plenty of Corsicans have settled here, and the local dialect is similar to that of southern Corsica.

Sights

When they're not on the beach, most people hang out in the town centre, lounging on the cafe-lined piazza and admiring the pastel-coloured houses. Otherwise you can wander up to the 16th-century Torre di Longonsardo, which overlooks a natural deep port on one side and the entrance to the town's idyllic (but crowded) Spiaggia Rena Bianca on the other. If you tire of the beach, head down to the **Porto Turistico**, a small enclave of whitewashed villas set around a cloistered courtyard and crowded marina.

Spiaggia Rena Bianca BEACH
The 'just like the Caribbean' comments come thick and fast when it comes to this bay – a glorious sweep of pale sand lapped by shallow, crystal-clear aquamarine water. From the eastern tip, a trail threads along the coastline past granite boulders and formations that fire the imagination with their incredible shapes.

Torre di Longonsardo TOWER
(€2; 10am-1pm & 4-8pm Jun-Sep) The 16th-century Torre di Longonsardo is in a magnificent position, overlooking the natural deep port on one side and the entrance to the town's idyllic (but crowded) Spiaggia Rena Bianca on the other.

Activities

★Capo Testa WALKING, SWIMMING
Four kilometres west of Santa Teresa, this extraordinary lighthouse-topped headland resembles a vast sculptural garden. Giant boulders lie strewn about the grassy slopes, their weird and wonderful forms the result of centuries of wind erosion. The Romans quarried granite (p164) here, as did the Pisans centuries later.

A couple of beaches lie to either side of the narrow isthmus that leads out to the headland: **Rena di Levante** and **Rena di Ponente**, where you can rent surfing gear, beach umbrellas and sunloungers.

Follow Via Capo Testa west of town and it's around an hour's hike to the cape. The walk itself is stunning, passing through boulder-strewn scrub and affording magnificent views of rock formations, rocky coves and the cobalt Mediterranean. You can stop en route for a swim and to admire the views of not-so-distant Corsica.

Consorzio delle Bocche BOATING
(0789 75 51 12; www.consorziobocche.com; Piazza Vittorio Emanuele; 9am-1pm & 5pm-7.30pm May, Jun & Sep, to 12.30am Jul & Aug) This outfit runs various excursions, including trips to the Maddalena islands and down the Costa Smeralda (summer only). These cost around €45/25 per adult/child and include lunch (excluding drinks).

Blu Dive Center DIVING
(338 6808576, 328 7173499; www.bludivecenter.com; Via Nazionale 73; 8am-9pm summer) This professional and super-friendly dive centre offers two-tank dives, wreck dives and snorkelling excursions, as well as the whole shebang of PADI courses – from Discover Scuba Diving to Divemaster. You'll be taken to the gorgeously clear waters around La Maddalena marine park, Capo Testa and off the coast of Corsica.

Santa Teresa di Gallura

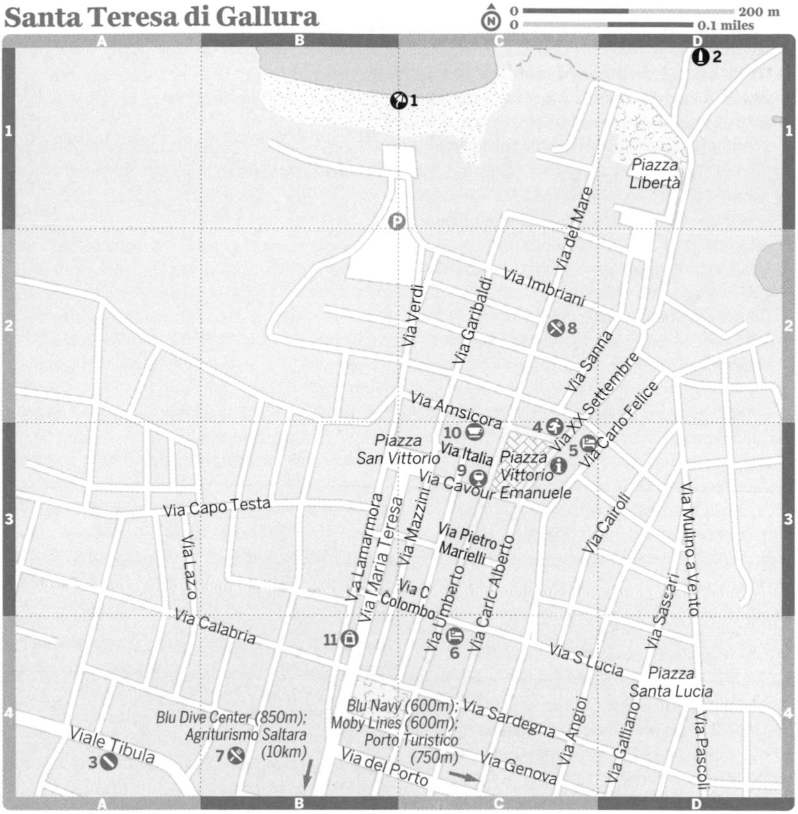

Centro Sub Marina di Longone DIVING
(☎338 6270054; www.marinadilongone.it; Viale Tibula 11; ⏰9am-7pm) For an adventure in the deep blue, check out the offerings at this PADI-accredited dive centre. Single dives start at €40 and a 'sea baptism' discovery course costs €70.

Eating

Restaurants and pizzerias are sprinkled throughout the town centre, from Via Eleonora d'Arborea north to the port. There's another cluster down by the Porto Turistico. Most open daily in summer and then close completely in winter.

Il Grottino MEDITERRANEAN €€
(☎0789 75 42 32; Via del Mare 14; pizzas €5-14, meals €35-45; ⏰noon-3pm & 7-11.30pm summer) Il Grottino sets a rustic picture with bare, grey stone walls and warm, low lighting. In keeping with the look, the food is

Santa Teresa di Gallura

Sights
1 Spiaggia Rena Bianca C1
2 Torre di Longonsardo D1

Activities, Courses & Tours
3 Centro Sub Marina di Longone A4
4 Consorzio delle Bocche C3

Sleeping
5 B&B Domus de Janas C3
6 Hotel Moderno C4

Eating
7 Da Thomas B4
8 Il Grottino C2

Drinking & Nightlife
9 Bar Central 80 .... C3
10 Caffè Mediterraneo C3

Shopping
11 Mascheras B4

OFF THE BEATEN TRACK

THE ANCIENT QUARRIES OF CAPO TESTA

These days Gallura's fame revolves around its splendid beaches, but centuries ago the region was just as famous for its quarries, which yielded granite for some of Italy's greatest monuments.

For a fascinating glimpse of this lesser-known past, head to Zia Columba beach, 4km west of Santa Teresa, at the foot of Capo Testa. Shortly after the main road crosses the isthmus onto Capo Testa, look for Tampanama Market Bar on your left and descend to the beach directly opposite. A five-minute walk north along the sand brings you to a lone granite column standing upright at the water's edge – you've just discovered the remnants of what was once a thriving Roman quarry. The ancient Romans valued the granite here for two reasons: first, the massive size of the local deposits allowed colossal columns to be carved from a single block of stone; second, the proximity of the quarry to the Strait of Bonifacio allowed columns to be easily loaded onto ships bound for Rome.

Continue walking northwest along the beach here, and you'll find dozens of additional column fragments lying haphazardly about in the water and strewn along the shoreline – the graveyard of an ancient, long-abandoned enterprise. Further on, you can still make out a series of giant chutes carved into the rock by Roman stonemasons to facilitate the transport of finished columns. According to some historians, granite quarried here was used to construct the columns of Rome's Pantheon.

Capo Testa stone was similarly prized by the medieval Pisans, who extracted granite from a separate quarry on the west side of the cape in 1162 for use in the beautiful Romanesque baptistery and cathedral of Pisa (yep, the one with the leaning tower!).

wholesome and hearty with no-nonsense pastas, fresh seafood, juicy grilled meats and wood-fired pizzas.

La Locanda dei Mori SEAFOOD €€
(☎0789 75 51 68; www.locandadeimori.com; SP90, Km 5; menus €33-43; ⏰8-11pm Jun-Sep) Immersed in a country setting just off the main road 6km south of Santa Teresa, this lovely *agriturismo* spreads a sea of tables onto its open-air terrace each summer. Guests come from miles around for the Locanda's multicourse menu of fresh seafood. Wine, water, coffee and after-dinner drinks are all included in the price.

★ **Agriturismo Saltara** SARDINIAN €€€
(☎0789 75 55 97; www.agriturismosaltara.it; Località Saltara; meals €40-60; ⏰7-11pm; 👪) Natalia and Gian Mario welcome you warmly at this *agriturismo,* 10km south of town off the SP90 (follow signs up a dirt track). Tables are scenically positioned under the trees for a home-cooked feast. Wood-fired bread and garden-vegetable antipasti are a delicious lead to dishes such as *pulilgioni* (ricotta-filled ravioli with orange zest) and roast suckling pig or wild boar.

Vegetarian menus are available on request.

Da Thomas SARDINIAN €€€
(☎349 6929613, 0789 75 51 33; www.ristorantedathomas.com; Via Valle d'Aosta 22; meals €35-50) Santa Teresa's go-to spot for romantic dinners and special occasions, this sleek eatery with wrap-around windows and a cool white interior serves some of the best food in town, accompanied by an excellent (and generally expensive) wine list.

Drinking & Nightlife

Hang out with the locals at the cafe-bars on Piazza Vittorio Emanuele. Between May and October regular concerts are staged at the Porto Turistico among the boutiques and expensive cafes.

Caffè Mediterraneo CAFE
(Via Amsicora 7; ⏰8am-midnight Mon-Thu, 7am-3.30am Fri-Sun) With its arched windows, polished-wood bar and jazzy beats, this stylish cafe attracts a young, good-looking crowd. Join them for morning coffee or a cool evening cocktail. Mediterraneo also doubles as a restaurant, serving pricey meals and some of Santa Teresa's best pizza.

Bar Central 80 BAR
(Piazza Vittorio Emanuele; ⏰6am-3am) Right on the main square, this central hub swells with happy holidaymakers until the early hours. Grab an outside table and enjoy ringside views of the piazza with your drink.

Estasi's CLUB
(www.facebook.com/estasisdiscoclub; Località Buoncammino; ⏲11pm-6am) Towards Palau, 3km south of town, is Santa Teresa's nightlife hub, centred on this outdoor club, where DJs and the occasional band crank up the party vibe in summer.

Shopping

Mascheras ARTS & CRAFTS
(Via Maria Teresa 54; ⏲9.30am-1pm & 4.30-7.30pm) Watch Signor Maura at work, skilfully carving traditional Sardinian carnival masks, at this tiny shop. His intricate masks include the wooden *boes* and *merdules* (character masks; from €130) typical of Ottana. There's also a range of cheaper wooden knick-knacks.

Information

Tourist Office (☎0789 75 41 27; www.comunesantateresagallura.it; Piazza Vittorio Emanuele 24; ⏲9am-1pm & 4-6pm) Very helpful, with loads of information.

Getting There & Away

BOAT

Santa Teresa is the main embarkation point for Corsica. Two companies run car ferries on the 50-minute crossing to Bonifacio, although between November and March services are drastically reduced.

In summer, **Moby Lines** (☎0789 75 14 49, 199 30 30 40; www.mobylines.it) has four daily departures in each direction, while **Blu Navy** (☎0789 75 55 70; www.blunavytraghetti.com) operates three to four daily crossings. The two companies offer slightly different prices, but a one-way adult fare averages about €25 and a small car around €55.

BUS

Departing from the bus terminus on Via Eleonora d'Arborea, ARST buses run to/from Arzachena (€3.10, 1¼ hours, five daily), Olbia (€4.30, two hours, seven daily), Castelsardo (€4.90, 1½ hours, two daily) and Sassari (€6.70, 2½ hours, three daily).

Turmo Travel (☎0789 2 14 87; www.grupoturmotravel.com) operates a daily service to/from Cagliari (€19.50, six hours), as well as a summer service to Olbia airport (€4.30, 1½ hours, six daily June to September) via Arzachena and Palau.

Other summer services are provided by **Caramelli** (☎079 67 06 13; www.caramellitours.it), which runs a daily bus to/from Porto Cervo (€4.90, 1¼ hours) via Palau (€2.50, 30 minutes) and Baia Sardinia (€4.30, one hour).

CAR & MOTORCYCLE

Santa Teresa di Gallura is at the northernmost end of the SS133b and on the SP90, which runs southwest to Castelsardo.

There are numerous rental agencies in Santa Teresa di Gallura, including **Just Sardinia** (☎0789 75 43 43; www.justsardinia.it; Via Maria Teresa 60), which has bikes (from €10 per day), scooters (€25) and cars (from €50).

Palau

☎0789 / POP 4210

Palau is a lively summer resort, its streets lined with surf shops, boutiques, bars and restaurants. It's also the main gateway to Arcipelago di La Maddalena's granite islands and jewel-coloured waters. Out of town, the coast is famous for its bizarre weather-beaten rocks, such as the Roccia dell'Orso, 6km east of Palau.

Sights & Activities

Fortezza di Monte Altura FORT
(adult/reduced €5/2.50; ⏲guided tours 9.15am-12.15pm & 5.15-7.15pm Jun-Aug, 10.15am-12.15pm & 3.15-5.15pm Apr, May & Sep–mid-Oct) Standing sentinel on a rocky crag, this sturdy 19th-century bastion was built to help defend the north coast and Arcipelago di La Maddalena from invasion – something it was never called on to do. A guided 45-minute tour leads you to watchtowers and battlements with panoramic views out to sea. The fortress is signposted off the SS125, 3km west of town.

Roccia dell'Orso VIEWPOINT
(trail adult/reduced €3/2, parking €3; ⏲9am-sunset; 👪) This weather-beaten granite sculpture sits on a high point 6km east of Palau. The Roccia dell'Orso (Bear Rock) looks considerably less bearlike up close, resembling more – dare we say it? – a dragon. Analogies aside, the granite formations are extraordinary, as are the far-reaching views of the coast from up here. From the parking lot it's a 10- to 15-minute climb.

Nautilus DIVING
(☎340 6339006, 0789 70 90 58; www.divesardegna.com; Piazza Fresi 8) There's some excellent diving in the marine park. This PADI five-star dive centre runs dives to 40 sites, with single dives starting at around €55. Kids' Bubblemaker courses are available.

Tours

Sardinia Island Tours/Natour Sardinia BOATING
(☎Kevin 391 7327232, Rodolfo 339 4774472; www.sardiniaislandtours.com; Via Guerrazzi 4; full-day tour €60) Sharing an office near the port, these two companies work in tandem to provide excellent multilingual tours of the Maddalena archipelago. In addition to visiting local beaches, guides Kevin and Rodolfo offer hikes to local fortresses dating back to WWII and Napoleon's ill-fated attempt to take over Isola Maddalena in 1793. Lunch, wine and water are included in the tour price.

Dea del Mare BOATING
(☎334 7882993, 349 4909260; www.deadelmare.com; Via Fonte Vecchia 76; day trips €65-110; ⏲office 9am-5pm) Down near the port, this outfit offers boat excursions around the Maddalena islands, with a chipper crew and passenger numbers limited to 20. Trips include lunch with wine and time to swim on well-known beaches.

Eating

The area around the port is packed with eateries for every budget. As elsewhere along the coast, nearly all restaurants close their doors from November to Easter.

Del Porticciolo SARDINIAN €
(☎0789 70 70 51; Via Omero; pizzas €4-9, meals €25-35; ⏲12.15-2pm & 7.15-10.30pm Sat-Thu) Locals swear by the authentic antipasti, pasta and fresh fish at this no-frills restaurant just south of the harbour. Stop by for a good-value lunch, or in the evening when chefs fire up the pizza ovens.

C'era una Volta ITALIAN €€
(☎0789 70 83 59; www.ristoranteceraunavoltapalau.it; Piazza del Molo 22; meals €25-50; ⏲noon-2.30pm & 7-11pm) On the road down to the harbour, C'era una Volta makes a convenient spot for a fixed-price lunch: €25 gets you a starter, a main course, wine, water and coffee. Dinner will set you back considerably more, though the food is some of Palau's best – follow fresh pasta with the simply grilled catch of the day and homemade desserts.

La Gritta ITALIAN €€€
(☎0789 70 80 45; www.ristorantelagritta.it; Località Porto Faro; meals €70-80; ⏲12.30-2.30pm & 7.30-10.30pm Thu-Tue Apr-Oct) One for special occasions, La Gritta is a memorable place to dine. Floor-to-ceiling windows and a terrace allow you to take in the wondrous coastal scenery, while the superbly presented seafood combines modern techniques with Italian ingredients. Cheese buffs will enjoy a selection of up to 20 different cheeses, while everyone will appreciate the classic Sardinian desserts.

Information

Tourist Office (☎0789 70 70 25; www.palauturismo.com; Palazzo Fresi, Piazza Fresi; ⏲9am-1pm & 4-7pm Mon-Fri, from 10am Sat) The multilingual staff at the tourist office can provide information about the surrounding area, including the Arcipelago di La Maddalena.

Getting There & Away

BOAT

Car ferries to Isola Maddalena are operated by **Delcomar** (☎0789 70 92 28; www.delcomar.it) and **Maddalena Lines** (☎0789 73 91 65; www.maddalenalines.it). Boats run every 15 to 30 minutes during daylight hours, then roughly hourly from midnight to 5.30am, with Delcomar offering the most frequent service. The 15-minute crossing costs between €3.40 and €5 per passenger and €7.30 to €12.50 per car (one way).

BUS

There are ARST buses connecting Palau with Olbia (€3.10, 1¼ hours, eight daily), Santa Teresa di Gallura (€2.50, 45 minutes, five daily) and Arzachena (€1.90, 30 minutes, five daily).

Turmo Travel (☎0789 2 14 87; www.gruppoturmotravel.com) offers year-round bus service from Palau to Olbia airport (€6, 50 minutes) and Santa Teresa di Gallura (€4, 35 minutes). Buses run six times daily from June through September, and once daily October to May.

In summer, **Caramelli** (p158) runs frequent buses to other nearby destinations such as Isola dei Gabbiani, Porto Pollo, Capo d'Orso, Baia Sardinia, Poltu Quatu and Porto Cervo.

TRAIN

The **trenino verde** (p268) runs from Palau port to Tempio Pausania (one way/return €14/21, 2¼ hours) Tuesday through Saturday from mid-June to early September. It's a slow ride along a narrow-gauge line through some great countryside.

Arcipelago di La Maddalena

One of Sardinia's most ravishing beauty spots, the Arcipelago di La Maddalena provides some spectacular, windswept seascapes. Nelson and Napoleon knew the archipelago well, as did that old warhorse Giuseppe Garibaldi, who bought Isola Caprera for his retirement.

Parco Nazionale dell'Arcipelago di La Maddalena (www.lamaddalenapark.it), established in 1996, consists of seven main islands and several smaller granite islets off Sardinia's northeastern coast. The seven principal islands are the high points of a valley, now underwater, that once joined Sardinia and Corsica. When the two split into separate islands, waters filled the strait now called the Bocche di Bonifacio. Over the centuries the prevailing *maestrale* (northwesterly wind) has helped to mould the granite into the bizarre natural sculptures that festoon the archipelago.

The area is an important natural habitat, and the ecosystem remains fragile. For this reason efforts have been launched to create a joint Italian-French marine park.

Isola Maddalena

Just over the water from Palau, the pink-granite island of Maddalena lies at the heart of the archipelago. From the moment you dock, you'll be taken by the urbane character of the place, its cobbled piazzas and infectious holiday atmosphere.

Until the end of the 17th century, the island's small population lived mainly in the interior, farming a meagre living out of the poor soil. But when the Sardo-Piedmontese navy arrived in 1767 to establish a naval base, residents gladly gave up their hilltops and relocated to the growing village around Cala Gavetta, now La Maddalena's main port.

Sights & Activities

Beyond the harbour, the island's drawcard is its startlingly lovely seascapes. Divers sing the praises of the sapphire waters here, which are among the cleanest in the Med and teem with marine life. A 20km panoramic road circles the island, allowing easy access to several attractive bays such as **Giardinelli**, **Monti della Rena**, **Lo Strangolato** and **Cala Spalmatore**.

Museo Archeologico Navale MUSEUM
(☎0789 79 06 33; Località Mongiardino; admission €4) About 1km out of town, on the road to Cala Spalmatore, this museum exhibits finds from a 1st-century shipwreck. The two modest rooms are presided over by an impressive reconstructed cross-section of the Roman vessel containing more than 200 amphorae. At the time of research, the museum was closed indefinitely for renovation; check locally for current status.

Elena Tour Navigazioni BOATING
(☎380 3032664; www.elenatournavigazioni.com; Lungomare Amendola) Elena Tour runs relaxed cruises to the hidden beaches and smaller, lesser-known islands of Arcipelago di La Maddalena, with plenty of time for chilling and swimming. Reckon on €35 to €40 per person for a full-day tour, including lunch. Itinerary details are given on the website.

Fratelli Cuccu CYCLING
(☎0789 73 85 28; www.fratellicuccu.it; Via Amendola 8; ⏰9am-8pm) Rental companies line up along Via Amendola on the waterfront. Among them is Fratelli Cuccu, which rents out bikes, scooters, cars and dinghy boats. Quad excursions are also available.

Saint Tropez WATER SPORTS
(☎335 6545214, 0789 72 77 68; Via Benvenuto Cellini 36) If larking around on waterskis, a wakeboard or a canoe in the calm waters of the Passo della Moneta appeals, try Saint Tropez, located near the bridge to Isola Caprera.

Eating

The best eating options are in La Maddalena town. Nearly every place closes from November to March.

Trattoria Vecchia Ilva SARDINIAN €€
(☎0789 73 73 72; www.facebook.com/vecchiailvalamaddalena; Largo Matteotti 1; meals €30-40; ⏰noon-2.30pm & 7.30-11pm) Buzzing with youthful energy and a welcoming vibe, this newly hatched restaurant breaks with its Mediterranean island surroundings, specialising in recipes from Sardinia's mountainous interior. Fregola pasta with tomato, sausage and porcini mushrooms, *culurgiones* (ricotta-stuffed pasta pockets) with orange-sage butter, or beef with Cannonau wine serve as preludes for unique desserts such as cinnamon-scented ricotta in a *carasau* bread nest. Delicious!

Parco Nazionale dell'Arcipelago di La Maddalena

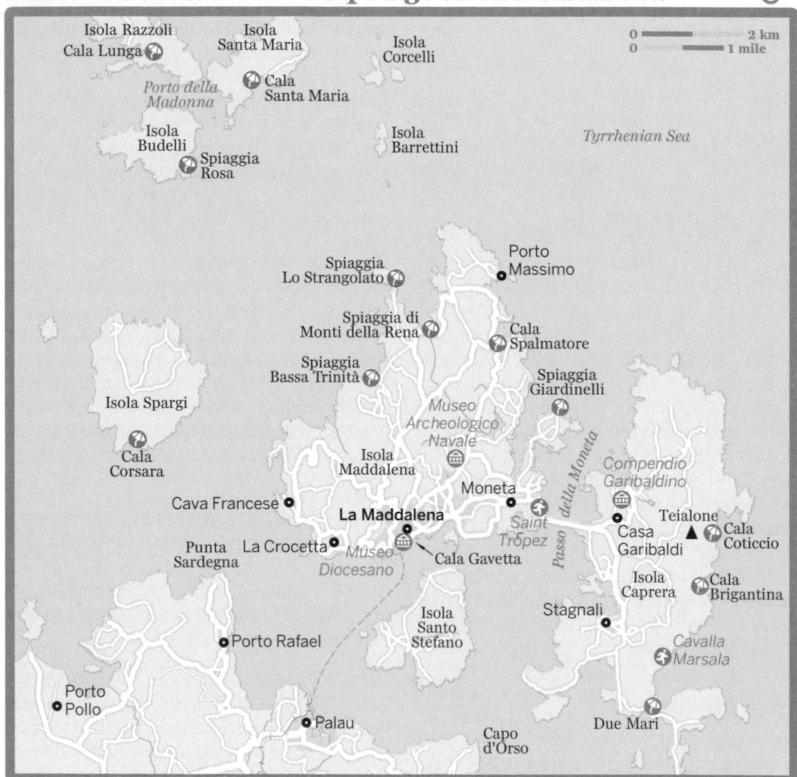

Sottovento SEAFOOD €€
(☎0789 73 77 49; www.ristorantilamaddalena.it; Via E Dandolo 9; meals €35-45; ⏰12.30-3pm & 7.30-11pm, closed lunch Mon in winter) Sardinian home cooking is on the menu at bistro-style Sottovento, a short stroll north of the harbour. Go for seafood antipasti, handmade pasta and fresh fish and you won't be disappointed.

Information

Tourist Office (☎0789 73 63 21; www.facebook.com/pg/lamaddalenaturismo; Via XX Settembre; ⏰9am-1.30pm & 3-7.30pm) The tourist office, just east of the Cala Gavetta ferry port, has limited information on the archipelago. Opening hours should be taken with a pinch of salt as they change frequently.

Getting There & Away

Car ferries operated by **Delcomar** (p166) and **Maddalena Lines** (p166) run between Isola Maddalena and Palau. Boats run every 15 to 30 minutes during daylight hours, then roughly hourly from midnight to 5.30am, with Delcomar offering the most frequent service. The 15-minute crossing costs between €3.40 and €5 per passenger and €7.30 to €12.50 per car (one way).

Getting Around

Turmo Travel (p166) operates two island bus services, both departing from Via Amendola on the waterfront. One goes to the Compendio Garibaldi complex on Isola Caprera, and the other circles Isola Maddalena, passing the Museo Archeologico Navale and several beaches, including Cala Spalmatore and Spiaggia Bassa Trinita.

Isola Caprera

Giuseppe Garibaldi's 'Eden', Isola Caprera is a wild, wonderfully serene island, covered in green pine trees that look stunning against the ever-present seascape and ragged granite cliffs.

Green, shady Caprera is ideal for walking, and there are plenty of trails weaving through the pine forests. There's a stairway right up to the top of the island (212m) where you'll find the Teialone lookout tower. As you wander, keep an eye out for seabirds such as royal seagulls, cormorants and peregrine falcons.

The island's rugged coast is indented with several tempting coves. Many people head south to the fine sands and turquoise-blue waters of **Due Mari** and **Spiaggia del Relitto**. You could, however, head north of the Compendio Garibaldino for about 1.5km and look for the walking trail that drops down to beautifully secluded **Cala Coticcio**. Marginally easier is **Cala Brigantina** (signposted), southeast of the Garibaldi complex.

Sights & Activities

★Compendio Garibaldino MUSEUM

(www.compendiogaribaldino.it; adult/reduced €7/3.50; ⏲9am-8pm Tue-Sun) Giuseppe Garibaldi, professional revolutionary and all-round Italian hero, bought half of Caprera in 1855 (he got the rest 10 years later). He made it his home and refuge, the place he would return to after yet another daring campaign in the pursuit of liberty. The Compendio Garibaldino is an object of pilgrimage for many Italians. Visits, by guided tour in Italian only, take in the rustic elegant rooms, the garden cemetery and a small but touching collection of Garibaldi memorabilia.

The red-shirted revolutionary first lived in a hut that still stands in the courtyard, while building his main residence, the **Casa Bianca**. You enter the house proper by an atrium adorned with his portrait, a flag from the days of Peru's war of independence and a reclining wheelchair donated to him by the city of Milan when he became infirm a couple of years before his death. You then proceed through a series of bedrooms where he and family members slept. The kitchen had its own freshwater pump, a feat of high technology in such a place in the 1870s. In what was the main dining room are now displayed all sorts of odds and ends, from binoculars to the general's own red shirt. The last room contains his death bed, facing the window and the sea, across which he would look longingly, dreaming until the end that he might return to his native Nice.

Outside in the **gardens** are his rough-hewn granite tomb and those of several family members (he had seven children by his three wives and one by a governess).

Cavalla Marsala HORSE RIDING

(☎347 2359064; Località Stagnali, Isola di Caprera) Cavalla Marsala's hacks along the beach and through the fragrant *macchia* are particularly atmospheric in the early evening. Reckon on €35 for a 1½-hour ride.

Getting There & Away

With your own wheels, Isola Caprera is a short, 6km hop from Isola Maddalena. The road east out of La Maddalena town takes you through desolate urban relics to the narrow causeway that spans the Passo della Moneta between the two islands.

Turmo Travel (p166) offers bus service from La Maddalena to Isola Caprera, stopping at Compendio Garibaldi year-round and continuing to the beach at Due Mari between mid-June and mid-September. There are four to five daily buses in winter, and 11 in summer.

Other Islands

Isola Budelli ISLAND

This small island near the northwestern corner of the Maddalena archipelago is best known for its **Spiaggia Rosa** (Pink Beach), so-called because of the sand's unique pink tinge. The beach is now protected and access to its environmentally threatened sands and waters is forbidden, though most boat trips will pause offshore, allowing you to enjoy a distant glimpse.

Isola Santa Maria ISLAND

The most exciting part of a visit to Isola Santa Maria is the journey across the crystal-clear aquamarine waters that lap its southern shores – known as **Porto della Madonna** or Porto Madonna, this area is renowned as one of the world's most gorgeous seascapes. On the island itself, boats typically stop at the often-crowded **Cala Santa Maria**.

Isola Spargi ISLAND

West of Isola Maddalena, Isola Spargi is necklaced by sandy coves and inlets. One of the best is **Cala Corsara**, where the sea is topaz blue.

Isola Santo Stefano ISLAND

Since NATO bid Isola Santo Stefano farewell in 2008, it has once again become a green, tranquil escape. Hikers can visit the fort

THE OLD MAN & THE SEA

Travellers on a day trip through the Maddalena archipelago may be surprised to discover that not all of the outer islands are uninhabited. Indeed, the tiny isle of Budelli boasts a whopping population of one – yes, you read that right: one.

For the past three decades, Budelli's lone resident has been septuagenarian Mauro Morandi, a former teacher and intrepid round-the-world sailor who took to these shores in 1989 and has since assumed the role of the island's caretaker. Living year-round in his simple home here, Morandi helps maintain Budelli's pristine beauty, picking up garbage that drifts in from the sea and intervening whenever wayward skippers attempt to land illegally on Budelli's legendary Spiaggia Rosa, designated a protected area since 1994 to safeguard its rare pink sands.

In early 2016, Morandi's unique way of life was threatened when Italy's Minister of the Environment, Gian Luca Galletti, made a move to have him evicted from the island. An internet firestorm quickly ensued, with friends launching a petition on Change.org to protect Morandi's right to remain. The petition, which, among other things, cited his important role in preserving the island's environment, quickly garnered 18,298 signatures, prompting the Italian government to back down, at least for now.

Meanwhile, Morandi's own intentions seem clear enough: his Facebook page bears the straightforward name 'Mauro Da Budelli' (Mauro from Budelli), signalling to all the world that this one man and his island remain essentially inseparable.

So if you find yourself sailing past Budelli, look for the distinctive profile of Morandi's island home, and don't forget to say a word of thanks to its solitary inhabitant.

used by Napoleon during his unsuccessful quest to capture Isola Maddalena in 1793.

Isola Razzoli ISLAND

The northwesternmost island in the archipelago, Isola Razzoli is a popular destination for boat tours, which ply the waters of its fjord-like **Cala Lunga**.

Porto Pollo & Isola Dei Gabbiani

Seven kilometres west of Palau, windsurfers and kitesurfers converge on Porto Pollo and the adjacent Isola dei Gabbiani (connected to Porto Pollo by a narrow isthmus), where stiff breezes and crystalline waters create the best conditions in Sardinia.

Along the beachfront you'll find various outfits offering lessons and supplying gear for a whole slew of water sports, including windsurfing, kitesurfing, sailing, kayaking and stand-up paddleboarding.

Activities

MB Pro Center WATER SPORTS

(☎0789 70 42 06, 335 6379949; www.procenter.it; Baia dei Delfini) MB Pro Center offers a vast range of services for windsurfers, kitesurfers, stand-up paddleboarders, sailors and kayakers. Two-hour windsurfing/kitesurfing taster sessions cost €69/120, and multiday courses, including equipment hire and lessons, start at €195/250 for two days. It also has a wide range of windsurfing courses for kids, as well as kite, windsurf, SUP, kayak and sailboat hire.

Sporting Club Sardinia WATER SPORTS

(☎0789 70 40 16; www.portopollo.it) Sporting Club Sardinia takes you windsurfing, kitesurfing and sailing, and has a chilled bar for post-water-sport drinks and gigs. Expect to pay €50 for a 1½-hour windsurfing lesson, €250 for a five-lesson introductory sailing course, or €280 for a block of six kitesurfing lessons, and €20/25/30 for an hour's windsurf/sailboat/kite rental. Kids' lessons are also available.

Getting There & Away

From Palau it's a 10-minute drive west to Porto Pollo. Buses on the Palau–Santa Teresa di Gallura route stop off at the signposted road junction, from where you have to walk about 2km.

THE INTERIOR

Away from the preening millionaires on the beach, Gallura's granite interior is remote and resolutely rural. In fact, it was this fertile hinterland that attracted the waves of

Corsican migrants who settled here to farm the cork forests and plant the extensive Vermentino vineyards. Cork has long been a mainstay of the local economy.

Tempio Pausania

☎079 / POP 14,240

Elevated above the hot Gallurese plain and surrounded by dense cork woods, Tempio Pausania (known to locals simply as 'Tempio') stays cool and calm even in the height of summer. Joint capital of the Olbia-Tempio province, it's an unpretentious spot with a rustic historic centre and a laid-back pace of life.

The town was founded by the Romans in the 2nd century BC, and was developed to become an administrative centre of the medieval Giudicato di Gallura. Tempio Pausania's heyday came under the Spanish and then the Savoys, when many of the churches that adorn the town's grey stone centre were constructed. These days it's a relaxed place to hang out, and the surrounding countryside is perfect for touring. Nearby Monte Limbara provides numerous trekking opportunities.

Sights

Nuraghe Maiori ARCHAEOLOGICAL SITE

(☎SS133, Km2; with/without guided visit €3.50/3; ⏲9.30am-7pm) Signposted 2km north of Tempio Pausania along the SS133, this *nuraghe* is more substantial than the many other ruins that dot the surrounding countryside. A trail leads through fragrant herb gardens to the tower, flanked by chambers on either side. Borrow a headlight at the ticket office to spot clusters of rare lesser horseshoe bats in the pitch-black left-hand chambers. A ramp climbs to an open room at the back, with stairs continuing to the top.

Fonti di Rinaggiu SPRING

Since Roman days Tempio has been known for its mineral-rich springs, said to have a curative effect on all who drink from them. Locals still come to fill their bottles at the Fonti di Rinaggiu, a pair of springs 1km southwest of the centre; take the shady Viale San Lorenzo and follow the 'Alle Terme' signs.

Cantina Gallura WINERY

(☎079 63 12 41; www.cantinagallura.com; Via Val di Cossu 9; ⏲8am-noon & 2-6pm Mon-Fri, 9am-1pm Sat) This cantina 1.5km east of town is the perfect place to stock up on the local DOCG Vermentino di Gallura.

Chiesa del Purgatorio CHURCH

(Piazza del Purgatorio; ⏲9am-noon) This modest 17th-century church, presiding over Piazza del Purgatorio, has an intriguing history. The story goes that a member of the noble Misorro family was found guilty of carrying out a massacre on this very spot. To expiate his sins, the pope ordered the man to fund the building of this church, where to this day it's the custom of townspeople to come and pray after a funeral.

Cattedrale di San Pietro CHURCH

(Duomo; Piazza San Pietro; ⏲8am-12.30pm & 3-8pm) This granite cathedral is the town's imposing centrepiece. All that remains of the 15th-century original is the bell tower and main entrance.

Monte Limbara MOUNTAIN

Some 17km southeast of Tempio, the jagged summit of Monte Limbara (1359m) dominates the landscape. The easiest way to reach it is to drive. From Tempio, head south past the train station and follow the SS392 road for Oschiri. After 8km you will hit the left turn-off for the mountain. Up top, the air is cool and refreshing, even on a midsummer's day, and the views west towards Sassari and north to Corsica are breathtaking.

From the turn-off, the initial drive takes you through thick pine woods. As you emerge above the treeline, a couple of *punti panoramici* (viewing spots) are indicated, from where you have terrific views across all of northern Sardinia. One is marked by a statue of the Virgin Mary and child, near the simple Chiesa di Santa Maria della Neve. The road then flattens out to reach the viewing point of Punta Balistreri (1359m), where the RAI national TV network has stacked its relay and communication towers.

Festivals & Events

Tempio's events calendar includes everything from concerts to religious and folkloric festivals.

Carnevale (in February) is big here, with flamboyant costumed parades in the build up to Lent, as is **Easter Week**. On Good Friday members of *confraternite* (religious brotherhoods) dress up in sinister-looking robes and hoods for the **Via Crucis** night procession. From mid-June to

PHILIP BIRD LRPS CPAGB/SHUTTERSTOCK ©

1. Tempio Pausania (p171)
A church in the rustic, historic centre of this unpretentious town.

2. Capo Testa (p162)
This boulder-strewn headland attracts hikers and climbers.

3. Porto Pollo (p170)
Stiff breezes and crystalline waters draw windsurfers to this coastal town.

2

ALESSANDRO ZAPPALORTO/SHUTTERSTOCK ©

Tempio Pausania

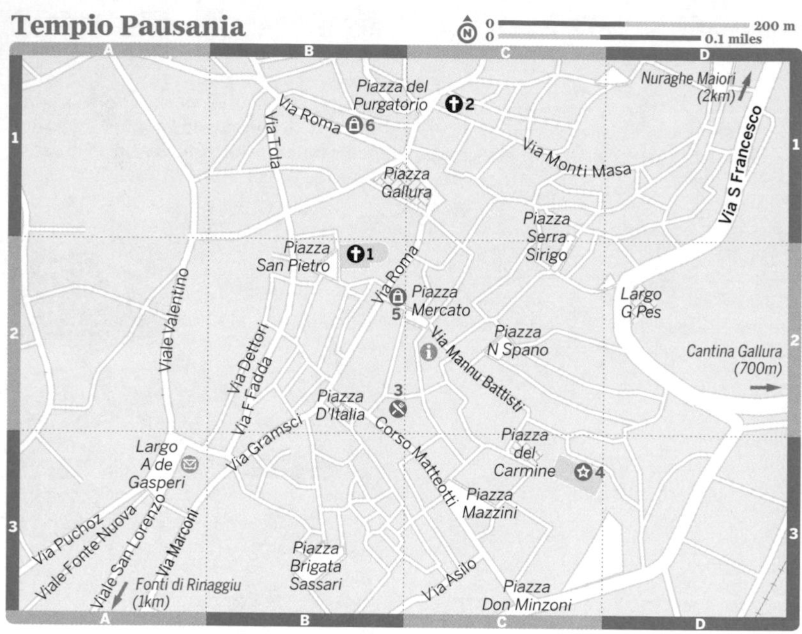

Tempio Pausania

Sights
1 Cattedrale di San Pietro....B2
2 Chiesa del Purgatorio....C1

Eating
3 Trattoria Gallurese....B2

Entertainment
4 Teatro del Carmine....C3

Shopping
5 Anna Grindi Atelier....B2
6 Casa Mundula....B1

mid-September, **l'Estate Tempiese** brings a variety of summer events to the historic centre, from symphonic and choral music concerts to folkloric processions.

Eating & Drinking

You can sample the region's hearty mountain cuisine at Tempio's handful of traditional restaurants. Local specialities worth trying include wild boar or mutton with Cannonau wine and olives, *pane frattau* (*carasau* bread with tomato sauce, *pecorino* cheese and fried egg) and *chiusoni alla gallurese* (handmade pasta with tomato-meat sauce).

On tree-shaded Piazza d'Italia and Piazza Gallura you'll find cafes with al fresco seating where you can grab an espresso or an early evening *aperitivo*.

★Trattoria Gallurese SARDINIAN €
(☎079 639 30 12; Via Novara 2; meals €20-25; ⏲noon-3.15pm & 7-10.15pm) This simple homespun trattoria serves a warm welcome and genuine Gallurese soul food. Go traditional with *cinghiale* (wild boar) slow-cooked in Cannonau red wine or *pecora alla gallurese* (Gallurese-style lamb). Delicious tiramisu with a shot of homemade *mirto* liqueur is the perfect coda to a meal.

Punto di Ristoro Nuraghe Majori GRILL €
(☎320 3060634; SS133, Km2; meals €15; ⏲9.30am-7pm Mar-Nov) With tables spilling onto a flowery open-air patio, this makes a lovely spot for an economical lunch of grilled meat, roast potatoes and salad, or plates of local cheese and charcuterie. Look for it 100m south of the Nuraghe Maiori archaeological site, via a cork-tree-lined path.

Entertainment

Teatro del Carmine THEATRE
(☎079 63 03 77, 388 3503817; Piazza del Carmine) A variety of performances, ranging from operetta to classical concerts, can be enjoyed

here, especially during the summer Festival d'Estate.

Shopping

Anna Grindi Atelier CLOTHING
(☎340 8630671; Via Roma 34; ⏲by arrangement) Tempio native Anna Grindi works magic in this innovative shop, which sells dresses, shoes and bags made entirely of native Sardinian cork. Using a process developed and patented by Grindi herself, cork from local oak trees is converted into the waterproof, fireproof, supple and light-as-silk fabric that you see displayed throughout the store.

Casa Mundula ARTS & CRAFTS
(Via Roma 102; ⏲10am-1pm & 4-8pm Mon-Sat) This store is a one-stop shop for cork-based knick-knacks, ceramics, filigree jewellery and hand-crafted knives, as well as Sardinian specialities such as *pane carasau*, local honey and wine and Carloforte tuna.

Information

Post Office (Largo A de Gasperi; ⏲8.20am-7.05pm Mon-Fri, to 12.35pm Sat)

Tourist Office (☎079 639 00 80; www.visit-tempio.it; Piazza Mercato 3; ⏲9am-7pm Mon-Fri, 10am-2pm & 3-7pm Sat & Sun) Run by helpful, multilingual staff.

Getting There & Away

There are good road connections from Tempio to Olbia (47km via the SS127), Palau (49km via the SS133) and Arzachena (42km via the SS427).

From Olbia (€3.70, 1¼ hours) there are seven daily ARST buses on weekdays to Tempio and three on Sunday.

The train station, a downhill walk from the centre, comes to life for the summertime **trenino verde** (☎070 2 65 71; www.treninoverde.com) to/from Sassari (€16, 2¾ hours, Thursday) and Palau (€14, 1¾ hours, Tuesday to Saturday).

Aggius

☎079 / POP 1520

Cowering at the foot of granite peaks, Aggius is a deeply traditional village, clustered around a historic centre of twisting lanes and squat stone houses. It's known throughout Sardinia for its choral music and carpets. A more sinister side of Aggius' past is its long-standing history as a hotbed of banditry, dating back to the 16th century. A pair of museums in the heart of town celebrate this multi-faceted cultural heritage.

Sights

★Museo Etnografico 'Olivia Carta Cannas' MUSEUM
(www.museodiaggius.it; Via Monti di Lizu 6; adult/reduced €4/3; ⏲10am-1pm & 3-7pm May–mid-Oct, 10am-1pm & 3.30-5.30pm Tue-Sat rest of year) Aggius is famous for its carpets, with a tradition dating back to the 1900s, when 4000 looms were busy in the area. This excellent museum showcases a fine collection of looms and the richly brocaded costumes worn for festive occasions, alongside a new wing opened in 2017 that uses inventive multimedia displays to document the town's proud tradition of vocal music.

Museo del Banditismo MUSEUM
(www.museodiaggius.it; Via Pretura; adult/reduced €4/3; ⏲10am-1pm & 3.30-6.30pm May-Oct, by appointment Nov-Apr) For a sinister peek at Aggius' past, stop by the new Museo del Banditismo. Housed in the former magistrate's court, the museum zooms in on banditry in Gallura (still a problem until the 1990s), with a collection of arms, police reports and snapshots of the island's most wanted outlaws.

WORTH A TRIP

THE SCENIC DRIVE FROM TEMPIO TO BERCHIDDA

One of northeastern Sardinia's most scenic drives follows the SS392 across the mountains from Tempio Pausania to Berchidda. The road skirts the western side of the Limbara massif, passing through cork-oak and pine woods, crests the Passo del Limbara (646m) and then begins its descent towards Oschiri. After about 12km the green gives way to scorched straw-coloured fields and the blue mirror of the artificial Lago di Coghinas comes into view. Just before the bridge over the lake, a narrow asphalted road breaks off east towards Berchidda. Total travel time from Tempio to Berchidda is about 50 minutes. You'll need your own vehicle, as there is no public transport along this route.

WORTH A TRIP

MUSEO ETNOGRAFICO GALLURAS

Housed in a reconstructed village dwelling in the small town of Luras, the fascinating **Museo Etnografico Galluras** (☎368 3376321; www.galluras.it; Via Nazionale 35a; guided tour €5; ⊙by appointment) celebrates inland Gallura's rural traditions. Guided tours take visitors through a half-dozen rooms filled with countless cultural artefacts: agrarian tools, wine presses, cheese-making equipment, traditional wedding breads, antique pharmacy shelves, forceps for catching eels, and much more.

The museum's crowning glory is its display dedicated to Sa Femina Accabadora, the midwife who in traditional Sardinian culture assumed the duty of putting terminally ill patients out of their misery with a gruesome hammer – a form of rural euthanasia practised into the 20th century. The last recorded use of the hammer here in Luras was in 1929, with the last confirmed case anywhere in Sardinia at Orgosolo in 1952. Less certain are the rumours of a woman in a small village near Bosa who confessed to her priest of having finished off a terminal cancer patient with the traditional hammer as recently as 2003.

Valle della Luna NATURAL FEATURE

A few kilometres northwest of Aggius towards Trinita d'Agultu, you reach the Valle della Luna. It's a surreal and evocative landscape, where huge granite boulders spill across rolling hills and farmland like giants' marbles. The **lookout** point on the SP74 commands fantastic views of the surrounding countryside, honeycombed with bizarrely sculpted rocks. The valley is a fantastic place for a bike ride, and the road through here down to the coast is tremendously scenic.

Getting There & Away

Aggius is 7km northwest of Tempio Pausania via the SP27. Other nearby destinations include Santa Teresa di Gallura (50km, 50 minutes) and Olbia (54km, one hour).

ARST runs three daily buses from Aggius to Palau (€3.70, 1½ hours) and several to Tempio (€1.30, 15 minutes). Connections to Olbia require a change of buses in Tempio.

Berchidda & Monti

Backed by the slopes of Monte Acuto (493m), the woody hill where Eleonora d'Arborea hid out for a period in the 14th century, Berchidda is a fairly nondescript farming town with a strong viticultural tradition, which you can delve into at the local wine museum.

Just over 15km east of Berchidda, surrounded by cork-oak forests and vineyards, the village of Monti is another well-known wine producer, famous for its production of Vermentino di Gallura, Sardinia's only DOCG-rated wine.

Sights & Activities

Museo del Vino MUSEUM

(www.muvisardegna.it; Via Giangiorgio Casu 5, Berchidda; adult/reduced €3/2.50; ⊙9am-1pm & 3-6pm Tue-Fri, to 7pm Sat & Sun) You can find out about local winemaking and taste some of the area's Vermentino at the modern Museo del Vino right at the top of town.

Cantina del Vermentino WINE

(☎0789 4 40 12; www.vermentinomonti.it; Via San Paolo 2, Monti; ⊙9am-1pm & 2-6pm Mon-Fri, 8.30am-12.30pm Sat) At the Cantina del Vermentino, taste and buy some of the region's finest wines, including the crisp Vermentino di Gallura, Sardinia's only DOCG-rated wine.

Festivals & Events

Time in Jazz MUSIC

(www.timeinjazz.it; ⊙Aug) In the second week of August, Berchidda's multicultural music festival lights up the town with jazz jams, dance happenings and concerts featuring everything from string quartets to piano soloists to saxophonists.

Getting There & Away

From Olbia, it's a straightforward drive west on the SS729 to Monti (25 minutes) and Berchidda (30 minutes).

Nuoro & the East

Includes ➡

Best Places to Eat

- ➡ Il Portico (p182)
- ➡ Su Bullicciu (p206)
- ➡ Santa Rughe (p188)
- ➡ Ristorante Ispinigoli (p201)
- ➡ Agriturismo Testone (p183)

Best Places to Sleep

- ➡ Agriturismo Guthiddai (p223)
- ➡ Casa Solotti (p221)
- ➡ Albergo Diffuso Mannois (p223)
- ➡ Agriturismo Codula Fuili (p222)
- ➡ Su Gologone (p223)

Why Go?

Nowhere else in Sardinia is nature such an overwhelming force as in the wild, wild east, where the Supramonte's imperious limestone mountains roll down to the Golfo di Orosei's cliffs and startling aquamarine waters. Who knows where that winding country road might lead you? Perhaps to deep valleys concealing prehistoric caves and Bronze Age *nuraghi*, to the lonesome villages of the Barbagia steeped in bandit legends, or to forests where wild pigs snuffle amid centuries-old holm oaks. Neither time nor trend obsessed, this region is refreshingly authentic.

Outdoor action is everywhere: along the coast where you can drop anchor in a string of pearly white bays, upon the cliffs where you can multi-pitch climb above the sea, on old mule trails best explored by mountain bike, and atop peaks and ravines only reachable on foot. True, the Costa Smeralda attracts more celebrities, but the real rock stars and rolling stones are right here.

When to Go

- ➡ Bonfires and masked dancers fill Mamoiada's streets during the Festa di Sant'Antonio Abate in January.
- ➡ In June, explore the magnificent cliffs and coves of Golfo di Orosei before temperatures and prices soar.
- ➡ Tackle the classic Selvaggio Blu trek or ride the *trenino verde* through Sorgono's vineyards in September.

Nuoro & the East Highlights

❶ **Gola Su Gorropu** (p199) Walking on the wild side in Europe's Grand Canyon.

❷ **Golfo di Orosei** (p191) Dropping anchor among the hidden coves and secluded beaches of Sardinia's most magnificent bay.

❸ **SS125** (p202) Taking a scenic drive along this serpentine road for captivating views of the mountains and the Med.

❹ **Tiscali** (p200) Marvelling at mysterious nuraghic ruins high in the Supramonte's limestone mountains.

❺ **Altopiano del Golgo** (p201) Leaving the world behind as you explore this weird highland plateau.

6 Cala Gonone (p191) Enjoying exhilarating coastal walks before cooling off with a dip in the bluest of seas.

7 Ulassai (p205) Scaling the hidden heights in this up-and-coming rock-climbing destination.

NUORO

0784 / POP 37,100

Once an isolated hilltop village and a byword for banditry, Nuoro had its cultural renaissance in the 19th and early 20th centuries when it became a hotbed of artistic talent. Today museums in the historic centre pay homage to local legends including Nobel Prize–winning author Grazia Deledda, acclaimed poet Sebastiano Satta, novelist Salvatore Satta and sculptor Francesco Ciusa. Further enhancing Nuoro's modern-day cultural vitality are the local university, with its graduate program in environmental studies and sustainable development, and the city's recently renovated ethnographic museum.

Nuoro's spectacular backdrop is the granite peak of Monte Ortobene (955m), capped by a 7m-high bronze statue of the Redentore (Christ the Redeemer). The thickly wooded summit commands dress-circle views of the valley below and the limestone mountains enshrouding Oliena opposite.

History

Archaeologists have unearthed evidence of prehistoric nuraghic settlements in the Nuoro area. A popular theory maintains that the city was established when locals opposed to Roman rule grouped together around Monte Ortobene. But little is known of the city before the Middle Ages, when it was passed from one feudal family to another under the Aragonese and, later, Spain.

By the 18th century the town, now under Piedmontese control, had a population of around 3000, mostly farmers and shepherds. A tough, often violent, place, it rose in rebellion in 1868 when citizens burned down the town hall to protest attempts to privatise public land (and thus hand it to the rich landowners). This action, known as Su Connuttu, no doubt confirmed the new

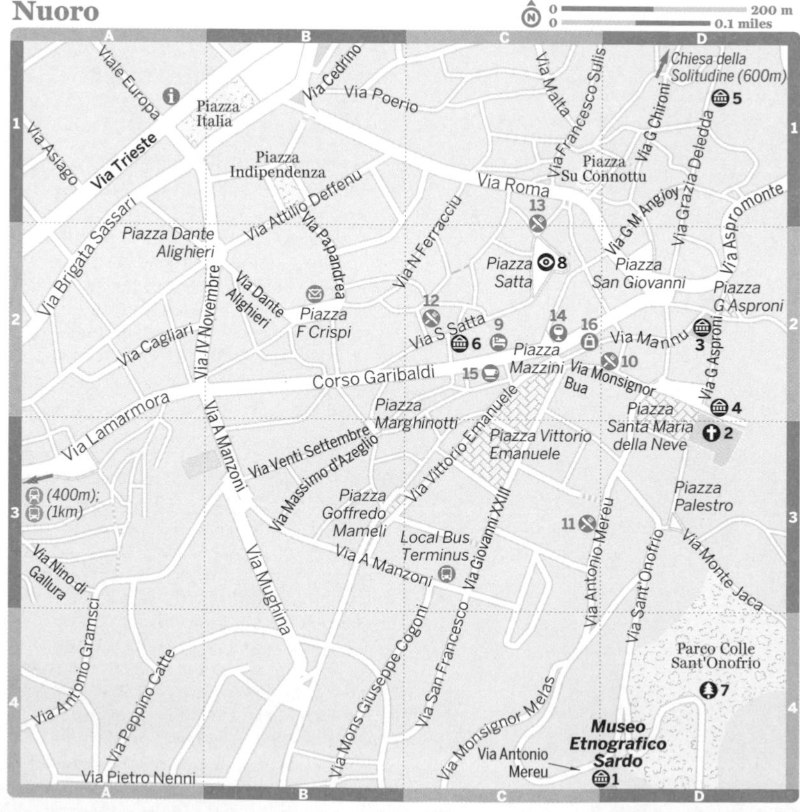

Italian nation's view of the whole Nuoro district as a 'crime zone', an attitude reflected in its treatment of the area, which only served to further alienate the Nuoresi and cement their mistrust of authority.

Nuoro was appointed a provincial capital in 1927. It quickly developed into a bustling administrative centre. Although the traditional problem of banditry has long since subsided and the town presents a cheerful enough visage, Nuoro remains troubled, as high unemployment forces many young people to leave in search of work.

Sights

★Museo Etnografico Sardo MUSEUM

(Museo del Costume; www.isresardegna.it; Via Antonio Mereu 56; adult/reduced €5/3; ⏲10am-1pm & 3-8pm Tue-Sun mid-Mar–Sep, 10am-1pm & 3-7pm Oct–mid-Mar) Beautifully renovated in 2016, this museum zooms in on Sardinian folklore, harbouring a peerless collection of filigree jewellery, carpets, tapestries, rich embroidery, musical instruments, weapons and masks. The highlight is the traditional costume display – the styles, colours and patterns speaking volumes about the people and their villages. Look out for fiery red skirts from the fiercely independent mountain villages, the Armenian-influenced dresses of Orgosolo and Desulo finished with a blue-and-yellow silk border, and the burkalike headdresses of Ittiri and Osilo.

Other rooms display life-size exhibits from the region's more unusual festivals. These include Mamoiada's sinister *mamuthones* (costumed characters), with their shaggy sheepskins and scowling masks, and Ottana's *boes* (men masked as cattle), with their tiny antelopelike masks, huge capes and furry boots. At the time of research, the masks and festivals section remained closed for renovation, with reopening tentatively scheduled for 2018. Check with the museum for its current status.

Museo Ciusa MUSEUM

(Museo Tribu; Piazza Santa Maria della Neve; adult/reduced €3/2; ⏲10am-8pm Tue-Sun Jun-Sep, 10am-1pm & 3-7pm Tue-Sun Oct-May) This recently reopened space has an entire wing devoted to the works of renowned Nuoro-born sculptor Francesco Ciusa. It also houses the permanent collection of Nuoro's excellent art museum, displaying works by the island's top 20th-century artists, including painters Antonio Ballero, Giovanni Ciusa-Romagna and Mario Delitalia, abstract artist Mauro Manca and sculptor Costantino Nivola.

Monte Ortobene MOUNTAIN

About 7km east of Nuoro is the granite peak of Monte Ortobene (955m), covered in thick woods of ilex, pine, fir and poplar, and capped by a 7m-high bronze statue of the Redentore (Christ the Redeemer). A favourite picnic spot, the mountain is the focus of Nuoro's annual Sagra del Redentore festival. On 29 August, the brightly clothed faithful make a pilgrimage here from the cathedral, stopping for Mass at Chiesa di Nostra Signora del Monte, and again under the statue.

The statue was raised in 1901 in response to a call by Pope Leo XIII to raise 19 statues of Christ around Italy to represent the 19 centuries of Christianity. Since then the statue, which shows Christ trampling the devil underfoot, has been an object of devotion for pilgrims who attribute all manner of cures and interventions to it.

The views across the valley to Oliena and Monte Corrasi are at their most breathtaking from the viewpoint near the summit, particularly at dusk when the last light makes the limestone peaks blush pink. To get to the summit by public transport, take local bus 8 from Via A Manzoni in Nuoro.

Nuoro

Top Sights

1 Museo Etnografico Sardo ... D4

Sights

2 Cattedrale di Santa Maria della Neve ... D3
3 Museo Archeologico Nazionale ... D2
4 Museo Ciusa ... D2
5 Museo Deleddiano ... D1
6 Museo MAN ... C2
7 Parco Colle Sant'Onofrio ... D4
8 Piazza Satta ... C2

Sleeping

9 Silvia e Paolo ... C2

Eating

10 Il Portico ... D2
11 Il Rifugio ... C3
12 La Locanda Pili Monica ... C2
13 Montiblu ... C1

Drinking & Nightlife

14 Bar Nuovo ... C2
15 Caffè Tettamanzi Bar Mayore ... C2

Shopping

16 Coltelli Sardi ... C2

Museo Deleddiano MUSEUM

(www.isresardegna.it; Via Grazia Deledda 44; adult/reduced €3/2; ⏲9am-1pm & 3-6pm Tue-Sun) FREE Up in the oldest part of town, the birthplace of Grazia Deledda (1871–1936) has been converted into this lovely little museum. The rooms, full of Deledda memorabilia, have been carefully restored to show what a well-to-do 19th-century Nuorese house looked like. Best of all is the material relating to her Nobel Prize – a congratulatory telegram from Italian king Vittorio Emanuele III and photos of the prize-giving ceremony, which show her, proud and tiny, surrounded by a group of stiffly suited men.

Piazza Satta PIAZZA

This small square is dedicated to the great poet Sebastiano Satta (1867–1914), who was born in a house here. To celebrate the centenary of Satta's birth, sculptor Costantino Nivola gave the square a complete makeover, whitewashing the surrounding houses to provide a blank backdrop for a series of granite sculptures planted in the piazza like menhirs. Each sculpture has a carved niche containing a bronze figurine (a clear wink at Sardinia's prehistoric *bronzetti*) depicting a character from Satta's poems.

Chiesa della Solitudine CHURCH

(Viale della Solitudine) Nobel Prize–winning author Grazia Deledda (1871–1936) was consumed by Nuoro and its essential dramas. Although she lived 36 of her 65 years in Rome, she was fittingly brought home to be buried in the plain granite church of the Chiesa della Solitudine. You will find her granite sarcophagus to the right of the altar.

Museo Archeologico Nazionale MUSEUM

(www.museoarcheologiconuoro.beniculturali.it; Via Mannu 1; adult/reduced €2/1; ⏲9am-6.30pm Wed-Sat, plus 1st Sun of month) This museum presents a romp through the region's archaeological sites. Finds from the surrounding province range from ancient ceramics and *bronzetti* to a drilled skull from 1600 BC and Roman and early-medieval artefacts. Anyone with more than a passing interest in nuraghic culture will enjoy the reconstruction of a prehistoric temple and ancient bronze laboratory.

Museo MAN GALLERY

(www.museoman.it; Via S Satta 27; adult/reduced €5/3, incl Museo Ciusa €6/4; ⏲10am-8pm Tue-Sun Jun-Sep, to 10am-1pm & 3-7pm Tue-Sun Oct-May) Housed in a restored 19th-century townhouse, this serious contemporary-art gallery hosts a wide range of rotating temporary exhibits.

Cattedrale di Santa Maria della Neve CATHEDRAL

(Piazza Santa Maria della Neve) A big, dusky peach-coloured wedding cake of a church, the 19th-century Cattedrale di Santa Maria della Neve is one of 300 or so Italian churches dedicated to the Madonna della Neve. The cathedral's facade is a big flouncing neoclassical spread, giving onto a single-nave interior.

Parco Colle Sant'Onofrio PARK

(Via Sant'Onofrio) A short wander uphill from the centre of town brings you to the quiet Parco Colle Sant'Onofrio, which commands broad mountain views. From the highest point you can see across to Monte Ortobene and, further south, to Oliena and Orgosolo.

Festivals & Events

Sagra del Redentore RELIGIOUS

(Festa del Redentore; ⏲Aug) The Sagra del Redentore (Feast of Christ the Redeemer) in the last week of August is Nuoro's main event and one of Sardinia's most exuberant folkloric festivals, attracting costumed participants from across the island for parades, music-making and dancing. On the evening of 28 August a torchlit procession, starting at the Chiesa della Solitudine, winds its way through the city.

Eating

The main street is Corso Garibaldi, which bisects a warren of tidy lanes, where you'll find several restaurants and popular cafes.

La Locanda Pili Monica TRATTORIA €

(☎0784 3 10 32; Via Brofferio 31; meals €20-25; ⏲12.30-2.45pm & 8.30-10.30pm Mon-Sat) It's all about the food at this friendly, down-to-earth trattoria. Bag a table and you're in for a treat – think fresh pastas, mains of grilled steak or seafood, and highly quaffable house wine.

★**Il Portico** SARDINIAN €€

(☎0784 21 76 41, 331 9294119; www.ilporticonuoro.it; Via Monsignor Bua 13; meals €35-45; ⏲12.30-2.30pm & 8-10.30pm Tue-Sat, 12.30-2.30pm Sun) You'll receive a warm welcome at this restaurant, where abstract paintings grace the walls and jazzy music plays. Behind the scenes, the talented Graziano and Vania rustle up a feast of local fare such as *spaghetti ai ricci* (spaghetti with sea urchins) and fresh gnocchi with lamb *ragù*. Save room for the delectable caramel-nougat semifreddo.

★Agriturismo Testone SARDINIAN €€
(☎328 3150592, 329 4115168; www.agriturismotestone.com; Via Verdi 49, Testone; meals €30;) You'll feel immediately part of *la famiglia* at this *agriturismo*, which rests in peaceful solitude in the countryside, 20km northwest of Nuoro. The welcome is heartfelt, mealtimes are cheerful and communal affairs, and the mostly home-grown food is terrific. The farm rears lamb and produces its own *formaggi, salumi,* honey, sweets, olive oil and wine. Advance reservations are obligatory.

Il Rifugio SARDINIAN €€
(☎0784 23 23 55; Via Antonio Mereu 28-36; meals €25-35, pizzas €6-10; ⊙12.45-3pm & 7.45-11.30pm Thu-Tue) One of Nuoro's most popular eateries, this jovial restaurant has won a faithful following for its creative brand of local cooking. Typical dishes include *capretto* (roasted kid) with artichokes and *pecora alla nuorese con cipolline* (Nuoro lamb with onions). And all at very reasonable prices.

Montiblu MEDITERRANEAN €€
(☎0784 23 14 43; www.montiblunuoro.com; Piazza Satta 8; meals €30-40; ⊙1-2.45pm & 8-11pm Tue-Sun) Clean, bright Mediterranean flavours shine through in regional dishes such as *tagliata di tonno* (sliced tuna steak with rocket and *pecorino*) at this stylish little restaurant. You can round out a meal in the tea room and stock up on *pecorino*, salami and preserves in the deli.

Drinking & Nightlife

Nuoro has a lively cafe scene. Take your pick of the pavement terraces in the historic centre for drinks and light bites.

Caffè Tettamanzi Bar Mayore CAFE
(Corso Garibaldi 71; ⊙6am-2am Mon-Sat) Going strong since 1875, Nuoro's oldest cafe is something of a local institution. The interior recalls a more glamorous age, with frescoed cherubs, marble tables and a deep velvet sofa where you can read works by Grazia Deledda and poet Sebastiano Satta. Snag a chair outside for crowd-watching and *panini*.

Bar Nuovo BAR
(Piazza Mazzini 6; ⊙7am-midnight) Right on Piazza Mazzini, this is an excellent place to park yourself with a cool beer and watch the world go by. It's equally good for the morning paper, midday gelato and evening *aperitivo*.

Shopping

Corso Garibaldi is studded with Italian fashion boutiques, and springs to life with an antiques market on the second Saturday of the month.

Coltelli Sardi ARTS & CRAFTS
(www.coltellisardi.com; Corso Garibaldi 53; ⊙9am-1pm & 4.30-7.30pm) True to Nuoro's pastoral heritage (not to mention those dastardly bandits), Franco Piredda crafts exquisite Sardinian knives, including the famous Pattada jackknife with a myrtle-leaf-shaped blade and a handle carved from mouflon or ram horn. They'll set you back between €50 and €750.

Information

Main Post Office (Piazza Crispi; ⊙8.20am-7.05pm Mon-Fri, to 12.35pm Sat)

Tourist Office (☎0784 44 18 23; www.provincia.nuoro.it; Piazza Italia 8; ⊙8.30am-2pm Mon-Fri, plus 3.30-7pm Tue) Multilingual staff provide plenty of useful information on Nuoro and environs.

Getting There & Away

The **bus station** (Viale Sardegna) is west of the centre, as is the train station, which is on Via Lamarmora (the westward extension of Corso Garibaldi).

BUS

ARST (☎0784 29 08 00; www.arst.sardegna.it) buses run from the bus station on Viale Sardegna to destinations throughout the province and beyond. These include Dorgali (€2.50, 45 minutes, six daily), Orosei (€3.70, 55 minutes, 10 daily), San Teodoro (€6.10, two hours, five daily), Olbia (€8.10, 2¾ to 3½ hours, three daily) and Tortolì (€5.50, two hours, five daily). There are also regular buses to Oliena (€1.90, 20 minutes) and Orgosolo (€2.50, 35 minutes). Two daily nonstop buses connect with Cagliari (€12.50, 2¾ hours).

Deplano (☎0784 29 50 30; www.deplanobus.it) also runs up to five daily buses to Olbia airport (€8.10, 1¾ hours) via San Teodoro (€6.10, 1¼ hours).

OFF THE BEATEN TRACK

ANCIENT SITES OF NUORO'S HINTERLAND

North of Nuoro, the forgotten and lonely countryside harbours some wonderful archaeological sites. They're not easy to get to – even with a car you'll be wondering where on earth you're heading – but persevere and you'll be amply rewarded. Few people make it out here, and there are no better places to experience the mystery and isolation of Sardinia's silent interior.

Fonte Sacra Su Tempiesu (www.sutempiesu.it; €3; 9am-7pm Apr-Sep, to 5pm Oct-Mar) Set in dramatic hill country near the dusty town of **Orune**, this sophisticated and elegant nuraghic well temple dates from the 2nd millennium BC. Reached by a steadily descending 800m nature trail with signposts offering background on local flora and fauna, the temple has a distinctive keyhole-shaped entrance, with stairs leading down to the well bottom – all oriented in such a way that on the day of the summer, solstice sunlight shines directly down the well shaft.

Complesso Nuragico Romanzesu (€4; 9.15am-1pm & 3-7pm Apr-Oct, to 5.30pm Nov-Mar) Spread over a 7-hectare site in a thick cork and oak wood, this 17th-century-BC nuraghic sanctuary comprises several religious buildings and circular village huts. The highlight is the sacred well temple, covered by a typical *tholos* (beehive-shaped dome) and connected to a semi-elliptic amphitheatre. Up to six daily guided tours help visitors make sense of the ruins; most are in Italian but tours in English and German are also offered. It's about 13km northwest of Bitti – follow the road towards Budduso.

For Alghero, **Redentours** (0784 3 03 25; www.redentours.com) has two daily buses (€18, 2¼ hours), for which bookings are required.

CAR & MOTORCYCLE

The dual-carriage SS131dcn highway skirts Nuoro to the north, running between Olbia and Abbasanta (where it joins the north–south SS131 Carlo Felice highway). The SS129 is the quickest road east to Orosei and Dorgali. Other roads head south for Oliena, Orgosolo and Mamoiada.

TRAIN

The train station is west of the town centre on the corner of Via Lamarmora and Via G Ciusa Romagna. ARST operates trains from Nuoro to Macomer (€4.90, 70 minutes, six daily Monday to Saturday), where you can connect with main-line Trenitalia trains to Cagliari (from Macomer €11, 1½ to 2¼ hours, eight daily).

Getting Around

Local **ATP** (0784 3 51 95; www.atpnuoro.it) buses 2 and 3 can be useful for the train station and the ARST bus station, and bus 8 from Via Manzoni for heading up to Monte Ortobene (€1.50). Tickets for city routes cost €1 and are valid for 90 minutes.

You can call for a **taxi** (368 7187232) or try to grab one along Via Lamarmora.

BARBAGIA

Sardinia's geographic and spiritual heartland is a tough, mountainous area known as the Barbagia. The name derives from the Latin term 'Barbaria' (itself derived from the Greek word *barbaros* – foreign person, barbarian), which the Romans gave the area after repeatedly failing to subdue it. The dramatic topography and tough-as-hobnail-boots locals kept the legionaries out, just as they have since kept the outside world at arm's length with their fierce inward-looking pride. Sardinian dialects are widely spoken in the Barbagia villages, traditional Sardinian music and Sardinian-language news are still broadcast on Radio Barbagia (FM103), and age-old festivities are celebrated with fervour. It's not uncommon to see older women walking down the street wearing traditional black vestments.

At the region's heart are the bald, windswept peaks of the Gennargentu massif, including Sardinia's highest mountain, Punta La Marmora (1834m) – and the Parco Nazionale del Golfo di Orosei e del Gennargentu, Sardinia's largest national park.

Orgosolo

0784 / POP 4230

High in the brooding mountains, Orgosolo is Sardinia's most notorious town, its name long a byword for the banditry and violence that blighted this part of the island for so long. More recently the town has attempted, with some success, to reinvent itself as an alternative tourist attraction. Nowadays, it's not unusual to see visitors walking down the main strip photographing the vibrant graffiti-style murals that adorn the village's buildings. But once the day-trippers have gone, the villagers come out to reclaim their streets – the old boys to sit staring at anyone they don't recognise and the lads with crew-cuts to race up and down in their mud-splattered cars.

Sights

Five kilometres to the south of the town, the SP48 local road heads up to the Montes heights, where cows, sheep and goats graze freely on communal land with a splendid mountain backdrop. Another 13km south is the **Funtana Bona**, the spring at the source of the Cedrino river. On the way you pass through the tall holm oaks of the **Foresta de Montes**.

Corso Repubblica AREA

WWII, the creation of the atomic bomb, the miners strikes of the Iglesiente, the evils of capitalism, women's liberation – Orgosolo is a giant canvas for emotionally charged graffiti. The majority of murals line the main thoroughfare, Corso Repubblica, and were initiated by Professor Francesco del Casino in 1975 as a school project to celebrate the 30th anniversary of the Liberation of Italy. There are now some 200 murals, many of them executed by Casino. Other notable artists include Pasquale Buesca and Vincenzo Floris.

The styles vary wildly according to the artists: some are naturalistic, others are like cartoons, and some, such as those on the Fotostudio Kikinu, are wonderfully reminiscent of Picasso. Like satirical caricatures, they depict all the big political events of the 20th and 21st centuries and vividly document the struggle of the underdog in the face of a powerful, and sometimes corrupt, establishment. Italy's own political failings are writ large, including the corruption of the Cassa del Mezzogiorno and Prime Minister Giulio Andreotti's trials for collusion with the Mafia, where speech bubbles mock his court refrain of 'I don't remember'. Even more interesting are the murals depicting recent events. On the corner of Via Monni there are portrayals of the destruction of the two World Trade Center towers (dated 28 September 2001) and the fall of Baghdad (dated 17 April 2003).

South of Corso Repubblica, the corner of Via Morti di Bugerru and Via Gramsci is festooned with colourful depictions of revolutionary fighter Che Guevara and the fathers of Communism: Marx, Engels and Lenin.

For a self-guided tour of the murals, get a multilingual audio guide from Orgosolo's tourist office (p187).

Festivals & Events

Festa dell'Assunta RELIGIOUS

(15 Aug) You'll catch Orgosolo at its best during the Festa dell'Assunta (Feast of the Assumption) on 15 August, when folk from all around the Barbagia converge on the town for one of the region's most colourful processions.

DON'T MISS

BARBAGIA'S VILLAGE FESTIVALS

Shrove Tuesday in Ottana The village of Ottana, near the geographic centre of Sardinia, is home to some of the island's most dramatic carnival celebrations, rivalling those of Mamoiada. Shrove Tuesday festivities here culminate in a parade of costumed *boes* (men masked as cattle) herded down the streets by their masters, the *merdules* (masked men symbolising our prehistoric ancestors).

Festa dell'Incoronazione della Madonna di Gonare Horse races, singing and dancing mark this lively religious festival, held every year between 5 and 8 September at the important pilgrimage site of Santuario di Nostra Signora di Gonare, a grey buttressed 17th-century church sitting atop a lone conical hill east of the village of Sarule, near the foot of 1083m Monte Gonare.

Sagra del Torrone Forget Easter eggs: on Easter Monday, Tonara (in the Barbargia di Belvi region) gorges on the region's deliciously nutty local *torrone* (nougat).

DON'T MISS

EASTERN SARDINIA'S TOP CLIMBS

Maurizio Oviglia's comprehensive *Pietra di Luna* (€50) climbing guide, available in local bookshops and online, is a useful resource.

Cala Fuili Easily accessible bay and good for beginners, with 190 routes from 5a to 8b+, including cliffs above the beach and scores of overhangs in the gorge for all tastes and exposures.

La Poltrona A massive limestone amphitheatre close to central Cala Gonone, with compact rock, 75 bolted routes from grades 4 to 8a and a maximum height of 175m. Mornings get too hot here in summer, so wait until late afternoon.

Cala Luna Fabulous climbing above a beautiful bay, accessed on a two-hour coastal walk from Cala Gonone or by boat. The 57 routes ranging from 5c and 8b+ include some tricky single-pitches in limestone caves with overhangs. Bonus: the rock faces are in the shade most of the day.

Hotel Supramonte Part of the fun is arriving at this breathtakingly sheer 400m cliff face, which is at the narrowest point of the Gola Su Gorropu canyon. A tough 8b multipitch climb, this is one best left to climbers with plenty of experience under their belts.

S'atta Ruia A Dorgali favourite, consisting of a long limestone cliff with vertical walls and overhangs. There are 81 routes from grades 5a to 7b. Climb in the morning for shade.

Biddiriscottai Just before the bay of Cartoe, Biddiriscottai has a stunning mountain setting with dramatic sea views. The sea cliffs and crags rise above a cave. Technical climbing on 50 well-bolted routes ranging from 5b to 8a+.

Ulassai Climbers have a high time of it in Ulassai. The sheer rock faces of the Bruncu Pranedda canyon and the Lecori cliffs provide some 80 routes, including a number of pretty tough ascents.

Aguglia This pinnacle towering above Cala Goloritzè is a superb introduction to multipitch climbing. The real challenge is the overhang – the toughest move is a 6b+.

Vascone (big pool) South of Cala 'e Luas, this is ideal for deep-water soloing (DWS), with lots of gorgeous granite to play on.

Isili Famous for its crags and overhangs, Isili is also a magnet for serious rock climbers, with 250 single-pitch sports routes ranging from 5a to 8b.

Eating

Corso Repubblica has a few inexpensive cafes and pizzerias.

Cortile del Formaggio DELI €
(☎340 9289415; www.facebook.com/ilcortiledelformaggioorgosolo; Corso Repubblica 216; ⏰10am-1pm & 3-8pm Mon-Fri May-Sep) The Cortile del Formaggio is a tiny courtyard house where you can buy fresh, smoked and roasted varieties of *fiore sardo* – Sardinian *pecorino* made from raw ewe's milk and matured for a minimum of three months.

Il Portico PIZZA €
(☎0784 40 29 29; www.ristoranteorgosolo.it; Via Giovanni XXIII 34; pizza €4-7, meals €15-20; ⏰noon-3pm daily, 7.30-10pm Mon-Sat) An excellent pizzeria/restaurant serving flavoursome pizzas and superb local vegetables and meats, such as *cinghiale in umido* (wild boar stew) with olives. The airy dining room and friendly, smiling service add to the pleasure.

Ai Monti del Gennargentu AGRITURISMO €€
(☎0784 40 23 74; http://aimontidelgennargentu.todosmart.net; Località Settiles; meals €35; ⏰12.30-3.30pm & 7.30-10.30pm Easter-Sep) For a memorable meal in pastoral surroundings, climb to this charming white farmhouse on the high Montes plateau (6km south of Orgosolo). Meals start with appetisers of home-cured meats, *pecorino* cheese and vegetables, followed by homemade pasta and Sardinia's classic *porcetto* (spit-roast suckling pig garnished with myrtle leaves). For dessert don't miss the *seadas* (cheese-filled fried dough drizzled with honey).

Information

Tourist Office (☎393 9044056; scoprior-gosolo@gmail.com; Piazza Caduti, Guerra; ⏲10.30am-6.30pm) Has a multilingual audio guide to Orgosolo's murals.

Getting There & Away

Regular buses make the run to/from Nuoro (€2.50, 35 minutes, six daily Monday to Saturday, three on Sunday). With your own vehicle, it's a 30-minute drive via the SP58.

Mamoiada

☎0784 / POP 2560

Just 14km south of Nuoro, the small stone-and-stucco village of Mamoiada stages Sardinia's most compelling carnival celebrations.

Mamuthones wearing shaggy sheepskins and beastly wooden masks run riot in Mamoiada during February's carnival festivities. If you can't be here then, you can get an idea of what it's all about at the Museo delle Maschere Mediterranee (p187). The exhibit includes a multimedia presentation and garbed mannequins wearing the famous sheepskins.

There are a couple of shops in the village selling the wooden masks worn by the *mamuthones*. Don't expect to pay less than €100 for a good one.

Sights

Museo delle Maschere Mediterranee MUSEUM
(www.museodellemaschere.it; Piazza Europa 15; adult/reduced €5/3; ⏲9am-1pm & 3-7pm) Get a firsthand feel for Mamoida's carnival at this small but engaging museum. The three-part exhibit starts with a film that allows you to vicariously experience carnival preparations such as the making of masks and bells, followed by the processions and bonfires that mark the big day itself. The second room displays masks and costumes from three traditional Sardinian carnivals (Mamoiada, Ovoda and Ottana), while the third room focuses on carnival attire from throughout the Alpine and Mediterranean regions.

Festivals & Events

★**Festa di Sant'Antonio Abate** CARNIVAL
(⏲mid-Jan) Bonfires rage throughout Mamoiada for two nights starting on 16 January as half-human, half-animal *mamuthones* parade through the streets – clad in sheepskins and shaking heavy bells – accompanied by white-masked, red-jacketed *issohadores* who go about town lassoing young women. This is one of Sardinia's most characteristic festivals, with deep pagan roots.

Eating

Locanda Sa Rosada SARDINIAN **€€**
(☎0784 5 67 13, 320 2306462; www.sarosada.com; Piazza Europa 2; meals €25-35; ⏲12.30-2.30pm & 8-10.30pm Thu-Tue) The perfect lunch stop after a visit to Mamoiada's mask museum, this Slow Food–recommended eatery has a pretty stone courtyard overhung with vines and a stone-vaulted interior dining room. The menus, built around seasonal produce, change regularly, but perennial standouts include Sa Rosada's roast meats, *culurgiones* (pasta pouches stuffed with *pecorino*, mint and potatoes) and locally produced Cannonau wine.

CARNIVAL IN MAMOIADA

Mamoiada's carnival festivities kick off with the **Festa di Sant'Antonio** on 16 and 17 January. According to myth, Sant'Antonio stole fire from hell to give to humankind, and to commemorate the fact, bonfires are lit across the village. But more than the fireworks, it's the appearance of the *mamuthones*, the costumed characters for which the village is famous, that gives the festival its sinister edge. These monstrous figures re-emerge on Shrove Tuesday and the preceding Sunday for the main Carnevale celebrations. Up to 200 men don shaggy brown sheepskins and primitive wooden masks to take on the form of the *mamuthones*. Weighed down by up to 30kg of *campanacci* (cowbells), they make a frightening spectacle. Anthropologists believe that the *mamuthones* embodied all the untold horrors that rural people feared, and that the ritual parade was an attempt to exorcise these demons before the new spring. The *mamuthones* are walked on a long leash held by the *issohadores*, dressed in the guise of outmoded gendarmes, whose job it is to drive them out of town.

Getting There & Away

Infrequent ARST buses connect with Nuoro (€1.90, 20 minutes, five daily Monday to Saturday, one Sunday). By car, it's an easy 20-minute shot up to Nuoro via the SS389var.

Gavoi

0784 / POP 2690

Famous for its *fiore sardo* (Sardinian *pecorino* cheese) and literature festival, Gavoi is one of Barbagia's prettier villages. It has a pristine historic centre, with a small web of narrow lanes hemmed in by attractive stone houses. Three kilometres to the south, **Lago di Gusana** shimmers amid thick woods of cork, ilex and oak.

Sights & Activities

A popular fishing spot, the lake and surrounding countryside provide plenty of sporting opportunities.

Chiesa di San Gavino CHURCH
In Gavoi village centre, the Chiesa di San Gavino was built in the 16th century to a Gothic-Catalan design, as evidenced by the plain red trachyte facade and splendid rose window. From the piazza outside the church, cobbled alleyways lead up through the medieval *borgo* (village).

Barbagia No Limits ADVENTURE SPORTS
(0784 182 03 73; www.barbagianolimits.it; Via Cagliari 186) Barbagia No Limits is a local operator that can organise a whole range of outdoor activities, including trekking, kayaking, canyoning, caving and jeep tours.

WORTH A TRIP

MUSEO NIVOLA

The main reason to make a stop in the grey, sleepy village of Orani is the **Museo Nivola** (www.museonivola.it; Via Gonare 2, Orani; adult/reduced €5/3; 10am-1pm & 3.30-7pm Thu-Tue). This museum celebrates the original sculpture and sand-casting techniques of Costantino Nivola, the son of a local stonemason, who fled Sardinia under Fascist persecution in 1938 and subsequently spent most of his life working in America.

Festivals & Events

L'Isola delle Storie CULTURAL
(www.isoladellestorie.it; early Jul) A rare success story, L'Isola delle Storie has gone from strength to strength since it was inaugurated in 2003. For four days in early July, the village of Gavoi is transformed into an outdoor stage, hosting readings, concerts, theatrical performances, screenings and seminars.

Eating

★ **Ristorante Santa Rughe** SARDINIAN €€
(0784 5 37 74; www.santarughe.it; Via Carlo Felice 2; meals €20-35; 12.45-2.30pm & 7.45-10.30pm Thu-Tue) Up in the village proper, this rustic restaurant serves hearty local fare such as roast veal, grilled pork chops and *gnocchetti* with saffron, mint and fresh ricotta. Also worth inquiring about (though not always on the menu) is *su erbuzzu*, a heart-warming soup of bacon, sausage, cheese and beans flavoured with wild herbs. Pizzas (evenings only) are also excellent.

Getting There & Away

ARST has a bus stop on Via Roma, just north of the medieval centre; there are four weekday connections to Nuoro (€3.10, 70 minutes) and one on Sunday. With your own wheels, it's a 40-minute drive.

Fonni

0784 / POP 3940

At 1000m Fonni is the highest town in Sardinia and has a sizeable rural community. It's also a popular base for hikers, who come to explore Sardinia's highest peaks – the Bruncu Spina (1829m) and the Punta La Marmora (1834m).

Sights

From Fonni, a scenic country road (SP7) wriggles south through parkland and oak forests, with grandiose views of limestone peaks rising out of deeply folded valleys. After 25km you hit **Desulo**, a long string of a town that was once three separate villages. There's nothing much to see, but like Fonni it provides a good base for hikers, given its proximity to the Gennargentu.

Basilica Santa Maria dei Martiri BASILICA
(off Piazza Europa) At Fonni's highest point is the imposing 17th-century Basilica della Madonna dei Martiri, one of Barbagia's most important baroque churches. Surrounded

OFF THE BEATEN TRACK

PEAK BAGGER

It's relatively easy to reach Sardinia's two highest peaks from either Fonni or Desulo. You'll find the turn-off for the **Bruncu Spina** trailhead 5km out of Fonni, on the road to Desulo. From here a 10km road winds through treeless territory to the base of a ski lift. One kilometre before the lift you'll see a steep dirt trail to the right, from where a 3km track leads right to the summit (1829m). From here you have broad, sweeping views across the island in all directions. If you're here in winter, there's some modest skiing on these slopes, and a daily lift pass and ski hire costs around €30. For details, see www.bruncuspina.com (in Italian).

For a view from 5m higher you need to march about 1½ hours south to **Punta La Marmora** (1834m). Although it looks easy enough from Bruncu Spina, you need a good walking map or a guide, as well as sufficient water in summer.

by *cumbessias* (pilgrims' huts), it's famous for a revered image of the Madonna that's said to be made from the crushed bones of martyrs. In June it's the focus of Fonni's two main feast days, the Festa della Madonna dei Martiri on the Monday after the first Sunday in June and the Festa di San Giovanni on 24 June.

Eating

Ristorante Albergo Il Cinghialetto SARDINIAN €€
(☎0784 5 76 60; www.ilcinghialetto.it; Via Grazia Deledda 193; pizza €5-10, meals €25-30; ⌚12.30-2.30pm & 7.30-10pm Tue-Sun) Down in the modern part of the village is this simple, friendly pick, dishing up meaty Sardinian fare and pizza. An open fire keeps things toasty in winter.

Getting There & Away

ARST buses run from Nuoro to Fonni (€3.10, 40 minutes, eight daily Monday to Saturday, two Sunday). With your own car, the same journey takes only 30 minutes.

Aritzo

A vivacious mountain retreat, Aritzo has been attracting visitors since the 19th century. Its cool climate and alpine character (its elevation is 796m) caught the imagination of the Piedmontese nobility, who came here to hunt boar in its forests. There are plenty of marked walking trails around the village, most of which are fine to walk along alone.

The lucrative business of snow gathering put Aritzo on the map. For some five centuries the village held a monopoly on snow collection and supplied the whole of Sardinia with ice. Snow farmers, known as *niargios*, collected the white stuff from Punta di Funtana Cungiada (1458m) and stored it in straw-lined wooden chests before sending it off to the high tables of Cagliari.

Sights

Ecomuseo della Montagna Sarda e del Gennargentu MUSEUM
(Parco Comunale Pastissu; incl Sa Bovida €3; ⌚10am-1pm & 4-7pm Tue-Sun Jun-Sep, to 6pm Oct-May) Newly expanded and relocated to Aritzo's town park in 2016, this ethnographic museum has rooms full of tools and artefacts from the rural, mountainous Gennargentu region.

Sa Bovida HISTORIC BUILDING
(Prigione Spagnola; Via Guglielmo Marconi; incl Ecomuseo della Montagna Sarda €3; ⌚10am-1pm & 4-7pm Tue-Sun Jun-Sep, to 6pm Oct-May) Just off the main drag is this chilling 16th-century prison, built of dark grey schist stone and used as a maximum-security facility right up until 1936. New prisoners, duly manacled, were lowered into the lone cell through a hole in the ceiling, which you can observe from above and below during the brief tour.

Festivals & Events

Sagra della Carapigna FOOD & DRINK
(⌚Aug) This two-day mid-August festival celebrates Aritzo's famous *carapigna*, a tangy lemon sorbet with origins dating back to the early days of commercial ice production in the surrounding mountains.

Sagra delle Castagne FOOD & DRINK
(⌚Oct) On the last Sunday of October, people crowd Aritzo's streets to sample chestnuts, live music and shows.

Getting There & Away

Aritzo is on the SS295, about 90 minutes south of Nuoro. There are some limited ARST bus services to neighbouring towns, but you'll need your own vehicle to do any serious exploring.

SARCIDANO

Southwest of Aritzo the rugged mountains flatten out to the broad Sarcidano plain, littered with *nuraghi* and other mysterious prehistoric sites.

Laconi

0782 / POP 1910

Straddling the SS128 as it twists south, Laconi is a low-key mountain town, with a slow pace of life and views of green, rolling countryside. Its cobbled lanes hide a few attractions, including an intriguing archaeological museum and a castle-topped woodland park.

Sights

Menhir Museum MUSEUM
(Museo della Statuaria Preistorica in Sardegna; www.menhirmuseum.it; Palazzo Aymerich, Piazza Marconi 10; adult/reduced €5/3; 10am-1pm & 3.30-7pm Tue-Sun Apr-Sep, 10am-1pm & 3.30-6pm Oct-Mar) Occupying an elegant 19th-century *palazzo*, this delightful museum exhibits a collection of 40 menhirs (billed as the largest such collection in the Mediterranean region). Taken from sites across the surrounding area, these stark anthropomorphic slabs are strangely compelling. Little is known of their function, but it's thought that they were connected with prehistoric funerary rites. In the backlit gloom they appear all the more mysterious, the shadows emphasising the faded sculptural relief that suggests whether they are 'male' or 'female'.

If you find this interesting, you may want to detour to Pranu Mutteddu (p191), 56km further south, where you can see them in situ.

Parco Aymerich PARK
(8am-8pm summer, to 4pm winter) Turn left off Via Sant'Ignazio to reach this smashing 22-hectare park, noted for sheltering Sardinia's widest variety of native orchid species. Among the exotic trees (including an impressive cedar of Lebanon and several eucalyptuses), springs, lakes and grottoes, you'll find the remains of an 11th-century castle, the **Castello Aymerich**. From here you have wonderful views across the park and the greenery surrounding Laconi.

Information

Tourist Office (0782 86 70 13; Palazzo Aymerich, Piazza Marconi; 9am-1pm Tue-Fri) Laconi's tourist office, inside Palazzo Aymerich in the heart of town, keeps limited hours. When it's closed you can get tourist info at the adjacent Menhir Museum.

Getting There & Away

With your own vehicle, Laconi is an hour from Oristano (via the SS442) or 1¾ hours from Nuoro (via Ghilarza on the SS131dcn).

Bus services to Laconi are fairly limited. There are daily connections with Isili (€1.90, 25 to 35 minutes), Aritzo (€2.50, 40 minutes), and Oristano (€4.30, 1¾ hours). Most run very early in the morning or in the late afternoon.

On Sundays in summer, the *trenino verde* calls in here on its way north from Mandas (€12, 1½ hours). The station is about 1km west of the town centre.

South of Laconi

Sights

Santuario Santa Vittoria ARCHAEOLOGICAL SITE
(adult/reduced €4/2, incl Nuraghe Arrubiu & Prano Mutteddu €10/5; 9.30am-sunset) Beyond the small village of Serri, the Santuario Santa Vittoria is one of Sardinia's most important nuraghic settlements. It was first studied in 1907 and later excavated in 1962. What you see today is divided roughly into three zones. The central area, the Recinto delle Riunioni (Meeting Area), is a unique enclave thought to have been the seat of civil power. A grand oval space is ringed by a wall within which are towers and various rooms.

Beyond it is the religious area, which includes a Tempietto a Pozzo (Well Temple), a second temple, a structure thought to have been the Capanna del Sacerdote (Priest's Hut), defensive trenches, and a much later addition, the Chiesa di Santa Vittoria, a little country church after which the whole site is now named. Separated from both areas is the Casa del Capo (Chief's House), so-called perhaps because it is the most intact habitation, with walls still up to 3m high. Finally, a separate area, made up of several circular dwellings, is thought to have been the main

WORTH A TRIP

SORGONO

As much for the getting there as the being there, Sorgono rewards a detour. Deep in the heart of the Mandrolisai, the remote hilly area to the west of the Gennargentu, the village is surrounded by vineyards and huge tracts of forest, full of ilex, cork, chestnut and hazel trees. In town, the **Cantina del Mandrolisai** (☎0784 6 01 13; www.cantinadelmandrolisai.com; Corso IV Novembre 20; ⏲8am-1pm & 2.30-5.30pm Mon-Fri, 9am-1pm Sat) is one of the area's most important wine producers.

Make a point of trying the local Mandrolisai DOC, a well-regarded red made from Cannonau, Muristeddu and Monica grapes.

Sorgono is a twisty 35-minute drive north from Aritzo via the SS295, or a 1¼-hour drive south from Nuoro via the SS131dcn. ARST also runs occasional buses from Sorgono to Aritzo (€2.50, 45 minutes) and Nuoro (€4.90, 1¾ hours).

From late June through early September, train enthusiasts can catch the *trenino verde* through the wine country between Sorgono and Mandas (€16, four hours).

residential quarter. Still, only four of about 22 hectares have been fully uncovered.

Santuario Santa Vittoria is at the end of a scenic road (on one side you look over La Giara di Gesturi (p88), on the other the land rises up towards the Gennargentu).

Pranu Mutteddu ARCHAEOLOGICAL SITE
(www.pranumuttedu.com; adult/reduced €5/3, incl Nuraghe Arrubiu & Santuario Santa Vittoria €10/5; ⏲8.30am-8pm May-Sep, to 6pm Oct-Apr) Near the village of Goni, Pranu Mutteddu is a unique funerary site dating to the neolithic Ozieri culture (between the 3rd and 4th millennia BC). The site is dominated by a series of *domus de janas* (literally 'fairy houses'; tombs cut into rock) and some 50 menhirs, 20 of them lined up east to west, presumably in symbolic reflection of the sun's trajectory. The scene is reminiscent of similar sites in Corsica and is unique in Sardinia.

Pranu Mutteddu is a 20km drive east of Senorbì and the SS128, close to the tiny village of Goni. The website pinpoints its exact location.

Nuraghe Is Paras ARCHAEOLOGICAL SITE
(☎0782 80 26 41; adult/reduced €3/2; ⏲10am-1pm & 3pm-sunset Apr-Oct; by arrangement Nov-Mar) About 20km south of Laconi, by the sports centre in Isili, the Nuraghe Is Paras is notable for its striking *tholos* (beehive-shaped cone), which at 11.8m is the highest in Sardinia.

Nuraghe Arrubiu ARCHAEOLOGICAL SITE
(☎346 6544747, 0782 84 72 69; www.nuraghearrubiu.it; adult/reduced €4/2, incl Santuario Santa Vittoria & Prano Mutteddu €10/5; ⏲9.30am-sunset) Rising out of the Sarcidano plain, about 10km south of Orroli and off the SP10, is the Nuraghe Arrubiu, which takes its Sardinian name from the red colour of the trachyte stone. This impressive structure, centred on a tower, now about 16m high, is thought to have once reached 30m. Surrounding it is a five-tower defensive perimeter and the remains of an outer wall and settlement. The artefacts found here indicate that the Romans made good use of it.

ℹ Getting There & Away

You'll need your own vehicle to reach the area's archaeological sites. From Laconi, the SS128 leads south towards Is Paras (18km), Santa Vittoria (30km) and Pranu Mutteddu (56km). For Nuraghe Arrubiu (45km), take the SP52.

GOLFO DI OROSEI

For sheer stop-dead-in-your-tracks beauty, there's no place like this gulf, forming the seaward section of the **Parco Nazionale del Golfo di Orosei e del Gennargentu** (www.parcogennargentu.it). Here the high mountains of the Gennargentu abruptly meet the sea, forming a crescent of dramatic cliffs riven by false inlets, scattered with horseshoe-shaped bays and lapped by exquisitely aquamarine waters. Beach space is at a premium in summer, but there's room for everyone, especially in the rugged, elemental hinterland.

Cala Gonone

☎0784 / POP 1280

Climbers, divers, sea kayakers, beachcombers and hikers all find their thrill in Cala Gonone. Why? Just look around you: imperious limestone peaks frame grandstand

DON'T MISS

SELVAGGIO BLU

For serious hikers, the **Selvaggio Blu** (www.selvaggioblu.it) is the stuff of myth: an epic seven-day, 45km trek along the Golfo di Orosei's wild and imperious coastline, traversing thickly wooded ravines and taking in bizarre limestone formations, caves and staggeringly sheer cliffs. Both the scenery and the walking are breathtaking (in every sense of the word!) on what is often hailed as Italy's toughest trek.

The trail follows the starkly eroded – and often invisible – trails of goatherds and charcoal burners, teetering around cliffs that plunge into the dazzlingly blue sea. Because of its challenging terrain, the trek requires a good level of fitness and some climbing experience for the short climbs and abseiling involved. The seven-day duration is based on the assumption that you will walk six to eight hours a day. You'll also need to come prepared with a bivi bag or an ultralight tent, climbing gear (including two 45m ropes), a roll mat, sturdy boots, a compass, map and ample food.

A guide is recommended as the trail is not well signposted and there's no water en route (guides can arrange for it to be dropped off by boat). The website www.selvaggioblu.it (in Italian) will give you itchy feet.

The author of *Arrampicare a Cala Gonone* (€18) and *Il Sentiero Selvaggio Blu* (€16), **Corrado Conca** (☎347 2903101; www.corradoconca.it; Via Barzini 15, Sassari) is Sardinia's hiking and climbing guru, and a brilliant guide for the trek. Bank on paying around €500 per person. Corrado is often up in the hills climbing, so give him plenty of notice.

views of the Golfo di Orosei, sheer cliffs dip into the brilliant-blue sea, trails wriggle through emerald-green ravines to pearly-white beaches. It is quite magnificent. Even getting here is an adventure, with each hairpin bend bringing you ever closer to a sea that spreads out before you like a giant liquid mirror.

Gathered along a pine-shaded promenade, this seaside resort still has the low-key, family-friendly vibe of the small fishing village it once was. August aside, the beaches tend to be uncrowded and the room rates affordable. Bear in mind that the resort slumbers in winter, closing from October until Easter.

Sights

Cala Gonone is the perfect launchpad for exploring the gulf's most alluring bays, which are scattered like horseshoes along the coast. The fact that the best beaches and grottoes can only be reached by hiking or dropping anchor gives them added castaway appeal.

Cala Fuili BEACH

About 3.5km south of town (follow Viale del Bue Marino) is this captivating rocky inlet backed by a deep green valley. From here you can hike over the cliff tops to Cala Luna (p192), about two hours (4km) away on foot. The trail cuts a scenic path through juniper and mastic trees and is easy to navigate, with triangle-circle symbols marking handy rocks. The coastal views are breathtaking as you approach Cala Luna.

Grotta del Bue Marino CAVE

(adult/reduced €8/5; ⏰guided tours hourly 10am-noon & 3-5pm summer, 11am-3pm winter, groups only Oct-Mar) It's a scenic 40-minute hike from Cala Fuili, or a speedy boat ride from Cala Gonone, to this enchanting grotto. It was the last island refuge of the rare monk seal (*'bue marino'* or 'sea ox' as it was known by local fishermen). The watery gallery is impressive, with shimmering light playing on the strange shapes and neolithic petroglyphs within the cave. Guided visits take place up to seven times a day. In peak season you may need to book.

Cala Luna BEACH

A favourite with rock climbers, this wildly beautiful crescent-shaped bay is backed by a lush ravine, framed by cave-pitted cliffs and pummelled by exquisite turquoise waters. Access is by foot or boat only. Linger after the tour boats have gone and you'll pretty much have the bay to yourself. If your navigation skills are good, you could continue along a tough, unmarked trail to the striking **Arco Lupiru** rock arch (4km; around 1½ hours) or **Cala Sisine** (11km; four hours).

Wild camping on the beaches is not permitted, but the authorities have been known to turn a blind eye to discreet campers.

Nuraghe Mannu ARCHAEOLOGICAL SITE
(adult/reduced €3/2; ⏲9am-noon & 5-8pm Jul & Aug, 9am-noon & 4-7pm May, Jun & Sep, 10am-1pm & 3-6pm Apr & Oct) To get an eagle-eye view over the coast, follow the signs off the Cala Gonone–Dorgali road to this *nuraghe*. After 3km the rocky track peters out at a wild headland where you can see nearly the entire curve of the gulf. The location is romantic, set above a lush gorge and with silver-grey blocks strewn beneath the olive trees. First inhabited around 1600 BC, the tower is a modest ruin, but you can still see niches in the central chamber.

The Romans took a shine to the *nuraghe*, and looking at the traces of former dwellings, you can contrast the geometric forms made by the Romans with the elliptical shapes made by their predecessors.

Acquario di Cala Gonone AQUARIUM
(www.acquariocalagonone.it; Via La Favorita; adult/reduced €10/6.50; ⏲10am-6pm daily May-Sep, Wed-Sun Apr-Oct) Check out the local marine life before taking the plunge at this shiny new aquarium, designed by architects Peter Chermayeff and Sebastiano Gaias. The 25 tanks bubble with seahorses, jellyfish, rays and – moving into more tropical waters – clownfish and anemones.

Spiaggia Sos Dorroles BEACH
About 1km south of Cala Gonone, backed by a striking yellow-orange rock wall, Spiaggia Sos Dorroles is one of the prettiest spots near town for splashing around in the aquamarine sea.

Spiaggia Palmasera BEACH
Just south of Cala Gonone, this narrow sandy strip is interrupted by rocky stretches (watch out for sea urchins).

Spiaggia Centrale BEACH
In town, the small shingle Spiaggia Centrale is good for a quick dip, though the finest beaches lie further south.

Activities

La Poltrona CLIMBING
This massive limestone amphitheatre close to Cala Gonone has compact rock and 75 bolted routes from grades 4 to 8a. Mornings get too hot here in summer, so wait until late afternoon.

Prima Sardegna ADVENTURE SPORTS
(☎0784 9 33 67; www.primasardegna.com; Viale Lungomare Palmasera 32; ⏲9am-1pm & 4-8pm summer) Prima Sardegna arranges guided excursions to Tiscali and Gorropu (€45), as well as hikes and 4WD tours in the Supramonte. Daily bike/scooter/single kayak/double kayak rental costs €30/48/36/65 respectively. Mini-cruises along the Golfo di Orosei cost between €35 and €45.

Dolmen ADVENTURE SPORTS
(☎347 6698192; www.sardegnadascoprire.it; Piazza del Porto 3) Dolmen is a reliable operator running 4WD tours into the Supramonte, canyoning excursions to the Gorropu and boat trips to the Grotta del Bue Marino and other points along the gulf. Bikes, scooters and dinghies are also available for hire. Call ahead for times and prices.

Argonauta DIVING
(☎347 5304097; www.argonauta.it; cnr Viale del Bue Marino & Via dell'Erica) PADI-accredited, Argonauta offers a range of water-based activities, including snorkelling tours (€40 adults, €35 kids), scuba-diving taster sessions (€65), cavern and wreck dives (€80 to €95) and canyoning excursions (€50). It also runs PADI Bubblemaker courses for children (€65).

Tours

Nuovo Consorzio Trasporti Marittimi BOATING
(☎0784 9 33 05; www.calagononecrociere.it; Piazza del Porto 1) This outfit offers tours including return trips to Cala Luna (€15), Cala Sisine (€22), Cala Mariolu (€30) and Cala Gabbiani (€30). A trip to the Grotta del Bue Marino costs €20, including entry to the cave. All tours are €5 to €10 more in July and August. See the website for timetables.

Cielomar BOATING
(☎0784 92 00 14; www.cielomar.it; Piazza del Porto 6) This outfit runs day-long tours along the gulf, costing from €35 to €55 per person, as well as hiring out *gommoni* (motorised dinghies) for €80 to €250 per day, excluding petrol, which usually costs an extra €25 or so.

Eating

There are plenty of snack bars, gelaterias and pizzerias on or near the waterfront. Most places close from November to March.

Gelateria Fancello GELATO €
(Viale Lungomare Palmasera 26; ice cream from €2; ⏲2-10.30pm) Hazelnut, fig, yoghurt and lemon – the gelati and sorbetti here are the real

DON'T MISS

THE BLUE CRESCENT

If you do nothing else in Sardinia, you should try to make an excursion along the 20km southern stretch of the Golfo di Orosei by boat. Intimidating limestone cliffs plunge headlong into the sea, scalloped by pretty beaches, coves and grottoes. With an ever-changing palette of sand, rocks, pebbles, seashells and crystal-clear water, the unfathomable forces of nature have conspired to create a sublime taste of paradise. The colours are at their best until about 3pm, when the sun starts to drop behind the higher cliffs.

From the port of Cala Gonone you head south to the **Grotta del Bue Marino** (p192). The first beach after the cave is **Cala Luna** (p192), a crescent-shaped strand closed off by high cliffs to the south. **Cala Sisine** is the next beach of any size, also a mix of sand and pebbles and backed by a deep, verdant valley. **Cala Biriola** quickly follows, and then several enchanting spots where you can bob below the soaring cliffs – look out for the patches of celestial-blue water.

Cala Mariolu is arguably one of the most sublime spots on the coast. Split in two by a cluster of bright limestone rocks, it has virtually no sand. Don't let the smooth white pebbles put you off, though. The water that laps these beaches ranges from a kind of transparent white at water's edge through every shade of light and sky blue and on to a deep purplish hue.

deal. Stop by for a cone to lick as you stroll the promenade.

★Agriturismo Nuraghe Mannu SARDINIAN €€
(☎0784 9 32 64; www.agriturismonuraghemannu.com; off the SP26/Dorgali-Cala Gonone Rd; meals €26; ⏲dinner from 8pm) Scenically perched above the gulf and nestled amid silvery olive groves, this *agriturismo* puts on a mouthwatering spread. Loosen a belt notch for a feast of home-produced *pecorino,* salami, olives and wine, followed by handmade pasta, succulent roast kid or lamb and (phew!) Sardinian sweets.

Il Pescatore SEAFOOD €€
(☎0784 9 31 74; www.ristoranteilpescatorecalagonone.com; Via Acqua Dolce 7; meals €30-45; ⏲noon-2.30pm & 7-10.30pm; 👪) Fresh seafood is what this authentic place is about. Sit on the terrace for sea breezes and fishy delights, such as pasta with *ricci* (sea urchins) and spaghetti with clams and *bottarga* (mullet roe). It also does a kids' menu (€15).

La Favorita ITALIAN €€
(☎0784 9 31 69; www.facebook.com/lafavorita-calagonone; Viale Lungomare Palmasera 30; pizzas €6-10, meals €25-35; ⏲12.15-3pm & 7-11pm) There's always a good buzz at this incredibly popular restaurant and pizzeria with a lovely sea-facing terrace. Snag a table to dig into excellent wood-oven pizzas, or go for fish dishes including ceviche with lemon, chilli and sweet potato and whatever is the catch that day.

Shopping

Namaste BOOKS
(Viale Colombo 11; ⏲6.30am-1pm & 4-8pm) For trekking and climbing maps and guides, check out Namaste. It stocks Maurizio Oviglia's *Pietra di Luna* (€50), a comprehensive rock-climbing guide covering the Cala Gonone, Jerzu and Baunei areas; Corrado Conca's *Arrampicare a Cala Gonone* (€20) and *Sentiero Selvaggio Blu* (€17), covering the stunning seven-day Selvaggio Blu hike; and *La Sardegna in Bicicletta* (€13.90) detailing 1000km of cycling routes.

You can also pick up walking maps and travel guides here.

Information

Tourist Office (☎0784 9 36 96; www.dorgali.it; Viale del Bue Marino 1a; ⏲9am-1pm & 3-7pm May-Sep, to 1pm Oct-Apr) A very helpful office in the small park off to the right as you enter town.

Getting There & Away

Buses run to Cala Gonone from Dorgali (€1.30, 20 minutes, seven daily Monday to Saturday, four Sunday) and Nuoro (€3.10, 1¼ hours, six daily Monday to Saturday, three Sunday).

Orosei

☎0784 / POP 7020

Scenically positioned at the gulf's northernmost point and surrounded by marble quarries and fruit orchards, Orosei is an unsung treasure. Over centuries the silting of the Rio Cedrino (Cedrino river), Spanish neglect, malaria and pirate raids took their toll on the town, once an important Pisan port. Today the atmospheric historic centre is laced with cobbled lanes that twist to pretty stone-built houses, medieval churches and leafy piazzas for kicking back and watching the world go slowly by.

Orosei's beachfront satellite, Marina di Orosei, is 2.5km east of the town proper. The beach marks the northern end of the Golfo di Orosei; from here you can see the gulf arched in all its magnificence to the south. The Marina di Orosei beach is closed off to the north by the Rio Cedrino and behind the beaches stretch the Stagni di Cedrino lagoons.

Sights

Chiesa del Rosario CHURCH
(Via del Rosario) Just off Orosei's main square (Piazza del Popolo), the baroque ochre-hued Chiesa del Rosario, with its trio of wooden crosses, wouldn't look out of place in a spaghetti Western. The lane leading up from its left-hand side takes you to Piazza Sas Animas and the stone church of the same name, with a vaguely Iberian feel about it.

Chiesa di San Giacomo CHURCH
(Piazza San Giacomo) Presiding over Piazza del Popolo is this Spanish-style church, with its imposing neoclassical facade and a series of tiled domes. Its terrace commands views of the mountains rising above a jumble of terracotta rooftops.

Chiesa di San Sebastiano CHURCH
(Piazza San Sebastiano) The most appealing of all Orosei's churches, the humble yet highly atmospheric 8th-century Chiesa di San Sebastiano is on Piazza San Sebastiano, with a trio of stone arches and a reed-woven ceiling.

Chiesa di San Antonio CHURCH
(Piazza San Antonio) On the fringes of the historic centre, this church dates largely from the 15th century. The broad, uneven courtyard surrounding it is lined with squat *cumbessias* (pilgrims' huts) and has a solitary Pisan watchtower.

Prigione Vecchia CASTLE
(Piazza Sas Animas) On the southern edge of Piazza Sas Animas rises the 15m-high hulk of the Prigione Vecchia, also known as the Castello, a tower left over from a medieval castle.

Eating & Drinking

Downtown Orosei and the northern beaches both offer a wide assortment of eating options, from bars and pizzerias to fancier seafood places.

Trattoria Manu TRATTORIA €
(☎0784 99 93 77; Piazza del Popolo 16; meals €25; ⏰12.30-10.30pm) This cafe-trattoria has two things going for it: first, a perfect location on Orosei's pretty main square; second, non-stop afternoon opening hours, so you can drop in for a snack any time of day. Aside from that, the food is just so-so.

Da Mario SEAFOOD, PIZZA
(☎0784 9 81 48; Via del Mare 27; ⏰noon-3pm & 7-11pm) Locals love this centrally located

FINDING YOUR PERFECT BEACH IN OROSEI

Just east of Orosei, a strip of pale-golden sand fringed by topaz waters runs 5km south and undergoes several name changes along the way: **Spiaggia Su Barone**, **Spiaggia Isporoddai** and **Spiaggia Osalla**. All are equally tempting and are mostly backed by pine stands, giving you the option of retreating to the shade for a picnic or even a barbecue (facilities are scattered about the pines). Past a big breakwater you can wander from Spiaggia Osalla around to **Caletta di Osalla**, the second stretch of sand after the main beach.

More fabulous beaches necklace the coast to the north of Marina di Orosei, including pine-backed **Cala Liberotto** and **Cala Ginepro**, which appeals to families with its shallow water and campground. Further north still is **Spiaggia Bidderosa**, which forms part of a nature reserve and never gets too busy because visitor numbers are restricted. A 4km trail leads down to the beach, a dreamy vision of sugar-white sand, flanked by lush pines, eucalypts and juniper, and lapped by cobalt-blue waters. The northern stretch sidles up to another fine beach, **Berchida**.

WORTH A TRIP

CALA GOLORITZÈ

The last beachette of the gulf, Cala Goloritzè rivals the best. At the southern end, bizarre limestone formations soar away from the cliffside. Among them is jaw-dropping Monte Caroddi or the Aguglia, a 148m-high needle of rock beloved of climbers. Many boat trips will take you here, or you can hike in from the Altopiano del Golgo on the beautiful, 3.5km **Cala Goloritzè Trail** (p202). Note that the beach itself is rather small and can get crowded in summer.

restaurant for its buzzing atmosphere, its welcoming terrace and its versatility. Whether you're after a full-on seafood dinner or just a great pizza, you'll find something to suit your mood. Beyond the classics – seafood pastas and risottos, platters of grilled fish – you can also get steaks and even some vegetarian fare.

Yesterday Bar BAR

(Via Nazionale 48; ⌚5pm-1am) Troubles indeed seem far away at this arty Beatles-themed bar, set around a pocket-sized courtyard. It's a chilled spot for a snack, cold beer or cocktail.

Information

Tourist Office (☎0784 99 81 84; Piazza del Popolo 12; ⌚9am-1pm & 5-9pm daily Jul & Aug, 10am-noon & 3-5pm Mon-Sat Sep-Jun) Once in town, follow signs for the *centro* to wind up in Piazza del Popolo, where you'll find the local tourist office.

Getting There & Away

Several daily buses run to Orosei from Nuoro (€3.70, 55 minutes, five daily Monday to Saturday, three daily Sunday) and Dorgali (€1.90, 30 minutes, two daily Monday to Saturday, one Sunday). From Orosei, it's a 30-minute drive to Dorgali, or a 40-minute drive to either Nuoro or Cala Gonone.

Galtelli

☎0784 / POP 2470

Crouched at the foot of Monte Tuttavista and hemmed in by olive groves, vineyards and sheep-nibbled pastures, Galtelli is quite the village idyll. Its tiny medieval centre is a joy to wander, with narrow lanes twisting to old stone houses and sun-dappled piazzas. If you fancy tiptoeing off the map for a while, this is the place.

Sights & Activities

Museo Etnografico Sa Domo 'e sos Marras MUSEUM

(Via Garibaldi 14; adult/reduced €3/2; ⌚10am-1pm & 4-7pm Tue-Sun Jun-Sep, to 1pm Thu-Sun Oct-May) Housed in an 18th-century noble villa, the Museo Etnografico Sa Domo 'e sos Marras contains a fascinating collection of rural paraphernalia. There's a loom made out of juniper wood, a donkey-drawn millstone and a small display of children's toys. Upstairs, rooms have been decorated in their original 18th-century style.

Grazia Deledda Trail WALKING

(www.parchiletterari.com/parchi/grazia-deledda/vita.php) The town's main claim to fame is its mention in Grazia Deledda's most famous novel *Canne al Vento* (Reeds in the Wind). The tourist office can advise on Grazia Deledda itineraries, which take in the **Chiesa di San Pietro**, a Romanesque-Pisan church near the town cemetery, and the 17th-century **Casa delle Dame Pintor**, the fictional home of the Pintor sisters in *Reeds in the Wind,* a passionate tale about the demise of a family of aristocratic landowners.

Information

Tourist Office (☎0784 9 01 50; www.galtellicomunitaospitale.it; Piazza SS Crocifisso; ⌚9am-noon & 4-7pm summer, 10am-noon Tue-Sun winter) Information is available from the tourist office in the old town.

Getting There & Away

Up to five daily buses connect Galtelli and Orosei (€1.30, 15 minutes). With your own vehicle, it's about a 10-minute drive.

SUPRAMONTE

Southeast of Nuoro rises the great limestone massif of the Supramonte, its sheer walls like an iron curtain just beyond Oliena. Despite its intimidating aspect, it's actually not as high as it seems – its peak, Monte Corrasi, only reaches 1463m – but it is impressively wild, the bare limestone plateau pitted with ravines and ragged defiles. The raw, uncompromising landscape is made all the more thrilling by its one-time notoriety as the heart of Sardinia's bandit country.

The Supramonte provides some magnificent hiking. But because much of the walking is over limestone, there are often few discernible tracks to follow, and in spring and autumn you should carefully check the weather conditions. You can engage a local guide in towns throughout the region, including Oliena, Dorgali and Baunei.

Oliena

☎0784 / POP 7140

Few images in Sardinia are as arresting as the magnificent peak of Monte Corrasi (1463m) when the dusky light makes its limestone summit glow. From Nuoro you can see Oliena's multicoloured rooftops cupped in the mountain's palm. The village itself is an unassuming place with a grey-stone centre, and is a handy base for exploring the Supramonte.

Oliena was probably founded in Roman times, although its name is a reference to the Ilienses people, descendants of a group of Trojans who supposedly escaped Troy and settled in the area. The arrival of the Jesuits in the 17th century was better documented and set the scene for the village's modern fame. The eager fathers helped promote the local silk industry and encouraged farmers to cultivate the surrounding slopes. The lessons were learnt well, and now Oliena is famous for its beautiful silk embroidery and its blood-red Cannonau wine, Nepente di Oliena. Oliena is also the home town of Gianfranco Zola, English football's favourite Sardinian import, who was born here in 1966.

Sights & Activities

The 13th-century **Chiesa di Santa Maria** rises above Piazza Santa Maria, the village's focal point and the site of the Saturday **market**. As you wander the steep grey streets, look out for **murals**, including one of a notorious bandit and local lad, Giovanni Corbeddu Sali (1844–98); on a pink house near Via Cavour, another mural depicts an old lady dressed in black and bearing a rifle, symbolising Oliena's Easter S'Incontru celebrations, during which shots are traditionally fired to celebrate Christ's resurrection.

The countryside surrounding Oliena provides some awesome trekking for enthusiasts.

★**Su Gologone** SPRING

(www.sorgentisugologone.it; adult/reduced €2/1.50; ⏲9am-7pm) Tucked beneath sheer limestone cliffs, this gorgeous mountain spring is the final outflow point for Italy's largest underground river system. Water percolating through the countless fissures and sinkholes in the Supramonte's high country eventually gathers here and flows out to join the Cedrino river. The spring is beautiful any time, but try to catch it around 1pm when the sun passes directly overhead, turning the water brilliant green. Afterwards, the adjacent

WORTH A TRIP

VALLE DI LANAITTU

Immerse yourself in the karst wilderness of the Supramonte by hiking, cycling or driving through this enchanting 7km valley, signposted off the Oliena–Dorgali road. Towering limestone mountains, cliffs and caves lord it over the narrow valley, scattered with natural and archaeological wonders. Rosemary and mastic, grapes and olives flourish in the valley, which attracts wildlife such as martens, birds of prey, wild boar and goats.

Archaeology buffs will be in their element discovering sites that have been inhabited since the Middle Neolithic period. Near the valley's southern end, it's possible to visit a pair of caves – **Grotta di Sa Ohe** (€2; ⏲9am-6pm Apr-Sep) and **Grotta Corbeddu** (€5; ⏲9am-7pm Apr-Sep) – and the nuraghic site of **Sa Sedda 'e Sos Carros** (p201), dating back to 1300 BC; buy tickets for all three sites at Rifugio Sa Ohe, a whitewashed hut down a signposted dirt road.

You'll need your own wheels to travel into the valley. Note that the road is mostly unpaved but generally suitable for 2WD vehicles; inquire locally if unsure about current conditions. The valley's northern entrance is 10km east of Oliena. Leaving Oliena, initially follow signs to Su Gologone, then branch right at the signposted turn-off for Valle di Lanaittu.

tree-shaded park is perfect for a picnic or an afternoon swim.

Scientists have only recently begun unravelling Su Gologone's mysteries. In a 1999 experiment designed to trace the flow of water through the Supramonte, researchers injected fluorescent dye into the waters of S'Edera cave near the mountain village of Urzulei. After waiting nearly a month, they discovered the dye finally flowing out right here at Su Gologone. The spring's normal flow has been measured at 500L per second, though it's estimated to increase to 10,000L per second during rainy periods. And the total volume of the Supramonte's underground water system is estimated to be about 100 million cubic metres. Any way you slice it, there's a lot of water in there: in 2010 Italian diver Alberto Cavedon explored the spring to a depth of 135m – but still didn't reach the bottom!

To get here from Oliena, follow the SP46 east 6km towards Dorgali, then turn right following signs for Su Gologone until the road dead ends into a parking lot.

Cooperativa Enis ADVENTURE SPORTS
(☎0784 28 83 63; www.coopenis.it; Località Monte Maccione) This highly regarded adventure-sports company offers guided treks and 4WD excursions into the Supramonte and along the Golfo di Orosei. Destinations include Tiscali, Gola Su Gorropu, Cala Luna and the Supramonte di Orgosolo and Murales, with prices starting at €37 for a half-day trek or €43 for a full day. A packed lunch bumps up the cost by €5.

Sardegna Nascosta HIKING
(☎349 4434665, 0784 28 85 50; www.sardegnanascosta.it; Via Masiloghi 35) Arranges trips and treks (€35 to €55 including lunch) with a cultural focus, from hikes to Monte Corrasi, Gola Su Gorropu and the Valle di Lanaittu to canoeing, climbing and caving excursions.

Festivals & Events

Autunno in Barbagia CULTURAL
From September to December, 27 mountain villages in Barbagia take it in turns to host a weekend of events, from cheese-making workshops to exhibitions and craft demonstrations. Residents open their doors to visitors and put on a feast of local fare. It's a great opportunity to buy local produce.

Settimana Santa CULTURAL
(Easter) The village is a hive of festive activity during Easter week. The culmination of the weeklong celebrations is the *S'Incontru* (The Meeting), a boisterous procession on Easter Sunday in which bearers carry a statue of Christ to meet a statue of the Virgin Mary in Piazza Santa Maria.

Eating

Some of the region's best eateries are outside Oliena along the road to Su Gologone gorge. Head out of town towards Dorgali, then turn right towards Valle di Lanaittu (follow the signs).

Agriturismo Guthiddai SARDINIAN €€
(☎0784 28 60 17; www.agriturismoguthiddai.com; Località Guthiddai; meals €28-35; 7.30-10.30pm;) Guests are welcomed like family members at this whitewashed *agriturismo*, romantically set between vineyards and olive groves. Home-grown wine, olive oil and vegetables appear on the dinner table, and the house speciality is flavoursome *pecora in cappotto* (ewe stew).

★**Su Gologone** SARDINIAN €€€
(☎0784 28 75 12; www.sugologone.it; Località Su Gologone; meals €35-45; 12.30-3pm & 8-10pm) Nestled at the foot of mountains, this rural retreat is a delight, with a bougainvillea-draped terrace for balmy evenings. The local Cannonau red goes well with the Sardinian classics on the menu – *culurgiones* (Sardinian ravioli), *porcetto* roasted to crackling perfection on a big open fire, and *seadas al miele* (light pastries with ricotta and bitter honey).

Getting There & Away

ARST runs frequent buses from Via Roma to Nuoro (€1.90, 20 minutes, up to 12 daily Monday to Saturday, six on Sunday).

It's a 15-minute drive from Nuoro to Oliena via the SP22.

Dorgali & Around

☎0784 / POP 8550

Dorgali is a down-to-earth town with a grandiose backdrop, nestled at the foot of Monte Bardia and framed by vineyards and olive groves. Limestone peaks rear above the centre's pastel-coloured houses and steep, narrow streets, luring hikers and climbers to their summits.

DON'T MISS

TREKKING TO TISCALI

The hike to the archaeological site of **Tiscali** (p200) is pure drama, striking into the heart of the limestone Supramonte. The trailhead is at the **Sa Barva bridge** over the green Rio Flumineddu, the same starting point as the route to **Gola Su Gorropu** (p199). You'll need sturdy footwear for some easy rock-hopping, but most of the path – marked with red arrows – is easygoing, and canopies of juniper and cork oaks afford shady respite. The 7km trail is signposted and takes between 1½ and two hours; allow five hours for the return hike, breaks and a visit to Tiscali. Time permitting, you can visit the **Domus de Jana Biduai** (dawn-dusk) FREE on the road back to Dorgali. Stepping stones cross the river to this ancient nuraghic tomb.

Alternatively, you can hike into Tiscali from the west, passing through the gorgeous Valle di Lanaittu. This approach involves driving the dirt road south from Su Gologone through the Valle di Lanaittu and parking at road's end. From here, a trail switchbacks up the mountainside before climbing along the base of a reddish-orange rock face and passing through a natural cleft to reach the final descent into Tiscali. The entire climb, alternately signposted with red-and-white blazes and cairns, takes about 1½ hours. To turn this into a scenic loop on the way back, follow signs for Sa Barva bridge on your initial descent from Tiscali, but then turn left at the bottom, looping around the base of the mountain to return to the Valle di Lanaittu parking area. This route is a bit harder to follow than the classic Sa Barva trail, so inquire locally before departing, or consider hiring a guide.

There are many companies in Oliena, Dorgali and Cala Gonone offering guided tours to Tiscali. Typically these cost around €40 per person and sometimes include lunch.

For more outdoor escapades, the dramatic Golfo di Orosei and spectacularly rugged Supramonte are within easy striking distance.

Sights

★Gola Su Gorropu CANYON

(328 8976563; www.gorropu.info; adult/reduced €5/3.50; 10.30am-5pm) Sardinia's most spectacular gorge is flanked by limestone walls towering up to 500m in height. The endemic (and endangered) *Aquilegia nuragica* plant grows here, and at quieter times it's possible to spot mouflon and golden eagles. From the Rio Flumineddu riverbed you can wander about 1km into the boulder-strewn ravine without climbing gear; follow the markers. Near the narrowest point (just 4m wide) you reach the formidable **Hotel Supramonte**, a tough 8b multipitch climb up a vertical 400m rock face.

To hike into the gorge, you'll need sturdy shoes and sufficient water. There are two main routes. The most dramatic begins from the car park opposite Hotel Silana at the **Genna 'e Silana** pass on the SS125 at Km 183. The 8km trail takes 1½ to two hours one way, so allow at least four hours for the return trek, longer if you plan to spend time exploring the gorge itself. While the descent is mostly easygoing, the climb back up is considerably tougher.

The hike weaves through holm oak woods, boulder-strewn slopes and cave-riddled cliffs. For a bird's-eye perspective of the gorge, you could take the 6km ridge trail from the car park to 888m **Punta Cucuttos**. It takes around 1½ hours one way.

The second and slightly easier hiking route (14km) to Gorropu is via the **Sa Barva bridge**, about 15km from Dorgali. To get to the bridge, take the SS125 and look for the sign on the right for the Gola Su Gorropu and Tiscali between Km 200 and Km 201. Follow this road for 10.5km until the asphalt finishes (about 20 minutes). Park here and cross the Sa Barva bridge, after which you'll see the trail for the Gola signposted off to the left. From here it's a scenic two-hour hike along the Rio Flumineddu to the mouth of the gorge (four hours return).

If you'd prefer to go with a guide, Sandra and Franco at the **Cooperativa Gorropu** (Franco 347 4233650, Sandra 333 8507157; www.gorropu.com; Passo Silana SS125, Km 183, Urzulei) arrange all sorts of excursions and activities, from trekking and canyoning to caving and cookery courses; see the website for prices. Their base is in Urzulei, but they also run a small info centre at Genna 'e Silana pass.

WORTH A TRIP

DAY TRIPS FROM DORGALI, OROSEI & CALA GONONE

Several attractions in the countryside north of Dorgali make perfect day trips from Dorgali, Orosei or Cala Gonone.

Grotta di Ispinigoli (adult/reduced €7.50/3.50; ⏲ hourly tours 10am-6pm Jul & Aug, to 5pm Jun & Sep, 10am-noon & 3-5pm Apr, May & Oct) A short drive north of Dorgali, the fairytale-like Grotta di Ispinigoli is a veritable forest of glittering rock formations, including the world's second-tallest stalagmite (the highest is in Mexico and stands at 40m). Unlike most caves of this type, which you enter from the side, here you descend 60m inside a giant 'well', at whose centre stands the magnificent 38m-high stalagmite. You can admire the tremendous rock formations, many of them sprouting from the walls like giant mushrooms and broccoli.

Discovered by a shepherd in 1950, the caves weren't explored in earnest until the 1960s. A deep network of 15km of caves with eight subterranean rivers has since been found. Cavers can book tours of up to 8km through one of the various tour organisers in Dorgali or Cala Gonone. *Nuraghe* artefacts were discovered on the floor of the main well, and Phoenician jewellery on the floor of the second main 'well', another 40m below. On the standard tour you can just peer into the hole that leads into this second cavity, known also as the **Abbisso delle Vergini** (Abyss of the Virgins). The ancient jewellery found has led some to believe that the Phoenicians launched young girls into the pit in rites of human sacrifice.

Forget the souvenir snapshots – photography is not permitted.

S'Abba Frisca (☎335 6569072; www.sabbafrisca.com; adult/reduced €7.50/5; ⏲ 9am-noon & 3-7pm Apr-Sep, by appointment Oct-Mar) Around 5km from Grotta di Ispinigoli, on the country road towards Cala Gonone, S'Abba Frisca is an ethnographic treasure trove. Centred on a lake and waterfalls, its gardens bristle with centuries-old olive trees, *macchia* and medicinal plants. As you wander, look out for rare Sardinian tortoises milling around. Other displays bringing Sardinia's cultural heritage to life include a shepherd's hut built from basalt and juniper, old olive and wine presses, a *pane carasau* bread oven, traditional costumes and blacksmith tools.

Cala Cartoe Secluded at the end of a remote back road, this lovely sweep of sand makes a pleasant day trip from Cala Gonone, 11km to the south.

Serra Orrios (adult/reduced €5/2.50; ⏲ hourly tours 9am-1pm & 3-6pm, shorter hours winter) Eleven kilometres northwest of Dorgali, at Km 25 on the SP38, is Serra Orrios, a ruined nuraghic village inhabited between 1500 BC and 250 BC. Nestled among olive groves, the remains comprise a cluster of 70 or so horseshoe-shaped huts grouped around two basalt-hewn temples: Tempietto A, thought to be used by visiting pilgrims, and Tempietto B, for the villagers. There's a diagram near the entrance, which helps to understand the site, as the guided tours are in Italian only.

S'Ena 'e Thomes (⏲ dawn-dusk) Signposted 3km north of the intersection of the SP38 and the SS129 (Nuoro–Orosei road), S'Ena 'e Thomes is a fine example of a *tomba di gigante* (literally 'giants' tomb'; ancient mass grave) built at the height of the nuraghic period. A narrow path winds through marshy farmland to the central, oval-shaped stone stele (3.65m tall and 2.10m wide), which closes off the ancient burial chamber.

★Tiscali ARCHAEOLOGICAL SITE

(www.museoarcheologicodorgali.it/wp/Reperto_Sito/tiscali; adult/reduced €5/2; ⏲ 9am-7pm daily May-Sep, to 5pm Oct-Apr, closed in rainy weather) Hidden in a mountain-top cave deep in the Valle Lanaittu, the mysterious nuraghic village of Tiscali is one of Sardinia's must-see archaeological highlights. Dating from the 6th century BC and populated until Roman times, the village was discovered in the late 19th century. At the time it was relatively intact, but since then grave robbers have done a pretty good job of looting the place, stripping the conical stone-and-mud huts down to the skeletal remains that you see today.

Despite the fragmentary condition of the ruins themselves, Tiscali is an awe-inspiring sight: jumbled stone foundations amid holm oak and turpentine trees huddled in the eerie twilight of the limestone overhang. The inhabitants of nearby **Sa Sedda 'e Sos Carros** (☎333 5808844; €5; ⊙9am-7pm Apr-Sep) used it as a hiding place from the Romans, and its inaccessibility ensured that the Sards were able to hold out here until well into the 2nd century BC.

Museo Archeologico MUSEUM
(www.museoarcheologicodorgali.it; Via Vittorio Emanuele; adult/reduced €3/1.50; ⊙9.30am-1pm & 3.30-6pm Oct-Apr, 9.30am-1pm & 4-7pm May-Sep, closed Mon Nov-Feb) This modest archaeology museum spells out the region's past in artefacts, from pre-nuraghic to medieval times.

Activities

There are several outfits in Dorgali that organise 4WD excursions, hikes and caving expeditions in the great limestone wilderness just outside town.

Cooperative Ghivine ADVENTURE SPORTS
(☎338 8341618; www.ghivine.com; Via Lamarmora 31) A one-stop action shop, arranging treks to places including Gola Su Gorropu and Tiscali. Trekking packages including accommodation are also available.

Eating

Inexpensive snack bars, pizzarias and *pasticcerie* dot the main drag, Via Lamarmora.

Ristorante Colibrì SARDINIAN €€
(☎340 7211564; www.ristorantecolibridorgali.it; Via Floris 7; meals €30-35; ⊙12.30-2.30pm & 7-10.30pm, closed Sun Sep-Jun) Hidden away in an incongruous residential area (follow the numerous signs), this lemon-walled restaurant is the real McCoy for meat eaters. Stars of the menu include *cinghiale al rosmarino* (wild boar with rosemary), *capra alla selvatiza* (goat with thyme) and *porcetto*.

★**Ristorante Ispinigoli** SARDINIAN €€
(☎0784 9 52 68; www.hotelispinigoli.com; meals €30-36; ⊙12.30-2.30pm & 7.30-9.30pm) Linger for dinner and panoramic sunset views at the Ristorante Ispinigoli, just below the entrance to the Grotta di Ispinigoli. Located in Hotel Ispinigoli, the well-known restaurant rolls out local delights such as stone bass-stuffed black ravioli with mullet roe, herb-infused roast kid and a waistline-expanding selection of *formaggi*.

Shopping

Cantina Sociale Dorgali FOOD & DRINKS
(www.cantinadorgali.it; Via Piemonte 11; ⊙8.30am-1.30pm & 3-7pm Mon-Fri, 9am-1pm Sat) For tastings and sales of the region's fine local Cannonau (and other Sardinian varietals), stop in at this wine shop in the heart of town.

Information

Tourist Office (☎0784 92 72 35; www.enjoy-dorgali.it; Corso Umberto 37; ⊙10am-1pm & 4-8pm Mon-Fri) Can provide information on Dorgali and Cala Gonone, including contact details for local trekking outfits and accommodation lists.

Getting There & Away

ARST buses serve Nuoro (€2.50, 50 minutes, eight daily Monday to Saturday, four Sunday). Up to seven (four on Sundays) shuttle back and forth between Dorgali and Cala Gonone (€1.30, 20 minutes). You can pick up buses at several stops along Via Lamarmora. Buy tickets at the bar at the junction of Via Lamarmora and Corso Umberto.

By car or motorcycle, Dorgali is 15 minutes from Cala Gonone via the SP26, 35 minutes from Orosei via the SS125, and 45 minutes from Nuoro via the SP46 or SS129.

Baunei & the Altopiano del Golgo

Clinging to a precipitous rocky ridge on the long, tortuous road between Arbatax and Dorgali, the old stone shepherd's village of Baunei is an agreeable mountain outpost and a welcome oasis in the middle of the rugged Supramonte.

Whether or not you linger in town, be sure not to miss the region's uncontested highlight: the 10km detour up to the Altopiano del Golgo, a strange, other-worldly plateau where goats, pigs and donkeys graze in the *macchia* (Mediterranean scrub) and woodland. From here, one of Sardinia's best hiking trails descends to the coast at Cala Goloritzè, while a hardscrabble road snakes down to the rock spike of Pedra Longa, a natural monument and also the starting point for Sardinia's star coastal trek, the Selvaggio Blu.

Sights & Activities

Il Golgo LANDMARK
FREE Follow the signs from Baunei up a 2km climb of impossibly steep switchbacks

WORTH A TRIP

DRIVING THE SS125

It's well worth getting behind the wheel for the sheer pleasure of driving the 60km of road snaking from **Dorgali** to **Santa Maria Navarrese**. The serpentine, and at times hair-raising, SS125 threads through the mountaintops and the scenery is distractingly lovely: to the right the ragged limestone peaks of the Supramonte rear above the woods, and gorges carve up the broad valley; to the left the mountains tumble down to the bright-blue sea. The views are tremendous as you crest the vertiginous **Genna 'e Silana** pass at 1017m. Shortly afterwards, near the turn-off for Urzulei, you'll spot the sign for **Formaggi Gruthas** (www.gruthas.it; SS125, Km 175, Località Giustizieri), where you can stop to buy farm-fresh *pecorino*, goats' cheese and ricotta. The buttress-like peak of 647m Monte Scoine marks the approach to Santa Maria Navarrese. For a great detour on the return trip, follow signs from Lotzorai towards Talana, then Urzulei. The road twists through a canyon-like valley, shadowing a river and passing reddish granite outcrops, vineyards and cactus-dotted slopes, before looping back up to the SS125 at Urzulei.

The drive is perhaps most beautiful in spring when wildflowers cloak the hills and broom adds a splash of gold to the landscape. Aside from the odd hell-for-leather Fiat, traffic is sparse, but you should take care at dusk when wild pigs, goats, sheep and cows rule the road and bring down loose rocks from the heights.

to the plateau, then continue 6km north on pavement before taking the signposted turn-off for the final unpaved 1km to Su Sterru (Il Golgo). From the car park, walk five minutes to this remarkable feat of nature – a 270m abyss just 40m wide at its base. Its funnel-like opening is now fenced off, but just peering into the dark opening is enough to bring on the vertigo.

Chiesa di San Pietro CHURCH

Standing lonesome on the Golgo plateau amid ancient olive trees, this humble late-16th-century church with its striking whitewashed facade is flanked by *cumbessias* – rough, open stone structures that traditionally house pilgrims, who come here to celebrate the saint's day.

The church is a 10km drive north of Baunei. Turn off the SS125 at Via San Pietro, following signs for the Altopiano; after a steep and tortuous initial climb, it's a relatively straight shot to the church across high plateau country.

Cala Goloritzè Trail HIKING

(€6; ⏲trailhead 7.30am-4pm, beach to 6pm) Few experiences in Sardinia compare with this thrilling trek to Cala Goloritzè (p196), one of the Mediterranean's most spectacular beaches. Suitable for families, the easygoing, well-signposted (if rocky and occasionally steep) hike along an old mule trail takes you through a gorgeous limestone canyon shaded by juniper and holm oaks, passing cliffs honeycombed with caves, dramatic rock arches, overhangs and pinnacles. From the trailhead at Bar Su Porteddu on the Altopiano del Golgo, it's 3.5km down to the beach (about 1¼ hours).

After an initial 15-minute climb, you'll get your first tantalising glimpses of the bay and a sea so blue it will make you gasp. Keep an eye out for a traditional sheepfold and the idiosyncratic spike of the Aguglia as you approach the bay. Steps lead down to the half-moon of bone-white pebbles; this is a perfect picnic spot. Bring along your bathers for a dip in the deliciously warm, astonishingly blue waters. Allow 1½ hours for the slightly more challenging, uphill return trip.

To reach the trailhead from downtown Baunei, drive up Via San Pietro, following signs for the Altopiano. After travelling 8.4km north on pavement, continue another 1.2km east on the signposted dirt road to the parking lot at Bar Su Porteddu.

★Punta Salinas HIKING

For spellbinding views of the Golfo di Orosei coastline, climb to this viewpoint 466m up the mountainside from Cala Goloritzè. It's reachable as a side trip from the main Cala Goloritzè trail (p202), adding an extra hour of hiking time – but due to lack of signposting you're better off tackling this route with a guide, or inquiring at the trailhead near Bar Su Porteddu before setting off.

Salinas Escursioni WALKING

(☎340 5665739, 360 692431; www.supramonte-selvaggio.it; Via Pisa 4, Baunei; 🐾) If you want to strike out on foot on the old mule trails, into holm oak and juniper woods and along the limestone cliffs of the Supramonte, this operator will help you do it. It organises guided walks ranging from two-hour hikes to Pedra Longa to the six-day Selvaggio Blu (p192) trek.

Cooperativa Goloritzè HIKING

(☎368 7028980; www.coopgoloritze.com; Località Golgo) This highly regarded cooperative organises excursions ranging from trekking to 4WD trips. Many treks involve a descent through canyons to the Golfo di Orosei's dreamy beaches. Staff at the refuge also arrange guides and logistical support for walkers attempting Sardinia's once-in-a-lifetime Selvaggio Blu (p192) trek.

Eating & Drinking

Bar-Pizzeria Pisaneddu PIZZERIA €

(☎0782 61 06 04; SS125, Baunei; pizzas €4-8; ⊙8am-midnight) Just north of town, the brightly lit front terrace of this roadside eatery makes a festive spot to linger over wood-fired pizzas after a long day on the trail.

Locanda Il Rifugio SARDINIAN €€

(☎368 7028980; www.coopgoloritze.com; Località Golgo; meals €25-35; ⊙12.30-3pm & 7.30-11pm Easter-Oct) Managed by Cooperativa Goloritzè, this converted farmstead puts on a generous spread of regional fare such as *laded-dos* (potato gnocchi) and spit-roasted kid and suckling pig, washed down with local Cannonau red. Afterwards, spare yourself the nail-biting drive back down to Baunei by camping (per person €7) or staying in one of the refuge's simple rooms (double including breakfast €60).

Bar Su Porteddu BAR

(☎320 7481158; www.facebook.com/pg/suporteddu; Altopiano del Golgo; ⊙7am-2am) High on the Altopiano, this simple bar with a huge parking lot opposite the trailhead for Cala Goritzè makes a welcome stop for morning cappuccinos or afternoon snacks. There are also basic camping facilities if you want to get an early start on your hike to the beach.

Getting There & Away

Baunei sits astride the SS125, about 20km north of Tortolì/Arbatax and 48km south of Dorgali. Several daily ARST buses run south to Tortolì (€1.90, 35 minutes), but for travel north to Dorgali or up to the Altopiano del Golgo, you're much better off with your own wheels.

OGLIASTRA

Wedged in between Nuoro and Cagliari, the Ogliastra region boasts some of the island's most spectacular scenery. Inland, it's a vertical land of unspoilt valleys, silent woods and windswept rock faces, while the coastal stretches become increasingly dramatic the nearer you get to the Golfo di Orosei.

Tortolì & Arbatax

☎0782 / POP 11,100

Your impressions of Tortolì, Ogliastra's bustling provincial capital, depend on where you've arrived from. If you've just disembarked from the mainland you might be disappointed with the town's mundane, modern appearance. But if you've just emerged from the heavy silences of the interior, you

KAYAKING IN CARDEDU

There's no better way to explore Ogliastra's coves, grottoes and rock formations than with Francesco Muntoni, who knows the area like the back of his hand.

In Cardedu, 16km south of Tortolì, you'll find **Cardedu Kayak** (☎348 9369401, 0782 7 51 85; www.cardedu-kayak.com; Località Perda Rubia, SS125, Km 121.6, Cardedu), where you can spend the day with your paddle slicing rhythmically through the turquoise waters. Francesco caters to kayakers of all levels. His courses cost between €150 and €200 for five two-hour lessons. If you would prefer to go it alone, daily kayak rental starts at €25 per person. Be sure to bring your swimming gear in summer. Francesco can help organise longer tours and 'nautical camping' if you fancy fishing from the kayak and sleeping on the secluded beaches.

Francesco also arranges cycling tours into the fertile valleys surrounding Cardedu through his spin-off company **MTB Sardinia** (www.mtbsardinia.com), as well as hikes along the striking red granite coastline, and walks up into the surrounding hills, which are littered with fine examples of *domus de janas* (prehistoric chamber tombs).

might find the cheery souvenir shops and large roadside hotels a welcome change.

Ferries from Civitavecchia, Genoa, Olbia and Cagliari arrive at Arbatax port, about 4km away down Viale Monsignor Virgilio. You can also arrange boat tours up the coast to the Golfo di Orosei from here. In summer you can catch the *trenino verde* from the train station in Arbatax.

Sights

Tortolì and Arbatax are resort towns and sights are few and far between.

Rocce Rosse LANDMARK

If you have a moment in Arbatax, head across the road from the port and behind the petrol station to the Rocce Rosse (red rocks). Like the ruins of some fairy-tale castle, these bizarre, weather-beaten rock formations dropping into the sea are well worth a camera shot or two, framed in the distance by the imperious cliffs of the southern Ogliastra and Golfo di Orosei.

Spiaggia delle Rose BEACH

To reach this glorious beach – in Lotzorai, about 6km north of Tortolì – follow signs for the three camping grounds that are clustered just behind it. Even in peak summer season, it doesn't get all that crowded.

Eating

You'll find a handful of so-so pizzerias and snack bars by the port in Arbatax; nearly all are closed from November to March.

Ittiturismo La Peschiera SEAFOOD €€

(☎0782 66 44 15; Spiaggia della Cartiera, Arbatax; meals €35; ⏰1-8.30pm Apr-Oct) What swims in the Med in the morning lands on plates by lunchtime at this *ittiturismo,* run by Tortolì's fishing cooperative. The fixed-price menu includes copious seafood antipasti, followed by pasta, a main course, fruit, water, wine and coffee. Follow the signs as you enter town and walk five minutes along a river bank. Reservations are essential.

The humble shack may be in the back of beyond, but it's worth going the extra mile for fish this fresh.

La Bitta SEAFOOD €€€

(☎0782 66 70 80; www.hotellabitta.it; Località Porto Frailis; meals €35-50; ⏰12.30-2.30pm & 7.30-10pm) For fine dining with a gorgeous sea view, you can't beat La Bitta, down by the beach in Porto Frailis. Dress up for exquisitely prepared seafood – think handmade fregola (couscous-like Sardinian pasta) with fresh clams and lime, or tuna steak with fennel-orange salad and anchovies.

Information

Info Point Arbatax (☎339 8992939; www.arbatax.eu; Via Lungomare 89; ⏰9am-1pm & 6-8pm)

Getting There & Away

BOAT

The main ferry company serving Arbatax is **Tirrenia** (☎0782 66 70 67; www.tirrenia.it; Via Venezia 10). Ferries sail to/from Genoa (from €72, 15½ hours) and Civitavecchia (from €43, nine to 10½ hours). There are also connections with Cagliari and Olbia.

BUS

ARST buses connect Tortolì with Santa Maria Navarrese (€1.30, 15 minutes, 11 daily Monday to Saturday, two Sunday), Dorgali (€4.90, one hour 50 minutes, daily Monday to Saturday) and Nuoro (€5.50, 1½ hours, four daily Monday to Saturday), as well as many inland villages. Local buses 1 and 2 run from Arbatax to Tortolì and, in the case of the latter service, to the beach and hotels at nearby Porto Frailis.

TRAIN

Near the port, you'll find the terminus for the **trenino verde** (☎070 2 65 71; www.treninoverde.com), a scenic train that runs from Arbatax to Gairo (€14, 2½ hours) daily, except Tuesday, from mid-June to mid-September.

DON'T MISS

ARBATAX BEACHES

You can hit the beach on either side of Arbatax. You'll find the fine sandy bays and crystal waters of **Spiaggia Orri**, **Spiaggia Musculedda** and **Spiaggia Is Scogliu Arrubius** about 4km south of hotel-dotted Porto Frailis. Or continue even further south to the pristine cliff-flanked cove of **Spiaggia Cala Francese** at **Marina di Gairo**.

North of Tortolì & Arbatax

Santa Maria Navarrese

☎0782 / POP 1450

At the southern end of the Golfo di Orosei sits the unpretentious and attractive beach resort of Santa Maria Navarrese. Shipwrecked Basque sailors built a small church here in 1052, and then dedicated it to Santa Maria di Navarra on the orders of the Princess of Navarre, who happened to be one of the shipwreck's survivors. The church was set in the shade of a grand olive tree that is still standing – some say it's nearly 2000 years old.

Sights & Activities

Lofty pines and eucalyptus trees back the lovely town beach, lapped by transparent water and crowned at its northern end by a watchtower built to look out for raiding Saracens; there are more sandy stretches to the south.

About 500m further north of the centre is the small pleasure port, where various operators run cruises up the increasingly wild coastline.

Monte Scoine MOUNTAIN
Rearing above the landscape like a bishop's mitre, the crag of Monte Scoine attracts climbers to its bolted routes (4b to 6b), especially in summer when it stays shady until midafternoon.

Isolotto di Ogliastra LANDMARK
Offshore are several islets, including the Isolotto di Ogliastra, a giant hunk of pink porphyritic rock rising 47m out of the water.

Consorzio Marittimo Ogliastra BOATING
(0782 61 51 73; www.mareogliastra.com; Via Lungomare) The Consorzio Marittimo Ogliastra charges between €40 and €50 per person for tours that take in sea caves and several stunning swimming spots, such as Cala Goloritzè, Cala Mariolu and Cala Sisine. Children pay half-price or less.

Eating & Drinking

Pizzerias and seafood restaurants are scattered around the main church square and down by the waterfront.

Nascar SARDINIAN €€
(0782 61 53 14; www.nascarhotel.eu/ristorante; Via Pedras 1; meals €30-35; 7.30-10.30pm) A family-run affair, Nascar stands head and shoulders above most places in town, with its romantic garden terrace, slick vaulted interior and faultless service. The food is superb, too, with antipasti, fresh pasta and just-caught fish on the menu, all expertly paired with wines from local vineyards.

DON'T MISS

ON THE TRAIL IN ULASSAI

The dramatic limestone and dolomite cliffs, or *tacchi*, that rear above Ulassai make this fabulous hiking and climbing territory. Trekkers can strike out on foot into the **Bruncu Pranedda** canyon or head 7km southwest to view the totally arresting **Cascata Lequarci waterfall**, with wispy threads that plummet almost 100m over a vertical rock face. The waterfall is at its most spectacular after heavy rainfall. You can make a day of it by bringing a picnic to enjoy in the verdant surrounds of the **Santuario di Santa Barbara**, a quaint Romanesque chapel.

Bar L'Olivastro BAR
(0782 61 55 13; www.lolivastrobar.it; Via Lungomare Montesanto 1; 8am-1am) Offering lovely sea views from its shady terrace below the spreading branches of an ancient olive tree, Bar L'Olivastro is a relaxed spot for a coffee and snack by day, or a cocktail by night. There is occasional live music.

Inland Ogliastra

Ulassai

0782 / POP 1460

Heading inland from Arbatax you're in for some scenic treats as the road licks a tortuous path around the titanic mountains to Ulassai, which is dwarfed by the rocky pinnacles of Bruncu Pranedda and Bruncu Matzei. A popular destination for hikers and climbers, this small village is surrounded by some of Sardinia's most thrilling and impenetrable countryside, a vast natural playground for outdoor enthusiasts.

Sights & Activities

★**Grotta di Su Marmuri** CAVE
(www.grottasumarmuri.it; €10; tours 11am, 2pm, 4pm & 6pm May-July & Sep, less frequent Apr & Oct, more frequent Aug) High above Ulassai, the mammoth Grotta di Su Marmuri is a 35m-high cave complex. Visits are by guided tour only (minimum of four people), which take you on a one-hour, 1km walk through an underground wonderland festooned with stalactites and stalagmites – some like

humongous drip candles, others as delicate as coral. Whatever the temperature outside, it is always chilly down here, so be sure to bring some extra layers.

Scala di San Giorgio VIEWPOINT

Accessible from the village of Osini, the Scala di San Giorgio is a vertical gully that takes its name from the 12th-century saint who is said to have divided the rock as he walked through the area proselytising in 1117. From the top you get vast views over the valley to the abandoned villages of **Osini Vecchio** and **Gairo Vecchio**, both destroyed by landslides in 1951.

Stazione dell'Arte Maria Lai GALLERY

(www.stazionedellarte.com; Ex Stazione Ferroviaria; €5; 9am-8.30pm May-Sep, to 7pm Oct-Apr) Housed in the old railway station, the outstanding Stazione dell'Arte Maria Lai showcases the emotive works of the late artist Maria Lai. Born in Ulassai in 1919, Maria was one of Sardinia's most important contemporary artists.

Festivals & Events

Ulassai Climbing Festival SPORTS

(www.climbingulassai.com/festival; Jun) Launched in 2017 by a group of international climbers who have permanently relocated to Ulassai, this festival is a big four-day party for climbers and like-minded adventure-sports enthusiasts, with climbing and cycling competitions, highlining demos and – just to keep everyone limber – daily yoga sessions.

Eating

★ Su Bullicciu SARDINIAN €€

(0782 7 98 59; Località Su Marmuri; meals €25-30; 12.30-2.30pm & 7.30-10.30pm) Perched high on the hillside near the Su Marmuri caves, this restaurant serves up delicious home cooking, with an emphasis on traditional mountain fare such as spit-roasted meats, grilled vegetables, *pecorino* cheese, and *malloreddus* (homemade pasta) with tomato and meat sauce.

Shopping

Su Marmuri Cooperative Tessile Artigiana HOMEWARES

(www.sumarmuri.it; Via Funtana Serì; 8am-noon & 2-6pm Mon-Fri Sep-Jun, 8am-1pm & 2.30-8pm daily Jul & Aug) For rugs, towels, curtains and bedspreads bearing Maria's naturalistic designs, head to the Su Marmuri Cooperative Tessile Artigiana. Here you'll find a group of dedicated ladies keeping alive traditional hand-looming techniques and you can see the noisy looms in action. Prices start at around €20 for a hand towel.

Getting There & Away

ARST bus service from Tortolì to Ulassai (€3.10, 1¼ to 3½ hours) is very limited, always requiring a change of buses and usually a long wait. You're much better off with your own vehicle. The 36km drive from Tortolì via the SS125 and SP11 takes about 45 minutes.

Jerzu

0782 / POP 3170

Known as the Citta del Vino (Wine Town), Jerzu is famous for its full-bodied Cannonau red wine. The town is set precariously on a mountainside, its steeply stacked buildings surrounded by imposing limestone towers, known as *tacchi* (heels), and some 650 hectares of vineyards.

Sights

Antichi Poderi di Jerzu WINERY

(0782 7 00 28; www.jerzuantichipoderi.it; Via Umberto 1; 8.30am-1pm & 2.30-6.30pm Mon-Sat) Each year about 50,000 quintals of grapes are harvested to make two million bottles of wine at the Antichi Poderi di Jerzu, the town's modern cantina. Guided visits and tastings can be arranged by calling in advance.

Getting There & Away

ARST runs a couple of direct buses daily from Jerzu to Tortolì (€2.50, 50 minutes), but you're generally better off with your own vehicle. The drive from Tortolì takes about 35 minutes via the SS125 and SP11.

Accommodation

Includes ➡

Best Places to Sleep

- Casa Solotti (p221)
- Hotel Nautilus (p209)
- Hotel El Faro (p216)
- Agriturismo Codula Fuili (p222)

Best B&Bs

- B&B Benebenniu (p215)
- B&B Mare Monti Miniere (p210)
- B&B Domus de Janas (p220)

Best Boutique Hotels

- Nichotel (p211)
- Hotel Miramare (p209)
- Hotel Regina d'Arborea (p214)

Where to Stay

So what's it to be? A B&B housed in a restored *palazzo* in Nuoro, a chic apartment in Cagliari's medieval Il Castello district, or a back-to-nature *agriturismo* (farm-stay) snuggled in the depths of Gallura's holm oak forests? With so many atmospheric places to stay, deciding where to base yourself in Sardinia involves so much more than just choosing a bed for the night.

If you are here for the beaches, the island's your oyster – whether it's the serene Costa Verde in the southwest, the the Costa del Sud in the south, or the celebrity-style glamour of the Costa Smeralda in the northeast. Up for an adventure? Base yourself in laid-back Cala Gonone, Dorgali or Santa Maria Navarrese in the east for rock climbing, high-altitude hiking, water sports and sensational coastal walks.

With a little careful planning, accommodation need not be eye-wateringly expensive. Outside of high season (mid-June to August) and school holidays, rates invariably drop, often by as much as 50%, and it's much easier to find something on the spur of the moment. Generally, the further you are from the sea, the cheaper it gets. Note that most hotels close from mid-October to Easter.

Pricing

The price indicators (€, €€, €€€) used in reviews throughout this chapter refer to the cost of a double room with private bathroom. Unless otherwise stated, breakfast is included in the price. Reviews may also list prices for half-board and/or full-board where available.

€ less than €110
€€ €110 to €200
€€€ more than €200

Agriturismi

Bracing country hikes, sundowners under the olive trees, and braying donkeys as your wake-up call – if this appeals, you'll feel at home in an *agriturismo*. Often immersed in

BOOK YOUR STAY ONLINE

For more accommodation reviews by Lonely Planet authors, check out hotels.lonelyplanet.com. You'll find independent reviews, as well as recommendations on the best places to stay. Best of all, you can book online.

greenery at the end of long dirt tracks, these family-friendly working farms are for those who value peace and quiet over creature comforts.

Housed in a traditional *stazzo* (farmstead) or stone cottage, rooms are simple and snug – expect to pay between €70 and €100 for a double – and breakfasts are copious. Many *agriturismi* give you the choice of half-board (€60 to €80 per person) and dinner tends to be a communal affair, with a feast of farm-fresh vegetables, cheese, meat and wine. The only catch is that you'll almost certainly need your own wheels.

B&Bs

Like *agriturismi,* B&Bs often offer a family welcome and good value for money. The plushest boutique picks can rival hotels in comfort but obviously come at a higher price. There is no island-wide umbrella group for B&Bs, but tourist offices can usually provide contact details.

On average, budget for about €25 to €45 per person per night in a B&B.

Camping

Campers are well catered for in Sardinia, with most campgrounds scenically located on the coast and offering top-notch facilities such as swimming pools, restaurants, supermarkets and kids clubs. If inflatable mattresses are not your thing, many campgrounds have well-equipped bungalows. Prices can be surprisingly high in July and August, when advance bookings are recommended. Expect to pay between €30 and €40 for a site for two people, a car and a tent, and extra for showers and electricity. Campgrounds usually open from Easter to mid-October.

Wild camping is officially not permitted, but out of the main season and away from the resorts, you can often get away with it, providing you keep the noise down and don't light fires. Always get permission to camp on private property.

Hostels

Sardinia's six youth hostels are run by the **Italian Youth Hostel Association** (Associazione Italiana Alberghi per la Gioventù; ☎06 487 11 52; http://aighostels.it), which is affiliated with Hostelling International (www.hihostels.com). You'll need to have a HI card to stay at these hostels. Dorm rates range from €15 to €25, including breakfast. All the hostels also have beds in private rooms, typically costing around €20 per person.

Hotels

Hotels in Sardinia (and their rates) vary wildly, from small, family-run *pensioni* (guesthouses) with just a couple of no-frills rooms to the mammoth resort-style villages on the coast with private beaches, tennis courts, spas, the works. Quality varies enormously and the official star system should be taken with a pinch of salt.

Tourist offices have booklets listing all local accommodation, including prices.

CAGLIARI & THE SARRABUS

Cagliari

Il Cagliarese B&B €

(Map p52; ☎339 6544083; www.ilcagliarese.com; Via Vittorio Porcile 19; s €45-60, d €60-75; ❄@🛜) Bang in the heart of the Marina district, this snug B&B is a real find. It has three immaculate rooms, each with homey touches such as embroidered fabrics and carved wooden furnishings. Breakfast is scrumptious, and Mauro, your welcoming host, bends over backwards to please.

Maison Savoia GUESTHOUSE €

(Map p52; ☎334 2088478, 070 67 81 81; www.maisonsavoia.it; Piazza Savoia 2; s €60-70, d €80-90; ❄🛜) This discreet guesthouse is brilliantly placed right in the heart of the action. It's surrounded by restaurants, bars and shops, yet its decently sized rooms are quiet. Decor is old school with parquet floors, framed prints and heavy wood furniture. Note that breakfast is not always included in your room rate.

Locanda dei Buonoi e Cattivi PENSION €

(Map p48; ☎070 734 52 23; www.locandadeibuoniecattivi.it; Via Vittorio Veneto 96; s €55-65, d

€75-95; ❄📶) Some way out of the centre, but still walkable, this modest pension is a great budget option. It's a homey affair with five modest guest rooms and a salon decorated with antiques and paintings by local artists. Downstairs, its restaurant is highly rated locally.

Casa Marina B&B €

(Map p52; ☎327 3042552; www.bandbcasamarina.it; Via Cavour 52; d €60; 📶) Casa Marina offers handsome home-style comfort and a super-central location at bargain prices. Just paces from the sights and waterfront, the two roomy, light-drenched guest rooms have been decked out with minimalist flair, and there's a shared kitchen should you wish to rustle up a snack. Alberto is your affable host. Breakfast is available for €5.

Residenza Kastrum B&B €

(Map p52; ☎348 0012280; www.kastrum.eu; Via Nicolò Canelles 78; s €45-60, d €55-85, q €120-160; ❄📶) Escape the hurly-burly of the centre at this cosy B&B in the hilltop Castello district. Its simple white rooms are comfortable enough, with parquet floors and classic dark wood furniture, but what sets it apart are the memorable views from the small rooftop terrace. The quad rooms are ideal for families.

Il Girasole B&B €

(Map p52; ☎348 1097278, 070 65 19 17; www.ilgirasole.sardegna.it; Vico Barcellona 6; s €40-50, d €60-90; ❄📶) As bright and cheery as a *girasole* (sunflower), this boho three-room B&B is crammed with ethnic knick-knacks and African art. It's a relaxed set-up and Luca, your friendly host, puts on a decent spread at breakfast. You're welcome to use the kitchen and unwind in the living room or on the terrace.

Marina di Castello B&B €

(Map p52; ☎335 8125881; www.bedandbreakfastcagliaricity.it; Via Roma 75a; d €75-120; ❄📶) Sabrina makes you feel instantly at ease at this B&B on Cagliari's main seafront boulevard. There's a clean, modern feel about the place with rooms tastefully done out in silver, bronze and gold, while patches of exposed brick and artistic flourishes add a boutique touch. Up top, the roof terrace overlooking the marina is a panoramic spot for a summer sundowner.

Hostel Marina HOSTEL €

(Map p52; ☎070 67 08 18; www.hostelmarinacagliari.it; Scalette San Sepolcro 2; dm/d/q €22/60/100; ❄📶) Housed in a converted 16th-century monastery, Cagliari's official HI hostel has oodles of historic charm and original features such as vaulting and beams. Its dorms, doubles and family rooms are fairly spartan, but all come with en-suite bathrooms and they're spacious and well kept. Outside, there's a popular courtyard bar.

Suite sul Corso B&B €

(Map p52; ☎349 4469789, 070 68 02 50; www.lesuitesulcorso.it; Corso Vittorio Emanuele 8; s/d/ste €70/90/130; ❄📶) Sleep in style at this boutique B&B just off Piazza Yenne. Exposed stone, floaty fabrics and glass mosaics lend warmth to the minimalist-chic rooms, all with flat-screen TVs and kettles; one even has its own whirlpool bath. The owner's quirky photography jazzes up the corridors.

La Ghirlanda GUESTHOUSE €

(Map p52; ☎070 204 06 10; www.bnblaghirlanda.com; Via Baylle 7; s €55-70, d €70-90, tr €95-110, q €120-135; ❄📶) Antiques and frescoes whisk you back in time at this handsome 19th-century townhouse in the Marina district. The five bright, high-ceilinged rooms are tastefully done out in pastel colours and wooden floors. Breakfast at a nearby bar is included.

★**Hotel Nautilus** HOTEL €€

(☎070 37 00 91; www.hotelnautiluspoetto.com; Viale Poetto 158; d €150-210, tr €170-225; ❄📶) Nothing shouts holiday as much as the sight of sea and sand on your doorstep. This gleaming three-star hotel is one of the best on the Poetto beachfront, offering summery blue and white rooms, balconies and sea views. Rates plummet in the low season, meaning there are some real off-season bargains to be had.

★**Hotel Miramare** BOUTIQUE HOTEL €€€

(Map p52; ☎070 66 40 21; www.hotelmiramarecagliari.it; Via Roma 59; r €195-500; ❄📶) A fashion magazine spread waiting to happen, this boutique four-star exudes effortless chic with its artistic interiors and classy rooms. Located on sea-facing Via Roma, it has individually styled rooms whose decor ranges from pared-down contemporary cool to full-on belle-époque glamour, with crimson walls, zebra-print chairs, pop art and art-deco furniture.

The Sarrabus

Villasimius & Capo Carbonara

Villaggio Camping Spiaggia del Riso CAMPGROUND €

(☎070 79 10 52; www.villaggiospiaggiadelriso.it; Via Degli Aranci 2; 2 people, car & tent €23-42, 4-bed bungalows €100-160; ⌚mid-Apr–Oct; 📶) 🍃 Set in a pine grove near the Porto Turistico, this big, well-equipped beachside campground has tent pitches, bungalows, food shops and a children's play area. Booking is absolutely essential in summer. There's a two-week minimum stay in July and August.

Hotel Mariposas HOTEL €€

(☎070 79 00 84; www.hotelmariposas.it; Via Mar Nero 1; s €75-190, d €100-250, ste €125-280; P❄📶🏊). Situated about halfway between the town centre and Spiaggia Simius, this lovely stone-clad hotel is set in glorious flower-strewn gardens. Its sunny spacious rooms all have their own terrace or balcony, and there's an attractive pool for whiling away those lazy afternoons.

Stella Maris HOTEL €€€

(☎070 79 71 00; www.stella-maris.com; Via dei Cedri 3, Località Campulongu; r €200-650; P❄📶🏊) Off the road to the Porto Turistico, this is a beautiful four-star resort hotel set in a pine wood on a frost-white beach. Its stylish rooms, the best of which have sea views, are decorated with Sardinian fabrics, tasteful furniture and splashes of colour. Outside the gardens and split-level pool are perfect for some R&R. A seven-night minimum stay is required for July and August.

Costa Rei

Villaggio Camping Capo Ferrato CAMPGROUND €

(☎070 99 10 12; www.campingcapoferrato.it; Località Costa Rei; 2 people, car & tent €17-45; ⌚Apr-Oct; P📶) Pitch a tent under eucalyptus and mimosa trees at this well-organised campground by the southern entrance to Capo Rei. Facilities include a small food shop, tennis court, kids' playground and direct access to the adjacent beach.

Albaruja Hotel HOTEL €€

(☎070 99 15 57; www.albaruja.it; Via C Colombo; s €70-120, d €115-175; ⌚May–mid-Oct; P❄@📶🏊) The Albaruja is a cut above most of the hotels on the Costa Rei. As well as attractive summery rooms and flowery gardens, it has a bistrot, kids' playground and palm-rimmed swimming pool. It's just a two-minute walk from the beach.

ROOM WITH A VIEW

Ca' La Somara (p220)

Borgo Alba Barona (p218)

Residenza Kastrum (p209)

Agriturismo Codula Fuili (p222)

Casa Doria (p216)

IGLESIAS & THE SOUTHWEST

The Iglesiente

Iglesias

★**B&B Mare Monti Miniere** B&B €

(Map p70; ☎348 3310585, 0781 4 17 65; www.maremontiminiere-bb.it; Via Trento 10; s €35-40, d €45-50, tr €65-75; ❄📶) A warm welcome awaits at this cracking B&B. Situated in a quiet side street near the historic centre, it has two cheery and immaculately kept rooms in the main house and an independent studio with its own kitchen facilities. Thoughtful extras include beach towels and a regular supply of home-baked cakes and biscuits.

★**La Babbajola B&B** B&B €

(Map p70; ☎349 7074383; www.lababbajola.com; Via Giordano 13; r €55-65; ❄📶) Housed in an aristocratic 19th-century townhouse, this characterful B&B offers homey accommodation in the heart of the *centro storico*. Its three double rooms are spacious and tastefully furnished with patterned floor tiles, bold colours and heavy wood furniture. There's also a kitchen, where the ample breakfast is served, and a communal TV room.

Buggerru & Portixeddu

Hotel Golfo del Leone HOTEL €

(☎0781 5 49 52; www.hotelgolfodelleone.it; Località Portixeddu; s €50-60, d €70-90, tr €90-120, q €110-145; P❄📶) Set in its own tranquil grounds about 1.5km inland from Portixeddu beach, this relaxed year-round hotel has 14 bright, modestly furnished rooms. Service is friendly and there's a convenient in-house restaurant, open from May to October, where you can dine on local seafood for about €25 per head. Half-board is available.

Agriturismo Fighezia AGRITURISMO €
(☎348 069 83 03; www.agriturismofighezia.it; s €65-70, d €80-90, tr €105-120, half-board per person €55-90; P 📶) One of several *agriturismi* in the lush green hills behind Portixeddu, this tranquil farm-stay boasts soothing views, almost complete silence, and 10 rustic cabin-style rooms with terracotta tiles, solid wooden fixtures and private terraces. Dinner is served on large communal tables in the covered verandah of the main house.

Costa Verde

Agriturismo L'Aquila AGRITURISMO €
(☎347 822 24 26; www.agriturismolaquila.com; Località Is Gennas, Montevecchio; r per person €35-40, half-board per person €55-60; P ❄) A welcoming oasis in the green wilderness of the Costa Verde, this authentic *agriturismo* offers modest, no-frills rooms, earthy farmhouse food (p76), and stunning views of the surrounding peaks. To get there from Montevecchio, head towards Torre dei Corsari, then take the signposted exit and follow the dirt track for a couple of bumpy kilometres.

Agriturismo L'Oasi del Cervo AGRITURISMO €
(☎347 3011318; www.oasidelcervo.com; Località Is Gennas, Montevecchio; d €60-70, half-board per person €55-60; P 📶) With 12 modest rooms and a remote location in the midst of *macchia*-cloaked hills, this working farm is a genuine country hideaway. It's all very down to earth but the rooms are comfortable enough, the views are uplifting, and the homemade food (p76) is delicious. You'll see a sign for the *agriturismo* off the SP65 between Montevecchio and Torre dei Corsari.

Sulcis

Carbonia & Around

Lu Hotel HOTEL €€
(☎0781 66 50 20; www.luhotel.it; Via Costituente; s €40-135, d €80-190; P ❄ 📶 🏊) Near Carbonia train station in the modern lower town, this recently opened four-star makes for a convenient base. It's a smart operation with jacketed reception staff, corporate-styled rooms and excellent facilities, including a restaurant, spa and outdoor pool.

Villaggio Minerario Rosas HOTEL €
(☎0781 185 51 39; www.ecomuseominiererosas.it; Località Rosas, Narcao; s €30-35, d €44-54; P 📶) This one-time pit village near Narcao has been resurrected as a museum-complex-cum-hotel with guest rooms in the former miners' cottages. Rooms are basic but well sized and rustic with plenty of wood, brick and exposed stone in evidence; cottages come with kitchen facilities. There's an on-site bar for breakfast, which is not included in room rates.

Carloforte & Isola di San Pietro

Hotel California PENSION €
(☎333 7392868, 0781 85 44 70; www.hotelcaliforniacarloforte.com; Via Cavallera 15; s €40-60, d €60-100; ❄ 📶) This super-friendly family-run *pensione* is situated in a quiet residential street a few blocks back from the *lungomare* (seafront). It's a modest affair but it's open year-round and the 16 sun-filled rooms are tastefully decorated and exceptional value.

★Nichotel HOTEL €€
(☎0781 85 56 74; http://nichotel.it; Via Garibaldi 7; d €60-255, ste €95-300; ❄ 📶) Style, comfort and a warm welcome await at this great little hotel. Located just off the main seafront strip, it has lovely, spacious rooms with quietly elegant modern decor and gleaming designer bathrooms; some also boast balconies and rooftop views over to the port. Capping everything is the excellent abundant breakfast.

Hotel Riviera HOTEL €€
(☎0781 85 32 34; www.hotelriviera-carloforte.com; Corso Battellieri 26; d €90-190, ste €140-210; ❄ 📶) Housed in a red seafront villa, this landmark four-star exudes Mediterranean chic. The rooms are cool and light, with tiled floors, traditional Sardinian fabrics and marble-clad bathrooms. Some also have sea views and balconies, though these cost extra.

Hotel Hieracon HOTEL €€€
(☎0781 85 40 28; www.hotelhieracon.com; Corso Cavour 62; s €70-110, d €90-270, tr €120-270;

⌚May-Nov; ❄📶) A throwback to a smarter age, this seafront hotel occupies a grand art-nouveau mansion. Period furniture and oil paintings set the tone, rooms are spacious, if rather functional, and there's a tranquil internal garden.

Isola di Sant'Antioco

Hotel Moderno HOTEL €
(☎0781 8 31 05; www.hotel-moderno-sant-antioco.it; Via Nazionale 82; s €50-70, d €80-120, tr €105-145, q €120-155; ❄📶) A bright, year-round hotel on the main road into Sant'Antioco town. Rooms are agreeable with beige colours, minimal decor and big, comfy beds. Downstairs, the in-house seafood restaurant, Ristorante da Achille, has an excellent local reputation. Room rates drop during the winter months.

Hotel del Corso HOTEL €
(☎0781 80 02 65; www.hoteldelcorso.it; Corso Vittorio Emanuele 32; s €55-70, d €80-110, tr €90-120; ❄📶) Conveniently positioned on the main drag into the town centre, this friendly three-star sits above the Cafè del Corso, one of Sant'Antioco's most popular drinking spots. Its nine rooms are well appointed with polished wooden floors and en-suite designer bathrooms.

Campeggio Tonnara CAMPGROUND €
(☎0781 80 90 58; www.campingtonnara.it; Località Cala Sapone; 2 people, car & tent €16-54; ⌚Apr-Oct; P📶🏊) Near the tiny little beach at Cala Sapone, this is a well-equipped campground on the island's west coast. As well as tent pitches it also has bungalows to rent and an extensive list of services, including a swimming pool, tennis court, on-site shop and pizzeria.

★**Hotel Luci del Faro** HOTEL €€
(☎0781 81 00 89; www.hotelucidelfaro.com; Località Mangiabarche, Calasetta; d €110-225, half-board per person €85-140; ⌚mid-Apr–early Nov; P❄📶🏊) Only a few kilometres outside Calasetta, this delightful retreat stands in glorious solitude on an exposed plain near Spiaggia Grande, the island's best-known beach. It's a relaxed, family-friendly place with sunny, summery rooms, an in-house restaurant and sweeping views. Extras include free shuttle buses to the beach and free bike hire.

Costa del Sud

Campeggio Torre Chia CAMPGROUND €
(☎070 923 00 54; www.campeggiotorrechia.it; Via del Porto 21, Chia; 2 people, car & tent €24-32, 4-person cottage €65-130; ⌚May-Oct) At the popular summer resort of Chia, this busy campground enjoys a prime location near the beach. It's fairly spartan with minimal facilities, tent pitches under pine trees and basic four-person cottages.

Porto Pino & Around

Camping Sardegna CAMPGROUND €
(☎0781 96 70 13; Via della Prima Spiaggia 1, Località Porto Pino; 2 people, car & tent €20-27.50, 4-person caravan €64-80; ⌚Jun-Sep; 📶) This seasonal campground offers basic facilities and sheltered pitches in a pine grove at Porto Pino. There are few frills but the location is great and the beach is right on your doorstep.

Pula & Around

B&B Fiore B&B €
(☎070 924 60 10, 340 8761821; www.bedandbreakfastfiore.it; SS195, Km31; d €75-95; P❄📶) Some 2km southwest of Pula, this homey B&B is set amid fruit and palm trees in its own grounds just off the SS195. It has three bright, simply furnished rooms, each with its independent entrance and verandah. From here, it's about an 800m walk to the pale-sand beach of Porto d'Agumu.

Hotel Villa Madau HOTEL €€
(☎070 924 90 33; www.villamadau.it; Via Nora 84; s €70-95, d €80-150, tr €90-195; ❄📶) This friendly three-star is in Pula's historic centre, a short hop from Piazza del Popolo. Rooms are individually decorated but the overall feel is summery boho with cheerful blue and yellows, traditional Sardinian fabrics, and cool polished tiles. Try to get an internal room to avoid the pealing of the local church bells.

★**Hotel Baia di Nora** HOTEL €€€
(☎070 924 55 51; www.hotelbaiadinora.com; Località Su Guventeddu; d €190-435; ⌚Apr–mid-Oct; P❄📶🏊) On the main road from Pula to Nora, this is a swish four-star resort hotel with all the trimmings – a lush garden, swimming pool, restaurant and private beach space. Rooms, which come with patios or balconies, are cool and summery with tiled floors and understated furnishings.

Forte Village RESORT €€€

(☎070 921 88 18; www.fortevillage.com; Santa Margherita di Pula; r from €480; P ❄ 🛜 🏊) Hidden in a wooded grove near Santa Margherita di Pula, Forte Village is one of Sardinia's most celebrated resorts. An unapologetic bastion of luxury, it has bungalows, villas and several four- and five-star hotels. Facilities include swimming pools, restaurants, a cooking school, shops, a nightclub and up to 1km of beach frontage.

La Marmilla

Barumini & Nuraghe Su Nuraxi

Hotel Su Nuraxi HOTEL €

(☎070 936 83 05; www.hotelsunuraxi.it; Viale Su Nuraxi 6; s €50, d €70-80, half-board per person €40-75; P ❄ 🛜) This family-run hotel near the Nuraghe Su Nuraxi makes an ideal base for exploring the area. Rooms, which come with tiled floors and plain wooden furniture, are set hacienda-style around a central courtyard. There's a lovely restaurant where you can dine on filling farmhouse food.

Villanovaforru & Nuraghe Genna Maria

★**Agriturismo Su Boschettu** AGRITURISMO €

(☎333 4797401, 070 93 98 84; www.suboschettu.it; Località Pranu Laccu, Pauli Arbarei; s/d €60/80, tr €100-105, q €120-140; P ❄ 🛜 🏊) Guests are met with a warm Sardinian welcome at this charming farm-stay, nestled amid olive groves and fruit trees near Pauli Arbarei. Its sunny, simply attired rooms offer soothing views over the surrounding greenery, while outside, there's plenty of space to sit and contemplate the pastoral setting. If you can muster the energy there's even a pool to splash around in.

Hotel Funtana Noa HOTEL €

(☎070 933 10 20; www.hotelfuntananoa.it; Via Vittorio Emanuele III 66-68, Villanovaforru; d €55-65, tr/q €80/95; ❄) A tasteful three-star housed in a large *palazzo* just down from the centre of Villanovaforru. Rooms are spacious if unspectacular, and communal spaces, including an in-house restaurant, feature plenty of heavy timber, antique-style furniture and brick arches.

ORISTANO & THE WEST

Oristano

★**Eleonora B&B** B&B €

(Map p94; ☎347 4817976, 0783 7 04 35; www.eleonora-bed-and-breakfast.com; Piazza Eleonora d'Arborea 12; s €40-60, d €70-90, tr €80-110; ❄ 🛜) This charming B&B scores on all counts: location – it's in a medieval *palazzo* on Oristano's central piazza; decor – rooms are tastefully decorated with a mix of antique furniture, exposed brick walls and gorgeous old tiles; and hospitality – owners Andrea and Paola are helpful and hospitable hosts. All this and it's excellent value for money.

APARTMENT & VILLA RENTALS

If you plan to stay in one place for a week or more, self-catering accommodation can be excellent value. For a two- to four-bed apartment, rates are typically between €350 and €600 per week in low season, €500 to €900 in high season. You'll pay double that for a more luxurious villa with a swimming pool and sea views. Be sure to read the small print for additional charges such as electricity, water, bed linen and final cleaning.

Apartments are generally well located and equipped with kitchenettes and terraces or balconies. Seven nights is usually the minimum stay and some apartments have fixed change-over days. You may be required to pay a deposit of around 30% by credit card or bank transfer when you book, and some places require the balance to be settled before arrival.

Costa Smeralda Villas (www.destinationcostasmeralda.com) Blow-the-budget villas on Sardinia's glammest stretch of coast.

Rent Sardinia (www.rent-sardinia.com) A good selection of 1000 villas and apartments scattered across the island, searchable by location and other criteria.

Sardegne (www.sardegne.com) Lists apartment rentals alongside B&Bs, agriturismi and hotels.

★**Hotel Regina d'Arborea** BOUTIQUE HOTEL €€
(Map p94; ☎0783 30 21 01; www.hotelregina darborea.com; Piazza Eleonora 4; r €130-180) Palatial elegance and prime location are the twin attractions at this relative newcomer on Oristano's main square. Four of the seven rooms are downright magnificent, with 7m-high ceilings, restored ceiling frescoes and original patterned floors. Book ahead for the Sofia room, crowned with a hexagonal cupola and wraparound windows that offer a bird's-eye views of Oristano's famous Eleonora d'Arborea statue.

Duomo Albergo HOTEL €€
(Map p94; ☎0783 77 80 61; www.hotelduomo.org; Via Vittorio Emanuele II 34; s €65-80, d €80-110; ❄@📶) Behind the discreet facade of this centrally located four-star, guest rooms reveal a low-key look with traditional fabrics and cooling white tones. In summer, breakfast is served in an internal courtyard, while gourmets can dine on creative Sardinian cuisine at the hotel's highly rated restaurant, Grekà.

Arborea

Horse Country Resort HOTEL €€
(☎0783 8 05 00; www.horsecountry.it; Strada a Mare 24, Marina di Arborea; r €100-148; ⏲Mar-early Nov; P❄📶🏊) This big four-star resort is part of Marina di Arborea's famous equestrian centre (p97). Set on a green site near the beach, it offers a full range of services with up to 1000 beds, two swimming pools, a health centre and excellent sporting facilities. Staff can arrange horse riding and excursions to nearby sites and the Costa Verde.

Sinis Peninsula

Agriturismo Sinis AGRITURISMO €
(☎328 9312508, 0783 39 26 53; www.agri turismoilsinis.it; Località San Salvatore; half-board per person €52-65; ❄) This working farm offers 12 guest rooms (including six constructed in 2017) and serves wonderful earthy food. Rooms are frill-free but clean and airy, and views of the lush garden can be enjoyed from chairs on the patio.

Camping Is Aruttas CAMPGROUND €
(☎0783 192 54 61; www.campingisaruttas.it; Località Marina Is Aruttas; 2 people, car & tent €25-42; ⏲mid-Apr–Sep; 📶) Within walking distance of the beach, Camping Is Aruttas has modest facilities set amid olive trees and Mediterranean shrubbery.

★**Hotel Lucrezia** HOTEL €€
(☎0783 41 20 78; www.hotellucrezia.it; Via Roma 14a, Riola Sardo; r €164-184, ste €264-284; ❄@) Housed in a 17th-century *cortile* (courtyard house), this elegant hideaway has rooms surrounding an inner garden complete with wisteria-draped pergola, fig and citrus trees. The decor is rustic-chic, with high 18th-century antique beds, period furniture and eye-catching tiled bathrooms. Bikes are provided, and the welcoming staff regularly organise cooking classes. Note that there's a three-night minimum stay in August.

Montiferru

Santu Lussurgiu

★**Antica Dimora Del Gruccione** HOTEL €
(☎0783 55 20 35; www.anticadimora.com; Via Michele Obinu 31; s/d €60/90, half-board per person €75; ❄📶) It's worth overnighting in Santu Lussurgiu just to stay at this charming hotel. Its rooms are spread over multiple buildings: those in the main 17th-century mansion come with high ceilings, creaking parquet floors and heavy brocade fabrics, while others boast a more modern look with art deco–style furniture and rooftop views. Don't miss the sumptuous breakfasts and multi-course dinners.

★**Eremo del Cavaliere** B&B €
(☎345 5156501; www.eremodelcavaliere.it; Via del Castagno 1, San Leonardo de Siete Fuentes; r per person incl breakfast/half-board/full board €40/65/90) Surrounding a verdant courtyard directly adjacent to the 12th-century stone church of San Leonardo de Siete Fuentes (p102), this six-room B&B is a lovely place to savour the Montiferru region's tranquil beauty. Half- and full board are available on request, with all meals served in a spacious dining room overlooking the garden.

Santa Caterina di Pittinuri

Campeggio Nurapolis CAMPGROUND €
(☎0783 5 22 83; www.nurapolis.it; Località Is Arenas; 2 people, car & tent €28-33) This end-of-the-road spot offers low-key camping within a

stone's throw of one of western Sardinia's longest beaches, with pine-shaded sites and solar-heated showers.

Inland Oristano Province

Mandra Edera HOTEL €€
(☎320 1515170; www.mandraedera.cc; Località Mandra Edera; r per person €61-81, half-board per person €81-101; ⊙Mar-Dec; P❄≋) The welcoming, family-friendly Mandra Edera is a lovely ranch-style hotel set amid towering oak trees and fruit orchards. Rooms are in bungalows laid out on neat lawns and there's a smart restaurant as well as a pool and the opportunity for horse riding. The hotel is signposted off the SS131 north of Paulilatino.

Bosa

★La Torre di Alice B&B €
(Map p108; ☎347 6671785, 329 8570064; www.latorredialice.it; Via del Carmine 7; s/d/tr €60/75/95; ❄📶) This great budget choice is set in a wonderful old tower house in Bosa's medieval centre, within easy walking distance of everything. Its five rooms are neat and comfortable, with low brick-vaulted ceilings, wrought-iron beds and electric kettles. Owners Alice and Marco offer oodles of local information and serve a tasty breakfast at the rustic communal table downstairs.

Hotel Sa Pischedda HOTEL €€
(Map p108; ☎0785 37 30 65; www.hotelsapischedda.com; Via Roma 8; d €95-170; ❄@📶) The apricot facade of this restored 1890s hotel greets you just south of the Ponte Vecchio. Several rooms retain original frescoed ceilings, some are split-level, and a few (such as 305) have terraces overlooking the river. Additional perks include friendly staff, an excellent restaurant and thoughtful touches for families (witness the 4th-floor suite with its own elevator for easy stroller access).

Corte Fiorita HOTEL €€
(Map p108; ☎0785 37 70 58; www.albergo-diffuso.it; Via Lungo Temo de Gasperi 45; s €69-119, d €89-179; ❄@) A so-called *albergo diffuso*, Corte Fiorita has beautiful, spacious rooms in three *palazzi* across town, including its main building on the riverfront. No two rooms are exactly the same, but the overall look is rustic-chic with plenty of exposed stonework, wooden beams and vaulted ceilings.

ALGHERO & THE NORTHWEST

Alghero

B&B Benebenniu B&B €
(Map p120; ☎380 1746726; www.benebenniu.com; Via Carlo Alberto 70; r €50-105; ❄📶) A home away from home, this laid-back B&B exudes warmth and familiarity. It's wonderfully located on a lively *centro storico* piazza and has three generously sized rooms with simple furnishings and plenty of natural light. Hosts Katya and Valeria are more than happy to share their local tips and recommendations.

Camping La Mariposa CAMPGROUND €
(Map p126; ☎079 95 04 80; www.lamariposa.it; Via Lido 22; 2 people, car & tent €34-46, 4-person bungalows €60-80; ⊙late Apr–mid-Oct; @) About 2km north of central Alghero, on the road to Fertilia, this busy site is the nearest campground to town. It enjoys a prime beachside location with tent sites and bungalows set amid pine and eucalyptus trees. Decent facilities include reserved beach space, bike hire and a diving centre.

Lloc d'Or B&B €
(Map p118; ☎391 1726083; www.llocdor.com; Via Logudoro 26; s €45-55, d €60-80; ❄📶) A cute budget B&B just a couple of minutes' walk from the seafront and harbour. Its two rooms and apartment are bright and simply furnished, and hosts Gemma and Giovanni go that extra mile to make you feel welcome – be it with beach towels, delicious breakfasts or tips on getting about town.

★Angedras Hotel HOTEL €€
(Map p118; ☎079 973 50 34; www.angedras.it; Via Frank 2; s €74-110, d €90-200; P❄📶) A 15-minute walk from the historic centre, the Angedras – Sardegna backwards – is a model of whitewashed Mediterranean elegance. Rooms, which come with their own small balcony, are decorated in an understated Sardinian style with cool white tiles and aquamarine-blue touches. There's also an airy terrace, good for iced drinks on hot summer evenings.

BOOKING SERVICES

Agriturismi di Sardegna (www.agriturismodisardegna.it) Organic farm-stays and campgrounds in Sardinia.

Agriturismo (www.agriturismo.it) Italian farm-stay specialist listing a wide range of *agriturismi* across the island.

Bed and Breakfast Italia (www.bed-and-breakfast.it) Online listings of B&Bs in Italy and Sardinia.

Campeggi (www.campeggi.com) Search for campgrounds in Sardinia by region on this specialist site.

Charme e Relax (www.charmerelax.it) This Italian association specialises in small to midsized hotels with character and boutique style, usually in unique buildings (monasteries, castles, old inns and so on).

Domus Karalitanae (www.domuskaralitanae.it) A comprehensive listing of B&Bs in Cagliari and around the island.

Sardegna Camping (www.sardegna.camping.it) Links to campgrounds up and down the island.

★Villa Las Tronas HERITAGE HOTEL €€€
(Map p118; 079 98 18 18; www.hotelvillalastronas.it; Via Lungomare Valencia 1; s €227-297, d €257-519; P❄🛜🏊) Live like royalty at this palatial seafront hotel. Housed in a 19th-century palace once used by holidaying royals, it's set in its own lush gardens on a private headland. The individually styled rooms are pure fin de siècle, with elegant antiques, oil paintings and glorious sea views. A spa with an indoor pool, sauna, hydro-massage and gym invites lingering.

Castelsardo

Casa Doria B&B €
(349 3557882; www.casadoria.it; Via Garibaldi 10; r €50-82; ❄🛜) One of a number of B&Bs in the hilltop historic centre, this homey place has all the trappings of a rustic guesthouse: period furniture, wrought-iron bedsteads and wooden ceilings. There are three simply decorated rooms, two sharing a bathroom, and an upstairs breakfast room with fantastic sea views.

Riviera del Corallo

Capo Galera Diving Centre B&B €
(Map p126; 079 94 21 10; http://diving.capogalera.com; Località Capo Galera, Fertilia; d €75-110, apt €140-180; 🛜) This popular diving centre provides simple accommodation in a white cliffside villa near Fertilia. As well as an enchanting setting and laid-back atmosphere, it offers several double rooms and apartments for two or six people. Note that there's a four-night minimum stay between July and September.

★Agriturismo Sa Mandra AGRITURISMO €€
(Map p126; 079 99 91 50; www.aziendasamandra.it; Strada Aeroporto Civile 21; d €80-120; P❄🛜) Set on a working farm, this terrific *agriturismo* is a veritable museum to the country way of life, with displays of old farming machines and five comfortable guest rooms. These are styled in traditional Sardinian fashion and come with thoughtful extras such as toiletries made from locally foraged herbs.

Agriturismo Porticciolo AGRITURISMO €€
(Map p126; 079 91 80 00, 347 5231024; www.agriturismoporticciolo.it; Località Porticciolo; per person B&B €39-60, 4-person apt per week €600-1000; ❄) This smart country set-up – and 24-hectare working farm – offers decent year-round accommodation in a series of independent lodges peppered around a large lawn. Rooms are clean and functionally furnished, while the rustic-styled apartments come with their own kitchen facilities. To find the *agriturismo* take the Porticciolo road from the SP55 and follow the signs.

★Hotel El Faro HOTEL €€€
(Map p126; 079 94 20 10; www.elfarohotel.it; Località Porto Conte 52; d €200-400; Apr-Oct; P❄🛜🏊) You'll find this gorgeous, whitewashed enclave at the southern tip of Porto

Conte. Facilities, which include two pools, a private jetty, spa and gym, are superb, while rooms are coolly stylish. Many have their own balconies, the best offering heavenly views over the Bay of Nymphs. Note that rates drop considerably outside the main summer months of June to August.

Stintino & Isola dell'Asinara

Albergo Silvestrino HOTEL €

(☎079 52 30 07; www.hotelsilvestrino.it; Via Sassari 14; s €45-70, d €60-130; ⊙closed Dec & Jan; ❄📶) Stintino's oldest hotel is still one of its best. Housed in a hard-to-miss red villa at the sea end of the main street, it offers summery rooms with cool aquamarine tiled floors, colourful paintings and unfussy furniture; some also have their own terrace. Downstairs, the excellent in-house restaurant specialises in local seafood.

La Pelosetta Residence Hotel HOTEL €€

(☎079 52 71 88; www.lapelosetta.it; Capo Falcone; s €74-110, d €97-194, 4-person apt €143-211; ⊙May-Sep; ❄@) A stunning location and easy access to one of Sardinia's most celebrated beaches are the key selling points of this seasonal three-star. Its rooms and small self-catering apartments are functional but the sea views are sensational and you only need to cross the road to get to the Spiaggia della Pelosa.

Sassari

★Tanina B&B B&B €

(Map p138; ☎346 1812404; www.taninabandb.com; Viale Trento 14; s/d/tr €30/50/70; 📶) About 500m from Piazza Italia, this is a model B&B. Its three large guest rooms are lovingly maintained and decked out in old-school Italian style with original tiled floors, antique furniture and floral motifs. Each has its own external bathroom and there's a fully equipped communal kitchen for guest use.

I Tetti di Sassari B&B €

(☎347 3603184; www.bebsassari.it; Corso Trinità 193; s/d/tr €50/75/110; ❄📶) In a residential building above a furniture shop, this cute little B&B boasts gracious hosts (Patrizio and Daniella), comfy rooms, decent breakfasts and a terrace with cracking views over the city.

Hotel Vittorio Emanuele HOTEL €€

(Map p138; ☎079 23 55 38; www.hotelvittorioemanuele.ss.it; Corso Vittorio Emanuele II 100-102; s €44-54, d €54-150; ❄@📶) Occupying a renovated medieval *palazzo* (historic mansion), this friendly three-star provides corporate comfort at reasonable rates. Rooms are decent enough, if anonymous, and the location, on the main drag in the historic centre, is convenient for pretty much everywhere.

Valle dei Nuraghi

Agriturismo Sas Abbilas AGRITURISMO €

(☎347 6758725; www.sasabbilas.it; Località Mariani, Bonorva; d €70-80, half-board per person €55-60; P❄📶) If you really want to get away from it, this bucolic *agriturismo* offers modest guest rooms deep in the heart of the Bonorva countryside. With little to disturb your peace except birdsong and the sound of grazing goats, it's as tranquil a spot as you'll find.

OLBIA, THE COSTA SMERALDA & GALLURA

Olbia

★Porto Romano B&B €

(Map p149; ☎349 1927996; www.bedandbreakfastportoromano.it; Via A Nanni 2; d €65-90; ❄📶) We love the chilled vibe and the heartfelt *benvenuto* at this welcoming B&B in an old family home near the train station. Light, spacious and well kept, the rooms have tiled floors and wood furnishings, and some come with balconies. Homey touches include the shared kitchen and barbecue area, and the friendly reception from owner Simonetta and her lovable dog Lilly.

Hotel Panorama HOTEL €€

(Map p149; ☎0789 2 66 56; www.hotelpanoramaolbia.it; Via Giuseppe Mazzini 7; s €95-140, d €110-200, ste €170-300; P❄📶) The name says it all: the roof terrace and 5th-floor superior rooms at this friendly, central hotel enjoy peerless views over the rooftops of Olbia to the sea and Monte Limbara. Even the standard rooms are fresh and elegant, with gleaming wooden floors and marble bathrooms, and there's a whirlpool and sauna for quiet moments.

La Locanda del Conte Mameli BOUTIQUE HOTEL €€

(Map p149; ☎0789 2 30 08; www.lalocandadelcontemameli.com; Via delle Terme 8; r €89-159; P ❄ ☎) Raising the style stakes is this boutique hotel, housed in an 18th-century *locanda* (inn) built for Count Mameli. A wrought-iron balustrade twists up to chic caramel-cream rooms with Orosei marble bathrooms. The vaulted breakfast room boasts a pair of unique treasures: an original Roman well and a 1960s-vintage Lambretta motorcycle.

Golfo Aranci

★**Borgo Alba Barona** B&B €

(☎347 4141292; www.borgoalbabarona.com; Via Sa Curi 25, Località Donigheddu; d €69-120; P ❄ ☎) High above the Golfo Aranci, Francesca and Angelo's welcoming Gallurese *stazzo* (farmhouse) stands in blissful isolation on a hilltop with 360-degree views. The simple, tile-floored bungalows have spirit-lifting perspectives on the glittering sea and granite mountains, and there's a wonderful breakfast spread featuring typical local products. It's up a winding country road off the SP16 between Olbia and Golfo Aranci.

Hotel Gabbiano Azzurro HOTEL €€€

(☎0789 4 69 29; www.hotelgabbianoazzurro.com; Via dei Gabbiani; s €210-300, d €300-410; P ❄ ≋) Overlooking the aquamarine waters of Spiaggia Terza, the Gabbiano Azzurro is a big, anonymous hotel. But that shouldn't put you off, as the benefits are many: a pool with jetted seats, a sea-view restaurant and a pretty private beach to name a few. Activities, from cookery classes to wine tastings, sport fishing and trekking, can be arranged.

Porto San Paolo & Isola Tavolara

Agriturismo L'Aglientu AGRITURISMO €

(☎0789 4 10 91; www.turismorurale.org; Via l'Aglientu 1, Porto San Paolo; s €50-80, d €70-100, tr €90-135; P ❄ ☎) Serene and delightfully green, this farmstead 20km west of Porto San Paolo is a fine country escape – you can even buy home-grown organic vegetables. The rooms are bright

TOP 10 AGRITURISMI

The best way to experience authentic Sardinian food is to eat at an *agriturismo* (farmstay accommodation). There are hundreds dotted around the island, but these are our faves:

Agriturismo Sinis (p214) A genuine working farm on the wild, peaceful Sinis Peninsula, with a relaxed vibe, rustic rooms and superb food.

Agriturismo Testone (p222) Surrounded by oak woods, this is a silent retreat, offering a warm welcome and a feast of home-grown food.

Agriturismo Porticciolo (p216) A friendly 24-hectare farm near Alghero, with 100 pigs.

Agriturismo Su Boschettu (p213) A blissfully relaxed farmstead nestled amid olive and fruit trees.

Agriturismo L'Oasi del Cervo (p211) A charming country abode with gorgeous beaches close by and mood-lifting mountain views.

Agriturismo Guthiddai (p223) A delightful whitewashed retreat in the granite Supramonte.

Agriturismo Nuraghe Mannu (p222) Look over the spectacular Orosei coast at this terraced jewel.

Agriturismo L'Aquila (p211) Drop off the tourist trail for a spell at this comfortable and rustic working farm, dishing up a feast of home-grown fare.

Agriturismo Sa Mandra (p216) An enticing country hideaway within easy striking distance of Alghero.

Agriturismo Muto Di Gallura (p221) Farm animals bray and bleat a greeting to you at this welcoming *agriturismo*, tucked in cork-oak woods near Aggius.

and rustic, with colour-scheme themes such as lemon, olive and lilac. There's a laid-back vibe in the living room, where you can peruse the books and games.

San Teodoro

Camping San Teodoro La Cinta CAMPGROUND €
(0784 86 57 77; www.campingsanteodoro.com; Via del Tirreno; 2 people, car & tent €32-41, 4-person bungalows €105-120; May-Oct;) About 800m from the town centre, this popular campground sits in a huge tree-filled plot right on the southern end of La Cinta beach.

Agriturismo Li Scopi AGRITURISMO €€
(338 9766350; www.agriturismoliscopi.com; Li Scopi; d €85-138;) Only the rustle of the olive trees and birdsong interrupt the pin-drop peace at this lovely *agriturismo* on the fringes of San Teodoro. The bright, spacious tiled-floor rooms open onto verandahs overlooking the well-tended gardens. La Cinta beach is 1.5km away. Breakfast costs €5 extra.

Costa Smeralda

★S'Astore BOUTIQUE HOTEL €€
(0789 3 00 00; www.hotelsastore.it; Via Monte Ladu 36, Porto Rotondo; d €100-200) With sweeping perspectives over the sea far below, this whitewashed honeycomb of 26 rooms sits amid beautifully landscaped grounds on a rocky hilltop between Golfo Aranci and Porto Rotondo. All but four rooms enjoy magnificent Mediterranean views, as does the gorgeous central lawn and pool area – a dreamy spot for parents to lounge while kids frolic at the adjacent playground.

Hotel Capriccioli HOTEL €€€
(0789 9 60 04; www.hotelcapriccioli.it; Località Capriccioli; d incl half-board €300-380, full-board €340-420;) In an area dominated by luxury hotel chains, it's a pleasure to find a welcoming family-run place like Hotel Capriccioli. Only 200m from beautiful Capriccioli beach, it offers bright rooms furnished in typical Sardinian style with wrought-iron beds and classical island fabrics.

Porto Cervo

Hotel Le Ginestre LUXURY HOTEL €€€
(0789 9 20 30; www.leginestrehotel.com; Località Porto Cervo; d incl half-board €244-614;) In typical Costa style, this hotel has rooms in low-lying ochre buildings interwoven with perfect lawns, palms and bougainvillea. Uniformed staff provide impeccable service, rooms are light and elegant and there's a pool and beauty centre for R&R. It's 1km south of Porto Cervo.

Poltu Quatu

B&B Smeralda B&B €€
(0789 9 98 11; www.bbsmeralda.com; Villaggio Faras; d €80-140;) Straddling a steep hillside 1km above Poltu Quatu's fjord-like harbour, this charming B&B offers three comfortable bedrooms with pretty tiled bathrooms. The real stars here are the outdoor whirlpool tub surrounded by sculpted rocks and the tantalising sea views from the verandah, where you can enjoy Luciana's freshly made breads and pastries at breakfast.

Baia Sardinia

★La Murichessa B&B €
(339 5316532; www.lamurichessa.it; Località Vaddimala; d €75-100, tr €100-130;) Planning a peaceful escape? This bucolic country house delivers with views of mountains, centuries-old olive trees and the glinting sea. The big, sunny rooms bear artistic touches such as shell-shaped lights. Anna Lisa is a great cook – be sure to try her homemade marmalade at breakfast. Take the SP59 Porto Cervo–Arzachena road and look carefully for the wooden sign.

La Rocca Resort & Spa LUXURY HOTEL €€€
(0789 93 31 31; www.laroccaresort.com; Località Pulicino, Baia Sardinia; d incl breakfast/half-board from €279/314;) A postcard ensemble of pastel-pink villas, green lawns and flower-lined walkways, La Rocca is a plush five-star retreat with cool, summery rooms and excellent facilities. The pool has a natural rocky fountain and there's a free shuttle bus to take you to the private beach 800m away.

Arzachena

B&B La MeSenda B&B €
(0789 8 19 50; www.lamesenda.com; Loc Malchittu; d €70-100) Immersed in peaceful countryside along the Tempio di Malchittu trail, this converted stone and stucco farmhouse makes an idyllic spot for an

overnight stay. Simple rooms with exposed beams face onto a courtyard with a 500-year-old olive tree, a hot tub and comfortable spaces for lounging. Owners Judith (from French Polynesia) and Mario (from Sardinia) serve a delicious homemade breakfast.

★B&B Lu Pastruccialeddu B&B €€
(☎0789 8 17 77; www.pastruccialeddu.com; Località Lu Pastruccialeddu, Arzachena; s €70-100, d €90-120, ste €120-150; P 🏊) This is the real McCoy, a smashing B&B housed in a typical stone farmstead, with pristine rooms, a beautiful pool and two resident donkeys. It's run by the ultra-hospitable Caterina Ruzittu, who prepares the sumptuous breakfasts – a vast spread of biscuits, yoghurt, freshly baked cakes, salami, cheese and cereals.

★Surrau Turismo Rurale B&B €€
(☎339 6788556; www.bebsurrau.it; SS125, Località Surrau; s €65-90, d €90-118) Dreamily set above vineyards, with views of granite peaks, this B&B combines rustic touches – tiled floors, wrought-iron bedsteads – with modern simplicity in its peaceful rooms. The ever-charming Emanuele is on hand to prepare breakfast, give tips or serve you a glass of local wine on the verandah at sundown. Heading north from Arzachena, find it at Km 347 on the SS125.

Hotel Stazzo Lu Ciaccaru HOTEL €€€
(☎0789 84 40 01, 0789 8 19 47; www.stazzoluciaccaru.it; Località Lu Ciaccaru; d €159-269, ste €199-329; P ❄ 📶 🏊) Hotel Stazzo Lu Ciaccaru is rural romance in a nutshell, with granite-and-wood dwellings sprinkled across grounds planted with centuries-old olive trees. For extra luxury, there's a private villa complete with four-poster bed and its own pool – at a price, naturally. Nestled in glorious seclusion, the *stazzo* (farmhouse) sits 3km south of Arzachena (follow the signs on the SP427).

San Pantaleo

★Ca' La Somara B&B €€
(☎0789 9 89 69; www.calasomara.it; s €58-98, d €80-148; P 🏊) Follow the donkey signs to Laura Lagattolla's welcoming rural retreat, 1km north of San Pantaleo. A relaxed, ramshackle farm, it offers simple guest rooms and endless opportunities for downtime: swinging in a hammock, strolling the gardens, or lounging poolside surrounded by rocky crags. Marvellous breakfasts featuring home-grown produce are served in the rustic dining room.

Credit cards (and kids) not accepted.

Locanda Sant'Andrea HOTEL €€
(☎0789 6 52 05; www.locandasantandrea.com; Via Zara 36; s €105-170, d €110-220, tr €140-245, q €180-315; P ❄ 📶 🏊) Located near the heart of the village, this tranquil place has bright, well-kept rooms, including a few units recently remodeled with snazzy new bathrooms. Families will appreciate the two-room downstairs suite opening directly onto the bougainvillea-framed pool.

Northern Gallura Coast

Santa Teresa di Gallura

Camping La Liccia CAMPGROUND €
(☎0789 75 51 90; www.campinglaliccia.com; SP90, Km 59; 2 people, car & tent €22-33, 2-person bungalows €42-110; ⏱late May-Sep; 📶 🏊) This campground, 5km west of town on the road towards Castelsardo, has fab facilities, including a playground, pool and sports area.

★B&B Domus de Janas B&B €€
(Map p163; ☎338 4990221; www.bbdomusdejanas.it; Via Carlo Felice 20a; s €70-100, d €80-150, q €130-170; ❄ 📶) Daria and Simone are your affable hosts at this sumptuous six-room B&B smack in the centre of town (as photos on the wall attest, the rambling home has belonged to Daria's family since her great-great-grandmother's days). The colourfully decorated rooms are spacious and regally comfortable, the rooftop terrace enjoys cracking sea views, and guests rave about the varied, abundant self-service breakfast.

Hotel Moderno HOTEL €€
(Map p163; ☎393 9177814, 0789 75 42 33; www.modernohotel.eu; Via Umberto 39; s €65-80, d €75-150, tr €105-180; ❄) This is a homey, family-run pick near the piazza. Rooms are bright and airy with little overt decor but traditional blue-and-white Gallurese bedspreads and tiny balconies.

Palau

L'Orso e Il Mare B&B €
(☎331 2222000; www.orsoeilmare.com; Vicolo Diaz 1; d €55-110, tr €85-145; ❄) Pietro gives his

guests a genuinely warm welcome at this two-room B&B, just steps from Piazza Fresi. The spacious rooms sport cool blue-and-white colour schemes and homey amenities such as fridges, kettles and corkscrews in each room. Breakfast is a fine spread of cakes, biscuits and fresh fruit salad.

Camping Baia Saraceno CAMPGROUND € (☎0789 70 94 03; www.baiasaraceno.com; Punta Nera, Palau; 2 people, car & tent €30-36, 2-person bungalows €65-115; ⏲Mar-Oct; 📶) Beautifully located on the beach east of Palau and shaded by pine trees, this campground has an on-site pizzeria, playground and dive centre.

Isola Maddalena

★**B&B Petite Maison** B&B € (☎0789 73 84 32, 340 6463722; www.lapetitmaison.net; Via Livenza 7, La Maddalena; d €85-110; 📶) Liberally sprinkled with paintings and art-deco furnishings, this B&B is a five-minute amble from the main square. Miriam's artistically presented breakfasts, with fresh homemade goodies, are served in a bougainvillea-draped garden. Credit cards not accepted.

The Interior

Tempio Pausania

★**Agriturismo La Cerra** AGRITURISMO € (☎347 5606462; www.agriturismolacerra.it; Località Stazzo La Cerra, SS133, Km 12.5; r per person incl breakfast €33-38, half-board €55-60) About 13km north of Tempio Pausania, this *agriturismo* in an old stone farmhouse sits on a gorgeous 75-hectare estate surrounded by cork oaks, olive trees and rocky outcrops. The Pesenti family welcomes travellers with a library and game area, hammocks, spectacular views and delicious meals made with home-grown organic produce. The six guest rooms are complemented by a small campground.

Aggius

La Vignaredda Residenza d'Epoca HOTEL € (☎079 62 08 18, 335 8018240; www.lavignaredda.it; Via Gallura 14; d €50-79, apt €70-155, breakfast per person €8.50; P📶) To really appreciate the region's tranquility, stay at this beautifully converted manor house at the town's edge. Exposed granite, cosy nooks, traditional furnishings and family heirlooms lend character without spilling over into chintz, and everything is done with care and love – from the flowery gardens to the homemade cakes at breakfast. Excursions with local guides can be arranged on request.

Agriturismo Muto Di Gallura AGRITURISMO €€ (☎079 62 05 59; www.mutodigallura.com; Località Fraiga; d €100-110, half-/full-board per person €84/96; P🏊) 🌿 Free-roaming donkeys, cows, goats, sheep and hens, beautiful stone cottages nestled in cork-oak woods, bucolic views, a quiet pool – what more could you want from an *agriturismo*? Nothing, except perhaps the delicious home-produced organic cheese, meat, vegetables and wine that land on the dinner table (menus €35 to €50). You can also organise horse riding, 4WD excursions and donkey trekking.

Berchidda & Monti

B&B Domo De Resteblas B&B € (☎340 8208482; www.bbdomoderesteblas.it; Località Restelies, Berchidda; s €35-50, d €54-70, tr €70-95; P📶🏊) Tucked into the folds of vine and olive-cloaked hills west of Berchidda, this B&B's three rooms are split between a century-old farmhouse and a more modern addition. The apartments have kitchens and balconies overlooking the central swimming pool and surrounding countryside. Local cheeses and homemade cakes feature at breakfast, and affable host Mauro offers tastes of his home-produced Vermentino wine.

NUORO & THE EAST

Nuoro

★**Casa Solotti** B&B € (☎328 6028975, 0784 3 39 54; www.casasolotti.it; Località Monte Ortobene; per person €26-35; P❄📶) This B&B reclines in a rambling garden amid woods and walking trails near the top of Monte Ortobene, 5km from central Nuoro. Decorated with stone and beams, the elegantly rustic rooms have tremendous views of the surrounding valley and the Golfo di Orosei in the distance. Staying here is a delight.

Nothing is too much trouble for your hosts, Mario and Frédérique, who can arrange everything from horse riding to packed lunches and guided hikes in the Supramonte.

Silvia e Paolo B&B €
(Map p180; ☎0784 3 12 80; www.silviaepaolo.it; Corso Garibaldi 58; s €33-40, d €55-65, tr €77; ❄📶) Silvia and Paolo run this sweet B&B in the historic centre. Cheerful family decor makes you feel right at home in the bright, spacious rooms, while up top there's a roof terrace for observing the action on Corso Garibaldi by day and stargazing by night. Note that two of the three guest rooms share a bathroom.

Agristurismo Testone AGRITURISMO €
(☎328 3150592, 329 4115168; www.agriturismotestone.com; Località Testone; r per person incl breakfast/half-board €45/65; P) About 20km from Nuoro, deep in a cork-oak forest, is this fabulously rustic farm-stay, with exposed walls, heavy wooden furniture, hanging pots and pans, and wide-open vistas of the surrounding countryside. The farm has been in the same family for many generations, as black-and-white photos on the wall attest, and guests are made to feel immediately welcome.

Barbagia

Gavoi

Albergo Gusana HOTEL €
(☎0784 5 30 00; www.albergogusana.it; Località Lago di Gusana, Gavoi; s/d €60/80; 📶🏊) A slice of civilisation in Barbagia's wild, forest-cloaked mountains, this bright, well-kept hotel (run by the same family for more than 60 years) enjoys a picturesque perch above Lago di Gusana, 4km from Gavoi's centre. The surrounding silence ensures a good night's sleep, the attached restaurant serves tasty traditional fare, and families love the swimming pool, stables and playground.

Aritzo

Sa Muvara HOTEL €€
(☎0784 62 93 36; www.samuvarahotel.com; Via Kennedy 33, Aritzo; s/d/q €95/140/220, half-board per person €95-115; P❄📶🏊) On a leafy hillside near Aritzo's southern entrance, this terraced hotel complex immersed in flowery gardens offers large, airy rooms (many with balconies) decorated with carved wood furniture. The spring-water pool and mini spa invite relaxation, the helpful front desk provides info on local walks, and the restaurant serves up a feast of local fare (meals €30 to €40).

Golfo di Orosei

Cala Gonone

★ **Agriturismo Codula Fuili** AGRITURISMO €
(☎340 2546208, 328 7340863; www.codulafuili.com; r per person incl breakfast €35-60, half-board €65-90, camping 2 people, car & tent €16-20) You could be excused for fainting when you first see the spellbinding views from this end-of-the-road *agriturismo*. Perched high on the slopes above Nuraghe Mannu and Cala Fuili, it offers four rooms, campsites, a bungalow and a panoramic terrace. Dinners (€30) feature cheese from the family's free-ranging goats, plus homegrown olives, olive oil, meats and veggies.

Agriturismo Nuraghe Mannu AGRITURISMO €
(☎0784 9 32 64, 328 8685824; www.agriturismonuraghemannu.com; Località Pranos; r per person incl breakfast €28-35, half-board €46-53, camping 2 people, car & tent €18-24) 🍃 Immersed in greenery and with blissful sea views, this is an authentic, ecofriendly working farm with five simple rooms, a restaurant open to all, and home-produced bread, milk, ricotta and sweets at breakfast. For campers, there are also five tent pitches available.

Hotel Bue Marino HOTEL €€
(☎0784 92 00 78; www.hotelbuemarino.it; Via Vespucci 8; s €82-108, d €108-180) Conveniently located just steps above the port, this blindingly white hotel has pleasant, cool blue rooms done up in traditional Sardinian fabrics. Adding to its appeal are friendly staff and magnificent sea views from many guest rooms, as well as from the upper-floor breakfast area, solarium and hot tub.

Hotel Nuraghe Arvu HOTEL €€
(☎0784 92 00 75; www.hotelnuraghearvu.com; Viale del Bue Marino; d €150-272, tr €214-388; P❄📶🏊) A terrific pick for families, Nuraghe Arvu has neat white bungalows, which are decorated in natural materials and open onto verandahs. These are gathered around an attractive pool, with massage jets to pummel you into relaxation. The friendly staff can help arrange excursions and wine-tasting tours.

Hotel L'Oasi B&B €€
(☎0784 9 31 11; www.loasihotel.it; Via Garcia Lorca 13; s €60-102, d €75-138; P ❄ 📶) Perched on the cliffs above Cala Gonone and nestling in flowery gardens, this B&B offers enticing sea views from many of its breezy rooms. The friendly Carlesso family can advise on activities from climbing to diving. L'Oasi is a 700m uphill walk from the harbour.

Hotel Miramare HOTEL €€
(☎0784 9 31 40; www.htlmiramare.it; Piazza Gigardini 12; s €72-98, d €104-146; ❄ 📶) Cala Gonone's oldest hotel, opened in 1955, is definitely showing its age, but the harbourside location can't be beaten, and it does have a certain retro appeal. Sea breezes cool the simple, tiled-floor rooms; the best have terraces overlooking the Med, while cheaper rooms face inland. Snag a lounger on the rooftop terrace to kick back and enjoy the view.

Orosei

B&B Marzellinu B&B €
(☎339 6000590; http://marzellinu.wordpress.com; Viale Sas Linnas Siccas 96, Cala Liberotto; d €60-100; P 📶) Reclining among pines and lawns, this B&B close to Cala Liberotto is a delight. The bright, cheerful rooms are kept immaculate – ask for La Peonia for a sea view. A footpath threads down to a secluded bay with crystal-clear water, perfect for snorkelling. Kids will love the kittens prowling around the grounds. There is a three-night minimum stay.

★ **Albergo Diffuso Mannois** B&B €€
(☎0784 99 10 40; www.mannois.it; Via G Angioy 32; s €70-120, d €80-150; ❄ 📶) Spread across three lovingly restored buildings in the medieval centre of Orosei, Albergo Diffuso Mannois is very special. Each of the light-filled, pastel-hued rooms is individually decorated, with lovely touches such as exposed stone, Sardinian fabrics and juniper-wood beams. Various excursions, including horse riding and diving, can be arranged here.

Anticos Palathos HOTEL €€
(☎0784 9 86 04; www.anticospalathos.com; Via Nazionale 51; s €60-150, d €75-220; P ❄ 📶) Centred on a beautiful courtyard, this stone townhouse keeps it rustic with a vaulted breakfast room and characterful rooms featuring wrought-iron bedsteads and ornamental fireplaces. Freshly baked bread and pastries are served at breakfast.

Supramonte

Oliena

★ **Agriturismo Guthiddai** AGRITURISMO €
(☎0784 28 60 17; www.agriturismoguthiddai.com; Nuoro-Dorgali bivio Su Gologone; d €98-115, half-board per person €70-80; ❄ 📶) On the road to Su Gologone, this bucolic, whitewashed farmstead sits at the foot of rugged mountains, surrounded by fig, olive and fruit trees. Olive oil, Cannonau wine and fruit and veg are all home produced. Rooms are tiled in pale greens and cobalt blues. From Oliena, head to Dorgali, taking the turn-off right towards Valle di Lanaittu.

Hotel Monte Maccione HOTEL, CAMPGROUND €
(☎0784 28 83 63; www.coopenis.it; Località Monte Maccione; s €44-55, d €76-90, q €136-164, camping 2 people & tent €20; P 📶) Run by the Cooperativa Enis, this place offers simple, rustic rooms, campsites and astonishingly lovely views from its hilltop location, 4km south of Oliena up a steep series of switchbacks off the SP22. This back-to-nature retreat is a great choice if you want to strike out into the mountains on foot.

Su Gologone HOTEL €€€
(☎0784 28 75 12; www.sugologone.it; Località Su Gologone; d incl half-board €254-392; P ❄ 📶 🏊) Treat yourself to a spot of rural luxury at Su Gologone, nestled in glorious countryside 7km east of Oliena. Rooms are decorated with original artworks and handicrafts, and the facilities are top notch – it has a pool, a spa, a wine cellar and a restaurant (p198), which is considered one of Sardinia's best.

Dorgali

Sa Corte Antica B&B €
(☎349 8401371; www.sacorteantica.it; Via Mannu 17; d €50-60, tr €75-90; ❄ 📶) Gathered around an old stone courtyard, this B&B housed in an 18th-century townhouse oozes charm from every brick and beam. The rooms are traditional and peaceful, with reed ceilings and wrought-iron bedsteads. Enjoy homemade bread and *biscotti* at breakfast.

Hotel S'Adde HOTEL €
(☎0784 9 44 12; www.hotelsadde.it; Via Concordia 38; s/d €36/63, half-board €61/113; P ❄ 📶) Only a short, signposted walk up from the main thoroughfare, this welcoming chalet has pine-clad rooms with terraces and green

views. The restaurant-pizzeria (meals €25 to €30) opens onto a 1st-floor terrace. Breakfast costs an extra €5.

Hotel Il Querceto HOTEL €€
(☎0784 9 65 09; www.ilquerceto.com; Via Alfonso Lamarmora 4; s €68-114, d €73-163, ste €221-325; P ❄ ≋) An ecofriendly hotel using solar and geothermal energy, Il Querceto boasts nicely low-key rooms with lashings of cream linen and honey-coloured tiles. The pools and oak-shaded garden invite relaxation, while the restaurant emphasises seasonal cuisine. It's just northwest of town.

Baunei & the Altopiano del Golgo

Hotel Bia Maore B&B €€
(☎0782 61 10 33; www.biamaore.it; Via San Pietro 19, Baunei; s €55-85, d €82-130, tr €107-150; P ❄ 📶) Perched like an eyrie above Baunei, this B&B has compelling views of the mountains and coast. The warm-hued rooms are decked out with handmade furnishings and Sardinian fabrics – the pick of them with a balcony overlooking the mountains and the Gulf of Ogliastra.

Ogliastra

Santa Maria Navarrese

Lemon House B&B €
(☎333 3862210; www.lemonhouse.eu; Via Dante 19, Lotzorai; r per person €33-43; 📶) New owners Riky and Elena have kept the same great vibe alive at this long-time favourite for hikers, climbers and cyclists. The lime-hued B&B makes a terrific base for outdoor escapades, with a bouldering wall, a relaxing roof terrace, a great library of outdoors-themed guidebooks, and plenty of invaluable tips on hiking, climbing, mountain biking and kayaking in the area.

It's 7km north of Tortolì and 10km south of Baunei, just off the SS125.

Albergo Santa Maria HOTEL €€
(☎0782 61 53 15; www.albergosantamaria.it; Via Plammas 30; s €65-85, d €115-155, half-board per person €76-95; P ❄ 📶) It's just a short amble from the beach to this low-rise, whitewashed hotel, where a warm welcome extends to all. The colourful rooms open onto balconies overlooking the courtyard or flower-dotted gardens. Substantial breakfasts and a gym (to work them off) are other pluses.

Tortolì & Arbatax

Camping La Pineta CAMPGROUND €
(☎0782 2 93 72; www.campingbungalowlapineta.it; Località Planargia, Barisardo; 2 people, car & tent €15-31.50, bungalows €45-115; P 📶) Hidden among the pine trees, a 400m walk from a fabulous beach, this family-run campsite is a real find, though you will need your own wheels to find it. Pitches have plenty of tree shade and there are also well-equipped bungalows, a little bar-restaurant and a playground. It is situated near the town of Barisardo, 12km south of Tortolì.

La Bitta HOTEL €€€
(☎0782 66 70 80; www.hotellabitta.it; Località Porto Frailis; d €129-305, incl half-board €179-355; P ❄ 📶 ≋) Right on the beach in Porto Frailis, this is a luxurious affair with palatial, vaulted rooms (sea views cost extra), a seafront pool and beauty treatments ranging from shiatsu to lymph drainage. Have a drink at the swish lounge bar while admiring close-ups of local marine life splashing around in an enormous aquarium.

Ulassai

★ **Hotel Su Marmuri** HOTEL €
(☎0782 7 90 03; www.hotelsumarmuri.com; Corso Vittorio Emanuele 20; s €30-40, d €60-80, tr €75-90, q €90-120) The delightful Lai family presides over this well-known village institution, which offers simple, neat rooms and stupendous views. Husband-wife team Tonino and Elena, together with their son Massimiliano, offer all the advice you need about the surrounding area, and delight in showing visitors its hidden corners – from nearby caves to scenic picnic spots.

Nannai Climbing Home GUESTHOUSE €
(www.climbingulassai.com; Via Monsignor Depau; dm €10, d €60, without bathroom €50; 📶) As the name implies, this unique accommodation in Ulassai is all about creating a welcoming atmosphere for climbers. Guests can choose between dorms or private doubles; either way, the real fun is sharing tips and stories in the cosy, well-equipped kitchen/lounge – or out on the inspirational roof terrace with views of the surrounding cliffs and the distant Mediterranean.

Understand Sardinia

Sardinia Today

Tourism is booming and unemployment is slowly dropping, but there are still some niggling worries that are stopping Sardinia from walking into the sunset. The high cost of travel to the mainland, the economic struggle between development and sustainable tourism, and the military presence on the island's coastline are all flagged as causes for concern. But that didn't stop the island from throwing one heck of a party when the Giro d'Italia kicked off in Alghero in May 2017, celebrating its 100th edition.

Best on Film

Padre Padrone (Father and Master; 1977) The true story of Gavino Ledda's harsh life as a shepherd.

Ballu a Tre Passi (Three-Step Dance; 2003) Four snapshots of life in Sardinia, with some beautiful shots of the Costa del Sud.

La Destinazione (The Destination; 2003) The story of a young Italian *carabiniere* (police officer) sent to a remote Sardinian village in Barbagia to investigate the murder of a shepherd.

Best Blogs

Sardegna in Blog (http://sardegnainblog.it) All things Sardinia feature on this island-focused blog.

Sardegna Cultura (www.sardegnacultura.it) For the inside scoop on the island's cultural life.

Sardegna.com (www.sardegna.com/it/blog) Interesting insights into island trails, arts, food and lifestyle.

SardegnaBlogger (www.sardegnablogger.it) Articles devoted to Sardinian current affairs and more.

Transport Connections

Sardinians are feeling the brunt of the high cost of travel to and from the island. While island's tourism economy depends on low-cost flights, many of these don't operate daily year-round leaving the locals in the hands of the big ferry companies such as Moby and Tirrenia. With a number competitors recently becoming defunct – among them Saremar and Go in Sardinia – the ferries remain expensive (around €180 one way between Naples and Cagliari, for instance), a bone of contention for residents in terms of feeling disconnected from the mainland. To mitigate this, the island has requested support from the Italian government and the EU to bring prices down for locals.

Their calls have to some extent been answered: in 2017 a decree for '*continuità territoriale*' (territorial continuity) was passed, ensuring Sardinians can reach the mainland without leaving the country borders. This entails capping fares for residents until 2021, ensuring they receive preferential rates on airline and ferry services to the mainland, especially for the most-travelled routes between Olbia, Alghero and Cagliari and Milan and Rome.

Sustainable Tourism vs Development

Striking the right balance between development and sustainable tourism remains an ongoing issue. Sardinia's progressive Salvacoste (Save the Coastline) law, first introduced in 2004, was a controversial ban on building within 2km of the coast, considered by many the best environmental protection measure ever passed in Italy. But it has run up against challenges in the wake of more recent economic crises. Recently the Sardinian government has been working on a new *'legge urbanistica'* (town planning law) that aims to allow further development of existing properties while still protecting especially sensitive areas, such as those directly adjoining the waterfront. The minutiae of the new law and how it will synchronise with the Salvacoste law remains to be seen.

In response, many local communities are now taking steps, either individually or in groups of neighbouring towns, to establish protected areas in the hope of getting official recognition at the national or even Unesco level that will let them prioritise sustainable tourism as the backbone of their economies.

Military in the Med

There is more to this picturesque island than meets the eye. Sardinia is home to more than 50% of Italy's military bases, including Salto di Quirra, the largest military range in the country. According to a February 2016 article in the news magazine *L'Espresso*, 80% of the military explosives in Italy are used in Sardinia. The deaths of six soldiers between December 2015 and January 2016 provoked protests and concern.

Once-beautiful stretches of coastline, such as Cala Zafferano, near Capo Teulada on the island's southwestern tip, are now no-go zones according to newspaper *L'Unione Sarda*. And in January 2017 daily newspaper *La Stampa* reported on protests from fishermen and other local residents about the military testing and war games at Capo Teulada, as well as potential corruption in the process to pay compensation to fishermen for lost earnings.

Rising Employment & Booming Tourism

Sardinia is finally emerging from the gloom of the economic crisis. Although unemployment in Sardinia remained higher (15.9%) than the national average (10.9%) in the last quarter of 2016, this still indicated a slight improvement compared to the previous year's figure of 16.7%, proof that slowly but surely the job market is picking up.

Tourism numbers have rocketed in recent years, with ISTAT figures showing an increase of around 20%. Airlines have responded to the upsurge in tourism by launching additional flights to the island in 2017, among them the new BMI route from Bristol to Cagliari and new Ryanair connections from Luton and Stansted to Cagliari.

Given that tourism is the driving force behind growth, booming tourist numbers have largely been a cause for island-wide celebration. However, some holiday hot spots – the Costa Smeralda, for instance – are struggling with the surge in visitors during peak summer months. And while the coast is overcrowded, vast areas of the interior receive just a trickle of visitors by comparison. In 2017, the Giro d'Italia cycling race turned the spotlight on the island's less-discovered interior. Going forward the key to sustainable, year-round tourism may be to get the message out that there's more to Sardinia beyond the beach.

POPULATION: **1.67 MILLION**

AREA: **24,090 SQ KM**

GDP PER CAPITA: **€17,800**

INFLATION: **0.6%**

UNEMPLOYMENT: **15.9%**

if Sardinia were 100 people

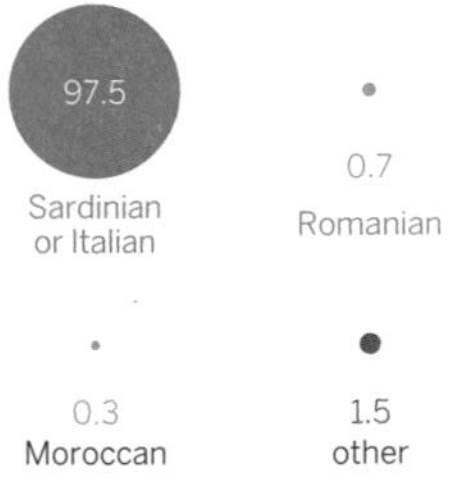

the land

(%)

population per sq km

History

Sitting between Europe and Africa, Sardinia's strategic position and rich mineral reserves have brought tidal waves of power-hungry invaders to its shores, and its rugged, impenetrable mountains have attracted everyone from Stone Age men to 19th-century bandits in hiding. Thanks to a certain inward-looking pride and nostalgic spirit, the Sards have not allowed time and the elements to erase their story. Travellers can easily dip into the chapters of the island's past by exploring tombs, towers, forts and churches.

Mysteries of the Ancients

Palaeolithic & Neolithic Ages

When the first islanders arrived and where they came from are questions that have been puzzling researchers for centuries. The most likely hypothesis is that they landed on Sardinia's northern shores sometime during the lower Palaeolithic period (Old Stone Age). When flint tools were found at Perfugas in 1979, archaeologists muttered excitedly about primitive humans crossing from mainland Italy as far back as 350,000 BC. It's thought they came from Tuscany, although it's possible that other waves arrived from North Africa and the Iberian Peninsula via the Balearic Islands. Geneticists have attempted to solve the riddle by researching the island's curious genetic make-up – in certain parts of the interior a particular gene mutation is found in concentrations only otherwise present in Scandinavia, Bosnia & Hercegovina and Croatia. However, in spite of this research, the geneticists seem just as puzzled as the rest of us.

Five Neolithic Wonders

- *Pranu Muttedu (Goni)*
- *Museo delle Statue Menhir (Laconi)*
- *Caves in the Valle Lanaittu (Nuoro province)*
- *Museo Archeologico Ozieri))*
- *Dolmen Sa Coveccada (Mores)*

Wherever the early settlers came from, they were apparently happy with what they found, because by the neolithic period (8000 BC to 3000 BC), Sardinia was home to several thriving tribal communities. The island would have been a perfect home for the average neolithic family – it was covered with dense forests that were full of animals, there were caves for shelter, and the land was suitable for grazing and cultivation. Underlying everything were rich veins of obsidian, a volcanic black stone that was used for making tools and arrow tips. This black gold became the Mediterranean's most coveted commodity, and

TIMELINE

350,000 BC

Fragments of basic flint tools indicate the first traces of human culture on the island.

4000–2700 BC

Thriving Copper Age communities form around the town of Ozieri. Copper was smelted into ingots and traded, and the first *domus de janas* (rock tombs) appear.

1800–1500 BC

The nuraghic period: most of the stone ruins that litter Sardinia date back to this time. Some 30,000 fortified stone towers are built.

was traded across the area – shards of Sardinian obsidian have been found as far away as France.

Most of what we know of this period, known as the Ozieri (or San Michele) culture, comes from findings unearthed in caves around Ozieri and in the Valle Lanaittu. Fragments of ceramics, tools and copper ingots attest to knowledge of smelting techniques and artistic awareness, while early *domus de janas* (literally 'fairy houses'; tombs cut into rock) tell of complex funerary rituals. Their menhirs and ancient rock tombs still stand today.

The funerary site of Pranu Muttedu on the central Sarcidano plain offers a deeper insight into Sardinia's neolithic Ozieri culture, strewn with *domus de janas* and around 50 menhirs. Another megalithic wonder is Biru 'e Concas in the Mandrolisai, one of Sardinia's largest collections of menhirs, with some 200 standing stones in situ. Around 30 of them are lined up east to west, presumably as a symbolic representation of the sun's trajectory.

Best Nuraghic Sites

- *Nuraghe Su Nuraxi*
- *Tiscali*
- *Nuraghe Losa*
- *Santuario Santa Vittoria*
- *Nuraghe di Palmavera*
- *S'Ena 'e Thomes and Serra Orrios*

Nuraghic Civilisation

A millennium or so after the Ozieri culture came the nuraghic people, whose 7000 *nuraghi* (Bronze Age towers and fortified settlements) are scattered across the island like pieces of a hard-to-solve puzzle. But according to archaeologists this is just tip of the iceberg stuff, with at least the same number of *nuraghi* estimated to lie beneath the ground, yet to be discovered. Most of these *nuraghi* were built between 1800 and 500 BC. These Bronze Age fortified settlements were used as watchtowers, sacred areas for religious rites, and meeting places, and provide some of the few insights into nuraghic civilisation.

The discovery of Mycenaean ceramics in Sardinia and nuraghic pottery in Crete suggest an early trade in tableware and contact with other cultures. Evidence of pagan religious practices are provided by *pozzi sacri* (well temples). Built from around 1000 BC, these were often constructed so as to capture light at the yearly equinoxes, hinting at a naturalistic religion. The well temple at Santa Cristina is a prime example.

But perhaps the most revealing insights into nuraghic culture come from the *bronzetti* (bronze figurines) that populate many of Sardinia's archaeological museums, most notably those in Cagliari and Sassari. Scholars reckon that these primitive depictions of shepherd kings, warriors, farmers and sailors were used as decorative offerings in nuraghic temples.

Head to www.sardegnaturismo.it for historic itineraries of the island, taking you in the footsteps of the nuraghic people, Phoenicians, Romans and the giudicati.

One thing is certain: Sardinia's mysterious, unfathomable *nuraghi* reveal a highly cultured civilisation. The nuraghic people were sophisticated builders, constructing their temples with precisely cut stones and no mortar; they travelled and exchanged (as revealed by the discovery

1500 BC

Sardinia's most important *nuraghe*, Nuraghe Su Nuraxi, is built near Barumini.

1100 BC

The Phoenicians establish the town of Nora on the southwest coast, one of a series of important trading posts along with Karalis (Cagliari) and Tharros.

1000 BC

The nuraghic people begin to build elaborate *pozzi sacri* (sacred wells).

650 BC

Phoenicians build their first inland fortress on Monte Sirai following clashes with Sardinians.

of seal remains and mussel shells inland); and they had the time, skills and resources to stop and build villages, and to dedicate to arts such as ceramics and jewellery.

Masters of the Mediterranean

The Phoenicians

Some historians argue that the nuraghic populace of Sardinia were the Shardana, a piratical seafaring people who appear in early Egyptian inscriptions.

Sardinia's strategic position and its rich natural resources (silver and lead reserves) and fertile arable land have long made the island a target of the Mediterranean's big powers.

The first foreigners on the scene were the enterprising, seafaring Phoenicians (from modern-day Lebanon). The master mariners of their day, they were primarily interested in Sardinia as a staging post – they had colonies on Sicily, Malta, Cyprus and Corsica – so Sardinia was an obvious addition. The exact date of their arrival is unclear, although Semitic inscriptions suggest that Spain-based Phoenicians may have set up at Nora, on the south coast of Sardinia, as early as 1100 BC.

In the early days the Phoenicians lived in relative harmony with the local nuraghic people, who seemed happy enough to leave the newcomers to their coastal settlements – Karalis (Cagliari), Bithia (near modern Chia), Sulci (modern Sant'Antioco), Tharros and Bosa. However, when the outsiders ventured inland and took over the lucrative silver and lead mines in the southwest, the locals took umbrage. Clashes ensued and the Phoenicians built their first inland fortress on Monte Sirai in 650 BC. This proved wise, as disgruntled Sardinians attacked several Phoenician bases in 509 BC.

In his book Le Colonne d'Ercole: Un' inchiesta (The Pillars of Hercules: An investigation), Sergio Frau stakes a claim for Sardinia as the lost civilisation of Atlantis. The debate is reflective of an island whose origins lie beyond the reach of traditional history.

Against the ropes, the Phoenicians appealed to Carthage for aid. The Carthaginians were happy to oblige and joined Phoenician forces in conquering most of the island. Most, though, not all. As the Carthaginians found out to their cost, and the Romans would discover to theirs, the tough, mountainous area now known as the Barbagia didn't take kindly to foreign intrusion.

Set against the backdrop of the glittering Mediterranean, the archaeological remains of the mighty Phoenician port Tharros, founded in 730 BC, are one of Sardinia's most stunning sights. More tangible vestiges of the Phoenicians are visible in Sant'Antioco's historic centre, littered with necropolises and with an intact *tophet,* a sanctuary where the Phoenicians and Carthaginians buried their stillborn babies. Monti Sirai near Carbonia also offers a glimpse into the island's past with its ruined Phoenician fort, built in 650 BC.

Carthaginians & Romans

It was the Carthaginians, rather than the Phoenicians, who first dragged Sardinia into the Mediterranean's territorial disputes. By the 6th century

550 BC

The Carthaginians take control of this neck of the Mediterranean. Their influence extends to the island's west and south coast.

227 BC

More than a decade after victory in the First Punic War (264–241 BC), Sardinia becomes a Roman province.

216 BC

The Carthaginians are defeated. The Romans build roads and develop centres at Karalis (Cagliari), Nora, Sulcis, Tharros, Olbia and Turris Libisonis (Porto Torres).

177 BC

Some 12,000 Sardinians die under Roman rule, and some 50,000 are sent to Rome as slaves.

BC, Greek dominion over the Mediterranean was being challenged by the North African Carthaginians. So when the Greeks established a base on Corsica, the Carthaginians were happy to accept Phoenician invitations to help them subdue the by-now rebellious Sardinians. It was the foot in the door that the Carthaginians needed to take control of the island and boost their defences against the growing threat from Rome.

The ambitious Roman Republic faced two main challenges to their desire to control the southern Mediterranean: the Greeks and the Carthaginians. The Romans saw off the Greeks first, and then, in 241 BC, turned their attention to Carthaginian-controlled Sardinia.

The Romans arrived in Sardinia buoyed by victory over Carthage in the First Punic War (264–241 BC). But if the legionnaires thought they were in for an easy ride, they were in for a shock. The new team of the Sards and their former enemies, the Carthaginians, were in no mood for warm welcomes. The Romans found themselves frequently battling insurgents, especially in the mountainous Gennargentu area, which they dubbed Barbaria in reluctant homage to the sheer bloody-minded courage of the region's shepherd inhabitants.

In 215 BC Sardinian tribesmen, under their chieftain Ampsicora, joined the Carthaginians in the Second Punic War and revolted against

Phoenician & Roman Must-Sees

Tharros (Sinis Peninsula)

Nora (Pula)

Villa di Tigellio (Cagliari)

Sant'Antioco (Isola di Sant'Antioco)

Monte Sirai (Carbonia)

Anfiteatro Romano (Cagliari)

SARDONIC: THE LAST LAUGH

When Homer wrote about hero Odysseus smiling 'sardonically' when being attacked by one of his wife's former suitors, he was surely alluding to a grin in the face of danger. Yet the word sardonic, from the Greek root *sardánios,* has come to mean simply 'scornful' or 'grimly mocking' in today's usage.

If recent scientific findings are anything to go by, Homer may have been on the right track with his hint at danger. Studies carried out by scientists at the University of Eastern Piedmont in 2009 identified hemlock water dropwort *(Oenanthe crocata)* as being responsible for the sardonic smile from, of course, Sardinia. It seems that in pre-Roman times, ritual killings were carried out using the toxic perennial (known locally as 'water celery'). The elderly, infirm and indeed anyone who had become a burden to society were intoxicated with the poisonous brew, which made their facial muscles contract into a maniacal sardonic grin, before being finished off by being pushed from a steep rock or savagely beaten.

Regardless of whether the word sardonic refers to this sinister prehistoric malpractice, it seems that the findings could have positive implications in the field of medicine. Some scientists believe that the molecule in hemlock water dropwort could be modified by pharmaceutical companies to have the opposite effect, working as a muscle relaxant to help people to recover from facial paralysis.

456 AD

In the wake of the fall of the Roman Empire, the Vandals land on Sardinia.

456–534

Byzantine chroniclers, not the most objective, record the almost 80 years of Vandal rule as a time of misery for islanders.

600

Christianity is finally imposed on the Barbagia region, the last to succumb to Byzantine proselytising.

705

Saracens begin a spate of attacks on the island's coastal cities. Sardinia is subjected to raids for several centuries.

MALARIA

Sardinia has endured millennia of invasion and foreign control, but until 1946 the island's single-most dangerous enemy was malaria.

Although scientists believe that the disease was probably present in prehistoric times – some maintain that *nuraghi* were built as defence against weak-flying mosquitoes – it became a serious problem with the arrival of the Carthaginians in the 5th century BC. Keen to exploit the island's agricultural potential, the colonists cut down swathes of lowland forest to free land for wheat cultivation. One of the effects of this was to increase flooding and create areas of free-standing water, perfect mosquito breeding grounds. The problem was exacerbated by the arrival of imported soldiers from North Africa, many of whom were infected.

By the time the Romans took control of the island in the 3rd century BC, Sardinia was a malarial hothouse, its *mal aria* (bad air) thought to bring certain death. Despite this, the Romans followed the Carthaginian lead and continued to exploit the island's fertile terrain. The Campidano plain became, along with Sicily and occupied North Africa, the granary of the entire Roman Empire.

The Rockefeller Foundation Sardinian Project (1946–51) enlisted 32,000 DDT workers to spray 10,000 tons of DDT over the island, which finally wiped out malaria entirely. The effects are still being researched.

their Roman masters. But it was a short-lived rebellion, and the following year the rebels were crushed at the second battle of Cornus.

Once they had Sardinia in their hands, the Romans set about shaping it to suit their own needs. Despite endemic malaria and frequent harassment from locals, they expanded the Carthaginian cities, built a road network to facilitate communications and organised a hugely efficient agricultural system. The Romans also severely decreased the island's population – in 177 BC around 12,000 Sardinians died and as many as 50,000 were sent to Rome as slaves. Many noble families managed to survive and gain Roman-citizen status and learnt to speak Latin, but on the whole, the island remained an underdeveloped and overexploited subject territory.

Raids & Resistance: Medieval Sardinia

Pisa vs Genoa

By the 9th century, the Arabs had emerged as a major force in the Mediterranean. They had conquered much of Spain, North Africa and Sicily, and were intent on further expansion. Sardinia, with its rich natural resources and absentee Byzantine rulers, made for an inviting target and the island was repeatedly raided in the 9th and 10th centuries. But as

1000–1400

Sardinia is divided into four *giudicati* (provinces), the most famous being the Giudicato d'Arborea, centred on Oristano. The *giudicati* are eventually incorporated into Pisan and Genoese spheres.

1015

Pisa and Genoa begin their long struggle for control of the island. By the late 13th century, the mainlanders control three-quarters of the island.

1297

In the face of Catalan pressure, Pope Boniface VIII creates the Regnum Sardiniae et Corsicae (Kingdom of Sardinia and Corsica) and declares Jaume II of Aragon its king.

1323

The Aragonese invade the southwest coast and take actual possession of the island.

Arab power began to wane in the early 11th century, so Christian ambition flourished, and in 1015 Pope Benedict VIII asked the republics of Pisa and Genoa to lend Sardinia a hand against the common Islamic enemy. The ambitious princes of Pisa and Genoa were quick to sniff an opportunity and gladly acquiesced to the pope's requests.

At the time Sardinia was split into four self-governing *giudicati* (provinces), but for much of the 300-year period between the 11th and 14th centuries, the island was fought over by the rival mainlanders. Initially the Pisans had the upper hand in the north of the island, while the Genoese carried favour in the south, particularly around Cagliari. But Genoese influence was also strong in Porto Torres, and the *giudicati* swapped allegiances at the drop of a hat. Against this background of intrigue and rivalry, the period was strangely prosperous. The island absorbed the cultural mores of medieval Europe, and powerful monasteries ensured that islanders received the message of Roman Christianity loud and clear. The Pisan-Romanesque basalt churches of the Logudoro in the northwest remain a striking legacy of the period.

Medieval Marvels

Torre dell'Elefante (Cagliari)

Basilica della Santissima Trinità di Saccargia (Logudoro)

Chiesa di San Simplicio (Olbia)

Castello Malaspina (Bosa)

Centro storico (Iglesias)

Torre Porta a Terra (Alghero)

Fighting Spirit & Spanish Conquerors

Described as Sardinia's Boudicca or Joan of Arc, Eleonora d'Arborea (1340–1404) was the talismanic figure of Sardinia's medieval history and embodies the islanders' deep-rooted fighting soul. As the island's most inspirational ruler, she is remembered for her wisdom, moderation and enlightened humanity.

Queen of the Giudicato d'Arborea, one of four *giudicati* – the others were Cagliari, Logudoro (or Torres) in the northwest and Gallura in the northeast – into which the island had been divided, she became

ELEONORA'S CARTA DE LOGU

Eleonora d'Arborea's greatest legacy was the Carta de Logu, which she published in 1392. This progressive code, based on Roman law, was far ahead of the social legislation of the period. The code was drafted by her father, Mariano, but Eleonora revised and completed it. To the delight of the islanders, it was published in Sardinian, thus forming the cornerstone of a nascent national consciousness. For the first time the big issues of land use and the right to appeal were codified, and women were granted a whole raft of rights, including the right to refuse marriage and – significantly in a rural society – property rights. Alfonso V was so impressed that he extended its laws throughout the island in 1421, and this remained so until 1871.

Eleonora never saw how influential her Carta de Logu became. She died of the plague in 1404, and the Aragonese took control of Arborea only 16 years after her death. Eleonora remains the most respected historical figure on the island.

1392
Sardinia's great heroine and ruler of the Giudicato d'Arborea, Eleonora d'Arborea, publishes the Carta de Logu, the island's first code of common law.

1400–1500
Under Catalan-Aragonese control, absentee landlords impose devastating taxes and leave the rural population to struggle against famine and plagues, which claim 50% of the island's population.

1478
On 19 May Sardinian resistance to Aragonese control is crushed at the Battle of Macomer. Led by the Marquis of Oristano, Leonardo de Alagon, Sard forces prove no match for the Iberian army.

1700
The death of the heirless Habsburg ruler Carlos II puts Sardinia up for grabs once again.

a symbol of Sardinian resistance for her unyielding opposition to the Pisans, Genoese and Catalan-Aragonese.

By the end of the 13th century, Arborea was the only *giudicato* not in the hands of the Pisans and Genoese. The Arboreans, however, toughed it out and actually increased their sphere of influence. At its height under King Marianus IV (1329–76) and Eleonora, the kingdom encompassed all of the modern-day provinces of Oristano and Medio Campidano, as well as much of the Barbagia mountain country.

Initially Arborea had supported the Catalan-Aragonese in their conquering of Cagliari and Iglesias, but when they realised that their allies were bent on controlling the whole island, their support for the foreigners quickly dried up. Eleonora became Giudicessa of Arborea in 1383, when her venal brother, Hugo III, was murdered along with his daughter. Surrounded by enemies within and without (her husband was imprisoned in Aragon), she silenced the rebels and for the next 20 years worked to maintain Arborea's independence in an uncertain world.

From 1383 to 1404, Eleonora bitterly opposed the Catalan-Aragonese. But she couldn't live forever and her death in 1404 paved the way for defeat. In 1409 the Sardinians were defeated at the Battle of Sanluri, in 1410 Oristano fell, and in 1420 the exhausted Arborean rulers of the *giudicato* finally gave in to the inevitable and sold their provinces to the Catalans.

Spain & the Savoys

Aragonese Invaders

Sardinia's Spanish chapter makes for some grim reading. Spanish involvement in Sardinia dates back as far as the early 14th century. In 1297 Pope Boniface VIII created the Regnum Sardiniae e Corsicae (Kingdom of Sardinia and Corsica) and granted it to the Catalan-Aragonese as an inducement to the Spaniards to relinquish their claims on Sicily. Unfortunately, however, the kingdom only existed on paper and the Aragonese were forced to wrench control of Sardinia from the hands of its stubborn islanders. In 1323 the Aragonese invaded the southwest coast, the first act in a chapter that was to last some 400 years.

Under the Catalan-Aragonese and the Spanish, the desperately poor Sardinian population was largely abandoned to itself – albeit on the crippling condition that it pay its taxes – and the island remained underdeveloped. But Spanish power faded in the latter half of the 17th century and the death of the heirless Habsburg ruler Carlos II in 1700 once again put Sardinia up for grabs.

Habsburgs & Piedmontese

The death of Carlos II triggered the War of the Spanish Succession, which set pro-Habsburg Austrian forces against pro-Bourbon French factions

1708

English and Austrian forces seize Sardinia from King Felipe V of Spain during the War of the Spanish Succession, a European-wide scramble for the spoils of the rudderless Habsburg Empire.

1720

Duke Vittorio Amedeo II of Savoy becomes King of Piedmont and Sardinia after the island is yo-yoed between competing powers: Austria, then Spain, Austria again, Spain for a second time and finally the Savoys.

1795–99

After Piedmontese authorities deny requests for greater self-rule, angry mobs take to the streets of Cagliari, killing senior Savoy administrators. By 1799 the revolutionary flame has burnt itself out.

1823

Intended to promote land ownership among the rural poor, the Enclosures Act sees the sale of centuries-old communal land and the abolition of communal rights. It's not popular and riots result.

in a battle for the spoils of the Habsburg empire. In 1708 Austrian forces backed by English warships occupied Sardinia. There followed a period of intense politicking as the island was repeatedly passed back and forth between the Austrians and the Spanish, before ending up in the hands of the Duchy of Savoy.

Piedmontese rule (from 1720 to Italian unification in 1861) was no bed of roses, either, but in contrast to their Spanish predecessors, the Savoy authorities did actually visit the areas they were governing. The island was ruled by a viceroy who, by and large, managed to maintain control.

In 1847 the island's status as a separate entity ruled through a viceroy came to an end. Tempted by reforms that had been introduced in the Savoys' mainland territories, a delegation requested the 'perfect union' of the Kingdom of Sardinia with Piedmont, in the hope of acquiring more equitable rule. The request was granted. At the same time, events were moving quickly elsewhere on the Italian peninsula. In a series of daring military campaigns that were led by Giuseppe Garibaldi and encouraged by King Carlo Emanuele, Sardinia managed to annexe the Italian mainland to create the united Kingdom of Italy in 1861.

Nowhere is the Spanish influence more palpable than in Alghero, which fell to Spanish invaders in 1353 after 30 years of resistance. Even today Catalan is still spoken, and street signs and menus are often in both languages.

Italy's revolutionary hero, Giuseppe Garibaldi, died on 2 June 1882 on the Isola Caprera, his private island in the Arcipelago di La Maddalena. Today you can visit his home, the Compendio Garibaldino, for an insight into the man who succeeded in uniting Italy.

Buried Treasures

Boom Years

Although all but extinct, Sardinia's mining industry has played a significant role in the island's history. Southwest Sardinia is riddled with empty mine shafts and abandoned mine works, hollow reminders of a once-booming sector.

Sardinia's rich mineral reserves were being tapped as far back as the 6th millennium BC. Obsidian was a major earner for early Ozieri communities and a much sought-after commodity. Later, the Romans and Pisans tapped into rich veins of lead and silver in the Iglesias and Sarrabus areas.

The history of Sardinian mining really took off in the mid-19th century. In 1840 legislation was introduced that gave the state (the ruling Savoys) control of underground resources, while allowing surface land to remain in private hands. This, combined with an increased demand for raw materials fuelled by European industrial expansion, started a mining boom on the island.

By the late 1860s there were 467 lead, iron and zinc mines in Sardinia, and at its peak the island was producing up to 10% of the world's zinc.

Iglesiente miners only went on strike in September, when the wild prickly pear came into fruit. This meant their families would have something to eat while the miners weren't earning a wage.

1840

Legislation is introduced giving the state (the ruling Savoys) control of underground resources, which starts a mining boom.

1847

Requests for the Kingdom of Sardinia, up to this point a separate entity ruled by a viceroy, to be merged with the Kingdom of Piedmont are granted. From this point on, Sardinia is governed from Turin.

1861

In a series of military campaigns led by Giuseppe Garibaldi, King Carlo Emanuele annexes the Italian mainland to create the united Kingdom of Italy.

1915

The Brigata Sassari (Sassari Brigade) is founded and sent into WWI action in the northeastern Alps. Its Sardinian soldiers earn a reputation for valour and suffer heavy losses – 2164 deaths, 12,858 wounded or lost.

Inward investment had spillover effects. The birth of new towns, the introduction of electricity, construction of schools and hospitals – these were all made possible thanks to mining money.

But however much material conditions improved, the life of a miner was still desperately hard, and labour unrest was not uncommon – strikes were recorded in southwest Sardinia at Montevecchio in 1903, and a year later at Buggerru. The burgeoning post-WWI socialist movement attempted to further politicise Sardinia's mine workers, but without any great success.

Fascism & Failure

Following the worldwide recession sparked off by the 1929 Wall Street Crash, the Sardinian mining industry enjoyed something of a boom under the Fascists. Production was increased at Montevecchio, and the Sulcis coalmines were set to maximum output. In 1938 the town of Carbonia in southwest Sardinia was built to house workers from the Sirai-Serbariu coalfield.

Mining output remained high throughout Italy's post-WWII boom years, but demand started to decline rapidly in the years that followed. Regular injections of public money couldn't stop the rot, which was further exacerbated by high production costs, the poor quality of the minerals and falling metal prices. One by one the mines were closed and, as of 2008, Sardinia's only operative mine is Nuraxi Figus, near Carbonia.

THE RISE AND FALL OF SORU

Dubbed the Sardinian Bill Gates, self-made billionaire Renato Soru has been central to tourism in the island's recent past. He founded the internet company Tiscali in 1998, was listed as one of the world's richest people by Forbes in 2001, entered politics in 2003 and was voted regional president a year later, a position he held until February 2009. But away from the controversial 'luxury tax' and *Salvacoste* (Save the Coast) ban on coastal development, Soru's lasting achievements include overseeing the withdrawal of US atomic naval forces from the environmentally sensitive Arcipelago di La Maddalena after 35 years. This divided local opinion, with environmentalists and Soru fans applauding the move, and business owners mourning the loss of free-spending American sailors.

The tides turned, however, in May 2016 when the high-flying entrepreneur and leftist politician was given a three-year jail sentence by a court in Cagliari for tax evasion amounting to €2.6 million.

1921

The Partito Sardo d'Azione (PSd'Az; Sardinian Action Party) is formed by veterans of the Brigata Sassari. It aims to pursue regional autonomy and politicise the Sardinian public.

1926

Sardinian writer Grazia Deledda wins the Nobel Prize for Literature.

1928–38

As part of Mussolini's plans to make Italy economically self-sufficient, Sardinia is given a makeover. Large-scale irrigation, infrastructure and land-reclamation projects begin and new towns are established.

1943

Allied bombing raids destroy three-quarters of Cagliari.

Bravery, Banditry & Identity

WWI Heroes

Sardinia's martial spirit found recognition on a wider stage in the early 20th century. The island's contributions to Italy's campaigns in WWI are legendary. In 1915 the Brigata Sassari was formed and immediately dispatched to the northeastern Alps. The regiment was made up entirely of Sards, who quickly distinguished themselves in the merciless slaughter of the trenches. It is reckoned that Sardinia lost more young men per capita on the front than any other Italian region, and the regiment was decorated with four gold medals.

Kidnap Country

A less salubrious chapter is the island's tradition of banditry, which had reached epidemic proportions by the late 19th and early 20th centuries, especially in the Province of Sassari. The crusade to bring the bandits to justice was one the government was destined to lose as poverty and an inhospitable environment fuelled banditry throughout the 20th century.

The town of Orgosolo, deep in Barbagia hill country, earned a reputation as a hotbed of lawlessness, and as recently as the 1990s gangs of kidnappers were still operating in its impenetrable countryside. Between 1960 and 1992, 621 people were kidnapped in Italy, 178 of them in Sardinia. Though Orgosolo has left this dark chapter of its past behind it, the town is now a canvas for vibrant, politically charged murals.

A Political Awakening

WWI was a watershed for Sardinia. Not only in terms of lives lost and horrors endured, but also as a political awakening. When Sardinian soldiers returned from the fighting in 1918, they were changed men. They had departed as illiterate farmers and returned as a politically conscious force. Many joined the new Partito Sardo d'Azione (PSd'Az; Sardinian Action Party), founded in Oristano in 1921 by Emilio Lussu and fellow veterans of the Brigata Sassari (the Sardinian regiment that served in WWI).

The party's central policy was administrative autonomy, embracing the burgeoning sense of regional identity that was spreading throughout the island. This led many to start viewing Sardinia as a region with its own distinct culture, aspirations and identity.

But a call for autonomy was just one of the cornerstones of the party's political manifesto. Combining socialist themes (a call for social justice and development of agricultural cooperatives) with

Vittorio de Seta's 1961 classic film, *Banditi a Orgosolo* (Bandits of Orgosolo), brilliantly captures the harsh realities of rural life in mid-20th-century Sardinia.

1948

Sardinia becomes a semi-autonomous region with a regional assembly, the Giunta Consultativa Sarda, that has control over agriculture, forestry, town planning, tourism and the police.

1946–51

The sinister-sounding Sardinia Project finally rids the island of malaria. The US Army sprays 10,000 tonnes of DDT over the countryside.

1950–70

Sardinia benefits from the Cassa per il Mezzogiorno, a development fund for southern Italy. But improvements in agriculture, education, industry, transport and banking cannot prevent widespread emigration.

1962

The Aga Khan forms the Consorzio della Costa Smeralda to develop a short stretch of northeastern coast. The resulting Emerald Coast kick-starts tourism on the island.

A SWISS SARDINIA

One is landlocked and famous for its mountains, the other is an island and renowned for its coastline. Apart from both being small and beautiful, Switzerland and Sardinia, some 1000km apart, appear to have little in common on the face of things. But that hasn't stopped Andrea Caruso, the co-founder of the Canton Marittimo (Maritime Canton) movement, from garnering support from independence seekers who would like the island to become the 27th Swiss canton.

Disillusioned with the island's future in the face of high unemployment, bureaucracy and a system that they claim has 'squandered economic potential and disenfranchised the ordinary citizen', the movement says that Sardinia becoming part of Switzerland would be 'common sense'. They believe that Switzerland would bring the island the efficiency, economic wealth and direct democracy it needs.

Dismissed by some as bonkers and hailed by others as a brainwave, the plea for Rome to sell the island to Switzerland has certainly caught the attention of the public and the press and, at the time of writing, the Canton Marittimo Facebook page had more than 10,000 'likes' and counting. But though an online poll of 4000 German-speaking Swiss found that 93% would be in favour of Sardinia becoming the 27th canton, the Costa del Alps is, in real terms, still a distant dream.

free-market ideology (the need for economic liberalism and the removal of state protectionism), it created a distinct brand of Sardinian social-democratic thought.

Isolation to Autonomy

WWII left Sardinia shattered. The island was never actually invaded, but Allied bombing raids in 1943 destroyed three-quarters of Cagliari. Worse still, war isolated the island. The ferry between the mainland and Olbia was knocked out of action and did not return to daily operation until 1947. As a result of the political upheavals that rocked Italy in the aftermath of the war – in a 1946 referendum the nation voted to dump the monarchy and create a parliamentary republic – Sardinia was granted autonomy in 1948.

In 1921 DH Lawrence spent six days travelling from Cagliari to Olbia. The result was *Sea and Sardinia*, his celebrated travelogue full of amusing and grumpy musings.

Sun, Sea & the Rise of Tourism

Until malaria was eradicated in the mid-20th century, visitors (at least those with peaceful intent) were few and far between. DH Lawrence famously grumped his way round the island in 1921, and his words paint a fairly depressing picture of poverty and isolation. Were he to return today, he'd find a very different island. Poverty still exists, particularly in the rural interior, and unemployment remains a serious issue (in 2016 it

1985

Sassari-born Francesco Cossiga is elected President of the Republic of Italy. He was Minister of the Interior when the Red Brigade (extreme-left terrorists) kidnapped and killed ex-PM Aldo Moro in 1978.

1999

The EU identifies Sardinia as one of a handful of places in Europe in dire need of investment for 'development and structural upgrading'.

2004

Self-made billionaire Renato Soru is elected president of Sardinia. He sets the cat among the pigeons by banning building within 2km of the coast and taxing holiday homes and mega-yachts.

2008

After 36 years, the US Navy withdraws from the Arcipelago di La Maddalena. It had long divided opinion: friends pointed to the money it brought while critics highlighted the risks of hosting atomic submarines.

stood at 15.9%), but despite that the island has changed almost beyond recognition.

Before the Aga Khan 'discovered' the Costa Smeralda in the late 1950s and developed it together with a consortium of international high-rollers in the 1960s, Gallura's northeastern coast was a rocky backwater, barely capable of supporting the few shepherds who lived there. Now the Costa Smeralda (Emerald Coast) is one of the world's glitziest destinations; its beaches are a playground for Russian oligarchs, celebrities, supermodels and VIPs, including former Formula One racing manager Flavio Briatore.

2009

Renato Soru is defeated in the February regional election by centre-right candidate Ugo Cappellacci.

2011

In a May referendum, 98% of Sardinians vote against nuclear power. Enel gets the green light to build a 90 megawatt wind farm at Portoscuso.

2013

Cyclone Cleopatra tears across the island, bringing apocalyptic flash floods and storms that kill 18 people and leave thousands homeless. Olbia is the worst affected area.

2014

Fabrizio Aru comes third in the Giro d'Italia in May 2014 – the first time a Sard has ever been on the podium.

The Sardinian Way of Life

History might suggest otherwise, but centuries of colonial oppression have done little to dent Sardinians' fierce local pride and their patient, melancholic resolve. A strong sense of fraternity, respect for tradition and passion for a good *festa* – these are what unite the islanders. But to speak of a regional identity is to overlook Sardinia's geography.

Above Grocery store, Cagliari (p41)

Isolation & Introspection

By modern roads, Bitti Bitti, a dusty inland town north of Nuoro, is only about 50km from the sea, but until relatively recently it was a world unto itself, cut off from the rest of the island by inhospitable mountains and a lack of infrastructure.

The same could be said of any one of hundreds of inland communities, left to fend for themselves by island authorities unable or unwilling to reach them. Such isolation nurtured introspection and a diffidence towards outsiders, while also preserving local traditions – many towns speak their own dialects, cook their own recipes and celebrate their own festivals that have been developed without any outside interference. It also exacerbated the ever-increasing divide between coast and interior. The advent of tourism and industrial development has had a far greater impact on coastal towns than on the island's hinterland, and there's still a world of difference between the modern-minded cities of Alghero, Sassari, Olbia and Cagliari and the traditional lifestyles of inland villages.

Sardinia is an island of shepherds, home to around four million sheep (around 2.5 per capita)..

Yet for all the hardship isolation has inflicted on the islanders, it has left Sardinia with some unique qualities. In recent years, researchers have been falling over themselves to study the island's uncontaminated gene pool, and musicologists have long appreciated the island's strange and unique musical traditions.

On the surface, Sardinians display none of the exuberance usually associated with mainland Italians, nor their malleability or lightness of heart. They come across as friendly and hospitable, but modest and quietly reserved. Unlike other islanders, they don't look outwards, longing for escape and opportunity; instead they appear becalmed in the past, gripped by an inward-looking intensity.

Life in the Slow Lane

Perhaps a reason for the Sardinians' celebrated longevity is the island's laid-back, unhurried approach to life. After all, who cares if you are a little late in the grand scheme of things? There are far more important matters in life, such as friends and family, enjoying your free time, and stopping to chat with the baker, the newsagent, the neighbour and his dog, and just about anyone else who crosses your path. Friendliness is paramount.

This go-slow approach comes naturally to Sardinians. Never mind if Massimo is waffling on about the economy for the umpteenth time that day, while the queue snakes to the back of his grocery store – you know he always has a big smile for you. Or that Silvia is deeply embroiled in conversation at the post office counter – everyone knows that she could talk the hind leg off a donkey.

A major mental shift, however, happens when Sardinians slip behind the wheel of their cars – then patience goes straight out the

GENE GENIES

A kent'annos, may you live to be 100. This traditional greeting may sound like wishful thinking but, then again, maybe not – the odds are good in Sardinia. Forget super-foods, macrobiotic diets and 10-years-younger supplements, this island holds the secret to longevity, apparently, with almost 500 centenarians out of a population of 1.67 million, more than twice the normal level. Ask Sardinians why and you'll get a different answer every time – the air, the outdoor living, eating and drinking well, God.

Previous studies have highlighted environmental and lifestyle factors (local Cannonau wines are rich in procyanidins, chemicals that contribute to red wine's heart-protecting qualities) as the main reasons for this longevity, but researchers from the University of Sassari remain convinced that there's a fundamental genetic element. The inhabitants of the mountainous province of Ogliastra have long been undisturbed by the outside world. As a result intermarriage has produced a remarkably pure gene pool, a veritable goldmine of genetic raw material – and of great interest to scientists.

window. A tourist on the SS125 is driving at only 30km/h, braking on every bend and has now – *incredibile!* – stopped to take photos of a passing shepherd and his flock. The frustration mounts in such cases as Sardinians don't like to dawdle on the road and will sometimes drive 2cm behind your rear bumper, just to give you a little nudge on. So in the driving seat, they reveal their Italian side.

La Famiglia

'My 32-year-old son is too fat. Should I put him on a diet?' It's the typical agony-aunt conundrum in the problem pages of Sardinia's magazines and newspapers. Paolo may be 32, but he will always be a boy in the eyes of his doting *mamma*. Like Italy, Sardinia can come across as something of a matriarchal society at times, with around 25% of men staying at home well into their 30s, and a smaller percentage of women following suit. While their decision to fly the nest late, typically not until they marry, is the subject of much ridicule, it is often an economic decision – many young people, particularly with unemployment at around 15.9%, simply can't afford to leave home.

In 2007 Italy's oldest woman, Rafaella Monni, died in Arzana in the province of Ogliastra, at 109. Five years earlier the 112-year-old Antonio Todde, the oldest man in the world, had died in Tiana, province of Nuoro.

Whichever way you look at it, the family is central to life in Sardinia, and so it comes as something of a surprise that the average rate of fertility is an incredibly low 1.1% (the EU average is 1.6%). The latest figures show that Sardinians are also waiting longer to have a family, with 32.5 being the average age for a woman to have her first baby.

La Donna

Attitudes are changing, but many families still live according to the classic model, with women staying at home and men going out to earn. These gender roles were originally dictated by the practical division of labour – with the men away from home pasturing their flocks, women were left running the house and raising the children – although nowadays they're as much about tradition and convention as practical necessity.

Girls might have once been under the watchful eye of their elders until they reached marriage age, but today men and women are in many respects equal, as Sardinia opens up to tourism and new media.

Faith & La Festa

Conservative and for much of the year politely reserved, Sardinians let go with a bang during their great festivals. These boisterous and spectacular occasions reveal much about the islanders' long-held beliefs, mixing myth with faith and folklore.

MOTHER TONGUE

Sardo (or Sardu), Sardinia's first language, is the largest minority language in Italy. Originally derived from the Latin brought over by the Romans in the 3rd century BC, it has four main dialects: Logudorese (from the northwest), Campidanese (from the south), Gallurese (from the northeast) and Sassarese (from the Sassari area). These dialects are further complicated by the incorporation of distinct local influences, so in Alghero residents speak a variation of Catalan, and on the Isola di San Pietro locals converse in a 16th-century version of Genoese. The Gallura and Sassari dialects also reflect the proximity of Corsica.

Recent studies on the usage of Sardo brought to light some humorous facts: apparently 60.2% use the mother tongue when they're angry and 64% when they want to be funny, but only 26.5% to discuss politics and a mere 16.5% to speak about the kids.

Women in traditional costume, Festa di Sant'Efisio (p54), Cagliari

Religious belief has deep roots in Sardinia. The presence of *sacri pozzi* (well temples) in nuraghic settlements attests to naturalistic religious practices dating to the 2nd millennium BC. Christianity arrived in the 6th century and quickly established itself. Today Sardinian faith finds form in street parties as much as church services, and many of the island's biggest festivities are dedicated to much-loved saints. The greatest of them all, St Ephisius, an early Christian martyr and Sardinia's patron saint, is the star of Cagliari's huge May Day carnival.

Elsewhere on the island, you'll find a number of *chiese novenari* – small countryside chapels that are only opened for several days of the year to host saints' day celebrations. These churches are often surrounded by *cumbessias* (also known as *muristenes*), simple lodgings to house the pilgrims who come to venerate the saint honoured in the church.

Easter is an important event in Sardinia, marked by island-wide celebrations, many of which reflect Spanish influence. Castelsardo, Iglesias and Tempio Pausania all put on night processions featuring hooded members of religious brotherhoods more readily associated with Spain.

The Island of the Ancients, by Ben Hills, features interviews with Sardinia's most extraordinary centenarians and reveals their life elixir.

The Arts

Sardinia's arts have been tempered by the island's rich culture and rugged topography. Shielded from outside influences, Sardinian musical traditions are like nothing else on the planet and they fuel a contemporary fusion scene. Literary legends such as Nobel-prize-winning Grazia Deledda reel you into the intrigues of small-town life in the wilds of mountainous Barbagia. Up and down the island you will encounter festivals where folk dancing, hand-carved masks and flamboyant costumes keep Sardinia's one-of-a-kind heritage very much alive.

Above *Launeddas* players, Festa di Sant'Efisio, Cagliari (p54)

Music

Canto a Tenore

If ever music could encapsulate the spirit of Sardinia's rugged mountains and pastoral landscapes, it is *canto a tenore*. This traditional male harmony singing is one of the oldest known forms of vocal polyphony. It is performed by a four-part male choir, the *tenores,* made up of *sa oghe* (the soloist and lead voice), *su bassu* (bass), *sa contra* (contralto) and *sa mesu oghe* (countertenor). Little is known of the *canto's* origins but it's thought that the voices were originally inspired by the sounds of nature – the *contra* based on a sheep's bleat, the *bassu* on a cow's moo and the *mesu oghe* on the sound of the wind. The *canto* is performed in a tight circle, with the soloist singing a poem to choral accompaniment.

Read up about Sardinia's best-known traditional group and listen to them in action at www.tenores-dibitti.com.

Canto a tenore is most popular in the centre and north of the island, with the best-known groups coming from the Barbagia region. The most famous is the Tenores di Bitti, which has recorded on Peter Gabriel's Real World record label and performed at Womad festivals. Other well-known choirs hail from Oniferi, Orune and Orgosolo. In 2008, the *canto a tenore* was inscribed on the Unesco Representative List of the Intangible Cultural Heritage of Humanity.

A similar style, although more liturgical in nature, is the *canto a cuncordu,* again performed by four-part male groups. To hear this head for Castelsardo, Orosei and Santu Lussurgiu.

Launeddas

The *launeddas* is Sardinia's trademark musical instrument. A rudimentary wind instrument made of three reed canes and played using circular breathing, it is particularly popular at village festivals in the south. If you can't attend a festival, listen to the legendary recordings *Launeddas,* by Efisio Melis and Antonio Lara. Other names to look out for on the *launeddas* circuit are Franco Melis, Luigi Lai, Andria Pisu and Franco Orlando Mascia.

For an insight into Sardinian music, visit Sardegna Cultura (www.sardegnacultura.it), which has recordings of traditional island music.

Poetry

Like many of the island's art forms, Sardinian poetry is a much-felt part of local culture, which in the 19th century gave rise to an early form of rap duelling, the so-called *gare poetiche* (poetry duels). At village festivals, villagers would gather to watch two verbal adversaries improvise rhyming repartee that was sarcastic, ironic or simply insulting. The audience loved it and would chime in with their own improvised shots! Little of this was ever written down, but you can find CDs featuring a classic duo from the mid-20th century: Remundo Piras and Peppe Sozu.

In the 1930s the Fascists banned the Sardinian *cantadores* (poets), whose attacks on church and state they deemed dangerous and subversive.

Bardic contests still take place in the mountain villages and there are two important poetry competitions: Ozieri's Premio di Ozieri and the Settembre dei Poeti in Seneghe.

Sardinia's most famous poet is Sebastiano Satta (1867–1914), who celebrated the wild beauty of the island in his poetry *Versi Ribelli* and *Canti Barbaricini.*

SEA AND SARDINIA

Sardinia's wild, untamed landscapes, sense of space and age-old traditions sparked the fervent imagination of 20th-century literary giant DH Lawrence. The nine days he spent travelling the island with his wife Frieda inspired one of his most impassioned travel books, *Sea and Sardinia*.

Travelling on the Trenino Verde (p268), the Lawrences visited Cagliari, Mandas, Sorgono and Nuoro before taking a boat back to Sicily, where DH Lawrence dashed off the book entirely from memory in just six weeks. His rapturous prose beautifully captures the spirit and timelessness of the island.

If you're planning a slow journey through Sardinia by narrow-gauge train, the book is the perfect literary travel companion.

Each of the 370 villages and towns on the island has its own traditional costume.

Folk dancing, Assemini

Dance & Festivals

Ballo Sardo

No Sardinian festival or celebration would be complete without folk dancing, referred to as *ballo sardo* (Sardinian dance) or *su ballu tundu* (dancing in the round), which is interpreted slightly differently from region to region. It generally involves a group of dancers or couples in a line or open circle, who hold hands or link arms and move gracefully across the floor with agile steps, twists and turns. Their movements often become sprightlier as the music quickens.

Launeddas is often performed during the dance, while a *canto a tenore* might accompany slower pieces. Like the *launeddas,* it is thought that *ballo sardo* dates back to nuraghic times. There has been much speculation on the connections between *ballo sardo* and the similar *sardana* (circular folk dance) of Catalonia in northeastern Spain.

The Art of Celebration

Sardinia has produced some fine female vocalists, most notably Maria Carta, a 20th-century island legend. The folksy tunes of Elena Ledda are also widely known.

Sardinians find expression for their heritage, history, faith and identity through folk music, dance and intricately embroidered costumes at their rich and varied festivals. Many festivals have a religious origin, such as the numerous holy or feast days, the solemn Easter processions, and pilgrimages like the Festa di Sant'Efisio in Cagliari and the Festa del Redentore in Nuoro. As an agricultural island, seasonal products from cherries to asparagus, chestnuts, wine and tuna are another cause for celebration (and indulgence).

In the west, horse races and parades bring historic triumphs to life, from Sassari's spirited Cavalcata Sarda marking victory over the Saracens in AD 1000 to the fiery S'Ardia horse race in Sedilo, trumpeting the victory of Roman Emperor Constantine over Maxentius in AD 312.

Handmade traditional mask

Literature

Sardinia's rural society had no great literary tradition, but the early 20th century marked a watershed. Grazia Deledda (1871–1936) won the 1926 Nobel Prize and a series of talented scribes began to emerge from the shadows. Their work provides an unsentimental picture of island life, as well as a fascinating insight into how the islanders see themselves.

Taking inspiration from the petty jealousies and harsh realities of the Nuoro society in which she grew up, Grazia Deledda towers above the world of Sardinian literature. Her best-known novel is *Canne al vento* (Reeds in the Wind), which recounts the slide into poverty of the aristocratic Pintor family, but all her works share a strong local flavour.

Also Nuoro born, Salvatore Satta (1902–75) is best known for *Il giorno del giudizio* (The Day of Judgement), a biting portrayal of small-town life.

A contemporary of Satta, Giuseppe Dessì (1909–77) found fame with *Il disertore*, the story of a shepherd who deserts his WWI army unit and returns to his native Sardinia where he finds himself caught between a sense of duty and his own moral code.

One of the most famous works to have emerged from postwar Sardinia is *Padre Padrone*, Gavino Ledda's bleak autobiographical depiction of his early life as a shepherd. Later made into a critically acclaimed but little-known film by the Taviani brothers, it paints a harrowing picture of the relentlessness of poverty and the hardships it provokes.

The intractability of political and social life in postwar Italy is the central theme of *Il figlio di Bakunin* (Bakunin's Son), the one translated work of Sergio Atzeni (1952–95). One of the giants of Sardinia's recent literary past, Atzeni, like Deledda before him, depicts a society that resists the simple reductions of comfortable moral and political assumptions.

Get the lowdown on Sardinia's top literary event, Gavoi's Festa Letterario di Sardegna, at www.isoladellestorie.it.

Six Sardinian authors contributed to the book *Sei per la Sardegna* (Six for Sardinia; Marcello Fois). The anthology was written to raise money for victims of the 2013 floods.

SARDINIAN HANDICRAFTS

Filigree jewellery Cagliari, Alghero and Dorgali are the best places to purchase exquisitely crafted gold and silver *filigrana* (filigree work).

Red coral Top-quality coral is harvested off Alghero's Riviera del Corallo (Coral Riviera). In many cases coral is combined with filigree work.

Ceramics Oristano, Sassari and Assemini (north of Cagliari) are famous for their ceramics, glazed in blue or white or yellow and green, and embellished with naturalistic motifs such as birds and flowers.

Wool carpets Aggius and Tempio Pausania have a strong cottage industry in wool carpets, decorated with traditional geometric designs.

Basketry In the north, around Castelsardo and in Oristano, women still make traditional baskets from asphodel, rush, willow and dwarf palm leaves.

Festival masks The festival masks handcrafted in the Nuoro region are real works of art. Look out for Mamoiada's *mamuthones* and Ottana's *boes* and *merdules* masks.

Textiles Traditional hand-looming techniques are used in Ulassai to make one-of-a-kind towels, curtains and bedspreads.

Cork In Gallura, cork wood is used to make everything from decorative bowls to stools and chopping boards.

Pocket knives Handmade pocket knives with horn-carved handles are produced in Pattada and Arbus by a handful of remaining master craftsmen.

In recent times Sardinia has produced a good crop of noir writers, including Flavio Soriga (b 1975), whose *Diavolù di Nuraio* (The Devil from Nuraio) won the Premio Italo Calvino prize in 2000. His more recent book *Nuraghe Beach* (2011) takes an entertaining look at the island's prehistoric wonders, ancient cities and celebrity-studded coastline.

Traditional Crafts

As befits an agricultural island, Sardinia has a long tradition of handicrafts, many of which make the most of local materials from cork wood to coral. But where objects were originally made for practical, everyday use, they are now largely made for decoration. Local ironworkers around Santu Lussurgiu, for example, have adapted to the modern market by replacing agricultural tools, the mainstay of their traditional income, with decorative lamps, gates and bedsteads.

Quality still remains high, however, and you can find some excellent deals. To be sure of reasonable prices and quality, head for the local Istituto Sardo Organizzazione Lavoro Artigiano (ISOLA) shop, which authenticates each piece it sells.

Modern & Contemporary Art

The Art-Culture section of www.marenostrum.it details up-and-coming cultural events and festivals, including art retrospectives and cinema events.

Though Sardinia's modern art scene has kept something of a low profile on the international stage, there are a few galleries where you can view the work of important modern artists. A good starting point is Cagliari's Galleria Comunale d'Arte, which showcases the work of leading 20th-century Sardinian artists, among them Nuoro-born Francesco Ciusa and neorealist painter Foiso Fois.

Contemporary Sardinian art is presented in an attractively restored 19th-century townhouse at Nuoro's Museo d'Arte, which harbours some 400 works by the island's foremost 20th-century painters, including Giovanni Ciusa-Romagna, Mario Delitalia, Antonio Ballero and abstract artist Mauro Manca.

The Sardinian Kitchen

Sweet, buttery ricotta, lobster, red prawns and mullet from the Med, wild thyme, rosemary, myrtle and juniper, sun-ripened olives and citrus fruits, farm-raised lamb and suckling pig cooked on an open spit – nowhere does slow food like Sardinia. Throw in mountain and sea views, fine home-produced wines, own takes on pasta and winningly fresh farm produce and you are looking at a great culinary experience. Simple but great.

A Day at Sardinia's Table

Like most Italians, Sardinians rarely eat a sit-down *colazione* (breakfast), preferring a swift cappuccino and *cornetto* (croissant) standing at a bar. Out in the wilds, shepherds would start the day with a handful of bread and a slice of hard *pecorino* (sheep's milk cheese).

Above *Culurgiones*, Sardinian-style ravioli (p252)

Civraxiu takes its name from *cibaria*, the word for 'flour' during the Roman occupation when Sardinia was one of the major grain suppliers to the Empire.

Pranzo (lunch) remains a ritual observed by many Sardinians and is still considered the most important meal of the day. Workers can't always get home, but across the island shops and businesses close for three to four hours to ensure lunch is properly taken and digested. A full meal will consist of an antipasto (starter) followed by a *primo* – usually a thick soup, pasta or risotto – and a *secondo* of meat or fish. Inlanders will invariably prefer meat, often served roasted or in thick stews. To finish *alla sarda* (in Sardinian style) go for cheese and a *digestivo,* perhaps a shot of grappa, although it is now usual to wind up with dessert and coffee. Look out for the good-value *piatto del giorno* (dish of the day).

Postwork *aperitivo* is taken between 5pm and 8pm, with an array of often-complimentary snacks to whet the appetite for dinner.

Cena (the evening meal) was traditionally a simpler affair, but as work habits change and fewer people eat lunch at home, it increasingly becomes the main meal of the day.

Sardinian Cuisine

Daily Bread

Few experiences in Sardinia beat walking into a neighbourhood *panetteria* (bakery) in the morning, breathing in the yeasty aromas and feasting your eyes on the loaves of freshly baked bread. The Sardinians hold the humble loaf in high esteem and have come up with literally hundreds of types of bread, each one particular to its region and town. Traditional bakeries pride themselves on using durum wheat of the best quality and age-old kneading techniques.

For special occasions such as weddings and religious feast days, bread is elevated to an art form called *su coccoi,* with intricate floral wreaths, hearts and animals that are impossibly delicate and almost too pretty to eat.

Music Paper

As crisp as a cracker, as light as a wafer and thin enough for the sun to shine through, *pane carasau,* also known as *carta da musica* (music paper), is the star of Sardinia's bread basket. It is ubiquitous in the rural interior, particularly in the Gallura, Logudoro and Nuoro regions, where it is still made by hand using the simplest of ingredients – durum wheat, water and a pinch of salt – and twice baked in a wood-fired oven to achieve its distinctive crispness. For centuries this long-lasting bread has been ideal for shepherds out in the pasture.

WE DARE YOU TO TRY...

Casumarzu If you can find it, try this rotten *pecorino* alive with maggots.

Cordula Lamb tripe grilled, fried or stewed with peas.

Granelle Calf's testicles sliced, covered in batter and lightly fried.

Salsiccia or salame di cavallo/d'asino Horsemeat or donkey sausages.

Tataliu or trattalia A mix of kidney, liver and intestines stewed or grilled on skewers. The dish is made with veal, lamb, kid or suckling pig.

Zimino russo A selection of roasted offal, usually from a calf, including the heart, diaphragm, liver, kidney and other red innards.

Zurrette A black pudding made of sheep's blood cooked, like haggis, in a sheep's stomach with herbs and fennel.

MAGGOTY CHEESE, ANYONE?

Ask Sardinians about the island's infamous *casumarzu,* 'rotten cheese' alive with maggots, and watch them raise a knowing eyebrow, snigger at hilarious memories of trying to eat the stuff, or else swiftly change the subject. Everyone, it seems, has a story or an opinion about the *formaggio che salta* (cheese that jumps). It's creamier and tastier than anything you've ever tried, say some; it makes your skin crawl and festers in the gut, warn others.

If you were a horror-movie scriptwriter with a passion for *pecorino* you couldn't make it up: *pecorino* deliberately infested with the larvae of the *piophila casei* cheese fly, whose digestive acids break down the cheese fats, advancing fermentation and rapidly leading to decomposition. The pungent liquid that oozes out of the cheese is called the *lagrima* (tear). When eating the cheese, locals cover it with one hand to stop the sprightly little larvae from jumping into their face – they can leap up to 15cm, apparently. Others prefer to remove the maggots by placing the cheese into a paper bag and letting them starve of oxygen.

Tempted? Well, even if you are, you would have to be pretty determined to find the cheese. Though considered a 'traditional food' exempt from EU health regulations, it is still illegal to sell and serve *casumarzu,* and most is produced for private consumption. Its elusiveness adds to its mystery: ask those same Sardinians where to find *casumarzu* and they will probably make a wide, sweeping gesture and tell you in the mountains...maybe. Head to the lonesome Barbagia in summer and with a little luck and one very strong stomach, you might just find a farmer willing to reveal his secret stash.

Brushed with olive oil and sprinkled with salt, *pane carasau* becomes a moreish snack known as *pane guttiau.* A fancier version often served as a first course is *pane frattau,* where *pane carasau* is topped with tomato sauce, grated *pecorino* and a soft-boiled egg.

Antipasti

A tasty Italian import, antipasti appear on almost every menu as a lead to *primi* (first courses). *Antipasti di terra* ('of the land') is often a mouthwatering assortment of homemade bread, cured ham, tangy Sardinian salami, olives and a range of cooked, raw and marinated vegetables such as artichokes and eggplant. There is also *frittelle di zucchine* (an omelette stuffed with zucchini, breadcrumbs and cheese). Along the coast you'll find *antipasti di mare* ('of the sea'), such as thinly sliced *bottarga* (mullet or tuna roe), the best of which comes from the lagoon town of Cabras. Cagliari is famous for its *burrida* (marinated dogfish).

Cheese, Glorious Cheese

Sardinia is an island of shepherds, so it's hardly surprising that cheese-making is a fine art here. Cheese has been produced on the island for nearly 5000 years, and Sardinia makes about 80% of Italy's *pecorino* (sheep's milk cheese). Gourmands will delight in flavours and textures, from tangy *pecorino sardo* to smoked varieties, creamy goat cheeses (such as *ircano* and *caprino*), ricotta and speciality cheeses like *canestrati,* with peppercorns and herbs.

Fiore sardo, a centuries-old cheese recipe, is eaten fresh, smoked or roasted and packs a fair punch. It is traditionally made from ewe's milk, but varieties such as *fresa* and *peretta* are made from cow's milk. The most popular goat cheese is *caprino,* and the soft *crema del Gerrei* is a combination of goat milk and ricotta.

Only the bravest connoisseurs will want to sample *formaggio marcio* or *casumarzu,* quite literally a 'rotten cheese' alive with maggots!

Porceddu (suckling pig)

Sardinian Pasta

Sardinia generally has an individual way of doing things, and the island's pasta is no different.

Malloreddus, dense shell-shaped pasta made of semolina and flavoured with saffron, is usually served with *salsa alla campidanese* (sausage and tomato sauce) and is sometimes called *gnocchetti sardi.* Another uniquely Sardinian creation is *fregola,* a granular pasta similar to couscous, which is often served in soups and broths.

Culurgiones (spelled in various ways) is a ravioli-like pasta that appears on many menus. Typically it has a ricotta or *pecorino* filling and is coated in a tomato and herb sauce.

Maccarones furriaos are strips of pasta folded and topped with a sauce (often tomato-based) and melted cheese. *Maccarones de busa,* or just plain *busa,* is shaped by wrapping the pasta around knitting needles.

Other pastas you may come across are *pillus,* a small ribbon pasta, and *filindeu,* a threadlike noodle usually served in soups.

To discover the nuances of Sardinian cuisine, consult www.sardegnaturismo.it, which gives a great overview of the specialities of each region.

On the Spit

Sardinia's carnivorous heart beats to its own unique drum. Three specialities stand out: *porceddu* (suckling pig), *agnello* (lamb) and *capretto* (kid). These dishes are flavoured with Mediterranean herbs and spit-roasted.

The most famous of this culinary triumvirate is the *porceddu* (also spelled *porcheddu*), which is slow roasted until the skin crackles and the meat is meltingly tender, then left to stand on a bed of myrtle leaves.

Agnello is particularly popular around December, although it's served year-round. *Capretto* is harder to find on menus, but it gets more common up in the mountains, where it is flavoured with thyme.

A country classic – and a rarity – is *su carraxiu* (literally 'of the buried') – the meat is compressed between two layers of hot stones, covered in myrtle and left to cook slowly in a hole dug in the ground.

Sards also have a penchant for game birds, rabbit and wild boar. A wonderful local sauce for any meat dish is *al mirto* – made with red myrtle, it is a tangy addition.

To hide evidence of their crime, bandits would slow roast stolen pigs in underground holes under bonfires. The technique is known as *su carraxiu*.

Fish & Seafood

Sardinians point out that they are by tradition *pastori, non pescatori* (shepherds, not fishermen). There is some tradition of seafood in Cagliari, Alghero, Cabras and other coastal towns, but elsewhere the phenomenon has arrived from beyond Sardinia.

At the top end of the scale, lobster (legally in season from March to August) is *the* local speciality, particularly in Alghero, where it's served as *aragosta alla catalana* with tomato and onion. *Muggine* (mullet) is popular on the Oristano coast, and *tonno* (tuna) dishes abound around the Isola di San Pietro.

Cagliari also has a long tradition of seafood recipes that run the gamut from sea bream to bass, although the most famous is based on the local *gattucio di mare* (dogfish). Clams, cockles, octopus and crab also feature, as do eels around the marshes of Cabras. For something more adventurous, try *orziadas* (deep-fried sea anemones) and *ricci* (sea urchins).

Room for Dessert

Sardinia's sweet trolley has always been constrained by the natural flavours of the island. Take the recipe for *amarettes* (almond biscuits): there are just three ingredients – almonds, sugar and eggs – but the biscuits are delightfully fluffy and moist.

Though traditionally an Easter recipe, you might spot *pardulas* (also known as *casadinas* and *formagelle*) in cake shops at other times of the year. These delectable mini cheesecakes are made from ricotta or *pecorino,* flavoured with saffron and baked in a crisp shell.

Other sweets and biscuits are strictly seasonal. *Ossus de mortu* (dead men's bones) biscuits, infused with cinnamon and studded with almonds, are served on All Saints' Day in November. After the grape harvest you'll start to see *papassinos de Vitzi* (almond and sultana biscuits) and *pabassinas cun saba,* mixed with almonds, honey, candied and grape must. At festivities you may well come across *sospiri di Ozieri,* rich patties of minced almonds, sugar, honey and lemon glazed with icing, and *coffettura,* tiny baskets of finely shaved orange peel and almonds drenched in honey.

The island's most famous dessert, however, is the *seadas* (or *sebadas*), a deliciously light pastry (vaguely like a turnover) stuffed with bran, orange peel and ricotta or sour cheese and then drenched in *miele amaro* (bitter honey).

CHEAP TREATS

These are our favourite snacks to nibble in Sardinia – yours for a fistful of change.

Fainè Chickpea-flour flatbread with pizza-like toppings. Particularly popular in Alghero and the island's northwest.

Gelato Ice cream for a piazza-side slurp.

Pane carasau Crisp, cracker-like flatbread. The perfect picnic companion.

Pizza al taglio Pizza by the slice.

Pecorino Hard, nutty sheep's milk cheese. Goes well with fresh, crunchy bread.

A Sweet for Every Town

Sweets, tarts, cakes and biscuits – Sardinia's dessert menu is rich and varied. Alongside the island staples, there's a never-ending list of local specialities.

Every town has its own recipes in Sardinia. There is, for instance, a *dolce* (sweet) called *papassino* (from *papassa*, which means raisin) made all over Sardinia, but there many local variations, such as the one from Selargius which uses cinnamon and *vino cotto* (mulled wine).

These variations can reflect an area's history, incorporating foreign influences into traditional recipes. Middle Eastern flavours predominate in the centre and south of Sardinia, where orange blossom, cinnamon and vanilla are used a lot. In the north, *vino cotto* and *vino selvatico* (wine from wild plants) are often used, while the agricultural centre uses *pecorino* to make *casatinas*. In Cagliari, sweets are made from ricotta and often infused with saffron.

Torrone (nougat), also made in Sicily, is found in Sardinia without the addition of sugar, so just with honey, egg whites, almonds and walnuts.

Many of Sardinia's regional sweets can be sampled and purchased at the wonderful Durke (p60) in Cagliari.

Sardinian Drinks

Coffee

The espresso is the standard coffee drink in Sardinia and is what you get if you ask for *un caffè. Doppio espresso* is a double shot and a *caffè americano* is a watered-down version. If you prefer your coffee with milk,

WINE TASTING

You can buy and drink Sardinian wines at any *enoteca* (wine bar), but you'll get far more out of a proper tasting. Here is our pick of the best wineries and cellars that open their doors for tastings.

Sella e Mosca (p127) Sardinia's top wine producer has free guided tours of its museum. Sample wines such as pale, crisp Vermentinos and ruby red Cannonaus with a hint of oak.

Cantine Surrau (p159) A strikingly contemporary winery near Arzachena, with guided tours, art exhibitions and tastings. Be sure to try the intense, fruity Cannonau reds and the mineral-rich Vermentino whites.

Cantina del Vermentino (p176) Pass through the arch to descend to this winery, where you can taste and buy some of the finest Vermentino whites to be found in the Gallura.

Antichi Poderi di Jerzu (p206) Sip beefy Cannonau red wines in the town nicknamed the Citta del Vino (Wine Town), surrounded by fabulous scenery.

Cantina del Mandrolisai (p191) In the heart of the hilly Mandrolisa, this *cantina* is famous for its beefy reds.

Cantine Argiolas (p62) Just a short detour north from Cagliari brings you to this award-winning winery in vine-strewn Serdiana. Stop by for a guided tour and tasting.

Cantina Santadi (p78) The biggest winery in the southwest whose reds include the highly rated Terre Brune and Grotta Rossa. Book a visit online.

Cantina Sociale di Santa Maria la Palma (p129) South of Lago Baratz, Santa Maria la Palma is home to this winery. Stock up on fine wines at the *enoteca* or take a guided tour.

Tenute Olbios (p151) A wine estate on the fringes of Olbia, producing excellent Vermentino whites. Go for tastings and guided vineyard tours.

Ricotta-stuffed *pardulas* (p253)

there are various options. A *caffè latte,* regarded by locals as a breakfast drink, is coffee with a reasonable amount of milk. A *caffè macchiato* is an espresso with a dash of hot milk, and a *latte macchiato* is a glass of hot milk with a dash of coffee. The cappuccino is a frothy version of the *caffè latte.*

Wine

Sardinian wines might not be as venerated as those from Italy, but times are changing, as vintners push for a higher profile and quality gets better and better. Contemporary producers have started taming the mighty alcoholic content of their traditional blends and are now producing some light, dry whites and more sophisticated reds.

The best winegrowing regions for visitors are the Gallura for Vermentino whites; the Ogliastra, Baronia, Barbagia and Mandrolisai for Cannonau reds; and Sulcis in southwest Sardinia for Carignano reds and rosés.

On the whole Sardinian wine is very reasonably priced, with quality labels often available from around €10 to €15 per bottle. You can buy wine directly from the producer or from a *cantina sociale* (wine-producers' cooperative). Lots of these organisations offer a *degustazione* (tasting). Many *agriturismi* (farm-stay accommodation) also produce their own wine, much of which is surprisingly good value. When dining out, house wine is inexpensive at between €5 and €10 for a litre; it generally comes in quarter-, half- and full-litre carafes.

Italian Wines, published by Gambero Rosso and Slow Food Editore, is the definitive annual guide to Italian wines. Producers and their labels are reviewed in encyclopaedic detail.

Vermentino Whites

Introduced to Sardinia in the 18th century, the Vermentino grape flourishes on the sandy granite-based soil in the northeast. The area's best wine is the Vermentino di Gallura, Sardinia's only DOCG. A crisp

TABLE MANNERS

- Drinking cappuccino after a meal is a no-no for locals; after noon it's espresso only.
- Sardinians don't generally eat on the hoof (unless it's gelato).
- Eat spaghetti with a fork, not a spoon.
- Locals never season their food without trying it first.
- Don't finish the bread before the food arrives; it's for mopping up delicious sauces.
- Make eye contact when toasting.
- Some, but not all, restaurants will provide *acqua di rubinetto* (tap water) if you ask for it, but locals tend to order a bottle of *acqua frizzante* (sparkling mineral water).
- If you are invited to someone's home for a meal, always take wine, chocolates or flowers.
- The person who invites usually pays, though splitting *il conto* (the bill) is becoming more common.
- On a restaurant or trattoria bill you can expect to be charged for *pane e coperto* (bread and a cover charge). Typically it ranges from €1 to €4.
- *Servizio* (service charge) of 10% to 15% may or may not be included in the bill; if it's not, round up the bill or leave a 10% tip.

aromatic white with a slightly bitter almond aftertaste, it's best drunk young as an aperitif or with fish. But Vermentino is not confined to the Gallura DOCG area, although the Vermentino di Sardegna produced elsewhere only carries the DOC rating.

Cannonau Reds

The island's best-known red wines are made from the Cannonau vine. This is cultivated across the island, although it's particularly widespread on the mountains around Oliena and Jerzu. Especially good paired with roasted meats, Cannonau reds are a rich, heavy drop that have been sustaining locals for centuries. Research has revealed that Cannonau wines are particularly rich in procyanidins, one of the chemicals that is reputed to give red wine its heart-protecting qualities, which may go some way to explaining the exceptional longevity of people in the Nuoro province.

Vernaccia & Malvasia

Produced since Roman times on the alluvial plains around Oristano, Vernaccia is one of Sardinia's most famous wines. It's best known as an amber sherry-like drop usually taken as an aperitif or to accompany pastries like *mustazzolus*. There are nine Vernaccia wines, however, ranging from dry still whites to aged fortified wines.

Malvasia (Malmsey) is another excellent tipple produced in the Planaragia hills near Bosa, but it's also made around Cagliari (Malvasia di Cagliari). The Malvasia di Bosa, a delicious honey-coloured dessert wine, is widely available in the Bosa area.

To avoid taxes Sardinians hid their homemade *acquavita*. They'd mark the hideout with an iron wire (the *filu e ferru*), from which the drink derives its name.

Spirits

Mirto is Sardinia's national drink, a smooth, powerful liqueur distilled from the fragrant purple fruit of the myrtle bush. In its most common form it's a purplish berry-red, although a less common white version is also made.

But *mirto* is just the tip of the iceberg for Sardinian spirits. Islanders have developed a range of local firewaters made using easily found ingredients, such as *corbezzolo* (an autumnal plant that is similar to wild strawberry), prickly pears and basil. There's even a local form of *limoncello,* a sweet lemon-based tipple, similar to the better-known Amalfi Coast drink.

The strangely named *filu e ferru* (the iron wire) provides quite a kick. Similar to grappa, it is made from a distillate of grape skins and positively roars down the throat – the alcohol content hovers around 40%, with some home brews reaching an eye-watering 60%.

Zedda Piras is a reliable brand of *mirto* and *filu e ferru.*

Eating Out in Sardinia

Sardinia has a range of eating options (p249). Booking on the day of your meal is usually fine, but reserve at least a week ahead for popular places.

Agriturismi Dinner at a wonderfully atmospheric working farm will usually be a set fixed-price feast.

Enoteche Wine bars usually serve snacks and/or tasting plates to accompany drinks.

Pizzerias Cheap and cheerful, the best have wood-fired ovens and long queues.

Ristoranti From simple affairs by the sea to plush gourmet restaurants with extensive wine lists.

Tavola calda Basic sit-down eatery (literally 'hot table'), generally offering canteen-style food.

Trattorias Traditionally family-run places serving a basic menu of affordable local dishes.

Vegetarians & Vegans

Sardinia is a robustly meat-eating island. But the good news is that vegetables are of a universally high standard and appear in many antipasti and *contorni* (side dishes). However, note that even apparently meat-free food such as risotto or soup is often prepared with meat stock. Vegans will find it even harder as so many dishes feature some sort of animal product, be it dairy, eggs or animal stock.

Cookery Classes

Sardinia is not as well endowed with cooking schools as many Italian regions are, but there are a handful of places where you can get behind the stove. These include the Cooperativa Gorropu (p199), based in the highlands around Dorgali; Hotel Gabbiano Azzurro (p218), a seafront resort hotel in Golfo Aranci; and Hotel Lucrezia (p214), in the flatlands north of Oristano. At Cantine Argiolas (p62) you can learn to cook Sardinian specialities such as *fregola* and enjoy them with Argiolas wines.

There are a number of specialist operators selling cooking holidays to Sardinia, including Ciao Laura (www.ciaolaura.com), an American outfit arranging culinary breaks in Orosei. A four-day course costs €625, including accommodation.

Top Sardinian Cookbooks

The Foods of Sicily and Sardinia, by Giuliano Bugialli

Sweet Myrtle and Bitter Honey: The Mediterranean Flavours of Sardinia, by Efisio Farris

Gastronomia in Sardegna, by Gian Paolo Caredda

A Sardinian Cookbook, by Giovanni Pilu and Roberta Muir

The Sardinian Cookbook: The Cooking and Culture of a Mediterranean Island, by Viktorija Todorovska

TOP FIVE DINING EXPERIENCES

Trattoria Lo Romanì (p119) Meltingly tender spit-roasted pork at an intimate Alghero trattoria.

Agriturismo Su Boschettu (p213) Farm-fresh food served with love among the olive groves and orchards.

Luigi Pomata (p58) Buzzy choice in Cagliari for winningly fresh seafood in minimalist surrounds.

Su Gologone (p198) Rustic-chic mountain escape with beautiful grounds for alfresco feasts of classic Sardinian food.

Il Portolano (p153) Spot-on seafood and zingy flavours shine at this seafront number, with sunset views to Isola Tavolara.

WHEN IN ... TRY ...

Cagliari *Burrida*, dogfish marinated in walnuts, garlic, vinegar and spices.

Gallura *Zuppa cuata* or *zuppa gallurese*, a heart-warming casserole comprising layers of bread, cheese and meat *ragù*, drenched in broth and baked to a crispy crust.

Olbia *Zuppa di cozze* e *vongole* (garlicky clam and mussel soup), *ricci* (sea urchins) and *ortidas* (fried sea anemones).

Barbagia *Pecora in capoto*, a hearty, flavoursome ewe stew.

Alghero *Aragosta alla catalana*, lobster with tomato and onion, and *ricci* (sea urchins) when in season – March to April.

Cabras *Muggini* (mullet) and *bottarga* (mullet roe).

Nuoro & Ogliastra *Fiore sardo pecorino*, suckling lamb and pig, and wild boar.

Seasonal Food & Wine Festivals

A history of rural isolation has led to a fierce pride in local traditions, many of which find form in extravagant celebrations and food-based *sagre* (festivals dedicated to a particular food). Traditionally these were based on the farming calendar and provided a rare occasion for villagers to meet up, show off their most splendid costumes and prepare their finest recipes. Here's our pick of the best:

Sagra del Bogamarì (p117) In Alghero, an ode to the humble *ricci* (sea urchin), held on several weekends in March.

Sagra degli Agrumi (p63) Muravera's folksy Citrus Fair, held on the second or third weekend in April.

Sagra del Torrone (p185) Located in Tonara in the Barbagia di Belvi, a sweet tribute to nougat; held on Easter Monday.

Girotonno (p80) In Carloforte, this is a four-day festival celebrating the island's famous *mattanza* (tuna catch) in early June.

Sagra delle Castagne (p189) An autumnal feast of chestnuts in the mountain town of the Aritzo, held on the last Sunday of October.

Rassegna del Vino Novello (p105) In Milis, one of Sardinia's top wine festivals, where new wine is sniffed, tasted and sold; held in mid-November.

Survival Guide

Directory A–Z

Customs Regulations

Most articles you take into Sardinia for personal use can be imported free of duty and tax. The following allowances apply to duty-free goods purchased in a non-EU country. In addition you can bring in other products up to a value of €430.

Alcohol 1L spirits (or 2L fortified wine), 4L still wine

Other goods 60mL perfume, 16L beer, 200 cigarettes

Cash Up to €10,000

Discount Cards

➡ Those under 18 years and over 65 are often entitled to free or discounted admission to state-run museums and cultural sights. To claim your discount take proof of your age, ideally an ID card or passport.

➡ International Student Identity Card (ISIC; www.isic.org) entitles students to various shopping, accommodation and museum discounts in Cagliari, Sassari and Nuoro. A similar card is available to non-students under 26 years, the International Youth Travel Card. The cost varies depending on where you get it, but reckon on about €15.

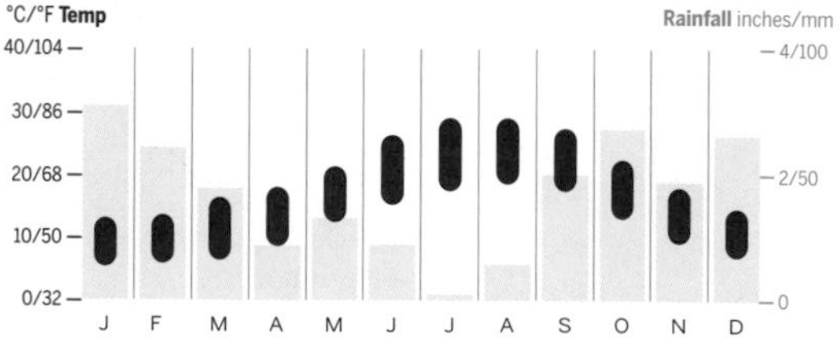

➡ European Youth Card (www.euro26.org) offers a wide range of discounts across Europe. Cardholders do not need to be European citizens. It costs €11 if bought in Italy.

➡ Student cards are issued by student unions, hostelling organisations and some youth travel agencies. In Cagliari, Sassari and Nuoro, the **Centro Turistico Studentesco e Giovanile** (www.cts.it) youth travel agency can issue ISIC and IYTC cards and the European Youth Card.

Climate

Cagliari

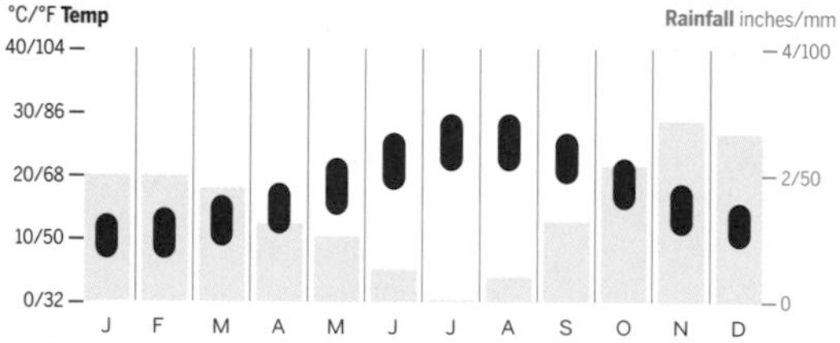

°C/°F **Temp** — **Rainfall** inches/mm

40/104 – 30/86 – 20/68 – 10/50 – 0/32; 4/100 – 2/50 – 0

J F M A M J J A S O N D

Olbia

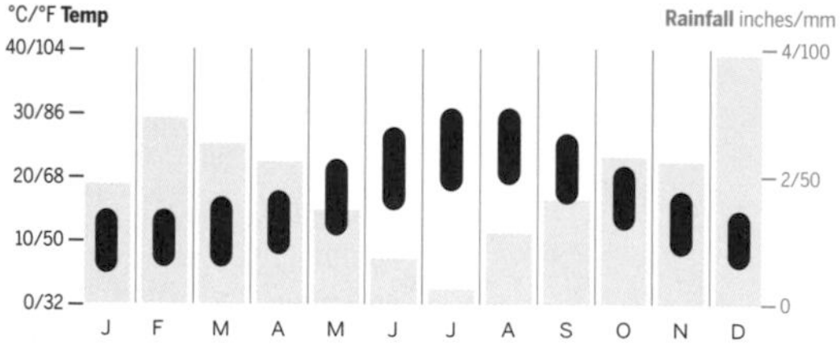

°C/°F **Temp** — **Rainfall** inches/mm

40/104 – 30/86 – 20/68 – 10/50 – 0/32; 4/100 – 2/50 – 0

J F M A M J J A S O N D

Oristano

°C/°F **Temp** — **Rainfall** inches/mm

40/104 – 30/86 – 20/68 – 10/50 – 0/32; 4/100 – 2/50 – 0

J F M A M J J A S O N D

Electricity

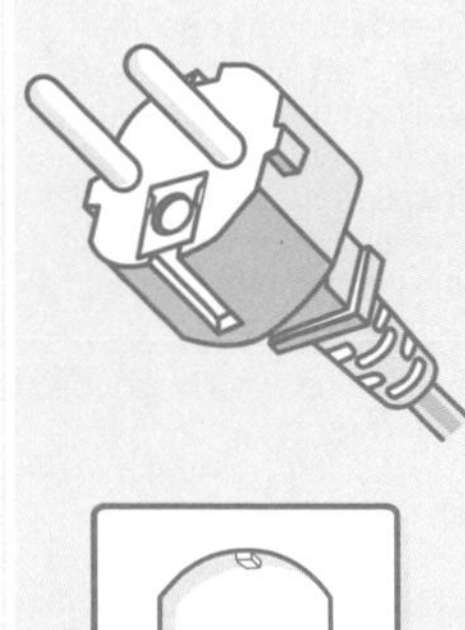

Type F
230V/50Hz

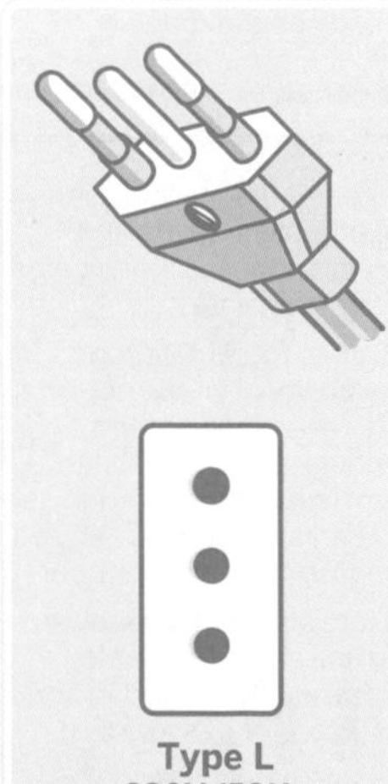

Type L
230V/50Hz

Embassies & Consulates

Most countries have an embassy in Rome, and several also maintain an honorary consulate in Cagliari. Passport inquiries should be addressed to Rome-based offices.

Australian Embassy (☎06 85 27 21, emergencies 800 877790; www.italy.embassy.gov.au; Via Antonio Bosio 5; ⏰9am-5pm Mon-Fri; 🚌Via Nomentana)

British Embassy (☎06 4220 0001; www.ukinitaly.fco.gov.uk; Via XX Settembre 80a, Rome)

Canadian Embassy (☎06 8 5444 2911; www.canadainternational.gc.ca/italy-italie; Via Zara 30; ⏰9am-noon Mon-Fri; 🚌Via Nomentana)

Dutch Embassy (☎06 3228 6001; www.olanda.it; Via Michele Mercati 8; ⏰9am-noon Mon-Wed & Fri, 10am-noon & 2-4pm Thu; 🚋Via Ulisse Aldrovandi)

French Embassy (☎06 68 6011; www.ambafrance-it.org; Piazza Farnese 67) Housed in the Renaissance Palazzo Farnese.

German Embassy (☎06 49 21 31; www.rom.diplo.de; Via San Martino della Battaglia 4, Rome)

Irish Embassy (☎06 585 23 81; www.ambasciata-irlanda.it; Via Giacomo Medici 1, Villa Spada)

New Zealand Embassy (☎06 853 75 01; www.mfat.govt.nz/en/countries-and-regions/europe/italy/new-zealand-embassy; Via Clitunno 44; ⏰8.30am-12.30pm & 1.30-5pm Mon-Fri; 🚌Corso Trieste)

US Embassy (☎06 4 67 41; www.italy.usembassy.gov; Via Vittorio Veneto 121, Rome)

Food & Drink

For detailed information on eating and drinking in Sardinia, see The Sardinian Kitchen (p249).

EATING PRICE RANGES

The following price ranges refer to a two-course meal including a glass of house wine and *coperto* (cover charge) for one person.

€ less than €25

€€ €25 to €45

€€€ more than €45

Gay & Lesbian Travellers

Although homosexuality is legal, Sardinian attitudes remain largely conservative. There is practically no open gay scene on the island and overt displays of affection could attract unpleasant attention, especially in the rural interior.

➡ The most tolerant places are the island's two largest cities, Sassari and Cagliari.

➡ The island's most high-profile gay activist organisation is the Sassari-based **Movimento Omosessuale Sardo** (MOS; ☎079 21 90 24; www.movimentomosessualesardo.org; Via Rockfeller 16c). Check out its website for listings and information on gay-friendly accommodation, clubs and beaches.

➡ Also useful is the national gay organisation Arcigay (www.arcigay.it).

➡ **Sardegna Pride** (www.sardegnapride.org; ⏰Jun) takes to the seafront streets of Cagliari in June.

Health

Before You Go

HEALTH INSURANCE

➡ The European Health Insurance Card (EHIC) entitles EU citizens and nationals of Switzerland, Iceland, Norway and Liechtenstein to free or reduced-cost state-provided health care for emergency treatment in Sardinia or other parts of Italy.

➡ The card is available from health centres and, in some countries, online. For more information see https://ehicdirect.org.uk. In the UK, get application forms from post offices or download them from the Department of Health (www.dh.gov.uk) website.

➡ The EHIC does not cover private health care, so make sure that you are treated by a state health-care provider. You will need to pay directly and fill in a treatment form; keep the form to claim any refunds. In general, you can claim back around 70% of the standard treatment cost.

➡ Citizens from other countries should check if there is a reciprocal arrangement for free medical care between their country and Italy. Australia, for instance, has such an agreement – carry your Medicare card.

➡ If you need health insurance, make sure you get a policy that covers you for the worst possible scenario, such as an accident requiring an emergency flight home.

➡ Find out in advance if your insurance plan will make payments directly to providers or reimburse you later for overseas health expenditures.

VACCINATIONS

No vaccinations are required to travel to Sardinia, though the World Health Organization (WHO) recommends that all travellers should be covered for diphtheria, tetanus, the measles, mumps, rubella, polio and hepatitis B.

In Sardinia

AVAILABILITY & COST OF HEALTH CARE

Health care is readily available throughout Sardinia, but standards can vary. Pharmacists are able to advise when more specialised help is required and point you in the right direction.

➡ *Farmacie* (pharmacies), marked by a green cross, can give medical advice and sell over-the-counter medication for minor illnesses. They can advise when more specialised help is required and point you in the right direction.

➡ Pharmacies generally keep the same hours as shops, from around 9am to 1pm and 4.30pm to 8pm Monday to Friday and on Saturday mornings. Closed pharmacies display a list of the nearest open ones.

➡ For emergency treatment, go to the *pronto soccorso* (casualty) section of a public hospital, where you can also get emergency dental treatment.

➡ Available in most towns, the on-call Guardia Medica service offers assistance throughout the night (8pm to 8am) on weekends and on public holidays. It does not provide emergency care (for that go to the *pronto soccorso*).

ENVIRONMENTAL HAZARDS

➡ Mosquitoes are a real nuisance around low-lying marshy areas such as Cabras and Olbia, especially if you are camping. Pack mosquito repellent in summer as a matter of course.

➡ Jellyfish are not uncommon in Sardinian waters. But while their stings are painful, they're not dangerous. Dousing in vinegar will deactivate stingers that have not fired. Calamine lotion, antihistamines and analgesics may reduce the reaction and relieve pain.

TAP WATER

Tap water is safe to drink in Sardinia, although many islanders prefer to buy bottled *acqua minerale* (mineral water), either *frizzante* (sparkling) or *naturale* (still).

Insurance

➡ Travel insurance to cover theft, loss and medical problems is highly recommended. It may also cover you for cancellation, delays to your travel arrangements or an emergency flight home.

➡ Check your policy covers any activities you might be planning such as diving, motorcycling, climbing, even trekking.

➡ Find out in advance if your insurance plan will make payments directly to providers or reimburse you later. If the latter, make sure you keep all documentation.

➡ Worldwide travel insurance is available at www.lonelyplanet.com/travel-insurance. You can buy, extend and claim online anytime – even if you're already on the road.

Internet Access

➡ Free wi-fi is available in most hostels, B&Bs and hotels, as well as many cafes and restaurants.

➡ Due to the widespread availability of wi-fi, internet cafes are a dying breed, although you can still find them in major cities such as Cagliari and Alghero. Access typically costs €5 per hour.

➡ Note also that whenever you use an internet cafe you're legally obliged to show an ID card or passport.

➡ Some hotels provide a computer for guest use.

Legal Matters

➡ Italy has tough drug laws. If caught with 5g of cannabis you can, in theory, be prosecuted as a trafficker. Those caught with amounts below this threshold can be subject to minor penalties.

➡ The legal limit for a driver's blood-alcohol reading is

0.05%. Random breath tests do occur.

➡ If you are detained for any alleged offence, you should be given verbal and written notice of the charges laid against you within 24 hours.

➡ You have no right to a phone call upon arrest, but you can choose not to respond to questions without the presence of a lawyer.

Maps

For travelling around the island, a good-quality map is very useful. The Touring Club Italiano's Touring Editore (www.touringclub.com) does an excellent island map at a scale of 1:200,000. It's available online or at bookshops in Sardinia.

Money

➡ Sardinia's unit of currency is the euro (€), which is divided into 100 cents.

➡ Coin denominations are one, two, five, 10, 20 and 50 cents and €1 and €2. The euro notes come in denominations of €5, €10, €20, €50, €100, €200 and €500.

➡ Exchange money in banks, post offices and exchange offices.

➡ Banks generally offer the best rates, but shop around as rates tend to fluctuate considerably.

➡ Credit cards are not always accepted, especially in many B&Bs, cheaper trattorias and other smaller establishments, so bring enough cash.

ATMs

➡ ATMs (known as 'Bancomat' in Italy) are widely available throughout Italy, and most will accept cards tied into the Visa, MasterCard, Cirrus and Maestro systems.

➡ Beware of transaction fees. Every time you withdraw cash, you'll be hit by charges – typically your home bank will charge a foreign-exchange fee (usually around 1%) as well as a transaction fee of around 1% to 3%. Fees can sometimes be reduced by withdrawing cash from banks affiliated with your home bank; check with it.

➡ If an ATM rejects your card, try another one before assuming the problem is with your card.

➡ If your card is lost, stolen or swallowed by an ATM, you can telephone toll-free to have an immediate stop put on its use:

American Express (Amex; ☎06 7290 0347)

Diners Club (☎800 393939)

MasterCard (☎800 870866)

Visa (☎800 819014)

Credit Cards

➡ Major cards such as Visa, MasterCard, Eurocard, Cirrus and Eurocheques are widely accepted. Amex is also recognised, although it's less common than Visa or MasterCard.

➡ Virtually all midrange and top-end hotels accept credit cards, as do most restaurants and large shops. Some cheaper *pensioni*, trattorias and pizzerias only accept cash.

➡ Do not rely on credit cards at museums or galleries.

➡ Note that using your credit card in ATMs can be costly. On every transaction there's a fee, which can reach US$10 with some credit-card issuers, as well as interest per withdrawal. Check with your issuer before leaving home.

➡ Always inform your bank of your travel plans to avoid your card being blocked for payments made in unusual locations.

Taxes & Refunds

Value-added-tax (VAT) is a 22% sales tax levied on most goods and services. To reclaim VAT on purchases made in tax-free shops, visit www.globalblue.com.

Tipping

Italians are not big tippers. Use the following as a rough guide:

Taxis Optional, but most people round up to the nearest euro.

Hotels Tip porters about €5 at high-end hotels.

Restaurants Service (*servizio*) is generally included in restaurants – if it's not, a euro or two is fine in pizzerias, 10% in restaurants.

Bars Optional, though many Italians leave small change on the bar when ordering coffee (usually €0.10 per coffee). If drinks are brought to your table, a small tip is generally appreciated.

Opening Hours

➡ Opening hours vary throughout the year depending on season and location. In some smaller, more out-of-the-way places, business hours might simply depend on how long the owner decides to stay open.

➡ Hours listed in reviews are generally high-season opening hours; hours will generally decrease in the shoulder and low seasons. 'Summer' times generally refer to the period from May to September or October.

Post

➡ Italy's, and by association Sardinia's, postal system **Poste Italiane** (☎803 160; www.poste.it) is reasonably reliable.

➡ *Francobolli* (stamps) are available at post offices and *tabacchi* (tobacconists) – look for the official sign, a big white 'T' against a blue-black background.

➡ Post offices are widespread in towns and cities, and most villages and resorts have *tabacchi*.

Public Holidays

Most Italians take their annual holiday in August. Settimana Santa (Easter Week) is another busy holiday period. National public holidays:

Capodanno (New Year's Day) 1 January

Epifania (Epiphany) 6 January

Pasqua (Easter Sunday) March/April

Pasquetta (Easter Monday) March/April

Giorno della Liberazione (Liberation Day) 25 April

Festa del Lavoro (Labour Day) 1 May

Festa della Repubblica (Republic Day) 2 June

Ferragosto (Feast of the Assumption) 15 August

Ognissanti (All Saints' Day) 1 November

Immacolata Concezione (Feast of the Immaculate Conception) 8 December

Natale (Christmas Day) 25 December

Festa di Santo Stefano (Boxing Day) 26 December

Safe Travel

Sardinia is a safe island, but use common sense.

➡ Stash away your valuables and lock hire cars.

➡ In case of theft or loss, report the incident at the *questura* (municipal police station) within 24 hours and ask for a statement, otherwise your travel-insurance firm won't pay up.

Telephone

➡ To call Sardinia from abroad, dial your international access number, Italy's country code ☎(39) and then the local number (including the area code with the leading 0).

➡ To call abroad from Sardinia, dial ☎00 and then the relevant country and area codes, followed by the telephone number.

➡ Mobile phone numbers begin with a three-figure prefix, typically 330, 331 etc.

➡ Sardinian area codes all begin with 0 and consist of up to four digits. Always dial the area code, even when calling locally. Toll-free numbers, known as *numeri verdi*, usually start with 800.

➡ The cheapest way to place international calls from Sardinia is via free or low-cost apps such as Skype and Viber, connecting by using the wi-fi at your hotel or at a cafe or other venue offering free wi-fi.

Mobile Phones

➡ As of June 2017, roaming charges no longer apply in the EU. Australian mobiles must be set up for international roaming.

➡ US cell phones that operate on the 900 MHz and 1800 MHz frequencies work in Sardinia.

➡ The cheapest way of using your mobile is to buy a prepaid *(prepagato)* Italian SIM card, readily available at phone and electronic stores throughout Sardinia. TIM (www.tim.it), Wind (www.wind.it), Vodafone (www.vodafone.it) and Tre (www.tre.it) all offer SIM cards. These must be officially registered at time of purchase, so make sure you have a passport or ID card with you when you buy one.

➡ You can top up your Italian SIM with a recharge card *(ricarica)*, available at most tobacconists, some bars, supermarkets and banks.

Time

➡ Sardinian time is one hour ahead of GMT/UTC.

➡ Daylight-saving time, when clocks are moved forward one hour, commences on the last Sunday in March. Clocks are put back an hour on the last Sunday in October.

➡ Italy operates on a 24-hour clock, so 6pm is written as 18.00.

➡ The following times do not take daylight-saving time into account.

City	Noon in Cagliari
Auckland	11pm
Berlin	noon
Cape Town	noon
London	11am
New York	6am
San Francisco	3am
Sydney	9pm
Tokyo	8pm

Toilets

➡ Most toilets in Sardinia are of the Western-style, sit-down variety.

➡ Public toilets are not widespread. If you're caught short, nip into a cafe or bar, all of which are required by law to have a toilet.

Tourist Information

Tourist information is widely available in Sardinia, although the quality varies tremendously. On the whole, offices in important tourist centres such as Alghero, Cala Gonone, Santa Teresa di Gallura and Villasimius are efficient and helpful, with English-speaking staff.

Sardegna Turismo (www.sardegnaturismo.it) For the lowdown on the island online.

Italia (www.italia.it) Multilingual site of the Italian State Tourist Office.

Alghero (Map p120; ☎079 97 90 54; www.algheroturismo.eu; Largo Lo Quarter; ⊙9am-1pm & 3.30-6.30pm Mon-Fri, 9am-1pm & 4-7pm Sat year-round, plus 10am-1pm Sun summer

PRACTICALITIES

Weights & Measures The metric system is used.

Smoking Banned in all enclosed public spaces.

Newspapers Key newspapers include Cagliari's L'Unione Sarda (www.unionesarda.it) and Sassari's La Nuova Sardegna (lanuovasardegna.gelocal.it).

Radio Radiolina (www.radiolina.it) is a popular local radio station. National stations RAI-1, RAI-2 and RAI-3 (www.rai.it) play a mix of phone-ins, sport, news and music.

TV Local TV channels, Videolina (www.videolina.it) and Sardegna 1 (www.sardegna1.tv) are usually pretty dire, pumping out news, football and traditional costumed dancing. National channels include the state-run RAI-1, RAI-2 and RAI-3.

only) Helpful tourist office in the town's centre.

Cagliari (Map p48; ☎070 677 81 73; www.cagliariturismo.it; Via Roma 145, Palazzo Civico; ⏰9am-8pm summer, 10am-1pm & 2-5pm Mon-Sat winter) Main island tourist office in the capital.

Olbia (Map p149; ☎0789 5 22 06; www.olbiaturismo.it; Piazza Terranova Pausania; ⏰9am-8pm Apr-Sep, reduced hours Oct-Mar) This should be your first port of call for information on Olbia.

Travellers with Disabilities

Sardinia has little infrastructure to ease the way for travellers with disabilities, and few museums and monuments are wheelchair accessible. Footpaths are generally well maintained, though the access to some of the more remote beaches is on rough, off-road dirt tracks.

Rete Ferroviaria Italiana (RFI; ☎800 90 60 60, 02 32 32 32; www.rfi.it) Provides assistance for train travel; two dedicated telephone lines are active between 6.45am and 9.30pm daily.

Italia (www.italia.it) The Italian State Tourist Office's official site may be able to provide advice on associations for travellers with disabilities.

Accessible Italy (www.accessibleitaly.com) Specialises in holiday services for travellers with disabilities, including tours and hiring adapted transport.

For more information download Lonely Planet's free Accessible Travel guide from http://lptravel.to/AccessibleTravel.

Visas

➡ Italy is part of the Schengen area. There are no customs controls when travelling between Schengen countries, so the visa rules that apply to Italy apply to all Schengen countries.

➡ The standard tourist visa for a Schengen country is valid for 90 days and allows unlimited travel within the entire Schengen zone. You must apply for it in the country of your residence and you cannot apply for more than two in any 12-month period. They are not renewable within Italy.

➡ EU citizens do not need a visa to enter Italy. A valid ID card or passport is sufficient.

➡ Nationals of some other countries, including Australia, Canada, Israel, Japan, New Zealand, Norway, Switzerland and the US do not need a visa for stays of up to 90 days.

Volunteering

➡ Volunteering opportunities are fairly limited in Sardinia.

➡ Websites such as www.transitionsabroad.com have links to organisations offering volunteering positions in Italy and Sardinia. A common request is for mother-tongue English speakers to work at summer schools/camps.

➡ Some seasonal farm work may be available through organisations such as WWOOF.

Women Travellers

Sardinians are almost universally polite to women, and it is unlikely that you will suffer the sort of harassment that you might in parts of mainland Italy. It is wise – and polite – to dress modestly in inland Sardinia, however. Communities here are very conservative, and you will still see older women wearing the traditional long, pleated skirts and shawls. Take your cue from the local women.

Work

➡ High unemployment in Sardinia, particularly among young people, means job opportunities are scarce.

➡ Seasonal work in resorts, bars, restaurants and hotels does exist but most jobs are snapped up by young Sardinians or Italians coming over from the mainland.

➡ Other possibilities include English-language teaching – in a company, language school or through private lessons – and working as an au pair.

➡ A useful online resource is Season Workers (www.seasonworkers.com), listing job opportunities on summer resorts.

Transport

GETTING THERE & AWAY

Entering the Region

➡ EU and Swiss citizens can travel to Italy with their national ID card alone. People from countries that do not issue ID cards must carry a valid passport. All other nationalities must have a full valid passport and may be required to fill out a landing card on arrival in Italy.

➡ If you are flying to Sardinia via the Italian mainland, all customs and immigration formalities will take place at the mainland airport. The Sardinian leg of your journey will be considered an internal flight.

➡ You should carry your ID card or passport when travelling on internal flights or ferry crossings.

➡ Technically all foreign visitors to Sardinia are supposed to register with the local police within eight days of their arrival. However, if you are staying in a hotel, the hotel does this for you – which is why they always take your passport details.

Air

Airports & Airlines

Flights from Italian and European cities serve Sardinia's three main airports:

Cagliari Elmas Airport (☎070 21 12 11; www.cagliariairport.it)

Aeroporto di Olbia Costa Smeralda (☎0789 56 34 44; www.geasar.it)

Alghero Airport (Fertilia; Map p126;☎079 93 50 11; www.aeroportodialghero.it)

International airlines operate year-round flights from cities across Europe including Barcelona, Brussels, Dortmund, Dublin, Düsseldorf, Eindhoven, Frankfurt, London, Madrid, Munich, Oslo, Paris and Stockholm.

Domestic flights connect with mainland Italian airports including Rome, Milan, Naples, Bari, Bologna, Turin, Venice and Verona.

Note that there's a marked increase in flights to and from Sardinia in summer, with many seasonal flights operating between June and September. Some low-cost European carriers only operate seasonal flights, typically between May and October.

Italian airlines serving Sardinia:

Alitalia (www.alitalia.it) Italy's national carrier.

Meridiana (www.meridiana.it)

Budget airlines serving Sardinia:

easyJet (www.easyjet.com)

Ryanair (www.ryanair.com)

Wizz (www.wizzair.com)

CLIMATE CHANGE & TRAVEL

Every form of transport that relies on carbon-based fuel generates CO_2, the main cause of human-induced climate change. Modern travel is dependent on aeroplanes, which might use less fuel per kilometre per person than most cars but travel much greater distances. The altitude at which aircraft emit gases (including CO_2) and particles also contributes to their climate change impact. Many websites offer 'carbon calculators' that allow people to estimate the carbon emissions generated by their journey and, for those who wish to do so, to offset the impact of the greenhouse gases emitted with contributions to portfolios of climate-friendly initiatives throughout the world. Lonely Planet offsets the carbon footprint of all staff and author travel.

Land

Sardinia is the most isolated island in the Mediterranean, some 200km from the nearest land mass. Car ferries are available at all major ferry crossings. The shortest ferry crossing from the Italian mainland is from Civitavecchia to Olbia on Sardinia's northeast coast, though there are various alternatives.

If you are travelling by bus, train or car to Italy, check whether you require visas for the countries you intend to pass through.

Sea

Sardinia is accessible by ferry from ports in Spain, France and Italy.

- The arrival points in Sardinia are Olbia, Golfo Aranci, Santa Teresa di Gallura and Porto Torres in the north; Arbatax on the east coast; and Cagliari in the south.
- Services are most frequent between mid-June and mid-September, when it is advisable to book well ahead.
- You can book tickets at travel agents throughout Italy or directly online.

Useful ferry websites:

AFerry (www.aferry.co.uk) Information on routes, ferry operators and online booking.

Traghetti Web (www.traghettiweb.it) Comprehensive site listing major routes and ferry companies. Also has online booking.

From Mainland Italy & Sicily

Year-round ferries sail from Genoa, Livorno, Civitavecchia, Naples and Palermo. Seasonal services run from Piombino in Tuscany.

- Seasonal crossings generally operate from mid-April to the end of September.
- As well as reclinable seats, most ferries also offer cabins with en-suite bathrooms. Prices vary according to the number of occupants (generally one to four) and position (with or without window). Note that cabins don't always cost a lot more than a reclinable seat, particularly in the low season – it's always worth checking.
- Most companies offer discounts on return trips and other deals – check the website or ask your travel agent.

From Corsica

The main crossing from Corsica to Sardinia is between Bonifacio and Santa Teresa di Gallura on the northern coast, though ferries also depart from Bastia, Ajaccio and Propriano. **Corsica Ferries, Sardinia Ferries** (☎0495 32 95 95; www.corsica-ferries.co.uk) operates these services.

From Mainland France

La Méridionale (☎in France 0970 83 20 20; www.lameridionale.fr) operates ferries from Marseille to Porto Torres (via Corsica). Crossing time is around 10 hours. Tickets for a reclinable seat cost roughly €44 and for a small car €98 in high season.

From Spain

Grimaldi Lines (☎081 496 444; www.grimaldi-lines.com) operate ferries from Barcelona to Porto Torres. Tickets for a reclining seat cost around €59 per person or €115 with a car. Journey time is 11¾ hours. Services run from mid-April to October with up to five weekly sailings between mid-June and early September.

Ferries to Sardinia

Three main ferry operators serve Sardinia from mainland Italy.

Grandi Navi Veloci (☎010 209 45 91; www.gnv.it) From Genoa to Porto Torres in northern Sardinia.

Moby Lines (☎+49 (0)611-14020; www.mobylines.com) From Civitavecchia, Genoa, Livorno and Piombinoo to Olbia in northeastern Sardinia.

Tirrenia (☎199 30 30 40; www.tirrenia.it) To Cagliari from Civitavecchia, Naples, Palermo and Trapani; to Olbia from Civitavecchia and Genoa; to Arbatax from Civitavecchia and Genoa; and to Porto Torres from Genoa.

GETTING AROUND

Air

Internal flights are not available, nor are they necessary given the island's size.

Bicycle

- Bike hire is available in most major towns and resorts, including Alghero, Santa Teresa di Gallura, La Maddalena, Palau and Olbia.
- Rates range from around €10 per day to as much as €25 for mountain bikes.
- You cannot cycle on the SS131, Sardinia's principal road, which runs from Cagliari to Porto Torres.
- If cycling in summer, take plenty of water and sunblock as the heat can be exhausting.
- Bikes can be taken on regional trains but you'll need to buy a separate 24-hour ticket (€3.50).
- You can carry bikes with you on ferries to Sardinia for a small fee, usually €3 to €10.

Boat

- Boat tours generally run from late March or early April to October. They are an excellent way to see Sardinia's more inaccessible coastal highlights.
- Services are cut back considerably over the winter months, so always check

ahead. If taking a car in summer, try to arrive in good time as boats fill up quickly.

➡ The most popular tours include trips out of Cala Gonone and Santa Maria Navarrese along the majestic Golfo di Orosei. Also highly recommended is a cruise from Palau around the islands of the Maddalena archipelago.

➡ Boats frequently head out of Porto San Paolo, south of Olbia, for trips around Isola Tavolara and the nearby coast. From Alghero you can take boat trips up to Capo Caccia and the Grotta di Nettuno; from the Sinis Peninsula, boat tours head over to Isola di Mal di Ventre.

➡ Most trips are by motorboats or small ferries, but a handful of sailing vessels are also on hand.

➡ **Delcomar** (☎0781 85 71 23; www.delcomar.it) connects Palau with the Isola di La Maddalena. In summer services run every 30 minutes and cost €3.40 to €5 for the 15-minute crossing (depending on date and time of travel. A car costs €7.30 to €12.50, depending on vehicle size and date and time of travel.

➡ Delcomar also operates nightly crossings from Portovesme to Carloforte, as well as between Carloforte and Calasetta.

Bus

Bus services within Sardinia are provided by the **Azienda Regionale Sarda Trasporti** (ARST; ☎800 865042; www.arst.sardegna.it), which runs the majority of local and long-distance buses.

➡ ARST also operates a limited network of private *servizi ferroviari* (narrow-gauge railways), most notably the **Trenino Verde** (☎070 265 76 12; www.treninoverde.com; ⊙mid-Jun–Sep).

➡ In smaller towns and villages there will simply be a *fermata* (stop) for intercity buses, not always in an immediately apparent location.

➡ Tickets must usually be bought prior to boarding at stations or designated bars, *tabacchi* (tobacconists) or newsstands near the bus stop. On some services you can buy tickets on-board but they'll cost slightly extra.

➡ Timetables are sometimes posted next to the bus stop, but don't hold your breath.

➡ Tourist offices in bigger towns can usually provide timetables for their area. Alternatively ask at the bar or newsstand where you buy your ticket.

FERRY ROUTES

The following is a rundown of the main ferry routes to Sardinia, the companies that operate them and the route details. Fares are for a 2nd-class *poltrona* (reclinable seat) in high season and are intended as a rough guide only. Children aged four to 12 generally pay half-price, and under-fours travel free.

FROM	TO	COMPANY	FARE	CAR	DURATION (HR)	FREQUENCY
Civitavecchia	Arbatax	Tirrenia	€45	€141	10	2 weekly
Civitavecchia	Cagliari	Tirrenia	€53	€141	13	daily
Civitavecchia	Olbia	Tirrenia	€49	€92	5½	daily
Genoa	Arbatax	Tirrenia	€74	€186	15-18	2 weekly
Genoa	Olbia	Moby	€61	€121	10½	daily end-May–mid-Oct
Genoa	Olbia	Tirrenia	€71	€183	10-12	up to 5 weekly
Genoa	Porto Torres	GNV	€74	€124	11	up to 4 weekly end-May–mid-Sep
Genoa	Porto Torres	Tirrenia	€64	€109	12	daily
Livorno	Golfo Aranci	Sardinia Ferries	€80	€98	10	daily
Livorno	Olbia	Moby	€37	€79	6½	daily
Naples	Cagliari	Tirrenia	€50	€139	13½	2 weekly
Palermo	Cagliari	Tirrenia	€50	€138	12	2 weekly
Piombino	Olbia	Moby	€41	€87	5	daily end-May–Sep

+ Includes all taxes.

➡ Note that while services might be frequent on weekdays, they are cut back drastically on Sunday and holidays. Keep this in mind, as it is easy to get stranded in smaller places, especially on weekends.

Car & Motorcycle

Local drivers are fairly courteous and driving in Sardinia is reasonably stress-free. Traffic is only really a concern in the main towns (Cagliari, Sassari and Olbia) and in high summer. The main hazards you're likely to face are flocks of sheep.

➡ To really explore the island you'll need to use the system of smaller *strade provinciali* (provincial roads), marked as P or SP on maps. These are sometimes little more than country lanes, but they provide access to some of the more beautiful scenery and the many small towns and villages.

➡ Many spectacular beaches and rural *agriturismi* (farmstays) are only accessible by dirt tracks.

➡ Sardinia is very popular with motorcyclists who enjoy tearing around the island's scenic roads and hairpin bends.

➡ Unless you're touring it's probably easier to rent a motorbike once you're in Sardinia.

Automobile Associations

Italy's motoring organisation is the **Automobile Club d'Italia** (ACI; ☎803 116; www.aci.it). Foreigners do not have to join but instead pay a fee in case of breakdown assistance (€115 to €138, 20% more on weekends and holidays). Further charges apply if your car needs to be towed away. Check the website for details.

The UK's **AA** (www.theaa.com) and the **RAC** (☎0333 2000 999; www.rac.co.uk) both offer European breakdown cover.

Bringing Your Own Vehicle

When driving in Italy you'll need to have the following documents with you:

➡ your vehicle-registration certificate

➡ a valid driving licence

➡ proof of third-party liability insurance cover

You'll also need a warning triangle to use in case of an accident, and a fluorescent safety vest to be worn if you have to get out of your car in the event of a breakdown.

A first-aid kit, a spare-bulb kit and a fire extinguisher are also recommended.

Driving Licences

➡ All EU driving licences are recognised in Sardinia.

➡ Holders of non-EU licences are officially required to carry an International Driving Permit (IDP) or an Italian translation of their home country licence, though this policy is rarely enforced..

➡ No licence is required to ride a scooter under 50cc, but you must be 14 or over and you can't carry passengers. To ride a scooter up to 125cc, you must be 16 or over and have a licence (a car driving licence will do). For motorcycles over 125cc you must be 18 or over and have a motorcycle licence.

Fuel

➡ Smaller filling stations tend to close between about 1pm and 3.30pm and on Sunday afternoons.

➡ Many stations have self-service *(fai da te)* pumps that you can use 24 hours a day. To use one insert a bank note into the payment machine and press the number of the pump you want.

➡ Unleaded petrol is marked as *benzina senza piombo*, diesel as *gasolio*.

➡ Prices vary from one filling station to another but reckon on around €1.60 per litre for unleaded petrol and €1.50 per litre for diesel.

Hire

➡ It is *always* cheaper to arrange car hire before you arrive in Sardinia.

➡ All the major international car hire outlets have offices at the airports, where you usually pick up your car and deposit it at the end of your stay. You'll also find rental agencies in some of the main cities and in most coastal resorts.

➡ Age restrictions vary from agency to agency but generally you'll need to be 21 or over.

➡ If you're under 25, you'll probably have to pay a young driver's supplement on top of the usual rates.

➡ To hire, you'll need a credit card and a valid driving licence.

➡ In tourist hot spots such as Santa Teresa di Gallura and Alghero you'll find rental outlets offering motorcycles and scooters.

➡ Most agencies will not hire out motorcycles to people under 18.

➡ Note that many places require a sizeable deposit for a motorcycle and that you could be responsible for reimbursing part of the cost of the bike if it is stolen.

The main national and international agencies:

Avis (☎06 452 108 391; www.avisautonoleggio.it)

Budget (☎199 307 373; www.budgetautonoleggio.it)

Europcar (☎199 307 030; www.europcar.it)

Hertz (☎199 11 22 11; www.hertz.it)

Italy By Car (☎334 648 19 20; www.italybycar.it)

Maggiore (☎199 151 120; www.maggiore.it)

Insurance

➡ Third-party motor insurance is a minimum requirement in Italy.

➡ Residents of non-EU countries should check with their car insurer whether they need an International Insurance Certificate, known as a *Carta Verde* (Green Card).

➡ It's not obligatory but you could ask your insurer for a European Accident Statement form, which can simplify matters in the event of an accident.

➡ Similarly, a European breakdown-assistance policy will make life easier in the event of a breakdown.

Road Conditions & Rules

➡ The island's principal artery is the SS131 (known as the Carlo Felice), a mostly dual carriageway that runs from Cagliari to Porto Torres via Oristano, Macomer and Sassari.

➡ These and many roads in the more touristy coastal areas are reasonably well maintained but can be narrow and curvy.

➡ In summer, it is virtually impossible not to get caught in traffic jams along many roads. The area between Olbia and Santa Teresa di Gallura is particularly bad.

➡ Getting in and out of the cities, notably Cagliari and Sassari, can be a test of nerves as traffic chokes approach roads and exits.

➡ You will also be surprised by the number of unpaved and uneven roads on the island – a worry if in an expensive rental car. Many *agriturismi* (farm-stays), prehistoric sites and beaches are only accessible by dirt tracks.

➡ In Sardinia, as in the rest of continental Europe, drive on the right-hand side of the road and overtake on the left. Give way to cars entering an intersection from the right.

➡ Front and rear seatbelts are compulsory in cars, as are helmets on two-wheeled vehicles.

➡ Random breath tests take place and penalties can be severe. The blood-alcohol limit is 0.05%.

➡ Speed limits on main highways (there are no autostradas in Sardinia) are 110km/h, on secondary highways 90km/h, and in built-up areas 50km/h.

➡ Speeding fines follow EU standards and are proportionate to the number of kilometres you are driving over the limit.

➡ Drivers are obliged to keep headlights switched on day and night on all dual carriageways.

➡ There is no daytime lights-on requirement for motorcycles. On a motorcycle you can enter restricted traffic areas in cities and towns without any problems. Also traffic police generally turn a blind eye to motorcycles or scooters parked on footpaths.

Hitching

➡ Hitching is never entirely safe in any country, and we don't recommend it. Travellers who decide to hitch should understand that they are taking a small but potentially serious risk.

➡ Hitching is extremely uncommon in Sardinia. Sardinians can be wary of picking up strangers, which makes travelling this way a frustrating business.

➡ Look presentable, carry as little luggage as possible, and hold a sign in Italian indicating your destination.

➡ Do not use the normal thumbs-up signal, as this can offend (in these parts it means 'Up yours'!).

Tours

Across the island local operators offer all manner of guided excursions and tours. You'll also find hundreds of outfits running boat trips along Sardinia's coastal waters. Popular spots include Alghero, Cala Gonone, Stintino, Santa Maria Navarrese and Porto San Paolo.

Specialist tour agencies:

Agenzia La Nassa (☎079 52 00 60; www.agenzialanassa.it; Via Sassari 39; tours per person €18-65; ⏲8.30am-1pm & 4.30-8pm daily summer, Mon-Sat winter) Excursions to the Parco Nazionale dell'Asinara.

Barbagia No Limits (☎0784 182 03 73; www.barbagianolimits.it; Via Cagliari 186) This adventure-sports outfit organises all sorts of outdoor activities in the Barbagia area of eastern Sardinia, including caving trips, 4WD tours and survival courses.

Esedra Sardegna (Map p108; ☎0785 37 42 58; www.esedrasardegna.it; Corso Vittorio Emanuele 64; ⏲9.30am-1pm & 4.30-8pm Mon-Sat, 10.30am-1pm Sun) Runs excursions in and around Bosa. Packages range from river cruises and boat tours to guided birdwatching trips.

Linea del Parco (☎349 2605023; www.lineadelparco.it; Porto Mannu, Stintino; ⏲ticket office 9am-12.30pm, longer hours summer) Offers a number of tours by bus or 4WD, horse rides and boat excursions to the Parco Nazionale dell'Asinara.

Mare e Natura (☎339 9850435, 079 52 00 97; www.marenatura.it; Via Sassari 77, Stintino) One of several companies that organises land and boat tours of the Parco Nazionale dell'Asinara.

Parco della Giara Escursioni (☎348 2924983, 070 936 42 77; www.parcodellagiara.it; Via Tuveri 16, Tuili) Operating out of the tiny village of Tuili, this small local group leads guided tours of the Giara di Gesturi.

Sardinia Island Tours (☎Kevin 391 7327232, Rodolfo 339 4774472; www.sardiniaisland

tours.com; Via Guerrazzi 4; full-day tour €60) Terrific tours of the Maddalena archipelago, as well as excursions in the Golfo di Orosei, walking tours, and wine and archaeology tours.

Train

Sardinia's rail network, though cheap, is limited and on some routes a bus is quicker.

➡ You will find train *orari* (timetables) posted on station noticeboards. *Partenze* (departures) and *arrivi* (arrivals) are clearly indicated.

➡ Note that there are all sorts of permutations on schedules, with services much reduced on Sunday. Handy indicators to look out for are *feriale* (Monday to Saturday) and *festivo* (Sunday and holidays only).

➡ Only one type of train runs in Sardinia – the basic *regionale*. These tend to be chuggers that stop at every village on the way, so you won't get anywhere fast.

➡ Some trains offer 1st and 2nd class, but you won't find there's a big difference between them.

➡ It is not worth buying a Eurail or InterRail pass if you are only travelling in Sardinia. Italy's state-run train company **Trenitalia** (☎892021; www.trenitalia.com) runs the bulk of Sardinia's limited network. The main Trenitalia line runs from Cagliari to Oristano and on to Chilivano-Ozieri, where it divides into two branch lines: one heads northwest to Sassari and Porto Torres; the other goes northeast to Olbia and Golfo Aranci. Macomer is another important hub with connections to Nuoro.

The following train services also operate within Sardinia.

Azienda Regionale Sarda Trasporti (ARST; ☎800 865042; www.arst.sardegna.it) Sardinia's main bus company runs most local and long-distance services, but it also runs a limited network of private *servizi ferroviari* (narrow-gauge railways), including the slow-going **Trenino Verde** (☎070 265 76 12; www.treninoverde.com; ⏲mid-Jun–Sep).

Rete Ferroviaria Italiana (RFI; ☎800 90 60 60, 02 32 32 32; www.rfi.it) The company that oversees Italy's (and Sardinia's) rail network.

Language

In Italy, regional dialects are an important part of identity in many parts of the country, but you'll have no trouble being understood anywhere if you stick to standard Italian and this also holds true for Sardinia. Many Sardinians are bilingual, switching from Sardinian, the island tongue, to Italian with equal ease. Their pronunciation of Italian is refreshingly clear and easy to understand, even if you have only a limited command of the language.

The sounds used in spoken Italian can all be found in English. If you read our coloured pronunciation guides as if they were English, you'll be understood. The stressed syllables are indicated with italics. Note that ai is pronounced as in 'aisle', ay as in 'say', ow as in 'how', dz as the 'ds' in 'lids', and that r is a strong and rolled sound. Keep in mind that Italian consonants can have a stronger, emphatic pronunciation – if the consonant is written as a double letter, it should be pronounced a little stronger, eg *sonno* *son*·no (sleep) versus *sono* *so*·no (I am).

BASICS

Italian has two words for 'you' – use the polite form *Lei* lay if you're talking to strangers, officials or people older than you. With people familiar to you or younger than you, you can use the informal form *tu* too.

In Italian, all nouns and adjectives are either masculine or feminine, and so are the articles *il/la* eel/la (the) and *un/una* oon/*oo*·na (a) that go with the nouns.

WANT MORE?

For in-depth language information and handy phrases, check out Lonely Planet's *Italian Phrasebook*. You'll find it at **shop.lonelyplanet.com**, or you can buy Lonely Planet's iPhone phrasebooks at the Apple App Store.

In this chapter the polite/informal and masculine/feminine options are included where necessary, separated with a slash and indicated with 'pol/inf' and 'm/f'.

Hello.	*Buongiorno.*	bwon·*jor*·no
Goodbye.	*Arrivederci.*	a·ree·ve·*der*·chee
Yes./No.	*Sì./No.*	see/no
Excuse me.	*Mi scusi.* (pol) *Scusami.* (inf)	mee *skoo*·zee *skoo*·za·mee
Sorry.	*Mi dispiace.*	mee dees·*pya*·che
Please.	*Per favore.*	per fa·*vo*·re
Thank you.	*Grazie.*	*gra*·tsye
You're welcome.	*Prego.*	*pre*·go

How are you?
Come sta/stai? (pol/inf) *ko*·me sta/stai

Fine. And you?
Bene. E Lei/tu? (pol/inf) *be*·ne e lay/too

What's your name?
Come si chiama? pol *ko*·me see *kya*·ma

My name is ...
Mi chiamo ... mee *kya*·mo ...

Do you speak English?
Parla/Parli inglese? (pol/inf) *par*·la/*par*·lee een·*gle*·ze

I don't understand.
Non capisco. non ka·*pee*·sko

ACCOMMODATION

Do you have a ... room?	*Avete una camera ...?*	a·*ve*·te *oo*·na *ka*·me·ra ...
double	*doppia con letto matrimoniale*	*do*·pya kon *le*·to ma·tree·mo·*nya*·le
single	*singola*	*seen*·go·la
How much is it per ...?	*Quanto costa per ...?*	*kwan*·to *kos*·ta per ...
night	*una notte*	*oo*·na *no*·te
person	*persona*	per·*so*·na

Is breakfast included?

La colazione è compresa?	la ko·la·*tsyo*·ne e kom·*pre*·sa

air-con	*aria condizionata*	*a*·rya kon·dee·tsyo·*na*·ta
bathroom	*bagno*	*ba*·nyo
campsite	*campeggio*	kam·*pe*·jo
guesthouse	*pensione*	pen·*syo*·ne
hotel	*albergo*	al·*ber*·go
youth hostel	*ostello della gioventù*	os·*te*·lo de·la jo·ven·*too*
window	*finestra*	fee·*nes*·tra

DIRECTIONS

Where's ...?
Dov'è ...? — do·*ve* ...

What's the address?
Qual'è l'indirizzo? — kwa·*le* leen·dee·*ree*·tso

Could you please write it down?
Può scriverlo, per favore? — pwo *skree*·ver·lo per fa·*vo*·re

Can you show me (on the map)?
Può mostrarmi (sulla pianta)? — pwo mos·*trar*·mee (soo·la *pyan*·ta)

at the corner	*all'angolo*	a·*lan*·go·lo
at the traffic lights	*al semaforo*	al se·*ma*·fo·ro
behind	*dietro*	*dye*·tro
far	*lontano*	lon·*ta*·no
in front of	*davanti a*	da·*van*·tee a
left	*a sinistra*	a see·*nee*·stra
near	*vicino*	vee·*chee*·no
next to	*accanto a*	a·*kan*·to a
opposite	*di fronte a*	dee *fron*·te a
right	*a destra*	a *de*·stra
straight ahead	*sempre diritto*	*sem*·pre dee·*ree*·to

EATING & DRINKING

What would you recommend?
Cosa mi consiglia? — *ko*·za mee kon·*see*·lya

What's in that dish?
Quali ingredienti ci sono in questo piatto? — *kwa*·li een·gre·*dyen*·tee chee *so*·no een *kwe*·sto *pya*·to

What's the local speciality?
Qual'è la specialità di questa regione? — kwa·*le* la spe·cha·lee·*ta* dee *kwe*·sta re·*jo*·ne

That was delicious!
Era squisito! — *e*·ra skwee·*zee*·to

Cheers!
Salute! — sa·*loo*·te

Please bring the bill.
Mi porta il conto, per favore? — mee *por*·ta eel *kon*·to per fa·*vo*·re

I'd like to reserve a table for ...	*Vorrei prenotare un tavolo per ...*	vo·*ray* pre·no·*ta*·re oon *ta*·vo·lo per ...
(two) people	*(due) persone*	(*doo*·e) per·*so*·ne
(eight) o'clock	*le (otto)*	le (*o*·to)

I don't eat ...	*Non mangio ...*	non *man*·jo ...
eggs	*uova*	*wo*·va
fish	*pesce*	*pe*·she
nuts	*noci*	*no*·chee
(red) meat	*carne (rossa)*	*kar*·ne (*ro*·sa)

Key Words

bar	*locale*	lo·*ka*·le
bottle	*bottiglia*	bo·*tee*·lya
breakfast	*prima colazione*	*pree*·ma ko·la·*tsyo*·ne
cafe	*bar*	bar
cold	*freddo*	*fre*·do
dinner	*cena*	*che*·na
drink list	*lista delle bevande*	*lee*·sta *de*·le be·*van*·de
fork	*forchetta*	for·*ke*·ta
glass	*bicchiere*	bee·*kye*·re
grocery store	*alimentari*	a·lee·men·*ta*·ree
hot	*caldo*	*kal*·do
knife	*coltello*	kol·*te*·lo
lunch	*pranzo*	*pran*·dzo
market	*mercato*	mer·*ka*·to
menu	*menù*	me·*noo*
plate	*piatto*	*pya*·to
restaurant	*ristorante*	ree·sto·*ran*·te
spicy	*piccante*	pee·*kan*·te
spoon	*cucchiaio*	koo·*kya*·yo
vegetarian (food)	*vegetariano*	ve·je·ta·*rya*·no
with	*con*	kon
without	*senza*	*sen*·tsa

Meat & Fish

beef	*manzo*	*man*·dzo
chicken	*pollo*	*po*·lo
duck	*anatra*	*a*·na·tra
fish	*pesce*	*pe*·she
herring	*aringa*	a·*reen*·ga
lamb	*agnello*	a·*nye*·lo
lobster	*aragosta*	a·ra·*gos*·ta
meat	*carne*	*kar*·ne
mussels	*cozze*	*ko*·tse
oysters	*ostriche*	*o*·stree·ke
pork	*maiale*	ma·*ya*·le
prawn	*gambero*	*gam*·be·ro
salmon	*salmone*	sal·*mo*·ne
scallops	*capasante*	ka·pa·*san*·te
seafood	*frutti di mare*	*froo*·tee dee *ma*·re
shrimp	*gambero*	*gam*·be·ro
squid	*calamari*	ka·la·*ma*·ree
trout	*trota*	*tro*·ta
tuna	*tonno*	*to*·no
turkey	*tacchino*	ta·*kee*·no
veal	*vitello*	vee·*te*·lo

KEY PATTERNS

To get by in Italian, mix and match these simple patterns with words of your choice:

When's (the next flight)?
A che ora è (il prossimo volo)? — a ke *o*·ra e (eel *pro*·see·mo *vo*·lo)

Where's (the station)?
Dov'è (la stazione)? — do·*ve* (la sta·*tsyo*·ne)

I'm looking for (a hotel).
Sto cercando (un albergo). — sto cher·*kan*·do (oon al·*ber*·go)

Do you have (a map)?
Ha (una pianta)? — a (*oo*·na *pyan*·ta)

Is there (a toilet)?
C'è (un gabinetto)? — che (oon ga·bee·*ne*·to)

I'd like (a coffee).
Vorrei (un caffè). — vo·*ray* (oon ka·*fe*)

I'd like to (hire a car).
Vorrei (noleggiare una macchina). — vo·*ray* (no·le·*ja*·re oo·na *ma*·kee·na)

Can I (enter)?
Posso (entrare)? — *po*·so (en·*tra*·re)

Could you please (help me)?
Può (aiutarmi), per favore? — pwo (a·yoo·*tar*·mee) per fa·*vo*·re

Do I have to (book a seat)?
Devo (prenotare un posto)? — *de*·vo (pre·no·*ta*·re oon *po*·sto)

Fruit & Vegetables

apple	*mela*	*me*·la
beans	*fagioli*	fa·*jo*·lee
cabbage	*cavolo*	*ka*·vo·lo
capsicum	*peperone*	pe·pe·*ro*·ne
carrot	*carota*	ka·*ro*·ta
cauliflower	*cavolfiore*	ka·vol·*fyo*·re
cucumber	*cetriolo*	che·tree·*o*·lo
fruit	*frutta*	*froo*·ta
grapes	*uva*	*oo*·va
lemon	*limone*	lee·*mo*·ne
lentils	*lenticchie*	len·*tee*·kye
mushroom	*funghi*	*foon*·gee
nuts	*noci*	*no*·chee
onions	*cipolle*	chee·*po*·le
orange	*arancia*	a·*ran*·cha
peach	*pesca*	*pe*·ska
peas	*piselli*	pee·*ze*·lee
pineapple	*ananas*	*a*·na·nas
plum	*prugna*	*proo*·nya
potatoes	*patate*	pa·*ta*·te
spinach	*spinaci*	spee·*na*·chee
tomatoes	*pomodori*	po·mo·*do*·ree
vegetables	*verdura*	ver·*doo*·ra

Other

bread	*pane*	*pa*·ne
butter	*burro*	*boo*·ro
cheese	*formaggio*	for·*ma*·jo
eggs	*uova*	*wo*·va
honey	*miele*	*mye*·le
ice	*ghiaccio*	*gya*·cho
jam	*marmellata*	mar·me·*la*·ta
noodles	*pasta*	*pas*·ta
oil	*olio*	*o*·lyo
pepper	*pepe*	*pe*·pe
rice	*riso*	*ree*·zo
salt	*sale*	*sa*·le
soup	*minestra*	mee·*nes*·tra
soy sauce	*salsa di soia*	*sal*·sa dee *so*·ya
sugar	*zucchero*	*tsoo*·ke·ro
vinegar	*aceto*	a·*che*·to

Drinks

beer	*birra*	*bee*·ra
coffee	*caffè*	ka·*fe*
(orange) juice	*succo (d'arancia)*	*soo*·ko (da·*ran*·cha)
milk	*latte*	*la*·te
red wine	*vino rosso*	*vee*·no *ro*·so
soft drink	*bibita*	*bee*·bee·ta
tea	*tè*	te
(mineral) water	*acqua (minerale)*	*a*·kwa (mee·ne·*ra*·le)
white wine	*vino bianco*	*vee*·no *byan*·ko

EMERGENCIES

Help!
Aiuto! a·*yoo*·to

Leave me alone!
Lasciami in pace! *la*·sha·mee een *pa*·che

I'm lost.
Mi sono perso/a. (m/f) mee *so*·no *per*·so/a

There's been an accident.
C'è stato un incidente. che *sta*·to oon een·chee·*den*·te

Call the police!
Chiami la polizia! *kya*·mee la po·lee·*tsee*·a

Call a doctor!
Chiami un medico! *kya*·mee oon *me*·dee·ko

Where are the toilets?
Dove sono i gabinetti? *do*·ve *so*·no ee ga·bee·*ne*·tee

I'm sick.
Mi sento male. mee *sen*·to *ma*·le

It hurts here.
Mi fa male qui. mee fa *ma*·le kwee

I'm allergic to ...
Sono allergico/a a ... (m/f) *so*·no a·*ler*·jee·ko/a a ...

SHOPPING & SERVICES

I'd like to buy ...
Vorrei comprare ... vo·*ray* kom·*pra*·re ...

I'm just looking.
Sto solo guardando. sto *so*·lo gwar·*dan*·do

Can I look at it?
Posso dare un'occhiata? *po*·so *da*·re oo·no·*kya*·ta

How much is this?
Quanto costa questo? *kwan*·to *kos*·ta *kwe*·sto

It's too expensive.
È troppo caro/a. (m/f) e *tro*·po *ka*·ro/a

Can you lower the price?
Può farmi lo sconto? pwo *far*·mee lo *skon*·to

There's a mistake in the bill.
C'è un errore nel conto. che oo·ne·*ro*·re nel *kon*·to

SIGNS

Entrata/Ingresso	Entrance
Uscita	Exit
Aperto	Open
Chiuso	Closed
Informazioni	Information
Proibito/Vietato	Prohibited
Gabinetti/Servizi	Toilets
Uomini	Men
Donne	Women

ATM	*Bancomat*	*ban*·ko·mat
post office	*ufficio postale*	oo·*fee*·cho pos·*ta*·le
tourist office	*ufficio del turismo*	oo·*fee*·cho del too·*reez*·mo

TIME & DATES

What time is it?	*Che ora è?*	ke *o*·ra e
It's one o'clock.	*È l'una.*	e *loo*·na
It's (two) o'clock.	*Sono le (due).*	*so*·no le (*doo*·e)
Half past (one).	*(L'una) e mezza.*	(*loo*·na) e *me*·dza
in the morning	*di mattina*	dee ma·*tee*·na
in the afternoon	*di pomeriggio*	dee po·me·*ree*·jo
in the evening	*di sera*	dee *se*·ra
yesterday	*ieri*	*ye*·ree
today	*oggi*	*o*·jee
tomorrow	*domani*	do·*ma*·nee
Monday	*lunedì*	loo·ne·*dee*
Tuesday	*martedì*	mar·te·*dee*
Wednesday	*mercoledì*	mer·ko·le·*dee*
Thursday	*giovedì*	jo·ve·*dee*
Friday	*venerdì*	ve·ner·*dee*
Saturday	*sabato*	*sa*·ba·to
Sunday	*domenica*	do·*me*·nee·ka
January	*gennaio*	je·*na*·yo
February	*febbraio*	fe·*bra*·yo
March	*marzo*	*mar*·tso
April	*aprile*	a·*pree*·le
May	*maggio*	*ma*·jo
June	*giugno*	*joo*·nyo
July	*luglio*	*loo*·lyo

August	*agosto*	a·*gos*·to
September	*settembre*	se·*tem*·bre
October	*ottobre*	o·*to*·bre
November	*novembre*	no·*vem*·bre
December	*dicembre*	dee·*chem*·bre

TRANSPORT

Public Transport

At what time does the ... leave/arrive?	*A che ora parte/ arriva ...?*	a ke o·ra *par*·te/ a·*ree*·va ...
boat	*la nave*	la *na*·ve
bus	*l'autobus*	*low*·to·boos
ferry	*il traghetto*	eel tra·*ge*·to
metro	*la metro-politana*	la me·tro·po·lee·*ta*·na
plane	*l'aereo*	la·*e*·re·o
train	*il treno*	eel *tre*·no
... ticket	*un biglietto ...*	oon bee·*lye*·to
one-way	*di sola andata*	dee *so*·la an·*da*·ta
return	*di andata e ritorno*	dee an·*da*·ta e ree·*tor*·no

NUMBERS

1	*uno*	*oo*·no
2	*due*	*doo*·e
3	*tre*	tre
4	*quattro*	*kwa*·tro
5	*cinque*	*cheen*·kwe
6	*sei*	say
7	*sette*	*se*·te
8	*otto*	*o*·to
9	*nove*	*no*·ve
10	*dieci*	*dye*·chee
20	*venti*	*ven*·tee
30	*trenta*	*tren*·ta
40	*quaranta*	kwa·*ran*·ta
50	*cinquanta*	cheen·*kwan*·ta
60	*sessanta*	se·*san*·ta
70	*settanta*	se·*tan*·ta
80	*ottanta*	o·*tan*·ta
90	*novanta*	no·*van*·ta
100	*cento*	*chen*·to
1000	*mille*	*mee*·le

bus stop	*fermata dell'autobus*	fer·*ma*·ta del *ow*·to·boos
platform	*binario*	bee·*na*·ryo
ticket office	*biglietteria*	bee·lye·te·*ree*·a
timetable	*orario*	o·*ra*·ryo
train station	*stazione ferroviaria*	sta·*tsyo*·ne fe·ro·*vyar*·ya

Does it stop at ...?
Si ferma a ...? see *fer*·ma a ...

Please tell me when we get to ...
Mi dica per favore quando arriviamo a ... mee *dee*·ka per fa·*vo*·re *kwan*·do a·ree·*vya*·mo a ...

I want to get off here.
Voglio scendere qui. *vo*·lyo *shen*·de·re kwee

Driving and Cycling

I'd like to hire a/an ...	*Vorrei noleggiare un/una ...* (m/f)	vo·*ray* no·le·*ja*·re oon/*oo*·na ...
4WD	*fuoristrada* (m)	fwo·ree·*stra*·da
bicycle	*bicicletta* (f)	bee·chee·*kle*·ta
car	*macchina* (f)	*ma*·kee·na
motorbike	*moto* (f)	*mo*·to

bicycle pump	*pompa della bicicletta*	*pom*·pa *de*·la bee·chee·*kle*·ta
child seat	*seggiolino*	se·jo·*lee*·no
helmet	*casco*	*kas*·ko
mechanic	*meccanico*	me·*ka*·nee·ko
petrol/gas	*benzina*	ben·*dzee*·na
service station	*stazione di servizio*	sta·*tsyo*·ne dee ser·*vee*·tsyo

Is this the road to ...?
Questa strada porta a ...? *kwe*·sta *stra*·da *por*·ta a ...

(How long) Can I park here?
(Per quanto tempo) Posso parcheggiare qui? (per *kwan*·to *tem*·po) *po*·so par·ke·*ja*·re kwee

The car/motorbike has broken down (at ...).
La macchina/moto si è guastata (a ...). la *ma*·kee·na/*mo*·to see e gwas·*ta*·ta (a ...)

I have a flat tyre.
Ho una gomma bucata. o *oo*·na *go*·ma boo·*ka*·ta

I've run out of petrol.
Ho esaurito la benzina. o e·zow·*ree*·to la ben·*dzee*·na

GLOSSARY

AAST – Azienda Autonoma di Soggiorno e Turismo (tourist office)

ACI – Automobile Club d'Italia (Italian automobile club)

acqua – water

agnello – lamb

agriturismo – farm-stay accommodation

albergo – hotel (up to five stars)

albergo diffuso – hotel spread over more than one site, typically in the historic centre of a town

alimentari – food shops

alto – high

anfiteatro – amphitheatre

aperitivo – aperitif

aragosta – lobster

ARST – Azienda Regionale Sarda Trasporti (state bus company)

bancomat – ATM

benzina – petrol

benzina senza piombo – unleaded petrol

borgo – ancient town or village

bottarga – mullet roe

burrida – dogfish with pine nuts, parsley and garlic

calamari – squid

camera – room

campanile – bell tower

cappella – chapel

capretto – kid (goat)

carabinieri – military police (see *polizia*)

carciofi – artichokes

Carnevale – carnival period between Epiphany and Lent

castello – castle

cattedrale – cathedral

cena – evening meal

centro – centre

centro storico – literally 'historical centre'; old town

chiesa – church

colazione – breakfast

comune – equivalent to a municipality or county; town or city council

coperto – cover charge

cornetto – croissant

corso – main street, avenue

cortile – courtyard

cotto/a – cooked

cozze – mussels

CTS – Centro Turistico Studentesco e Giovanile (student/youth travel agency)

culurgiones – ravioli filled with cheese and/or potato

cumbessias – pilgrims' lodgings found in courtyards around churches, traditionally the scene of religious festivities (of up to nine days' duration) in honour of a particular saint

cupola – dome

digestivo – after-dinner liqueur

dolci – sweets

domus de janas – literally 'fairy house'; ancient tomb cut into rock

duomo – cathedral

ENIT – Ente Nazionale Italiano per il Turismo (Italian state tourist office)

enoteca – wine bar or wine shop

farmacia – pharmacy

festa – festival

fiume – (main) river

fontana – fountain

formaggio – cheese

fregola – a large couscouslike grain

fritto/a – fried

frutti di mare – seafood

funghi – mushrooms

gasolio – diesel

gelateria – ice-cream shop

giudicato – province; in medieval times Sardinia was divided into the Giudicato of Cagliari, Giudicato of Logudoro, Giudicato of Gallura and Giudicato of Arborea

golfo – gulf

grotta – cave

guardia medica – emergency call-out doctor service

insalata – salad

isola – island

lago – lake

largo – (small) square

latte – milk

libreria – bookshop

lido – managed section of beach

lungomare – seafront road; promenade

macchia – Mediterranean scrub

malloreddus – semolina dumplings

mare – sea

mattanza – literally 'slaughter'; the annual tuna catch in southwest Sardinia

miele – honey

mirto – myrtle berries; also a liqueur distilled from myrtle berries

monte – mountain, mount

muggine – mullet

municipio – town hall

muristenes – see *cumbessias*

Natale – Christmas

nuraghe – Bronze Age stone towers and fortified settlements

oratorio – oratory

ospedale – hospital

palazzo – palace; a large building of any type, including an apartment block

panadas – savoury pie

pane – bread

panino – bread roll

parco – park

Pasqua – Easter

passeggiata – traditional evening stroll

pasticceria – pastry shop

pensione – small hotel, often with board

piazza – square

pietà – literally 'pity or compassion'; sculpture, drawing or painting of the dead Christ supported by the Madonna

pinacoteca – art gallery

polizia – police

polpo – octopus

poltrona – literally 'armchair'; airline-type chair on a ferry

ponte – bridge
porceddu – suckling pig
porto – port
pronto soccorso – first aid, casualty ward
prosciutto – cured ham

questura – police station

rio – secondary river
riserva naturale – nature reserve
ristorante – restaurant

sagra – festival, usually dedicated to one culinary item, such as funghi (mushrooms), wine etc
saline – saltpans
santuario – sanctuary, often with a country chapel
scalette – 'little stairs' (as in Scalette di Santa Chiara, a steep stairway up into Cagliari's Il Castello district)
sebadas – fried pastry with ricotta
seppia – cuttlefish
servizio – service fee
spiaggia – beach
stagno – lagoon
stazione marittima – ferry terminal
stazzo/u – farmstead in the Gallura region
strada – street, road

tavola calda – canteen-style eatery
teatro – theatre
tempio – temple
terme – thermal baths
tholos – name used to describe the conical tower of a *nuraghe*
tomba di gigante – literally 'giant's tomb'; ancient mass grave
tonnara – tuna-processing plant
tonno – tuna
tophet – sacred Phoenician or Carthaginian burial ground for children and babies
torre – tower
trippa – tripe

via – street, road
viale – avenue
vicolo – alley, alleyway
vino (rosso/bianco) – wine (red/white)
vongole – clams

zucchero – sugar
zuppa – soup or broth

Behind the Scenes

SEND US YOUR FEEDBACK

We love to hear from travellers – your comments keep us on our toes and help make our books better. Our well-travelled team reads every word on what you loved or loathed about this book. Although we cannot reply individually to your submissions, we always guarantee that your feedback goes straight to the appropriate authors, in time for the next edition. Each person who sends us information is thanked in the next edition – the most useful submissions are rewarded with a selection of digital PDF chapters.

Visit **lonelyplanet.com/contact** to submit your updates and suggestions or to ask for help. Our award-winning website also features inspirational travel stories, news and discussions.

Note: We may edit, reproduce and incorporate your comments in Lonely Planet products such as guidebooks, websites and digital products, so let us know if you don't want your comments reproduced or your name acknowledged. For a copy of our privacy policy visit lonelyplanet.com/privacy.

OUR READERS

Many thanks to the travellers who used the last edition and wrote to us with helpful hints, useful advice and interesting anecdotes:

Andy Miller, Christer Törnemo, Fred Thomas, Henrik Ott, John and Roxanne McCaffrey, Julia van den Berg, Kirsten Lee, Linda Bottari, Matthias Schwarz, Melanie Snell, Nicoline Beglinger, Nora Rademacher, Pete Towler, Peter Sagal, Philippe Funken, Robert Schwartz, Sarah Matthews.

WRITER THANKS

Gregor Clark

Sincere thanks to the many Sardinians who so generously shared their time, insights and love of the island, particularly Mario and Frédérique in Nuoro, Daria in Santa Teresa, Simonetta in Olbia, Riky in Lotzorai, Laura in San Pantaleo, and Kevin and Rodolfo in Palau. Finally, hugs to my wife, Gaen, and daughters, Meigan and Chloe, who always make coming home the best part of the trip.

Kerry Christiani

Mille grazie to all the Sardinian locals, experts and tourism officials who made the road to research so smooth and provided such valuable insight for the Plan Your Trip and Understand chapters. Big thanks, too, go to my fellow authors – Duncan Garwood and Gregor Clark – for being such stars to work with.

Duncan Garwood

A big thank you to Giacomo Bassi for his brilliant tips and suggestions. In Sardinia *grazie* to everyone who helped and offered advice, in particular Luisa Besalduch, Agostino Rivano, Marianna Mascalchi, Valentina Sanna, Marco Vacca, and the tourist office teams at Alghero, Sassari and Castelsardo. At LP, thanks to Anna Tyler for all her support. And, as always, a big, heartfelt hug to Lidia and the boys, Ben and Nick.

ACKNOWLEDGEMENTS

Climate map data adapted from Peel MC, Finlayson BL & McMahon TA (2007) 'Updated World Map of the Köppen-Geiger Climate Classification', Hydrology and Earth System Sciences, 11, 163344.

Cover photograph: Costa del Sud, Pawel Kazmierczak/Shutterstock ©

THIS BOOK

This sixth edition of Lonely Planet's *Sardinia* guidebook was researched and written by Gregor Clark, Kerry Christiani and Duncan Garwood. The previous edition was written by Kerry Christiani and Duncan Garwood, and earlier editions were written by Duncan Garwood, Paula Hardy and Damien Simonis. This guidebook was produced by the following:

Destination Editor Anna Tyler

Product Editors Ronan Abayawickrema, Amanda Williamson

Regional Senior Cartographer Anthony Phelan

Senior Cartographer Corey Hutchison

Book Designer Gwen Cotter

Assisting Editors Andrew Bain, Heather Champion, Gabby Innes, Helen Koehne, Simon Williamson

Cover Researcher Naomi Parker

Thanks to Nigel Chin, Victoria Harrison, Lauren Keith, Sandie Kestell, Kate Kiely, Genna Patterson, Angela Tinson, Tony Wheeler

Index

Map Pages **000**
Photo Pages 000

Map Pages **000**
Photo Pages **000**

Map Legend

Sights

- Beach
- Bird Sanctuary
- Buddhist
- Castle/Palace
- Christian
- Confucian
- Hindu
- Islamic
- Jain
- Jewish
- Monument
- Museum/Gallery/Historic Building
- Ruin
- Shinto
- Sikh
- Taoist
- Winery/Vineyard
- Zoo/Wildlife Sanctuary
- Other Sight

Activities, Courses & Tours

- Bodysurfing
- Diving
- Canoeing/Kayaking
- Course/Tour
- Sento Hot Baths/Onsen
- Skiing
- Snorkelling
- Surfing
- Swimming/Pool
- Walking
- Windsurfing
- Other Activity

Sleeping

- Sleeping
- Camping
- Hut/Shelter

Eating

- Eating

Drinking & Nightlife

- Drinking & Nightlife
- Cafe

Entertainment

- Entertainment

Shopping

- Shopping

Information

- Bank
- Embassy/Consulate
- Hospital/Medical
- Internet
- Police
- Post Office
- Telephone
- Toilet
- Tourist Information
- Other Information

Geographic

- Beach
- Gate
- Hut/Shelter
- Lighthouse
- Lookout
- Mountain/Volcano
- Oasis
- Park
- Pass
- Picnic Area
- Waterfall

Population

- Capital (National)
- Capital (State/Province)
- City/Large Town
- Town/Village

Transport

- Airport
- Border crossing
- Bus
- Cable car/Funicular
- Cycling
- Ferry
- Metro station
- Monorail
- Parking
- Petrol station
- S-Bahn/Subway station
- Taxi
- T-bane/Tunnelbana station
- Train station/Railway
- Tram
- Tube station
- U-Bahn/Underground station
- Other Transport

Routes

- Tollway
- Freeway
- Primary
- Secondary
- Tertiary
- Lane
- Unsealed road
- Road under construction
- Plaza/Mall
- Steps
- Tunnel
- Pedestrian overpass
- Walking Tour
- Walking Tour detour
- Path/Walking Trail

Boundaries

- International
- State/Province
- Disputed
- Regional/Suburb
- Marine Park
- Cliff
- Wall

Hydrography

- River, Creek
- Intermittent River
- Canal
- Water
- Dry/Salt/Intermittent Lake
- Reef

Areas

- Airport/Runway
- Beach/Desert
- Cemetery (Christian)
- Cemetery (Other)
- Glacier
- Mudflat
- Park/Forest
- Sight (Building)
- Sportsground
- Swamp/Mangrove

Note: Not all symbols displayed above appear on the maps in this book

OUR STORY

A beat-up old car, a few dollars in the pocket and a sense of adventure. In 1972 that's all Tony and Maureen Wheeler needed for the trip of a lifetime – across Europe and Asia overland to Australia. It took several months, and at the end – broke but inspired – they sat at their kitchen table writing and stapling together their first travel guide, *Across Asia on the Cheap*. Within a week they'd sold 1500 copies. Lonely Planet was born.

Today, Lonely Planet has offices in Franklin, London, Melbourne, Oakland, Dublin, Beijing and Delhi, with more than 600 staff and writers. We share Tony's belief that 'a great guidebook should do three things: inform, educate and amuse'.

OUR WRITERS

Gregor Clark

Curator, Oristano & the West; Olbia, Costa Smeralda & Gallura; Nuoro & the East

Gregor is a US-based writer whose love of foreign languages and curiosity about what's around the next bend have taken him to dozens of countries on five continents. Chronic wanderlust has also led him to visit all 50 states and most Canadian provinces on countless road trips through his native North America. Since 2000, Gregor has regularly contributed to Lonely Planet guides, with a focus on Europe and the Americas. Titles include *Italy*, *France*, *Brazil*, *Costa Rica*, *Argentina*, *Portugal*, and *New England's Best Trips*, as well as coffee-table pictorials such as *Food Trails*, *The USA Book* and *The LP Guide to the Middle of Nowhere*.

Kerry Christiani

Kerry is an award-winning travel writer, photographer and Lonely Planet author, specialising in Central and Southern Europe. Based in Wales, she has authored/co-authored more than a dozen Lonely Planet titles. An adventure addict, she loves mountains, cold places and true wilderness. She features her latest work at https://its-a-small-world.com and tweets @kerrychristiani. Kerry's insatiable wanderlust has taken her to all seven continents – from the frozen wilderness of Antarctica to the Australian Outback – and shows no sign of waning. Her writing appears regularly in publications like *Adventure Travel* magazine and she is a *Telegraph* travel expert for Austria and Wales. Kerry wrote the Plan Your Trip, Understand and Survival Guide chapters.

Duncan Garwood

Cagliari & the Sarrabus, Iglesias & the Southwest, Alghero & the Northwest

From facing fast bowlers in Barbados to sidestepping hungry pigs in Goa, Duncan's travels have thrown up many unique experiences. These days he largely dedicates himself to Italy, his adopted homeland, where's he's been living since 1997. From his base in the Castelli Romani hills outside Rome, he's clocked up endless kilometres exploring the country's well-known destinations and far-flung reaches, working on the guidebooks *Rome*, *Sardinia*, *Sicily*, *Piedmont* and *Naples & the Amalfi Coast*. Other LP titles include *Italy's Best Trips*, *The Food Lover's Guide to the World* and *Pocket Bilbao & San Sebastian*. He also writes on Italy for newspapers, websites and magazines.

Published by Lonely Planet Global Limited
CRN 554153
6th edition – January 2018
ISBN 978 1 78657 255 4

10 9 8 7 6 5 4 3 2 1
Printed in China